CHARACTER AND

Character and Person

JOHN FROW

OXFORD
UNIVERSITY PRESS

OXFORD
UNIVERSITY PRESS

Great Clarendon Street, Oxford, OX2 6DP,
United Kingdom

Oxford University Press is a department of the University of Oxford.
It furthers the University's objective of excellence in research, scholarship,
and education by publishing worldwide. Oxford is a registered trade mark of
Oxford University Press in the UK and in certain other countries

First published 2014
First published in paperback 2016

Published in the United States of America by Oxford University Press
198 Madison Avenue, New York, NY 10016, United States of America

British Library Cataloguing in Publication Data
Data available

Library of Congress Cataloging in Publication Data
Data available

ISBN 978–0–19–870451–5 (Hbk.)
ISBN 978–0–19–877855–4 (Pbk.)

Preface

A well-known film by Alfred Hitchcock stars Anthony Perkins as Norman Bates: a person (an actor), and a character.[1] 'Norman Bates' is made up of two dissociated and conflicted personae: that of a shy young man with repressed sexual desires, and that of Mother, who murders the young women who provoke those desires in him. Norman as a young man seems plausibly real to us, in part because he is constructed on the real frame of Anthony Perkins; as Mother, however, he is a crude semblance of a person, an acted character badly acting another character. But the bad acting is part of the point: the splitting of Norman as he assumes 'the vesture of cross-dressing hell' is part of his characterization.[2] He belongs to a recognizable type: the psycho, the split personality, the pathologically dependent child. We know the type from popular psychology, and it is summarized for us at the end of the movie by the forensic psychiatrist who laboriously explains Norman's pathology. We also know it from elsewhere in the movies: Hitchcock's *Psycho* belongs to the subgenre of the psychological horror movie, and it has many of the trappings of the cinematic gothic: the creepy old house, the sinister stuffed birds, the music shrieking at moments of terror, the atmosphere of lurking evil. Norman is an effect of projected light and darkness, of camera angles, of the dated popular psychology of the time, of the conventions of the genre. He tells us something about what it means to be a character, and something about what it means, within a particular culture, to be a human being (including what it might mean to be more than one person within a single body: to be at once a man and his mother).

If we were to ask about the sort of thing human beings are we would probably start by making a distinction between people and animals, between people and inanimate things, and between people and other intelligent entities such as computers or perhaps gods or angels or spirits, and we would then qualify these distinctions by pointing to the qualities human beings have in common with animals and things and computers or spirits, and to the relations that tie them together. We would also need to specify the relation between living and dead human beings, as well as what it means to be 'fully' human. But another way of thinking about the sorts of things people are is to distinguish between real people and imaginary people, and then to ask how they differ, about the conditions that allow each of these kinds of being to exist, and about the interplay between them. This distinction has to do with the kinds or degrees of reality of persons (I use the word 'person' to designate a slightly more abstract and structural way of talking about people) and with the social institutions that define and support that reality—such things as legal and religious codifications of what it means to be a person, or practices of self-shaping, or fictional genres and the character types that are peculiar to each of them.

[1] Alfred Hitchcock, dir., *Psycho* (1960).
[2] Don DeLillo, *Point Omega* (London: Picador, 2010), p. 141.

The argument of this book can be briefly stated: persons exist across a range of modalities. Some people are real and physically present to us; others are real but we know them only by repute—by the stories that are told about them or the reports we have of their existence or our assumption that they must exist or have once existed—or they exist in our memories; others may or may not be real, or imaginary qualities may be grafted onto real people; and others may be fictitious, with varying degrees of resemblance to real people. The argument itself is neither original nor particularly interesting; it becomes interesting, I think, when we begin to examine the way these different modes of existence relate to each other. I try to do this here by investigating some of the many culturally and historically specific schemata by which real and imaginary persons are assigned their particular ways of being, and I take fictional character as the starting point from which to examine the spectrum of modalities along which persons exist. I do this because fictional characters have a more clearly modal existence than real people do (they are more clearly constructs of the imagination), and in that sense they are exemplary of the way a mode of reality is ascribed to persons of all sorts.

What kinds of things are literary characters? To the extent that there is a consensus among literary theorists about this most inadequately theorized of literary concepts,[3] it is that neither of the classes of answer that have traditionally been given to this question—the 'ethical' answer that characters are to be treated and analysed as though they were persons, having lives that transcend the texts they appear in, or the 'structuralist' answer that characters are to be treated purely as textual constructs—deals satisfactorily with the theoretical problem. The first tends to conflate textually formed entities with persons, and privileges the forms of character construction that are specific to the classic European novel and to much film and television drama; the second tends to have no way of dealing with the processes of affective engagement by which textual constructs acquire their hold on readers, acting on us *as though* they were real.

But to say that there is a general agreement about the nature of the problem is of little help in framing a positive understanding of this ontologically ambivalent construct which lies at the heart of the life of textual fictions of all kinds. How can we understand fictional character both as a formal construct, made out of words or images and having a fully textual existence, and as a set of effects which are modelled on the form of the human person? The danger of thinking of it in terms of this modelling is that we commit the category error of abstracting character from its textual existence and treating it as though it had an independent presence. We think of Omar in *The Wire*, say, as a psychologically complex person, we admire him or we don't, we may know that he is based on a number of actual Baltimore gangsters, and Wikipedia gives a detailed biography.[4] He's a kind of acquaintance.

[3] Many years ago I wrote that 'the concept of character is perhaps the most problematic and the most undertheorized of the basic categories of narrative theory', whilst also being perhaps the most widely used tool we have for thinking about fictional texts. John Frow, 'Spectacle, Binding: On Character', *Poetics Today* 7: 2 (1986), p. 227. That article is the germ from which this book has sprouted, and I draw on it in Chapter 1.

[4] <http://en.wikipedia.org/wiki/Omar_Little>. Last accessed 28 June 2013.

Yet to describe this sense of the reality of textual constructs as a category err doesn't mean we can escape that kind of recognition of quasi-human being, even in the case of the least anthropomorphic characters, since the character form makes no sense in abstraction from the form of the person. The problem, to put it simply, is that characters and persons are at once ontologically discontinuous (they have different manners of being) and logically interdependent. You can get around this problem in one of two ways: either by viewing fictional characters as somewhat similar to persons, or by viewing persons as somewhat similar to fictional characters. In a sense these two moves amount to the same thing, but the problem with the former is that it assumes the self-evident reality of persons: it gives away too much to an understanding of persons as substantial, consistent, coherent subjects of being. The second move looks to me like a better one, since it allows us to understand persons not as ontological givens but as constructs, which are in part made out of the same materials as fictional characters.

The first task that this book addresses is to investigate not only the kind of thing character is but how it works to engage readers and the range of typologies which shape and organize it in a number of very different periods, media, and genres. The second task of the book, however, is to explore the ways in which character is person-like, and, through that, the question of what it means to be a social person. I seek both to keep the categories of character and person distinct and specific to the fields in which they operate, and to explore the interaction and overlapping of those fields. This means that I need to understand not only how characters work as quasi-persons across a range of media and genres, but also how social personhood works as a kind of fiction: that is, as a model shaped by particular social practices and institutions (legal and religious frameworks, for example), but also by the schemata that underpin fictional personhood. In the chapters on 'Person' and 'Type' I explore social personhood across a range of legal, religious, medical, ethical, civic, and socioeconomic institutions and organizations of practice. In the chapters on 'Voice' and 'Name' I explore the articulation of personhood through the pronoun system and the order of the name. In the final two chapters, 'Face' and 'Body', I turn to the somatic organization of personhood and the symbolic dimensions of embodiment.

In one sense, then, the book evolves into a kind of phenomenology of social and fictive personhood, exploring the constitutive categories (name, pronoun, body, face) that are common to each. But its focus is always on the dialectical interaction between its two major categories, character and person, and its method involves a constant play back and forth between them: from neurophilosophical theories of embodiment to an account of the cinematic body; from an exploration of medieval beliefs about the body's existence in the afterlife to a reading of Dante's *Purgatorio*; from the history of humoral medicine to the figure of the melancholic in Jacobean drama; from eighteenth-century theories of sympathy to the novels of Richardson and Sade.

The methodological consequence of focusing on the interplay between different ways of being a person is that the weight of the book falls not on a linear exposition of a progressively developing argument but, rather, on the exploration of juxtaposed materials and the threads that tie them together. The form of the book as a whole is something like that of a prolonged essay. As I wrote in the introduction to an earlier book, 'I take it as axiomatic that cultural things cannot be understood in isolation from economic and political and technological things, and that the analytic objects I construct will be ontologically heterogeneous.'[5] Each chapter typically dwells on literary or dramatic or cinematic materials and on the corresponding forms of theory, on accounts of its topic which are philosophical or historical or sociological or anthropological, and at times on scientific accounts; and I use these shifting perspectives to explore different dimensions of a conceptual field. Thus, Chapter 7, 'Face', for example, begins with a reading of a Japanese novel in order to develop an argument about the contrasting figures of the face as window to the soul and the face as mask. I explore these figures through the work of an anthropologist (Michael Taussig), a sociologist (Georg Simmel), and a pair of philosophers (Gilles Deleuze and Félix Guattari) and then read an account of a face in Proust that is not unique, is not singular, is not the property or the manifestation of its wearer, and is neither spatially nor temporally coherent. The notion that the face is expressive of inner character is theorized by Darwin and by a number of contemporary evolutionary psychologists; I argue that the face should be understood in terms of display rather than expression, and I then seek to recast that opposition at a different level of abstraction as a contrast between Emmanuel Levinas's ethical conception of the face and Erving Goffman's concept of facework. From the face I turn to its counterpart in this chapter, the mask, using an essay of Claude Lévi-Strauss's on facial tattoos and Florence Dupont's account of the Roman *imago*, the death mask that represents the venerated ancestor. Both the *imago* and the early Christian icon are understood within their respective cultures as manifestations of a real, not a fictional, presence; the portrait, by contrast, is ambivalently understood within an aesthetic regime both as a conventional form and as a way of capturing inner character, and the self-portrait is dependent on the mirror in which the self is seen as other. I finish by analysing the masking theatre of the Hellenistic and Roman New Comedy and the typologies of character built around its system of masks.

The path I follow is thus often a twisting one, like the one Donne describes in his third satire:

> On a huge hill,
> Cragged and steep, Truth stands, and he that will
> Reach her, about must and about must go…

The book's coherence consists precisely in that process of going about and about over long stretches of argument: in the knotting of the threads of thematic patterning across the book as a whole. That is what I mean by invoking the genre of the essay, a genre that is defined by a double movement: on the one hand towards the

[5] John Frow, *Time and Commodity Culture: Essays in Cultural Theory and Postmodernity* (Oxford: Clarendon Press, 1997), p. 11.

coherence of a systematic argument, but on the other towards a desire to dwell in the moment, giving it its full weight and letting the argument proceed by indirection. My argument develops from within and through other arguments, which I allow, as far as possible, to speak for themselves before moving beyond them. As Adorno puts it, the essay differs from discursive logic in that it 'neither makes deductions from a principle nor draws conclusions from coherent individual observations. It coordinates elements instead of subordinating them'.[6] It proceeds, that is to say, paratactically, and it 'becomes true in its progress'.[7]

Amongst the book's recurrent arguments are the following:

- Character is not a substance but the literary or dramatic or filmic instance of an operation within a social assemblage, by means of which the reader is inscribed into the terms of a particular formation of personhood. It is a moment of an apparatus for the mobilization of subjectivity within the terms of an ethical or legal or religious or civic mode of action and understanding.
- Character is specific to the genres in which it is formed, but generic typologies are built on the basis of folk taxonomies of personhood.
- Two of the crucial mechanisms by which the form of the person is constructed are the pronoun system and the system of social nomenclature; these figure crucially in the way person effects are shaped in fictional texts, and in the way the reader or viewer is induced to identify and to relate to the text's quasi-persons.
- Identification with fictional characters takes place both at the level of the character represented in a text and at the level of an explicit or implicit enunciative instance; Freud's account of the dispersal of ego-identifications through the dream serves as a model for the general structure of identification. The processes of identification *of* and identification *with* are mutually implicated; the latter, which defines a text's affective interest, takes place through a series of layered positionings that inscribe the reader or viewer or game player into a text or game.
- Central to the definition of persons and characters is the fact of their embodiment; but embodiment is not a matter of fact. The body is at once real (its reality being that of the articulation and layering of numerous physiological and neurological systems) and imaginary. Its key coordinates are the boundaries between the inside and the outside; between the self and the other; between male and female; between the clean and the polluted; and between the living and the dead.

[6] Theodor W. Adorno, 'The Essay as Form', in *Notes to Literature*, vol. 1, trans. Shierry Weber Nicholsen (New York: Columbia University Press, 1991), p. 22.

[7] Adorno, 'The Essay as Form', p. 13.

- The face (like the voice) is part of the body, but in most cultures is also imagined separately from it. It tends to work as that part of the body that is most expressive of inner character, but it is better understood as a semiotic instrument for the display of messages, and it is thus, in principle, akin to the mask, to which it is often opposed.
- Character is shadowed by a daemonic other, the 'associated' and uncanny figure that I call the paredros: the familiar who accompanies a group, the non-human but figured absence from which all narrative figuration emerges. One name for this daemonic other is the reader.

'Character' is a concept of form. By 'form' I mean patterns of transtextual repetition which organize textuality into meaningful units. In writing about character I work within a formalist tradition that takes the textual construction of character seriously; but this is a formalism which then tries to think about the social life of forms, including the discursive regimes and technical apparatuses in which they develop and their role in the construction of personhood. The book is thus intended as a contribution to a sociological poetics concerned with the social force of representations.

I focus for much of the book, although by no means exclusively, on the genre of the novel, not only because so much of the literature on character takes the novel as its exemplary form but because I take it that it is the novel that constructs, in the eighteenth century, the affective and moral technologies of self-shaping inwardness that, together with those mobilized in the later narrative genres of film and television, inform much of our contemporary understanding of what it means to be a person. But my object is character and personhood in all of their many forms. What technologies of selfhood will emerge with the development of digital media is an open question, although I touch on it in my treatment of the role of avatars in digital games in Chapter 2.

I don't try to deliver a history of the concept of character, let alone a history of fictional characterization; and although the book has a wide historical sweep, its choices of times are driven by the logic of the argument and the pertinent case, and by a focus on the interaction between complex systems. (Although the formal logic of character is always historically and generically particular, I am wary of reducing it to historicist specifications of the more or less homogeneous structure of the period, just as I am wary of grand narratives of the successive transformations of selfhood.)[8] Nor am I just doing literary theory, partly because the book covers other domains of representation (film, theatre, visual art, digital games) but, more importantly, because it is concerned with the relation between the formal category

[8] Eric Hayot writes tellingly of the way the integration of New Historicist methodologies into the disciplinary common sense has 'inculcated a strong unstated theory of the *era* as the final goal and subtending force of the intimacies of literary criticism, which reifies at an ideological level a powerful theory of periods as social wholes', instantiating 'more or less untheorised and inherited notions of totality'. Eric Hayot, *On Literary Worlds* (New York: Oxford University Press, 2012), pp. 151–2.

and particular forms of life. Nor, finally, is it an exercise in psychology, although one of the things it has in its sights is the singular, complex madness that drives each one of us. It is, above all, a book about reading: about the kinds of knowledge and emotional investment that you need to do it well, and about the centrality of fictional character—and, by extension, of social models of personhood—to reading of almost any kind.

Acknowledgements

This book, like every book, is the work of many hands. I have been thinking about fictional character and about questions of personhood for a number of years, and many friends, colleagues, and writers known and unknown to me have helped clarify my thinking about them. The book took shape within particular institutions of learning, but also within the invisible college of my peers, past and present. I have talked with my students about much of the material that has been worked into this book, and have learned much of what I know from them. As it came into being, this book had many readers, some of whom were voices in my head, readers over my shoulder, of whose virtual cautions and (I hope) at times approval I have been constantly aware. Tony Bennett, Anne Freadman, Nick Heron, Noel King, Grace Moore, and Lesley Stern read sections of the book and made suggestions that were sometimes detailed, always immensely helpful, and of some of which I took heed. Anonymous readers for Oxford University Press and another publisher gave helpful advice. Victoria Reeve acted as a research assistant in the early stages of the project and uncovered texts I would not otherwise have found. Colleagues at the various universities in which I have worked or which I visited listened to presentations of some of the material and asked the difficult questions that pushed me to think harder. But let me single out two people in particular who played a major role in helping me find a form for my argument and understand it better than I had before. Justin Clemens was an exemplary interlocutor. Whenever I gave him chunks of text to read, he came back quickly with carefully considered responses; he had always read everything I had and always had suggestions for other things I might read; and he helped me see both what was wrong with an argument, and how it might work better. Bruce Robbins read an earlier draft of the book for another publisher, and later identified himself to me. He had grappled with the book as a whole (or most of a whole) and wrote a report that was generous, perceptive, and acute in picking out how the book's argument might look if I changed perspective here or took a particular train of thought in another direction or thought through the implications of an argument a little more deeply. To them and to all the readers who helped me write this book I owe a profound debt of gratitude.

Parts of the book were previously published in *Poetics Today, New Literary History, Cultural Studies Review*, and *Affirmations: Of the Modern*. A three-year Discovery grant from the Australian Research Council gave me the most valuable of research resources, time free of other responsibilities, which helped make the book possible.

I dedicate this book to three people. First, with love, to my partner Sandra Hawker. Second, to the memory of my mother, Nola Frow, who gave me unstinting and unselfish love throughout my life, and who died in August 2013. And third, to Kai Motum, born on 22 October 2013.

Sydney
October 2013

Contents

1
Figure

I

'It would be pointless for the author to try to convince the reader that his characters once actually lived,' writes the barely visible character who narrates Milan Kundera's *The Unbearable Lightness of Being*. 'They were not born of a mother's womb; they were born of a stimulating phrase or two or from a basic situation. Tomas was born of the saying "*Einmal ist keinmal*". Tereza was born of the rumbling of a stomach.'[1]

This is the first part of the problem we encounter when we try to understand the nature of fictional character: these figures are made of words, of images, of imaginings; they are not real in the way that people are real. The second part of the problem is this: why and how do we endow these sketched-in figures with a semblance of reality? Why are we moved by these ontologically hybrid beings that people the pages of novels or the space of the theatre or the storyline of films? What makes us imagine that these clusters of words or images are in some way like persons?

We first come across the two central characters of this novel, 'Tomas' and 'Tereza', after several pages of reflection on Nietzsche's concept of eternal return and the gravity it gives to human being:

> I have been thinking about Tomas for many years. But only in the light of these reflections did I see him clearly. I saw him standing at the window of his flat and looking across the courtyard at the opposite walls, not knowing what to do.
>
> He had first met Tereza about three weeks earlier . . .[2]

The hesitation before the introduction of the character, his emergence, in the shift from 'did I see him' to 'I saw him', out of the act of imagining that brings him into being, makes explicit the fragile 'let's pretend' moment that precedes all narration, and which all narrative texts have devices to handle, from open proclamation of the pretence, to invocation of a Muse to take responsibility for it, to modulation from abstract statement to concrete case, to direct suppression of it. At the moment we begin reading, say, *Emma*, we must imagine an implied predicate of

[1] Milan Kundera, *The Unbearable Lightness of Being*, trans. Michael Henry Heim (London: Faber, 1984), p. 39.

[2] Kundera, *Unbearable Lightness*, p. 6.

existence: '[Let us suppose that there was once a person called Emma Woodhouse such that] Emma Woodhouse, handsome, clever, and rich, with a comfortable home and happy disposition, seemed to unite some of the best blessings of existence; and had lived nearly twenty-one years in the world with very little to distress or vex her.'[3] Not only do the explicit entities 'Tomas' or 'Emma Woodhouse' (and the entirety of the fictional worlds that encompass them) arise from such an implicit act of predication, but so does the voice that speaks of them, whether that voice speaks as an 'I', as in Kundera's novel, or is kept firmly in the background, as in *Emma*, or—an important limit case of the quietly personified source of enunciation—as in the position from which a lyric poem is enunciated, or the perspectival focus of a film.

In this and the following chapters I explore the tension between thinking of characters as pieces of writing or imaging and thinking of them as person-like entities, and I seek to resolve that tension by proposing that fictional character must—in ways that I think are logically difficult to hold together—be seen to be both at once. Before beginning that discussion, however, I ask a preliminary question about whether and to what extent character must be seen as unified and coherent ('handsome, clever, and rich'), and, indeed, whether and to what extent it must look like a person at all; this question is a prelude to my later consideration of whether persons are unified and coherent selves, and whether persons need to be human at all.

Again, let me proceed by way of examples.

Chapter 62 of Julio Cortázar's novel *Hopscotch* summarizes 'a few scattered notes' in which the writer Morelli speaks of a book he had planned.[4] His starting point is the research of a Swedish neurobiologist into the chemical basis of mental processes (the idea doubtless sounded more radical in 1963), and Morelli's note reads in part:

> Chemistry, electromagnetism, the secret flow of living matter, everything returns strangely to evoke the idea of mana; in a like manner, on the edge of social behaviour, one might suspect an interaction of a different nature, a billiard game that certain individuals play or are played at, a drama with no Oedipuses, no Rastignacs, no Phaedras, an *impersonal* drama to the extent that the consciences and the passions of the characters cannot be seen as having been involved except a posteriori.[5] As if the subliminal levels were those that wind and unravel the ball of yarn which is the group that has been involved in the play. Or to please the Swede: as if certain individuals had cut into the deep chemistry of others without having meant to and vice versa, so that the most curious and interesting chain reactions, fissions, and transmutations would result. (pp. 361–2)

[3] Jane Austen, *Emma*, ed. Stephen M. Parrish (New York: Norton Critical Edition, 2000), p. 1.

[4] Julio Cortázar, *Hopscotch*, trans. Gregory Rabassa (London: Collins and Harvill Press, 1967), p. 361; hereafter cited in the text. Julio Cortázar, *Rayuela* (Buenos Aires: Editorial Sudamericana, 1963), p. 415.

[5] Rabassa translates '*comprometidas*' as 'compromised', but the word has the sense in this case of something being committed or at stake, so I have modified the translation here and in the next sentence to read 'involved'.

In this book—had it been written—a group of people would think that its actions were psychologically motivated, but these actions would merely represent 'an instance in that flow of animated matter, in the infinite interactions of what we formerly called desires, sympathies, wills, convictions', a flow which is governed by some 'dark necessity' beyond them (pp. 362–3). Although these characters would think of themselves as acting in accordance with psychological motivations, in fact 'psychological causality would yield disconcertedly, and those puppets would destroy each other or love each other or recognise each other without suspecting too much that life is trying to change its key in and through and by them...' (p. 363).

The programme Morelli maps out here is taken up (although to put the connection so directly is problematic) in a later novel of Cortázar's, *62: A Model Kit*. In this novel things happen in the usual way: friends talk, characters love and are or are not loved, they move from hotel to hotel, there are seductions, an old woman is outraged, vampires suck the blood of their victims, a dead boy haunts Hélène, and 'a doll began to complete its disgraceful destiny',[6] circulating relentlessly between the characters. In structural terms, a series of dyads ('Juan and Hélène in Paris, Juan and Tell in Vienna, Marrast and Nicole in London, Celia and Austin in London, Celia and Hélène in Paris, Frau Marta and the English girl in Vienna') is overlaid by 'the triangles of desire that bind these figures together (Juan–Tell–Hélène, Hélène–Celia–Austin, Marrast–Nicole–Juan)'.[7] But nothing hangs together: the logic of the story is like that of a dream or a shaggy dog story; things happen without apparent reason, the patterns formed by the characters reform again and again, kaleidoscopically. Places dissolve into each other, the narration switches randomly between first and third person and from the actions of characters to the flight of insects around a lamp or a statue of Vercingetorix. The cities—Paris, London, Vienna, Buenos Aires—overlap to form a single, uncanny 'zone' of psychic energy.

Accompanying the characters, as a kind of collective double,[8] is the figure of 'my paredros', a word derived from the Athenian legal system where it designates an assistant, but with a later secondary sense of a 'familiar spirit',[9] and in that sense part of the Gothic apparatus that helps form the texture of the novel. 'Texture' is a key term: in the later story 'The Broken Doll', in which Cortázar reflects on *62*, he quotes a line from John Shade's poem in Nabokov's *Pale Fire*, which he had been reading at the time of writing his own book, a line that speaks of 'not text, but texture', a pattern of coincidences that make up 'some kind/Of correlated pattern in the game', and

[6] Julio Cortázar, 'The Broken Doll', in *Around the Day in Eighty Worlds*, trans. Thomas Christensen (San Francisco: North Point Press, 1986), p. 204.

[7] Lucille Kerr, 'Betwixt Reading and Repetition (apropos of Cortázar's *62: A Model Kit*)', in Carlos J. Alonso (ed.), *Julio Cortázar: New Readings* (Cambridge: Cambridge University Press, 1998), p. 97.

[8] Steven Boldy, *The Novels of Julio Cortázar* (Cambridge: Cambridge University Press, 1980), p. 105.

[9] Victor Sage, '"[T]he privileged horror...of the constellation": Cortázar's use of the Gothic in *62: A Model Kit*', *E-rea* 5: 2 (2007), p. 2. The OED gives the word as 'paredrus'.

> ... [c]oordinating there
> Events and objects with remote events
> And vanished objects. Making ornaments
> Of accidents and possibilities.[10]

That patterning of narrative by coincidence is central to the surrealist ethos with which Cortázar was so deeply imbued: the compositional technique of the 'exquisite corpse', or of Breton's *Nadja* in which random happenings are repeatedly endowed with a deeper meaning. It is the novel's central formal structure, and it is directly connected to the dissolution of 'character' as a distinct entity.

The figure of the paredros is the most explicit figure of this dissolution. It is explained, early in the novel, as

> a routine in the sense that among us there was always something we called my paredros, a term introduced by Calac and which we used without the slightest feeling of a joke because the quality of paredros alluded, as can be seen, to an associated entity, a kind of buddy [*compadre*] or substitute or babysitter for the exceptional, and, by extension, a delegating of what was one's own to that momentary alien dignity without losing anything of ours underneath it all...[11]

A little later we read that

> the attribution of the exalted condition of paredros fluctuated and depended on the momentary decision of each one with no one being able to know for certain when he was or was not the paredros of others present or absent in the zone, or whether he had been and had just stopped being. The condition of paredros seemed to consist above all in the fact that certain things we did or said were always done or said by my paredros, not so much to avoid responsibilities but as if underneath it all my paredros was a kind of modesty... [A]nyone could be the paredros of another or of all and being it gave him something like the value of a joker in cards... (pp. 29–30)

The 'delegat[ion] of what was one's own' to this uncanny double is part of a broader movement where character, place, and recurrent motifs, such as the doll and the basilisk, transfer their properties to the 'associated' and uncanny realm of the 'zone', which functions, in one sense, as the place where Juan and the others are caught up in the ineluctable clichés of a vampire novel, and, in another sense, as the realm of textuality itself, a structure of resemblances, correspondences, repetitions, and variations striving for but never achieving narrative coherence, and where the appearance of temporal succession is negated by a purely thematic ordering of events 'in which different times are intertwined and consumed like smoke from different cigarettes in the same ashtray'.[12]

The postulation of a 'dark necessity' lying deep beneath character motivations lies at the core of one of the greatest of European novels. I have previously written

[10] Vladimir Nabokov, *Pale Fire, Novels 1955–1962* (1962; rpt. New York: The Library of America, 1996), pp. 479–80; quoted in Cortázar, 'The Broken Doll', p. 205.

[11] Julio Cortázar, *62: A Model Kit*, trans. Gregory Rabassa (1972; rpt. New York: Bard Books, 1973), p. 24; hereafter cited in the text. The Spanish text is Julio Cortázar, *62: Modelo para armar* (Buenos Aires: Editorial Sudamericana, 1968), p. 23; 'babysitter' is in English in the original.

[12] Cortázar, 'The Broken Doll', p. 205.

about Goethe's *Elective Affinities* (*Die Wahlverwandtschaften*, 1809) as a text which sets up a reflexive internal model of its generic structure and then transforms that model in quite complex ways.[13] Here I want to mention, more briefly, its fulfilment *avant la lettre* of Morelli's plan for a novel that would exemplify the chemical workings of character and dispense with psychological motivation and differentiation in favour of a narrative of underlying and impersonal forces.

The novel tells the story of a couple, Eduard and Charlotte, who fall in love, respectively, with Charlotte's niece Ottilie and with Eduard's friend the Captain. A child is born to Eduard and Charlotte after he has left home to fight as a soldier; it drowns while in Ottilie's care, Ottilie renounces Eduard, and first Ottilie and then Eduard dies. The names I have given the characters is misleading, however: Eduard was christened Otto, but gave the name up in favour of the Captain, whose name it is too; the name Charlotte is often abbreviated in German to Lotte; and the child's name is, of course, Otto. At the level of the name, then, there is an almost complete lack of differentiation between the five major characters (Otto, Otto, Lotte, Ottilie, Otto). The other, minor characters in the novel are known either by their title—'the Count', 'the architect', 'the schoolteacher'—or by a surname such as Mittler ('mediator') which is allegorical of their character.

This set of relations between persons is retold early in the novel by analogy with the relations of affinity between chemical elements. Eduard and the Captain explain to Charlotte that each element has an adherence to itself and a relation of attraction or antipathy towards other elements; yet through the mediation of a third element, antipathetic elements may be made to combine. When elements separate from an existing union in order to recombine in this way, one can talk of an 'elective affinity', a relationship which is at once given in the order of things and yet in some sense 'chosen'; and when a fourth element is introduced, to pair with the 'divorced' element, then

> one can actually demonstrate attraction and relatedness, this as it were crosswise parting and uniting [*dieses Verlassen, dieses Vereinigen gleichsam übers Kreuz*]: where four entities, previously joined together in two pairs, are brought into contact, abandon their previous union, and join together afresh. In this relinquishment and seizing, in this fleeing and seeking, one can really believe one is witnessing a higher determination; one credits such entities with a species of will and choice, and regards the technical term 'elective affinities' as entirely justified.[14]

The two men then illustrate this process with letters of the alphabet:

> Imagine an A intimately united with a B, so that no force is able to sunder them; imagine a C likewise related to a D; now bring the two couples into contact: A will throw itself at D, C at B, without our being able to say which first deserted its partner, which first embraced the other's partner. (p. 56)

[13] John Frow, *Genre* (London: Routledge, 2006), pp. 116–23.

[14] Johann Wolfgang von Goethe, *Elective Affinities*, trans. R. J. Hollingdale (Harmondsworth: Penguin, 1971), p. 55; hereafter cited in the text. Goethe, *Die Wahlverwandtschaften: Ein Roman, Werke III* (Frankfurt am Main: Insel-Verlag, 1966), p. 374.

Not only is this, in a nutshell, the story of the adulterous liaison at the heart of the novel, it also exemplifies—and calls attention to—one of the book's narrative strategies, the reduction of human relationships to formal patterning, such that the world of social differentiations is subordinated to another where identities are transformed or exchanged just as letters are rearranged in a shifting equation. As the plot develops, first Eduard and Charlotte discuss the possibility that their closed relationship will be disrupted by the introduction of a third and then a fourth term; then Eduard and the Captain are drawn to each other and Charlotte is excluded; then the fourth term, Ottilie, is introduced into the equation and is paired first with Charlotte and then with Eduard; then Eduard and Charlotte, each in love with one of the outsiders, make love to each other in a union which is physically conjugal but emotionally adulterous; and finally the child is born bearing the features not of its genetic parents but of the other partners at the lovemaking, the Captain and Ottilie.

In thematic terms, this formal patterning works on a number of different levels, each of which is richly organized through sets of symbolic oppositions. The play of chemical or human elements works through processes of splitting and uniting; the older term for chemist, cited in the novel, is *Scheidekünstler*, 'artist in division', a term which plays on the word for divorce, *Scheidung*, and on the notion of art as a process of bringing things together (as does metaphor) but also as a kind of violence of the imagination. In its strongest sense, formal pattern is dehumanizing; it belongs to the realm of the daemonic. Eduard and Ottilie's relationship works primarily at this level: each gets headaches on, respectively, the right and left side; Ottilie responds strongly to magnetism and to the pull of mineral deposits beneath the earth; when she copies a document her handwriting gradually becomes identical to Eduard's; and the two exert an 'almost magical attraction upon one another' (p. 286). The world of the daemonic, of the 'monstrous forces' (p. 274) that drive them, is a world of attraction and antipathy at a level deeper than the moral and the social. It is a world of random patterning, the quasi-chemical 'relationships' (or 'affinities') which are beyond human control but which nevertheless seem like 'choices'; a world of natural forces, of fate and of the omens in which Eduard so superstitiously trusts, of poetry and metaphor, and ultimately of death.

One way of understanding the dissolution of the distinctness and unity of character in *62* and *Elective Affinities* is to say that character here becomes a compositional device, part of the patterning of the text—and that these two novels merely take to its logical extreme an understanding of character that goes back to Aristotle, for whom character is a function of narrative structure.[15] Another way of approaching it would be in terms of the transpersonal forces that make up individual human beings: the web of connections through which they belong to a generational structure, for example, which joins them to a past and a future, or to the 'horizontal' patternings of the age cohort, of gender, of social class, of race

15 Aristotle, *Poetics* (*De Poetica*), trans. Ingram Bywater, in *The Basic Works of Aristotle*, ed. Richard McKeon (New York: Random House, 1941), §1450b, p. 1461: 'Tragedy is an imitation of action, and . . . it is mainly for the sake of the action that it imitates the personal agents.'

and ethnicity. And a third form of understanding would be in terms of a more specifically modern questioning of the coherence of the ego, which D. H. Lawrence famously expresses, once again, by means of a chemical analogy:

> You mustn't look in my novel for the old stable ego of the character. There is another ego, according to whose action the individual is unrecognisable, and passes through, as it were, allotropic states which it needs a deeper sense than any we've been used to exercise, to discover are states of the same single radically-unchanged element. (Like as diamond and coal are the same pure single element of carbon. The ordinary novel would trace the history of the diamond—but I say 'diamond, what! This is carbon.' And my diamond might be coal or soot, and my theme is carbon.)[16]

Lawrence's metaphor anticipates Freud's equation, in *Beyond the Pleasure Principle*, of the ego instincts with the drive towards death, the 'universal endeavour of all living substance . . . to return to the quiescence of the inorganic world'.[17] The tension expressed here is that between differentiation and the striving towards a state of indifferentiation, in each of which the ego partakes. And we might note that Freud characterizes the repetition compulsion, which he associates with the instinctual drive towards death, with the 'daemonic',[18] a term that Goethe, in turn, associates with the inhuman forces acting through Eduard and Ottilie, and that we could take as one possible translation of the figure of the paredros.

II

Like the hero of Franz Kafka's *The Castle* and *The Trial*, or like the characters in Heinrich von Kleist's novella *The Marquise of O–*, the central characters of *Elective Affinities* are designated by *characters*, letters of the alphabet. This is one of the root meanings of the English word 'character', whose etymology follows a well-trodden path. It enters English from French *caractere*, derived from the Latin *character*, which derives from the Greek *kharakter* (χαρακτηρ), an instrument for marking or stamping a distinctive mark, which in turn derives from the verb *kharattein* (χαραττ-ειυ), 'to make sharp, cut furrows in, engrave' (OED). When *kharakter* first appears in Greek literature, in Aeschylus's *Suppliants*, where it means the impression stamped on a coin, there is already a semantic transfer from the instrument to the mark, and the notion of the distinctive mark then generates a series of moral equivalents: 'to Herodotus "character" was a speech characteristic; to Aristophanes, style as spoken expression; to Euripides, abstract entities like virtue and noble descent; to Plato, an individuating quality'.[19] But it is only with

[16] D. H. Lawrence, *The Letters of D. H. Lawrence*, vol. 2: *June 1913–October 1916*, ed. George J. Zytaruk and James T. Boulton (Cambridge: Cambridge University Press, 1981), p. 183 (letter of 5 June 1914 to Edward Garnett).

[17] Sigmund Freud, *Beyond the Pleasure Principle: The Standard Edition of The Complete Psychological Works of Sigmund Freud*, vol. 18, trans. James Strachey (London: The Hogarth Press, 1955), p. 62.

[18] Freud, *Beyond the Pleasure Principle*, p. 35.

[19] Warren Ginsberg, *The Cast of Character: The Representation of Personality in Ancient and Medieval Literature* (Toronto: University of Toronto Press, 1983), p. 14.

Menander and the New Comedy that it comes to denote 'the individual nature of a single person'.[20]

That trajectory, from distinctive *symbolic* mark to distinctive spoken or written style, to a distinctive set of moral qualities, and, beyond this to the representation of those qualities (in a reference or in public report) and, finally, quite late in this sequence, to the sense of 'a personality invested with distinctive attributes and qualities, by a novelist or dramatist; also, the personality or "part" assumed by an actor on the stage' (OED 17a), involves a series of metonymic transfers from the more concrete to the more abstract, without ever quite losing the sense of the impressed physical mark;[21] 'character' as letter of the alphabet or as the repeatable and combinable unit of printer's type which both represents and imprints it (a singularity that produces distinctiveness through repetition) carries through to a sense of character as something imprinted on the features— 'characters graven on thy brows';[22] 'this thy faire and outward charracter'[23] —suggesting the external, physiognomic traits of an inwardly figured personality. Hillis Miller notes a series of paradoxes in the way this semantic complex is organized. The first is that the dictionary's designation of the first seven of its nineteen meanings as 'literal' is complicated by the fact that these 'literal' marks are symbols standing for something else and are thus 'irreducibly figurative', and, conversely, 'all the so-called figurative senses distinguished by the OED are extensions, variations, or reformulations of this initial figuration'.[24] Second, and particularly in the senses that cluster around print or handwriting, there is the paradox that 'a character is both peculiar, particular, distinctive, and at the same time it is repeatable, generalizable, able to be used and reused in a variety of circumstances'.[25] And third, that initial semantic transfer between the instrument and the mark it makes is repeated in the endless flow of meanings between the moral person and the things that express it, such that 'the originally figurative meaning, in a personality or character, becomes the literal meaning of which other visible, physical meanings are the figures or projected transfers, in a perpetual round in which the *other* meaning is always the literal one and the present one a displaced, that is, nonpresent figure'.[26]

'Character' is a figure, then; at once a figure of speech and a figural representation, the figure that stands out from a narrative ground and, more generally, the human shape or form. If character is a mark made by engraving or impressing, 'figure', by contrast, is originally a shape that emerges from a hollow mould (*forma*), although it then comes (by a similar transfer from instrument to effect)

[20] Ginsberg, *Cast of Character*, p. 17.

[21] If Pope can subscribe to a reported comment that '"Most women have no Characters at all"', it is because he believes them to be made of 'Matter too soft a lasting Mark to bear.' 'Of the Characters of Women', *Moral Essays*, 'Epistle II: To a Lady', in *The Poems of Alexander Pope*, ed. John Butt (1963; rpt. London: Methuen, 1965), p. 260.

[22] Christopher Marlowe, *Tamburlaine The Great*, First Part, I.ii, cited in OED entry 1b.

[23] William Shakespeare, *Twelfth Night*, I.ii.51, cited in OED entry 10.

[24] J. Hillis Miller, *Ariadne's Thread: Story Lines* (New Haven: Yale University Press, 1992), p. 57.

[25] Miller, *Ariadne's Thread*, p. 58.

[26] Miller, *Ariadne's Thread*, p. 59.

to mean form or shape in the sense of outline, a body that stands in relief against a ground. Erich Auerbach traces the development of a more abstract sense of the Latin *figura*, in part under the influence of the Greek *schema* (σχημα), so that 'side by side with the original plastic signification and overshadowing it, there appeared a far more general concept of grammatical, rhetorical, logical, mathematical—and later even of musical and choreographic—form'.[27] Figure as shape moves in one direction towards the meanings of 'statue', 'image', and 'portrait', in another towards that of 'appearance' and of 'the deceptive likenesses that walk in dreams',[28] and, in Lucretius, it shifts from the form to its imitation, from model to copy. For Quintilian it takes on the sense of rhetorical trope, and this lays the ground for the hermeneutic meaning it acquires with the Church Fathers: that of the prefiguring of one theologically significant historical event or personage by another.

All of these senses are registered in the English word 'figure'. The first cluster (OED senses 1 through 8) covers form in the sense of outline or shape, including bodily shape and 'an embodied (human) form; a person considered with regard to visible form or appearance' (5a), as well as appearance, impression, position, distinction. The second cluster (senses 9 through 12) refers to figure as *represented* form, including fantasms; the key senses here are found in 10, 'an artificial representation of the human form', in sculpture (a statue, an image, an effigy) and in painting or drawing, where it refers to 'a representation of human form (as opposed to landscape, still life, etc.)'; and in the obsolete forms of 11, '*represented character; part enacted; hence, position, capacity*'. The third cluster (senses 13 through 16) has to do with figure as design or pattern. The fourth (senses 18 through 20) designates written characters: letters of the alphabet, musical notes, mathematical symbols, and numerical symbols. Finally, the fifth cluster (senses 21 through 24) carries the sense of the Greek *schema*: figures of speech, of language, and of logic.

In the language of heraldry, 'figure' designates the likeness of the human face (French *figure*). When we speak of figurative painting we speak of a representation of bodies, of which the face is at once necessarily a part, and yet separately the subject of its own genre, the portrait. Character in narrative fiction (which is the central concern of this book, although I look from time to time at other manifestations) is both figural and figurative: both a figure standing out from a ground and a person-shaped entity which is the subject of narrative action. Roland Barthes distinguishes the *character*, a stable cluster of meanings cumulatively assembled around the proper name and referring virtually to a body, or around the pronoun 'I', which functions like a name in assigning a biographical duration to the one who speaks it, from the *figure*, which

> is not a combination of semes concentrated in a legal Name, nor can biography, psychology, or time encompass it: it is an illegal, impersonal, anachronistic configuration of symbolic relationships. As figure, the character can oscillate between two roles, without this oscillation having any meaning, for it occurs outside biographical time

[27] Erich Auerbach, 'Figura', trans. Ralph Manheim, in *Scenes from the Drama of European Literature* (Minneapolis: University of Minnesota Press, 1984), p. 15.

[28] Auerbach, 'Figura', p. 21.

> (outside chronology): the symbolic structure is completely reversible: it can be read in any direction...As a symbolic ideality, the character has no chronological or biographical standing; he has no Name; he is nothing but a site for the passage (and return) of the figure.[29]

A similar distinction—one that engages the 'daemonic' or 'allotropic' dimensions of fictional character—is at the heart of Gilles Deleuze's essay on Francis Bacon, which explores the limits of figurative representation.

'A round area,' Deleuze writes, 'often delimits the place where the person—that is to say, the Figure —is seated, lying down, doubled over, or in some other position.'[30] This is a technique for isolating the Figure from its surroundings; others that Bacon uses include placing the Figure in a cube, or against a bar, or combining some or all of these three spaces. The isolation of the Figure is a strategy 'to avoid the *figurative, illustrative*, and *narrative* character the Figure would necessarily have if it were not isolated'; if painting is not to embrace 'pure form through abstraction', it will oppose 'the 'figural' to the figurative' (p. 6).

In Deleuze's analysis, figuration is at once a structure of representation (the relation of an image to an object that it supposedly illustrates) and, since it implies the relation of one image to another, a structure of causality or narration. The isolation of the Figure is a way of thwarting this tendency of images to form chains and to imply a structural whole. The entire work of a painter like Bacon who eschews pure abstraction is one of extracting the Figure from the figurative: of refusing narrative and a representational aesthetic. Yet figuration as such never disappears: there is a 'secondary figuration' (the image of a screaming Pope, for example) which nevertheless 'depends on the neutralization of all primary figuration' (p. 34): a neutralization of the representational and narrative clichés which are the starting point of the painter's work. Thus,

> we never cease to trip over the objection of fact: the Figure is still figurative; it still represents someone (a screaming man, a smiling man, a seated man), it still narrates something, even if it is a surrealistic tale (head-umbrella-meat, howling meat...). We can now say that the opposition of the Figure to the figurative exists in a very complex relationship, and yet is not practically compromised or even attenuated by this relationship. There is a first, prepictorial figuration: it is on the canvas and in the painter's head, in what the painter wants to do, before the painter begins, in the form of clichés and probabilities. This first figuration cannot be completely eliminated; something of it is always conserved. But there is a second figuration: the one that the painter obtains, this time as a result of the Figure, as an effect of the pictorial act. (p. 79)

Between the two there is a 'deformation', a qualitative change in which the Figure emerges in its own, non-figurative right.

If we were to extrapolate from the pictorial to narrative fiction, we might say that the Figure corresponds to the textual ground of narration, underpinning and preceding it; it would be a pre-mimetic ontological level, not in contradiction with

[29] Roland Barthes, *S/Z*, trans. Richard Howard (New York: Hill and Wang, 1974), p. 68.

[30] Gilles Deleuze, *Francis Bacon: The Logic of Sensation*, trans. Daniel W. Smith (Minneapolis: University of Minnesota Press, 2003), p. 5. Hereafter cited in the text.

narration or representation but of a different order. In terms of character, it would correspond to that allotropic state—the elemental carbon—that lies deeper than the forms of individuated selfhood that bear the names of the quasi-persons of fiction. Another way of putting this would be to define the figure, as Stephen Heath does for cinema, in contradistinction to the *agent* (an entity defined functionally at the level of plot), the *character* (the individualized expression of agency and the bearer of a set of moral qualities), the *person* who, in cinema or the theatre, actualizes character (usually an actor), and the *image* ('the person, the body, in its conversion into the luminous sense of its film presence').[31] The figure then would be 'the circulation between agent, character, person and image, none of which is able simply and uniquely to contain, to *settle* that circulation, the figure it makes in a film. What obtain are specific regimes of the articulation of the different instances'.[32] It is these instances and their articulation that are the subject of the remainder of this chapter.

III

Think of a map; then draw a line to designate a particular passage across it. The map, and pathways designating the kinds of route that can be taken across it, are spatial and achronic, but once an actual route is charted we can ask questions about the time frame within which someone or something travels relative to the time frame of the observer, and we can also ask questions about the kind of reality defining its path. The map and the path across it, says Jurij Lotman, are a model of a narrative text, and this model has three levels: the level of the plotless semantic structure, the level of possible actions in relation to it, and the level of concrete action. Action is undertaken by a persona who is the intersection of a number of structural functions. Thus,

> the mandatory elements of any plot will include: 1) some semantic field divided into two mutually complementary subsets; 2) the border between these subsets, which, under normal circumstances, is impenetrable, though in a given instance (a text with a plot always deals with a *given* instance) it proves to be penetrable for the hero-agent; 3) the hero-agent.[33]

The initial moment of any plot is a differentiation of the agent from the semantic field surrounding it; the plot is set in motion when the agent crosses the edge of that field, which takes the form of an obstacle to be overcome: 'The "adversaries" in a fairy tale, the waves and winds and currents hostile to Odysseus, the false friends in a picaresque novel or the false clues in a detective novel' are structurally identical in functioning as impediments to movement from one semantic field to another.[34]

[31] Stephen Heath, 'Body, Voice', in *Questions of Cinema* (London: Macmillan, 1981), p. 181.

[32] Heath, 'Body, Voice', p. 182.

[33] Jurij Lotman, *The Structure of the Artistic Text*, trans. Ronald Vroon (Ann Arbor: Michigan Slavic Contributions, University of Michigan, 1977), p. 240.

[34] Lotman, *Structure of the Artistic Text*, pp. 240–1.

Once the agent has crossed the border it enters another semantic field, and either merges with it, becoming immobile (in marriage, victory, or death, for example), or continues to be mobile in relation to this new field. Plot functions are usually given human shape, but they may be inanimate or non-human; human agents may be seen to be driven by forces beyond them: the gods, Satan, unconscious desires.[35] Similarly, the obstacles to be overcome may be physical, or they may be other human beings.

If the persona (the agent) is a bundle of plot functions, a character is a paradigm constructed cumulatively across the length of a text as successive sets of semantic differentiation from other characters, generated in relation to culturally specific typologies, defined both by the words the character speaks and by words spoken about him, and unified as a composite and complex entity.[36] The agent is defined by the actions it undertakes; the character by the way these actions are endowed with meaning as the agent acts or is acted upon, speaks or is spoken about in the network of relations that the text establishes.

Lotman's analysis draws directly on the tradition of structuralist analysis that derives from Vladimir Propp's account of the fusion of roles and actions in the *motif* and from the Russian Formalists' concept of the motivation of the device.[37] Propp's *Morphology of the Folk Tale*, published in 1928, analysed the basic elements of folkloric narrative into thirty-one functions (generalized forms of action such as interdiction, interrogation, or flight, considered in abstraction from the characters who perform them) and seven basic character types: the *hero*; the *villain*; the *donor*, who prepares the hero for his quest; the *helper*, who assists the hero; the *princess* and her *father* (the two are structurally merged) who set the hero on his quest and reward him with marriage when it is completed; the *dispatcher*, who sends the hero on his way; and the *false hero* or *usurper*.[38] Propp's argument, influenced by the linguistic model of grammatical categories working as empty slots that are filled with variable lexical content in sentences, is that the multiplicity of characters appearing in folk tales can be reduced to this underlying typology, not all of the elements of which will necessarily be present, and some of which may be merged: 'The number of functions is extremely small, whereas the number of personages is extremely large.'[39] Although Propp's typology is, by definition, reductive, and thus doesn't attempt to do justice to the texture, tone, and particularity of the tales he analyses, the power of this reading lies in its capacity to isolate general patterns in narrative: to move beyond the detail of a text to the abstract formal structures composing it.

[35] On the relation between persons and forces in narrative, cf. Didier Coste, *Narrative as Communication* (Minneapolis: University of Minnesota Press, 1989), pp. 148–50.

[36] Lotman, *Structure of the Artistic Text*, pp. 254–5.

[37] E.g. Boris Tomashevsky, 'Thematics' (1925), in L. Lemon and M. Reis (trans. and eds), *Russian Formalist Criticism* (Lincoln: University of Nebraska Press, 1965), pp. 61–95.

[38] Vladimir Propp, *Morphology of the Folktale*, trans. Lawrence Scott (2nd edn, Austin: University of Texas Press, 1968).

[39] Propp, *Morphology of the Folktale*, p. 20.

Following Propp, writers such as A. J. Greimas, Claude Bremond, Philippe Souriau, Roland Barthes, and Tzvetan Todorov sought to construct a grammar of narrative which would specify a typology of roles from which characters are generated. The dominant tone is caught in Charles Grivel's thesis that '*le personnage (comme le nom l'indique) n'est personne*':[40] character is no one/is not a person. Grivel's Aristotelian reduction of character to a function of plot generates a demystificatory rhetoric in which the role of the character form is to introduce compositional non-conformity or disturbance, but also to enable the restoration of compositional order. That reduction is also evident in Greimas's influential concept of the *actant*: the slot or character-class defined by a permanent group of functions and qualities and by their distribution through a narrative; the term carefully refuses to distinguish between human and non-human actors. His schema posits the following general narrative logic:[41]

sender → object → receiver
↑
helper → subject ← opponent

In its focus on a logic of actions, however, this unpromisingly general typology lacks the universality it claims, and, like Propp's, it neglects all of those thematic and structural functions performed by narrative agents—such as thinking and perceiving—that are ancillary to the movement of the plot, serving to qualify the agent rather than to develop the action. Paul Ricoeur notes, too, the epistemological problems associated with 'the enterprise of dechronologizing narrative structures'.[42]

An associated strand of analysis works with syntactic models for the construction of a (metaphoric) grammar of narrative. Thus, Todorov defines character in terms of the proper name, which is initially 'blank' and is then filled with semes or predications.[43] Later versions of this model have tended to deal either with the anaphoric or co-referential function of proper names and pronouns,[44] or with the propositional logic of predication and attribution.[45] Pierre Glaudes and Yves Reuter's model of a narrative 'kernel' is built around the modal structure of the verb, and specifically the modalities of wanting and being-able (*vouloir/pouvoir*).[46] Philippe Hamon's synthetic account of a structuralist theory of fictional character, 'Pour un statut sémiologique du personnage', on which Glaudes and Reuter partly draw, offers an initial definition of the 'textual character effect' in terms of three modes of existence of character, corresponding to referential, deictic, and

40 Charles Grivel, *Production de l'intérêt romanesque* (The Hague: Mouton, 1973), p. 113.

41 A. J. Greimas, 1986. 'Réflexions sur les modèles actantiels', in *Sémantique structurale* (Paris: Larousse, 1966), p. 180.

42 Paul Ricoeur, *Oneself as Another*, trans. Kathleen Blamey (Chicago: University of Chicago Press, 1992), p. 146, n. 10.

43 Tzvetan Todorov, *Grammaire du Décaméron* (The Hague: Mouton, 1969), p. 28.

44 For example, François Corblin, 'Les désignateurs dans les romans', *Poétique* 54 (1983), pp. 199–211.

45 For example, James Garvey, 'Characterisation in Narrative', *Poetics* 7 (1978), pp. 63–78.

46 Pierre Glaudes and Yves Reuter, *Le Personnage* (Paris: PUF, 1998), pp. 53–4.

anaphoric forms of signification. *Referential* signs designate historical, mythological, or allegorical figures, or social types; *deictic* signs, or shifters, are the marks of the presence of the author, the reader, or their delegates: narrators, chorus figures, 'ficelles' who convey information to or receive it from the protagonist, and so on; and *anaphoric* reference ties a narrative together both through reference back to established figures and through time-shifting devices such as flashbacks and anticipations.[47] The signified of character, its 'value', is constituted not only by repetition, accumulation, and transformation, but also by its oppositional relation to other characters (p. 128). This definition—purely formal as it is—sets up the possibility of establishing a calculus of the features, the 'characteristics' which represent the basic components of character. To this end Hamon constructs a number of tables which yield a differential analysis of qualities, functions, and modes of determination of character. Let me paraphrase his summary. A character can be defined:

(a) by the way it relates to the functions it fulfils;
(b) by its simple or complex integration in classes of character types, or *actants*;
(c) as an *actant*, by the way it relates to other *actants* within well-defined types of sequences and figures (for example, 'quest' or 'contract');
(d) by its relation to a series of modalities ('wanting', 'knowing', 'being able' [*pouvoir*]);
(e) by its distribution within the whole narrative;
(f) by the bundle of qualities and thematic 'roles' which it supports.

The theoretical consequence of this definition is that, insofar as character is 'a recurrent element, a permanent support of distinctive features and narrative transformations, it combines both the factors which are indispensable to the *coherence* and *readability* of any text, and the factors which are indispensable to its stylistic *interest*' (pp. 141–2). This then leads to a final definition of character: as 'a system of rule-governed equivalences intended to ensure the readability of the text' (p. 144); and the question of the system of values which make a text readable is dealt with through a definition of the hero as the bearer of restrictions and combinations at the stylistic and cultural levels (p. 151).

In fact, this remains a purely formal definition. The proliferation of combinatories in Hamon's text indicates that the theory is additive rather than analytic, and this lack of economy is one reason why it does not, in fact, account for the way character works to ensure the readability of texts. In short, the theory does not account for the textual conditions of existence of characters as quasi-subjects, and for the activity of the reader in the constitution of these represented subjects. Hamon does argue that character 'is as much a reconstruction by the reader as it

[47] Philippe Hamon, 'Pour un statut sémiologique du personnage', in Roland Barthes, Wolfgang Kayser, Wayne Booth, and Philippe Hamon, *Poétique du récit* (Paris: Seuil, 1977), pp. 122–4. Hereafter cited in the text, in my translation.

is a textual construct' (p. 119), but, like later cognitive theories of text processing,[48] his model does little to explain the affective force of the imaginary unities of character.

Structuralist narratology now looks dated; its attempt to construct a rigorous account of textual functions on the basis of linguistic models which were themselves rapidly becoming obsolete is no longer a theoretically viable or, indeed, interesting project. Its insistence upon the textuality of character and its assertion of the irreducibility of character to person rest upon an assumption that the two are quite different: the person or subject cannot itself be thought in textual terms. And Jonathan Culler's criticism seems unanswerable: structuralist theorists view the usual primacy given to character as an ideological prejudice, rather than trying to *account* for it.[49]

Yet that insistence upon the verbal conditions of existence of narrative personae was, we should not forget, the consequence of a refusal of the representational criticism that went before it (and still survives it): a criticism that asked what kind of person Emma Woodhouse was, or whether Werther was to be pitied or condemned. This is that dominant mode of criticism that Fredric Jameson calls 'ethical', by which he means an 'essentially psychological or psychologizing' mode of interpretation, 'even where it appeals for its authority to this or that version of psychoanalysis',[50] and which deals in notions of personal identity, of the quest for self,[51] and of the unification (or, I would add, the scattering) of the self understood as a self-contained entity.[52] The methodology of ethical analysis is, at its simplest (for example in the 'character appreciation' that is at the heart of much of the literature syllabus in secondary schools), the discussion of the moral make-up (the

[48] For example, Catherine Emmott, *Narrative Comprehension: A Discourse Perspective* (Oxford: Oxford University Press, 1997); Jonathan Culpepper, *Language and Characterisation: People in Plays and Other Texts* (London: Longman, 2001); Aleide Fokkema, *Postmodern Characters: A Study of Characterization in British and American Postmodern Fiction* (Amsterdam: Rodopi, 1991); Fotis Jannidis, *Figur und Person: Beitrag zu einer historischen Narratologie* (Berlin: de Gruyter, 2004).

[49] Jonathan Culler, *Structuralist Poetics* (Ithaca: Cornell University Press, 1975), p. 230. Cf. Alexander Gelley, 'Character and Person: On the Presentation of Self in the Novel', in *Narrative Crossings: Theory and Pragmatics of Prose Fiction* (Baltimore: Johns Hopkins University Press, 1987), p. 60: '[I]f the notion of the existential autonomy and psychological fullness of characters in the novel represents an illusion, it is one that has not been simply manufactured by critics but that has been inextricably bound up with the evolution of the genre since the eighteenth century.'

[50] Fredric Jameson, *The Political Unconscious: Narrative as a Socially Symbolic Act* (London: Methuen, 1981), p. 60.

[51] Thus, Arnold Weinstein describes the thematics of the seventeenth- and eighteenth-century novel as 'the varieties and problems of self-realization; the search for freedom against the constraints of society and contingency', and all novels subsequent to *Lazarillo de Tormes* as 'fictions of self-realization' which 'constitute a tribute to the self's powers of creation and preservation' and 'aggrandize our sense of the human'. Arnold Weinstein, *Fictions of the Self: 1550–1800* (Princeton: Princeton University Press, 1981), pp. vii, 10, 11.

[52] Martin Price, one of the more thoughtful humanist critics, draws upon Clark's distinction between nudity and nakedness to establish the conventionality of character, even as he stresses the (organic) body as the source of perceptions of 'the wholeness of the self'. Martin Price, *Forms of Life: Character and Moral Imagination in the Novel* (New Haven: Yale University Press, 1983), pp. 38–9.

ēthos) of characters, as though they were acquaintances whose virtues and shortcomings one were dissecting.

One face of ethical criticism involves the widespread use of the notion of 'story' or 'narrative' to define the formation and coherence of the self: 'Man is in his actions and practice, as well as in his fictions, essentially a story-telling animal,' writes Alasdair MacIntyre in *After Virtue*,[53] and it is a line that is repeated in philosophical and psychological texts by Oliver Sacks, Jerome Bruner, Charles Taylor, Paul Ricoeur, and innumerable others.[54] The other face is that of the liberal doctrine of the freely self-governing and self-shaping individual, with its positing of a direct continuity between moral and literary character. John Stuart Mill writes in *On Liberty* that 'a person whose desires and impulses are his own—are the expression of his own nature, as it has been developed and modified by his own culture—is said to have a character. One whose desires and impulses are not his own, has no character, no more than a steam-engine has a character'.[55] Character here is predicated on the ownership and control of the self, and this classically liberal conception of the moral self underlies the understanding of literary character as the representation of autonomous, unified, and self-identical subjects (or, in 'transgressive' versions of the doxa, as representations of a dispersed, decentred self which is, nevertheless, still the narrative core and the central object of analysis).[56] Character in this sense is a resource for moral analysis and is closely tied to literary pedagogies in which the analysis of ethical issues and dilemmas relating to literary figures—'what was the fatal flaw in Hamlet's character?'—forms the basis of an institutionalized practice for constructing 'moral selves or good personal character'.[57] The moral selves of fictional characters reflect and help shape our own; there is 'full congruity between the way we perceive people in literature and the way we perceive them in life'.[58] The theoretical challenge to which this post-Kantian understanding of character responds is that of establishing a set of analytic categories which will have explanatory validity both in terms of the constitution of moral subjects and in terms of the effects of unity which are the precondition of literary character. Its genre of choice is the novel, which, more than any other genre, facilitates the detachment of the represented self from the events in which it is embedded, and thus allows that represented self to be the point of the stories told about it. The price paid for the continuity between character and person is that

[53] Alasdair MacIntyre, *After Virtue: A Study in Moral Theory* (3rd edn, Notre Dame, IN: University of Notre Dame Press, 2007), p. 216.

[54] Oliver Sacks, *The Man Who Mistook his Wife for a Hat* (London: Duckworth, 1985); Jerome Bruner, 'Life as Narrative', *Social Research* 54 (1987), pp. 11–32; Charles Taylor, *Sources of the Self: The Making of the Modern Identity* (Cambridge, MA: Harvard University Press, 1989); Paul Ricoeur, *Oneself as Another*. For a critique, cf. Galen Strawson, 'Against Narrativity', *Ratio* (new series) 17 (2004), pp. 428–52.

[55] Cited in the OED entry on 'character', 12a.

[56] For example, Hélène Cixous, 'The Character of "Character"', trans. Keith Cohen, *New Literary History* 5: 2 (1974), pp. 383–402.

[57] Ian Hunter, 'Reading Character', *Southern Review* 16: 2 (1983), p. 233.

[58] Baruch Hochman, *Character in Literature* (Ithaca: Cornell University Press, 1985), p. 44.

both must be thought in terms of presence—of 'real' personhood—rather than in terms of textuality.

The other main assumption of ethical theory is that of the excess of character over the formal means of its representation. This is the concept of that 'immense residue' that Culler finds left over in the structuralist analysis of narrative roles,[59] and it is the source of Shlomith Rimmon-Kenan's question as to whether changing notions of character 'can... be seen as nevertheless leaving some constitutive characteristics recognisable'.[60] The effect of supplementarity is theorized by Barthes in *S/Z*, where it is identified precisely as an ideology of the person, one which allows the whole to be perceived as greater than its parts:

> What gives the illusion that the sum [of attributes] is supplemented by a precious remainder (something like *individuality*, in that, qualitative and ineffable, it may escape the vulgar bookkeeping of compositional characters) is the Proper Name, the difference completed by what is proper to it. The proper name enables the person to exist outside the semes, whose sum nonetheless constitutes it entirely.[61]

Yet Barthes does not simply dismiss the residue effect, the illusion of plenitude conveyed by the proper name, but rather seeks to explain the quasi-autonomy of fictional subjects in terms of the codes which constitute it and the texts which traverse it. Chatman, who quotes this passage, misses its critical point completely, taking the effect of the proper name to be 'the identity or quintessence of selfhood property' (sic), 'a kind of ultimate residence of personality'.[62] In this he repeats a certain mysticism of the self which is characteristic of humanist theory and which is precisely spelled out in a manual for writers of fiction: 'Characterization is a complex and elusive art and cannot be reduced to exact rules or to a comprehensive statement. The more we talk about it, the more we feel has been left out, and this is necessarily so because the human personality remains a mystery, subject to obscure forces; it is a universe in itself and we are strangers even to ourselves...'[63]

IV

One way of moving beyond the tied dichotomy of structuralist reduction and humanist plenitude (of the *actant* and the fully human character) is to recognize that these models of fictional agency apply to different objects, and thus to recast them as distinct *levels* of analysis. This is the strategy Mieke Bal follows in positing three distinct levels at which fictional figures can be studied: as ' "actor" in the

[59] Culler, *Structuralist Poetics*, p. 232.

[60] Shlomith Rimmon-Kenan, *Narrative Fiction: Contemporary Poetics* (London: Methuen, 1983), p. 31.

[61] Barthes, *S/Z*, p. 191.

[62] Seymour Chatman, *Story and Discourse: Narrative Structure in Fiction and Film* (Ithaca: Cornell University Press, 1978), p. 131.

[63] Leon Surmelian, *Techniques of Fiction Writing: Measure and Madness* (New York: Doubleday, 1968), p. 139.

study of the fabula, "character" in the study of the story, and "speaker" in the study of the text' (where 'fabula' is the simple chronological sequence reconstructed in reading from the 'story').[64] Like Lotman, she understands actors (agents) as plot functions, whereas 'a character is the effect that occurs when an actor is endowed with distinctive human characteristics. In this view, an actor is a structural position, while a character is a complex semantic unit. But as readers, we "see" characters, only reducible to actors in a process of abstraction'.[65]

A similar functional differentiation of modes of analysis is made by Uri Margolin in the series of papers written over more than twenty years in which he has elaborated an account of fictional character on the basis of modal logic and the semantics of possible worlds. Part of the strength of Margolin's theoretical frame is its ability to situate itself in relation to, and to incorporate, a number of other models, including text linguistics, aesthetics, pragmatics, semiotics, and the theory of action. Distinguishing between the mimetic and the non-mimetic, he writes that non-mimetic theories 'refuse to go beyond the textual, intensional, or semiotic profile of the narrative discourse'.[66] The major mimetic paradigms, by contrast, focus on the ways in which character functions as a human or human-like entity; Margolin identifies them as *cognitive* (the construction of mental models of person-like characters), *communicative* (character as narrative instance or level), and *semantic* (possible-worlds theory).[67] These theories, he writes, are semantically heterogeneous and thus irreducible to a common denominator or a synthesis; each has its own legitimacy. Each serves distinct analytic interests, and each tends to work best when applied to particular genres. If his own preference is for a semantic account of characters as non-actual individuals, this is because it 'is arguably the closest to our cultural intuition', it is able (unlike the structuralist model of the *actant*) to deal with mental states and states of affairs, and yet it is, nevertheless, not naïvely mimetic since it insists on the non-actual ontological status of character.[68]

Margolin's theoretical starting point is thus a description of the ontological conditions of possibility of imagined and imaginary beings, from which he then derives the logical scaffolding that sustains them:

> Fictive entities are... the product of the discourse which posits or projects them and are essentially dependent on their textual constitutive conditions: logico-semantic, epistemic, and text-grammatical. The existence of a text is an essential enabling condition for imagining any literary entity, and the specific selection and combination of textual elements confers on it existence and determines its nature. At the same time, and with the exception of meta-fictional texts, literary narratives are structured in such a way as to create an illusion that they are reports about individuals and domains of

[64] Mieke Bal, *Narratology: Introduction to the Theory of Narrative* (2nd edn, Toronto: University of Toronto Press, 1997), p. 9.

[65] Bal, *Narratology*, p. 115.

[66] Uri Margolin, 'Character', in David Herman, Manfred Jahn, and Marie-Laure Ryan (eds), *Routledge Encyclopedia of Narrative Theory* (London: Routledge, 2005), p. 56.

[67] Margolin, 'Character', *Routledge Encyclopedia*, p. 53.

[68] Uri Margolin, 'Structuralist Approaches to Character in Narrative: The State of the Art', *Semiotica* 75: 1/2 (1989), p. 10.

> reference which are not themselves linguistic and which have been in existence prior to these texts, separately from them, and independently of them.[69]

The use of the preterite tense in narrative, for example, generates this effect of pre- and extratextual existence, but so does using a range of devices which mimic the operation of reference in actual worlds. Singular referring expressions (personal pronouns, definite descriptions, and proper names) play a key role in establishing the existence of non-actual individuals.[70] Possible-worlds semantics thus deals with the operations (on the part of the text and, correspondingly, on the part of the reader) by which properties are ascribed to these quasi-persons who are members of some non-actual state of affairs, which may be 'very close or very far from the actual world in terms of properties and regularities'.[71] Unlike actual individuals, fictional characters are schematic, radically incomplete, and thus 'underdetermined':[72] the text of *Anna Karenin* gives us all the information about its heroine that we will ever have.

If fictive entities are to be brought into being and sustained through one or more states of affairs (and narrative, by definition, involves more than a single state), a set of minimal conditions of representation must be observed. First, a set of referring expressions must ascribe existence and modal status within a given narrative domain and, second, the narrative acts of identification and qualification of that entity must ascribe to it (with more or less authority and reliability) a set of properties (minimally, one property) which establish the character's identity. Third, the character must be differentiated from other characters. Fourth, the properties ascribed to the character must be organized to form a coherent set. Finally, the character must be shown to be continuous across different states of affairs.[73] Each of these conditions may be breached: 'realist' narratives satisfy all five, 'modernist' narratives only the first three, and 'postmodernist' narratives may satisfy none. In J. M. G. Le Clézio's novels, for example, the continuity of the proper name may be associated with semantic discontinuity and thus the absence of any stable set of coherent properties. In Virginia Woolf's *The Waves*, 'at each story state the six narrative agents involved are interchangeable in terms of their inner states, while the properties of all of them are radically discontinuous between successive states'.[74] And in Samuel Beckett's *Trilogy*,

[69] Uri Margolin, 'Characters in Literary Narrative: Representation and Signification', *Semiotica* 106: 3/4 (1995), p. 383.

[70] Uri Margolin, 'Naming and Believing: Practices of the Proper Name in Narrative Fiction', *Narrative* 10: 2 (2002), p. 108.

[71] Uri Margolin, 'Character', in David Herman (ed.), *The Cambridge Companion to Narrative* (Cambridge: Cambridge University Press, 2007), p. 71.

[72] Uri Margolin, 'Introducing and Sustaining Characters in Literary Narrative: A Set of Conditions', *Style* 21: 1 (1987), p. 108.

[73] Margolin, 'Introducing and Sustaining Characters', pp. 111–21. This is the fullest account of these conditions; later papers give more summary versions, and I have silently incorporated several modifications of the base model.

[74] Margolin, 'Introducing and Sustaining Characters', p. 121.

> the puzzling narrative agents... are subject to the twin operations of fission and fusion. In the first, a single individual persists over a series of states, where he is endowed with a proper name and a property set. But at one particular story state the property set is split into two or more subjects, each of which is given from this point onwards a label or proper name of its own, turning it into a separate individual. Conversely, two or more separate individuals, each with his own unique name and property set, are fused at some point in the narrative sequence into a single individual, possessing from this point onward one proper name, as well as the conjunction of their property sets.[75]

Each of the five conditions of representation corresponds to a set of operations performed by readers processing schematic information to infer patterns which are both general (cultural or generic character types) and specific (a coherent organization of inferences to build up a more or less unified character construct through operations of naming, sorting, the inferring of second-order properties, the determination of the temporal extent and intensity of traits or the significant absence of traits, the rank ordering of features, the hierarchization of categories, and the construction of a global frame).[76] The reader's mapping of character is integrated within knowledge structures which include scripts, schemata, and stereotypes drawn from both cultural and literary spheres, and these spheres may be in tension with each other.[77] The resulting construct is then integrated through successive frames with one of a number of modalities of change: an *absence* of change as successive states of affairs extend and diversify the character's property set; singular progressive change, as in the *Bildungsroman* where a character develops continuously and incrementally; an abrupt but semantically related change through, for example, religious conversion; and 'abrupt, iterative, and semantically unrestricted (random) change of most or all core properties of a narrative agent' in a way that establishes no coherent pattern and makes character 'unreadable'.[78]

In addition to temporal continuity or discontinuity within a storyworld, a character may have an existence across a plurality of storyworlds or in another domain of the same storyworld:[79] Eugène de Rastignac is a minor character in Balzac's *Les Illusions Perdues* but a primary character in *Le Père Goriot* and a number of other novels in the *Comédie Humaine* series. Don Juan and Faust are the protagonists of innumerable literary and operatic texts. The name Napoleon designates both an actual person (a person designated by historical texts with a claim to truth status) and a character in Tolstoy's *War and Peace* and in countless other fictional texts. Sherlock Holmes is a character both in a series of stories by Arthur Conan Doyle and in numerous film adaptations and literary parodies. In each case what matters is both the storyworld within which the character is constructed and the intra-,

75 Margolin, 'Introducing and Sustaining Characters', p. 121.

76 Margolin, 'Structuralist Approaches to Character in Narrative', p. 17.

77 Margolin, 'Character', *Routledge Encyclopedia*, p. 55.

78 Margolin, 'Structuralist Approaches to Character in Narrative', p. 19.

79 Uri Margolin, 'Characters and their Versions', in Calin-Andrei Mihailescu and Walid Hamarneh (eds), *Fiction Updated: Theories of Fictionality, Narratology, and Poetics* (Toronto: University of Toronto Press, 1996), p. 113.

inter-, and extratextual relations that storyworld maintains with other possible worlds.

The ontological foundation which underpins this model is, Margolin insists, essential to any modelling of fictional character.[80] Yet the strengths of his approach—its heuristic distinction between the actual and the non-actual—are exactly its point of weakness: necessary and fruitful as that distinction is, it makes it ultimately impossible to think of 'actual' persons as in some, very real sense 'fictional', imaginary or at least imagined. It assumes the actual as a stable ontological horizon, and it thereby makes the 'fictional'—paradoxically—more fictive, less actual, than it needs to be.

Establishing the representational conditions of existence of a fictional world allows us to understand it as a compositional domain which sustains a represented world, and thus to raise the question of the role played by characters in shaping its compositional coherence. The question is at the heart of Henry James's attempt to replace the shapelessness of the 'loose baggy monsters' of nineteenth-century fiction by a restriction of the flow of information to the perspective of a single character, as well as by the symmetrical patterning of characters that becomes a hallmark of his late novels. But the question of formal coherence is already an issue for Aristotle in his analysis of the differences in the way fictional and historical narratives are shaped:

> As to the poetic imitation which is narrative in form ... [it] should have for its subject a single action, whole and complete, with a beginning, a middle and an end. It will thus resemble a living organism in all its unity, and produce the pleasure appropriate to it. It will differ in structure from historical compositions, which of necessity present not a single action, but a single period, and all that happened in that period to one person or to many (ενα η πλειουζ), little connected as the events may be.[81]

In his commentary on this passage, Alex Woloch notes that beneath the formal question—'how can a single composition have many parts?'—there is a second question about how a multiplicity of represented persons can be contained within a coherent narrative: a question that concerns 'not only the textual arrangement of multiple elements but also the social balancing and comprehension of multiple characters or persons' (p. 1). This is a question about what it means for a character to be central to the plot (the 'hero') or to be secondary (a 'minor' character). The simple answer to this question is that a narrative like the *Iliad*, which is Aristotle's reference point here, tells a story about *both* the one *and* the many: both Achilles and the multitude of participants in the Trojan War. But this answer, says Woloch, obscures, on the one hand, the flows of attention and neglect which position characters in the narrative, and, on the other, the fact that to be a 'minor' character is not simply to have a lesser role but is a kind of identity: Thersites, 'perhaps the

[80] Uri Margolin, 'Individuals in Narrative Worlds: An Ontological Perspective', *Poetics Today* 11: 4 (1990), p. 845.

[81] Aristotle, *Poetics*, §1459a; cited in Alex Woloch, *The One vs. the Many: Minor Characters and the Space of the Protagonist in the Novel* (Princeton: Princeton University Press, 2003), p. 1. Hereafter cited in the text.

first truly minor character in Western literature' (p. 4), is defined by characteristics (his disruptive talkativeness, his physical ugliness) which mark his narrative subordination as thematic: he represents something like the potential disruptiveness of the crowd.

Woloch proposes two categories, the *character space* and the *character system*, as tools for analysing the distribution of narrative attention. The first holds in tension 'our sense of the character as an actual human placed within an imagined world and the space of the character within the narrative structure', and thus carries with it a sense that 'the implied person behind any character is never directly reflected in the literary text but only partially inflected' (p. 13). This is that effect of supplementarity, the excess of character over the formal means of its representation, that Barthes says has the function precisely of disguising the textuality of character; and Woloch's vocabulary oscillates between the two poles that make up the character space: the anthropomorphic and the structural, the 'individual human personality' and the 'determined space and position within the narrative as a whole' (p. 14). The second category, the character system, has as its object 'the arrangement of multiple and differentiated character-spaces—differentiated configurations and manipulations of the human figure—into a unified narrative structure' (p. 14). These two terms open up an extended analysis of the distribution of attention between protagonist and minor characters in three bodies of novelistic work: those of Jane Austen, Charles Dickens, and Honoré de Balzac.[82]

The central feature of the character system of the nineteenth-century novel is that 'any character *can* be a protagonist, but only one character is',[83] and this fact gives rise either to an asymmetrical division or to an interchangeability of central and peripheral places. Jane Austen's work exemplifies the former: the authority of her omniscient and impersonal narrative style allows her to construct a pattern of psychological and moral contrasts in which human beings come to function as abstract qualities, in such a way that the inwardness of the protagonist comes at the expense of the minor characters who are 'ever more distorted, and diminished' (p. 68), compressed into a synecdoche which represents the sum of their being. Such a compression is also a feature of Dickens's 'panoply of eccentrics and grotesques', but his novels seek to bring them to the centre of attention by increasing their distortion. Balzac, by contrast, 'in an attempt to give every character potential roundness, bursts apart the seams of *La Comédie humaine*', with a minor character in one novel becoming a major character in another (p. 35).

It is in the systematic analysis of Dickens' work that Woloch's approach is most successful, since the notion of a character system allows him to pose the question, not of what specific characters 'stand for' but rather: '*why are minor characters made to stand for so much in the first place*?' (p. 127; emphasis in original). Certainly the minor characters (of which the two prototypes are the automaton or worker, and

[82] The concept of a character system had previously been articulated by Fredric Jameson in *The Political Unconscious* (pp. 161, 166–7), where it designates an underlying 'semic system', analysable by means of a Greimasian semiotic rectangle, from which surface character effects are generated.

[83] Woloch, *The One vs. the Many*, p. 31.

the eccentric) fulfil a range of structural and thematic functions, but more important is the way Dickens 'dramatizes the *écartement* between a minor character's function and his or her own fictional being, showing how the very subordinated nature of minor characters catalyses new kinds of affective presence' (p. 128): it is precisely the insignificance of minor characters that gives them their force vis-à-vis the protagonist. Unlike both Austen and Balzac, where characters *become* minor—that is, are always endowed with the potential *not* to be minor—a Dickensian character like Uriah Heep is 'always already flat, eccentric, exaggerated, a parody of himself' (p. 146); in a world of rigid segmentation and specialization, social processes harden into substantive physical phenomena: twisted bodies, facial features, characteristic gestures, but, above all, the eccentricity of language. This substantialization is, at the same time, a removal of character from history: a reflection of the division of labour which is at once homologous with character and concealed by it.[84]

Underlying Woloch's systemic attempt to overcome the poles of structuralist reduction and humanist plenitude, however, is a deeply problematic insistence on the fullness of being that underlies character, a sense that the asymmetry of attention to major and minor characters somehow represents a repression of the 'potentially full human beings' of narrative (p. 44). In formal terms this is expressed as the opposition between discourse and story (the hypothetical sequence of events reconstructed from the actual narrative: what Mieke Bal follows the Russian Formalists in calling the 'fabula'), where story is taken to be a state of potentiality which is then restricted and impoverished by its realization in discourse. In the tension between these two moments, narratives invite us to reconstruct a pattern of attention which 'is at odds with, or divergent from, the formed pattern of attention in the discourse', in such a way that the text 'creates... disjunctions between the attention the discourse grants certain characters and the attention that they would grant themselves—that the reader might grant them' (p. 41): might grant them, that is, were they *in fact* persons. The restriction of potential that is the operative condition of minor status opens up a 'gap between a minor character's implied being and the manifestation of this being in the fictional universe' (p. 24). But, of course, that 'implied being' is no more than a function of the fictional universe; and Woloch's constant slide from the concept of character to that of person repeats the gesture of ethical criticism that imagines the quasi-persons of narrative to be somehow extricable from the texts in which they fully exist.

Philippe Hamon similarly works with a notion of the systemic organization of character in his reading of the 'système des personnages' in Zola's Rougon-Macquart series, and similarly seeks to distance his analysis both from a conflation of a psychological and personalizing conception of the fictional character with the person understood as individual subject, and from the temptations of a purely formal (logical or mathematical) metalanguage.[85] One of the difficulties of theorizing

[84] Woloch appeals in a footnote (p. 349, n. 11) to Lucien Goldmann's postulation of a 'rigorous homology' between the structure of capitalism and the novel as a narrative form.

[85] Philippe Hamon, *Le Personnel du roman: Le système des personnages dans les* Rougon-Macquart *d'Émile Zola* (Geneva: Droz, 1983), pp. 10–18.

character is that it cannot easily be isolated from its textual embedding: it is not an autonomous and distinct textual unit but, rather, the site of a diffuse semantic effect. Any text is made up of a multiplicity of characters, some of them fleeting and barely visible, and each of them built up progressively through numerous fragments of information about what he or she or it is and does; if character is a bundle of differential elements it is, nevertheless (unlike the linguistic morpheme), not a stable given which can be recognized, but rather a construct which evolves through the course of a reading.[86] Only an analysis which can account for this dynamic force of character can get beyond being a simple catalogue of types or an inventory of regularities.

Yet Hamon's systemic analysis is structural rather than syntagmatic: his primary interest is in functional typologies, on the one hand, and, on the other, in the machinery of naming, predication, grouping, and structures of action by which the 'character effect' is constructed. The Rougon-Macquart series offers him a large and homogeneous corpus of texts which lack both a single central character and any strong individuation of characters. Following Roman Jakobson, who finds in Pasternak a decomposition of the hero into a series of metonymic elements (his own objectified states of mind, the objects which surround him), Hamon finds in Zola a form of character which has crumbled into discontinuity and metonymic displacement.[87] On this corpus he deploys the apparatus that he had earlier elaborated in his essay 'Pour un statut sémiologique du personnage', concentrating on those nodal points where a range of semantic axes are concentrated: the activities of seeing, saying, and working; the axes of gender and territory; the modal roles of desire (*vouloir*), power or capacity (*pouvoir*), and knowing (*savoir*). The effect, quite deliberately, is to dissolve the illusive unity of characters as quasi-persons into the differential components which make up the thematic, axiological, and narrative codes of a global text: the allotropic layers that lie beneath and extend beyond the named individuals of the novels' interlocking stories.

V

Fictional character is a person-shaped figure made salient by a narrative ground. As figure, it is a dimension of the compositional structure of a text, a moment of an action sequence which both drives and acquires attributes from the sequence. Through that process of attribution of qualities character takes the form of a semantic cluster, accumulating (progressively or discontinuously, coherently or incoherently) through the course of a text. But character is, in certain respects, also the analogue of 'real' persons, conforming more or less closely and more or less fully to the schemata that govern, in any particular society, what it means to be a person and to have a physical body, a moral character, a sense of self, and a

[86] Hamon, *Le Personnel du roman*, pp. 20–1.

[87] Hamon, *Le Personnel du roman*, p. 25; citing Roman Jakobson, 'Notes marginales sur la prose de Pasternak', in *Questions de Poétique* (Paris: Seuil, 1973), pp. 127ff.

capacity for action. I say 'in certain respects' because fictional character happens in accordance with the modes of being specified by particular genres; it is of the order of representation rather than of the order of the real. It is, in another sense, a particular kind of experience and a particular translation of interest: an affective recognition induced in readers or viewers or players by the rhetorical action of texts.[88] And, as a complex conceptual entity, character is the set of relations formed by the interaction of all of these dimensions.

In the chapters that follow I explore the dimensions of this complex conceptual entity, and my focus is on the tension that I identified between thinking of characters as pieces of writing or imaging, and thinking of them as person-like entities. I wrote that these two ways of thinking about character are logically difficult to hold together; and yet we do so in our every encounter with fictional character: the problem is to find a language in which to convey this ontological hybridity.

This is not a problem that lends itself to a progressive unfolding of concepts, with appropriately illustrative cases; rather, I work through a series of cases in order, first, to allow a conceptual language to emerge from within the problem itself, and second, to allow the problem to unfold with an adequate measure of complexity. I try to tease out the dimensions of the problem across a range of texts, and I try to complicate and mutually to implicate both of its poles, the textual and the person-like. What is at stake in this is not just the theoretical adequacy of the concept of fictional character—which I take to be both the central category of literary theory and its least adequately understood piece of equipment—but the category of the human person itself.

Let me conclude this introductory chapter by considering another text, Vladimir Nabokov's *Pale Fire*, which I will then use to map out the later development of the conceptual apparatus introduced here.

Pale Fire was published in 1962, two years before Nabokov's great edition of Pushkin's *Eugene Onegin*;[89] but that edition was substantially completed by 1957, and its four-part structure (Foreword, Poem, Commentary, Index) serves as a model for the novel. *Pale Fire*'s primary narrative develops parasitically through the paratextual material, with the frame engulfing the poem it is supposed to serve. Within the novel, 'Pale Fire' is also the title of one of the sections, the poem in four cantos written by the distinguished American poet John Shade (the title is taken from *Timon of Athens*, IV, 3: 'The moon's an arrant thief/And her pale fire she snatches from the sun'; the Foreword, written by the commentator Charles Kinbote, who misses the Shakespearean allusion because he has only a Zemblan translation of *Timon* available to him, refers to the 'pale fire of the incinerator'

[88] Susan Manning thus argues that what is at stake in the analysis of character is 'not primarily existential questions about whether character "is" innate, self-fashioned, or merely linguistic, but rather critical or representational issues of how literary character has been evoked so as to create certain responses in readers'. Susan Manning, 'Did Human Character Change? Representing Women and Fiction from Shakespeare to Virginia Woolf', *Partial Answers* 11: 1 (2013), p. 29.

[89] Aleksandr Pushkin, *Eugene Onegin, a Novel in Verse*; translated from the Russian, with a Commentary, by Vladimir Nabokov, Bollingen Series (New York: Pantheon, 1964).

in which Shade used to burn his drafts, the scraps of burnt paper turning into 'wind-borne black butterflies').[90]

Shade's poem—an autobiographical meditation in heroic couplets, with stylistic debts to Robert Frost and Wallace Stevens and with its central emotional focus the death of Shade's daughter Hazel—is not, strictly speaking, a poem but rather the imitation of a poem: it could not, for example, be anthologized in a collection of American poetry of the 1950s, despite the fact that it has passages of great beauty and complexity, because of its functional subordination to the novel where its role is to characterize John Shade. In the same way, the Commentary has only a parodic relation to its genre: it is, rather, a counter-genre to the poem (not Foucault's author-forming commentary but a direct attack on the poem which opportunistically incorporates the story Kinbote thinks it ought to have told), and a self-undermining component of the characterization of Kinbote.

The Foreword sets up the antagonistic relation that develops between text and Commentary. Beginning as a conventional critical apparatus with textual and biographical detail, it quickly veers into invective against scholarly enemies, extraneous insertions ('There is a very loud amusement park right in front of my present lodging') (p. 443), and a combative assertion of the priority of the Commentary over the poem. Referring to the placing of the notes after the text, Kinbote helpfully advises the reader 'to consult them first and then study the poem with their help, rereading them of course as he goes through its text, and perhaps, after having done with the poem, consulting them a third time so as to complete the picture' (p. 454). Without the notes, he contends, the poem 'simply has no human reality at all', since only the notes can provide 'the reality of its author and his surroundings, attachments and so forth... To this statement my dear poet would probably not have subscribed, but, for better or worse, it is the commentator who has the last word' (p. 445).

There are two basic versions of the story that is told through the paratextual material (Foreword, Commentary, and Index). The first goes like this: Kinbote, the scholarly commentator, is in reality King Charles the Beloved of Zembla, who, following a revolution in his remote northern country, has escaped from his palace and now lives disguised as a professor of literature at Wordsmith College in New Wye, Appalachia (a thinly disguised Cornell University in Ithaca, New York). Kinbote has supplied Shade with the story of his heroic escape from Zembla and expects that it will be the poem's theme; the Commentary registers his disappointment that it is not, but manages to tell the story at length under the guise of annotations to the text. A central part of the story is that Kinbote/King Charles is being pursued by a group of fanatical revolutionaries, the Shadows, and their henchman Jakob Gradus; the notes chart the progress of Gradus's pursuit of the king to the moment where, attempting to assassinate Charles outside his house in New Wye, he mistakenly shoots Shade.

[90] Nabokov, *Pale Fire*, p. 445. Hereafter cited in the text.

The second version of the story is one that the reader is led to deduce from the first. Kinbote is not King Charles but is a frustrated and unhappy man suffering paranoid delusions and compensating for his unhappy life with an elaborate fantasy. The man who shoots Shade is an escaped homicidal maniac, Jack Grey, who mistakes Shade for the owner of the house Kinbote is renting, Judge Goldsworth, in revenge for the Judge's having sentenced Grey to the Institute for the Criminally Insane.

A number of mechanisms facilitate the translation of the first story into the second. One is Kinbote's telling of stories in self-vindication, which work against the image he seeks to project: his account of his extortion from Shade's distraught widow of the right to edit and publish the poem is meant to justify him against her later change of heart, but in fact looks morally ugly; a story he tells of lunching with colleagues at the staff club, where he delivers a diatribe against eating food that had been 'handled by a fellow-creature' (such as the 'pulpous' girl who serves them) is followed by his noting, implausibly, that 'my free and simple demeanor put everyone at ease' (p. 449). Another is his use of delusional language, as when, referring to a boarder who has introduced a 'whore' into the house, he says that he 'can forgive everything save treason' (p. 453): it is Kinbote's paranoia, we deduce, that makes him a king. A third is the evidence of reported remarks by others, as when Kinbote hears Shade saying, in the context of a note about madness: 'That is the wrong word... One should not apply it to a person who deliberately peels off a drab and unhappy past and replaces it with a brilliant invention' (p. 610). On this occasion Kinbote fails to apply the reference to himself, but on others he comes close to doing so. One such moment happens when he complains that 'It is so easy for a cruel person to make the victim of his ingenuity believe that he has persecution mania, or is really being stalked by a killer, or is suffering from hallucinations' (p. 505). Another concerns a variant line about minds that die before arriving in the afterlife—'Poor old man Swift, poor . . . , poor Baudelaire' (p. 558)—where the commentator has 'dark, disturbing thoughts' (p. 558) that the blank trochaic name might refer to him (in the Index this line is simply listed under *Kinbote*). Elsewhere Kinbote compares himself directly to Swift: 'I too am a desponder in my nature, an uneasy, peevish, and suspicious man, although I have my moments of volatility and *fou rire*' (p. 562).

A further mechanism by which the first story is undermined is a set of curious correspondences between Zembla and the world of Wordsmith College. Brian Boyd notes that the names of the four Goldsworth girls whose photos Kinbote finds (and stores away) in the house he is renting—'Alphina (9), Betty (10), Candida (12), and Dee (14)'—correspond closely to the four members of two generations of the Zemblan royal family—King Alfin, Queen Blenda, King Charles, and Queen Disa.[91] An Index entry under *Kinbote*—'his loathing for a person who makes advances, and then betrays a noble and naïve heart, telling foul stories about

[91] Brian Boyd, *Nabokov's* Pale Fire: *The Magic of Artistic Discovery* (Princeton: Princeton University Press, 1999), p. 96.

his victim and pursuing him with practical jokes'[92] refers us to the commentary on line 741. This entry must refer to Gerald Emerald, a loathed colleague from the English Department who is repeatedly described as wearing a green jacket; but the actual commentary on line 741 describes only 'one of the greater Shadows, whom he had thought to be *onhava-onhava* ("far, far away"), in wild, misty, almost legendary Zembla!'—a 'merry, perhaps overmerry, fellow, in a green velvet jacket' (p. 623). Not only is this particular Shadow a delusional projection of Gerald Emerald, then, but the group of scholars to whom Kinbote refers disdainfully as the Shadeans are clearly the source of the evil cabal of Shadows who are hunting down the fallen king. At the most general level, we are led to make the translation from one story to another because Zembla is described in the language of fantasy appropriate to a historical romance, and we will note a discrepancy if we read this novel within the framework of a more 'realist' genre. Finally, we see Kinbote on several occasions not as the proud king in exile but as a man in spiritual agony: one lengthy descriptive entry ends abruptly with the words 'Dear Jesus, do something' (p. 501); and at a later moment we see the commentator in religious mood, hoping for salvation 'despite the frozen mud and horror in my heart' (p. 626).

This reduction of the first story to the second yields a perfectly satisfactory reading of the novel, then. It is, of course, a reductionist reading, made at the level of the diegesis (the represented reality), and it gives an essentially psychological reading of the character of Kinbote. There are, however, three good reasons to look further. The first is that the final paragraph of the Commentary concedes the fictional status of *both* stories: Kinbote announces that, after the publication of this edition, he may

> cook up a stage play, an old-fashioned melodrama with three principles [sc. principals]: a lunatic who intends to kill an imaginary king, another lunatic who imagines himself to be that king, and a distinguished old poet who stumbles by chance into the line of fire, and perishes in the clash between the two figments. (pp. 657–8)

The tale is a fiction; but the second premise here contradicts the first.

The second reason is the unification of the two disparate moments of the poem and the paratextual material as mirror reflections of each other. Shade's poem begins by describing the death of a bird against a glass window and the *trompe l'oeil* illusions created by windows in a lighted room, when inside is superimposed on outside. That imagery of reflection and deception is continued through both poem and Commentary. The assassin Gradus is a former glass-maker who had first worked in 'the famous Glass Factory' where mirrors were made and where the Zemblan revolution 'had flickered first' (p. 522); an explosion at the 'Glass Works' is mentioned several times; it is what supposedly scarred the face of the hideous cripple met by the fleeing king, who turns out to be the actor Odon (brother of Nodo) in disguise (pp. 589, 542). The mirror in which Fleur de Fyler contemplates herself is 'signed with a diamond by its maker, Sudarg of Bokay' (p. 516): 'Yakob Gradus' reversed. The escaping king is startled by a false reflection

92 Nabokov, *Pale Fire*, p. 662.

in a pool, creating 'a counterfeit king' (p. 540). Zemblan, we learn, is 'the tongue of the mirror' (p. 613), and the name Zembla 'is a corruption ... of Semblerland, a land of reflections, of "resemblers"' (p. 630). The looking-glass worlds of the novel shape its structure from deep within, and the question of character looks rather different at this thematic level. I return to this shortly, but let me cite one final passage that I think is relevant to the imagery of the looking glass. After the shooting of Shade, Kinbote conceals the manuscript of the poem in the closet where he had previously stored the photographs of the Goldsworth girls, and then emerges from it 'as if it had been the end of the secret passage that had taken me all the way out of my enchanted castle and right from Zembla to *this* Arcady' (p. 653). His way has taken him from one fantasy world to another, from the end to the beginning of the alphabet, and to that pastoral world where death announces that it, too, shall be found.

The third reason has to do with a series of clues buried throughout the text but, above all, in the Index, which tell a somewhat different story from the first two, and perhaps set a classically Nabokovian trap. A full account would require a knowledge, which I don't possess, of both formal and colloquial Russian, of lepidoptery, of chess strategy, of astronomy, of the history of Russian exile groups, and much more. Let me concentrate on only one of them, well documented in the secondary literature: the fleeting appearance in the novel of one V. Botkin. The Index entry for *Botkin, V.* is as follows: 'American scholar of Russian descent, *894*; king-bot, maggot of extinct fly that once bred in mammoths and is thought to have hastened their phylogenetic end, *247*; bottekin-maker, *71; bot*, plop, and *botelïy*, big-bellied (Russ.); botkin or bodkin, a Danish stiletto' (p. 659). The reference to the commentary on line 894 is not, however, to a Russian-American scholar but to a suggestion made to Kinbote that his name is 'a kind of anagram of Botkin or Botkine', a suggestion he angrily refutes (p. 632); the reference to the king-bot maggot is to Shade's wife Sybil having called Kinbote 'an elephantine tick; a king-sized botfly; a macaco worm; the monstrous parasite of a genius' (p. 561); and the references to the name Botkin, meaning 'bottekin-maker', and to botkin/bodkin as a stiletto, are quite gratuitous insertions into the narrative. The only actual (and very brief) reference in the main body of the text to Professor Botkin is absent from the Index; and, as Barton Johnson notes, 'this mysteriously unindexed passage suggests that there is indeed a real Professor Botkin on campus. Inasmuch as the V. Botkin index references actually concern Kinbote and two of them point out the Kinbote/Botkin(e) anagram, it seems certain that Kinbote is Botkin'.[93]

Perhaps it does, at least at the diegetic level—although it is also possible that these games may be a deliberate decoy on the part of Kinbote (at the diegetic level)

[93] D. Barton Johnson, *Worlds in Regression: Some Novels of Vladimir Nabokov* (Ann Arbor: Ardis, 1985), p. 70. Nabokov himself identified Kinbote with Professor V. Botkin in an interview with Maurice Dolbier: 'Books and Authors: Nabokov's Plums', *New York Herald Tribune*, 17 June 1962, p. 5. Brian Boyd cites a 1962 diary entry by Nabokov, wondering if any reader will notice that the commentator is neither an ex-king nor Kinbote but 'Prof. Vseslav Botkin, a Russian and a madman ...' Brian Boyd, *Vladimir Nabokov: The American Years* (Princeton: Princeton University Press, 1991), p. 709, n. 4.

or of whoever has invented Kinbote; there is never certainty in a novel that plays, as Nabokov does, with modal plurality. Johnson gives a precise account of how this works:

> Each Nabokov novel contains at least two fictive worlds. This 'two world' model accounts (in a formal sense) for much of what happens in many Nabokov novels. It describes their underlying cosmology. The patterns, the webs of coincidence that pervade the world of the characters, are but an imperfect mirroring of events on a second, controlling world. Although the characters of a given universe regard the intuited next higher world as the ultimate, self-defining one, it in turn stands in the same subordinate position vis-à-vis a still more all-encompassing world.[94]

We can see how this layering of modal worlds works in practice by following the two hypotheses that Johnson draws from the identification of Kinbote with Botkin. Either a 'real' V. Botkin is writing a novel about the fictional characters Shade, Gradus, and Kinbote: let us say then that fiction (1) refers to fiction (2); or 'Shade, his poem, and his killer are all real, as is V. Botkin, a drab Wordsmith faculty member, who creates a new identity for himself as the exotic Zemblan exile, King Charles the Beloved, who is passing himself off as Charles Kinbote.'[95] In this case Shade, Gradus, and V. Botkin count as fiction (1), referring to King Charles the Beloved as fiction (2), referring in turn to Charles Kinbote as fiction (3). In both cases fiction (1) counts within the text as the level of the 'real'.

This hierarchization of nested fictional worlds is, I think, true to our sense of the layering of realities in the novel; yet it remains reductive, positing the reality of a textual character rather than that of the textual game. And this is more generally true of the many sophisticated attempts to establish who the (implied) 'author' of *Pale Fire* actually is. Andrew Field contends that, because poem and Commentary are thematically unified by the topic of death, 'the primary author . . . must be John Shade'.[96] This is the first of the three possibilities that William Dowling summarizes: that 'the real narrator is the person corresponding to John Shade, who does not really die but composes a work in which he makes his own death an incident so that he can go on and compose a commentary to his own completed poem: "Man's life as commentary to abstruse/Unfinished poem."' The second possibility is that 'the real narrator is the person corresponding to Kinbote (Botkin), who writes a poem and imagines the death of the poet so as to have an excuse to tell the story he is really interested in—the magical tale of his lost kingdom of Zembla and his escape and exile'. And the third is that 'there really are two narrators in *Pale Fire*, one corresponding to Shade, one to Kinbote'.[97] Dowling himself—demonstrating from a brief allusion to the commentator's looking up references in 'WUL' (that is, Wordsmith University Library), when we know that Kinbote doesn't have access to a library, that the author of the Commentary must be someone else—opts for

[94] Johnson, *Worlds in Regression*, pp. 1–2.
[95] Johnson, *Worlds in Regression*, p. 71.
[96] Andrew Field, *Nabokov: His Life in Art* (Boston: Little, Brown, 1967), p. 300.
[97] William C. Dowling, 'Who's the Narrator of Nabokov's *Pale Fire*?', <http://www.rci.rutgers.edu/~wcd/palenarr.htm>. Last accessed 28 June 2013.

an author called 'Vladimir Nabokov', a textual identity who is not identical to the 'real' Nabokov. Johnson comes to much the same conclusion by adducing the anagrammatic similarity of 'V. Botkin' to 'Nabokov', and pointing to Kinbote's speculation that he might return elsewhere as 'an old, happy, healthy, heterosexual Russian, a writer in exile, sans fame, sans future, sans audience, sans anything but his art' (p. 337).[98]

The most audacious speculation is perhaps that of the doyen of Nabokov commentators, Brian Boyd, who asks: 'How can we explain the stealthy signals between part and part [that is, poem and Commentary], when the central irony of the novel appears to depend precisely on the *lack* of communication between part and part?'[99] Examining and rejecting psychologically based arguments for either Shade or Kinbote as the sole author, he opts—on the basis of intricate clues embedded in the text—for a reading which posits that it is the ghost of Shade's daughter Hazel that gives Kinbote his inspiration for the story of Zembla ('because she senses an affinity with him, because she wants to offer him an imaginative consolation for his anguish and loneliness, and because she can turn Zembla into a chance both to express and to ironize her own experience as a woman spurned') and that inspires her father 'to the great poem that she can see forms part of destiny's rough draft'.[100] Not stopping there, Boyd goes on to suggest that 'Shade's shade, his ghost' similarly gives guidance to Kinbote's paranoia, shaping the Gradus story into 'a complex narrative counterpoint to the composition of the poem'.[101] It is an act of kindness on Shade's part (or rather, that of his ghost) that allows Kinbote to write a text that will keep him from suicide a little longer as he writes the commentary that will keep him the centre of attention.[102]

As I suggested before, Nabokov the chess player sets traps for his commentators. But the issue here is not so much the inherent absurdity of such readings as their inability to move beyond diegetic accounts of character in order to treat characters as textually based effects. That move, I believe, should take place by shifting to the compositional level where characters work as allotropes, no longer fully distinct but forming patterns of interaction and of thematic connection,

> Some kind of link-and-bobolink, some kind
> Of correlated pattern in the game,
> Plexed artistry... (pp. 479–80)

At this level we would notice that Kinbote and Shade have, in some respects, the identity of self and anti-self: Kinbote is Shade's antagonist as commentator to author; he is his own antagonist as failed person and fantasy king; he is his own assassin: Shade mentions that Kinbote has told him 'that *kinbote* means regicide

98 Johnson, *Worlds in Regression*, p. 72; Nabokov, he writes, has a 'penchant for incorporating himself into his novels, sometimes by description, sometimes by initials, and often by anagrams such as Vivian Darkbloom, Baron Klim Avidov, Blavdak Vinomori, or Adam von Librikov'.

99 Boyd, *Nabokov's* Pale Fire, p. 114.

100 Boyd, *Nabokov's* Pale Fire, p. 173.

101 Boyd, *Nabokov's* Pale Fire, p. 211.

102 Boyd, *Nabokov's* Pale Fire, pp. 218–9.

in your language'; '"Yes, a king's destroyer," I said (longing to explain that a king who sinks his identity in the mirror of exile is in a sense just that)' (p. 632); seeing Gradus with gun in hand, Kinbote feels a 'tremor of recognition', as though of his mirror image (p. 652); Gradus's murder of Shade rather than Kinbote reinforces the role of the commentator as assassin; and Shade, the uxorious heterosexual, is both the opposite of the homosexual Kinbote and the counterpart of the uxorious Nabokov.

Within this patterned play we can notice a further thematic opposition between the poem and the novel. 'I have no desire to twist and batter an unambiguous *apparatus criticus* into the monstrous semblance of a novel,' writes the commentator at one point (p. 495); but that is precisely what he is doing when he carefully stages his descriptions of Gradus from the most to the least vague (p. 546), or displays a detailed knowledge of scenes at which he was not present, or allows himself to be carried away in his salacious description of a young man (pp. 582–3). Kinbote is a component of the struggle between poem and novel in this torn, agonistic text; and, like Gradus, whose deathly reality cannot be distinguished from 'the magic action of Shade's poem itself' (p. 534), Kinbote is made of words: 'My notes and self are petering out,' he says in the final pages (p. 657). At this level of structure, his reality is an effect of the modality of the textual world to which he belongs, and of the intermodal play between the novel's worlds.

VI

The following chapters of this book explore these questions across a range of dimensions. Chapter 2, 'Interest', asks about the affective work that is done by fictional character. Without privileging the forms of empathetic identification that have been at the heart of the classic European novel, I seek to specify the minimal conditions for character to exist and have effect, and to understand how the reader is positioned in relation both to the central and minor characters and to an implicit narrative voice. I develop my analysis of identification by examining its progressive elaboration in Freud's work, and I use Freud's notions of the fantasmatic structure of selfhood and the dispersal of ego-identifications as the basis for understanding the binding-in of the reader to fictional works. *Pale Fire* might involve relatively conventional modes of identification: with Shade as autobiographical narrator, and with the pathos of Hazel's suicide; but these are subsumed within our complex positioning in relation to Kinbote. We see the world as he sees it, but we also see that world as an imaginary construct which characterizes him in particular ways, and we are positioned metadiscursively in relation to the novel's joking parody of scholarly conventions. The novel is rich in dispersed ego-identifications: those of Nabokov at one level (the murder of Shade—possibly by mistake for Kinbote—closely recalls the assassination of Nabokov's father as he got in the way of a bullet intended for someone else; and we note that Vladimir Nabokov senior was replaced as head of Russian émigré organizations in Berlin by one S. D. Botkin);[103]

[103] Boyd, *Vladimir Nabokov: The American Years*, p. 456.

at another level, and pervasively, those of Kinbote, whose monstrous self-obsession stands as a parodic figure for the reader, deeply attached to the text he wishes to appropriate, 'especially when it is the underside of the weave that entrances the beholder and only begetter, whose own past intercoils there with the fate of the innocent author' (p. 446).

Chapter 3, 'Person', makes explicit the assumption running through the two previous chapters that the category of fictional character depends upon the prior category of human being. Of the various related concepts that express it (the self, the subject, the soul, the individual, the person, *Dasein*, the agent or actor or *actant*, and so on), the most useful for my purposes is that of the person, which is formed less by a history of philosophical elaboration than by a set of changing social practices that distinguish human from non-human being and bring together religious, legal, medical, ethical, civic, and socioeconomic taxonomies in a single point. The initial question to ask here about *Pale Fire* concerns the core identity of characters: what modal status is to be assigned to a fictional person? What kind of person is a king, what kind of person is a hallucinatory maniac? And then: how do we make sense of Kinbote—what mode of personhood do we assign to him? As he flees after Shade's assassination, Kinbote is holding on to the manuscript of the poem, 'still clutching the inviolable shade' (p. 329); this 'shade' (the quotation is from Matthew Arnold's 'The Scholar Gypsy') is Dido in Hades, and the word is an indirect translation of Dante's *ombra*, the ghostly body, which I discuss at some length in relation to medieval theories of the persistence of the soul in the afterlife and of the body in resurrection. Personhood is a vast topic, and what I seek to do in this chapter is merely to adumbrate the dimensions of the concept, while emphasizing its centrality to any consideration of the frameworks within which the quasi-persons of fiction are constructed and become recognizable.

My fourth chapter, 'Type', begins by deploying Elizabeth Fowler's concept of social persons, which she uses to understand how characters in Chaucer and other medieval and early modern writers are built up as composite figures out of the raw materials of preformed social typologies. I modify her argument somewhat to extend the discussion of the frameworks within which personhood is constructed, positing that fictional character is formed on the basis of folk taxonomies, including popular psychologies, physiognomies, and characterologies, as well as models of social hierarchy and legal and religious order. *Pale Fire* activates a range of typologies which straddle real and fictional realms: the academic poet, the scholar, the deranged scholar, the assassin, the escaped lunatic, and so on, each inhabiting a conventional plot that defines its scope. My two major case studies in this chapter—of Hamlet as melancholic, and of the family romance in Dickens—are reflected thematically in *Pale Fire*: melancholy through the parallel drawn between Kinbote and Swift, and through the preoccupation of both Kinbote and Hazel with suicide; and the family romance through the various versions of it that Kinbote projects, as well as—less fantasmatically, more tragically—through the Shades' sheltering of their physically unattractive daughter and their extended grieving after her death.

Chapter 5, 'Voice', begins by arguing that to be a fictional character is to be both an agent and an object of discourse; at once a speaker, a person spoken to, and a person referred to. I undertake a lengthy analysis of the first-person pronoun, initially through discussions in analytical philosophy and then through an exploration of Émile Benveniste's notion of the performative constitution of the subject in discourse The archetypal performative is promising, and it underlies contractual notions of the person as will and intention: I analyse it through readings of works by Searle, Agamben, Nietzsche, Ricoeur, and Derrida, before returning to the account of deixis mooted in Benveniste. Charles Fillmore's work on deixis, together with Goffman's notion of 'footing', help me develop an account of the first-person pronoun as structurally riven, positional and alienable yet embodied, a reference point in time and space and yet movable from discursive point to point; and I extend this analysis to questions of narrative voice and of the positions that underlie it. The primary forms of the 'I' running through *Pale Fire*, and in tension within it, are those of the autobiographical poet and the obtrusive commentator; but it is clear that certain moments of discourse—certain voices—are not contained by those two first-person speakers. These are the moments in which the novel opens up, and in which the characters merge into something more impersonal.

Charles Kinbote is, we are told at one point, the author of a book on surnames; and *Pale Fire* foregrounds the role of names in establishing and underpinning fictional worlds. Its deranged Index, which introduces stories and characters unmentioned in the body of the text, provides a kind of semantic summation of named characters (Kinbote above all, of course; Shade to a lesser extent, and in large part through his association with Kinbote; Sybil Shade is dismissed with a terse 'passim'; and scholarly enemies are noted as not being mentioned in the Index). The free-flowing recombinations of characters' names throughout the text (Jakob Gradus/Jack Degree/Jacques de Grey/James de Gray/Ravus/Ravenstone/Jacques d'Argus; Kinbote/Botkin/Nabokov; Campbell/Beauchamp; Radomir/Mirador; Odon/Nodo) indicate the fluidity of the entities they designate. In Chapter 6, 'Name', I take the process of nomination to be at once a central condition for the existence and recognition of fictional character and a central dimension of narrative structure, worked out differently in different genres. The medieval romance (my example is Chrétien's *Le Conte du Graal*) frequently involves a quest for the true name, the recovery of which will conclude the story, whereas the hero or heroine of the novel is more likely to pass through a series of nominations, none of which is necessarily definitive; I read the failure of self-nomination in *Don Quixote* as the exemplary beginning of the novel's account of a disenchanted world. In this chapter I examine the anthropological literature on systems of nomenclature, the philosophical literature on naming (Frege, Kripke), the role played by names in the construction of fictional worlds, and Proust's account of the magical structure of the proper name, and conclude the chapter with a reading of the function of the heteronym in the work of Fernando Pessoa in order to think more fully about the grounding of textuality in the act of naming.

The final two chapters of the book turn from the linguistic to the bodily schemata that inform personhood. I begin Chapter 7, 'Face', with a reading of Kōbō

Abe's novel *The Face of Another*, and from it develop an argument about the topoi of the face as window to the soul and the face as mask. The extended thread of analysis of Albertine's face in Proust's *À la recherche du temps perdu* is, in contrast to both these tropes, an account of a face that is not unique, is not singular, is not the property or the manifestation of its wearer, and is neither spatially nor temporally coherent. Turning to arguments about facial expression, in Charles Darwin and in a number of contemporary evolutionary psychologists (Silvan Tomkins, Paul Ekman, Alan Fridlund), I argue that the face should be understood in terms of display rather than expression, and I then seek to recast that opposition at a different level of abstraction as a contrast between an ethical conception of the face (Levinas) and the sociological concept of facework. I examine the relation of icon to portrait and of the self-portrait to the mirror, before concluding the chapter with a long analysis of the masking theatre of the Greek and Roman New Comedy. Here, the relevant dimensions of *Pale Fire* have to do with the recurrent theme of masking, mirroring, and concealment, in particular the donning of disguise not only by the king as he escapes from Zembla, but also by hundreds of his followers who disguise themselves as him. Conversely, the novel is preoccupied with disgrace, the loss of face that accompanies Kinbote's humiliations, and with sad Hazel's suffering for the face that she bears. Her father, too, is defined by the discrepancy between face and character: his face is that of 'a fleshy Hogarthian tippler of indeterminate sex... He was his own cancellation' (p. 453).

What turns Kinbote into a vegetarian for life is his reading, when young, a story about an Italian despot who is 'tied, naked and howling, to a plank in the public square and killed piecemeal by the people who cut slices out, and eat them, and distribute his living body among themselves' (p. 548). Although the king has two bodies, one of them, the mortal one, is prey to cannibalism; the underlying fantasy here is that what you eat could be your own body. In Chapter 8, entitled 'Body', I pull the threads of the book's argument together through an account of the fantasmatic structure of embodied selfhood. I begin with a reading of Thomas Mann's story *The Transposed Heads*, which wittily explores body/mind dualism in ways that have a strong resonance with contemporary analytic philosophy (Derek Parfit's disembodied minds in *Reasons and Persons*, for example, and P. F. Strawson's meditation on embodied personhood in *Individuals*), and I also read Richard Powers' novel *Galatea 2.2* to extend some of these paradoxes. I take the fictional and the fantasmatic to be closely related, and fictional character to be integral to the ways in which we form selves. But bodies are equally fantasmatic, deeply informing the way we think the world through language, and existing experientially as schemata that organize our socio-spatial relation to ourselves and others. I develop these arguments in relation to previous arguments about personhood as place or 'office', and make the link between proprioception and self-shaping—between 'perceptions' and 'technologies'. Finally, I extend the argument to cinematic bodies, looking at the way *Blade Runner* uses the figure of the replicant to problematize the relation between the human and its simulation. Fictional character is here understood in terms of the thesis that runs through the book: that the non-personal insists at the very heart of the personal.

2
Interest

I

The work done by fictional character is a function of its ability to engage its interlocutor: to do emotional as well as representational work. Always in some sense shaped like a person, a figural pattern asks us to respond to a form of life that we recognize: what happens next, what will its fate be? Because its work is that of engaging the reader's interest, it is 'as much a reconstruction by the reader as it is a textual construct'.[1] You can put this negatively: without the awakening of an interest in a figure that in some way resembles us, we won't engage as fully or deeply with the process of the text. It's arguable that even discursive prose—a conceptual argument dealing with abstract forces, say—can't be dissociated from our sense of a speaking self onto whom we project characteristics, and perhaps even from our tendency to conceive of abstract forces as actors working at human scale and involved in the fundamental narrative patterns of quest and antagonism. To say this is not to privilege the forms of empathetic identification that have been at the heart of the classic European novel or of Hollywood cinema, and the ethical accounts of character that have accompanied them: it is to set out one of the conditions for the existence of fictional character.

Those conditions are minimal because we have the capacity to turn just about anything into a quasi-person. Usually a character is a human person; it has a name; it speaks; it is embodied, unitary, and persistent over time; and it performs an action or a series of actions, on the basis of which we impute intentionality to it. But even these minimal conditions need not all be met. The narrators and central characters of the eighteenth-century genre of the 'it-narrative' are things in circulation: a coin or a banknote, a coat, a coach, a walking stick.[2] From Aesop through La Fontaine to Beatrix Potter, Walt Disney, and George Orwell, animals have been

[1] Philippe Hamon, 'Pour un statut sémiologique du personnage', in Roland Barthes, Wolfgang Kayser, Wayne Booth, and Philippe Hamon, *Poétique du récit* (Paris: Seuil, 1977), p. 119 (my translation).

[2] Cf. Deirdre Lynch, 'Fictions of Social Circulation, 1742–1782', in *The Economy of Character: Novels, Market Culture, and the Business of Inner Meaning* (Chicago: University of Chicago Press, 1998), pp. 80–119; Jonathan Lamb, 'Things as Authors', in *The Things Things Say* (Princeton: Princeton University Press, 2011), pp. 201–29; Mark Blackwell (ed.), *The Secret Life of Things: Animals, Objects, and It-Narratives in Eighteenth-Century England* (Lewisburg: Bucknell University Press, 2007).

fully realized characters.[3] The transmigratory soul in David Mitchell's *Ghostwritten* has no name and no fixed body (it passes through and is instantiated as a series of characters); Bertha Mason, the madwoman in *Jane Eyre*'s attic, never speaks; an anonymous, featureless Beckett character neck-deep in mud or garbage performs no action other than talking, and Godot is absent in all but name. Some or all of the characters in Juan Rulfo's *Pedro Páramo* and Patrice Chaplin's *Siesta* (to say nothing of Dante's *Commedia*) are dead, as is the central figure in Hitchcock's *The Trouble with Harry*.[4] Neither the gods of the Homeric epics nor the figures of animated cartoons act in accordance with the laws of embodied physical being. What counts is less what they are than what we do with them: the historically, culturally, and generically various ways in which the reader or spectator or listener endows them with a specular personhood, and on that basis finds them of interest.

Philippe Hamon divides the study of character into three strands, each of which is the site of particular effects: the study of figuration, where fictional reality effects are generated; of anthropomorphization, where the particular kinds of reality effect that relate to the human figure—a 'moral effect', a 'person effect', a 'psychological effect'—come into play; and of intersecting projections ('*un carrefour projectionnel*') on the part of the author and of the reader and critic, who like or dislike and recognize themselves or not in a particular character.[5] Each of these strands is a moment in a process of recognition which brings characters into being. More precisely, recognition is at once an effect generated by fictional character, and a process by which we activate that effect.[6] It is only through such a process of recognition that characters become interesting to us, in the double sense that we find a frame for understanding what kind of being they are, and that in some way we see ourselves in these figures and make an affective investment in them.

That affective investment is often called 'identification': a term that has traditionally been central to theories of character because of its ability to mediate between character as a formal textual structure and the reader's structured investment in it. The term is, however, in many ways problematic, particularly because, in assuming a general structure of relations between fictional characters and readers or spectators, it underestimates the complexity and specificity of modes of response (I detail some of these later in this chapter).[7] The force of the concept has been strongly

[3] Cf. Bruce Boehrer, 'Animal Characters and the Deconstruction of Character', *PMLA* 124: 2 (2009), pp. 542–7; Boehrer, *Animal Characters: Nonhuman Beings in Early Modern Literature* (Philadelphia: University of Pennsylvania Press, 2010).

[4] On the narrative role of dead bodies in cinema, cf. Lesley Stern, *Dead and Alive: The Body as Cinematic Thing* (Montreal: Caboose, 2012).

[5] Philippe Hamon, *Le Personnel du roman: Le système des personnages dans les* Rougon-Macquart *d'Émile Zola* (Geneva: Droz, 1983), p. 9.

[6] This is the force of Vincent Jouve's argument for a reorientation of the study of character to a systematic focus on the 'aesthetic' pole of its concretization in the act of reading. Vincent Jouve, *L'effet-personnage dans le roman* (Paris: PUF, 1992).

[7] Julian Murphet describes identification as 'the moral engagement of a fictive "one" by the "one" that I hypothetically am', and argues that it thereby functions as a disavowal of 'the inherent multiplicity of a complex structure of signification'. 'The Mole and the Multiple: A Chiasmus of Character', *New Literary History* 42: 2 (2011), p. 256.

influenced by eighteenth-century theories of sympathy and by later accounts of empathetic identification;[8] but affective investment may be positive or negative, and indeed encompasses a range of possible relations to characters, including dislike and indifference. Dostoevsky's *Notes from Underground* is an extended exercise in negative identification: to what extent, it asks, can the reader's interest be held in a character who goes out of his way to be unlikeable? And reality television works above all by a discrimination of identifications, inviting its viewers to work out whom they like and dislike, and to carry those emotions through into the talk that complements viewing.

Identification has two relevant and closely linked senses: identification *of* a character, and identification *with* a character. Identification 'of' is generated by triggers such as a name or a personal pronoun, a body or a mask or (in radio drama) a voice, and it has to do with the separation of a character from all others in the storyworld and with the sense that the character is self-identical over time (this is the form of continuity of the self that Paul Ricoeur calls *idem*, a mode of invariance of the person).[9] Identification 'with' has to do with the filling of that initial moment of identification with an affective content. But these are not two separate moments: the act of recognition that identifies a figure in a text is, at the same time, a way of relating to that figure. And this act of recognition and response is dual: it goes at once to the position of an enunciating subject and to that of an enunciated object, who is at the same time a subject (of action, of thought, of talk) in his or her own right.

Here is a narrating voice speaking of a character, in Henry James's 1895 story 'The Altar of the Dead':

> He had a mortal dislike, poor Stransom, to lean anniversaries, and loved them still less when they made a pretence of a figure. Celebrations and suppressions were equally painful to him, and but one of the former found a place in his life. He had kept each year in his own fashion the date of Mary Antrim's death. It would be more to the point perhaps to say that this occasion kept *him*: it kept him at least effectually from doing anything else. It took hold of him again and again with a hand of which time had softened but never loosened the touch. He waked to his feast of memory as consciously as he would have waked to his marriage-morn. Marriage had had of old but too little to say to the matter: for the girl who was to have been his bride there had been no bridal embrace. She had died of a malignant fever after the wedding-day had been fixed, and he had lost before fairly tasting it an affection that promised to fill his life to the brim.[10]

Introducing Stransom as though in mid-conversation with an anaphora ('he... Stransom') that reverses the usual order of proper name and pronoun, the voice that narrates is at once a colloquial and evaluative presence ('poor Stransom')

[8] Cf. Suzanne Keen, *Empathy and the Novel* (Oxford: Oxford University Press, 2007).

[9] Paul Ricoeur, *Oneself as Another*, trans. Kathleen Blamey (Chicago: University of Chicago Press, 1992), p. 119.

[10] Henry James, 'The Altar of the Dead', in *The Short Stories of Henry James*, ed. Clifton Fadiman (New York: Modern Library, 1945), p. 319.

and yet effaced as a present figure. Before we focus our attention on Stransom we occupy, however lightly, the position from which Stransom's story can make sense. That positioning situates us in a place which is like that of a speaking person, a place from which the existence and the qualities of Stransom are posited and judged as though by a fellow human being; this narrative instance, this disembodied voice, has few personal qualities beyond its attitude to the character and a precise, self-conscious deployment of syntax and trope.

Yet this voice, this minimally specified subject, is unlikely to be the source of another layer of enunciation which logically precedes and qualifies it: a layer which works, for example, by giving an ironic inflection, in this story of ghosts, to the word 'mortal', and to that ghostly hand 'of which time had softened but never loosened the touch'. That irony takes place at a different level, as a prior instance which is voiceless and featureless, yet which guides our reading of textual patterns, including our hearing of the voice that condescends to 'poor Stransom'. This bare, featureless place is the necessary condition for any more structured recognition and identification to occur.

It is from these layered initial positionings that we place ourselves in relation to Stransom, the central character of this story; and we do so by entering into his dislike of lean anniversaries and his feast of memory. We need not share his feelings, or approve of the choices he has made in his life: we must merely be able to imagine doing so, and, with whatever reservations, to enter into his world and the moral dilemma that comes to shape it. This is scarcely the case with Mary Antrim: having little presence in the storyworld other than as a part of Stransom's story, she can be identified as a distinct character but barely evokes an affective response on the reader's part; she is one of Stransom's ghosts. We could perhaps say that she is a postulate of his world as he is a postulate of the narrator's, who is, in turn, postulated by the textual first instance.

I return in Chapter 5 to a more technical discussion of that first narrative instance; here I want merely to make the argument that identification—but perhaps the more neutral 'positioning' would be a better way of describing this process—takes place initially in relation to an enunciative instance, whether overt or covert, as a precondition of its taking place in relation to a definite character. At its simplest, this positioning is dual: we occupy the place of an enunciating subject (however weakly specified as a quasi-person), and the place of a character who is spoken of. That schema can then be complicated in numerous ways: there may be multiple levels of narration, narrators may be foregrounded or entirely inconspicuous, and in homodiegetic narration (where the narrator is part of the narrated world) the narrator may be identical to the central character, or may play a subordinate role in the storyworld.[11] There may be no one 'central' character, or there may be multiple central characters, simultaneously or successively; and the relation between 'central' and 'minor' characters distributes the reader's

[11] The concept of homodiegesis is taken from Gérard Genette, *Narrative Discourse*, trans. Jane Lewin (Ithaca: Cornell University Press, 1980).

affective involvement in complex ways. In the case of film, Vivian Sobchack suggests identification should be understood at an even deeper, 'prepersonal' level, related 'not to our secondary engagement with and recognition of either "subject positions" or characters but rather to our primary engagement (and the film's) with the sense and sensibility of materiality itself', including the 'subjective matter' that we ourselves are.[12]

What of texts such as lyric poems, which may be characterized by the absence of figural representation of the kind that narrative texts deploy? In the case of texts with a first-person speaker there is little difficulty in defining that speaker as a persona, a quasi-person. But what of a text such as this, which seems to preclude ready identification?

Use No Flukes
Close to stand
Glitter with edge
Clouds, what's, but
Weather of devoid
Uses unwrapping
Lower the second
Gravity for allowing, but
Slowly, as if
Backward, falling
Folded.[13]

Not only is there little evidence here of a speaking self, but the fragmented syntax, with its mix of disconnected constatives, infinitives, participles, and subjectless verbs and its apparently disconnected nouns, offers little hold on either a coherent position of enunciation or a coherent represented world. A fluke is a variety of flat, triangular fish; a kind of worm; the pointy barb of an anchor or an arrow; or one of a whale's two tail fins. In billiards a fluke is a successful stroke made by accident or chance, and, by extension, it means something difficult that's pulled off by chance or luck. A fluke of wind is a chance breeze, and that meaning may connect with the words associated with the semantic domain 'weather' ('glitter', 'clouds'). The other possible semantic domain here has to do with 'falling' ('lower', 'gravity', 'backward', and perhaps, as a prelude to falling, 'stand' and 'edge'). It's not clear how these two domains could relate to each other (although an implicit suggestion of 'rain' might do it), and it may be that the poem should be read as an extreme form either of ellipsis (hence the syntactically isolated 'what's' and 'but', and the absence of a connected sentence structure) or of a scrambled syntax which could be reconstructed ('stand close to the edge', 'weather devoid of uses'), or else as a

[12] Vivian Sobchack, *Carnal Thoughts: Embodiment and Moving Image Culture* (Berkeley: University of California Press, 2004), p. 65.

[13] Charles Bernstein, 'Use no Flukes'. Reprinted with the permission of the author from *The Sophist* (Los Angeles: Sun & Moon Press, 1987; rpt. Cambridge: Salt Publishing, 2004), p. 133.

poem about, precisely, the difficulty of making coherent meaning out of fragmented pieces of language.

A text such as this raises in acute form the question of whether there can be character in the absence of recognition or identification; yet the mere institutional existence of this text as a poem (its inclusion in a volume described on the jacket as a collection of poetry, its lineation, and its enclosure by white space on the page) requires us to suppose both the possibility of sense and, therefore, the possibility of a coherent position of enunciation, however lacking in personal characteristics that position may be. The poem gives little hold for affective involvement on the part of the reader, but to the extent that we are interested enough to read it and to struggle with it (this is an open question, of course), it binds the reader in to its difficult world. As H. R. Jauss puts it, 'identification with the hero does not exhaust the possibilities of aesthetic identification. Identification with what is being portrayed may occur through other relevant figures or through a paradigmatic situation which characterizes especially a primary level of the lyrical experience'.[14] And that 'situation' may be entirely minimal.

Identification takes place in relation to positions of enunciation before it takes place in relation to characters; it may be either positive or negative, 'with' or 'against' (and usually the one implies the other); and identifications may shift during the course of a reading: the investment of affective energy in watching a film or reading a written text is typically diffuse and dynamic rather than punctual and static. Fictional character is textually constructed in the play between positions of enunciation and figural constructs in the storyworld, and these positions are cumulatively and complexly filled during the course of a prose narrative or a lyric or a film or gameplay.

The binding-in of the reading or viewing or speaking subject occurs above all in its slotting into these positions which constitute it as a subject in the very process of making sense. And, conversely, 'sense' is 'made' within a textual circuit articulating positions through processes of identification, 'the maintenance of these positions being the work effected by us as subjects each time we understand the meaning of a sentence, each time we "get" the joke, each time we "make" the film make sense'.[15]

II

In the worlds of digital gaming and screen-based virtual reality (and increasingly in military robotics),[16] the inscription of participants into discursive places happens through the manipulation of a representation called an avatar.[17] The avatar, a word

[14] H. R. Jauss, 'Interaction Patterns of Identification with the Hero', in *Aesthetic Experience and Literary Hermeneutics*, trans. Michael Shaw (Minneapolis: University of Minnesota Press, 1982), p. 153.

[15] Claire Pajaczkowska, 'The Heterosexual Presumption: A Contribution to the Debate on Pornography', *Screen* 22: 1 (1981), p. 83.

[16] Cf. Patrick Crogan, *Gameplay Mode: Between War, Simulation and Technoculture* (Minneapolis: University of Minnesota Press, 2011).

[17] I am indebted for much of the thinking and some of the formulations in this section to my colleagues Justin Clemens and Tom Apperley.

which in Vedic religion and its offshoots designates the incarnation of a deity (from the Sanskrit *avatāra*, a descent, a passing over or down), is the primary interface between the user and the screenworld,[18] and it may manifest any degree of incarnation along a spectrum running from the very abstract to the very concrete: from an onscreen cursor, a string of text, a name, a schematic cartoon figure, to a hyperreal three-dimensional graphic figure, a photograph, or a simulation of the body of the user itself, inscribed into the screenworld by means of voice- and face-recognition technologies and by motion sensors which set up kinaesthetic and proprioceptive feedback loops between the user and the screen.[19]

The avatar is a placeholder, an 'interactive, social representation of a user',[20] deployed in the majority of digital games to make possible 'the players' projections of intent and will into, as well as interaction and manipulation of, the gameworld'.[21] The simplest view of an avatar, then, is that it is a surrogate for the user, mediating between positions in the actual and the virtual worlds and often projecting an idealized alter ego.[22] Yet the avatar does not simply translate an intention from one world to the other. It is selected or designed in such a way that its abilities match the affordances of the game or universe: James Gee's example is that of the game *Thief: Deadly Shadows*, where the skills called for are those of sneaking and hiding, and the skills of overt confrontation needed in war games would be out of place.[23] Similarly, Marsha Kinder has found that boys would frequently choose the Princess Toadstool avatar in *Super Mario Bros. 2*, despite her gender and because of her powers of action (the Princess can float above the ground).[24] The mode of being of the avatar is bound up with the ends it serves, and these ends are both specific to each game or universe, and inherently social.

If the avatar is 'a prosthetic that replaces the entire body',[25] then—a set of capacities, a 'kinaesthetic grammar, with a limited set of actions for us to deploy'[26]—it is also 'a tool for regulating intimacy'.[27] Its most basic function in games which involve more than a single player is to make the player vicariously visible to the

[18] I use this term to cover the represented space-time coordinates of both digital games and virtual universes such as *Second Life*.

[19] Katherine Hayles writes about this process in relation to virtual reality technologies, many of which have now been incorporated into game design, in *How We Became Posthuman: Virtual Bodies in Cybernetics, Literature, and Informatics* (Chicago: University of Chicago Press, 1999), pp. 26–7 and passim.

[20] Mark Stephen Meadows, *I, Avatar: The Culture and Consequences of Having a Second Life* (Berkeley: New Riders, 2008), p. 13.

[21] Anders Tychsen, Michael Hitchens, and Thea Brolund, 'Character Play: The Use of Game Characters in Multi-Player Role-Playing Games across Platforms', *ACM Computers in Entertainment* 6: 2 (2008), article 22, p. 2.

[22] Robbie Cooper's *Alter Ego: Avatars and their Creators* (London: Chris Boot, 2007) revealingly juxtaposes images of users and their online selves.

[23] James Paul Gee, 'Video Games and Embodiment', *Games and Culture* 3: 3–4 (2008), p. 258.

[24] Marsha Kinder, *Playing with Power in Movies, Television, and Video Games: From Muppet Babies to Teenage Mutant Ninja Turtles* (Berkeley: University of California Press, 1993), p. 107.

[25] Meadows, *I, Avatar*, p. 92.

[26] Andrew Burn and Gareth Schott, 'Heavy Hero or Digital Dummy? Multimodal Player–Avatar Relations in *Final Fantasy 7*', *Visual Communication* 3: 2 (2004), p. 221.

[27] Meadows, *I, Avatar*, p. 36.

avatars of other players; it represents a user to other users within the screenworld, and thereby establishes a realm of mediated social interaction which is also, strictly speaking, a realm of social interaction in its own right.

This distinction between the instrumental and social functions of the avatar (functions which are, of course, never mutually exclusive) corresponds in part to that between first- and third-person perspectives. Lev Manovich argues that in computer space 'the standard interface... is the virtual camera modeled after the film camera rather than a simulation of unaided human sight'.[28] But this camera looks with subjective eyes: unlike film, where subjective perspective is a marginal technique used primarily 'to effect a sense of alienation, detachment, fear, or violence', in digital games it is the usual manner of achieving 'an intuitive sense of motion and action in game-play'.[29] In strongly rule-based systems this perspective, which is the characteristic one for genres such as the first-person shooter, may be a pure look or camera angle without objectification, or there may be minimal objectification (the cross-hairs of a gunsight, a protruding rifle barrel at the edge of the frame, a steering wheel). Similarly, real-time strategy games, such as *StarCraft*, and simulation games with a godlike perspective, such as *The Sims*, may operate from an invisible place which is, nevertheless, a point of presence and the source of actions. In role-based systems, by contrast, the user's presence in the game or world tends to be represented either as an over-the-shoulder rear view of the avatar, or, more usually, as a view of a fully visible figure.

Amongst those visible figures we can distinguish a continuum of modalities of avatar construction, from strongly defined and represented characters whose affective force lies in their hyperreal singularity, to minimally defined 'shell' characters whose identificatory force resides in a blankness of surface on which very diverse players may inscribe their own interests, fantasies, and even their empirical features. As a general rule, action games tend to work with invisible or shell characters,[30] while multiplayer games and virtual worlds tend to be driven by increasingly sophisticated technologies of graphic simulation to develop characters with both visual and psychological complexity. In massively multiplayer games such as *Ultima Online* or *World of Warcraft* avatars can take on additional skills and knowledge, as well as change their appearance, in the course of the game. This kind of gaming experience is thus strongly grounded in the identification of players with avatars functioning as 'affective sympathetic interfaces' between the actual and virtual worlds.[31]

[28] Lev Manovich, *The Language of New Media* (Cambridge, MA: MIT Press, 2001), p. 265.

[29] Alexander R. Galloway, *Gaming: Essays on Algorithmic Culture* (Minneapolis: University of Minnesota Press, 2006), p. 40.

[30] Cf. Celia Pearce, 'Towards a Game Theory of Game', in Noah Wardrip-Fruin and Pat Harrigan (eds), *FirstPerson: New Media as Story, Performance, and Game* (Cambridge, MA: MIT Press, 2004), pp. 146, 152.

[31] Ana Paiva, Gerd Andersson, Kristina Höök, Dário Mourão, Marco Costa, and Carlos Martinho, 'SenToy in FantasyA: Designing an Affective Sympathetic Interface to a Computer Game', *Personal and Ubiquitous Computing* 6 (2002), pp. 378–89.

That identification may have real emotional intensity. Julian Dibbell's account of the emotional trauma caused by the virtual rape of one avatar by another in the multiplayer dungeon LambdaMOO[32] is the classic study of the proposition that 'interaction in virtual worlds is real interaction with real emotions and real consequences':[33] that virtual worlds are imaginary gardens with real toads in them. Real lust and arousal are at play in sexual relations between avatars (just as they are in the represented sex of pornography),[34] and real ethical issues are raised by such actions as virtual sex with child avatars.[35] This is to say that, as with all fictions, the question of the ontological status of fictive entities is largely irrelevant to our ability and willingness to interact with them *as though* they were persons like ourselves.[36]

It is clear that that willingness is at the heart of the increasingly central role played by avatars in the commercial growth of the gaming industry. The impact of digital gaming upon globalized culture has depended, perhaps unexpectedly, upon a concerted attention in gaming R&D to the design of game characters which must be able to sustain the identifications of very large numbers of players if the game is to be commercially successful. Avatars are, moreover, the primary way by which gameworlds are embedded in a broader globalized commercial culture, enabling characters to cross genres and media:[37] avatars function not only as essential in-game doppelgangers, but as part of the game's branding strategies (including the sale of customized identities or identity attributes) and its associated media spin-offs. The Mario Brothers characters, which now drive films, television shows, and other kinds of merchandising, are the exemplars of this new design paradigm. At another level of gaming, *Angry Birds*, at the time of writing the most popular mobile phone application in the world, is integrated with the production of soft toys, short films, and so on, all available for purchase online. The marketing of games and of systems such as Xbox Live is thus heavily focused on avatar characterization; it is above all the avatar that enables digital games to develop and to exert a cultural dominance over an unprecedentedly complex system of interlinked online (and offline) media.

The intensity of affective investment that flows between the user and the avatar should not, however, mask the real discontinuity between the player/subject and

[32] Julian Dibbell, 'A Rape in Cyberspace', in *My Tiny Life: Crime and Passion in a Virtual World* (New York: Henry Holt & Co., 1998), pp. 11–30; first published in a slightly different form in *Village Voice*, 23 December 1993.

[33] Mikael Jakobsson, 'Rest in Peace, Bill the Bot: Death and Life in Virtual Worlds', in Ralph Schroeder (ed.), *The Social Life of Avatars: Presence and Interaction in Shared Virtual Environments* (London: Springer-Verlag, 2002), p. 71.

[34] Meadows, *I, Avatar*, p. 57.

[35] Andrew A. Adams, 'Virtual Sex with Child Avatars', in Charles Wankel and Shaun Malleck (eds), *Emerging Ethical Issues of Life in Virtual Worlds* (North Carolina: Information Age Publishing, 2010), pp. 55–72.

[36] Cf. Graham Priest, *Towards Non-Being: The Logic and Metaphysics of Intentionality* (Oxford: Clarendon Press, 2005), pp. 116–17.

[37] Cf. Tom Apperley, *Gaming Rhythms: Play and Counterplay from the Situated to the Global*, Theory on Demand #6 (Amsterdam: Institute of Networked Cultures, 2010), p. 12.

their online representative. One of the ways in which we can envisage the complexity of that relation of representation lies in the possibility that multiple selves might control a single avatar, or that a single self might have multiple avatars. The latter can happen in one of two ways: I can be represented by a homogeneous cohort of avatars, as in a game of chess; or I can use alternative avatars, or 'alts', either so that one of them can perform routine tasks while a primary avatar engages in more interesting interactions, or so that I can occupy and explore heterogeneous forms of surrogate selfhood. Tom Boellstorff argues that, if we accept that avatars in *Second Life* are 'not just placeholders for selfhood, but sites of self-making in their own right',[38] then the avatar has a degree of autonomy from the user, and, indeed, users may act in accord with their avatar's personality rather than the one they would think of as their 'own'. 'As a subject of technics,' writes Emily Apter, 'the avatar is not the idealized double of the player-subject (which is the naïve concept of avatar), but a transformer of fates, at once independent and mimetic of some modicum of subjective agency.'[39] The alt is an important index of this partial independence of the avatar from its user, and, as Boellstorff argues, of the way in which the gap between the actual and the virtual is operationalized so as to make it a resource for a sort of 'fractal subjectivity'.[40]

At the heart of the avatar's functions is that of building a sense of presence in a virtual world through the simulation of an embodied sociality. What does 'embodiment' mean in a virtual environment? In one sense the virtual avatar is the opposite of an incarnation: it is a movement from fleshly to digital being. Yet to put it this way is, as T. L. Taylor writes, to rely on 'an impoverished view of the nature of the body, both off- and online'.[41] Rather, we operate constantly with 'distributed bodies and selves'.[42] Taylor cites a distinction made by Frank Biocca between 'the virtual body, the physical body, and the phenomenal body', where the latter designates 'our body schema or the "mental or internal representation" of our body'[43] (I explore a similar set of distinctions in Chapter 8). In Biocca's argument,

> [i]t appears that embodiment can significantly alter body schema. Metaphorically, we might say that the virtual body competes with the physical body to influence the form of the phenomenal body. The result is a tug of war where the body schema may oscillate in the mind of the user of the interface.[44]

We can thus not assume 'that actual-world embodiment is the only real embodiment':[45] our sense of our body is influenced by each of the forms that it takes.

[38] Tom Boellstorff, *Coming of Age in Second Life: An Anthropologist Explores the Virtually Human* (Princeton: Princeton University Press, 2008), p. 149.

[39] Emily Apter, 'Technics of the Subject: The Avatar-Drive', *Postmodern Culture* 18: 2 (2008), n.p.

[40] Boellstorff, *Coming of Age in Second Life*, p. 150.

[41] T. L. Taylor, *Play between Worlds: Exploring Online Game Culture* (Cambridge, MA: MIT Press, 2006), p. 117.

[42] T. L. Taylor, 'Living Digitally: Embodiment in Virtual Worlds', in Schroeder (ed.), *The Social Life of Avatars*, p. 58.

[43] Frank Biocca, 'The Cyborg's Dilemma: Progressive Embodiment in Virtual Environments', *Journal of Computer-Mediated Communication* 3: 2 (1997), n.p.; cited in Taylor, 'Living Digitally', p. 57.

[44] Biocca, 'The Cyborg's Dilemma'.

[45] Boellstorff, *Coming of Age in Second Life*, p. 135.

The clearest demonstration that the phenomenal body carries over into the avatar is perhaps the way cultural norms of body space are partly but not completely consistent between actual and virtual worlds. The focal point for perception and action in a virtual world is centred on your avatar. What you see in *Second Life*, for example, is 'the view from your avatar's proximity... The virtual thirty-meter radius within which you "hear" the typed chat of other residents extends out from your avatar's body'.[46] The sense of being physically immersed in an environment includes a coherent sense of personal space: 'Just as we move away if someone comes too close to us, so players will move their avatars away if someone else's avatar invades their "personal" space, or move them close to signal aggression.'[47] Avatars thus organize space, time, and social interaction within the screenworld in ways that are analogous with the organization of actual space, time, and social interaction by and around our physical bodies.

What avatars generate, then, is a sense of a world that is coherent, centred, and present to itself and to the user. But virtual presence is no more self-identical than is our presence to ourselves in a primary reality. This non-self-identity is, I think, neatly demonstrated by a class of entities, signs, and states that shadow their positive counterparts. One is the concept of 'afk' or 'away from keyboard', a state in which a user is absent but their avatar remains present; this state, Boellstorff argues, introduces a constitutive absence, or 'a kind of ghostly absent presence', into a virtual world: 'residents never completely "come back" to a virtual world because they were never completely there in the first place'.[48] A second member of this class is the so-called 'ghost signs' that Peter Bogh Andersen describes, in his taxonomy of the computer signs deployed in games, as being without features and unable to be handled but nevertheless existing as a kind of trace because of their influence on the behaviour of other, functional signs.[49] A third is the machine-run entities called bots, logged on as players and used to perform routine functions or to annoy other players in multiplayer environments. And the fourth is the diegetic and non-diegetic machine acts described by Galloway: the steady-state loops that keep a game ticking over in the absence of players, or the issuing of commands such as 'game over'.[50] In each of these, it seems to me, we can recognize the figure

[46] Boellstorff, *Coming of Age in Second Life*, p. 129; I have taken the liberty of changing Boellstorff's ethnographic preterite into the present tense.

[47] Jessica Wolfendale, 'My Avatar, My Self: Virtual Harm and Attachment', *Ethics and Information Technology* 9 (2007), p. 114.

[48] Boellstorff, *Coming of Age in Second Life*, p. 117.

[49] Peter Bogh Andersen, *A Theory of Computer Semiotics: Semiotic Approaches to Construction and Assessment of Computer Systems* (Cambridge: Cambridge University Press, 1990), p. 211; cited in Espen J. Aarseth, *Cybertext: Perspectives on Ergodic Literature* (Baltimore: Johns Hopkins University Press, 1997), pp. 32–3.

[50] Galloway, *Gaming: Essays on Algorithmic Culture*, pp. 8–38. Each of these figures closely resembles the 'quasi-objects' that Michel Serres identifies as occupying the space between subjecthood and objecthood: an object that, without being a subject, 'marks or designates a subject who, without it, would not be a subject'. Michel Serres, *The Parasite*, trans. Lawrence R. Schehr (Baltimore: Johns Hopkins University Press, 1982), p. 225.

of *my paredros* that I discussed in Chapter 1: the unfigured other, the figured absence, which is at once the negation and the condition of existence of character.

Much of the literature on the avatar has been concerned with disputing the applicability of literary conceptions of character to digital games. Although many of these arguments rely on simplistic dichotomies—interpretation versus action, or identification versus instrumentality, or passive versus active uses of texts and games, respectively,[51] —there is, nevertheless, a core of truth to the distinction. Whereas narratives represent an activity of disordering that moves a 'world' from one state of equilibrium to another, games present an injunction to the player to make this movement happen. In this sense, avatars are more than 'displayed representations on the screen'; they 'exist as performed entities',[52] and Marie-Laure Ryan's conceptualization of games in dramatic rather than narrative terms is appropriate: in games,

> [t]he player pursues the goal specified by the game by performing a series of moves that determine the destiny of the gameworld. This destiny is created dramatically, by being enacted rather than diegetically, by being narrated. But, in contrast to standard drama, the enactment is autotelic, rather than being directed at an observer: performing actions is the point of the game and the main source of the player's pleasure.[53]

The avatar thus has the dual functions of being an element in an action sequence and a representative of the player in the gameworld. This duality of action and person corresponds to the Aristotelian distinction between *mythos and ēthos*, plot and character, together with his explicit subordination of the latter to the former.[54] If the avatar, like the tragic hero, is a function of plot (the game), then it is also the mechanism by which the player is inscribed, both functionally and affectively, into the game and by which the gameworld, in turn, is made to seem intuitively obvious.[55] The affective work of games differs from that of tragedy, but the central role of virtual death in digital gaming means that there are both points of contact with the generic norms of tragedy, and a fundamental dissimilarity because of the reversibility of death in virtual worlds.

[51] For example, Ken Perlin, 'Can There Be a Form Between a Game and a Story?', in Wardrip-Fruin and Harrigan (eds), *FirstPerson*, p. 14; James Newman, 'The Myth of the Ergodic Videogame', *Game Studies* 2: 1 (2002), n.p. <http://www.gamestudies.org/0102/newman/>. Last accessed 28 June 2013; Aarseth, *Cybertext*, p. 38.

[52] Alison Gazzard, 'The Avatar and the Player: Understanding the Relationship Beyond the Screen', in *2009 Conference in Games and Virtual Worlds for Serious Applications* (IEEE Computer Society, 2009), p. 190.

[53] Marie-Laure Ryan, 'Will New Media Produce New Narratives?', in Marie-Laure Ryan (ed.), *Narrative Across Media: The Languages of Storytelling* (Lincoln: University of Nebraska Press, 2004), p. 349.

[54] Aristotle, *Poetics (De Poetica)*, trans. Ingram Bywater, in *The Basic Works of Aristotle*, ed. Richard McKeon (New York: Random House, 1941), §1450a, p. 1460.

[55] Discussing Brenda Laurel's likening of graphical user interfaces to theatre (*Computers as Theatre*, Reading, MA: Addison-Wesley, 1991, 1993), Alan Liu writes that 'Software that characterizes the user by giving her or him an explicit game role constrains ensuing events to settings, actions, or tools that appear "intuitive" because they are unified around the character…' Alan Liu, *The Laws of Cool: Knowledge Work and the Culture of Information* (Chicago: University of Chicago Press, 2004), p. 170.

The pleasure of rule-based games is kinaesthetic in the first place—a pleasure of the body, a state of haptic absorption;[56] but beyond that it is immersive. One speaks of being in the grip of a game, of being absorbed in it; players repeat an action over and over, obsessed with getting it right (and repeating the action through the multiple deaths of their avatar: this is, precisely, a repetition compulsion). Puzzle, quest, and combat are the core structures of digital games,[57] and two types of action predominate: moving around the virtual world, and shooting.[58] If identification is involved here, it is less with the avatar than with the process of the game. Ted Friedman speaks of this as an identification with the computer itself, an internalization of the logic of the program in a way that helps explain

> the strange sense of self-dissolution created by computer games, the way games 'suck you in'. The pleasure of computer games is in entering into a computer-like mental state: responding as automatically as the computer, processing information as effortlessly, replacing sentient cognition with the blank hum of computation.[59]

But rather than positing a single point of identification (the avatar, kinaesthetic immersion, the logic of computation), we should perhaps posit instead a hierarchy of levels of identification, the 'layered positionings' that I proposed in section I. At the deepest level would be the process that Manovich describes as the use of spatialized representations to navigate a multimedia database and thereby immerse the user in an imaginary world.[60] Kinaesthetic positioning would be a moment of this level of identification. At the next level, but equally embedded in the logic of computation, is the simultaneous enactment and learning of an algorithm ('kill all the enemies on the current level, while collecting all the treasures it contains; go to the next level and so on until you reach the last level') which mimes computer algorithms in a manner 'too uncanny to be dismissed'.[61] At each of these levels the player identifies with a logic of movement through a world. At higher levels, identification takes place in relation to the objects that populate that world, including an avatar that corresponds to the placement of the user and to the fantasies of omnipotence or of perfected identity that direct it; and, depending on the genre of the game, these higher, figural levels may or may not be present.

Unlike traditional board, sports, and card games, which are relatively abstract, digital games tend to project worlds;[62] and worlds precede and suppose the avatars that negotiate them. In spatial terms, these worlds are a 'fully rendered, actionable

[56] Cf. Angela Ndalianis, *The Horror Sensorium: Media and the Senses* (Jefferson, NC: McFarland, 2012), p. 44; Ndalianis notes the intensification of that haptic absorption by the Xbox 360 Kinect, which 'requires that our whole body becomes the controller as our body motions are interpreted by the camera and, in turn, by the game' (p. 50).

[57] Pearce, 'Towards a Game Theory of Game', p. 156.

[58] Marie-Laure Ryan, *Avatars of Story* (Minneapolis: University of Minnesota Press, 2006), p. 118.

[59] Ted Friedman, '*Civilization* and Its Discontents: Simulation, Subjectivity, and Space', in Greg M. Smith (ed.), *On a Silver Platter: CD-ROMs and the Promises of a New Technology* (New York: New York University Press, 1999), p. 136.

[60] Manovich, *Language of New Media*, p. 215.

[61] Manovich, *Language of New Media*, p. 222.

[62] Jesper Juul, 'Introduction to Game Time', in Wardrip-Fruin and Harrigan (eds), *FirstPerson*, p. 139.

space', able to be explored exhaustively.[63] Yet they are also, as Manovich argues, structured by a binary ontology that distinguishes animate entities from a space which is discontinuous and aggregate rather than systematic and homogeneous.[64] Similarly, the temporal structure of gameworlds is split between the time of play and moments of suspended time in which the player arranges the framework of play (sets up actions, rearranges the disposition of characters, inspects statistics, and so on).[65] Game time itself can be described in terms of a 'basic duality' of the time taken to play the game and the time of events in the gameworld.[66] Action games are usually played in real time, whereas in strategy and simulation games time can be slowed down or speeded up.

The crucial point about the space-time coordinates of gameworlds is their malleability and their reversibility. Games can be endlessly replayed; the death of an avatar is (almost) always provisional. This death, says Aarseth, lays bare the logical distinction between (a) the character, (b) the internal addressee of the game, and (c) the player or user, and thus the epistemological hierarchy that governs the game: the character dies, is erased from the game, and begins again in another; the addressee or narratee is told of the death and invited to play again; and the user, 'aware of all this in a way denied to the narratee, learns from the mistakes and previous experience and is able to play in a different game'.[67] But the death of the avatar lays bare, too, the fantasmatic nature of identification with the gameworld: driven by a compulsive repetition, 'the purpose of a targeting game is the overcoming of death through the targeting of the other, freeing the self to be itself—temporarily. The goal, the target of the target, is to stop playing while still alive'.[68]

III

The reciprocal action by which the sense-making self is repeatedly constituted as a unified subject in its recognition of subject positions in the text is at the heart of the process of identification of and with characters. The most illuminating account of identification that I know—for all its incompleteness and its lack of coherence—is Freud's.

Freud struggled over many years with the concept of identification and its closely linked counterpart, narcissism. J. Laplanche and J.-B. Pontalis define identification as a 'psychological process whereby the subject assimilates an aspect, property or attribute of the other and is transformed, wholly or partially, after the model the other provides. It is by means of a series of identifications that the personality is constituted and specified'.[69] This definition, something of a miracle of concision,

[63] Galloway, *Gaming: Essays on Algorithmic Culture*, p. 63.

[64] Manovich, *Language of New Media*, pp. 253–4, 256.

[65] Galloway, *Gaming: Essays on Algorithmic Culture*, p. 65.

[66] Juul, 'Introduction to Game Time', p. 131.

[67] Espen J. Aarseth, 'Nonlinearity and Literary Theory', in George P. Landow (ed.), *Hyper/Text/Theory* (Baltimore: Johns Hopkins University Press, 1994), p. 74.

[68] McKenzie Wark, *Gamer Theory* (Cambridge, MA: Harvard University Press, 2007), p. 138.

[69] J. Laplanche and J.-B. Pontalis, *The Language of Psychoanalysis*, trans. Donald Nicholson-Smith (New York: Norton, 1973), p. 205.

deliberately simplifies the long process of development through which the concept passed.

In its initial formulation, in letters to Wilhelm Fliess written in the late 1890s, it has to do with a hysterical fantasy expressing an unconscious assimilation of oneself to another; in a letter of 17 December 1896, for example, Freud writes of agoraphobia as 'the repression of the impulse to take the first comer on the streets—envy of the prostitute and identification with her'. [70] This is a relatively opportunistic mode of identification, in which the unconscious formulates a trope of similitude and exploits it to generate a symptom. The identification is occasional rather than formative of the ego. Similarly, in the section of *The Interpretation of Dreams* on the dreamwork, identification is described, along with condensation and overdetermination, as one of the rhetorical devices through which the dream is constructed: this is the transitive sense of identification (identification of x *as* y) rather than the reflexive sense (identification of oneself *with*).

A major turn in Freud's thinking comes in the essays on narcissism and on mourning and melancholia, published during the First World War, in which identification figures as a mechanism by which the loved object is introjected into the ego, thereby splitting the ego into a part that loves or hates and a part that is loved or hated.[71] What brings the concepts of narcissism and identification together is the notion that object choice involves, at its most primitive and regressive, a desire to incorporate the other into one's own body, an oral fantasy which corresponds to the melancholic's identification with the lost and introjected other.[72] In the 'Introductory Lectures' of 1917 Freud writes that

> [W]e can conclude that the melancholic has, it is true, withdrawn his libido from the object, but that, by a process which we must call 'narcissistic identification', the object has been set up in the ego itself, has been, as it were, projected onto the ego…The subject's own ego is then treated like the object that has been abandoned.[73]

It is on the basis of these essays from the middle period of psychoanalysis that Freud comes to a view of the ego as a 'precipitate of abandoned object cathexes',[74] formed on the basis of the traces of past identifications and 'constituted from the beginning by an identification having oral incorporation as its prototype':[75] in Adam Phillips's paraphrase, 'character is constituted by identification—the ego likening itself to what it once loved'.[76]

[70] Sigmund Freud, *The Origins of Psychoanalysis: Letters to Wilhelm Fliess, Drafts and Notes: 1887–1902*, ed. Marie Bonaparte, Anna Freud, and Ernst Kris, trans. Eric Mosbacher and James Strachey (New York: Basic Books, 1954), p. 182.

[71] Sigmund Freud, 'On Narcissism: An Introduction (1914)', in *The Standard Edition of the Complete Psychological Works of Sigmund Freud* XIV, trans. James Strachey (London: Hogarth Press, 1955), pp. 73–102; 'Mourning and Melancholia (1917)', in *Standard Edition* XIV, pp. 239–58.

[72] Freud, 'Mourning and Melancholia', p. 249.

[73] Sigmund Freud, *Introductory Lectures on Psychoanalysis*, in *Standard Edition* XVI, p. 427.

[74] W. W. Meissner, 'Notes on Identification 1: Origins in Freud', *The Psychoanalytic Quarterly* 39 (1970), p. 579.

[75] Laplanche and Pontalis, *Language of Psychoanalysis*, p. 138.

[76] Adam Phillips, 'Keeping it Moving: Commentary on Judith Butler's "Melancholy Gender/Refused Identification"', in Judith Butler, *The Psychic Life of Power: Theories in Subjection* (Stanford: Stanford University Press, 1997), p. 151.

What the ego loves is, in the first instance, itself. What is striking and innovative in Freud's thought is not the postulation of a love of self, which in itself is a commonplace, but the fact that this is understood as occurring through the taking of the ego as a possible love object; and the fact that the actual positions of subject and object may be less important than the fantasized positions (which may indeed both be internal to the ego). Narcissism is one of Freud's major explanatory categories, and he takes it to constitute the real basis of every object choice: 'the libidinal energy is always borrowed from the ego, and always ready to return to it',[77] because 'the ego is to be regarded as a great reservoir of libido from which libido is sent out *to* objects and which is always ready to absorb libido flowing back *from* objects'.[78]

If the ego is formed by 'likening itself to what it once loved', this identification is always circular: the choice of an object of love is always in some sense narcissistic, and the relation to the other is thus preceded by and formed upon the ego's taking of itself as an object of love. Laplanche posits that the genesis of the ego through a process of identification 'must occur extremely early if it is true that its effect is to allow for the establishment of a boundary... rendering intelligible such primitive mechanisms as introjection and projection'.[79] The identifications through which the ego is formed and which give it its imaginary unity set up a relation between inside and outside, and thus take place by means of a superimposition of the boundary of the ego on the boundary of the body. Jacques Lacan's concept of the mirror stage accordingly theorizes this passage from auto-erotism to narcissism and the formation of the ego by positing a scenario of self-recognition in the bounded alterity of the body of another;[80] and Freud makes it clear that 'the ego is first and foremost a bodily ego; it is not merely a surface entity, but is itself the projection of a surface'.[81] From this, Laplanche concludes that, 'on the one hand, the ego is the surface of the psychical apparatus, gradually differentiated in and from that apparatus, a specialized organ continuous with it; on the other hand, it is the projection or metaphor of the body's surface, a metaphor in which the various perceptual systems have a role to play'.[82] Crucially, in relation to the fragmented body of auto-erotism, the ego functions as a metaphor of unity, albeit a unity which is made up of sedimented identifications with and incorporations of others (most notably, of course, the fantasy figures of the Mother and the Father as they are played out in the Oedipus complex).

Identification is thus not merely central to my relation to the other, but is constitutive of my relation to my self. At the same time, it is at the basis of the relations of

[77] Jean Laplanche, *Life and Death in Psychoanalysis*, trans. Jeffrey Mehlman (Baltimore: Johns Hopkins University Press, 1976), p. 77.

[78] Sigmund Freud, 'Two Encyclopaedia Articles (1923)', in *Standard Edition* XVIII, p. 257.

[79] Laplanche, *Life and Death in Psychoanalysis*, p. 80.

[80] Jacques Lacan, 'The Mirror Stage as Formative of the *I* Function as Revealed in Psychoanalytic Experience', in *Ecrits*, trans. Bruce Fink, in collaboration with Héloïse Fink and Russell Grigg (New York: Norton, 2006), pp. 75–81.

[81] Sigmund Freud, 'The Ego and the Id', in *Standard Edition* XIX, p. 26.

[82] Laplanche, *Life and Death in Psychoanalysis*, p. 81.

unity and dispersal and of introjection and projection by which my ego is formed as an imaginary unity. Let me give two examples.

The first is that of male homosexuality, in which 'the young man does not abandon his mother, but identifies himself with her; he transforms himself into her...A striking thing about this identification is its ample scale; it remoulds the ego in one of its important features—in its sexual character—upon the model of what has hitherto been the object'.[83] Laplanche adds to this the comment that 'these positions are by no means stable, but, on the contrary, are caught up in a see-sawlike movement which, at the slightest shift of the mirror, can cause an exchange of positions'.[84] It might, in fact, be more correct to say that two positions—a subject position and an object position—are occupied simultaneously, and that there is an unsteady balance between the primary and secondary position.[85]

The second example is that of melancholia. In analysing this neurosis Freud comes to the conclusion that the self-reproaches characteristic of melancholia are really 'reproaches against a loved object which have been shifted away from it on to the patient's own ego'.[86] This situation arises because of a withdrawal of libido from the object; but the emotional energy is not then transferred to another object, but is rather withdrawn into the ego. This causes a splitting of the ego, such that one part identifies itself with the abandoned object and is, in turn, judged and condemned by another part. The ego becomes the object of its own repudiation.[87] This model becomes the basis for Freud's later theorization of the splitting-off of parts of the ego (into ideal ego, ego-ideal, and super-ego).

It is to this dispersal of ego-identifications that I wish to liken the workings of fictional character. The 'recognition' or 'identification' of character that forms the basis of our dealings with a fictional text would involve a mirroring of the semantic and libidinal processes of 'self'-construction in an imaginary construction of 'other', quasi-unified selves. The character effect thus involves a kind of doubling, the shadowing of the other by my self and of my self by the figured other.

This process of the narcissistic dissemination of ego-libido, which I take to be the basis of all historically specific regimes of identification with fictional characters, is identified by Freud as characteristic of the language of dreams. The passage is worth quoting in full:

> It is my experience, and one to which I have found no exception, that every dream deals with the dreamer himself. Dreams are completely egoistic. Whenever my ego does not appear in the content of the dream, but only some extraneous person, I may safely assume that my own ego lies concealed, by identification, behind this other

[83] Sigmund Freud, *Group Psychology and the Analysis of the Ego*, in *Standard Edition* XVIII, p. 108.

[84] Laplanche, *Life and Death in Psychoanalysis*, p. 75.

[85] David Halperin takes two Joan Crawford melodramas, *Mildred Pierce* and *Mommie Dearest*, as models of the family romance of gay men; each represents a mother/daughter dyad, soliciting—through the screening mechanisms of camp—'a simultaneous emotional involvement with the rebellious child and the indignant parent'. David M. Halperin, *How To Be Gay* (Cambridge, MA: Harvard University Press, 2012), p. 223.

[86] Freud, 'Mourning and Melancholia', p. 248.

[87] Freud, 'Mourning and Melancholia', p. 249.

person; I can insert my ego into the context. On other occasions, when my own ego *does* appear in the dream, the situation in which it occurs may teach me that some other person lies concealed, by identification, behind my ego. In that case the dream should warn me to transfer on to myself, when I am interpreting the dream, the concealed common element attached to this other person. There are also dreams in which my ego appears along with other people, who, when the identification is resolved, are revealed once again as my ego. These identifications should then make it possible for me to bring into contact with my ego certain ideas whose acceptance has been forbidden by the censorship. Thus my ego may be represented in a dream several times over, now directly and now through identification with extraneous persons. By means of a number of such identifications it becomes possible to condense an extraordinary amount of thought-material. The fact that the dreamer's own ego appears several times, or in several forms, in a dream is at bottom no more remarkable than that the ego should be contained in a conscious thought several times or in different places or connections—e.g. in the sentence 'when I think what a healthy child I was'.[88]

Despite the disclaimer, this final sentence really is quite remarkable: first, because it demonstrates the dreamwork's dispersal and displacement of the ego by appealing to the grammatical disjunction between the *sujet de l'énonciation* and the *sujet de l'énoncé* (the speaking self and the self spoken of: 'I think... I was'): a repetition and splitting of the grammatical subject; and second, because it lays bare and denies in the same oddly naïve movement the whole problematic of infantile sexuality and of the 'perverse' foundations of normality. The dispersal of the 'I' thus occurs not only at the level of grammar but at the level of rhetoric. Here the relevant trope is that of negation, but Freud's work is rich in rhetorical transformations—for example, the analysis of the shifting subject positions in 'A Child is Being Beaten', where the title sentence is transformed back through 'my father is beating the child' and 'my father is beating the child whom I hate' to 'I am being beaten by my father' (with a corresponding shift from a sadistic to a masochistic position of enunciation).[89] Here the neutrality of the title sentence conceals the underlying fantasy, and the shifting identifications through which it is played out. It also conceals the inherent ambivalence of identification, which 'can turn into an expression of tenderness as easily as into a wish for someone's removal', since 'the object that we long for and prize is assimilated by eating and is in that way annihilated as such'.[90]

When we ask how character works to construct the 'interest' of a story, its affective hold, we are asking a question about the relation between the construction of character and the construction of the reader as reading subject, together with the forms of unity generated by their mutual recognition. What is at issue is character as an effect of desire, understood not as 'someone's' desire but as a structure forming the imaginary unity of subjects in their relation to the imaginary unity of

[88] Sigmund Freud, *The Interpretation of Dreams*, in *Standard Edition* IV, pp. 322–3.

[89] Sigmund Freud, 'A Child is Being Beaten', in *Standard Edition* XVII, p. 179. Laplanche describes this series in terms of the functional equivalence of four very different processes: 'introjecting the suffering object, fantasizing the suffering object, making the object suffer inside oneself, making oneself suffer'. *Life and Death in Psychoanalysis*, p. 97.

[90] Freud, *Group Psychology and the Analysis of the Ego*, p. 105.

objects. To say this is to argue that there can be no separation between an objective textual construct and something (desire) brought to it by a reader; rather, 'character' is an effect of the self-'recognition' of a subject in its dispersal through the multiple positions offered to it by a text.

IV

The question of the affective binding-in of readers to texts is inseparable from that of the historically shifting regimes that govern our identification with or against fictional characters or avatars: learning how to read character is directly bound up with the practice of the self, of recognition of other selves, and of forming an emotional bond with fictional 'selves', and these practices work in distinctively different ways in different genres and in different historical and cultural formations. The text that, more than any other in English, instituted a genre that would 'provide [...] useful training in the more or less official psychological language of our culture',[91] is Samuel Richardson's *Clarissa*, along with its predecessor *Pamela* and its successor, *Sir Charles Grandison*. Together, these novels established the mechanisms of sympathetic identification which have grounded the work of fiction to our day.

Rather than approaching these texts frontally, however, let me do so by indirection, with a text and a device that parodically exaggerate, and thereby elucidate, Richardson's innovations in the technopoetics of feeling and of mimetic identification. I begin with that most eccentric of punctuation marks, the variable-length dash in *The Life and Opinions of Tristram Shandy, Gentleman.*

This is Chapter XVII of Volume 5:

> ——'TWAS nothing,—I did not lose two drops of blood by it——'twas not worth calling in a surgeon, had he lived next door to us——thousands suffer by choice, what I did by accident.——Doctor *Slop* made ten times more of it, than there was occasion:——some men rise, by the art of hanging great weights upon small wires,—and I am this day (*August* the 10th, 1761) paying part of the price of this man's reputation.———O 'twould provoke a stone, to see how things are carried on in this world!——The chamber-maid had left no ******* *** under the bed:———Cannot you contrive, master, quoth *Susannah*, lifting up the sash with one hand, as she spoke, and helping me up into the window seat with the other,—cannot you manage, my dear, for a single time to **** *** ** *** ******?
>
> I was five years old.——*Susannah* did not consider that nothing was well hung in our family,——so slap came the sash down like lightning upon us;—Nothing is left,—cried *Susannah*,—nothing is left—but for me to run my country.——
>
> My uncle *Toby's* house was a much kinder sanctuary; and so *Susannah* fled to it.[92]

[91] Leo Bersani, *A Future for Astyanax: Character and Desire in Literature* (Boston: Little, Brown and Co., 1976), p. 20 (Bersani is here referring to the plays of Racine).

[92] Laurence Sterne, *The Life and Opinions of Tristram Shandy, Gentleman*, ed. Melvyn New and Joan New (London: Penguin, 2003), p. 339. This text is based on the definitive Florida Edition of 1978.

Sterne's use of the dash is heterogeneous, eccentric, and at odds with previous novelistic usage. In *Clarissa*, for example, it works representationally, as a marker of emotional stress and of the syntactic incoherence that accompanies it ('I see, I see, Mr Lovelace, in broken sentences she spoke—I see, I see—that at last—at last—I am ruined!—ruined—if *your* pity—Let me implore your pity!—').[93] Despite Jonathan Lamb's location of the origins of the dash in the pathos-laden punctuation of the 'preacherly sublime',[94] it works in this chapter from *Tristram Shandy* less as a marker of feeling than as a signal of the introduction of a new voice, as a pause introducing a punch line (but the shaggy dog story has no definitive punch line, only a series of digressive nudges), and as the site of a missing syntactic connection. Ian Watt notes this paratactic force of the dash: its most important strategic function 'is to serve Tristram as a non-logical junction between different kinds of discourse: between past and present; between narrative event and authorial address to the reader; between one train of thought and another in Tristram's mind'.[95]

Critics differ over whether Sterne's punctuation is a matter of rhetorical pointing, giving cues to timing and pace,[96] or rather a matter of visual spacing which sets up a tension between oral delivery and writing and between writing and meaning.[97] There is agreement, however, that it 'remains obstinately unassimilable by being a sign of a-logical thought',[98] expressing 'the jettisoned conjunctions of asyndeton'.[99] Another way of putting this is to say that the dash obeys and expresses the laws of the association of ideas, both in John Locke's sense of ingrained prejudice which, as the opposite of reason, 'is really Madness'[100] —a notion that (in a quite unLockean twist) forms the basis of Sterne's comedy—and in David Hume's more considered sense of relations of resemblance, of contiguity in time or place, and of causality.[101] Sterne's syntax is aligned less with association by cause and effect, in the form of the subordination and superordination of clauses, than with association by contiguity and by resemblance and contrast. This is Locke's 'Connexion of *Ideas* wholly

[93] Samuel Richardson, *Clarissa, or The History of a Young Lady*, ed. Angus Ross (London: Penguin, 1985), p. 881. The text is that of the first edition of 1747–8.

[94] Jonathan Lamb, *Sterne's Fiction and the Double Principle* (Cambridge: Cambridge University Press, 1989), p. 114.

[95] Ian Watt, 'The Comic Syntax of *Tristram Shandy*', in Howard Anderson and John S. Shea (eds), *Studies in Criticism and Aesthetics 1660–1800: Essays in Honour of Samuel Holt Monk* (Minneapolis: University of Minnesota Press, 1967), p. 321.

[96] Michael Vande Berg, '"Pictures of Pronunciation": Typographical Travels through *Tristram Shandy* and *Jacques le Fataliste*', *Eighteenth-Century Studies* 21: 1 (1987), p. 23.

[97] Roger B. Moss, 'Sterne's Punctuation', *Eighteenth-Century Studies* 15: 2 (1981–2), p. 184; cf. Christopher Fanning, 'On Sterne's Page: Spatial Layout, Spatial Form, and Social Spaces in *Tristram Shandy*', in Marcus Walsh (ed.), *Laurence Sterne* (London: Pearson Education, 2002), especially p. 199, n. 19.

[98] Moss, 'Sterne's Punctuation', p. 195, n. 13.

[99] Lamb, *Sterne's Fiction and the Double Principle*, p. 114. Asyndeton is a rhetorical figure designating the omission of the conjunction.

[100] John Locke, *An Essay Concerning Human Understanding*, ed. Peter H. Nidditch (Oxford: Clarendon Press, 1975), p. 395; Chapter XXXIII of Book II, '*Of the Association of* Ideas', was added to the fourth edition of 1700.

[101] David Hume, *A Treatise of Human Nature*, ed. David Fate Norton and Mary J. Norton (Oxford: Oxford University Press, 2000), p. 13.

owing to Chance or Custom', a manifestation of 'Trains of Motion in the Animal Spirits, which once set a going continue on in the same steps they have been used to, which by often treading are worn into a smooth path';[102] and it is thematized as the book's manner of moving forward by interruptions of and digressions from its tenuous narrative thread, with the digressions then tending to generate new narrative lines by means of further interruption and digression, tying together sequences of fortuitously connected events: the accident that befalls young Tristram is the final point in a quasi-causal chain that runs from his Uncle Toby's being wounded at the siege of Namur to the replication of the battlefield in miniature on Toby's bowling green, where the traumatic moment of his injury is constantly replayed, to Corporal Trim's removal of the sash window's lead weights and wheels in order to cast cannon for this field of play, to the chambermaid's absent-mindedness and the inevitable consequence that, in a household where 'nothing was well hung', Tristram's 'spout' ('——I wish, said *Trim*, as they entered the door,—instead of the sash-weights, I had cut off the church-spout, as I once thought to have done.—You have cut off spouts enow, replied Yorick.——')[103] suffers an unspecified but much speculated-on injury.

The fortuitous association of ideas is thematized as well in Toby's 'unsteady uses of words' (p. 78): Toby is in constant perplexity because of 'the almost insurmountable difficulties he found in telling his story intelligibly, and giving such clear ideas of the differences and distinctions between the scarp and counterscarp,——the glacis and covered way,——the half-moon and ravelin,——as to make his company fully comprehend where and what he was about' (p. 74). At the same time, his *idée fixe* forces him to return obsessively to the site of his wounding, reading a military significance into chance phrases of his brother's: a 'train' (of ideas) puts him at once in mind of 'a train of artillery' (p. 172); a metaphor of truth not yielding to the closest 'siege' transports him at once to Namur (p. 215). This is Toby's *hobby horse*: a pattern of eccentricity that is at once a liberation (from his brother Walter's heavy-handed commitment to Logos, on the one hand, and from the dark mysteries of sex on the other) and yet at the same time a compulsive repetition of the trauma in which he was either literally or symbolically (it's characteristic of the novel's narrative strategy that we don't know for sure) castrated.[104]

Compulsion and freedom are inextricably united in the chains of association that organize the narrative structure of *Tristram Shandy* and the behaviour of its characters. There is nothing fortuitous in the way these chains are formed: if for Toby language returns him constantly to the battlefield at Namur (and the traumatic and ultimately sexual meanings it represents for him), for everyone else, including, most especially, the narrator and the embedded reader, language, and the ideas and impressions which underpin it, are constantly torqued towards sexuality, shaped

[102] Locke, *An Essay Concerning Human Understanding*, pp. 395, 396.

[103] Sterne, *Tristram Shandy*, p. 344.

[104] For a counter-argument that Sterne in fact goes out of his way to make it clear that Toby is neither castrated nor impotent, cf. Mark Sinfield, 'Uncle Toby's Potency: Some Critical and Authorial Confusions in *Tristram Shandy*', *N&Q* 223 (1978), pp. 54–5.

by a curiosity which is urgent, unconscious, and always frustrated.[105] Even Toby is affected by this unconscious torqueing: taxed by Walter as to whether he knows 'the right end of a woman from the wrong', Toby

> look'd horizontally.—Right end,—quoth my uncle *Toby*, muttering the two words low to himself, and fixing his two eyes insensibly as he muttered them, upon a small crevice, form'd by a bad joint in the chimney-piece.—Right end of a woman!——I declare, quoth my uncle, I know no more which it is, than the man in the moon; —and if I was to think, continued my uncle *Toby*, (keeping his eye still fix'd upon the bad joint) this month together, I am sure I should not be able to find it out. (pp. 90–1)

Walter's language, like Toby's unconscious associations, is equally vulnerable to this skewing towards the sexual: defending the integrity of the sciences, he proclaims that '—The laws of nature will defend themselves;—but error—(he would add, looking earnestly at my mother)—error, Sir, creeps in thro' the minute-holes, and small crevices, which human nature leaves unguarded' (p. 130). The sexual meaning, like Poe's purloined letter, is at once invisible and plain to see, just as the asterisks in the chapter quoted above (******* ***; **** *** ** *** ******) spell out 'chamber pot' and 'piss out of the window' in a disguised form which conceals nothing, and which generates its comic force out of this non-concealment of the open secret. The compulsive nature of sexual associations (and the powerlessness of the reader to resist them) is spelled out in the prohibition on any wayward understanding of noses:

> I define a nose, as follows,——intreating only beforehand, and beseeching my readers, both male and female, of what age, complexion, and condition soever, for the love of God and their own souls, to guard against the temptations and suggestions of the devil, and suffer him by no art or wile to put any other ideas into their minds, than what I put into my definition.——For by the word *Nose*, throughout all this long chapter of noses, and in every other part of my work, where the word *Nose* occurs,—I declare, by that word I mean a Nose, and nothing more, or less. (p. 197)

The principle that wherever a sexual meaning can possibly be read into a word or phrase or action, it will be, governs the reading process like an iron law. Whiskers, fingers in pies, fur hats—a general contamination inexorably turns them into sexual objects: the narrator's 'infinite regard for our virtue' has the effect that the whole vocabulary of siege warfare becomes an extended sexual metaphor, and that

> few of the English nouns that are privileged to appear in the pages of his book remain intact. Ordinary domestic objects like button-holes and candles and empty bottles and sausages and old hats and sealing-wax and slippers and buttered buns start to look like articles in a sex-shop catalogue. Blameless locutions like 'rise up trumps' or 'get it out of him' or 'to make ends meet' turn into ideas we can scarcely permit ourselves to entertain.[106]

[105] For the Freudian sense of 'curiosity', cf. Gabriel Josipovici, 'The Body in the Library', in *Writing and the Body* (Brighton: The Harvester Press, 1982), p. 20.

[106] Jacques Berthaud, 'Shandeism and Sexuality', in Valerie Grosvenor Myer (ed.), *Laurence Sterne: Riddles and Mysteries* (London: Vision Press, 1984), p. 25.

The magnetic force of the double entendre is one of a set of determinisms that operate in the novel to constrain its much-damaged narrator. Another is represented by the Father, Walter Shandy, the representative in the novel of Lockean rationality and the 'gravity' of learning, of the Law, and (despite his own deep ambivalence) of male sexuality (his 'ass'—carefully distinguished from 'my hobby-horse'—is 'a beast concupiscent') (p. 530). Tristram's character is formed by a series of such determinisms: that of the clockwork universe which governs the time of his conception; that of the *coitus interruptus* in which his mother's thoughtless exclamation at the crucial moment causes a failure of the transmission of the soul to the sperm and thus the catastrophic weakening of the homunculus's animal spirits;[107] that of nomenclature, the 'strange kind of magick bias, which good or bad names' (in Walter Shandy's strongly held opinion) 'irresistibly impress'd upon our characters and conduct' (p. 47), with the name 'Tristram' being on a par with 'Judas' for its inevitable production of 'nothing *in rerum naturâ*, but what was extreamly mean and pitiful' (p. 50); and that of the various sexual catastrophes visited on Tristram, from the crushing of his nose at birth onwards.

To put a complex matter crudely: it is castration, or the asexuality that resembles it, that represents, for Toby and for Tristram, the possibility of freedom from and within this deterministic universe, just as the dash, with its air of being dashed off in the spontaneous flow of writing, is what allows escape from or at least interruption of the linear order of narrative. This is the realm of the hobby horse, of whimsical eccentricity. The activities that constitute it are displacements of a primal wound, 'palliative replays of an original experience of loss and pain';[108] when they take the form of language (including that of the novel) they exhibit 'a continual and repetitive movement from loss, interruption, or accident... to a restoration pursued through linguistic media'.[109] Yet that restoration, like any compulsive repetition, necessarily fails: the wound is reduplicated in language, not repaired by it. What it means for Tristram to be a character is just his occupation of this site of compulsive repetition of the past, in a present ('*August* the 10th, 1761') built on incompleteness, misnaming, and an act of narration made up of endless deferral and interruption.

But it is the reader, too, drawn into knowing complicity with the identification of the double entendre, who occupies this site. As Sterne wrote in a letter to a friend: 'A true feeler always brings half the entertainment along with him. His own ideas are only call'd forth by what he reads, and the vibrations within, so entirely correspond with those excited, 'tis like reading *himself* and not the *book*.'[110] *Tristram Shandy* is something like a laboratory for the evolution of novelistic character in

[107] Cf. Valerie Grosvenor Myer, 'Tristram and the Animal Spirits', in *Laurence Sterne: Riddles and Mysteries*, p. 100, quoting Nathaniel Highmore's *The History of Generation* (1651): 'In all involuntary emissions, the soul is not communicated to the seed.'

[108] Lamb, *Sterne's Fiction and the Double Principle*, p. 40.

[109] Ross King, '*Tristram Shandy* and the Wound of Language', *Studies in Philology* 92: 3 (1995), p. 293.

[110] Laurence Sterne, *Letters of Laurence Sterne*, ed. Lewis Perry Curtis (1935; rpt. Oxford: Clarendon Press, 1965), p. 411; cited in Lamb, *Sterne's Fiction and the Double Principle*, p. 83.

the eighteenth century. In its relation to the Humean doctrine of sympathy and the movement of sensibility it simultaneously builds on the model of identification most powerfully elaborated in Richardson's *Clarissa,* and parodically undermines it. Indeed, rather than being either a throwback to pre-novelistic modes of learned-wit satire or an anticipation of modernist techniques, it is directly engaged with the conventions of the novel in the crucial period of its formation, the decades of the 1740s and 1750s, responding to those conventions 'with witty parody, intricate elaboration, and occasional outright theft'.[111]

Its intervention takes place most directly in relation to the great novelistic achievement of those decades, that of Samuel Richardson. The revolution that Richardson instigates with *Pamela* (1740–1) and which culminates in *Clarissa* (1747–8) and *Sir Charles Grandison* (1753–4) consists in the construction of a writing machine designed to evoke sympathetic response to a minutely explored interiority—and, more precisely, of 'a technology designed to produce a reader in tears'.[112] Pathos, sympathy, pity—these emotions work as part of a narrative strategy of breaking down the distance between reader and character. Adam Smith's account of imaginative sympathy (published, of course, some years after Richardson's three novels) gives the example of our understanding of the suffering of 'our brother... upon the rack', which can come about only 'by conceiving what we ourselves should feel in the like situation'. Our senses can never 'carry us beyond our own person', and what we can imagine 'is the impressions of our own senses only, not those of his'.[113] In this sense sympathy is narcissistic, and Smith's argument repeats Hume's: 'In sympathy there is an evident conversion of an idea into an impression. This conversion arises from the relation of objects to ourself. Ourself is always intimately present to us.'[114] Yet, in Smith's argument, we also lose something of that primacy of the self, since in the act of imagination 'we place ourselves in his situation, we conceive ourselves enduring all the same torments, we enter as it were into his body, and become in some measure the same person with him'.[115] This is that sympathetic 'vibration' that Sterne speaks of ('tis like reading *himself*'), and Hume speaks of sympathy as a form of 'communication' passing as though by contagion from one person to another:[116] a 'communication' that situates feelings in a transsubjective space of circulation rather than 'within the private, inner lives of individual persons', as though our feelings were 'always

[111] Thomas Keymer, *Sterne, the Moderns, and the Novel* (Oxford: Oxford University Press, 2002), p. 8.

[112] Paul Scott Gordon, 'Disinterested Selves: *Clarissa* and the Tactics of Sentiment', *ELH* 64: 2 (1997), p. 496.

[113] Adam Smith, *The Theory of Moral Sentiments*, ed. Knud Haakonssen (Cambridge: Cambridge University Press, 2002), p. 11.

[114] Hume, *A Treatise of Human Nature*, p. 208. Adela Pinch notes the way this argument reverses the usual direction of the flow of force between the strength and immediacy of the impression and the weakness of the idea; it is by means of its narcissistic action that sympathy effects a paradoxical reverse conversion. Adela Pinch, *Strange Fits of Passion: Epistemologies of Emotion, Hume to Austen* (Stanford: Stanford University Press, 1996), p. 34.

[115] Smith, *The Theory of Moral Sentiments*, p. 12.

[116] Hume, *A Treatise of Human Nature*, p. 206.

really someone else's'.[117] Diderot records the workings of this effect in his eulogy for Richardson, published in 1762:

> Who has not been shaken by the character of a Lovelace or a Tomlinson? Who has not been struck with horror by the moving and truthful tone, the air of honesty and dignity, the deep art with which Tomlinson acts out all the virtues? Who has not said to himself deep in his heart that if there were men capable of such dissimulation, it would be necessary to flee society or to take refuge in the depths of the forests?... Oh Richardson, whatever our reticence, we take on a role in your works, we join in conversations, we approve or blame, admire, get irritated or indignant. How often have I not found myself, like a child being taken to the theatre for the first time, calling out *don't believe him, he's deceiving you!... If you go there, you're lost!* My soul was kept in perpetual agitation. How good I was! How just! How satisfied with myself! Coming away from reading you, I was like a man who's spent the day doing good.[118]

Diderot is, of course, Richardson's ideal reader: his heart is in the right place. But the reception of *Pamela* brought home to Richardson the fact that not every reader's heart was so situated. The anti-Pamelists, writes Paul Gordon, 'interpret *Pamela* according to expectations established by a generation of writers—Behn, Manley, Defoe, and, most thoroughly, Mandeville—who... construe the profession of "virtue" as a mask strategically adopted to further one's interest'.[119] The dilemma that Richardson faces in *Clarissa* is that of constructing a plausibly sincere character who cannot be accused of calculation, while writing in a perspectival form (exchanges of letters telling different versions of the one story) that accentuates precisely the conflict of interpretations and the instrumental nature of communication.

The first moment of the solution that Richardson adopts is to build this conflict of interpretations into the narrative itself. There is a key example of this at the family gathering held at Harlowe Place while Clarissa is gravely ill, where Colonel Morden reads an extract from a letter in which Clarissa takes leave of her close friend Anna Howe:

> Oh my child! my child! said your mamma, weeping, and clasping her hands.
>
> Dear madam, said your brother, be so good as to think you have more children than this ungrateful one.
>
> Yet your sister seemed affected.
>
> Your uncle Harlowe wiping his eyes, Oh cousin, said he, if one thought the poor girl was *really* so ill—
>
> She *must*, said your uncle Antony. This is written to her private friend. God forbid she should be quite lost!...[120]

After an exchange of angry words between Clarissa's brother James and Colonel Morden, the Colonel continues reading, inciting conflicting emotions:

[117] Pinch, *Strange Fits of Passion*, p. 19.

[118] Denis Diderot, 'Éloge de Richardson', in *Contes et romans*, ed. Michel Delon, Bibliothèque de la Pléïade (Paris: Gallimard, 2004), pp. 897–8 (my translation).

[119] Gordon, 'Disinterested Selves', pp. 475–6.

[120] Richardson, *Clarissa*, p. 1322. Hereafter cited in the text.

> Your sister called you sweet soul; but with a low voice: then grew hard-hearted again; yet said, nobody could help being affected by your pathetic grief—but that it was your talent.
>
> The colonel then went on to the good effect your airing had upon you; to your good wishes to Miss Howe and Mr Hickman; and to your concluding sentence, that when the happy life you wish *her* comes to be wound up, she may be as calm and as easy at quitting it as you hope in God you shall be. Your mamma could not stand this, but retired to a corner of the room and sobbed and wept. Your father for a few minutes could not speak, though he seemed inclined to say something.
>
> Your uncles were also both affected—but your brother went round to each; and again reminded your mamma that she had other children; what was there, he said, in what was read, but the result of the talent you had of moving the passions? And he blamed them for choosing to hear read what they knew their abused indulgence could not be proof against. (pp. 1322–3)

The accusation made against Clarissa by her brother and sister is that she has a 'talent' for 'moving the passions': that she uses pathos as a rhetorical device to achieve her own interests. The exchange crystallizes the antagonism within the novel between 'suspicious' and 'sentimental' readings of the character of Clarissa, a tension which is then echoed through the critical literature. Commenting on the novel's continually shifting and contested textual history, William Warner seeks to show 'that the textual field of *Clarissa*, with its intricate history, is like a vast plain where Clarissa and Lovelace, and their respective allies, and the two ways of interpreting world they embody, collide and contend'.[121] This is the process that Michel Callon calls *intéressement*: the recruiting of allies in the formation of networks which are at once semiotic and material,[122] and which, in the case of Richardson, have direct effects in the ideological struggles in which his novels so deeply engage. Warner himself (in ways that have been strongly criticized)[123] takes the side of Lovelace in arguing that 'Clarissa's two most characteristic activities—her mimetic narrative and her efforts at "self"-construction—are designed in and for Clarissa's struggle with her family and Lovelace':[124] the self we see is the effect of a rhetorical calculation on her part.

As Warner documents at length, Richardson sought to contain these interpretive conflicts by extensive editorial intervention from the second edition onwards, using prefaces and postscripts, an index-summary, and collections of pious sentiments gathered from the text of the novel to clarify its intended moral force. Amongst

[121] William Warner, 'Preface', in *Reading* Clarissa: *The Struggles of Interpretation* (New Haven: Yale University Press, 1979), p. viii.

[122] Michel Callon, 'Some Elements of a Sociology of Translation: Domestication of the Scallops and the Fishermen of St Brieuc Bay', in John Law (ed.), *Power, Action and Belief: A New Sociology of Knowledge*, (London: Routledge & Kegan Paul, 1986), pp. 196–223.

[123] Terry Castle, in *Clarissa's Ciphers: Meaning and Disruption in Richardson's 'Clarissa'* (Ithaca: Cornell University Press, 1982), p.193, notes, contra Warner, that the interpretive field is heavily weighted against Clarissa; Terry Eagleton, in *The Rape of Clarissa: Writing, Sexuality and Class Struggle in Samuel Richardson* (Oxford: Basil Blackwell, 1982), p. 65, describes Warner's book as 'a fashionably deconstructionist piece out to vilify Clarissa and sing the virtues of her rapist'.

[124] Warner, *Reading Clarissa*, p. ix.

other devices, he speaks directly in footnotes to a reader who 'will not have failed to notice' a point, or who has 'not paid a due attention to the story'—a device that Sterne directly parodies when he chides his reader ('Madam') for inattention and insists that, as a punishment, she should 'immediately turn back...and read the whole chapter over again'.[125] But Richardson's major weapon is not argument but a more fundamental manner of engaging the reader in the novel's moral *casus* by undermining the rhetorical force of argument and interpretation. This is the use of pathos as an instrument of sympathetic identification with a character, which allows us, in Smith's words, to 'enter as it were into his body, and become in some measure the same person with him'. The crucial word here is 'body': it is at the level of involuntary bodily response that our 'suspicious' judgement is overcome: the 'sensibility' of both the virtuous character and the reader 'is not so much spoken as displayed. Its instrument is a massively sensitized, feminine body; its vocabulary is that of gestures and palpitations, sighs and tears'.[126] In a sentence that lays bare the line of affiliation between the novels of Richardson and those of Sade, Gordon writes that 'Lovelace may be intellectually enchanting, but Clarissa seduces the *bodies* of readers to have a physical experience that they cannot deny.'[127]

Samuel Johnson wrote of the genre of the novel that its 'power of example is so great, as to take possession of the memory by a kind of violence, and produce effects almost without the intervention of the will'.[128] Richardson's strategy is to compel the reader, even despite herself, to weep at the spectacle of virtue in distress; he seeks to 'overwhelm the judging reader with feeling'.[129] The body of the reader enacts the pity and compassion that disprove the accusations made against Clarissa of rhetorical calculation: it is the reader's tears that prove the heroine's sincerity, and prove ours in pitying her.[130]

V

Deirdre Lynch's account of the transition from a neoclassical to a romantic regime of characterization seeks to flesh out that grounding of character in a set of newly developed affective technologies. Pitching her argument against histories of the novel in which the genre moves from the 'flat' and formulaic characters of Defoe or Fielding to achieve its full realization in the 'round', psychologically complex characters of Jane Austen, Lynch posits instead that what is at stake is the transition

[125] Sterne, *Tristram Shandy*, p. 52.

[126] John Mullan, *Sentiment and Sociability: The Language of Feeling in the Eighteenth Century* (Oxford: Clarendon Press, 1988), p. 61.

[127] Gordon, 'Disinterested Selves', pp. 495–6.

[128] Samuel Johnson, *The Rambler*, Issue no. 4 (1750); cited in Maureen Harkin, 'Smith's *The Theory of Moral Sentiments*: Sympathy, Women, and Emulation', *Studies in Eighteenth-Century Culture* 24 (1995), p. 182.

[129] Chad Loewen-Schmidt, 'Pity, or the Providence of the Body in Richardson's *Clarissa*', *Eighteenth-Century Fiction* 22: 1 (2009), p. 15.

[130] Cf. Gordon, 'Disinterested Selves', pp. 484–5.

from one set of material, rhetorical, and affective practices to another. Charting a set of changing practices of self-cultivation, of shopping, of fashion, of character 'appreciation', and many others, she posits that 'with the beginnings of the late eighteenth century's "affective revolution" and the advent of new linkages between novel reading, moral training, and self-culture, character reading was reinvented as an occasion when readers found themselves and plumbed their own interior resources of sensibility by plumbing characters' hidden depths'.[131] In Smollett, for example, we can see a gradual shift from viewing the protagonist as an empty position to seeing him as an object of identification, so that we come to be involved with 'a being that, through its capacity to prepossess, can train the reader in sympathizing and so in participating in a social world that was being reconceived as a transactional space, as a space that held together through the circulation of fellow feeling'.[132]

This shift in part reflects (and in part helps to form) that larger movement in the late eighteenth century in which the grounding of personal identity in 'an essential core of selfhood characterized by psychological depth, or interiority' becomes dominant,[133] in which childhood takes on a new status as the foundation of 'the unique, ingrained, enduring inner self',[134] and in which an organic model of the realization of an essential selfhood displaces an older model in which the self is less an essence than a set of publicly appropriate roles. This new understanding breaks radically with older presuppositions. As Charles Taylor puts it:

> We have come to think that we 'have' selves as we have heads. But the very idea that we have or are 'a self', that human agency is essentially defined as 'the self', is a linguistic reflection of our modern understanding and the radical reflexivity it involves. Being deeply embedded in this understanding, we cannot but reach for this language; but it was not always so.[135]

While character in the novel is not reducible to forms of social selfhood, since it is produced by means of specifically literary conventions of representation, it is, nevertheless, closely bound up with the transformations of selfhood over the last three hundred years. This is less a matter of reflection of a pre-existing reality than of the way the reading of character actively helps shape readers' understanding of what it might mean to be a person. In this sense, reading character is what Foucault calls a technology of the self: an aesthetico-ethical machine for modelling behaviour, an exercise in self-cultivation through a recognition of and identification with other (represented) selves.[136]

131 Lynch, *The Economy of Character*, p. 10.

132 Lynch, *The Economy of Character*, p. 89.

133 Dror Wahrman, *The Making of the Modern Self: Identity and Culture in Eighteenth-Century England* (New Haven: Yale University Press, 2004), p. xi.

134 Wahrman, *The Making of the Modern Self*, p. 282.

135 Charles Taylor, *Sources of the Self: The Making of the Modern Identity* (Cambridge, MA: Harvard University Press, 1989), p. 177.

136 Michel Foucault, 'Technologies of the Self', in Luther H. Martin, Huck Gutman, and Patrick H. Hutton (eds), *Technologies of the Self: A Seminar with Michel Foucault* (Amherst: University of Massachusetts Press, 1988); Michel Foucault, *The Hermeneutics of the Subject: Lectures at the Collège de France 1981–1982*, trans. Graham Burchell (New York: Picador, 2005).

Ian Hunter's 'Reading Character' takes as its object just this 'interface between literary conceptions of character and the formation of moral character'.[137] By contrasting two readings of *Hamlet* by George Stubbes (1736) and A. C. Bradley (1904), Hunter seeks to analyse the emergence of 'character' in the nineteenth century as 'a new literary-moral object'. In the eighteenth-century text character is 'primarily a rhetorical object rather than a moral one, and appears in a space opened by a rhetoric of dramatic representation', whereas in a nineteenth-century regime character appears rather 'as a projection or correlate of the reader's moral self-personality' (p. 230), and is linked to quite different practices of reading. These would include, for example, 'supplementing the text with a moral discourse on character-type'; the derivation of universal moral imperatives from the text; and the novelistic construction of character interiorities through techniques of 'character appreciation' (p. 231). This shift in the formation of 'character' 'is not a change in the reader's consciousness of the object "character". Instead, we are dealing with a change in the practical deployment of a public apparatus of reading, in which what is to count as character is determined' (p. 232). This change has specific institutional conditions of possibility, in particular the 'process of secularisation of techniques of moral interrogation and confession'. These techniques are embedded in a variety of institutions and practices, but Hunter suggests that 'the emergence of an apparatus of popular education in the nineteenth century is what finally establishes the technical connection between the rhetorical analysis of characterisation and the machinery for the construction of moral selves or good personal character' (p. 233).

There are problems with the historical detail of Hunter's argument. The use of character as a model of moral emulation, a machine for the construction of good moral selves, is not invented in the late nineteenth century: it runs through Greek *paideia*, Christian practices of 'imitation', and Renaissance modes of emulation of heroic models, and indeed it is present in some form in all literary cultures. It is certainly present in the early eighteenth century in the forms of moral training disseminated by the *Spectator* and *Tatler*; and Stubbes's reading precedes by a mere three years the writing of *Pamela*, the first great exercise in novelistic inwardness and novelistic perspective. Deirdre Lynch locates the genesis of the practice of 'character appreciation', which 'produces the depth that needs explicating and with it the textual effects that signal the psychological real', substantially earlier than Hunter does, in a series of essays on Shakespeare's characters published in the second half of the eighteenth century.[138] Nevertheless, the argument for a focus on the uses made of texts, and the institutional machinery that underpins those uses, usefully opens up the field of the rhetorical analysis of texts: of their embedding in practices of self-shaping which, through the paradoxical mechanisms of governmentality, acquire their affective force by virtue of the very freedom with which they are chosen. To feel with Clarissa is to take on the moral force of her exemplary

[137] Ian Hunter, 'Reading Character', *Southern Review* 16: 2 (1983), p. 226; hereafter cited in the text.
[138] Lynch, *The Economy of Character*, p. 135.

life and her even more exemplary death. Fictional character, in this perspective, is less a substance than a set of practices of self-shaping, operating around and making use of texts.

VI

Both the technologies of pathetic identification developed by Richardson and the practices of haptic and kinaesthetic identification that operate in digital gaming take place, in the first instance, at the level of bodily affect. My final study is of a rather different matrix of textual practices built around the bodily representations we label pornographic. There are strong reasons, I think, for insisting on 'the circumstantial character of pornography' as at once 'an eroticising device, a target of medical and pedagogical programmes, a tradable commodity, an aesthetic category, an object of feminist and governmental reforms, [and] a legal problem'.[139] It is circumstantial because the same representation of intimate body parts will have a quite different force on an adult website and in a medical textbook, and because its definition emerges on quite different social surfaces. Yet pornography is often, perhaps even usually, understood as being unified precisely by the relation it bears to actions and emotions. When Stephen Dedalus expounds his theory of the beautiful to his friend Lynch, he contrasts the action of the beautiful, which 'awakens, or ought to awaken, or induces, or ought to induce, an esthetic stasis, an ideal pity or an ideal terror, a stasis called forth, prolonged, and at last dissolved by what I call the rhythm of beauty', with 'the feelings excited by improper art', which are 'kinetic, desire or loathing. Desire urges us to possess, to go to something; loathing urges us to abandon, to go from something. The arts which excite them, pornographical or didactic, are therefore improper arts.'[140] That definition, in all its Kantian normativity, concisely summarizes the argument against which this chapter has been directed.

Pornography, I want to say, is an extreme but not atypical form of the affective working of texts. It raises again the question of the level at which the inscription of readers or viewers takes place, since it is structurally marked by the poverty of its characterization—those 'truck-drivers, airline hostesses, nurses or nuns, all of whom are deemed to be sexually more active than surveyors and accountants'.[141] Susan Sontag speaks of it as 'a theater of types, never of individuals'.[142] The only generalization we can make about characters in prose fiction, she writes, 'is that they are, in Henry James' phrase, "a compositional resource" ',[143] and the figures

[139] Ian Hunter, David Saunders, and Dugald Williamson, *On Pornography: Literature, Sexuality and Obscenity Law* (London: Macmillan, 1993), pp. ix, 229.

[140] James Joyce, *A Portrait of the Artist as a Young Man* (London: Penguin, 1960), pp. 206, 204–5.

[141] Bernard Arcand, *The Jaguar and the Anteater: Pornography Degree Zero*, trans. Wayne Grady (London: Verso, 1993), pp. 16–17.

[142] Susan Sontag, 'The Pornographic Imagination', in *Styles of Radical Will* (New York: Dell, 1970), p. 51.

[143] Sontag, 'The Pornographic Imagination', p. 42.

who act as sexual objects in pornography can be compared to one of the principal 'humours' of comedy, the naïf, the 'still center in the midst of outrage':[144] a Candide or a Buster Keaton, seen only from the outside and using a deadpan tone to generate, not the release of laughter but

> the release of a sexual reaction, originally voyeuristic but probably needing to be secured by an underlying direct identification with one of the participants in the sexual act. The emotional flatness of pornography is thus neither a failure of artistry nor an index of principled inhumanity. The arousal of a sexual response in the reader *requires* it. Only in the absence of directly stated emotions can the reader of pornography find room for his own responses.[145]

But is it true that a response to pornography is secured by 'an underlying identification with one of the participants in the sexual act'? An alternative view would be that the inscription of the reader or viewer takes place at the level of enunciation: the level of discursive address, or, in the case of visual media, of the look. Laura Mulvey argues for a distinction between voyeuristic and fetishistic modes of identification with the look, giving rise to distinct forms of narrativization: a voyeuristic regime will tend to be distanced, analytic, and sadistic, and to generate articulated and linear narratives; a fetishistic regime will attempt to abolish narrative distance and is therefore (in John Ellis's words) 'only capable of producing an attenuated narration, a constant repetition of scenarios of desire, where the repetition around certain neuralgic points outweighs any resolution of a narrative enigma, any discovery or reordering of facts'.[146] Hence the episodic structure of pornography, the anxiety of an act of looking which is serially repeated and which, in denying the very fact of its own existence, thereby inscribes the reader as its accomplice.[147] Pornography is organized by a curiosity about the body that can never be satisfied: no matter how hard and how often we look, the 'reality' of the body eludes us, precisely because it is fantasmatic—as is, therefore, our own placement before it.[148] The scenario happens over and over in Sade: when Justine, hidden in the bushes and silently protesting the acts committed by Bressac and his companion, nevertheless seems to witness every sordid detail of their tryst; or when Justine and Rosalie, hidden in a closet, peep out at the surgeon Rodin whipping and abusing a series of children (and when Justine explains that 'all takes place directly before us, not a detail can escape us'),[149] it is we who are positioned with her, complicit in her look and the anonymous, ownerless desire that fills it.

[144] Sontag, 'The Pornographic Imagination', p. 54.
[145] Sontag, 'The Pornographic Imagination', p. 54.
[146] John Ellis, 'Photography/Pornography/Art/Pornography', *Screen* 21: 1 (1980), p. 99; cf. Laura Mulvey, 'Visual Pleasure and Narrative Cinema', *Screen* 16: 3 (1975), pp. 13–14.
[147] Stephen Heath, 'Difference', *Screen* 19: 3 (1978), p. 91.
[148] Cf. Linda Williams, *Hard Core: Power, Pleasure, and the 'Frenzy of the Visible'* (Berkeley: University of California Press, 1989), p. 50: 'The animating male fantasy of hard-core cinema might...be described as the (impossible) attempt to capture visually this frenzy of the visible in a female body whose orgasmic excitement can never be objectively measured.'
[149] Donatien-Alphonse-François, Marquis de Sade, *Justine, Philosophy in the Bedroom, and Other Writings*, trans. Richard Seaver and Austryn Wainhouse (New York: Grove Press, 1965), p. 537.

With a greater sophistication, that other rewriter of Richardson's eroticized spectacle of virtue in distress, Pierre Choderlos de Laclos, endows the reader with a knowledge which is always guilty, as when we read a letter addressed by Valmont to the Présidente which, we have just been told, was written from the bed of the prostitute Émilie, using her back as a desk: a knowledge that allows us fully to grasp the letter's language of double entendre.[150] The equation the novel sets up is this: to be virtuous is to be innocent; to be innocent is to be ignorant, and therefore gullible, and therefore vulnerable; conversely, to have insight into others (and the very structure of the novel, its consistent clash of perspectives between those who know and those who are deceived, valorizes knowledge, insight, clarity of perception of the intricacy of motives and desires) is to be the opposite of innocent. We occupy every pronoun in the novel, and possess a knowledge that belongs to none and transcends each of them.

In the languages of the social sciences, and of the commissions of inquiry that draw upon them, the question of the inscription of readers or viewers into texts becomes the question of the effects of texts upon their audience. I won't rehearse here the detail of these numerous studies, which have been ably summarized and dissected elsewhere.[151] Their very framing in terms of distinct domains of representation and real-world consequences, with a more or less mechanical translation from the one to the other, renders them problematic. As a totality, the 'effects' research is contradictory and incoherent; the one area where there is some degree of consistent agreement is the study of convicted sex offenders, who 'tend to use less pornography than control groups' and, on average, 'come from sexually repressed backgrounds and are exposed to pornography at a later age'.[152] Beyond that, the scientific literature does little more than reflect the diversity of opinions concerning pornography in the larger society.

The more influential version of the notion of the 'effects' of pornography has doubtless been the radical–feminist coupling of pornography with the rape and degradation of women: pornography the theory, rape the practice.[153] In the writings of the most systematic exponent of this line, Catherine MacKinnon, pornography 'is a form of forced sex', closely akin to rape and prostitution, and, as such, it is the truth of 'the sexuality of male supremacy, which fuses the erotization of dominance and submission with the social construction of male and female. Gender is sexual. Pornography constitutes the meaning of that sexuality'.[154] The circle is seamless. Crucially, pornography is not a more or less conventional construction

[150] Pierre Choderlos de Laclos, *Les Liaisons Dangereuses*, trans. P. W. K. Stone (London: Penguin, 1961), pp. 110–11.

[151] For a small selection, cf. Edward Donnerstein, Daniel Linz, and Steven Penrod, *The Question of Pornography: Research Findings and Policy Implications* (New York: The Free Press, 1987); Arcand, *The Jaguar and the Anteater*, pp. 62–75; Alan McKee, Katherine Albury, and Catharine Lumby, *The Porn Report* (Melbourne: Melbourne University Press, 2008), pp. 74–97.

[152] McKee, Albury, and Lumby, *The Porn Report*, p. 77.

[153] Robin Morgan, 'Theory and Practice: Pornography and Rape', in Laura Lederer (ed.), *Take Back the Night* (New York: William Morrow Co., 1980), p. 139.

[154] Catherine A. MacKinnon, *Feminism Unmodified: Discourses on Life and Law* (Cambridge, MA: Harvard University Press, 1987), p. 148.

of the real: 'Pornography is not imagery in some relation to a reality elsewhere constructed. It is not a distortion, reflection, projection, expression, fantasy, representation, or symbol either. It is sexual reality', and the actors in a pornographic movie 'are real women to whom something real is being done'.[155] The harm done by pornography is thus not moral but political, and the 1983 anti-pornography ordinance drafted by MacKinnon and Andrea Dworkin for the city of Minneapolis couches this as 'a harm of gender inequality'.[156]

Many later feminists have attacked the literalism that underlies MacKinnon's collapsing of representation into the real, accusing her of adopting 'an especially narrow version of behaviorist psychology in equating images with actions and imagining a straightforward causal connection between the sight of images and one's subsequent behavior'.[157] But there is more to say about the ontological distinctions at issue here. In his long and perceptive reading of MacKinnon's argument J. M. Coetzee draws out something of what is most radically interesting about it:

> To MacKinnon, male sexuality is—and indeed is defined by—the possession and consumption of women as sexual objects. Visual pornography caters to male sexuality by creating for it accessible sexual objects, namely images of women. As objects of male desire, women and images of women are not categorically distinct: 'Sex in life is no less mediated than it is in art. Men have sex with their image of a woman.' Through this thoroughly Freudian insight MacKinnon draws into doubt and even collapses the distinction between the reality and the representation. The woman with whom a man has physical relations is only a vehicle through whom he strives to attain the ensemble of representations that make up her image for him.[158]

The radicalism is, in part, that of Puritan iconoclasm, but MacKinnon's 'thoroughly Freudian insight' is one that can be turned to other uses in an account of the saturation of the real by the fantasmatic.

Frances Ferguson is similarly persuaded that MacKinnon has something important to say about the performative structure of representations: 'Far from being naïve about representation,' she writes, 'or unable to tell the difference between an act and the representation of that act, the strength of MacKinnon's position is precisely its focus on the representation as act.'[159] Ferguson's claim is built on a broader argument that pornography is coeval with and integral to the emergence of utilitarian social structures in the late eighteenth century which, rather than

[155] MacKinnon, *Feminism Unmodified*, p. 149.

[156] MacKinnon, *Feminism Unmodified*, p. 177.

[157] Frances Ferguson, *Pornography the Theory: What Utilitarianism Did to Action* (Chicago: University of Chicago Press, 2004), p. 41, summarizing the arguments of Sara Diamond, Ann Snitow, Lisa Duggan, Nan Hunter, and Carole Vance in *Women Against Censorship*, ed. Varda Burstyn (Vancouver: Douglas and McIntyre, 1985). The other key feminist response to the work of Dworkin and MacKinnon is Carole S. Vance (ed.), *Pleasure and Danger: Exploring Female Sexuality* (1984; rpt. London: Pandora Press, 1992).

[158] J. M. Coetzee, 'The Harms of Pornography: Catherine MacKinnon', in *Giving Offense: Essays on Censorship* (Chicago: University of Chicago Press, 1996), pp. 71–2, citing Catherine MacKinnon, *Toward a Feminist Theory of the State* (Cambridge, MA: Harvard University Press, 1989), p. 199.

[159] Ferguson, *Pornography the Theory*, p. 44.

recognizing intrinsic merits, distribute value between individuals on the basis of objectively recognized actions: both the school and the prison work as such public distributive structures making use of explicit criteria of performance. So, she argues, does pornography: in the writings of Sade, sex and its representation are a perceptible mechanism for sorting out inequalities of power and for allowing the reader to decide about the costs for an individual of collective actions. Sade 'focuses on the evaluations that sexual games produce for all of the members of the community so as to insist on the hierarchy of hierarchy—so that one can know who's boss'.[160] But this is surely wrong: while it may be the case that the reader regards the costs of sexual scenarios as too high (think of Roland's slave Suzanne in *Justine*, her buttocks calloused from being whipped with a bull's pizzle, a cancer on her breast and an abscess in her womb as 'the fruit of his lecheries'),[161] this judgement in no way alters the collective structure: hierarchies in Sade are never the outcome of a distributive action, since they always precede sexual action as a rigid and unchanging demarcation between a libertine elite and its degraded victims.[162]

The 'representational collapse'[163] that Ferguson sees as a strength of MacKinnon's argument (the description, for example, of pornography 'not as a description of sex but as sex')[164] is what most closely aligns that argument with the characteristic truth effects of visual pornography: the money shots that prove the 'reality' of male orgasm. This is an 'empiricism of naïve realism: the real is what we can see',[165] and it ultimately works against any recognition of the fantasmatic structuring of the real. For MacKinnon and Dworkin, pornography is the record of a crime (since male sexuality is, by definition, an act of violence against women, and since the women who act in pornographic films do so, by definition, as the result of physical or economic coercion and—whether they know it or not—against their own real interests). The collapsing of representations into acts is thus equally a collapsing of the distinction between consensual and non-consensual sex—a distinction which is no less and no more important in the case of acted pornography than in other areas covered by criminal law.

Beverley Brown spells out the case against that representational collapse when she writes that 'the harms feminism wishes to mark do not depend for their seriousness on being or resulting directly in acts'; where pornographic images do have consequences for 'ordinary' behaviour, however, 'they will not be of the order of a literal re-enactment, but work through a general psychic economy as it orders and disorders conduct'.[166] Understanding the harms of pornography in this way

160 Ferguson, *Pornography the Theory*, p. 26.
161 Sade, *Justine*, p. 677.
162 Cf. Roland Barthes, *Sade/Fourier/Loyola*, trans. Richard Miller (Berkeley: University of California Press, 1976), p. 24: '[T]here are two great classes of Sadian society. These classes are set, one cannot emigrate from one to another: no social promotion.'
163 Ferguson, *Pornography the Theory*, p. 46.
164 Ferguson, *Pornography the Theory*, p. 44.
165 Coetzee, 'The Harms of Pornography', p. 75.
166 Beverley Brown, 'A Feminist Interest in Pornography: Some Modest Proposals', *m/f* 5–6 (1981), pp. 13–14.

underlines the importance of holding together in a single frame at once the ontological discontinuity which allows us to distinguish a representational act from other acts, and the ontological continuity that binds them to each other.

Ferguson writes of pornography as an intensification of what she calls, after Niklas Luhmann, the 'body-to-body analogy': an orientation of the reader's social and spatial experience in relation to that of the represented bodies of fictional characters, in such a way that personal memories come to look like 'representations of hypothetical or fictitious experience'.[167] Pornography, that is to say, is an intensification of the technologies of bodily affect that Richardson developed for the European novel and that constitute the properly mimetic dimension of drama. It touches on the taboo, the daemonic, what Sontag calls 'the extreme rather than the ordinary experiences of humanity'.[168] And it raises the paradox of how it is that an image, a narrative, a voice on a telephone—the most schematic outline of a representation of sexual desire—can invoke a corresponding desire in us, inducing in our body a state of physical arousal no matter what our will or our judgement might wish; the 'effects' of pornography are registered on the body. This is the paradox of fictional character: that there are real toads in its imaginary garden; its dream of passion comes true in our waking world.

[167] Ferguson, *Pornography the Theory*, p. x, citing Niklas Luhmann, *The Reality of the Mass Media*, trans. Kathleen Cross (Stanford: Stanford University Press, 2000), p. 59.
[168] Sontag, 'The Pornographic Imagination', p. 57.

3

Person

I

The category of fictional character depends upon the prior category of human being, which can be cast in the form of any of a number of related concepts with somewhat different histories and force: the self, the subject, the soul, the individual, the person, *Dasein*, the agent or *actant*, and so on. Of these, the concept of the person is by far the most useful for my purposes, since I take it to be formed less by a history of philosophical elaboration than by a rich set of changing socio-technical practices which distinguish human from non-human being and bring together religious, legal, medical, ethical, civic, and socioeconomic taxonomies in a single point. In Foucault's terms, the person is less a concept than a *dispositif*, an evolving apparatus for the shaping of social arrangements.[1]

I begin this chapter with a reading of an essay by Marcel Mauss, trying to bring out some of the complexities in his account of the category of the person, which are often glossed over in rapid summaries or paraphrases. The essay is 'A Category of the Human Mind: The Notion of Person; The Notion of Self', first delivered as a lecture in 1938.[2] Mauss writes as an anthropologist exploring a 'category of the mind' to which he wishes to restore a history that stretches in a process of continuous evolution from a 'prehistory' that is, in fact, the anthropological present,[3] through to the historical present. That notion of a progressive linear movement which, despite the 'delays' and 'obstacles' put in its path by the history of thought from the fourth century through to the Enlightenment, culminates triumphantly in the present state of self-consciousness and of recognition of 'the sacred character

[1] Michel Foucault, 'The Confession of the Flesh', in *Power/Knowledge: Selected Interviews and Other Writings, 1972–1977*, ed. Colin Gordon (New York: Pantheon, 1980), pp. 194–5; cf. Giorgio Agamben, 'What is an Apparatus?', in *What is an Apparatus and Other Essays*, trans. David Kishik and Stefan Pedatella (Stanford: Stanford University Press, 2009), pp. 1–24.

[2] The essay was published as section V of *Sociologie et anthropologie* (1950; rpt. Paris: PUF, 1973), and translated by Ben Brewster in Marcel Mauss, *Sociology and Psychology: Essays* (London: Routledge & Kegan Paul, 1979), pp. 57–94, and by W. D. Halls in Michael Carrithers, Steven Collins, and Steven Lukes (eds), *The Category of the Person: Anthropology, Philosophy, History* (Cambridge: Cambridge University Press, 1985), pp. 1–25. I have consulted both translations but followed the later one, which is clearer at several key points; page references (hereafter cited in the text) are therefore to this translation.

[3] Cf. Johannes Fabian, *Time and the Other: How Anthropology Makes its Object* (New York: Columbia University Press, 1983), p. 80.

of the human person' (p. 22),[4] is deeply problematic, as is the question about the extent to which this is properly a history, and what exactly it is a history of. Steven Lukes notes that Mauss's neo-Kantian view of the self as a 'category of the mind' supposes that 'a certain structure of thinking concerning the person is held to be fundamental, universal and necessary, but to take different forms in different contexts'.[5]

Mauss himself is cagey about the relation between 'the idea of "person" (*personne*)' and 'the idea of "self" (*moi*)' (p. 1),[6] terms which he places in apposition. The universality of the category of self is evidenced linguistically: Mauss makes no claim that any language has ever existed which lacked expressions for 'I' and 'me' and in which these forms have not 'expressed something clearly represented' (p. 3)—that is, as I read it, he argues that every language expresses a sense of selfhood as well as deploying it through the functional pronouns or inflections of the verb; and yet, although, in addition to the pronominal and verb forms, most languages have forms to express the spatio-temporal existence of the self, this omnipresent 'self' is, nevertheless, not necessarily understood as a distinct entity, 'a' self. Likewise, the fact of consciousness is taken to be universal: it is clear 'that there has never existed a human being who has not been aware, not only of his body, but also at the same time of his individuality, both spiritual and physical' (p. 3). What does vary historically is 'not the sense of the "self" (*moi*)—but the notion or concept that men in different ages have formed of it' (p. 3): the reflexive understanding of that intuitive sense of self, which, in turn (as I interpret Mauss's argument), is distinct from the mental *category* of the self.[7]

All of this, I think, begs more questions than it answers—and, indeed, the long history of mutual contamination of these categories perhaps makes any clear distinctions between them impossible, while Mauss's own usage is inconsistent. But the essay is so richly suggestive that for the moment I'd like to put these problems to one side and to explore what I think is its real strength: its account of personhood. This account takes place over three stages: that of tribal societies; that of archaic and classical Rome; and that of Christianity and of the history of philosophical thought concerning selfhood that flows from it.

Mauss begins his analysis by summarizing Frank Hamilton Cushing's work on the Zuñi Pueblo Indians, and particularly his examination of the relation between 'roles' (*personnages*) and 'persons' (*personnes*). Here there are two key facts: the existence of a limited repertoire of names in each clan, and the use of this repertoire to express a set of social roles. Names are associated with totems and act in a manner similar to titles; in addition, kinship terms refer to status and authority, and there is a hierarchical differentiation of modes of address by age and by rank in both the

4 Mauss, 'A Category of the Human Mind', p. 22.

5 Steven Lukes, 'Conclusion', in Carrithers, Collins, and Lukes (eds), *The Category of the Person*, p. 284.

6 Mauss, 'A Category of the Human Mind', p. 1.

7 This distinction between a *sense* of self, an evolving *concept* of self, and the Kantian *category* of the self is made by Martin Hollis, 'Of Masks and Men', in Carrithers, Collins, and Lukes (eds), *The Category of the Person*, p. 221.

clan and the fraternity. More generally, the individuals who bear these titles and privileges 'not only sustain the life of things and of the gods, but the "propriety" of things', and not only 'the life of men, both here and in the after-life, but also the rebirth of individuals (men), sole heirs of those that bear their forenames' (p. 6).[8] Thus, 'with the Pueblo we already see a notion of the "person" (*personne*) or individual, absorbed in his clan, but already detached from it in the ceremonial by the mask, his title, his rank, his role, his survival and his reappearance on earth in one of his descendants endowed with the same status, forenames, titles, rights and functions' (p. 6). Personhood, that is to say, is defined for the Pueblo by an identity with both ancestors and descendants, who are linked by a name, a ceremonial mask, and a set of social entitlements; these constitute a social person who is at once distinct from the social whole yet greater than the individual bearers of that personhood.

In the case of the Native Americans of the north-west, similar problems of the name, of entitlement, and of roles are posed in different terms. Here each individual has two sets of names, one profane linked to the summer and one sacred linked to the winter; these names are distributed among families. In addition, each clan disposes of two sets of names, everyday and secret, with the latter changing with the individual's age and age-related functions. What is at stake in naming is the existence both of the clan and of 'the ancestors reincarnated in their rightful successors, who live again in the bodies of those who bear their names, whose perpetuation is assured by the ritual in each of its phases. The perpetuation of things and spirits is only guaranteed by the perpetuating of the names of individuals, of persons' (p. 8). As Mauss remarks in a note on the potlatch, '*everything, even war and conflicts, takes place only between the bearers of these hereditary titles, who incarnate these souls*' (p. 23, n. 5; Mauss's emphasis). Individuals 'act only in their titular capacity' (p. 8), *ex officio*;[9] and this 'office', this complex fusion of rights and transgenerational personhood in the power of the name, is not only distributed by the clan but can also be acquired in war: it is sufficient either to kill the possessor of rank, religious or aesthetic entitlements, of a place in the dance and of the paraphernalia that go with it, or to seize his robes or masks, in order to inherit his names, his goods, his obligations, his ancestors, the 'person (*personne*) in the fullest sense of the word' (p. 9).

In moving to a very different case study, that of Indigenous Australians, Mauss points both to a continuity with the American tribes in the distribution of names to express the reincarnation of ancestors and of the associated ritual privileges in their bearers, and to a discontinuity in the use of temporary rather than permanent masks in the ceremonies in which 'men fashion for themselves a superimposed "personality" (*personnalité*), a true one in the case of ritual, a feigned one in the case of play-acting' (p. 12). But the difference is merely one of degree: 'in both cases,

[8] Mauss, 'A Category of the Human Mind', p. 6.

[9] This is the phrase used in Brewster's translation, *Sociology and Psychology*, p. 69; Mauss's phrase (*Sociologie et anthropologie*, p. 342) is '*ès qualités*', meaning 'in an official capacity' or *ex officio*.

all has ended in the enraptured representation of the ancestor' (p. 12). Thus, he concludes, it is clear that 'a whole immense group of societies have arrived at the notion of "role" (*personnage*), of the role played by the individual in sacred dramas, just as he plays a role in family life' (p. 12).

We might note, though, that the distinction between *personnage* and *personne* has slipped away in this concluding formulation. 'Role' has become the primary category to describe this phase of civilization; it expresses individual participation in a form of corporate identity without any moment of inwardness, and it moves from a quite literal sense of acting in a (sacred) drama to the sense that's conveyed by the Latin *officium* and the now somewhat archaic English 'office': 'a position or place to which certain duties are attached' (OED).

This concludes the first section of Mauss's discussion, and he moves from it to the Latin concept of *persona*, 'a mask, a tragic mask, a ritual mask, and the ancestral mask' (p. 13), from which the modern category of the person develops.

Before making this move, however, Mauss undertakes a detour by way of two ancient civilizations which 'invented' this 'category of the mind', but 'only to allow it to fade away almost irrevocably'—in both cases 'in the last centuries B.C.' (p. 13). The first of them, Brahmin and Buddhist India, 'appears to me indeed,' he writes, 'to have been the most ancient of civilisations aware of the notion of the individual, of his consciousness—may I say, of the "self" (*moi*). *Ahamkara*, the "creation of the 'I'" (*je*), is the name of the individual consciousness; *aham* equals "I" (*je*). It is the same Indo-European word as "ego"'. As for the second of these civilizations, China, just as with the American tribes of the north-west 'birth-order, rank and the interplay of social classes settle the names and life style of the individual, his "face"... His individuality is his *ming*, his name... The name, the *ming*, represents a collective noun, something springing from elsewhere: one's corresponding ancestor bore it, just as it will fall to the descendant of its present bearer' (p. 14).

It is in Rome, however, that the idea of the human person as 'a complete entity, independent of all others save God' (p. 14), originates. It does so because the Latin term *persona* 'is more than an organisational fact, more than a name or a right to assume a role and a ritual mask' (p. 14): it is a fundamental legal category in a system which recognizes only three entities, *personae, res*, and *actiones* (persons, property, and legal proceedings).

The word *persona* is probably of Etruscan origin and is perhaps borrowed from the Greek *prosōpon*, 'death mask'—Mauss notes that 'the Etruscans had a "mask" civilisation' (p. 15). But this primitive meaning then begins to acquire new layers. In the first place, there are traces among the Latins of totemic institutions: for example in the religious ritual of the Hirpi Sorani, the wolves of Soracte, which Sir James Frazer suggests is 'the remnants of an ancient clan, which had become a fraternity, bearing names, and wearing skins and masks' (p. 15). The connection is clear between such rituals and those of contemporary tribal civilizations: 'All in all, Samnites, Etruscans and Latins still lived in an environment we have just left, from *personae*, masks and names, and individual rights to rituals and privileges' (p. 16). From this point, however, a decisive step is taken away from corporate identity:

> I imagine that legends like that of the consul Brutus and his sons and the end of the right of the *pater* to kill his sons, his *sui*, signify the acquisition of the *persona* by the sons, even while their father was still alive. I believe that the revolt of the Plebs, the right to full citizenship that, following upon the sons of senatorial families, was gained by all the plebeian members of the *gentes*, was decisive. All freemen of Rome were Roman citizens, all had a civil *persona*; some became religious *personae*; some masks, names and rituals remained attached to some privileged families of the religious *collegia*. (p. 16)

Parallel to the institution of the civil and religious *persona* is the system of nomenclature. Roman citizens are entitled to the use of a *praenomen* denoting, for example, the birth-order of the ancestor who bore it (Primus, Secundus...), and which may be taken only from the list available to one's own *gens* (clan or tribe); a *nomen*, the sacred name of the *gens*; and a *cognomen* or nickname, referring to the attributes not of the individual but of his ancestor. The *cognomen*, Mauss writes, 'ended up being confused with the *imago*, the wax mask moulded on the face of the dead ancestor' (p. 16); the use of these masks and busts was confined to the patrician families, and 'to the very end the Roman Senate thought of itself as being made up of a determinate number of *patres* representing the "persons" (*personnes*), the "images" of their ancestors...It is to the *persona* that is attributed the property of the *simulacra* and the *imagines*' (p. 17).

What changes in these institutions is, on the one hand, the political movement Mauss describes, whereby the right to the *persona* is extended, at least in part, to all free citizens, and, on the other, that legal categorization by which 'the personal nature of the law had been established' (p. 17) and personhood becomes detached from a rigid taxonomy of status and privileges. But Mauss gives no account of the development and the semantic force of this legal category; it is likely that what he has in mind is something like the evolution of a sense of intention or of responsibility for acts in the law, but neither this nor any other argument about legal personhood is articulated. Instead, we have a brief mention of the splitting of the meaning of the word *persona* between the sense of 'an artificial "character" (*personnage*), the mask and role of comedy and tragedy, of trickery and hypocrisy—a stranger to the "self" (*moi*)', on the one hand, and, on the other, its becoming 'synonymous with the true nature of the individual' (p. 17). The only elaboration of the flat statement concerning the legal category of personhood—that 'the right to the *persona* had been established'—is made by negation:

> Only the slave is excluded from it. *Servus non habet personam*. He has no 'personality' (*personnalité*). He does not own his body, nor has he ancestors, name, *cognomen*, or personal belongings. Old Germanic law still distinguished him from the freeman, the *Leibeigen*, the owner of his body. But at the time when the laws of the Saxons and Swabians were drawn up, if the serfs did not possess their body, they already had a soul, which Christianity had given them. (p. 17)

II

This passage marks the transition to the third phase of Mauss's argument, in which he traces the crucial role of the Stoic philosophers in enriching the Roman notion of the person with their 'voluntarist and personal ethics' (p. 18) and in preparing the ground for Christianity's ethical conception of the person, 'no longer clad in a condition' (p. 19) but fully universal. Let me leave Mauss here, at the point where his argument becomes both teleological and contradictory, in order to stay a little longer with the legal category of the person, at the heart of which is a disjunction between its 'natural' and 'legal' forms. The core of the argument, as it is articulated in a modern legal reference work, is this:

> A person is such, not because he is human, but because rights and duties are ascribed to him. The person is the legal subject or substance of which the rights and duties are attributes...Every full citizen is a person; other human beings, namely, subjects who are not citizens, may be persons. But not every human being is necessarily a person, for a person is capable of rights and duties, and there may well be human beings having no legal rights, as was the case with slaves in English law.[10]

Roman law allows for one individual to have multiple *personae* according to the legal role he is playing (that of owner, of inheritor, of plaintiff...), or for several individuals to constitute a single person (as when a father and son jointly inherit); a slave jointly owned by two masters may be deemed to have two distinct persons (or more correctly *vicarious* persons) when he acts on behalf of one master in relation to the other. Thus 'the law composes "persons" by effecting a veritable dissociation of subjects and bodies',[11] and rather than being equivalent to a physical or psychological subject, the unity of the person is essentially that of an estate (*un patrimoine*) and is of an administrative order: 'In Roman law it is the holder of an estate who is called a *persona*, together with the agents (sons or slaves) included in it and thus authorized to represent him juridically.'[12] The Roman *paterfamilias* 'is the only full person known to the law. His children, of whatever age, though they are citizens and therefore have rights in public law, are subject to his unfettered power of life and death. Again, only he can own property, and anything which his children acquire belongs to him alone'.[13] The Roman slave partakes only of the personhood of his master, and is categorized as a 'servile *persona*'; in this sense the slave is understood in Roman law as an *instrumentum*, a tool, rather than a person (although the slave is differentiated from animals as an *instrumentum vocale* rather than an *instrumentum mutum*).[14] Orlando Patterson's account of the

[10] *Black's Law Dictionary* (4th edn, St. Paul, MN: West Publishing Company, 1968), entry under 'person'.

[11] Yan Thomas, 'Le sujet de droit, la personne et la nature', *Le Débat* 100 (1998), p. 99, my translation.

[12] Thomas, 'Le sujet de droit', p. 100.

[13] Barry Nicholas, *An Introduction to Roman Law* (Oxford: Clarendon Press, 1962), p. 65.

[14] Marcus Terentius Varro, *Rerum Rusticarum Libri Tres*, in Marcus Porcius Cato and Marcus Terentius Varro, *On Agriculture*, trans. William Davis Hooper, Loeb Classical Library (Cambridge, MA: Harvard University Press, 1967), pp. 224-5: *Instrumenti genus vocale et semivocale et mutum, vocale in quo sunt servi, semivocale in quo sunt boves, mutum in quo sunt plaustra* ('there are three

'civil death' undergone by American slaves on entering their condition (a 'death' which involved separation from kin and renaming as an act of incorporation into the master's property) is a later example of this loss of personhood in the state of slavery,[15] although in practice American law in the slave-holding states remained inconsistent, criminalizing the killing of slaves but holding 'that the common law of assault and battery, which generally prohibited attacks on persons, did not apply to slaves'.[16] Roman citizens captured into slavery entered the limbo state of *postliminium*, in which their civil rights were suspended during their lifetime. If a prisoner returned, these rights 'revived automatically and retrospectively; if he died in captivity his death was deemed to have occurred at the moment of his capture'.[17] Christianity, formed in the context of slavery, by contrast fuses the legal and dramatic sources of the concept of person and thus makes 'every human being with a will, qualify as a person, in order to make them all equally qualified to receive divine judgment'.[18]

Finally, the insane have an ambivalent status in both ancient and modern law, with the criterion of autonomous will—of 'self-possession'—tending to deprive them of the status of person. It is possible to plot back from this exclusion to reconstruct the particular doctrines of responsibility and causality which give that status its force. Thus Goodrich writes that

> the legal individual or legal subject is a very specialized and distinct rhetorical person...a unity constructed upon the basis of its past actions. The legal subject cannot revoke or renounce its deeds, the legal subject is the straightforward cause of its deeds (acts) and it is morally and legally responsible for those deeds—utterances, actions and omissions. The legal subject is a static unity in the sense that it cannot avoid the legal imputation of a causal relation between past acts and present responsibility.[19]

In one of the few systematic sketches of the history of the legal concept of person Yan Thomas has charted its semantic vicissitudes since its initial conception in Roman law as an abstract function defined by the capacity to hold and exercise rights. In one sense these rights are united in an individual; but, in another, they are located not in a physical self but in a mode of identity imputed to any subject engaged in legal relationships. This second sense of *persona* emerges fully only in the fifth and sixth centuries AD, and designates not a role but a constant juridical personality, an inherent capacity to fill the appropriate legal roles. Thus, subjects

types of instrument, the class of instruments which is articulate, the inarticulate, and the mute; the articulate comprising the slaves, the inarticulate comprising the cattle, and the mute comprising the vehicles').

[15] Orlando Patterson, *Slavery and Social Death: A Comparative Study* (Cambridge, MA: Harvard University Press, 1982).

[16] Anon, 'Note: What We Talk About When We Talk About Persons: The Language of a Legal Fiction', *Harvard Law Review* 114: 6 (2001), p. 1749.

[17] Nicholas, *An Introduction to Roman Law*, pp. 71–2.

[18] Amélie Oksenberg Rorty, 'A Literary Postscript: Characters, Persons, Selves, Individuals', in Amélie Oksenberg Rorty (ed.), *The Identities of Persons* (Berkeley: University of California Press, 1976), p. 310.

[19] Peter Goodrich, *Reading the Law: A Critical Introduction to Legal Method and Techniques* (Oxford: Blackwell, 1986), p. 204.

'have' or 'don't have' a juridical personality (*personam habere*), and this personality is a permanent quality of men as long as they are deemed to have legal capacity; it has nothing to do with what they are 'independently of the law as living and social beings'.[20]

This conception changes in the Middle Ages under the influence of Christian theology, for which Christ is the archetype and fulfilment of human personhood, the redeemer in his own person of the fallen human nature of Adamic mankind. The essence of his being is that he is the incarnate form of God, consisting of two natures, human and divine, but having one person; and that person (the Greek term used at the First Council of Nicaea in 325 and again at the Council of Constantinople in 381 is *hypostasis*) is one of the three persons of the Trinity, distinct, co-equal, co-eternal, and consubstantial in the unity of substance of God.[21] Christ is, in brief, at once a fully human and suffering person and the promise of glorified personhood in its reunion with the God from which it has been separated. After many centuries of doctrinal debate about the person of Christ and the relation of the carnal to the spiritual, the person thus comes to be understood as the unity of the two distinct and irreducible substances of body and soul. The person and the biological human being are thenceforth fused in a unity in which the *persona* is an ontological rather than a functional entity, and is anchored in the body. As Christian doctrine and Roman law come to be reconciled from the thirteenth century onwards, however, this substantial unity leads to a dichotomization of the 'fictive' legal person and the 'real' natural person. The subject to whom rights are imputed is imaginary, having neither body nor soul; 'real' persons, by contrast, 'formed a blend of reality and fiction, a mix of concrete existence and law, a hybrid which could only with difficulty be disentangled'.[22]

When humanism subsequently undertakes a systematic and synthetic account of rights, the *persona* can thus easily be decomposed into its constitutive elements, emphasizing the juridical and functional value of the legal *persona*. At this point

[20] Yan Thomas, 'Le sujet concret et sa personne: Essai d'histoire juridique rétrospective', in Olivier Cayla and Yan Thomas, *Du droit de ne pas naître: À propos de l'affaire Perruche* (Paris: Gallimard, 2002), p. 129 (my translation).

[21] Boethius, defining the person as embodied, animate, rational, and particular, and thus as 'the individual substance of a rational nature', struggles to reconcile the Latin *persona*, derived from the mask which differentiates actors on the stage, with *hypostasis*: the former designates a substance, that which underlies accidental qualities; the latter designates the pure subsistence which is independent of accidental qualities, but corresponds to the former when it takes on particular form. Anicius Manlius Severinus Boethius, 'A Treatise Against Eutyches and Nestorius', in *Boethius: The Theological Tractates and The Consolation of Philosophy*, trans. H. F. Stewart and E. K. Rand, Loeb Classical Library (Cambridge, MA: Harvard University Press, 1968), pp. 85, 87–9. Thanks to Nick Heron for this reference.

[22] Thomas, 'Le sujet concret et sa personne', p. 133. Alain Boureau notes the convergence of the theological and juridical conceptions of the category of person in the thirteenth century, such that it now comes to designate 'the abstract instance endowed with enumerable juridical capacities such as owning property and bequeathing it or undergoing punishment; this instance does not necessarily coincide with the empirical individual ("this man") since a church or a prebend [the land from which a stipend is derived] can constitute a person; the individual can represent a fraction of a person or, conversely, comprise in himself several persons or elements of persons'. Alain Boureau, 'Droit et Théologie au XIIIe siècle', *Annales. Histoire, Sciences Sociales* 47: 6 (1992), p. 1117; my translation.

the opposition of *persona* to *homo* ('man' in the sense of human being), the latter term having been used in Roman law and through until the late Middle Ages to designate slaves, loses its pejorative connotation: each free-born adult male is both universally a 'man' and legally a 'person'. This simultaneous transformation and reconstitution of the categorical structure of Roman-law conceptions of personhood was accompanied by the elaboration of a dual temporality: the transient time of events and the timeless order of the law, which coincide fully only at two moments:

> From the Christian vision of a necessarily embodied law right through to modern legal systems, it remained necessary that between the concrete subject and the person, between life and law, between the natural temporality of a living being and the juridical temporality of a legal subject, a double convergence should be assured at the points of birth and death.[23]

Even these points of convergence can be disrupted, however, by the irreducibility of the law to 'natural' time: its ability to control time (by means of annulment, suspension, or retroactivity) or even to abolish it (as in the case of collective entities, which are not subject to human mortality). Indeed, contemporary biotechnologies have pushed the law to recognize the disjunction between 'sex and identity, sexuality and procreation, procreation and birth, birth and the establishment of the legal subject'.[24]

In addition to 'natural' persons, the concept of person is applied in modern legal systems to certain non-human entities—in particular, and subject to certain conditions of registration and jurisdiction, to corporations and to church and governmental associations. In his classic paper of 1938 Martin Wolff distinguishes four main doctrines on the nature of the juristic person. The first is the fiction theory, according to which only human beings can be persons and so the subjects of rights; as a consequence, 'corporations, States, foundations are not persons, but they are treated as if they were', by a legal fiction.[25] Maitland notes that this theory goes back to Pope Innocent IV in the thirteenth century, who proclaimed the personality of the corporation to be a gift of the Church (or, subsequently, the sovereign), and, in that sense, fictive.[26] The second theory is that enunciated by Henri Bekker, Aloys von Brinz, and Gustav Demelius, which 'declares that a so-called juristic person is no person at all, but is "subjectless property destined for a particular purpose" (*subjektloses Zweckvermögen*), that there is ownership but no owner. This theory, too, is based upon the assumption that only human beings

[23] Thomas, 'Le sujet concret et sa personne', p. 139.

[24] Thomas, 'Le sujet concret et sa personne', p. 141.

[25] Martin Wolff, 'On the Nature of Legal Persons', *Law Quarterly Review* 14 (October 1938), p. 496.

[26] Frederic Maitland, 'Moral Personality and Legal Personality', in *The Collected Papers of Frederic William Maitland*, ed. H. A. L. Fisher (Cambridge: Cambridge University Press, 1911), vol. 3, p. 309. Ernst Kantorowicz traces the transfer of the doctrine *de nullo potest aliquid facere*, 'something can be made out of nothing', to the secular state and thus to the theory of legal fictions, in 'The Sovereignty of the Artist: A Note on Legal Maxims and Renaissance Theories of Art', in *Selected Studies* (Locust Valley, NY: J. J. Augustin, 1965), pp. 352–65.

can have rights. As corporations and foundations are not humans, no subject exists in which the right can be vested'.[27] The third theory, developed in particular by Rudolf von Jhering, treats institutions in terms of the individuals (the members or shareholders of corporations, the beneficiaries of foundations) which make them up. Wolff argues that this account is unable adequately to explain the unity of will and the specificity of institutions vis-à-vis these individual agents. Finally, there is the organism doctrine, according to which

> a legal person is a real personality in an extra-juridical, pre-juridical sense of the word. In contradistinction to the others, this theory assumes that the subjects of rights need not be human beings, that every being which possesses a will and a life of its own may be the subject of rights and that States, corporations, foundations are beings just as alive and just as capable of having a will as are human beings. They are—so it says—social organisms just as humans are physical organisms. Their will ('common will') is different from the will of the members of the corporation or from the will of the founder. Their actions are their own, not carried out by agents or representatives like those of incapables (infants, lunatics), but in the same way as those of normal adults. Man uses his bodily organs for the purpose. Corporations use men.[28]

Each of these doctrines entails different judicial consequences, and each corresponds in some way to different modes of commercial practice and different conceptions of responsibility and capacity. Historically, the organicist conception of the corporation as an immortal autonomous entity with an interest separate from that of its corporators, and a will expressed by its management and carried out by its agents, coincided with the rise of corporate capitalism in the late nineteenth century. By the 1920s, 'the personified corporation had...completely absorbed the imagery which had suited the real person/real entity theorists only as an analogy',[29] allowing it to capture rights which had hitherto been reserved to natural persons (in the United States, for example, the right to freedom of expression, as well as certain, primarily financial, rights not available to natural persons).

In some sense, of course, the endowment of a non-human entity with rationality is always a fiction, an artifice. But the distinction between 'legal' persons and 'natural' persons cannot be mapped onto a simple dichotomy of nature and culture, because the status of the 'natural' person is itself constituted by a juridical demarcation of the problematic boundaries of the human: boundaries between foetus and child; between the living, the comatose, the brain-dead, and the dead; between the bodies and persons of Siamese twins; between the normal and the subnormal. The European Court of Human Rights, overruling the legal principle of the inalienability of juridical identity, has recently recognized the right of transsexuals to reassign their birth identity.[30] Moreover, 'natural' persons are not necessarily coextensive with their bodies. They may, for example, be represented by an

[27] Wolff, 'On the Nature of Legal Persons', p. 496.
[28] Wolff, 'On the Nature of Legal Persons', p. 498.
[29] Gregory A. Mark, 'The Personification of the Business Corporation in American Law', *University of Chicago Law Review* 54 (1987), p. 1479.
[30] Thomas, 'Le sujet de droit', pp. 90–1.

agent, acting as a legal extension of their status as person and able to create rights and incur duties on their behalf.

Both this constructedness of the natural person, then, and the distinction between legal and natural persons mean that there can be no general concept of 'person' with a necessary or unified form.[31] Processes of registration and certification control the 'recognition' of the status of both corporations and human beings. The natural person has distinct conditions of constitution (specific institutional and practical conditions), and is conceptually distinct from the juridically constituted person. Yet, while the clarity of this distinction matters deeply for and within the law, it has little purchase on everyday usage, where there is a constant leakage between the subject of rights and embodied individuals. As Thomas puts it, the complexity of the notion of person 'derives from the way a tool which was at first strictly juridical came over time and in its passage through Christian theology and humanism to be loaded with values incompatible with the narrowness of its original function'.[32] Mauss's essay had already made clear that that 'original function' was never simply legal: the concept of person is made up of multiple dimensions and multiple semantic layers.

III

At the heart of the juridical conception of the person is the premise that the self is a perduring identity responsible for all of its past states and able to make commitments with respect to its future states. This is the contractual or promissory dimension of selfhood that is most fully formulated in the market economies of early capitalism.[33] Yet contract, in the form of a solemnized affirmation, often accompanied by the swearing of an oath to assume an obligation, is among the most archaic foundations of human society.

Giorgio Agamben's discussion of the oath questions the 'endlessly repeated paradigm' according to which the force of the oath is to be sought in a supposedly more archaic magico-religious sphere;[34] rather, he argues, magic, religion, and law are what result from the fragmentation of the oath into its constituent elements, namely an affirmation, a calling of a god as witness, and a curse directed against the breaking of the oath. What is at stake in the oath is 'the very consistency of language and the very nature of humans as "speaking animals" ' (p. 8), and the god

[31] Paul Hirst, 'Introduction to Edelman', in Bernard Edelman, *Ownership of the Image: Elements for a Marxist Theory of Law*, trans. Elizabeth Kingdom (London: Routledge & Kegan Paul, 1979), pp. 13–14.

[32] Thomas, 'Le sujet concret et sa personne', p. 125.

[33] Morton Horwitz argues, however, that it was only in the late eighteenth and early nineteenth centuries that the grounding of contract law in 'the convergence of the wills of the contracting parties', rather than in equitable notions of substantive justice, was carried through to completion. Morton J. Horwitz, *The Transformation of American Law, 1780–1860* (Cambridge, MA: Harvard University Press, 1977), p. 160.

[34] Giorgio Agamben, *The Sacrament of Language: An Archaeology of the Oath*, trans. Adam Kotsko (Stanford: Stanford University Press, 2011), p. 12; hereafter cited in the text.

who is invoked is thus not external to it but, rather, names a potential for language to work successfully (to approximate the Logos of God). The curse is the negative counterpart of the oath (in English, the words 'oath' and 'swear' carry this ambivalence embedded within them), and it is closely linked to blasphemy, the taking of the name of the god in vain, expressing the failure of Logos. It is this possibility of failure that explains the work of religion and law, which 'do not preexist the performative experience of language that is in question in the oath, but rather... were invented to guarantee the truth and trustworthiness of the *logos* through a series of apparatuses' (p. 59). Both the performative nature of the oath, and the fact that language 'prepares within itself a hollowed-out form that the speaker must always assume in order to speak', constitute an ethical relation between the speaker and his language, determining 'the extraordinary implication of the subject in his word' (p. 71). The subject commits itself as subject in the oath's performance.

Promising is a performative transaction which commits me to act in the future as though I were to possess then the same intentions I now have.[35] It both presupposes and creates a will to act, and it thereby allows a series of consequences which include at once the accomplishment (or not) of the promise and my construction as the subject in the present of this performative act, a subject which is constant and continuous with itself. It is the translation of this subject form by way of the apparatus of the law into the characteristic property relations of modernity that gives rise to what Clifford Geertz famously called 'the Western conception of the person as a bounded, unique, more or less integrated motivational and cognitive universe, a dynamic center of awareness, emotion, judgment, and action organized into a distinctive whole and set contrastively both against other such wholes and against its social and natural background', a conception he described as 'a rather peculiar idea within the context of the world's cultures'.[36]

The juridical subject of will and intention is individual: bounded not only by its body but by its constitutive relation to persons and things understood as external to it. What Marilyn Strathern calls 'Western proprietism' finds expression in one of two complementary propositions: either the person is a unitary self with the power freely to alienate its possessions or to acquire possessions which become a separable component of its identity; or the person is conceived as identical with its activities and loses its unitary identity when the products of these activities are alienated from the person. In both cases the person is self-possessed and self-contained, separate from the world of social others; things have a singular value in relation to the person, and it is the external social world that gives things the plurality and diversity of their value. This assumption runs counter, however, to the supposition

[35] For an overview of the paradoxes involved in the promise's demand for 'assertiveness, commitment, and certainty at precisely the point where we are least able to give it', cf. William Vitek, *Promising* (Philadelphia: Temple University Press, 1993); the citation is from p. 1.

[36] Clifford Geertz, 'From the Native's Point of View: On the Nature of Anthropological Understanding', in *Local Knowledge: Further Essays in Interpretive Anthropology* (New York: Basic Books, 1983), p. 59.

of many traditional societies 'that persons are intrinsically plural and diverse in origin and in their acts'.[37]

That alternative supposition may be called *dividuality*, and it is, in some ways, already a component of Western personhood: on the one hand, although personhood is conceived in terms of a singular will expressively tied to the body, human time is nevertheless divided between the discontinuous domains of waking and sleep, consciousness and dream; and will is limited in sexual experience, in illness, in the drive of the body towards ageing and death. On the other hand, the primary locus of decision-making in advanced capitalist societies is, in many ways, not the individual but corporate entities—the state and its bureaucracies, corporations, and planning and administrative systems that take on person-like qualities and may have the legal status of a person. We could also think of the complex networks both of kinship, friendship, civic, and work relations, and of relations between persons and things, as undermining the boundedness of the individual subject. The relation between persons and things is complicated by the precarious nature of this distinction in the larger social world. Pottage cites the effects of technologies of *in vitro* reproduction on understandings of the human:

> Gene sequences are at once part of the genetic programme of the person and chemical templates from which drugs are manufactured; embryos are related to their parents by means of the commodifying forms of contract and property, and yet they are *also* persons; depending on the uses to which they are put, the acts of embryos produced by *in vitro* fertilisation might be seen as having either the 'natural' developmental potential of the human person or the technical 'pluripotentiality' that makes them such a valuable resource for research into gene therapies. In each of these cases, the categorisation of an entity as a person or a thing is dependent upon a contingent distinction rather than an embedded division.[38]

In general, as Chris Fowler argues, 'personhood is attained and maintained through relationships not only with other human beings but with things, places, animals and the spiritual features of the cosmos. Some of these may also emerge as persons through this engagement'.[39] In the mode of dividuality 'people are composed of social relations with others to the degree that they owe parts of themselves to others'.[40] Fowler distinguishes between two central modes of dividuality which he calls *partibility* and *permeability*. The concept of partibility is most closely associated with Marilyn Strathern's arguments about the relation between persons and things in the gift economies of Melanesia, where it is impossible to speak of an alienation

[37] Marilyn Strathern, *The Gender of the Gift: Problems with Women and Problems with Society in Melanesia* (Berkeley: University of California Press, 1988), p. 159. These sentences are adapted from my essay 'Gift and Commodity', in *Time and Commodity Culture: Essays in Cultural Theory and Postmodernity* (Oxford: Clarendon Press, 1997), p. 126.

[38] Alain Pottage, 'Introduction: The Fabrication of Persons and Things', in Alain Pottage and Martha Mundy (eds), *Law, Anthropology, and the Constitution of the Social* (Cambridge: Cambridge University Press, 2004), pp. 4–5.

[39] Chris Fowler, *The Archaeology of Personhood: An Anthropological Appraisal* (London: Routledge, 2004), p. 7.

[40] Fowler, *The Archaeology of Personhood*, p. 8.

of property since 'persons simply do not have alienable items, that is, property, at their disposal; they can only dispose of items by enchaining themselves in relations with others'.[41] Gift exchange must thus be understood as a recursive process in which objects are circulated in order to make the relations in which they can circulate: this is a 'personifying' mode of sociality 'in which the objects of relations are always other relations'.[42] Conversely, there is both a division of interests among persons and an inherent divisibility of personal identity: 'The partibility of the person (evinced in flows of wealth) is a counterpart to the person as a composite of the relations that compose him or her.'[43]

Whereas in partible relations both persons and things are divisible into metonymic states which then enter into relations of exchange and recomposition, in the mode of personhood that Fowler calls permeability the person's mode of being is affected by the flow of the substances they ingest and exchange. In Hindu thinking about persons, social transactions are formed by exchanges of what McKim Marriott calls 'substance codes': degrees of refinement of matter that carry codes of action and conduct and are correlated with rank within the caste system. The scale runs from relatively 'gross' substances such as cooked food or garbage, through more refined substances such as grain or land, still more refined substances such as money, and the most subtle (and most abstract) substances such as knowledge. Subtler substance codes emerge

> through processes of maturation or (what is considered to be the same thing) cooking. Thus subtler essences may sometimes be ripened, extracted, or distilled out of grosser ones (as fruit comes from plants, nectar from flowers, butter from milk); and grosser substance-codes may be generated or precipitated out of subtler ones (as plants come from seed, feces from food).[44]

All natural entities are composed of the substance codes that pass through them and are modified by combinations and separations of these substance codes; and 'what goes on *between* actors are the same connected processes of mixing and separation that go on *within* actors'.[45] Human existence involves the constant transfer and absorption of particles of heterogeneous matter through relations of kinship or exchange, through the giving of alms and gifts, and through commerce, as well as through 'subtler, but still substantial and powerful forms, such as perceived words, ideas, appearances, and so forth. Dividual persons, who must exchange in such ways, are therefore always composites of the substance-codes that they take in',[46] and are constantly reconstituted through these processes. The caste system is built

[41] Strathern, *The Gender of the Gift*, p. 161.
[42] Strathern, *The Gender of the Gift*, p. 221.
[43] Marilyn Strathern, *Property, Substance and Effect: Anthropological Essays on Persons and Things* (London: Athlone Press, 1999), p. 155.
[44] McKim Marriott, 'Hindu Transactions: Diversity without Dualism', in Bruce Kapferer (ed.), *Transaction and Meaning: Directions in the Anthropology of Exchange and Symbolic Behaviour* (Philadelphia: Institute for the Study of Human Issues, 1976), p. 110.
[45] Marriott, 'Hindu Transactions', p. 109.
[46] Marriott, 'Hindu Transactions', p. 111.

on the basis of transactions in substance codes between superiors, inferiors, equals, and those without a place in the system.

We might think of these relations of individuality, partibility, or permeability between persons and between persons and things as the lateral dimension of social being; it is complemented by a vertical, eschatological dimension in which persons are constituted by their relation to the generations of the dead from whom they inherit, to the gods, and to the unborn descendants to whom property and some of the components of kinship (a name, a status, a genetic inheritance) are to be passed on. These are virtual relations, which may yet possess a compelling concreteness.

All societies have at their heart the integration of the dead into the order of the living, typically through mortuary rites intended 'to keep the soul of the dead person (or, rather, his image or phantasm) from remaining a threatening presence in the world of the living (the *larva* of the Latins and the *eidolon* or *phantasma* of the Greeks)'.[47] Robert Hertz's description of the phenomenon of provisional burial, followed after a period by a set of final rites, draws attention to the marginal status of the soul between the two worlds, treated as an intruder if it ventures into the afterworld, and as an importunate guest among the living.[48] The period of mourning after death corresponds to this liminal state in which the soul belongs neither to the visible nor to the invisible community. Its passage from this world to the afterlife results in the formation of new communities, in which the dead either continue to mingle with the living or inhabit a quite separate space. While some anthropologists make a clear distinction between traditional and modern societies on the basis of the fusion or the separation of the quick and the dead,[49] this seems to me too simple a dichotomy. Funerary rites and the veneration of the dead are still a component of the societies of modernity, and new eschatological relations have emerged as the boundaries of the person have been problematized by technologies of the genetic or surgical transformation of the body, by its integration in a world populated by artificially intelligent entities and in new, virtual environments, and by its potential destruction as a consequence of catastrophic climate change (or, lest we forget, of nuclear holocaust). The body is never a simple presence: its lineage stretches into the past and the future, and those relations with the dead and the unborn, whether conceived spiritually, genetically, or socially, shape its present being.

[47] Giorgio Agamben, *Remnants of Auschwitz: The Witness and the Archive*, trans. Daniel Heller-Roazen (New York: Zone Books, 2002), p. 79.

[48] Robert Hertz, *Death and the Right Hand*, trans. Rodney and Claudia Needham (Glencoe: The Free Press, 1960), p. 36.

[49] Cf. Cécile Barraud, Daniel de Coppet, André Iteanu, and Raymond Jamous, *Of Relations and the Dead: Four Societies Viewed from the Angle of their Exchanges*, trans. Stephen J. Suffern (Oxford: Berg, 1994), p. 112.

IV

In Canto III of the *Purgatorio* Dante, journeying with his guide Virgil, turns his face to the mountain that rises from the sea, and notes that:

Lo sol, che dietro fiammeggiava roggio,
rotto m'era dinanzi a la figura,
ch'avëa in me de' suoi raggi l'appoggio.
Io mi volsi dallato con paura
d'essere abbandanato, quand'io vidi
solo dinanzi a me la terra oscura...

[*The sun, which was flaming red behind, was broken in front of me by the figure which was formed by the staying of its rays upon me. I turned to my side, fearing that I was abandoned, when I saw the ground darkened before me only.*][50]

Until this point in his journey through a sunless hell and the early stages of Purgatory, Dante has had no occasion to notice that the spirits of the dead do not cast a shadow. Virgil now reassures him, asking him not to wonder at the fact that there is no shadow in front of his own form. I am here with you and guide you, he says; but

Vespero è già colà dov'è sepolto
lo corpo dentro al quale io facea ombra;
Napoli l'ha, e da Brandizio è tolto.

[*It is now evening in the place where the body is buried within which I made a shadow: Naples has it, and it was taken from Brindisi.*][51]

Virgil's existence, like that of all the inhabitants of the afterlife, is split between his present state as a shade with the mere appearance of a human being, and his dead body, distant in space and present at a different time of day. Having his existence in the strange interval between two embodiments, and speaking of his former body as though it were a distant stranger or a lost acquaintance, Virgil is a shadow that casts no shadow, equivalent to the 'figure' formed in that absence of light that falls before Dante's solid and living body. In a later canto, the poet Statius seeks to embrace the feet of his master, Virgil, whom Dante here refers to as 'mio dottor', my teacher; but Virgil says to him:

'Frate,
non far, ché tu se' ombra e ombra vedi.'
Ed ei surgendo: 'Or puoi la quantitate
comprender de l'amor ch'a te mi scalda,

[50] Dante Alighieri, *Purgatorio 1: Italian Text and Translation, The Divine Comedy*, trans. Charles S. Singleton, Bollingen Series LXXX (Princeton: Princeton University Press, 1973), Canto III, ll. 16–21. Further references to the *Inferno, Purgatorio*, and *Paradiso* are to this edition.

[51] Dante, *Purgatorio*, III, ll. 25–7.

quand'io dismento nostra vanitate,
trattando l'ombre come cosa salda.'

[*'Brother, do not so, for you are a shade and a shade you see.' And he, rising, 'Now you may comprehend the measure of the love that burns in me for you, when I forget our emptiness and treat shades as solid things.'*][52]

Virgil has the appearance of substance, of a 'solid thing', but is insubstantial to the touch—as indeed Dante had realized in Canto II of the *Purgatorio*, when he sought to embrace the shade of his friend Casella:

Ohi ombre vane, fuor che ne l'aspetto!
tre volte dietro a lei le mani avvinsi,
e tante mi tornai con esse al petto.

[*O empty shades except in aspect! Three times I clasped my hands behind him and as often brought them back to my breast.*][53]

This state of shaped emptiness, 'vanità che par persona' [*an emptiness which seems like a person*],[54] embodies a paradox about the absence of bodies in the thickly populated realms through which Dante travels. The paradox is not that there are no bodies in the afterlife, since those bodies will remain buried and decaying until the resurrection; rather, it is that these disembodied spirits have human shape, that they suffer physical torments, and that they bear the characteristics of the persons they once were. The shape they have is that of 'aerial bodies, fictive replicas of their real bodies and exact reflections of the soul itself'.[55] Of course, this paradox is essential to the figural representation of disembodied souls: Dante's cosmos must be filled with perceptible, person-like entities in order to work as narrative, and the fictiveness of these replicas in one sense mirrors and performs the fiction of the poetic work. But it also responds to the puzzling theological issues associated both with the notion of hell and with the emergent doctrine of Purgatory, which Jacques Le Goff dates in its achieved form to the late twelfth century:[56] the question of how souls can be corporeally punished after death and before they are restored to their bodies at the resurrection; the 'materiality *sui generis*' with which the soul is endowed in Purgatory;[57] the ability of these quasi-bodies to be burned by and yet to withstand eternal flame; and the efficacy of prayer in affecting the fate of souls whose eternal sentence is passed both at the moment of their death and, in confirmation, at the Last Judgement.

[52] Dante, *Purgatorio*, XXI, ll. 131–6.
[53] Dante, *Purgatorio*, II, ll. 79–81.
[54] Dante, *Inferno*, VI, l. 36; I have modified Singleton's translation to give a literal reading of 'persona', which he here—correctly for the context—translates as 'real bodies'.
[55] John Freccero, 'Manfred's Wounds and the Poetics of the Purgatorio', in Rachel Jacoff (ed.), *Dante: The Poetics of Conversion* (Cambridge, MA: Harvard University Press, 1986), p. 196.
[56] Jacques Le Goff, *The Birth of Purgatory*, trans. Arthur Goldhammer (Chicago: University of Chicago Press, 1984), p. 4 and pp. 130ff.
[57] Le Goff, *The Birth of Purgatory*, p. 6.

The central discussion of the nature of the aerial bodies of the shades takes place in Canto XXV of the *Purgatorio*. Here Statius, responding to Dante's question about fictive bodies, replies with a long disquisition on the relation of body to soul, in a passage that Freccero has described as 'something of a scandal in the history of Dante criticism' because of its use of a complex technical vocabulary drawn from Aquinas and from Aristotle's *De generatione animalium*.[58]

Statius's argument, in brief, is that 'the embryogeny of the shades is one particular case of the embryogeny of human beings in general'.[59] The argument proceeds as follows: first, that portion of the 'perfect blood' of a man which is not used up in the nourishment of the body is distilled in the heart and acquires an 'informing power' (*virtute informativa*, l. 41); it then passes through further processes of digestion to become semen, the active force in generation, which, in interaction with the woman's passive blood, coagulates to form the embryo. The child in the womb passes through the stages of the vegetative and the sensitive souls, which are then subsumed in the intellective soul; the quickening of that third soul occurs when, in an act that mirrors the original creation of mankind,

> lo motor primo a lui si volge lieto
> sovra tant'arte di natura, e spira
> spirito novo, di vertù repleto,
> che ciò che trova attivo quivi, tira
> in sua sustanzia, e fassi un'alma sola,
> che vive e sente e sé in sé rigira.

[*the First Mover turns to it with joy over such art of nature, and breathes into it a new spirit replete with virtue, which absorbs that which is active there into its own substance, and makes one single soul which lives and feels and circles on itself.*][60]

The process of death and the acquisition of an aerial body then, says Statius, repeats this process of formation of the embryo. At the moment of death the soul falls 'of itself' (*per se stessa*, l. 85), as though of its own volition, to one of two shores, and thus learns whether its path leads it to hell or to Purgatory. At this moment the informing power that had shaped the earthly body in the womb begins to radiate into the air around it. The analogy is with a rainbow:

> E come l'aere, quand' è ben pïorno,
> per l'altrui raggio che 'n sé si reflette,
> di diversi color diventa addorno;
> così l'aere vicin quivi si mette
> e in quella forma ch'è in lui suggella
> virtüalmente l'alma che ristette...

[58] Freccero, 'Manfred's Wounds', p. 201.

[59] Etienne Gilson, 'Dante's Notion of a Shade: *Purgatorio* XXV', *Mediaeval Studies* 29 (1967), p. 128.

[60] Dante, *Purgatorio*, XXV, ll. 70–5.

[And as the air, when it is full of moisture, becomes adorned with various colours by another's [the sun's] rays which are reflected in it, so here the neighboring air shapes itself in that form which is virtually imprinted on it by the soul that stopped there...][61]

This imprinted form then follows the spirit wherever it moves (in lines 25–6 Dante had used the example of the way one's movements are repeated in a mirror image). The spirit is called a shade because it takes its appearance from this shaped emptiness; and the shade takes its form, figures itself (*l'ombra si figura*, l. 107), in accordance with the desires and other feelings that affect it.

Freccero notes that there is no substantive Christian precedent for such a doctrine, arguing that 'the Christian emphasis on the indissoluble unity of the human composite and the Aristotelian theory of hylomorphism to which Dante subscribed rule out the possibility that Dante means us to take the fiction seriously as metaphysics'.[62] Gilson similarly remarks that '[t]here are no shades of Hades in the world of Aristotle or in that of Thomas Aquinas. The new cycle of operations imagined by Dante has for its object to account for the existence of such shades in his own poetic universe'[63]—although Gilson emphasizes the 'scientific' nature of Statius's account, which closely follows Aristotelian biology and Galenic medicine. There is, moreover, a closely related theological doctrine to do with the aerial bodies of angels, although angels are not persons in the sense of being a unity of substantial soul and material body.

The important point is perhaps just that the shades of the dead, too, are not persons, being disembodied—and that, conversely, the notion of person in the Christian Middle Ages has everything to do with the fusion of soul and body. If soul is the form that infuses and gives being to the body, and if form has no being apart from the matter that it informs, then 'it is impossible (except by conceptual abstraction) to separate body and soul, and this applies to resurrected bodies as much as to anything else... The resurrection of the body will therefore remove the *contra naturam* condition of separated souls'.[64] The shade is an entirely provisional entity, longing for the time when it will be reunited with its lost companion.

That longing is strikingly expressed in a passage in the *Paradiso*, in which Solomon explains how it is that resurrected bodies will be able to bear the sight of the radiance with which they will be clothed. Just as a burning coal gives out a white glow that outshines the flame, he says, so the radiance of our present disembodied state in Paradise will be surpassed in brightness by 'la carne/che tutto dí la terra ricoperchia' [*the flesh which the earth still covers*], and the organs of our immortal body will have the strength to bear the sight of that splendour. As he says this,

[61] Dante, *Purgatorio*, XXV, ll. 91–6.
[62] Freccero, 'Manfred's Wounds', p. 203.
[63] Gilson, 'Dante's Notion of a Shade', p. 130.
[64] Fernando Vidal, 'Brains, Bodies, Selves, and Science: Anthropologies of Identity and the Resurrection of the Body', *Critical Inquiry* 28: 4 (2002), p. 946.

Tanto mi parver sùbiti e accorti
e l'uno e l'altro coro a dicer 'Amme!'
che ben mostrar disio d'i corpi morti...

[*So sudden and eager both the one and the other chorus seemed to me in saying 'Amen', that truly they showed desire for their dead bodies...*][65]

'Desire for dead bodies' sounds just as richly perverse in Dante's Italian as it does in English. This desire—which may not be for themselves alone but also for others who were dear to them 'before they became eternal flames' [*anzi che fosser sempiterne fiamme*]—reflects the central belief that the person is not whole without the body, in this world or the one to come: '[T]he body we will finally resume is not the shade-body of purgation but the beloved and whole body of earth, expressing the person in its every detail and sensual experience.'[66] The fascination with dead bodies, the affective and intellectual investment in the resurrection of every last particle of the flesh—strange as it is to modern sensibilities—lies at the core of the vision of the wholeness and fixity of the person that informs Dante's ordered cosmos.

If the shade-body is not yet a person, it nevertheless figures the moral essence of the person for whom it stands: the physical characteristics of the aerial body 'reflect the soul's eschatological condition',[67] representing character as it is given definite and eternal form in the time between death and the Last Judgement. In what Hegel calls the 'changeless existence' (*dies wechsellose Dasein*) of Dante's characters,[68] 'we behold an intensified image of the essence of their being, fixed for all eternity in gigantic dimensions, behold it in a purity and distinctness which could never for one moment have been possible during their lives upon earth'.[69] By virtue of God's judgement (which is also that of the omnipotent creator of this alternative universe, its First Mover, Dante Alighieri), each figure we encounter

> is involved in an eternal situation which is the sum and the result of all his actions and which at the same time tells him what were the decisive aspects of his life and his character. Thus his memory is led along a path which, though for the inhabitants of hell it is dreary and barren, is yet always the right path, the path which reveals what was decisive in the individual's life.[70]

[65] Dante, *Paradiso*, XIV, ll. 61–3.

[66] Caroline Walker Bynum, *The Resurrection of the Body in Western Christianity, 200–1336* (New York: Columbia University Press, 1995), p. 302.

[67] Manuele Gragnolati, *Experiencing the Afterlife: Soul and Body in Dante and Medieval Culture* (Notre Dame, IN: University of Notre Dame Press, 2005), p. 86.

[68] G. W. F. Hegel, *Vorlesungen über die Ästhetik III, Werke in zwanzig Bänden* (Frankfurt am Main: Suhrkamp Verlag, 1970), p. 406.

[69] Erich Auerbach, *Mimesis: The Representation of Reality in Western Literature*, trans. Willard R. Trask (Princeton: Princeton University Press, 1953), p. 192.

[70] Auerbach, *Mimesis*, p. 197. Cf. Erich Auerbach, *Dante: Poet of the Secular World*, trans. Ralph Manheim (Chicago: University of Chicago Press, 1961), p. 91: 'The earthly entelechy of each person was fused with the idea of his self.'

This is 'a temporality figurally preserved in timeless eternity',[71] in which each of the dead is transfigured into himself, 'tel qu'en Lui-même enfin l'éternité le change'.[72]

The question of the condition of the soul after death goes to the heart of the question of what it means, in the Christian Middle Ages, to be a person; it opens it as a theological question, which can only be resolved by the doctrine of resurrection, the Event that brings time to a close and unites us with our immortal bodies. By implication, however, this is always a question about the meaning of personhood in this world, and it is for this reason, writes Fernando Vidal, that 'discussions on the resurrection of the body may function as a *fil conducteur* for a history of notions of personal identity'.[73]

The most comprehensive account of those discussions is Caroline Walker Bynum's *The Resurrection of the Body*. Let me start where she does, with a text that has been the central biblical locus for the discussion of resurrection, the fifteenth chapter of Paul's first epistle to the Corinthians:

> 35 But some *man* will say, How are the dead raised up? and with what body do they come?
> 36 *Thou* fool, that which thou sowest is not quickened, except it die:
> 37 And that which thou sowest, thou sowest not that body that shall be, but bare grain, it may chance of wheat, or of some other *grain*:
> 38 But God giveth it a body as it hath pleased him, and to every seed his own body.
> 39 All flesh *is* not the same flesh: but *there is* one *kind of* flesh of men, another flesh of beasts, another of fishes, *and* another of birds...
> 42 So also *is* the resurrection of the dead. It is sown in corruption; it is raised in incorruption:
> 43 It is sown in dishonour; it is raised in glory: it is sown in weakness; it is raised in power.
> 44 It is sown a natural body; it is raised a spiritual body. There is a natural body, and there is a spiritual body...
> 50 Now this I say, brethren, that flesh and blood cannot inherit the kingdom of God; neither doth corruption inherit incorruption.
> 51 Behold, I shew you a mystery; We shall not all sleep, but we shall all be changed,
> 52 In a moment, in the twinkling of an eye, at the last trump: for the trumpet shall sound, and the dead shall be raised incorruptible, and we shall be changed.
> 53 For this corruptible must put on incorruption, and this mortal *must* put on immortality.
> 54 So when this corruptible shall have put on corruption, and this mortal shall have put on immortality, then shall be brought to pass the saying that is written, Death is swallowed up in victory.[74]

The central image of the seed that dies and is quickened again carries over into the figure of the resurrection of an incorruptible from a corrupted body in a process

[71] Auerbach, *Mimesis*, p. 198.
[72] Stéphane Mallarmé, 'Le Tombeau d'Edgar Poe', in *Oeuvres complètes*, vol. I, ed. Bertrand Marchal, Bibliothèque de la Pléïade (Paris: Gallimard, 1998), p. 38.
[73] Vidal, 'Brains, Bodies, Selves, and Science', p. 935.
[74] *The Bible: Authorized King James Version* (Oxford: Oxford University Press, 1997), pp. 220–1.

of transformation which constitutes a mystery. The tenor of Bynum's argument is, however, that the organic connotations of this metaphor are not, for the most part, taken up in later Christian doctrine. In the patristic debates of the late second to the early fifth centuries there is an increasing emphasis on material continuity between the earthly and the resurrection body, and in key later texts such as Peter Lombard's influential compilation, the *Four Books of Sentences*, 'the emphasis is on an identity guaranteed by material and formal continuity, not on an opportunity for growth, escape, or rebirth'.[75] The resurrection body for most of late antiquity and the early Middle Ages is a reassemblage of parts, a body reconstituted in its smallest detail from the bones and dust of which it is made. Yet this eschatological materialism does not involve the dualistic opposition of body to soul: rather, the idea of person developed through the Middle Ages made the flesh integral to the self in all its dimensions.

For the patristic period, Bynum suggests, the paradigmatic resurrection body is that of the tortured martyr, a body that triumphs over the dispersal of its parts and the putrefaction of the dishonoured corpse. In line with the relic cult, Augustine stresses the 'hardening of the body against change' (p. 104), just as later images of the impassibility of the resurrection body liken it to the reliquaries which display the relic in a hardened, jewel-like form. Bynum makes a connection, too, between such models of the resurrection body and Mediterranean funerary practice, with its refusal of the decaying body and privileging of 'hard, dry remains (bones and ashes)' (p. 52); at a later period the practice of boiling the flesh from bones and then dividing and distributing them for burial became widespread. In a cultural context in which bodily change is abhorrent and inexplicable, resurrection 'had to replace process with stasis, to bring matter (changeable by definition) to changelessness. It had to restore body qua body, while transforming it to permanence and impassibility' (p. 57).

The concept of resurrection is an endeavour to answer the question of 'what body is that it can return after death and what it adds to person that separated soul lacks' (p. 136); it goes to the heart of the question of what it means to be a person, in this world as in the next. Yet at the same time it brings forth its own impossibly complicated questions. Augustine poses some of them:

> Will aborted fetuses rise? Will Siamese twins be two people or one in the resurrection? Will we all be the same sex in heaven? the same height and weight? the same age? Will we have to eat? Will we be able to eat? Will deformities and mutilations appear in heaven? Will nail and hair clippings all return to the body to which they originally belonged? Will men have beards in their resurrected bodies? Will we 'see' in heaven only when our eyes are open? Will we rise with all our internal organs as well as our external ones? (pp. 97–8)

And so on. Once the resurrection comes to be seen as the reassemblage of the particles of matter that constitute us, even more difficult questions are raised—'to the

[75] Bynum, *The Resurrection of the Body*, p. 8; hereafter cited in the text.

modern reader's astonishment' (p. 124)—by considering the chain of matter that goes into that process of constitution:

> How can all humankind descend from the drops of Adam's semen—indeed how can any embryo grow into a child or any child into an adult—without taking in so much food that it becomes roast pig or bread instead of human nature? If we eat and grow and excrete for a lifetime, cutting our hair and fingernails and spilling our blood, how can God bring back our particles when the trumpet blows? If food adds nothing to human substance, how do we grow? And why did God provide the tree of life in the Garden of Eden to sustain us? If food *does* add to human substance, how can we avoid becoming what we eat? How, in cases of cannibalism or attacks by wild animals, can we remain ourselves when digested by others? What will happen to superfluity when we rise? (pp. 124–5)

Mastication, swallowing, digestion, regurgitation, excretion—these are the fantasmatic images that underpin anxiety about the fate of the body, which is inextricable from personal destiny. Yet the promise of resurrection is also both a refusal to contemplate disembodiment—a refusal to reject bodily process—and the belief that the death of the body is only a moment in a larger cycle. What is astonishing is the persistent materialism of Christian doctrine in late antiquity and the Middle Ages: those thinkers who sought to resolve the problem of identity in terms closer to the metaphor of the organic transfiguration of seed or the patterning of matter by form (Origen's postulation of the body as eidetic continuity through processes of material flux, and—picking up on the distinction in Corinthians between natural and spiritual bodies—of the resurrection body as spiritual and luminous; Aquinas's notion of the substantial soul which can subsist, although incompletely, without body) were castigated precisely for their failure of belief in the literal resurrection of the material body. And that doctrinal evolution has had profound effects on later understandings of what it means to be human and where its boundaries lie. Just as, in medieval legal doctrine, the *persona* comes to be conceived as an ontological fusion of body and soul, a psychosomatic unity, so does medieval theology lay the ground for current arguments about the nature of identity and embodiment, which 'have not a little in common with the abstruse speculations of medieval theologians about what exactly must be reassembled at the end of time in order to constitute a "person"' (p. 342). Not only the brain-dead patients, the organ recipients, the transsexuals, the foetuses, and the autonomous artificial intelligences of modernity, but the vampires, zombies, and replicants of popular culture bear witness to that continuity.

V

The category of personhood is given by the gods, by totemic ancestors, by ancestral law embedded in country, or by a more or less secular system of law. The category designates a bounded set of capacities, and is defined in part by a set of exclusions: it is distinct from the members of other species, and from inanimate things; it is distinct from the dead and the unborn. Roberto Esposito points to the way the *dispositif* of the person works with a kind of violence to perform an act of simultaneous inclusion and exclusion by distinguishing full persons from semi-persons and non-persons (in Roman law, the *paterfamilias* from the sons, the female members of the family, and the slaves, as well as the free-born from the emancipated; in contemporary ethics, the adult with full mental and physical capacities from children, the foetus, the terminally ill, the insane, and so on).[76] As a positive construct, the person is bounded by the human body. It bears rights and obligations, and is the subject of will and cognition; and it is something like a place defined by a social order. Yet each of these distinctions and capacities must be qualified. Persons are, and are continuous with, animals. Their mode of relation to the world may be individual or dividual, permeable or partible; their identity may be limited to this world, may continue into an afterlife, or may pass by a process of metempsychosis into the identity of another person. Persons are never discontinuous with things since they project their will and capacities into technological things, and their sociality is, in many ways and increasingly, a 'sociality with objects'.[77] The interaction of humans and machines can be understood as a mode of distributed intelligence, and the 'self' as no more than 'a small part of a much larger trial-and-error system which does the thinking, acting, and deciding'.[78] Persons are joined in culturally various ways to the dead who gave them birth and who live in their memories, to the world of spirits, and to the unborn to whom they bequeath their genes, their name, and the world they leave behind; they occupy a transient space between non-being and death. The personal body may be incomplete, is subject to constant continuous and discontinuous change, and may be prosthetically extended. The will is negated in sleep, in sexual passion, in dreams, in the logic of the unconscious; cognition is driven by metaphor and desire and by the body's complex chemistry. Rights and obligations are subject to the play of social power and the pressure of social forces. And, to the extent that the person is a place defined by a social order (a *taxis* or office), it is a different kind of thing in each society, differentially defined by a sociology, an anthropology, an ontology, and an eschatology.

How does the category of person relate to that of the self? Charles Taylor, who has written the most comprehensive account of the history in Western thought of the category of the self, speaks of its connection with 'modern inwardness, the sense of ourselves as beings with inner depth',[79] and notes that the self is necessarily experienced from within, not as 'an object in the usually understood sense. We are not selves in the way that we are organisms, or we don't have selves in the way we

[76] Roberto Esposito, 'The Dispositif of the Person', *Law, Culture and the Humanities* 8: 1 (2012), pp. 25–6.

[77] Karin Knorr Cetina, 'Sociality with Objects: Social Relations in Postsocial Knowledge Societies', *Theory, Culture and Society* 14: 1 (1997), pp. 1–30.

[78] Gregory Bateson, *Steps to an Ecology of Mind* (Chicago: University of Chicago Press, 2000), pp. 331–2.

[79] Charles Taylor, *Sources of the Self: The Making of the Modern Identity* (Cambridge, MA: Harvard University Press, 1989), p. x; hereafter cited in the text.

have hearts and livers' (p. 34); we are selves to the extent that things have a significance for us that is conveyed in language and in our relation to other selves. The story that Taylor tells is, with variations of emphasis, one that is familiar from constant retelling:[80] the heterogeneous and aggregative nature of the terms designating body and soul in the Homeric epics; Plato's assertion of an ethics of the self that is grounded in reason rather than in a warrior ethos or an ethos of manic inspiration; Augustine's understanding of the soul as the remembrance of God, and of the will as perverse desire which drives us to act against our reason and our interests; the Cartesian turn from belief in cosmic order towards a mechanistic conception of the universe, knowledge of which is secured by an act of representation constructed through clear and distinct perceptions; the domination, in Descartes's account, of a disenchanted world of material extension (including the body) by a distinct and immaterial rationality; the decline of magic and of the 'orders of ontic logos';[81] the proximity of the soul to God in Puritan practices of personal commitment and self-scrutiny; Locke's formulation of a self which is punctual, disengaged, and radically reflexive, and of a rationality which is procedural and utilitarian; the formation, above all in the eighteenth-century novel, of a new, individualist moral culture which prizes the feelings and locates them in the intimate world of the family; Rousseau's elaboration of a self which is deeply inward and radically autonomous; Romantic 'expressive individuation' (p. 376); and the many mutations of the Romantic self in the modern world.

To speak of this as a familiar story is not, of course, to say that it is wrong, and it is frequently insightful. Yet what is striking in this narrative of the emergence of the individual, reflexive self is just how many entrances this character makes in the process of emerging: each time a little less in disguise, a little more like what it truly is. Despite the historical differentiations he makes in charting the course of the self from classical antiquity, Taylor's notion of the self is—like Mauss's—a notion of the successive mutations of a continuously developing entity which reaches its fullest form in modernity. And just as Mauss runs together an account of religious practices of introspection with a purely philosophical history of the self, so Taylor intersperses what is a quintessentially philosophical history of concepts of the self with accounts of changing social structures and practices. The key methodological reflection on this occurs in the following passage:

> The modern identity arose because changes in the self-understandings connected with a wide range of practices—religious, political, economic, familial, intellectual, artistic—converged and reinforced each other to produce it: the practices, for instance, of religious prayer and ritual, of spiritual discipline as a member of a Christian congregation, of self-scrutiny as one of the regenerate, of the politics of consent, of the family life of the companionate marriage, of the new child-rearing which develops from the eighteenth century, of artistic creation under the demands of originality,

[80] Roy Porter describes such teleological narratives of the evolution of the category of the self as mythical. Roy Porter, 'Introduction', in Roy Porter (ed.), *Rewriting the Self: Histories from the Renaissance to the Present* (London: Routledge, 1997), p. 8.

[81] Taylor, *Sources of the Self*, p. 192. Hereafter quoted in the text.

> of the demarcation and defence of privacy, of markets and contracts, of voluntary associations, of the cultivation and display of sentiment, of the pursuit of scientific knowledge. (p. 206)

Ideas and practices are always linked, even if this connection does not have the form of a linear causality. Locke's version of possessive individualism, for example, is correlated with the economic practices of the capitalist market; the context for Descartes's discourses on method is the rise of neo-Stoicism among elite groups in the late sixteenth and early seventeenth centuries, seeking to remake the self by means of methodical and disciplined action and, in turn, applying that discipline in the military and administrative fields. Yet Taylor's attention to such practices is episodic rather than systematic; his focus is on a general and emergent philosophical category rather than on the shaping of selfhood within and as a contingent effect of networks of social practice: as a *dispositif*.[82]

One way of thinking about how the ethical substance of selfhood might take on a quite radically different shape, even in the broadly individualist cultures of the West, is by way of the notion of social office. The 'presupposition of office' that Conal Condren traces from its roots in classical antiquity through to early modern England supposes a world in which the agent or *persona* is 'an embodiment of a moral economy';[83] this world is not divided between an 'official' form of the self and a 'private' residue: rather, there is *only* the web of offices to which one is called or which one assumes, and these prescribe a space of action for the most personal spheres (those of close kinship relations or of religion) as much as for the public domain. Without office there is no freedom, only the lack of a voice and of a domain of responsibilities. As Knud Haakonssen puts it, '*Officia* in the broader sense are... not simply "duties", as the word is usually rendered in English. They are the offices of life which encompass clusters of specific duties and rights, and we are bound to them by an *obligatio*, or moral necessity.'[84] The office (shepherd or courtier, king or sheriff, cleric or parent) is thus at once a kind of 'ethical habitus'[85] (p. 24) and a constellation of rights and responsibilities manifested in a specified form of the person; it is 'given shape over time, in relation to adjacent offices, and by the patterns of its negation';[86] and it is marked by 'a degree of formality in demarcation, an expectation of social continuity and the presentation of a *persona*. In the early modern world, these aspects were frequently signalled 'by ceremonial

[82] The same holds true, *a fortiori*, of a more conventional 'history of theories of selfhood' such as Jerrold Seigel's *The Idea of the Self: Thought and Experience in Western Europe since the Seventeenth Century* (Cambridge: Cambridge University Press, 2005) (the citation is from p. 40), or Raymond Martin and John Barresi's *The Rise and Fall of Soul and Self: An Intellectual History of Personal Identity* (New York: Columbia University Press, 2006).

[83] Conal Condren, *Argument and Authority in Early Modern England: The Presupposition of Oaths and Offices* (Cambridge: Cambridge University Press, 2006), p. 26.

[84] Knud Haakonssen, *Natural Law and Moral Philosophy: From Grotius to the Scottish Enlightenment* (Cambridge: Cambridge University Press, 1996), pp. 41–2; cited in Ian Hunter, *Rival Enlightenments: Civil and Metaphysical Philosophy in Early Modern Germany* (Cambridge: Cambridge University Press, 2001), p. 167.

[85] Condren, *Argument and Authority*, p. 24.

[86] Condren, *Argument and Authority*, p. 29.

rites of passage into and out of office, of witnessed oaths cementing office-holder to the burdens of responsibility and frequently requiring semiotic markers to sustain the *persona*'.[87]

If this description is valid, then seeking to understand the early modern world in terms of the emergence of a self-fashioning modern subjectivity would be an exercise in anachronism. When Prince Hal brutally renounces Falstaff ('I know thee not, old man')[88] he is stepping fully into his kingly office: the dramatic moment is not a psychological one but a matter of exploring, as the Henriad as a whole does, 'the interplay and problematics of office-holding'.[89] And the point of such a description is just to make it clear that the world has changed: that the autonomous and reflexive self of modernity, with its strict demarcation between public and private space, has no place in the office-based culture of early modernity.

To make this argument is not, of course, to deny the existence of subjectivity in any human society, nor of its peculiarly inward modern form, which Borges describes as 'the certainty of being the isolated, individualized, and distinct thing that each of us feels in the depths of his soul';[90] it is to say that the forms in which that subjectivity is experienced and the relations it holds to that of fellow human beings and to the natural and spiritual world are always structured by networks of practice and technique—aesthetic, legal, ethical, religious, civic, and so on. In this sense, the category of the self (like that of the soul) is a subclass of the category of the person.[91] Rom Harré makes the point more strongly: 'The self, as the singularity we each feel ourselves to be, is not an entity. Rather it is a site, a site from which a person perceives the world and a place from which to act. There are only persons. Selves are grammatical fictions, necessary characteristics of person-oriented discourses.'[92] The sense of self is thus, on this construal, not a moment of self-intuition but a sense of location in relation to 'several arrays of other beings', as well as the sense of having a distinctive set of attributes; self is 'the collected attributes of a person'.[93]

That nominalist view of the self, which owes a substantial debt to Wittgenstein and to the anti-Romantic current in literary modernism, has close connections with the Foucauldian nominalism that takes the self as the object of technologies of self-fashioning: *paideia, Bildung* (for which Reinhart Koselleck suggests that the closest English approximation is Shaftesbury's 'self-formation'),[94] Confucian

[87] Condren, *Argument and Authority*, p. 25.

[88] William Shakespeare, *Henry IV, Part 2*, ed. A. R. Humphreys, The Arden Shakespeare, Second Series (London: Methuen Drama/Bloomsbury Publishing, 1981), 5.5.47.

[89] Condren, *Argument and Authority*, p. 136.

[90] Jorge Luis Borges, 'The Nothingness of Personality', in *The Total Library: Non-Fiction 1922–1986*, ed. Eliot Weinberger, trans. Esther Allen, Suzanne Jill Levine, and Eliot Weinberger (London: Penguin, 2007), p. 4.

[91] Cf. Elizabeth Fowler, *Literary Character: The Human Figure in Early English Writing* (Ithaca: Cornell University Press, 2003), p. 249, n. 2.

[92] Rom Harré, *The Singular Self: An Introduction to the Psychology of Personhood* (London: Sage, 1998), pp. 3–4.

[93] Harré, *The Singular Self*, p. 4.

[94] Reinhart Koselleck, 'On the Anthropological and Semantic Structure of *Bildung*', in *The Practice of Conceptual History: Timing History, Spacing Concepts*, trans. Todd Samuel Presner et al. (Stanford: Stanford University Press, 2001), p. 173.

hsiu-yang (self-cultivation), and Stoic *epimeleia heautou*, the care of the self. Foucault's theorization of the formation of selfhood is always posed in a double relation to the apparatuses of power and the protocols that govern the determination of truth; this is the couplet that he calls 'power/knowledge'. Yet within his work we can distinguish broadly between an earlier phase concerned with the normalizing technologies of governmentality, and a later phase concerned with ethical practices of care of the self.

These phases correspond to a concern with two distinct modes of government: in the former, the focus is on the effects on the governed of raison d'état exercised in the form of pastoral care, where the governed are at once a 'population' (a statistical construct) and a formation of 'individuals' (individuated precisely by bureaucratic procedures of registration and documentation). Here the key texts are the 1978 essay on governmentality,[95] and the two courses of lectures from 1977/8 and 1978/9 entitled *Security, Territory, Population* and *The Birth of Biopolitics*.[96] The mode of individuality that emerges in modernity is, in Foucault's argument, the effect of a distinctive mode of power in its interrelation with new ways of knowing, above all those statist or 'statistical' knowledges that are concerned with intervention in and the management of populations. These new forms of knowledge work both at the level of demographic regularities and 'aggregate effects',[97] and at the level of the detailed inscription of individuating information, obtained through a constant and dispassionate surveillance which ranks and orders its elements and which, in its generalizing concerns, 'is... completely different from the exercise of sovereignty over the fine grain of individual behaviors'.[98] We might take as an emblem of the system of governmentality Jeremy Bentham's proposal 'that a new centralized system of personal nomenclature be "so arranged, that, in a whole nation, every individual should have a proper name, which should belong to him alone"', and which should be tattooed on his or her wrist.[99] Individuation is not the opposite of the technologies of power but their effect: a side effect, one might say, of a 'proliferating apparatus for the verification of identities',[100] which is concerned above all with security and public order, with the ownership of property,

[95] Michel Foucault, 'Governmentality', in *Power: Essential Works of Foucault, 1954–1984*, vol. 3, ed. James D. Faubion, trans. Robert Hurley et al. (London: Penguin, 2002), pp. 201–22.

[96] Michel Foucault, *Security, Territory, Population: Lectures at the Collège de France, 1977–1978*, ed. Michel Senellart, trans. Graham Burchell (New York: Palgrave Macmillan, 2007); Michel Foucault, *The Birth of Biopolitics: Lectures at the Collège de France, 1978–1979*, ed. Michel Senellart, trans. Graham Burchell (New York: Palgrave Macmillan, 2008).

[97] Foucault, 'Governmentality', p. 219.

[98] Foucault, *Security, Territory, Population*, p. 66.

[99] Jeremy Bentham, *Principles of Penal Law, the Works of Jeremy Bentham*, vol. 1, ed. John Bowring (Edinburgh: William Tait, 1843), p. 557; cited in Dror Wahrman, *The Making of the Modern Self: Identity and Culture in Eighteenth-Century England* (New Haven: Yale University Press, 2004), p. 277.

[100] Jane Caplan and John Torpey, 'Introduction', in Jane Caplan and John Torpey (eds), *Documenting Individual Identity: The Development of State Practices in the Modern World* (Princeton: Princeton University Press, 2001), p. 2.

with public hygiene, and with taxation, and which generates rights and recognition to the same extent that it exercises administrative control.

In the later phase of Foucault's work, his attention turns increasingly to the government of the self. In a course of lectures given in 1981–2 and entitled *The Hermeneutics of the Subject*,[101] Foucault speaks of a complex of images of piloting or navigation which work, in classical antiquity, as a unitary metaphor for curing others, governing others, and governing oneself. In the sixteenth century, however, this metaphor is fragmented, as 'the definition of a new art of governing centered around raison d'État will make a radical distinction between government of oneself, medicine, and government of others' (p. 250).

What does government of the self mean for the philosophers of classical antiquity, and particularly for those in whom Foucault is most closely interested—the Epicureans, Stoics, and Cynics of the first two centuries AD? In the text he takes as the starting point for this course of lectures, Plato's *Alcibiades*, governing oneself and governing the city are closely linked: to be virtuous and self-controlled is to have the requisite capacities to command respect from one's fellow citizens. By the Hellenistic period, by contrast, government of the self becomes an end in itself, and while the government of others still flows from it, this is a secondary effect rather than a primary objective. This mode of self-government is best understood as *epimeleia heautou*, the care of the self, a moral norm that structurally precedes and underpins the Delphic injunction to know oneself (*gnōthi seauton*). Knowledge of the self corresponds to the central task of philosophy, that of establishing the determinants of truth and falsity and 'the conditions and limits of the subject's access to truth' (p. 15); care of the self, by contrast, corresponds to

> the search, practice, and experience through which the subject carries out the necessary transformations on himself in order to have access to the truth. We will call 'spirituality'... the set of these researches, practices, and experiences which may be purifications, ascetic exercises, renunciations, conversions of looking, modifications of existence, etc., which are, not for knowledge but for the subject, for the subject's very being, the price to be paid for access to the truth. (p. 15)

Care of the self has three dimensions: first, a relation to the self, to others, and to the world; second, a form of attention to what and how we think; and third, a set of practices and exercises in which the self is transformed: a set of 'techniques of meditation, of memorization of the past, of examination of conscience, of checking representations which appear in the mind, and so on' (p. 10). It is (with the major exception of Aristotle) the dominant mode of understanding the subject's access to truth throughout classical antiquity, whereas in modernity access to the truth is given by knowledge (*connaissance*) alone, with reference only to a set of intrinsic conditions (methodological protocols, the structure of the object), of extrinsic

[101] Michel Foucault, *The Hermeneutics of the Subject: Lectures at the Collège de France 1981–1982*, trans. Graham Burchell (New York: Picador, 2005); hereafter cited in the text. It is this volume, rather than the third volume of *The History of Sexuality* entitled *The Care of the Self*, that engages most directly and fully with the ethical formation of selfhood.

conditions (the sanity of the knowing subject, the scientific consensus of the time), and of moral conditions (the subject's disinterest), all of which 'only concern the individual in his concrete existence, and not the structure of the subject as such' (p. 18). (Let me note in passing that Foucault never breaks with the philosophical problematic of truth and the form of the subject—that is, of epistemology—and, indeed, returns to it with renewed intensity in his later work.)

In very general terms, says Foucault, we can distinguish three historical modes in which thought reflects upon itself. In Platonic thought the dominant mode is *memory*, the recognition of a truth which one did not know one knew and in which the subject thus comes to modify itself in its return to its own being; in Hellenistic thought it is *meditation*, a testing of the subject of thought in its thinking in order to transform it into 'an ethical subject of truth' (p. 460); and in the Cartesian break which initiates modernity (and which can be traced back to Aquinas) it is *method*, 'a form of reflexivity that makes it possible to fix the certainty that will serve as criterion for all possible truth and which, starting from this fixed point, will advance from truth to truth up to the organization and systematization of an objective knowledge' (p. 460).

The ethos of the care of the self passes through into modernity by way of Christianity's development and transformation of Stoic and Cynic practices of meditation: the exercises of the anticipation of misfortune, of meditation on death, and of the examination of conscience. Christianity shares with those philosophical traditions a refusal of the Platonic and gnostic model of the subject's self-recognition in its recollection of the truth. It shares, too, an understanding of life as a continuous testing of the self, a testing which is thematized both in the Greek novel of the first few centuries AD and in early Christian spirituality as the ordeal of virginity, which emerges in this period as 'a metaphysical figure of the relationship to self' (p. 450).[102] Where Christianity differs from those Hellenistic and Roman philosophical traditions is in the fact that its ascetic exercises, its care of the self, are framed not within an aesthetically conceived art of living (*tekhnē tou biou*) but within a technology whose method is 'the constant anxiety of suspicion' (p. 422), a deciphering of the secret movements of the soul in order to break with the world and to renounce the self.

In Letter 8 Seneca writes that philosophy 'spins the subject around on himself' (p. 213): it undertakes metaphorically the action by which a master performs the legal manumission of a slave. This action in philosophy is a kind of conversion, a 'turning around to the self' which frees the self from the constraints of the world. Yet this conversion is a matter of gradual and continuous work on the self, a break *for* the self but not *within* the self. It thus differs from the radical and abrupt

[102] Peter Brown's *The Body and Society* explores early Christian practices of permanent sexual renunciation—'continence, celibacy, life-long virginity'—in their differences from those of the pagan world; in this context virginity comes to stand for 'the original state in which every body and soul had joined', working as a concrete image of 'the pre-existing purity of the soul' and an assertion of human freedom. Peter Brown, *The Body and Society: Men, Women, and Sexual Renunciation in Early Christianity* (New York: Columbia University Press, 1988), pp. xiii, 170.

moment of Christian conversion in which the self is instantaneously reborn. It is in that belief in and practice of rebirth that Christianity invents, from the ashes of classical philosophy, a quite new model of the self.

VI

Yet that model is not a necessary stage on the path to modernity, or anything other than a particular modality of personhood. Despite Marcel Mauss's belief in the universality of awareness of individual selfhood, writes Nikolas Rose,

> 'the self' does not pre-exist the forms of its social recognition; it is a heterogeneous and shifting resultant of the social expectations targeted upon it, the social duties accorded it, the norms according to which it is judged, the pleasures and pains that entice and coerce it, the forms of self-inspection inculcated in it, the languages according to which it is spoken about and about which it learns to account for itself in thought and speech. Thus 'belief systems' concerning the self should not be construed as inhabiting a diffuse field of 'culture', but as embodied in institutional and technical practices—spiritual, medical, political, economic—through which forms of individuality are specified and governed. The history of the self should be written at this 'technological' level in terms of the techniques and evaluations for developing, evaluating, perfecting, managing the self, the ways it is rendered into words, made visible, inspected, judged, and reformed.[103]

Christianity, or rather the heterogeneous multitude of Christianities, is the history of a series of such institutional and technical practices, of varying persistence and impact, and of the forms of selfhood that correspond to them. By the same token, as Deirdre Lynch writes, 'it is only within particular series of reading formations that the distinctiveness of literary characters becomes legible and valuable':[104] fictional character has distinctive conditions of possibility, at once institutional, cultural, and generic, and that complex of conditions constructs both the regime within which character is readable and its differential relation to other regimes.

I conclude this chapter with an analysis of the modelling of fictional selfhood in Defoe's *Robinson Crusoe*, at a moment when confessional practices of truthful self-revelation to an authoritative listener have been displaced—in parts of Europe, among certain social classes, and through a long and violent history of religious struggle—by a Protestant mode of self-regulation that requires an intense accounting for the self and its conduct, in immediate relation to God and often by means of a writing-up of the daily moral account in a confessional diary. Stephen Greenblatt locates a key dramatization of this shift in the torture and execution in 1532 of the Protestant lawyer James Bainham, who, in embracing two books,

[103] Nikolas Rose, *Governing the Soul: The Shaping of the Private Self* (London: Routledge, 1989), p. 218.
[104] Deirdre Shauna Lynch, *The Economy of Character: Novels, Market Culture, and the Business of Inner Meaning* (Chicago: University of Chicago Press, 1998), p. 8.

the *New Testament* in English and WilliamTyndale's *Obedience of a Christian Man*, makes clear that the new mode of interiority he represents is intimately tied to the printed word. Tyndale's conduct manual, writes Greenblatt,

> is designed to be absorbed: one should not, in principle, be able to say where the book stops and identity begins. This absorption of the book at once provides a way of being in the world and shapes the reader's inner life; Christian obedience is simultaneously a form of action and an internal state. Such fashioning of action and identity is essential because in breaking images, radical Protestants have rejected a central Catholic mode of generating inward reflection...while in abandoning formal auricular confession, they have rejected the primary Catholic mode of maintaining the obedience of the Christian man by ordering his inward reflection.[105]

Tyndale's *Obedience of a Christian Man* is located at a liminal point in the fashioning of a Protestant discourse of the self, performative rather than descriptive, and thus unlike—and yet anticipating—the modes of formal autobiography and personal testimony found in later works such as John Bunyan's *Grace Abounding* (1666) and George Fox's *Journal* (1694).

We have learned to read Defoe's novels, particularly *Robinson Crusoe*, within that generic history of the manual of spiritual conduct and the spiritual autobiography; the work of George Starr and Paul Hunter in the 1960s turned attention from an earlier tradition that read the novel primarily in relation to the genre of fictionalized travel narrative towards an emphasis on 'a familiar Christian pattern of disobedience-punishment-repentance-deliverance' and on the workings of 'a watchful providence'.[106] And, indeed, this generic framework, which Peter Hulme reads as an 'attempted solution to critical difficulties about the coherence of Defoe's text',[107] does provide illuminating insight into one strand of the novel: Crusoe looks constantly for signs of the workings of providence, and exemplifies the fallibility of human understanding in his disregard of the signs he receives. There is, at times, an almost mystical sense of personal guidance: the 'secret Intimations of Providence, let them come from what invisible Intelligence they will,' Crusoe writes, are 'certainly...a Proof of the Converse of Spirits, and the secret Communication between those embody'd, and those unembody'd'.[108]

Yet either of those frameworks taken alone is surely inadequate to our sense of the generic complexity, and perhaps the generic incoherence, of *Robinson Crusoe*; there are, moreover, a number of other contextually relevant generic traditions, some of which are directly invoked in the novel. There is, for example, a discourse on sovereignty, which sees Crusoe installed as a tolerant monarch over his three

[105] Stephen Greenblatt, *Renaissance Self-Fashioning: From More to Shakespeare* (Chicago: University of Chicago Press, 1980), pp. 84–5.

[106] J. Paul Hunter, *The Reluctant Pilgrim: Defoe's Emblematic Method and Quest for Form in* Robinson Crusoe (Baltimore: Johns Hopkins University Press, 1966), p. 19; cf. G. A. Starr, *Defoe and Spiritual Autobiography* (Princeton: Princeton University Press, 1965).

[107] Peter Hulme, *Colonial Encounters: Europe and the Native Caribbean, 1492–1797* (London: Methuen, 1986), p. 176.

[108] Daniel Defoe, *Robinson Crusoe*, ed. Michael Shinagel (2nd edn, New York: Norton Critical Edition, 1994), p. 127; hereafter cited in the text.

subjects, and which is closely tied to an economic discourse: 'the whole Country was my own meer Property; so that I had an undoubted Right of Dominion' (p. 174). That economic discourse, tied to a more general discourse of capital accumulation (in Crusoe's case through the slave trade), in turn implicitly develops a Lockean allegory of the transformation of the state of nature into personal property by the act of labour: it is impossible to read Crusoe's account of his initial reduction to 'a meer State of Nature' (p. 86), and of his transformation of that mythical state through his industry, without recalling certain passages of Locke's *Second Treatise of Civil Government*:

> *As much Land* as a Man Tills, Plants, Improves, Cultivates, and can use the Product of, so much is his *Property*. He by his Labour does, as it were, inclose it from the Common... God gave the World to Men in Common; but since he gave it them for their benefit, and the greatest Conveniencies of life they were capable to draw from it, it cannot be supposed he meant it should always remain common and uncultivated. He gave it to the use of the Industrious and Rational, (and *Labour* was to be *his Title* to it;)...[109]

Nor, reading of Friday's binding himself to Crusoe as his slave 'in token of acknowledgement for my saving his Life' (p. 147),[110] can we forget Locke's famous caveat concerning slavery, that 'having, by his fault, forfeited his own Life, by some Act that deserves Death; he, to whom he has forfeited it, may (when he has him in his Power) delay to take it, and make use of him to his own Service'.[111]

All of this is a commonplace of a reading of the figure of Robinson Crusoe as the prototype of *homo œconomicus*; and it is as limited a reading as the others. The more interesting way of approaching the text is surely by recognizing the instability of his formation as a self and the often clashing intersection of the discourses of self-fashioning that he deploys. We might start with a central moment of self-reckoning, when

> I now began to consider seriously my Condition, and the Circumstance I was reduc'd to, and I drew up the State of my Affairs in Writing... I began to... set the good against the Evil, that I might have something to distinguish my Case from worse, and I stated it very impartially like Debtor and Creditor, the Comforts I enjoy'd, against the Miseries I suffer'd, Thus,

EVIL	GOOD
I am cast upon a horrible desolate Island, void of all Hope of Recovery.	But I am alive and not drown'd, as all my Ship's Company was.
I am singl'd out and separated, as it Were, from all the World to be Miserable.	But I am singl'd out too from all the Ship's Crew to be spar'd from Death; and he that miraculously sav'd me from Death, can deliver me from this Condition.

[109] John Locke, *The Second Treatise of Civil Government, Two Treatises of Government*, ed. Peter Laslett (Cambridge: Cambridge University Press, 1988), ch. 5, sections 32, 34.
[110] Defoe, *Robinson Crusoe*, p. 147.
[111] Locke, *The Second Treatise of Civil Government*, ch. 4, section 23.

I am divided from Mankind, a Solitaire, one banish'd from humane Society.	But I am not starv'd and perishing on a barren Place, affording no Sustenance.
I have not Clothes to cover me.	But I am in a hot Climate, where if I had Clothes I could hardly wear them.[112]

And so on. This is the discourse of double-entry bookkeeping, an economic balancing of assets and liabilities, which is here deployed for a spiritual reckoning. What is—to modern ears—incongruous in this passage is precisely the lack of incongruity Crusoe feels between the spiritual and the commercial. The calculus he enters into is a technology of self-inspection, derived at once from the Puritan tradition of introspection and from the daily practice of tradesmen; thus fusing two domains which, for Crusoe, are not in contradiction.

This act of spiritual reckoning partakes of a rationality that we might well read as a rationalization. This is surely part of what it means to be a character in a novel rather than a figure in a 'familiar Christian pattern': that acts are open to interpretation, and that patterns might emerge that escape our attempts to bind them to an origin. In the case of *Robinson Crusoe*, the patterns of figural instability are, I think, compelling: this is a novel of paranoid fantasies. Consider, first, the recurrent theme of enclosure. Crusoe builds his stockade as a double row of sharpened stakes, with a further row of stakes and lengths of cable to reinforce them, so that 'neither Man nor Beast could get into it or over it' (p. 44); the enclosure is doorless, able to be entered only by a ladder, which is drawn inside when Crusoe enters. Within this stockade he pitches two tents, one inside the other; and at the back of the stockade he digs out a hollow in the rock to form a cave. The cave is progressively enlarged until Crusoe builds a door out on the other side of the rock. After his discovery of the footprint of an unknown man, however,

> I began sorely to repent, that I had dug my Cave so large, as to bring a Door through again, which Door, as I said, came out beyond where my Fortification joyn'd to the Rock: upon maturely considering this therefore, I resolv'd to draw me a second Fortification, in the same Manner of a Semicircle, at a Distance from my Wall just where I had planted a double Row of Trees, about twelve Years before, of which I made mention: These Trees having been planted so thick before, they wanted but a few Piles to be driven between them, that they should be thicker, and stronger, and my Wall would be soon finish'd.
>
> So that I had now a double Wall, and my outer Wall was thickned with Pieces of Timber, old Cables, and every Thing I could think of, to make it strong; having in it seven little Holes, about as big as I might put my Arm out at: In the In-side of this, I thickned my Wall to above ten Foot thick, with continual bringing Earth out of my Cave, and laying it at the Foot of the Wall, and walking upon it; and through the seven Holes, I contriv'd to plant the Musquets, of which I took Notice, that I got

[112] Defoe, *Robinson Crusoe*, p. 49.

> seven on Shore out of the Ship; these I say, I planted like my Cannon, and fitted them into Frames that held them like a Carriage, that so I could fire all the seven Guns in two Minutes Time: This Wall I was many a weary Month a finishing, and yet never thought myself safe till it was done. (p. 117)

This movement of enclosure and reinforcement is subsequently repeated when Crusoe discovers a cave on the island, which he enters with difficulty and then sees within 'two broad shining Eyes of some Creature, whether Devil or Man I knew not' (p. 128). Deciding then 'that I durst to believe there was nothing in this Cave that was more frightful than my Self', he rushes in with a flaming torch and is at once 'almost as much frighted as I was before; for I heard a very loud Sigh, like that of a Man in some Pain, and it was follow'd by a broken Noise, *as if* of Words half express'd' (p. 129). This creature, this wounded double of himself, he discovers, is 'a most monstrous frightful old He-goat', dying 'of meer old Age' in its solitary enclosure (p. 129). But this is not the end of this movement inwards: at the far end of this cave he discovers a passage, 'so low, that it requir'd me to creep upon my Hands and Knees to go into it' (p. 129); returning the next day with candles, he passes through it for some ten yards, until

> When I was got through the Strait, I found the Roof rose higher up, I believe near twenty Foot; but never was such a glorious Sight seen in the Island, I dare say, as it was, to look around the Sides and Roof of this Vault, or Cave; the Walls reflected 100 thousand Lights to me from my two Candles; what it was in the Rock, whether Diamonds, or any other precious Stones, or Gold, which I rather suppos'd it to be, I knew not. (p. 129)

The counterpart in the novel to this movement towards an ever more enclosed and womb-like space is the encounter with the other, cast, above all, as a recurrent fantasy of cannibalism. This is the novel's most famous sentence: 'It happen'd one Day, about Noon going towards my Boat, I was exceedingly surpriz'd with the Print of a Man's naked Foot on the shore, which was very plain to be seen in the Sand' (p. 112). The encounter with the other 'happens', in the sheer contingency of an occasion, by way of the indexical trace of a foot—isolated, singular—which is clearly to be read, which (when he later tests it) is not his own, and which, being 'naked', must be that of a savage and thus, necessarily, of a cannibal—for the moment of encounter with cannibal savages has long been anticipated.[113] The distant land mass that he sights on a clear day is self-evidently inhabited by 'the worst of *Savages*; for they are Cannibals, or Men-eaters, and fail not to murther and devour all the humane Bodies that fall into their Hands' (p. 80); Crusoe later expresses the view that the 'barbarous Customs' of these people are 'a Token indeed of God's having left them, with the other Nations of that Part of the World, to such Stupidity, and to such inhumane Courses', as will lead to his punishing them 'as a People, for national Crimes' (p. 168). The discovery of the footprint on the sand intensifies Crusoe's apprehensions a hundredfold, leading him to build the

[113] The logic of the encounter is that either the solipsistic hypothesis is true, and I am alone in the world, or else the other exists, in which case he will eat me.

second wall around his stockade and inducing first a 'Dread and Terror of falling into the Hands of Savages and Canibals' and the 'Expectation every Night of being murther'd and devour'd before Morning' (p. 119), and then the actualization of his fantasy when he comes upon a shore 'spread with Skulls, Hands, Feet, and other Bones of humane Bodies', scattered around the remains of a fire 'where it is suppos'd the Savage Wretches had sat down to their inhumane Feastings upon the Bodies of their Fellow-Creatures' (pp. 119–20). At the sight of this image of the ingestion and scattering of human bodies, 'I turn'd away my Face from the horrid Spectacle; my Stomach grew sick, and I was just at the Point of Fainting, when Nature discharg'd the Disorder from my Stomach, and having vomited with an uncommon Violence, I was a little reliev'd' (p. 120): as though he himself had ingested his fellow men and must purify his contaminated body. This vomiting is repeated in mimicry when Friday suggests he and Crusoe should dig up and eat two men he has buried. The theme of cannibalism is perhaps reiterated in the oddly inconsequential scene towards the end of the novel when, travelling through the Pyrenees, Crusoe's party is attacked by wolves and come across the carcasses of a horse and two men, 'devour'd by the ravenous Creatures' (p. 216).

Enclosure, ingestion, vomiting: these fantasies of the instability and vulnerability of the self are surely at least as powerful as, and are intricately involved in, the more explicit thematics of Christian self-shaping and redemption, or of economic personhood, or of colonial sovereignty and its basis in slavery. Doubtless, there is an element of anachronism in reading the novel in this way—but this is not to say that these patterns are not there to be read. Perhaps, too, it relies on an expectation of psychological coherence in a text marked by narrative inconsistencies (the three different versions of Crusoe's being cast upon the island, for example) and by Crusoe's own moral inconsistency (his selling into captivity of the boy with whom he escapes his Moorish imprisonment; his duplicity about the value of money; his opportunistic use of religious doctrine). But my point is just that each of the interpretive regimes we bring to bear on the novel, and on the heterogeneous and incoherent character of Crusoe himself, reflects one of a number of sets of practices, beliefs, and fantasies about what it means to be a person, which jostle side by side for position in the text in just the same way as commercial and religious genres—corresponding to the two great transformative forces of Defoe's Protestant and early-capitalist world—crowd in upon each other in Crusoe's moral accounting, his complex practice of the self.

4
Type

I

Our recognition of the kind of thing fictional characters are depends on our prior knowledge of the kind of thing persons are. We understand characters as quasi-persons. But the modelling goes the other way as well: our understanding of persons is, in part, shaped by our experience of dealing with fictional characters.[1]

Both fictional characters and kinds of person are models of an aspect of the world, schemata which generalize and simplify human being in conventional ways and make it available to understanding and action. In this chapter I explore the relation between such general models of the human person and the general or typological models of character that obtain within particular genres at particular times.

All theories of character are to some degree typological, invoking a limited range of kinds of person subsuming actual named characters; this relation differs from typologies of action, although the two overlap in the Proppian notion of the basic character types (hero, helper, opponent, and so on) around which the folk tale is structured. Such highly formalized genres tend to work with highly formalized character typologies which are closely related to folk psychologies and characterologies (the doctrine of humours, of the ruling passion, of the racial or psychological or historical 'type'). In the case of the novel, typological abstraction works as an informal and secular operator of extrapolation through layers of 'sociological' generality. Age, gender, occupation, and social class are the characteristic markers that we read from the persons of the novel: Don Quixote is an hidalgo; Emma Woodhouse is a young woman and a member of the provincial gentry whose social position is finely calculated vis-à-vis every other person in her social orbit; Oedipa Maas is a suburban Californian housewife. It is for this reason that we tend not to describe narratives based solely on a religious typology, such as *Pilgrim's Progress*, as novels.

The critical literature on the concept of character is overwhelmingly elaborated in relation to the novel: a recent form in European literature, although it has

[1] Cf. Alexander Gelley, 'Character and Person: On the Presentation of Self in the Novel', in *Narrative Crossings: Theory and Pragmatics of Prose Fiction* (Baltimore: Johns Hopkins University Press, 1987), p. 63: fictional character 'derives from and, correlatively, helps to shape a variety of other concepts outside the province of fiction—"person", "self", "individual", "soul"...'

forerunners in the Greek romances of the Hellenistic period and close analogues in the great Chinese 'novels' of the Ming and early Qing periods (seventeenth and eighteenth centuries) and in the Japanese *monogatari* of the tenth and eleventh centuries. But novelistic character has its antecedents in a more specific set of genres.

Consider this sketch from Joyce's *Dubliners*:

> The fourth member of the party... was too excited to be happy.
>
> He was about twenty-six years of age, with a soft, light-brown moustache and rather innocent-looking grey eyes. His father, who had begun life as an advanced Nationalist, had modified his views early. He had made his money as a butcher in Kingstown, and by opening shops in Dublin and in the suburbs he had made his money many times over. He had also been fortunate enough to secure some of the police contracts and in the end he had become rich enough to be alluded to in the Dublin newspapers as a merchant prince. He had sent his son to England to be educated in a big Catholic college and had afterwards sent him to Dublin University to study law. Jimmy did not study very earnestly and took to bad courses for a while. He had money and he was popular; and he divided his time curiously between musical and motoring circles. Then he had been sent for a term to Cambridge to see a little life. His father, remonstrative, but covertly proud of the excess, had paid his bills and brought him home.[2]

This is a relatively self-contained sketch of a moral type, something like 'the spoiled son of a newly wealthy family'. But, far from being self-contained, this sketch is filled with a coiled-up narrative time that is ready to unfold: it is a story waiting to happen. Novelistic character of this kind (the example is taken from a short story, of course; but the genre of the short story perhaps intensifies the key schematic features of novelistic character) is minimally based on an asemantic proper name and the concrete and contingent predicates which fill it: what Michael McKeon calls the idea of 'concrete virtuality'.[3] The genre to which this sketch belongs has its origins in the *Characters* of Theophrastus, a pupil of Aristotle and his successor as head of the Lyceum, who lived from about 371 to 287 BC. Theophrastus follows the doctrine elaborated in the *Nicomachean Ethics*, according to which moral character, *ēthos*, is formed as a set of acquired dispositions but is manifested by choices made within the framework of these dispositions. Each 'character' begins with an abstract definition of a moral quality, and then describes the type who embodies it; the general formula is: 'He is the sort of person who will...' Here is number three, *The Chatterer*:

> Chatter is the churning-out of long-winded, unconsidered talk.
>
> The chatterer is the sort of man who sits down beside someone he doesn't know and begins by delivering a panegyric on his own wife; continues with an account of his dream of the night before; then describes in detail what he had for supper. Next, getting into his stride, he remarks how far inferior men of the present day are to the ancients; how reasonable wheat is now in the shops; how full of foreigners Athens is

[2] James Joyce, *Dubliners* (Harmondsworth: Penguin, 1993), p. 41.

[3] Michael McKeon, *The Secret History of Domesticity: Public, Private, and the Division of Knowledge* (Baltimore: Johns Hopkins University Press, 2005), p. 109.

> getting. He observes that since the Dionysia it has been good sailing weather; and that if only Zeus would send more rain it would be better for the farmers. Then he tells you what part of his land he will put down to crops next year; and how difficult it is to live; and that Damippus has set up an enormous torch at the Mysteries; and 'How many columns has the Odeion?' and 'I was violently sick yesterday'; and 'What day of the month is it today?' Then he tells you that the Mysteries are in September, the Apaturia in October, and the Rural Dionysia in December. In fact, if you put up with him, he will never stop.[4]

The flow of contingent detail here is subordinated to the generality of the principle: this is the *sort of thing* chatterers will go on about. Following Aristotle, Theophrastus understands character as the habitual actions which give character its consistency.[5] The pleasure we might take in the sketch is an effect of its sharp, slightly gossipy observation of detail and of our sense of recognition of the type. As it develops,[6] the Theophrastan genre becomes embedded in the rhetorical tradition and is passed on by way of Quintilian, Cicero's *Rhetorica ad Herennium*, and Rutilius Lupus to the Middle Ages (where it is fused with the hierarchical and classificatory imagination of the Christian cosmology), and is continued in the Renaissance through the educational instruments of the rhetorical exercise and the commonplace book, both of which involve the writing of 'characters'. This largely unreflexive tradition is revitalized in the early seventeenth century with an explicit return to Theophrastus and a less sententious mode of characterization. Joseph Hall's *Characters of Virtues and Vices*, published in 1608, initiates this return, and it flourishes in works like Thomas Overbury's *Characters* (1614) and John Earle's *Microcosmography* (1628). The major figure in the seventeenth-century renewal of the genre of the character is, however, Jean de La Bruyère, whose *Les Caractères de Théophraste traduits du grec avec les Caractères ou les Moeurs de ce Siècle* was published in 1688, and then in a substantially revised and enlarged form in 1694.

In La Bruyère, the apparent mix of genres (the aphorism, the reflective passage, the character, the example) is actually a sliding between different levels of generality: that of the *general principle*, that of the *generalized example* ('celui qui', 'un homme qui', 'il y a des gens qui...'), and that of the *personified example*—as in the following passage:

[4] Theophrastus, *The Characters*, trans. Philip Vellacott (1967; 2nd edn, rpt. Harmondsworth: Penguin, 1973), p. 35.

[5] Cf. Mary Springer, *A Rhetoric of Literary Character: Some Women of Henry James* (Chicago: University of Chicago Press, 1978), pp. 34, 38. Michael FitzGerald points out that nine of the thirty-two 'vices' making up the *Characters* are drawn directly from Aristotle's *Nicomachean Ethics*, but for only one of Aristotle's antithetical character types are both poles represented: those of *eironeia* and *alazoneia*, understatement and overstatement: two sets of qualities that become central to the characterology of the New Comedy. Michael FitzGerald, 'Character Evidence and the Literature of the Theophrastan Character: A Phenomenology of Testimony', *An Aesthetics of Law and Character: Texts, Images, Screens, Studies in Law, Politics, and Society* 34 (2004), p. 150.

[6] I follow here the account given in J. W. Smeed, *The Theophrastan 'Character': The History of a Literary Genre* (Oxford: Clarendon Press, 1985).

Passions tyrannize over mankind, but ambition keeps the others in abeyance, and for a while makes a man appear to possess every virtue.

I once believed that Tryphon, whom I now know to practice every vice, was sober, chaste, liberal, modest, and even pious; I might have believed so still if he had not made his fortune.[7]

[*Les passions tyrannisent l'homme; et l'ambition suspend en lui les autres passions, et lui donne pour un temps les apparences de toutes les vertus. Ce Tryphon qui a tous les vices, je l'ai cru sobre, chaste, libéral, humble et même dévot: je le croirais encore, s'il n'eût enfin fait sa fortune.*][8]

That slide from generality to personification—to the *naming* of the individual representing a type—is the crucial step taken beyond Theophrastus. Often in La Bruyère there is a juxtaposition of a named, personified type and a non-personified type; it is these personifications that eventually become the quasi-persons of the novel—which, however, still retains the tension between generality and particularity in the form of the 'moral fable',[9] where characters are read as metonyms of classes of person. Here are two types, personified and non-personified, of the provincial nobleman:

Of Mankind 129: Don Fernando resides in his province, and is idle, ignorant, slanderous, quarrelsome, knavish, intemperate, and impertinent; but he draws his sword against his neighbours, and exposes his life for the smallest trifle; he has killed several men, and will be killed in his turn.
130. A provincial nobleman, useless to his country, his family, and himself, often without a roof to cover himself, without clothes or the least merit, tells you ten times a day that he is of noble lineage, despises all graduates, doctors, and presidents of courts as upstarts, and spends all his time among parchments and old title-deeds, which he would not part with to be appointed chancellor.[10]

[De l'homme 129. *Don Fernand, dans sa province, est oisif, ignorant, médisant, querelleux, fourbe, intempérant, impertinent; mais il tire l'épée contre ses voisins, et pour un rien il expose sa vie; il a tué des hommes, il sera tué.*
[130. *Le noble de province, inutile à sa patrie, à sa famille et à lui-même, souvent sans toit, sans habits, et sans aucun mérite, répète dix fois le jour qu'il est gentilhomme, traite*

[7] Jean de La Bruyère, 'Of the Gifts of Fortune', in *Characters*, trans. Henri van Laun (Oxford: Oxford University Press 1963), pp. 94–5.

[8] Jean de La Bruyère, 'Des biens de fortune', in *Les Caractères ou les moeurs de ce siècle, Oeuvres Complètes*, ed. Julien Benda, Bibliothèque de la Pléïade (Paris: Gallimard, 1951), p. 190.

[9] I take the term from F. R. Leavis, *The Great Tradition* (1948; rpt. Harmondsworth: Penguin, 1972), who defines it by saying that 'in it the intention is peculiarly insistent, so that the representative significance of everything in the fable—character, episode, and so on—is immediately apparent as we read' (p. 259).

[10] La Bruyère, *Characters*, p. 206.

les fourrures et les mortiers de bourgeoisie, occupé toute sa vie de ses parchemins et de ses titres, qu'il ne changerait pas contre les masses d'un chancelier.][11]

The transition from general type to personified type is even more clearly evidenced in a sequence in *De l'homme*, numbers 115 to 120, which runs from the two indefinite forms in which generality is expressed, 'old men' and 'an old man', to the definite characterization of a proper name: 115, 'les vieillards'; 116, 'les vieillards'; 117, 'un vieillard est...'; 118, 'un vieillard qui...'; 119, 'les vieillards'; 120, '*Phidippe*, déjà vieux...'[12]

J.W. Smeed suggests that La Bruyère's subjects are posited as existing in a shared world, and are thus not illustrations but 'descriptions of typical but real persons'.[13] In this I think there is a clear line of connection to early eighteenth-century English typologies, particularly the characters of the *Tatler* and *Spectator*, where the concern is with social rather than moral types, as well as with the representation of eccentrics for their own sake. We might think of Steele's description of the members of the Spectator club, comprising Sir Roger de Coverley, an old-fashioned country squire; an unnamed lawyer; Sir Andrew Freeport, a merchant; a soldier, Captain Sentry; a gallant, Will Honeycomb; and an unnamed clergyman.[14] These are either directly professional and social types, or the allegorically named personifications of types. Yet in several cases, notably that of Sir Roger de Coverley, the figure goes through a process of narrative development which raises it to a different level of specificity. For all the static quality of these portraits, these, too, are stories waiting to be told, and the novel (if I can put it in this teleological form) is the genre that develops in order to tell them.

A number of recent scholars have pointed to the emergence in the first half of the eighteenth century of a particular form of the category of fiction, and of the type of fictional character we associate with the novel, in which twin processes that Mary Poovey calls factualization and fictionalization come to replace a relatively undifferentiated fact/fiction continuum that we might see exemplified in the epistemologically ambiguous status of Defoe's narratives. But fiction is not simply an alternative to the factual, but, rather, a third category that emerges as an alternative to the dichotomy of truth and lying: fiction, in this sense, is that which is neither truth nor a lie;[15] it is, of course, not a new category,[16] but rather a new function in relation to the emergent regime of empirical epistemology and its increasing differentiation between the factually true and the untrue: a process that Latour calls the 'modern settlement', and Poovey the regime of the 'modern fact'.[17]

[11] La Bruyère, *Les Caractères*, pp. 333–4.

[12] La Bruyère, *Les Caractères*, pp. 327–8.

[13] Smeed, *The Theophrastan 'Character'*, p. 52.

[14] *The Spectator*, 1 March 1711.

[15] Mary Poovey, *Genres of the Credit Economy* (Chicago: University of Chicago Press, 2008), p. 104.

[16] Sidney's assertion in the *Apology* that 'the poet, he nothing affirmeth, and therefore nothing lieth' is already fully a defence of the specificity of the fictional, and, like Tasso's account of poetic verisimilitude, it is indebted to Aristotle. Sir Philip Sidney, *An Apology for Poetry, or The Defense of Poesy*, ed. Geoffrey Shepherd (London: Thomas Nelson, 1965), p. 123.

[17] Bruno Latour, *We Have Never Been Modern*, trans. Catherine Porter (Cambridge, MA: Harvard University Press, 1993); Mary Poovey, *A History of the Modern Fact: Problems of Knowledge in the*

This new function of the category of fiction is built on the category of the *vraisemblable*, the seemingly true or the plausible, in which the force of the concept has to do with its balancing of the notions of the true and the seeming, such that each qualifies the other: this is an aesthetic truth which is based in a simulation of the real rather than directly reflecting it; and it is a seeming, a simulation, which is, nevertheless, in some way true.[18] One way of thinking about this emergence of a new modality of fiction is to see it, as Michael McKeon does, as an epistemological shift, bound up with the increasing differentiation of the public and the private spheres—a shift away from the singular truth of factuality to another truth of simulation, and thus to an acceptance of verisimilitude as constituting a form of truth. In the genre of the novel, which is where it is primarily worked out, this shift involves a separation of the fictional from the historical elements of the romance.[19] McKeon writes that

> what was new in the later seventeenth and eighteenth centuries was a sensitivity to the truth claims of empirical epistemology so intense that it fostered the growth of powerful naïve literalisms... in reaction to which critics like Dryden, Addison, Fielding, and Johnson began to elaborate the modern view of fiction, which differs from the traditional one not in kind but in the explicitness and precision with which it seeks to describe the psychological state of 'believing' a fiction, that is, 'believing in' a plausible character without believing his or her actual existence.[20]

This argument is taken up by Catherine Gallagher in *Nobody's Story*. In the early eighteenth century, she writes, 'narrative came in two forms: referential truth telling and lying';[21] and 'until the mid-eighteenth century, there was no widely employed means of distinguishing between a fiction and a lie... [F]iction writing cannot be said to exist as a marked and recognised category in a culture until it can be effortlessly distinguished from lying.' Although the raw materials for such a distinction existed in early eighteenth-century England, 'they were seldom used. The discourse of fiction, therefore, was awaiting not so much the requisite

Sciences of Wealth and Society (Chicago: University of Chicago Press, 1998). Catherine Gallagher writes that 'the absence of the category did not necessarily indicate the absence of the thing', but it was not recognized as a common trait between diverse genres 'that were not taken to be the literal truth but that apparently had no particular intention to deceive'; and 'that discursive category we now call fiction was a "wild space", unmapped and unarticulated'. Catherine Gallagher, *Nobody's Story: The Vanishing Acts of Women Writers in the Marketplace, 1670–1820* (Berkeley: University of California Press, 1994), p. xvi.

[18] Cf. Boileau, *L'Art Poétique* III (160): 'Le vrai peut quelquefois n'être pas vraisemblable'; Ronsard, *La Franciade*, 'Au Lecteur apprentif': 'Il a pour maxime très nécessaire en son art de ne suivre jamais pas à pas la verite, mais la vraisemblance et le possible; et sur le possible et sur ce qui se peut faire, il bâtit son ouvrage.' Cited in *Le Grand Robert*, entry for 'vraisemblable'.

[19] In *The Origins of the English Novel* McKeon traces out the complex process by which the medieval romance, objectified by print culture as a definite and coherent genre, justifies itself by appeal to an Aristotelian notion of verisimilitude, and then falls prey to a critique by naïve empiricism and then of both by scepticism—all of this in continually changing relation to the authority of the Scriptures. For the novel the romance plays a key role as an epistemological, not just a generic category. Michael McKeon, *The Origins of the English Novel, 1600–1740* (Baltimore: Johns Hopkins University Press, 1987), especially pp. 25–89.

[20] McKeon, The *Secret History*, p. 746, n. 159.

[21] Gallagher, *Nobody's Story*, p. xvi.

conceptual tools as some cultural imperative to use them'.[22] That cultural imperative, which is associated both with narrow legal requirements and with broader structural determinants in the organization of markets, in the abstraction of social relations, and in the growth of the public sphere, had direct epistemological effects: 'What Fielding had that Defoe lacked was not an excuse for fictionality but a use for it as a special way of shaping knowledge through the fabrication of particulars.'[23]

One can thus observe, according to Gallagher, a 'massive reorientation of textual referentiality taking place in the mid-eighteenth century novel around the figure of "Nobody"', by which she means 'a proper name explicitly without a physical referent in the real world'.[24] It was this 'widespread acceptance of verisimilitude as a form of truth, rather than a form of lying, [that] founded the novel as a genre... It also created the category of fiction'.[25]

For my purposes, what is important here is the emergence of a new mode of contingently specific fictional characterization in the emergent genre of the novel around this figure of 'Nobody', this asemantic and non-referential proper name.[26] It is because this non-referential name is an empty form that it opens up deeper possibilities of sympathetic identification,[27] and that impossible illusion of inwardness that gives novelistic characters their 'peculiar affective force'.[28] Gallagher concludes that

> the character came into *fictional* existence most fully only when he or she was developed as nobody *in particular*; that is, the particularities had to be fully specified to ensure the felt particularity of the character. A generalized character would too easily take on allegorical or symbolic reference, just as one rendered in mere 'hints' would have been read at the time as a scandalous libel. Thinness of detail almost always indicated specific extra-textual reference. But the more characters were loaded with circumstantial and seemingly insignificant properties, the more the readers were assured that the text was at once assuming and making up for its reference to nobody at all.[29]

[22] Gallagher, *Nobody's Story*, p. 163.

[23] Catherine Gallagher, 'The Rise of Fictionality', in Franco Moretti (ed.), *The Novel*, vol. I: *History, Geography, and Culture* (Princeton: Princeton University Press, 2006), p. 344.

[24] Gallagher, *Nobody's Story*, p. xv.

[25] Gallagher, 'The Rise of Fictionality', p. 341.

[26] The classic argument was made by Ian Watt: 'Logically the problem of individual identity is closely related to the epistemological status of proper names; for, in the words of Hobbes: "Proper names bring to mind one thing only; universals recall any one of many." Proper names have exactly the same function in social life: they are the verbal expressions of the particular identity of each individual person. In literature, however, this function of proper names was first fully established in the novel.' Ian Watt, *The Rise of the Novel: Studies in Defoe, Richardson, and Fielding* (1957; rpt. Harmondsworth: Penguin, 1963), p. 19. The citation from Thomas Hobbes is to *Leviathan*, ed. Noel Malcolm (Oxford: Clarendon Press, 2012) [1651], Pt. 1, ch. 4. The historical accuracy of the argument has been challenged by Alastair Fowler, *Literary Names: Personal Names in English Literature* (Oxford: Oxford University Press, 2012), pp. 14, 16–17. Fowler notes Chaucer's innovations in the introduction of 'realistic' names into fiction, and, conversely, the presence in Defoe of single, quasi-mythological names ('Roxana'), of Cratylic names in Fielding ('Allworthy'), and of semantically suggestive names in Richardson ('Lovelace').

[27] Human sympathy, Gallagher argues, converts otherness into sameness, your feeling into mine, a process which 'might be expected to aggrandize the self and its properties even as it unsettles the concept of a bounded, stable ego'. *Nobody's Story*, p. 170.

[28] Gallagher, 'The Rise of Fictionality', pp. 356–7.

[29] Gallagher, *Nobody's Story*, p. 174.

One starting point for both Gallagher and McKeon is the debates in the early eighteenth century over satire and its potential to become libellous of individuals; libel legislation contributed to the attractiveness of 'avowedly fictional narrative that resembles, and borrows the authority of, factuality'.[30] Both quote Henry Fielding's *Joseph Andrews*, Book 3, chapter 1: 'I question not but several of my readers will know the lawyer in the stage-coach, the moment they hear his voice . . . To prevent therefore any such malicious applications, I declare here, once for all, I describe not men, but manners; not an individual, but a species'; the narrator's aim is

> not to expose one pitiful wretch, to the small and contemptible circle of his acquaintance; but to hold the glass to thousands in their closets, that they may contemplate their deformity, and endeavour to reduce it, and thus by suffering private mortification may avoid public shame. This places the boundary between, and distinguishes the satirist from the libeller; for the former privately corrects the fault for the benefit of the person, like a parent; the latter publickly exposes the person himself, as an example to others, like an executioner.[31]

Thus, Fielding proposes to solve the legal and moral issues involved in writing satire by 'generalizing from the realm of the actual to a realm that is virtual but also concrete':[32] the particularity of the individual novelistic character. This category of concrete virtuality, McKeon argues, has become central to modern doctrines of realism and the aesthetic, equivalent to 'the emergence, not of fiction, but of our kind of fiction, which openly proclaims its fictionality against the backdrop of its apparent factuality'.[33]

That fictional figure of 'the lawyer' is, of course, a Theophrastan character, a generalized type (he stands for a more general figure of self-centred meanness); the development Fielding is proposing here, however, involves precisely the passage away from the generality of the Theophrastan character. In *Joseph Andrews* it is the step from the moral characteristic to the profession that exemplifies it; in the next, novelistic step in that process, however, the lawyer will be further personified by his acquisition of a name—a mundane name referring to nobody who really exists, and concealing no identity which might be hinted at, as in the *roman à clef*.

Yet, for all the contingency and particularity he may acquire, the lawyer remains, at the same time, a member of the class of lawyers. There is thus a continued tension between reading character as a contingent particularity and reading it as the representative of a larger class of persons. Much of the energy of the novel has gone into refusing allegorical or symbolic reference; yet to the extent that character is a structural moment of the semantic patterning of the novel, that refusal is almost impossible to achieve.

Novelistic character is thus a mechanism for scaling up and down between orders of generality. In the course of the nineteenth century questions of social

[30] McKeon, *The Secret History*, pp. 98–9.

[31] Henry Fielding, *Joseph Andrews*, ed. R. F. Brissenden (Harmondsworth: Penguin, 1977), Book 3, ch. 1, pp. 185–6.

[32] McKeon, *The Secret History*, p. 109.

[33] McKeon, *The Secret History*, p. 109.

typology come to lie at the heart of the European novel, and are closely intertwined with its accompanying critical doctrines and with the more general theorization of the novel as a genre. The doctrine of realism, which is elaborated as the key support of the nineteenth-century novel, is grounded in a notion of the correspondence of novelistic character with an objectively given social taxonomy; Balzac's 'Avant Propos' to the *Comédie Humaine*, conceiving his work by analogy with natural history's description of the zoological species,[34] understands it as portraying the system of social types that make up post-Napoleonic France, as does Zola at the end of the century with reference to the laws of heredity and to Claude Bernard's experimental method.[35] Friedrich Engels formulates the doctrine concisely when he writes, in a letter of April 1888, that '[r]ealism, to my mind, implies, beside truth of detail, the truthful reproduction of typical characters under typical circumstances'.[36] For the most important theorist of the realist novel, Georg Lukács, the force of novelistic character at its most fully achieved is to render in formal terms the dynamics of social class. Philosophically, this is expressed by the role of particularity ('Besonderheit') in mediating between singularity ('Einzelheit') and generality ('Allgemeinheit').[37] The 'concrete artistic embodiment' of particularity, and the central category of realist literature, is the *type*, by which Lukács means

> a peculiar synthesis which organically binds together the general and the particular both in characters and situations. What makes a type a type is not its average quality, not its mere individual being, however profoundly conceived; what makes it a type is that in it all the humanly and socially essential determinants are present on their highest level of development, in the ultimate unfolding of the possibilities latent in them, in extreme presentation of their extremes, rendering concrete the peaks and limits of men and epochs.[38]

Realistic representation of the type makes it possible for 'a typicality of a higher order' to arise: 'the aspect of a typical stage of development of human life, of its essence, its destiny, its perspectives'.[39] But this 'typicality of a higher order' is only ambivalently a product of the work, because the typical, 'like all elements of artistic content, is a category of life'.[40] Thus, the work possesses its own autonomy only insofar as it establishes a correspondence with the immanent meaningfulness of the world.[41] Any account of the process by which singular fictional characters work at

[34] 'Il a donc existé, il existera donc de tout temps des Espèces Sociales comme il y a des Espèces Zoologiques.' Honoré de Balzac, 'Avant Propos', *La Comédie Humaine* I, Bibliothèque de la Pléïade (Paris: Gallimard, 1951), p. 4.

[35] Émile Zola, 'On the Rougon-Macquart Series' and 'The Experimental Novel', in George J. Becker (ed.), *Documents of Modern Literary Realism* (Princeton: Princeton University Press, 1963), pp. 159–161 and 162–196.

[36] Friedrich Engels, draft letter to Margaret Harkness (April 1888), in [Karl] Marx and [Friedrich] Engels, *On Literature and Art* (Moscow: Progress Publishers, 1976), p. 90.

[37] Georg Lukács, 'Über die Besonderheit als Kategorie der Ästhetik', in *Probleme der Ästhetik, Werke*, vol. 10 (Neuwied: Luchterhand, 1969), p. 670 (my translation).

[38] Georg Lukács, *Studies in European Realism* (New York: Grosset and Dunlap, 1964), p. 6.

[39] Lukács, 'Über die Besonderheit . . .', p. 757.

[40] Lukács, 'Über die Besonderheit . . .', p. 755.

[41] Cf. Lukács, 'Über die Besonderheit . . .', p. 683: 'The independent form of the work is therefore a reflection of essential connections and forms of appearance of reality itself.'

one or more higher levels of generality must account for the algorithmic quality of that referral to social norms while avoiding the normative insistence in Lukács's later work on an immanent meaningfulness of the social world against which novelistic form is to be measured.[42]

II

Elizabeth Fowler defines literary character by way of its relation to the concept of 'social person', a term she derives, in part, from Mauss's essay on the category of the person. She means by it not just an occupation or role but something more abstract: a figuration of the human that acquires a more general status as a cultural paradigm through repeated use. The concept includes such things as legal persons, civic agents, corporate entities, economic agents, kinship designations, races and ethnicities, and literary types, and it thus has close connections with the notion of social typology. Literary characters, she writes, 'are largely cobbled together out of allusions to a number of social persons'.[43] I can best make clear how Fowler understands this relation by discussing two of her examples from Chaucer.

The first is the Knight, described in the General Prologue in terms of a number of *personae* drawn from a chivalric ethos: those of the crusader, the knight of courtly romance, the knight of the *chanson de geste*, and the feudal retainer. At the same time, however, and in partial contradiction to this ethos, he is described as a mercenary, and as being 'as meek as is a mayde'; and his character is further complicated by the tension between the *personae* of crusader and pilgrim. These diverse social persons are 'phantom templates' from which we construct the complex and, in part, contradictory character of the Knight, moving backwards and forwards between the individual figure and the social frameworks on which that figure draws as we endow it with increasing concreteness.

The second is the Pardoner, in the tale of that name, who personifies the tensions inherent in the institution of simony, the sale (in this case) of absolutions from sin. These are tensions between the spiritual and the commercial, between the two jurisdictions of canon law ('internal' and 'external'), and between the intention and the act. 'The social person called "the pardoner",' Fowler writes, 'was invented to help absorb the intentional conflicts in the commerce of salvation, to embody and preserve the gap between the internal and external fora'; what is at stake in his

[42] That insistence contrasts starkly with the account in his 1916 essay *The Theory of the Novel* of the senselessness of the fallen or 'demonic' world. The novel, on this reading, 'is the epic of a world that has been abandoned by God. The novel hero's psychology is demonic', and the formal structure that corresponds to this loss of immanent meaning is irony, 'a portrayal of the kindly and malicious workings of the demons' and 'a refusal to comprehend more than the mere fact of these workings' (Georg Lukács, *The Theory of the Novel: A Historico-Philosophical Essay on the Forms of Great Epic Literature*, trans. Anna Bostock (Cambridge, MA: MIT Press, 1971), pp. 88, 90). This is the world of which Nobody is the hero: the world of the uncanny double and its allotropic transformations.

[43] Elizabeth Fowler, *Literary Character: The Human Figure in Early English Writing* (Ithaca: Cornell University Press, 2003), p. 17. Hereafter cited in the text.

profession is the question: 'Can a sacrament be efficacious if its agents are in a state of sin? Can any act be efficacious if undertaken in an intentional state that contradicts its formal purpose?' Yet although the purpose of his office is precisely that of 'insulating the sacrament from the doubtful nature of intention' (on the part both of the priest and of the penitent), the Pardoner nevertheless 'repeatedly speaks in a framework that invites us to assess his intentions' (p. 64): Chaucer's personification of the office undermines precisely that bracketing of inner states that the theology requires. This rendering of the role as a subjective state is supplemented by a set of analogies to the animal world that work in much the same way as iconographic props do in portraiture, overlaying the Pardoner's character with metaphors of the bestial so that he is seen variously as

> the carousing seducer, the vain man, the fabricated effigy, the doll, the animal-like body from the fabliaux, the courtly eunuch. Figural details evoke the conventions of social persons, and at the same time set forth the specific variance of this complex Pardoner from each of those conventions.... Character is such a powerful fiction in *The Canterbury Tales* that it can stuff the most motley crowd of figurations into a single body, merely by unifying them under the rubric of a single name and a pronoun. (p. 69)

One of the advantages of the concept of social person is that it allows for an extrapolation from figural representations to social relations: the social person 'is best understood as the personification of social bonds' (p. 95), and of the institutions that sustain those bonds; indeed, 'the very construction of literary character from the material of social persons puts forth arguments about the nature of contemporary institutions and their attendant modes of thought' (p. 179). In the case of the Pardoner, the social person on which he is modelled is the point of concentration of a dense network of evolving theological norms and disputes, of popular images of sin and the afterlife derived from those theological norms, of a market in intangible spiritual goods sanctioned by the Church as an instrument for raising funds, of the apparatus of canon law which underpins the market and the powers of action of the Pardoner, and of a social order which fuses secular and religious hierarchies in complex patterns. Thus, the 'ghostly social person' of the Pardoner, evoking the ethical and political questions associated with these interlocking structures, 'brings with it values, standards of evaluation, a configuration of attributes, a sense of possible actions and plots, an orientation toward social institutions' (p. 72): a set of materials that combine with other social persons invoked by the figure of the Pardoner (that of the homosexual or the sodomite, for example), and with their concretization in the patchwork of ekphrastic conventions that make up his body, to produce a complex object of interpretation.

Literary character, Fowler writes, is 'a literary instance of the representation of persons more broadly construed' (p. 247):

> 'character' is to literary discourse what 'economic person' is to economics, what 'legal person' is to the law, what a 'Christian soul' is to theology, what the 'female nude' is to painting: each is a dominant model of person that has grown out of a social

> practice—a practice that has its own institutions, behaviors, artifacts, motives, social effects, audiences, and intellectual issues. (p. 28)

The formation of literary character from the raw materials of the social person is thus, in part, a question of the institution of literature, and of its relation not just to the particular types of social person but to the general category of person of which those types are instances.

Let me note in passing several problems with the concept of social person as Fowler uses it. The first is that the term is a tautology: persons are, by definition, social. But avoiding the oxymoron by using simply the term 'person' would be wrong too, since what Fowler is concerned with is metonyms of the person, particular types or qualities of personhood: 'social categories' might catch the sense better. But these social persons or social categories are not 'social' as opposed to 'literary': the Knight, for example, is composed of elements which include the stylized figures of the knight of courtly romance and the knight of the *chanson de geste*, and it is more generally the case that no social type is ever just one thing or the other, literary or social: the categories are constantly fused, constantly work upon each other.

In principle there is a closed set of social persons for any given culture; and Fowler's analysis works particularly well for a feudal order with its structural restriction of the range of possible social roles. Yet in practice, and especially in the more fluid societies of modernity, the concept of social person has little predictive power because it is never a limited class: rather, there are as many social persons as there are roles for people to assume, and roles exist at many levels of generality. It can thus only ever be a category applied a posteriori through an interpretive act, and, indeed, Fowler notes that social persons 'are better regarded as cumulative and changing sets of resemblances than as susceptible to definition by a list of features' (pp. 2–3). In contrast to mimetic typologies of character which evaluate it against a criterion given by social reality itself, however, this concept takes seriously the structuralist insight that '*le personnage... n'est personne*',[44] character is not a person. It makes it possible to apprehend *in the same terms* both the generically and culturally specific logic of character as it is formed in relation to a set of social (or socio-literary) raw materials, and the cultural logic of personhood itself.

III

Fictional characters are formed on the basis of folk taxonomies, including such forms of everyday knowledge as folk physiognomies with their 'system of strictly coded equivalences' (hooked nose = greed, fleshy lips = sensuality),[45] the psychological doctrine of the ruling passion, models of gender roles, or notions of the

[44] Charles Grivel, *Production de l'intérêt romanesque* (The Hague: Mouton, 1973), p. 113.

[45] Patrizia Magli, 'The Face and the Soul', in Michael Feher (ed.), *Fragments for a History of the Human Body, Part Two* (New York: Zone Books, 1989), p. 89.

racial or historical 'type'; on the basis of models of social hierarchy and legal and religious order such as the great chain of being or the social contract or the class system; and on the basis of specifically fictional taxonomies such as those of the New Comedy or the Baroque heroic opera or cinematic space opera or television sitcoms. (I describe the characterology of the New Comedy in some detail in Chapter 7.) The character typologies on which fictional texts draw and to which they contribute provide a ready-made model of personhood which is usable, on the one hand, for immediate recognition of characters in texts, and, on the other, for application to persons in the world.

Folk taxonomies differ, by definition, from scientific taxonomies. The abstract actantial categories used by Propp or Greimas to describe narrative functions, for example, have little in common with the archetypal figures of folk and fairy tales, with their religious origins and their strongly fantasmatic make-up. We can perhaps begin to clarify some of the features of character typologies by drawing an analogy with the most widely studied areas of folk taxonomization, which have to do with plant and animal species. Here, our primary classification tends to take place at the level of the genus rather than the species or the life form: 'maple' rather than 'sugar maple' or 'tree', the level of simple names and the single gestalt rather than of distinctive features.[46] As it happens, this is the same 'basic level' as that which makes up the 'natural kinds' of scientific taxonomy, because scientific classification builds upon folk classification: the Linnaean system is focused on the genus, which gives general characteristics, rather than the species, which differentiates. Both the folk and the scientific taxonomy are based on easily observable characteristics such as the shape of the fruit, and the basic level of categorization is thus 'primarily characterized by gestalt perception (the perception of overall shape), by imaging capacity (which depends on overall shape), and by motor interaction (the possibilities for which are also determined by overall shape)'.[47] There is a good fit between folk and scientific taxonomies at the level of the genus, then, but not at the other levels at which knowledge is organized.

Eleanor Rosch's argument that categorization happens by way of prototypes rather than by the construction of sets whose members all have equivalent properties similarly depends upon an observation that taxonomic hierarchies are organized around the middle of the set rather than being equally distributed across it: in the sequence 'animal–dog–retriever' it is the middle term that is culturally and perceptually most salient. This is the highest level at which category members have similarly perceived shapes; it is organized by a single mental image; it is the level at which similar motor actions are used for interaction with category members; it is the most quickly identified, has the most commonly used labels, is the first level named and understood by children, the first level to enter the lexicon of a language, has the shortest primary lexemes, is used in neutral contexts, and is 'the level at which most of our knowledge is organized'.[48] Basic-level categories are

[46] George Lakoff, *Women, Fire, and Dangerous Things: What Categories Reveal About the Mind* (Chicago: University of Chicago Press, 1987), pp. 32–4.

[47] Lakoff, *Women, Fire, and Dangerous Things*, p. 36.

[48] Lakoff, *Women, Fire, and Dangerous Things*, p. 46.

identified by the clusters of properties which allow for human interaction, and they operate at human scale.

Human scale is the distinguishing feature of the logic of everyday or practical reason, a concept I take from Pierre Bourdieu, who also uses the concept of a 'logic of practice' to designate the formal structure of an everyday dealing with the world which operates in time, and is therefore open-ended, based in uncertainty and strategic calculation; which is tactful, in that it works by constant adjustment to fluid interactions; which works with shared distributions of knowledges between a negotiable foreground and a background of commonsense assumptions; which depends upon a logic of analogy, and the forms of causality that flow from it; and which organizes its world by story rather than by syllogism.[49] The concept is analogous to Agnes Heller's account of everyday thinking, to which she attributes a number of characteristics.

The first is that everyday appropriations of the world are inescapably anthropocentric. Heller identifies three modes of human-centredness: one, which she calls 'anthropologicalness', has to do with the experiential basis of everyday practice: for most of our practical purposes the sun rises and sets in relation to an earth which is flat. Counter-intuitive knowledge (for example, that a spherical earth rotates around the sun) is not (necessarily) excluded from everyday practice or disbelieved, it is merely not relevant to it.[50] The second she calls anthropocentricity: since the everyday is directly involved with the reproduction of the person, its teleology 'is relative to, correlated with "the person"' (p. 51); everyday knowledge takes place on and in relation to a human scale, and it is narrative in form. Third, everyday knowledge is anthropomorphic: it apprehends the world by analogy to the body, the person, and immediate social relations. It is thus inherently mimetic, an imitation of action, behaviour, and affect.

The second dimension of Heller's description of everyday knowledge has to do with the principles of economy and repetition that structure it. These principles (the opposite of 'inventive thinking') are designed to make activity spontaneous and routine, and they are linked to the schematic organization of everyday thought. The schemata are rough guides to the processing of data and to translating it into action. They organize everyday thinking in terms of calculations of probability, of intuition and 'tact', of inference from analogy and precedent, and of generalization on the basis of particular cases. Everyday reason thus works by routine and formula and moves to generalization on the basis of a fuzzy logic of similarity and typicality: all this in contrast to the putatively more rigorous logic of the specialized knowledges.

A third dimension has to do with its pragmatic orientation. Again, we can understand this as an effect of the parsimonious use of cognitive resources: everyday

[49] Pierre Bourdieu, *The Logic of Practice*, trans. Richard Nice (Stanford: Stanford University Press, 1990). This and the following paragraphs draw on my essay '"Never Draw to an Inside Straight": The Critique of Everyday Reason', *New Literary History* 33: 4 (2002), pp. 623–38.

[50] Agnes Heller, *Everyday Life*, trans. G. L. Campbell (London: Routledge & Kegan Paul, 1984), pp. 50–1; hereafter cited in the text.

thinking is directed to the achievement of a task and minimizes theoretical reflection on process. This is not to say that theoretical reflection is absent: metalanguage always accompanies language in use, for example, and can be called on when needed for repair or problem-solving. A further component of this pragmatic economy is the conventional delimitation of signification in relation to customary contexts of use—the activation of meaning only within typified enunciative situations which, again, are rarely available for theoretical scrutiny.

Finally, Heller stresses the heterogeneity of everyday ways of knowing, a consequence of the heterogeneity of domains of activity and being which they must coordinate and by which they are shaped. But we could think of this as a matter not only of the diversity of spheres across which everyday knowledge moves, but also as a matter of the diversity of cognitive modalities which it incorporates. It is for this reason that Heller emphasizes that everyday life is not equivalent to Alfred Schutz's 'life world', since it involves not, as in Schutz, a single 'natural' attitude but can include reflexivity. More generally, this is why it is a relatively simple matter to refuse Heller's idealization of scientific or philosophical thought as non-pragmatic, non-particularist, absolute rather than probabilist, and not shaped around tropes, prototypes, and schemata. It is not only the case, as Heller concedes, that specialized knowledges are constantly folded into the everyday, but that the modes of thinking that she takes to characterize the everyday equally permeate scientific or philosophical or technical rationalities.

The idea of a singular mode of everyday knowledge—a practical reason, a non- or pre-reflective thought, a schematized *sensus communis*—is at once a dangerous fantasy of otherness (a not-so-remote descendant of imperialist anthropology's notion of a primitive mentality),[51] and a heuristic for thinking about the relations between a plurality of domains and modalities of knowledge within the common space of a culture. Stripped of its essentialism, it defines a transformational process by which macrostructural categories are continuously translated into manageable structures of sense at human scale. I use the concept of human scale to refer, in the first place, to the sphere of person-to-person relations, and I call this sphere a 'moral economy'. By 'moral' I mean the forms of action and imagining that are structured by *mores*, customary ways of doing things, the mode of being that Hegel called *Sittlichkeit*; and by 'economy' I mean to indicate the characteristic closure of this sphere.[52]

Moral economies are 'ordinary' ways of knowing and understanding at particular times and places. Like the 'universes of recognition' that Marc Augé describes as governing traditional societies,[53] they are organized by the spatio-temporality

[51] Lucien Lévy-Bruhl, *Primitive Mentality*, trans. Lilian A. Clare (New York: Macmillan, 1923); *How Natives Think*, trans. Lilian A. Clare (Princeton: Princeton University Press, 1985).

[52] My usage of the term 'moral economy' is cognate with but different from that of E. P. Thompson, who uses it to describe morally structured forms of economic activity. E. P. Thompson, 'The Moral Economy of the English Crowd in the Eighteenth Century', in *Customs in Common* (London: Penguin, 1993), pp. 185–258.

[53] Marc Augé, *Non-Places: Introduction to an Anthropology of Supermodernity*, trans. John Howe (London: Verso, 1995).

of a centred cosmos; by a narrative logic; and by human or quasi-human actors whose bodies are the focus of that logic. Mark Johnson and George Lakoff have argued, through a series of books, that the semantic primitives that underlie all human conceptualization correspond directly to the experience of spatially situated human bodies: metaphors of front and back, of spatial containers, of motion through space, of grasping and ingesting, and of the relation of one body to another, form the substrate for all conceptual apprehension of the world.[54] Human thought is at once contained and structured by the boundaries of the body and its relation to lived space.

The strategic logic of everyday reason reduces the multiplicity of real and virtual worlds to a manageably small number of narratives and actors, and it projects an embodied self at the centre of this reduced world.[55] It is the combination of these two moves that I call 'human scale', with the proviso that the notion of 'embodiment' here has to do not with an empirical corporeality but with an imaginary of the boundaries of the self, and that the 'human' refers less to an essence grounded in nature than to a fantasmatic coherence projected onto a social order. In the same way, the concrete immediacy, the taken-for-grantedness of the everyday (its quality of being looked past rather than directly seen)[56] obscure its abstractness: its schematic structuring by 'type, analogy and generality',[57] and its heterogeneous fusion of very diverse modalities of knowledge.

Fotis Jannidis speaks of the derivation of character typologies from an 'everyday anthropology' which deploys an extensive repertoire of types (the extravert, the *femme fatale*...) and an even more extensive range of moral characteristics (mean, lazy, smart...). Accompanying this everyday anthropology is an 'everyday sociology which describes occupations, social classes and roles and their associated habitus'.[58] These, in turn, depend upon a folk psychology that deals with basic intuitions about the structure of personhood, distinguishing between inner and outer, identifying mental states and models of motivation, and extrapolating from acts to an underlying and more or less fixed moral character. This is the logic that governs typologies of personhood and, by extension, of the kinds of world in which fictional characters act: a logic which uses the embodied human figure as the basis for the organization of knowledge, which (in the case of narratives) splits that figure between an experiential centre and a set of represented narrative personae, and which distributes those personae along a spectrum of human types constructed according to the logic of folk taxonomy.

[54] George Lakoff and Mark Johnson, *Metaphors We Live By* (Chicago: University of Chicago Press, 1980); Mark Johnson, *The Body in the Mind: The Bodily Basis of Meaning, Imagination, and Reason* (Chicago: University of Chicago Press, 1987); George Lakoff and Mark Johnson, *Philosophy in the Flesh: The Embodied Mind and its Challenge to Western Thought* (New York: Basic Books, 1999).

[55] Witold Kula's classic study of systems of measurement demonstrates the centrality of the human body to the taxonomic organization of the world. Witold Kula, *Measures and Men*, trans. R. Szreter (Princeton: Princeton University Press, 1986).

[56] Maurice Blanchot, 'Everyday Speech', *Yale French Studies* 73 (1987), p. 14.

[57] Rita Felski, 'The Invention of Everyday Life', *New Formations* 39 (1999), p. 29.

[58] Fotis Jannidis, *Figur und Person: Beitrag zu einer historischen Narratologie* (Berlin: de Gruyter, 2004), p. 187 (my translation).

IV

In Don DeLillo's short story 'Midnight in Dostoevsky', two boys in a remote college town, 'way upstate', invent lives for the teachers and townspeople they encounter.[59] This is a mundane affair, speculation growing out of late-adolescent boredom. Metaphors become literal: in streets where there is 'hardly a soul to be seen', the local people 'were souls, were transient spirits' (p. 119). And suppositions crystallize into facts. A woman transferring her groceries to a baby stroller is called Isabel, but then this is revised to Mary Frances ('*Mar-y Fran-ces*. Never just Mary'); Isabel is her sister. 'They're identical twins. Isabel's the alcoholic twin.' But the central question is not what her name is but 'Where's the baby that goes with the stroller? Whose baby is it?... What's the baby's name?' (p. 126). A whole genre of Hollywood movies (*Dark Mirror*, amongst others) is invoked without ever having to be named.

The central object of their game is an elderly man wearing a hooded coat. They argue over whether it's a loden coat, an anorak, or a parka, but they know that 'this was why the man had been born, to end up in this town wearing that coat' (p. 120), and from this detail they begin to construct a biography. He lives with 'a son or daughter, grandkids'; 'He's not from here... He's from somewhere in Europe. They brought him over. He couldn't take care of himself anymore. His wife died. They wanted to stay where they were, the two elderly people. But then she died' (p. 127). If he's wearing a hat beneath his hood, 'there's only one kind of hat he could conceivably wear. A hat with an earflap that reaches from one ear around the back of the head to the other ear. An old soiled cap. A peaked cap with a flap for the ears' (p. 128). When they move on to ask where he is from, the question is even more precisely about types: they know it's somewhere where the temperature is measured in Celsius rather than Fahrenheit, and

> 'There's something not too totally white about him. He's not Scandinavian.'
> 'Not Dutch or Irish.'
> I wondered about Andalusian. Where was Andalusia exactly? I didn't think I knew. Or an Uzbek, a Kazakh. But these seemed irresponsible.
> 'Middle Europe,' Todd said. 'Eastern Europe.' (p. 129)

They decide which house he must live in, and that 'his family allows him to take a walk now and then, provided he stays within a limited area'; he's not much bothered by the cold because 'he's used to colder', and in any case 'he has very little feeling in his extremities' (p. 129). He sits in his small room, 'on the edge of a narrow bed in his long johns, staring into space' (p. 130). And they try to reconstruct his story: the narrator proposes that he is 'a figure who escaped the war in the 1990s. Croatia, Serbia, Bosnia. Or who didn't leave until recently'. But Todd doesn't buy it: '"I don't feel that here," he said. "It's not the right model"' (p. 129).

[59] Don DeLillo, 'Midnight in Dostoevsky', in *The Angel Esmeralda: Nine Stories* (New York: Scribner, 2011), p. 119; hereafter cited in the text.

The tempo of the game changes when the narrator makes a connection (again, entirely speculative) between the man and their philosophy teacher, Professor Ilgauskas, for whom they have also constructed a story: Ilgauskas speaks as though in a kind of trance, and

> we'd decided, some of us, that he was suffering from a neurological condition. He was not bored but simply unbound, speaking freely and erratically out of a kind of stricken insight. It was a question of neurochemistry. We'd decided that the condition was not understood well enough to have been given a name. And if it did not have a name, we said, paraphrasing a proposition in logic, then it could not be treated. (p. 123).

Ilgauskas is rumoured to read Dostoevsky 'day and night' (p. 134), and this helps the narrator to pin down the old man further. The revelation he has had is that the man is Russian (his name is 'Pavel, Mikhail, Aleksei. Viktor with a *k*. His late wife was Tatiana'), and he lives in the town because his son lives there, teaching at the college—Ilgauskas, in short. 'They're Russian, father and son' (p. 137). Is Ilgauskas a Russian name? It must be, because he reads Dostoevsky, doubtless in the original (this is 'a feasible truth, a usable truth', p. 140); he even speaks with a slight accent, if you listen for it. 'I didn't know whether it was there or not... We worked spontaneous variations on the source material of our surroundings' (p. 138).

From this insight they are able to reconstruct the details of the old man's day:

> He drinks coffee black from a small cup, and spoons cereal out of a child's bowl. His head practically rests in the bowl when he bends to eat. He never looks at a newspaper. He goes back to his room after breakfast, where he sits and thinks. His daughter-in-law comes in and makes the bed, Irina, although Todd did not concede the binding nature of the name... There are two schoolchildren and one smaller girl, Irina's sister's child, here for reasons not yet determined, and the old man often passes the morning fitfully watching TV cartoons with the child, though not seated beside her. He occupies an armchair well away from the TV set, dozing now and then. Mouth open, we said. Head tilted and mouth hanging open. (pp. 139–40)

They build up a description of the food he eats for lunch (homemade soup, every day), the way Irina tries to help him button his parka or anorak when he goes out for his walk; they posit that 'he wears trousers with suspenders, until we decided he didn't; it was too close to stereotype' (p. 140). They know that he doesn't have a private toilet, sharing one with the children, that his mind roams back over 'the village, the hills, the family dead' (p. 141); and they know that 'he probably smells bad but the only one who seems to notice is the oldest child, a girl, thirteen. She makes faces now and then, passing behind his chair at the dinner table' (p. 141).

At times this imagined person intersects with the old man onto whom they have projected it, and it is then 'thrilling to see the thing happen, see it become three-dimensional' (p. 142); he is 'someone who could easily be the man we were in the process of imagining' (p. 143). Then Todd ruins the game by deciding that it is time to take the next step: to speak to him. This is the end of the story: the boys fight, the narrator is angry and bewildered. It is clear that something crucial has changed: perhaps because the narrator is more aware than Todd of the provisional basis of their fiction, perhaps because it is too fragile to be exposed to the possibility of falsification. Whichever it is, what is allegorized here is the process of imagining fictional characters into being, in both its self-confidence and its frailty. That act of imagining depends not on invention *ex nihilo* but on filling out the details of the type. The narrator and Todd are novelists, imitating a reality made up of *nothing but* types, stereotypes, the exemplary figures of their culture's stories, in a world covered by 'a fine grid of typifications, so detailed and precise that it preempts and contains contingency'.[60] Reading Dostoevsky, the narrator reflects that 'we seemed to assimilate each other, the characters and I';[61] fictional worlds and 'real' worlds penetrate each other almost completely.

V

Two kinds of knowledge are drawn on for the construction of fictional character in DeLillo's story: an encyclopaedic form of knowledge about social types, and knowledge about the typologies relevant to the modal worlds of genre. I move now to a discussion of what is perhaps the archetypal 'character' in Western literature, the figure of Hamlet: a figure that has been taken as the initiator of modern inwardness, explored for motive and for its absence, and abstracted from the play *Hamlet* or placed firmly back within its various versions and its multiplicity of contexts.

Every Shakespearean critic has his or her theory about what drives, or fails to drive, the melancholy prince. That's not quite the question I want to ask here; what I shall do is explore two typological commonplaces in the critical literature, one drawn from the wider culture and one more specifically generic: that Hamlet is portrayed as a melancholic; and that his character has a relation to that of the revenger in the Elizabethan genre of the revenge tragedy. *Hamlet*, I argue, improvises freely on these models to produce what has come, since the late eighteenth century, to figure as the very model of the inwardness of character; and my interest here is in working out how those cultural and generic typologies are brought into relation with each other to generate that effect of inwardness.

The first of these typological schemata, that of melancholy, lies at the core of A. C. Bradley's analysis of *Hamlet*, and he contrasts it with the 'Schlegel–Coleridge theory', which blames Hamlet's apparent delay in avenging his father on a state of irresolution resulting from an excess of reflection. For Bradley, Hamlet's 'state of profound melancholy' explains his sense of *taedium vitae*, his oscillation between energy and lassitude, his moments of intense interest and pleasure, his savage irritability, his self-absorption and callousness, his 'bursts of transitory, almost hysterical, and quite fruitless emotion', his apathy, and his inability to understand why it is that he defers his act of revenge.[62] What Bradley is interested in is a

[60] John Frow, 'The Last Things Before the Last: Notes on *White Noise*', in Frank Lentricchia (ed.), *Introducing Don DeLillo* (Durham: Duke University Press, 1991), p. 179.

[61] DeLillo, 'Midnight in Dostoevsky', p. 134.

[62] A. C. Bradley, *Shakespearean Tragedy* (1904; 2nd edn, London: Macmillan, 1962), pp. 85, 86, 99.

psychologically coherent account of a play in which 'the whole story turns upon the peculiar character of the hero',[63] and in offering the diagnosis Bradley seeks to circumvent the question of whether Hamlet's 'madness' is feigned or real. 'That Hamlet was not far from insanity,' he writes, 'is very probable. His adoption of the pretence of madness may well have been due in part to fear of the reality.'[64]

Hamlet's performance of melancholy is both a topic within the play and is evidenced by the way in which his figure reproduces (perhaps to the point of parody) the stock iconography of melancholia. Gertrude's remark: 'But look where sadly the poor wretch comes reading'[65] directs us to the 'distinctive mark of the studious stage melancholic',[66] as do Hamlet's 'inky cloak' and 'customary suits of solemn black' (1.2.77–8), worn long after the rest of the court has put off mourning; the soliloquy beginning 'I have of late, but wherefore I know not, lost all my mirth...' (2.2.261–2); and the terse comment that 'My wit's diseased' (3.2.313–4). Lyons compares 3.1.172–4:

> This something-settled matter in his heart
> Whereon his brains still beating puts him thus
> From fashion of himself

with a phrase from Stephen Batman, writing in 1582: 'When any obscure thing beteth the brain (as melancholy fleme)...'[67] Lines 27–8 in 1.4 (Second Quarto only) refer to blemishes caused either by a defect in men's birth or

> By their o'ergrowth of some complexion
> Oft breaking down the pales and forts of reason,

where the 'o'ergrowth of some complexion' refers to an imbalance in the bodily humours. And in 2.2.533–8, Hamlet soliloquizes that

> The spirit that I have seen
> May be a de'il, and the de'il hath power
> T'assume a pleasing shape. Yea, and perhaps,
> Out of my weakness and my melancholy,
> As he is very potent with such spirits,
> Abuses me to damn me!

[63] Bradley, *Shakespearean Tragedy*, p. 70.

[64] Bradley, *Shakespearean Tragedy*, p. 96. Bradley's use of the preterite tense here has the effect of treating Hamlet as a person who once really existed.

[65] William Shakespeare, *Hamlet*, ed. Ann Thompson and Neil Taylor, The Arden Shakespeare, Third Series (London: Thomson Learning, 2007), 2.2.165. This edition, which takes the Second Quarto as its basis, conforms to the current editorial preference for a single rather than a composite source text, and I follow it with some reluctance.

[66] Bridget Gellert Lyons, *Voices of Melancholy: Studies in Literary Treatments of Melancholy in Renaissance England* (London: Routledge & Kegan Paul, 1971), p. 26. Douglas Trevor reads Hamlet in terms of the paradigm of scholarly melancholy in *The Poetics of Melancholy in Early Modern England* (Cambridge: Cambridge University Press, 2004).

[67] Lyons, *Voices of Melancholy*, p. 85, quoting Stephen Batman, *Batman Upon Bartholme, His Book De Proprietatibus* (London, 1582), fol. 33^r.

—evoking the commonplace that the devil has particular influence over those whose spirits are weakened by melancholy. Each of these passages deploys the language of humoral medicine, and it is clear that Hamlet's disorderly and unkempt appearance, his manic mood swings, his loathing of bodily corruption, his bitter disaffection from the king, and his disgust with his own cowardice, dullness, and sloth—what Walter Benjamin calls his 'saturnine *acedia*'[68] —all mark him as a melancholic. The play uses the full gamut of melancholic iconography: Bridget Gellert notes that the figure of the solitary young man meditating on a skull in the graveyard scene amalgamates the medieval 'Vanity' motif with the more modern emblem of Melancholia; and the gravediggers, the animals, and the occupations and professions mentioned here all have Saturnine connotations, as does suicide and the general motif of the corruption of the body.[69]

The play thus assumes a familiarity with the doctrines of humoral medicine and with the melancholy temperament. There is some argument about the extent to which those doctrines remained fully in force in early modern England,[70] but it is clear that Shakespeare has invoked a broad popular understanding both of the basic humoral concepts and of the character typologies associated with them. Gail Kern Paster declares flatly that early modern bodies were humoral:

> Every subject grew up with a common understanding of his or her body as a semi-permeable, irrigated container in which humors moved sluggishly. People imagined that health consisted of a state of internal solubility to be perilously maintained, often through a variety of evacuations, either self-administered or in consultation with a healer...This body had a distinct set of internal procedures dependent on a differential calorific economy (most men being hotter than most women) and characterized by corporeal fluidity, openness, and porous boundaries.[71]

The authors of *Saturn and Melancholy* describe the doctrine of temperaments as 'one of the longest-lived and in some respects one of the most conservative parts of modern culture', stretching from the sixth century BC until well into the eighteenth century; for Kant, for example, the sublime was intimately connected to the figure of the melancholic, whose '"sadness without cause" was based on his possession of a moral scale which destroyed personal happiness by the merciless revelation of his own and others' worthlessness'.[72] And Lawrence Babb notes the many common phrases contributed to the language by the old physiology: 'ardent love', 'blazing

[68] Walter Benjamin, *The Origins of German Tragic Drama*, trans. John Osborne (London: New Left Books, 1977), p. 156.

[69] Bridget Gellert, 'The Iconography of Melancholy in the Graveyard Scene of "Hamlet"', *Studies in Philology* 67: 1 (1970), pp. 57–66. Cf. Roland Mushat Frye, 'Ladies, Gentlemen, and Skulls: *Hamlet* and the Iconographic Traditions', *Shakespearean Quarterly* 30: 1 (1979), pp. 15–28.

[70] Lyons sees them as becoming obsolescent in this period (*Voices of Melancholy*, p. xiii), whereas Trevor speaks of a 'reinvigorated Galenism' (*The Poetics of Melancholy*, p. 4) and Lawrence Babb of an 'epidemic' of melancholy at the time. Lawrence Babb, *The Elizabethan Malady: A Study of Melancholia in English Literature from 1580 to 1642* (East Lansing: Michigan State College Press, 1951), p. vii.

[71] Gail Kern Paster, *The Body Embarrassed: Drama and the Disciplines of Shame in Early Modern England* (Ithaca: Cornell University Press, 1993), p. 8.

[72] Raymond Klibansky, Erwin Panofsky, and Fritz Saxl, *Saturn and Melancholy: Studies in the History of Natural Philosophy, Religion and Art* (London: Thomas Nelson, 1964), pp. 120, 122.

anger', 'boiling blood', 'cold-blooded murder', 'broken heart', and so on; these expressions, he writes, 'were not figures of speech in Queen Elizabeth's day'.[73]

Humoral medicine had its origins in the Hippocratic Corpus, a body of medical treatises in the Ionic dialect, often mutually contradictory, dating for the most part from between 410 and 360 BC, and attributed to Hippocrates of Cos.[74] These texts originally recognize three key fluids: phlegm and choler (bile) are directly associated with disease, whereas the blood is both crucial for life and, in excess, a cause of illness. A fourth fluid, black bile (black choler, or melancholy) is later added, in accordance with the Pythagorean requirement of fourfold symmetry, and with 'a desire to match the number of humors with the number of elements and qualities'.[75] The four humours, which mingle in the bloodstream, are not related 'exactly and in all particulars to the relevant visible bodily fluids':[76] rather, they are logically deducible categories, a component of a system of correspondences between bodily fluids, the cosmic elements, the primary qualities of moisture and heat, the seasons, and the ages of humankind:

blood	air	warm & moist	spring	childhood
bile	fire	warm & dry	summer	youth
black bile	earth	cold & dry	autumn	adulthood
phlegm	water	cold & moist	winter	old age

To these correspondences were later added, in Galen's synthesis, a set of four temperaments (the sanguine, choleric, melancholic, and phlegmatic) corresponding to the balance of humours in the blood (the *crasis* or 'complexion') and the balance of qualities. This correspondence is more than an analogy: Paster writes that the temperaments or passions have a functional relation to the humours, and 'in an important sense the passions actually *were* liquid forces of nature', a 'part of the fabric of the body'.[77] As Charles Taylor puts it,

> black bile doesn't just cause melancholy; melancholy somehow resides in it. The substance embodies this significance... Black bile produces melancholy feelings, because these manifest what it is, its ontic-logical status. The psychic is one of the media in which it manifests itself, if one likes, but black bile *is* melancholy, and not just in virtue of a psycho-physical causal link.[78]

Humoral medicine is thus resolutely materialist: 'emotions flood the body not metaphorically but literally, as the humors course through the bloodstream'.[79] It is the preponderance of one humour over the others that generates distinctive

[73] Babb, *The Elizabethan Malady*, pp. 15–16.

[74] Vivian Nutton, 'Humoralism', in W. F. Bynum and Roy Porter (eds), *Companion Encyclopedia of the History of Medicine*, vol. I (London: Routledge, 1993), p. 283.

[75] Nancy G. Siraisi, *Medieval and Early Renaissance Medicine: An Introduction to Knowledge and Practice* (Chicago: University of Chicago Press, 1990), p. 105.

[76] Nutton, 'Humoralism', p. 287.

[77] Gail Kern Paster, *Humoring the Body: Emotions and the Shakespearean Stage* (Chicago: University of Chicago Press, 2004), pp. 4, 5.

[78] Charles Taylor, *Sources of the Self: The Making of the Modern Identity* (Cambridge, MA: Harvard University Press, 1989), p. 189; cited in part in Paster, *Humoring the Body*, p. 5.

[79] Paster, *Humoring the Body*, p. 14.

temperaments, understood either as 'pathological states or constitutional aptitudes'.[80] Disease is caused by an imbalance of the humours or by the presence of noxious forms of choler, phlegm, or melancholy, and is treated by adjustment of the balance of bodily fluids—by the letting of blood, by purgation, by means of dietary measures to heat or cool, thin or thicken the offending humour, and by regulation of the environment, to which the humoral body is open and with which it exchanges matter (it exudes excrement, menstrual blood, sweat, tears, milk, semen, and, in turn, replenishes itself from the outside world), as well as by the conversion of humours within the body, in what Thomas Laqueur calls a 'free trade economy of fluids'.[81]

Melancholy, or black bile, is 'cold and dry, thick, black, and sour, begotten of the more feculent part of nourishment'.[82] It nourishes the spleen and bones, and, in the words of the sixteenth-century physician Timothy Bright, it is

> for the most part...settled in the splene, and with the vapours annoyeth the heart, and passing up to the braine, counterfetteth terrible objects to the fantasie, and polluting both the substance, and spirits of the braine, causeth it, without externall occasion, to forge monstrous fictions, and terrible to the conceit...[83]

The 'clouds of melancholy vapours' exhaled from the 'puddle of the splene' give rise to 'perturbations' which 'are for the most part, sad and fearefull', but which may also be 'furious, and sometimes merry in apparence':[84] the bipolar symptoms of manic depression, in short. Melancholy is a physiologically normal humour, but it also exists in an abnormal form, 'melancholy adust' (the 'scorched' humour that comes from excessive heat), which exacerbates its normal manifestations. Either in its 'natural' or its adust form, and especially when it is heightened by excessive mental activity, poor digestion, or lack of physical exercise, it gives rise to potentially morbid effects, when 'the animal spirit becomes tainted with melancholy and the mind grows sorrowful and fearful'.[85]

In a long passage of development beginning with the Galenic synthesis in the second century AD, the doctrine of temperaments corresponding to the humours comes to be codified as a general theory of types of disposition or character;[86] and in the course of the Middle Ages, as humoral psychology is fused with the doctrine

[80] Klibansky, Panofsky, and Saxl, *Saturn and Melancholy*, p. 12.

[81] Thomas Laqueur, *Making Sex: Body and Gender from the Greeks to Freud* (Cambridge, MA: Harvard University Press, 1990), p. 35.

[82] Robert Burton, *The Anatomy of Melancholy*, Partition I, Section 1, Member 2, Subsection ii (1621; rpt. London: J.M. Dent, 1932), p. 148.

[83] Timothy Bright, *A Treatise of Melancholy. Containing the Causes Thereof, And Reasons of the strange effects it untieth in our minds and bodies: with the Physick Cure, and spiritual consolation for such as have thereto adjoined afflicted Conscience* (1586; rpt. London: William Stansby, 1615), pp. 124–5; I have modernized Bright's long *s* and his use of *v* for *u* and vice versa.

[84] Bright, *A Treatise of Melancholy*, pp. 124–5.

[85] Babb, *The Elizabethan Malady*, p. 25.

[86] The line of development passes through Galen's Arab commentators, including Avicenna and Hunain ibn Ishâq (known as Johannitius, author of the *Isagoge in artem parvam Galeni*) and the eleventh- and twelfth-century commentators on the *Isagoge* (in particular Constantinus Africanus). Cf. Klibansky, Panofsky, and Saxl, *Saturn and Melancholy*, pp. 98, 104.

of the seven deadly sins, melancholy comes to be associated with *acedia*, the 'noonday demon' affecting monks and causing weariness of spirit, indifference to salvation, despair, and neglect of one's proper tasks.[87]

If humoral medicine is shaped from the beginning by patterns of correspondence between cosmic elements, that patterning intensifies in the Renaissance with the 'increasingly common notion of an occult cosmic sympathy',[88] of a 'system of equivalences between macrocosm and microcosm';[89] medical thought comes to be permeated with astrological and magical notions. Benjamin notes the close connection of the humours with the 'doctrine of stellar influence',[90] and, in particular, with the baleful influence of Saturn, whose duality is grounded in the dual nature of his Greek counterpart Cronos, at once god of the golden age and the mournful god who is dethroned and dishonoured by his son. It is in the Renaissance, too, that the positive dimension of melancholia first posited in the pseudo-Aristotelian *Problemata* is revived. 'Whereas,' Benjamin writes, 'the Aristotelian insights into the psychical duality of the melancholic disposition and the antithetical nature of the influence of Saturn had given way, in the middle ages, to a purely demonic representation of both, such as conformed with Christian speculation' (and Saturn/Cronos, the god of the crops and the sickle, is transformed into Death the reaper), 'with the Renaissance the whole wealth of ancient meditations re-emerged from the sources'.[91] The *Problemata* associates eminence in philosophy, politics, poetry, or the arts with the 'natural' form of melancholy when it is present in moderation and combined with warmer humours; melancholy genius is thus a matter of 'thermodynamic ambivalence',[92] and Marsilio Ficino's revival of the thesis begins a lengthy vogue of melancholy in Italy and England.[93] 'For this age,' writes Benjamin, 'which was bent at all costs on gaining access to the sources of occult insight into nature, the melancholic posed the question of how it might be possible to discover for oneself the spiritual powers of Saturn and yet escape madness.'[94]

Alongside its technical humoral sense, however, the concept of melancholy came to mean something like a mood, a state of depression, rather than a stable temperament. Andreas Laurentius speaks of it as 'fere and sadness, without any apparent occasion';[95] Bright as a condition in which we 'lament, when no cause requireth it';[96] and Burton,

[87] Giorgio Agamben, *Stanzas: Word and Phantasm in Western Culture*, trans. Ronald L. Martinez (Minneapolis: University of Minnesota Press, 1993), p. 13.

[88] Nutton, 'Humoralism', p. 288.

[89] Magli, 'The Face and the Soul', p. 107, commenting on G. B. Della Porta's *Magia Naturalis* (1558).

[90] Benjamin, *The Origins of German Tragic Drama*, p. 148.

[91] Benjamin, *The Origins of German Tragic Drama*, p. 150.

[92] Klibansky, Panofsky, and Saxl, *Saturn and Melancholy*, p. 42.

[93] Klibansky, Panofsky, and Saxl, *Saturn and Melancholy*, p. 60; Ficino's revival of the *Problemata*, which were possibly written by Theophrastus, takes place in his *De Studiosorum Sanitate Tuenda*, the first book of *De Vita Libri Tres* (1482–9).

[94] Benjamin, *The Origins of German Tragic Drama*, p. 150.

[95] Andreas Laurentius, *A Discourse of the Preservation of the Sight: Of Melancholick Diseases: Of Rheumes, and of Old Age*, trans. Richard Surphlet (London, 1599), pp. 86–7; cited in Trevor, *The Poetics of Melancholy*, p. 16.

[96] Bright, *A Treatise of Melancholy*, p. 122.

in discussing this 'sadness without cause', distinguishes between the 'melancholy habit' or disease and a transitory melancholy disposition.[97] In post-medieval usage it is this sense that comes to predominate, and to be transferable from the subject to inanimate objects.[98]

Hamlet's melancholy is signalled not only by 'the trappings and the suits of woe' (1.2.86) but, above all, by his 'wild and whirling words' (1.5.132); Jacques Lacan writes that 'we must not neglect the *way* in which Hamlet feigns madness, his way of plucking ideas out of the air, opportunities for punning equivocation, to dazzle his enemies with the brilliance of an inspired moment—all of which give his speech an almost maniacal quality'.[99] Think of Hamlet's reference to his hands:

> ROSENCRANTZ: My lord, you once did love me.
> HAMLET: And do still, by these pickers and stealers
> (3.2.326–7)

(where the reference is to the promise made in the *Book of Common Prayer*'s Catechism to 'keep my hands from picking and stealing'). This punning speech frequently carries a thematic strain of free-floating loathing of bodily corruption, and of misogynistic sexual disgust. The imagery is both localized in Hamlet's discourse and transcends it, generating what Caroline Spurgeon calls a 'feeling of horror and disgust at foul disease' arising from the play's 'constant conception of a corrupt and hidden tumour or cancer which is the central imaginative symbol of the tragedy' and through which the play thematizes the corruption of the body politic.[100] That rottenness of 'Denmark' (the king's body and the body of the state) is played out, for example, in the exchange between Claudius and Hamlet over the dead Polonius:

> KING: Now, Hamlet, where's Polonius?
> HAMLET: At supper.
> KING: At supper! Where?
> HAMLET: Not where he eats but where 'a is eaten. A certain convocation of politic worms are e'en at him. Your worm is your only emperor for diet. We fat all creatures else to fat us, and we fat ourselves for maggots. Your fat king and your lean beggar is but variable service, two dishes but to one table. That's the end.
> KING: Alas, alas.
> HAMLET: A man may fish with the worm that hath eat of a king and eat of the fish that hath fed of that worm.
> KING: What dost thou mean by this?
> HAMLET: Nothing, but to show you how a king may go a progress through the guts of a beggar.
> (4.3.16–30)

97 Burton, *The Anatomy of Melancholy*, Partition 1, Section 1, Member 1, Subsection v (p. 142).

98 Klibansky, Panofsky, and Saxl, *Saturn and Melancholy*, p. 220.

99 Jacques Lacan, 'Desire and the Interpretation of Desire in *Hamlet*', in *Literature and Psychoanalysis: The Question of Reading: Otherwise, Yale French Studies* 55/6 (1977), p. 34.

100 Caroline Spurgeon, *Shakespeare's Imagery and What It Tells Us* (1935; rpt. Cambridge: Cambridge University Press, 1952), Chart VII.

Reading this passage as 'a grotesquely materialist reimagining of the Eucharist', Stephen Greenblatt relates it to the body of the old king, Hamlet's father, taken 'grossly full of bread/With all his crimes broad blown as flush as May' (4.3.80–1)—a grossness which is 'figured as well by drinking, sleeping, sexual intercourse, and above all perhaps by woman's flesh. The play enacts and reenacts queasy rituals of defilement and revulsion, an obsession with a corporeality that reduces everything to appetite and excretion'.[101] The king's ghost reports that, when he was poisoned by a 'leperous distilment',

> a most instant tetter barked about
> Most lazar-like with vile and loathsome crust
> All my smooth body.
>
> (1.5.64, 71–3)

The image of the corrupted body of the sovereign is repeated in the graveyard scene, where, shortly after the gravedigger's disquisition on the length of time it takes a body to rot ('your water is a sore decayer of your whoreson dead body') (5.1.161–2), Hamlet imagines tracing 'the noble dust of Alexander till 'a find it stopping a bung-hole' (5.1.193–4), and jokes that 'Imperious Caesar, dead and turned to clay,/Might stop a hole to keep the wind away' (5.1.202–3).

The other, current 'Denmark', Claudius, is also described—or rather describes himself—in terms of bodily corruption: 'O, my offence is rank,' he says in soliloquy: 'it smells to heaven;/It hath the primal eldest curse upon't —/A brother's murder' (3.3.36–8). Speaking of his failure to restrain Hamlet, who has just killed Polonius, he says to Gertrude that

> so much was our love
> We would not understand what was most fit,
> But like the owner of a foul disease,
> To keep it from divulging, let it feed
> Even on the pith of life.
>
> (4.1.19–23)

And he adjures the English king (who holds his office in fealty to him, 'Since yet thy cicatrice looks raw and red/After the Danish sword') to dispose of Hamlet: 'For like the hectic in my blood he rages/And thou must cure me' (4.3.58–9, 64–5).

It is as though Hamlet's imagining of the corruption of the king's two bodies moves outwards to infect others, and, in particular, to turn Claudius into his specular double. The sheer force of Hamlet's loathing of corruption is the energetic centre of the play, and it is even more virulent when directed against his mother and, to a lesser extent (but without any apparent motivation), against Ophelia. The key passages are in Act Three, Scene Four, where Hamlet accuses Gertrude of an incestuous act which 'takes off the rose/From the fair forehead of an innocent

[101] Stephen Greenblatt, *Hamlet in Purgatory* (Princeton: Princeton University Press, 2001), pp. 241, 243.

love/And sets a blister there' (3.4.40–2), as though she were a branded (but also syphilitic) prostitute.[102] 'Nay,' he continues,

> but to live
> In the rank sweat of an enseamed bed
> Stewed in corruption, honeying and making love
> Over the nasty sty—
>
> (3.4.89–92)

and here he breaks off in hysterical rage, and breaks off again a few lines later as he sees the ghostly figure of his father—and he alone sees it: Gertrude, who does not, exclaims that he is mad: 'This bodiless creation ecstasy/Is very cunning in' (3.4.136–7). But Hamlet asks her, in language with strong religious overtones, not to deceive herself that he is mad:

> Mother, for love of grace
> Lay not that flattering unction to your soul
> That not your trespass but my madness speaks.
> It will but skin and film the ulcerous place
> Whiles rank corruption mining all within
> Infects unseen. Confess yourself to heaven,
> Repent what's past, avoid what is to come,
> And do not spread the compost on the weeds
> To make them ranker.
>
> (3.4.142–50)

(where the metaphor repeats Hamlet's description of Denmark as 'an unweeded garden/That grows to seed, things rank and gross in nature/Possess it merely') (1.2.135–7). After some thirty lines of more temperate speech, and after almost taking his leave, Hamlet returns obsessively to his sexual loathing, bidding his mother *not* to do what he now bids her do—

> Let the bloat king tempt you again to bed,
> Pinch wanton on your cheeks, call you his mouse,
> Or paddling in your neck with his damned fingers,
> Make you to ravel all this matter out
> That I essentially am not in madness
> But mad in craft.
>
> (3.4.180–6)

It is of language such as this that T. S. Eliot writes that Hamlet 'is dominated by an emotion which is inexpressible because it is in *excess* of the facts as they appear…Hamlet is up against the difficulty that his disgust is occasioned by his mother, but that his mother is not an adequate equivalent for it; his disgust envelops

[102] Cf. Ann Thompson and John O. Thompson, *Shakespeare: Meaning and Metaphor* (Brighton: The Harvester Press, 1987), p. 109, and note 31, p. 129.

and exceeds her'.[103] His feigned madness, his levity, his repetitions, his puns are 'the buffoonery of an emotion which can find no outlet in action'; what he experiences is an 'intense feeling, ecstatic or terrible, without an object or exceeding its object':[104] the 'sadness without cause' of the melancholic.

Now, what is at stake in such a description is not, as Eliot proposes, what Hamlet's emotions might really have been, and certainly not the disturbed state of Shakespeare's emotions, on which Eliot speculates, but the effect of inwardness that is generated by the figure of Hamlet. It is the apparent causelessness of Hamlet's emotion, the perceived lack of a full and sufficient motivation in the plot, that generates the play's effect of interiority, making Hamlet 'the canonical text for establishing the possibility and terms of "inwardness" in the late sixteenth century',[105] and giving rise, in the late eighteenth century, to a Hamlet 'distinguished by an inner being so transcendent that it barely comes into contact with the play from which it emerges'.[106] The apparent incoherence of Hamlet's actions (the unexplained delay in avenging his father; his unmotivated sexual distrust of Ophelia; the failure of his feigned madness to do anything other than attract attention to him) means that the play is read as leaving something to be explained. Real madness behind the feigned madness is one possibility (Greenblatt follows Bradley in arguing that 'Hamlet's show of madness... seems a cover for something like madness').[107] Bert States posits that Shakespeare's use of 'the swinging sickness', melancholia, allows him to explore extremes of character 'within a perfectly coherent radius of behavior'.[108] More generally, Margreta De Grazia argues that what Hamlet comes to acquire after Goethe, Schlegel, and Coleridge is not an inner self as such, but rather 'an area of consciousness which he cannot reveal even to himself'.[109]

Hamlet thus comes to be a central text for the psychoanalytic tradition, and Hamlet's humoral melancholy is transformed into the terms of a different medical discourse. Freud reads the play as a seminal text, in a letter to Fliess outlining his development of the theory of the Oedipal complex,[110] and expands on his analysis in chapter V of *The Interpretation of Dreams*, where he writes that, whereas in *Oedipus Rex* the underlying phantasy is brought into the open, in *Hamlet* it remains repressed and

[103] T. S. Eliot, 'Hamlet', in *Selected Essays* (3rd edn, London: Faber and Faber, 1961), p. 145.

[104] Eliot, 'Hamlet', p. 146.

[105] Paster, *Humoring the Body*, p. 25; cf. K. Maus, *Inwardness and Theater in the English Renaissance* (Chicago: University of Chicago Press, 1995).

[106] Margreta De Grazia, Hamlet *Without Hamlet* (Cambridge: Cambridge University Press, 2007), p. 1.

[107] Stephen Greenblatt, *Will in the World: How Shakespeare Became Shakespeare* (London: Pimlico, 2004), p. 307.

[108] Bert O. States, Hamlet *and the Concept of Character* (Baltimore: Johns Hopkins University Press, 1992), pp. 65–6.

[109] De Grazia, Hamlet *Without Hamlet*, p. 164.

[110] Sigmund Freud, Letter of 15 October 1897, to Wilhelm Fliess, *The Origins of Psychoanalysis: Letters to Wilhelm Fliess, Drafts and Notes: 1887–1902*, ed. Marie Bonaparte, Anna Freud, and Ernst Kris, trans. Eric Mosbacher and James Strachey (New York: Basic Books, 1954), p. 224.

> we only learn of its existence from its inhibiting consequences. Strangely enough, the overwhelming effect produced by the more modern tragedy has turned out to be compatible with the fact that people have remained completely in the dark as to the hero's character. The play is built up on Hamlet's hesitations over fulfilling the task of revenge that is assigned to him; but its text offers no reasons or motives for these hesitations and an immense variety of attempts at interpreting them have failed to produce a result.[111]

It is psychoanalysis, it seems, which, because of its ability to postulate motives hidden from the person themself, can solve this riddle, and Ernest Jones who can extrapolate from Freud's account to formulate its definitive 'solution'.[112]

Lacan's reading of the play is at once confident that it 'knows' that the play is about the circulation and the absence of the phallus and yet posits the impossibility of interpretation, taking as one of its central emblems Ophelia's grave as a gap (*béance*) or 'hole in the real':[113] the site of a desire that cannot be represented on the stage, of a loss for which both Hamlet and the play are in mourning. His reading thus returns us to Freud's 'Mourning and Melancholia', where the two terms are in an inverse relation: melancholia is the failure of mourning, a withdrawal of libido from the loved object into the ego and 'an *identification* of the ego with the abandoned object'.[114] Like mourning, melancholia is a reaction to the loss of the loved one; but, as Agamben argues, whereas mourning takes place in relation to a real loss, 'in melancholia not only is it unclear what object has been lost, it is uncertain that one can speak of a loss at all'.[115] Just as the 'desperate paralysis of the soul' that is *acedia* is a 'persistence and exaltation of desire in the face of an object that the subject itself has rendered unobtainable',[116] in the same way melancholy works as a kind of strategic warding-off of loss by grieving in advance for an object which it never possessed:

> Covering its object with the funereal trappings of mourning, melancholy confers upon it the phantasmagorical reality of what is lost; but insofar as such mourning is for an unobtainable object, the strategy of melancholy opens a space for the existence of the unreal and marks out a scene in which the ego may enter into relation with it and attempt an appropriation such as no other possession could rival and no loss possibly threaten.[117]

We might say that 'in mourning it is the world which has become poor and empty; in melancholia it is the ego itself',[118] and Hamlet's cynicism about himself and everyone else ('Use every man after his desert and who shall scape whipping?')

[111] Sigmund Freud, *The Interpretation of Dreams*, in *The Standard Edition of the Complete Psychological Works of Sigmund Freud* IV, trans. James Strachey (London: Hogarth Press, 1955), pp. 264–5.
[112] Ernest Jones, *Hamlet and Oedipus* (1949; rpt. New York: W.W. Norton, 1976), chapter III: 'The Psychoanalytic Solution', pp. 45–70.
[113] Lacan, 'Desire and the Interpretation of Desire in *Hamlet*', pp. 40, 37.
[114] Sigmund Freud, 'Mourning and Melancholia (1917)', in *Standard Edition* XIV, p. 249.
[115] Agamben, *Stanzas*, p. 20.
[116] Agamben, *Stanzas*, pp. 6–7.
[117] Agamben, *Stanzas*, p. 20.
[118] Freud, 'Mourning and Melancholia', p. 246.

(2.2.467–8) exemplifies melancholic self-abasement.[119] Benjamin's description of Hamlet as being not a tragedy but a *Trauerspiel*, a mourning play, is thus, on this reading, only partially correct.[120]

The central interpretive fact about *Hamlet* is the mass of interpretive recuperations projected into that hole in the real. Two influential recent readings (amongst many others in the *Hamlet*-machine), seeking to avoid the imputation of an interiority to Hamlet, have sought to develop interpretive strategies which take that imputation as their object rather than their means. Francis Barker makes a historicist argument that 'pre-bourgeois subjection does not properly involve subjectivity at all, but a condition of dependent membership in which place and articulation are defined not by an interiorized self-recognition . . . but by incorporation in the body politic which is the king's body in its social form'.[121] It is for this reason that 'Hamlet's melancholic excess of mourning, and the Oedipal drama that begins to speak itself there', are invoked first within the Danish council of state, as an 'agenda item':[122] Hamlet's melancholy is not a 'private' matter. It is only in his evasions of position and typing that a form of subjectivity emerges, but this subjectivity remains gestural and obscure because it is historically premature: Hamlet's interiority is before its time, and at its heart 'there is, in short, nothing'.[123]

Stephen Greenblatt, in an alternative historicization of the play, argues that 'the psychological in Shakespeare's tragedy is constructed almost entirely out of the theological, and specifically out of the issue of remembrance that . . . lay at the heart of the crucial early-sixteenth-century debate about Purgatory'.[124] A series of puns lays the groundwork for this argument: the ghost of Hamlet's father is 'Doomed for a certain time to walk the night' until his 'foul crimes . . . /Are burnt and purged away' (1.5.10, 12–13). Hamlet steps back from killing Claudius 'in the purging of his soul/When he is fit and seasoned for his passage' (3.4.85–6). And when Guildenstern remarks that the king is 'distempered' with 'choler', Hamlet jokes that 'Your wisdom should show itself more richer to signify this to the doctor, for for me to put him to his purgation would perhaps plunge him into more choler' (3.2.295, 297–10). Greenblatt comments on the dual meanings of 'choler' here, literally a term belonging to humoral medicine but, in its last use, metaphorically designating 'the rage of infernal punishment and torture'.[125] A series of phrases—the old king having been sent to his death 'Unhouseled, disappointed, unaneled' (1.5.77); Hamlet's bidding him to 'Rest, rest, perturbed spirit' (1.5.180), and invoking Saint Patrick, the patron saint of Purgatory (1.5.135); and his use of the phrase '*Hic et ubique*' (1.5.156), which is used in a Catholic prayer for souls in Purgatory—all refer to a machinery of intercession which the Reformation has

[119] Freud, 'Mourning and Melancholia', pp. 246–7.
[120] Benjamin, *The Origins of German Tragic Drama*, pp. 136–7.
[121] Francis Barker, *The Tremulous Private Body: Essays on Subjection* (London: Methuen, 1984), p. 31.
[122] Barker, *The Tremulous Private Body*, p. 33.
[123] Barker, *The Tremulous Private Body*, p. 37.
[124] Greenblatt, *Hamlet in Purgatory*, p. 229.
[125] Greenblatt, *Hamlet in Purgatory*, p. 232.

made redundant, with the effect that all of the old rituals for managing grief for the dead have been disrupted, and the realm of the aesthetic itself—the *Trauerspiel*, the mourning play—must take over its tasks. Hamlet's 'corrosive inwardness'[126] is intimately bound up with that loss of institutional practices of mourning.

The strength and the weakness of any historicism is its reduction of a text to its context of origin, and thus its privileging of an interpretive paradigm which is salient and valid in the period it deals with—and that criticism holds true, too, for the reading of the play I have been making in terms of humoral medicine and the type of the melancholic. A different way of dealing with some of the central problems of the play—no less partial, perhaps, but working at a different level of textual structure—would lie in situating it in relation to the typological conventions of the revenge tragedy, and the particular way in which it blocks the plot progression that those conventions require. From this perspective, the question of whether Hamlet is 'really' mad or not is the wrong one to ask: Hamlet is mad because the conventions of the genre require it.

Those conventions are set for Elizabethan drama by Jasper Heywood's translation of Seneca's tragedies, in particular *Thyestes* (1560, republished in 1581), and by the huge popularity of Thomas Kyd's *Spanish Tragedy* (published in 1592 but written some years earlier). In brief, the conventions that evolve from these two texts, from John Marston's *Antonio's Revenge* (1600) and *The Malcontent* (1603–4), from *Hamlet* (and its lost prototype), and from later plays such as Thomas Middleton's *The Revenger's Tragedy* (1606–7) and John Webster's *The White Devil* (1612), involve some variant of the following: the murder of a benevolent ruler by a usurper; the appearance of a ghost to incite blood-revenge; the adoption of the disguise of a malcontent by the avenger in order to avoid detection, or else his feigned or real madness; a hesitation on the part of the avenger before he commits himself to revenge; a counterplot mounted by the usurper; a play or masque within the play used to entrap or to murder the usurper; and the final catastrophic death of many or all of the major characters.

Peter Mercer describes the Senecan and Elizabethan revenge tragedy as having a three-part structure: the appearance of the ghost to open the action of revenge; the 'making' of the revenge, in which the avenger moves 'from frustrated rage to horrible intention'; and 'the revenge itself—the acting of ingenious deceit, the plotting, disguising and dissembling with which the revenger translates his malevolent will into dreadful reality'.[127] The core of its structure is thus the shaping and accomplishment of a will-to-revenge; but that shaping of the will is fraught with difficulty, since it involves the transformation of the hero from a self bounded by the laws of social normality into 'a monster of revenging fury',[128] urged on by a malevolent ghost. It is likely, Mercer argues, that delay, and the pretence of madness that usually accompanies it, are intrinsic to the genre because revenge destroys the avenger's humanity: they register a resistance to a role that requires 'a quite

[126] Greenblatt, *Hamlet in Purgatory*, p. 208.
[127] Peter Mercer, Hamlet *and the Acting of Revenge* (London: Macmillan, 1987), p. 27.
[128] Mercer, Hamlet *and the Acting of Revenge*, p. 2.

appalling intensification', a 'transformation of the self that borders on insanity'[129] and that brings about an act of vengeance which is spectacular and excessive.

Madness is thus both an aspect of that moral transformation (the possession of the hero by a daemonic force) and a symptom of a deep-seated reluctance to undergo it. Typically the hero's transformation involves a reshaping of the self by means of the assumption of disguises, ranging

> from simple dissembling to the acting-out of the parts of clown, malcontent, misanthrope and madman. At once covertly expressive and overtly protective, these performances bristle with ambiguity, and all the more so because the acting can shift to a kind of wild distraction that may be no acting at all.[130]

Hamlet's manic-depressive melancholy (whether real or feigned or both) is thus structurally ambivalent. It is also political through and through, the site of a struggle for the will to act against the corruption of the state, and of a repugnance for the terms of that struggle. Melancholy, we might say, is a disease of state, or a mode of response to a diseased body politic.

Freud speaks of a symbiosis between the opposed moods of 'revolt' and 'the crushed state of melancholia', reflecting the alternation found in this condition between aggression towards others and towards the self.[131] The characteristic form in which melancholy appears on the stage when it involves aggression towards others is the figure of the malcontent:[132] a stock type of cynical disaffection and of self-proclaimed plain speaking, often combined with misogyny and satire against public corruption. The language of the malcontent, derived ultimately from that of the Vices of the medieval morality plays,[133] is impertinent, in both senses of the word: it is disrespectful of established authority, and it wilfully misses the point of polite conversation. Babb describes the figure as 'usually black-suited and dishevelled, unsociable, asperous, morosely meditative, taciturn yet prone to occasional railing',[134] with hat pulled low and arms folded. The primary type of the malcontent is 'the melancholy man who resents the world's neglect of his superior abilities',[135] and Hamlet's 'Sir, I lack advancement' (3.2.331), which is, on the face of it, absurd, since 'advancement' at the court is hardly what he lacks, is the parodic gesture by which he takes on the role of the malcontent, as he takes on the role of the melancholic, of the clown, of the frustrated lover, and, indeed, of the betrayed son of his mother and the avenger of his father's death.

129 Mercer, Hamlet *and the Acting of Revenge*, p. 58.

130 Mercer, Hamlet *and the Acting of Revenge*, p. 2.

131 Freud, 'Mourning and Melancholia', p. 248.

132 Cf. Adam H. Kitzes, *The Politics of Melancholy from Spenser to Milton* (New York: Routledge, 2006), p. 60; and James R. Keller, *Princes, Soldiers and Rogues: The Political Malcontent of Renaissance Drama* (New York: Peter Lang, 1993), p. 1.

133 Robert Weimann, *Shakespeare and the Popular Tradition in the Theater: Studies in the Social Dimension of Dramatic Form and Function*, ed. Robert Schwarz (Baltimore: Johns Hopkins University Press, 1978), p. 119.

134 Babb, *The Elizabethan Malady*, p. 75.

135 Babb, *The Elizabethan Malady*, p. 76.

If *Hamlet* is a play about the acting of roles, then this perhaps explains something of the peculiar emptiness of Hamlet's 'character'. Lacking the will to assume the mask of the blood-lusting avenger (as Fortinbras, Laertes, and the player narrating the fall of Troy are all able to do with apparent ease), Hamlet must try to whip himself into the required frenzy—to persuade himself that he can 'drink hot blood/And do such business as the bitter day/Would quake to look on' (3.2.380–2)—in order to pass from the morally structured world of human decision to the amorally intense world of 'a necessity *beyond* human will or intention'.[136] But the hyperbole he needs appears ludicrous to him each time he tries it on. The generic rules that are supposed to drive him are displaced into the play within the play, or rather its double staging, as dumbshow and as the broken-off *Murder of Gonzago*, the 'Mousetrap' designed to force the king into self-recognition. Shakespeare's solution to the aporias of the revenge plot, Mercer writes, is 'to release Hamlet from the unsupportable necessity of revenge'; but the cost of that release was to be

> the relegation of the whole business of revenge, all the rhetoric and all the acting, to the world of the stage. In the complex and unyielding reality of the world of Elsinore the ancient ritual of revenge could find no place except in the fictive gestures of professional players. Revenge there really was to become nothing but acting.[137]

Nothing but acting: the actions of the players have consequences within and only within their fictional world, as Hamlet's action and inaction (complexly layered as reality and pretence) have consequences only within his.

That layering of modal states is repeated in the spatial disposition of bodies between upstage and downstage positions in performance. Robert Weimann draws from medieval theatre a distinction between the *locus* and the *platea*: the inner space of dramatic illusion, and the outer rim where that space merges into the space of the audience. In Shakespeare's theatre the *platea* corresponds to the downstage position at the edges of the projecting platform, where an actor can interact directly with the audience (in soliloquy or in clowning, for example).[138] The distinction corresponds to that between the elevated main plot and the comic counterplot carried by clowns and fools; and Weimann suggests that Hamlet (who inherits the use of proverbs and wordplay from the Vice figure of the old morality plays) moves flexibly between the conventions of *locus* and *platea* stagecraft, dissociating himself from the *locus* of the court both physically and by his use of dissociated and 'impertinent' language;[139] he also shifts character-position *within* his own discourse, interrupting the mimetic illusion of the dialogue by means of wordplay, rhyming couplets, asides, and monologues. The paradox here is that

> Hamlet, who knows no 'seems', has to develop his *platea*-like *Figurenposition* [character-position] within the 'seems', that is, the illusionistic frame of the Renaissance play. So he is made to use the most traditional conventions of a *platea*-like

[136] Mercer, Hamlet *and the Acting of Revenge*, p. 14.
[137] Mercer, Hamlet *and the Acting of Revenge*, p. 89.
[138] Weimann, *Shakespeare and the Popular Tradition*, p. 74.
[139] Weimann, *Shakespeare and the Popular Tradition*, pp. 230–1.

> embodiment—here, the verbal modes of his antic disposition—as a deliberate 'show', a psychological illusion, a strategy for discovery and survival. Hamlet's madness has a function in the play only because he *seems* mad. The resulting contradictions are obvious; by not suiting the action to the words Hamlet reveals his dilemma to be both one of the theater and one of character.[140]

By *Figurenposition* Weimann means both the actor's physical position on the stage and 'the speech, action, and degree of stylization associated with that position';[141] it involves at once the relation between the actors, between actor and audience, between actor and character, and between characters. The concept is thus close to Stephen Heath's concept of the *figure* as 'the circulation between agent, character, person and image, none of which is able simply and uniquely to contain, to *settle* that circulation'.[142] Hamlet occupies a *Figurenposition* which is at once fluid and ambiguous.

Stephen Greenblatt notes a 'pervasive pattern' of forcing together 'radically incompatible accounts of almost everything that matters in *Hamlet*'.[143] Elsewhere he argues that the play's 'intense representation of inwardness' was 'called forth by a new technique of radical excision' of 'the rationale, motivation, or ethical principle that accounted for the action that was to unfold. The principle was not the making of a riddle to be solved, but the creation of a strategic opacity'.[144] While we might demur at the notion that this principle is necessarily 'strategic', the structural function of opacity seems clear. The figure of Hamlet is a paredros: a wildcard; a machine for generating interpretations.

VI

The psychosomatic schema of melancholy and the generically specific figure of the revenger are complementary algorithms for establishing a movement between generality and singularity in the person of Hamlet; they are typological templates. But the sharp distinction I have made between a 'cultural' and a 'generic' typology is to some extent misleading; the figure of the melancholic is a stock figure in the drama of the period, and the figure of the revenger reworks and stylizes a set of cultural stereotypes about obligations to the dead in a patriarchal world built around honour.[145] Cultural typing—here and more generally—is overdetermined by generic typing. I turn now to a rather different mode of typological extrapolation in the work of Charles Dickens, where the charged structure of the family makes possible a scaling up and down between the humanly particular and the social.

[140] Weimann, *Shakespeare and the Popular Tradition*, p. 233.
[141] Weimann, *Shakespeare and the Popular Tradition*, p. 224.
[142] Stephen Heath, 'Body, Voice', in *Questions of Cinema* (London: Macmillan, 1981), p. 182.
[143] Greenblatt, *Hamlet in Purgatory*, p. 240.
[144] Greenblatt, *Will in the World*, pp. 323–4.
[145] Cf. Robert L. Oprisky, *Honor: A Phenomenology* (London: Routledge, 2012).

Hamlet draws on humoral medicine to set up the melancholic dimension of Hamlet's character, but Hamlet is not a humour, in the sense that Ben Jonson uses the term: a character identified with a single characteristic,

> As when some one peculiar quality
> Doth so possess a man that it doth draw
> All his affects, his spirits, and his powers
> In their confluxions all to run one way...[146]

Many of the characters of Charles Dickens' novels, by contrast, can more properly be read as humours, as long as we keep in mind that their semantic range is not exhausted by the singularity of their 'character' but is, rather, a function of their compositional role within the daemonic universe of the novels. In Dickens' 'radical stylistics of characterization,' Alex Woloch writes, his characters 'famously tend to resemble one another, accruing features that thus seem to transcend any particular structure'.[147] It is one set of the structural typologies patterning the world of Dickens' novels that I want to analyse here—typologies that I take to be organized around what Freud calls the Family Romance (*der Familienroman*),[148] although I give this term a broader sense than he does in order to designate the way Dickens imagines the social order in terms of the fantasmatic and child-centred relations structuring the nuclear family.

Let me begin by looking at the way knowledge of the world and the self is organized in a passage from the first chapter of *Great Expectations*:

> Ours was the marsh country, down by the river, within, as the river wound, twenty miles of the sea. My first most vivid and broad impression of the identity of things, seems to me to have been gained on a memorable raw afternoon towards evening. At such a time I found out for certain, that this bleak place overgrown with nettles was the churchyard; and that Philip Pirrip, late of this parish, and also Georgiana wife of the above, were dead and buried; and that Alexander, Bartholomew, Abraham, Tobias, and Roger, infant children of the aforesaid, were also dead and buried; and that the dark flat wilderness beyond the churchyard, intersected with dykes and mounds and gates, with scattered cattle feeding on it, was the marshes; and that the low leaden line beyond, was the river; and that the distant savage lair from which the wind was rushing, was the sea; and that the small bundle of shivers growing afraid of it all and beginning to cry, was Pip.[149]

[146] Ben Jonson, 'Induction', in *Every Man Out of His Humour*, ed. Helen Ostovitch, The Revels Plays (Manchester: Manchester University Press, 2001), p. 118.

[147] Alex Woloch, *The One vs. the Many: Minor Characters and the Space of the Protagonist in the Novel* (Princeton: Princeton University Press, 2003), p. 125.

[148] Sigmund Freud, 'Family Romances' [*Der Familienroman der Neurotiker*, 1909], in *Standard Edition* XIX, pp. 235–41. Freud's concern in this essay is with the child's fantasy of having parents of noble birth in place of an actual and ordinary family; as the child comes to realize the uncertainty of paternity, it is particularly the father who is the object of this fantasy.

[149] Charles Dickens, *Great Expectations*, ed. Edgar Rosenberg (New York: Norton Critical Edition, 1999), pp. 9–10; hereafter cited in the text.

There are five phrases here that have to do with perception and knowledge: 'impression'; 'seems to me'; 'memorable'; 'I found out for certain'; and 'growing afraid'. Weaving together the present of narration ('seems to me', 'memorable') with the narrated past ('My first...impression [was] gained'; 'I found out for certain'; 'growing afraid'), these phrases map the shift from impression to certainty by moving through a series of tautological identity statements: 'this bleak place overgrown with nettles' is identical to 'the churchyard'; the dead members of Pip's family are 'dead and buried'; elements of the landscape are identical with the marshes, the river, and the sea; and the person perceiving all this is identical with 'Pip'.

That final identity statement adds depth to the nomination announced in the first paragraph: being unable to pronounce my name, the narrator says, 'I called myself Pip, and came to be called Pip' (p. 9): the narrated third person is identical with the first-person narrator, who is here both a speaker in the present and the culmination in the narrated past of the effect of this landscape upon him (the 'small bundle of shivers growing afraid of it all'). This identity of first and third person, of self-nomination and social recognition, and of the present with the past self (at once united and disunited here) is predicated upon another: 'Pip' is an abbreviation of the name that the narrator shares with his dead father, Philip Pirrip; he is the person who bears his father's name in diminutive form, and who can be spoken of in the third person. That continuity between the child and the dead father might remind us of the 'posthumous child' David Copperfield looking out at the 'white grave-stone in the churchyard...lying out alone there in the dark night' where his father is buried, and surviving not only him but also his fantasmal sister who 'was for ever in the land of dreams and shadows, the tremendous region whence I had so lately travelled'.[150] The living person is haunted by the realms of the dead and the virtual: Pip and David come to know who they are through their relation to those absent beings who shadow the rest of their lives.

I have grouped the word 'memorable' in the passage above with the present of narration, but in fact it belongs to a continuous time flowing back and forth between the narrated past and the present. It is intimately linked to Pip's finding out for certain and to his fear, because what gives this scene its memorability is the event that immediately follows it—indeed, that seems to respond to it[151]—and that works retroactively to sear it into his memory. This event, the novel's primal scene, is the apparition of a 'fearful man' crying out in a 'terrible voice', who threatens to cut Pip's throat, and perhaps to eat him (p. 10).[152] His appearance is 'primal' in the sense that this castrating figure haunts the rest of the novel, laying the traces both for Pip's misplaced expectations of moving from commonness into gentility and for the relationship with Estella that more immediately motivates the

[150] Charles Dickens, *David Copperfield*, ed. Jerome H. Buckley (New York: Norton Critical Edition, 1990), pp. 10, 18.

[151] Cf. Goldie Morgentaler, *Dickens and Heredity: When Like Begets Like* (London: Macmillan, 2000), p. 73: 'No sooner has the full impact of this existential loneliness impressed itself upon Pip than he begins to cry, and his crying rouses the terrible specter of the convict. Pip in a sense calls him forth, so that the convict rises from among the graves seemingly in answer to a need.'

[152] Dickens, *Great Expectations*, p. 10.

desire (the family romance) that drives those expectations. It is from his traumatic relation to this nameless convict—Magwitch, as we later know him—that Pip's self-consciousness arises, and, with it, his sense of guilt for his complicity in a chain of events that leads to the eventual murder of his sister and surrogate mother, Mrs Joe (Pip steals the file with which Magwitch cuts off the leg iron with which Orlick, many years later, attacks her). And it is the gift of gentility that Magwitch later and secretly offers him that corrupts Pip into the fantasy of rising above his station and the reality of despising Joe.

Dorothy Van Ghent says that there are two kinds of crime in Dickens' world, 'the crime against the child, and the calculated social crime', that they are formally analogous in treating persons as things, and that each partakes of the nature of the other.[153] Pip and Magwitch are bound to each other in a complicated relationship structured around a crime which is at once that of the father and the child:

> In Dickens's modification of the folk pattern of the fairy-wishing, Magwitch is Pip's 'fairy god-father', and like all the fathers, he uses the child as a thing, in order to obtain through him sensations of grandeur. In relation to society, however, Magwitch is the child, and society the prodigal father; from the time he was first taken for stealing turnips, the convict's career has duplicated brutally and in public the pathos of the ordinary child. Again, in relation to Pip, Magwitch is still the child; for, having been dedicated from the first to criminality, Pip has carried his criminal father within him, and is projectively responsible for Magwitch's existence and for his brutalization; so that Pip is the father of his father. Thus the ambiguities of each term of the relationship between Pip and Magwitch are such that each is both child and father...[154]

'Look'ee here, Pip', says Magwitch at the moment of recognition of their true relationship. 'I'm your second father. You're my son—more to me nor any son!' (p. 241)—' "more",' writes Hillis Miller, 'because in this case the son has been as much maker of his father as father the maker of son'.[155] Pip carries this second father within him as a sense of guilt that is later realized as the nightmare of finding out (again, and again in relation to Magwitch) who and what he really is.

In Dickens' novels the social order is imagined through and as a family, and family relations—seen, above all, from the perspective of the child—take on a charged intensity.[156] Northrop Frye understands this patterning in terms of the New Comedy structure of a collision between an 'obstructing' society of thwarting parents and a 'congenial' society built around the lovers and their allies, with a plot reversal showing one of the characters to be of nobler birth than had been believed. In this structure as Dickens deploys it (and as he partly reverses it in

[153] Dorothy Van Ghent, 'The Dickens World: A View from Todgers's', in *The Dickens Critics*, ed. George H. Ford and Lauriat Lane, Jr (Ithaca: Cornell University Press, 1961), p. 225.

[154] Van Ghent, 'The Dickens World', p. 231.

[155] J. Hillis Miller, *Charles Dickens: The World of His Novels* (1958; rpt. Bloomington: Indiana University Press, 1969), p. 273.

[156] Catherine Waters argues in *Dickens and the Politics of the Family* (Cambridge: Cambridge University Press, 1997), p. 27, that Dickens' novels 'record a historical shift in notions of the family away from an earlier stress upon lineage and blood towards a new ideal of domesticity assumed to be the natural form of the family'; this form is what I am calling the 'nuclear' family.

some of the darker late novels) there are three types of parental figures: the dead, absent, or weak actual parents; the wicked step-parents of the obstructing society; and the benevolent parental or avuncular figures of the congenial society.[157] The character system that they form can perhaps be seen in its most schematic form in *Nicholas Nickleby*, the action of which is initiated by the death of Nicholas's weak and profligate father, driven to misguided speculation by the foolish Mrs Nickleby. Arraigned against Nicholas is his miserly uncle, Ralph Nickleby, who is the source of the plots directed both against Nicholas and his sister Kate, and against his own abandoned natural son Smike, and the schoolmaster Wackford Squeers, who acts as a surrogate bad father both to Nicholas and to the boys in his care. Since there is no member of the family in the generation above Nicholas to protect him, that role is filled by the avuncular and benevolent Cheeryble brothers as well as by the substitute family of Vincent Crummles' theatrical company. The structure of Nicholas's family is repeated in that of the young woman who becomes his wife, Madeline Bray, whose mother is dead and whose father's profligacy exposes her to the threat of being married to the elderly miser Arthur Gride.

Each of the novels plays out a set of variations on this structure. The components of the structure are in no way unique to Dickens: virtually all nineteenth-century novels thematize social structure by way of the family, and such figures as the orphan or the dead mother or the eccentric benefactor are widely used in the period. Dickens draws his character types from the popular theatre,[158] from the picaresque and sentimental traditions of the eighteenth-century novel, and from the journalistic genre of the character sketch, amongst others, and he shares them with many contemporaries. All I want to claim here is that a particular configuration of roles can be found repeatedly—and for reasons that may have to do as much with market calculations as with Dickens' emotional make-up—in a number of the novels.[159] I exclude from consideration here the early *Sketches by Boz*, the unfinished *Mystery of Edwin Drood*, the stories and miscellanies, and Dickens' first novel, *The Pickwick Papers*, although that novel does construct the model for all of Dickens' avuncular benefactors in the person of Mr Pickwick: elderly, stout, sexually innocent, unworldly, and benevolent. The avuncular figure (usually only figuratively so) represents a sideways step from the nuclear family: a representative of the higher generation who provides care, affection, and protection without the negative charge that attaches to the dead or absent or improvident fathers who are the norm in this world.[160]

[157] Northrop Frye, 'Dickens and the Comedy of Humours', in *The Stubborn Structure: Essays on Criticism and Society* (London: Methuen, 1970), pp. 220, 231–2.

[158] Cf. in particular Paul Schlicke, *Dickens and Popular Entertainment* (London: Allen & Unwin, 1985).

[159] On Dickens' 'sensitivity to mass culture understood as commercial, market-driven culture, and…his emotional, imaginative, and political engagement with the idea of a mass audience', cf. Juliet John, *Dickens and Mass Culture* (Oxford: Oxford University Press, 2010), p. 29 and passim.

[160] But, as Branwen Pratt points out, although the benevolent Pickwick presides over the novel, the interpolated tales have to do with filial aggression against the wicked father. Branwen Baily Pratt, 'Dickens and Father: Notes on the Family Romance', *Hartford Studies in Literature* 8: 1 (1976), p. 10.

Schematically, we can envisage the following set of *actant*-roles as forming the core character system of the remaining eleven novels:

- The *orphan* designates the hero or heroine: either a child or a young man or woman, typically bereft or one or both parents, and having the innocence and the vulnerability of a child. Esther, Richard, and Ada in *Bleak House* occupy the structural position of orphans, although they enjoy the spurious protection of the court as well as the real protection of their benefactor, John Jarndyce, and Esther has a living but radically absent mother; Jo is the extreme case of the orphan, the predestined victim of the novel's worst harms (and carrying some of the type's structural ambivalence, at once deprived of and threatening the family).[161]
- The *father* is either dead, or absent, or weak, or profligate, or disinheriting; there are no good fathers (at least of the central characters) in Dickens. The *mother* is typically dead or foolish; there are no strong and mature mothers in Dickens (with a few marginal exceptions, such as Edith Dombey in *Dombey and Son*, who is loving towards her stepdaughter Florence but unable to act accordingly for fear of damaging her; or Mrs Rouncewell and Mrs Bagnet in *Bleak House*). This pattern follows that articulated by Carolyn Dever for Victorian fiction more generally, in which the death of the idealized mother, resolving the conundrum of female sexuality, generates a melancholic 'poetics of abandonment and ambivalence'.[162]
- *Surrogate fathers and mothers* may be either step-parents, almost always unloving, such as Murdstone and his sister Jane in *David Copperfield*, or Miss Barbary in *Bleak House*; or schoolmasters or landlords such as Wackford Squeers or Creakle, again almost always uncaring; or figures of a false authority such as Mr Bumble, Fagin, Pecksniff, or Mrs General. There are also instances of *institutional* and 'blocking' *surrogate parents* such as Chancery and the Circumlocution Office.
- The *benefactor* is typically an avuncular figure; in *Martin Chuzzlewit* and *Our Mutual Friend* the benefactor is disguised as an antagonist for the purposes of testing the hero. Mr Micawber in *David Copperfield* is simultaneously a figure of the profligate surrogate father and a would-be (and eventually actual) benefactor; John Jarndyce in *Bleak House* threatens to misrecognize the necessary asexuality of the figure, but draws back in time to preserve the role intact. Magwitch in *Great Expectations* wishes to be a benefactor to Pip but is instead, as Hillis Miller puts it, 'a nightmare permutation of Mr Brownlow and Mr Jarndyce'.[163] The figure of the

[161] Cf. Laura Peters, *Orphan Texts: Victorian Orphans, Culture and Empire* (Manchester: Manchester University Press, 2000), p. 22: the orphan 'is not a foreign invading threat but is actually produced by and hence is an essential component of the family itself'.

[162] Carolyn Dever, *Death and the Mother from Dickens to Freud: Victorian Fiction and the Anxiety of Origins* (Cambridge: Cambridge University Press, 1998), p. xi.

[163] Miller, *Charles Dickens: The World of His Novels*, p. 255.

benefactor is occasionally shadowed by its negative double, the false benefactor (Pumblechook, for example).

- Villains (*antagonists*) in Dickens' novels are of two kinds: those who are internal to the family, and—more commonly—an external villain;[164] the damage done by the family is more usually a matter of weakness or the absence of love than of direct evil, although this does occur in the early novels in the cases of Oliver Twist's half-brother Monks, Little Nell's brother Fred, and the bad uncles Ralph Nickleby and Jonas Chuzzlewit.
- In many of the novels there is a *congenial substitute family*, typically a theatrical company or a circus, but also nurturing individuals such as Mark Tapley and Polly Toodle, and the Peggotty and Meagles families.
- Finally, almost every novel contains a figure of *radical innocence* who is typically also simple-minded: Smike, Barnaby Rudge (where the figure is conflated with that of the orphan and titular hero), Tom Pinch, Uncle Dick, Miss Flite, Maggie, Sloppy…

This schematic mapping has the advantage of formalizing the fantasmatic structure of the family in Dickens' novels, and, of course, the disadvantage of reducing to a skeleton their rich proliferation of language and character. Let me note some of the ways in which we might move out from this formalization.

- Although the New Comedy convention is that what the obstructive family blocks is the union of lovers, it is often the case that what is more deeply blocked is knowledge of the child's true identity: this is straightforwardly so in *Oliver Twist*, but it is also the case in *Bleak House* and *Little Dorrit*, where Esther and Clennam discover their true parentage, and even in a sense in *Great Expectations*, where Pip comes to a knowledge of his relation to his 'second father' and his own moral identity.
- Weak fathers are often presented as children in relation to their own children: Little Nell cares for her drunken grandfather; Dombey is reduced to a child, to be cared for by Florence; Harold Skimpole survives on the strength of being as calculatedly naïve as a child; Little Dorrit is the head of her family in all but name. In *Great Expectations*, as we have seen, Pip and Magwitch are each both child and father to the other.
- Mothers in the Dickens world are, at one level, absent or insignificant; they tend to die early, and are charged with much less affective force than fathers. We might suspect, however, that this insignificance screens a deeper level at which the mother is *intensely* absent. This is perhaps clearest in *Dombey and Son*, where the foregrounded drama of longing for the

[164] On the melodramatic origins of Dickens' villains, cf. Juliet John, *Dickens's Villains: Melodrama, Character, Popular Culture* (Oxford: Oxford University Press, 2001). 'The out-and-out villain,' she writes (pp. 48–9), 'is a type before he is a character'; but 'the villains of nineteenth-century melodrama are, however, types struggling to become individuals'.

rejecting father is underpinned by a figuring of the absent mother in terms of the oceanic realm of death.

- The family romance in the Freudian sense of the desire for and fantasy of higher birth is rarely realized after *Oliver Twist*; it is inverted in *David Copperfield* (where David descends from his middle-class security to Murdstone's warehouse), refused in *Little Dorrit*, where happiness is achieved by the loss of wealth and status, and carefully dismantled in *Great Expectations*.
- Many of the novels posit a radical change of moral state through an experience of near-death—typically severe illness (Martin Chuzzlewit, Dombey, Esther Summerson, Pip), but also drowning. In *Our Mutual Friend*, John Harmon, Eugene Wrayburn, and Rogue Riderhood are all revived from death in the river, and the first two undergo a moral conversion.

That transformation of moral state is described by Frye as the passage of the hero or heroine through a 'hidden and private world of dream and death out of which all the energy of human life comes', the daemonic source from which life is renewed and which, at once Eros and Thanatos, is the basis for the division of the action between the worlds of the obstructing and the congenial societies.[165] That daemonic energy is also, however, what drives the humoral characters—Dickens' misers, hypochondriacs, parasites, braggarts, all those characters governed by an obsessive moral tic. 'Humours,' says Frye, 'are, so to speak, petrified by-products of the kind of energy that melodrama expresses more directly. Even the most contemptible humours, the miserly Fledgeby or the hypocritical Heep, are exuberantly miserly and hypocritical: their vices express an energy that possesses them because they cannot possess it.'[166] Because they are so entirely possessed by this daemonic energy, the ritual habits that they set up to deal with it transforms them into mechanical puppets, automatons engaged in the endless repetition of a mannerism.

Another way of putting this is to say that there is an exchange of energy and function between persons and things in this universe. Dorothy Van Ghent writes that 'the course of things demonically possessed is to imitate the human, while the course of human possession is to imitate the inhuman. This transposition of attributes, producing a world like that of ballet, is the principle of relationship between things and people in the novels of Dickens.'[167] The thinglike nature of Dickens' mechanical persons (the way in which Pancks, say, in *Little Dorrit*, is described as steaming around like a tug boat, or Mr F's Aunt as a battered doll whose face has been dented by the child who owns it) works against any possible imputation of psychological depth; but, as Van Ghent argues, if we focus on the 'total aesthetic occasion' rather than isolating characters from their environment, then 'there is a good deal of "inner life", transposed to other forms than that of character';[168]

[165] Frye, 'Dickens and the Comedy of Humours', p. 236.
[166] Frye, 'Dickens and the Comedy of Humours', p. 237.
[167] Van Ghent, 'The Dickens World', p. 213.
[168] Van Ghent, 'The Dickens World', p. 217.

conversely, in Dickens' novels the mode of existence of the world of things 'constantly exceeds its material limitations' as it is 'altered by the human purposes and deeds it circumscribes'.[169] The animate and the inanimate bleed into each other, and the boundary between them is constantly dissolved.[170] This continuous transposition of the qualities of persons and things is a function of what Van Ghent calls 'a thoroughly nervous universe, whose ganglia spread through things and people alike',[171] so that 'predications about persons or objects tend to be statements of a metabolic conversion of one into the other'.[172]

Nervous energy flows through Dickens' novels in two interconnected circuits. The first is that of the fantasmatic family which forms the primary system of typological resemblances in the Dickens world. The second is that of the channelling of energy into the rigid habits and tics of the humours which proliferate endlessly through the novels. The humours are characterized by means of a limited number of identifiers. In the first instance, they bear distinctive names which are either allegorical, like those of the morality Vices (Pyke and Pluck, Cheeryble, Wackford Squeers, Mr Mould the undertaker, Bounderby, Gradgrind, M'Choakumchild, Barnacle, Veneering), or are onomatopoeic or punning distortions of conventional names (Chuzzlewit, Chuffey, Sweedlepipe, Pecksniff, Gummidge, Murdstone, Guppy, Snagsby, Squod, Flintwinch, Merdle, Podsnap, Twemlow...). Second, their speech is formed by repetitive, obsessive mannerisms: Jingle's breathlessly distorted and verbless sentences, Sam Weller's Cockney wit, Sairey Gamp's rambling, projective, monstrously egocentric discourse, Joe Gargery's peculiar grammar. Third, they are described either by a metonymic reduction to parts of their own body or clothing (Silas Wegg's wooden leg, James Carker's teeth, Mrs Merdle's bosom, Mr Tulkinghorn's clothing, 'mute, close, irresponsive to any glancing light'),[173] or by being metaphorically converted into things: Chadband as a 'vessel' with 'a good deal of train oil in his system',[174] Krook as 'a bundle of old clothes, with a spirituous heat smouldering in it',[175] Grandfather Smallweed plumped up like a pillow. Underpinning these flows and the knotted ganglia in which they are concentrated is a language that is constantly alert to the penumbra of virtuality surrounding and interpenetrating the 'actual' that it constructs, a language that converts metaphor and metonymy and prosopopoeia into literal statement and vice versa. Character in Dickens is a function of the thickening of these flows of language into effects of personhood and into the affective intensities it carries: into types, and into their constant transformations into selves.

[169] Van Ghent, 'The Dickens World', p. 218.

[170] Cf. Herbert Sussman and Gerhard Joseph, 'Prefiguring the Posthuman: Dickens and Prosthesis', *Victorian Literature and Culture* (2004), p. 617.

[171] Van Ghent, 'The Dickens World', p. 222.

[172] Van Ghent, 'The Dickens World', p. 221.

[173] Charles Dickens, *Bleak House*, ed. George Ford and Sylvère Monod (New York: Norton Critical Edition, 1977), p. 14.

[174] Dickens, *Bleak House*, p. 235.

[175] Dickens, *Bleak House*, p. 253.

5

Voice

I

But what are the mechanisms by which selves are represented in discourse, and how do we recognize them? I use the concept of 'voice' in this chapter as a shorthand for the processes by which such representation and recognition happen, and as a way of broaching the questions of the situational positioning (or 'deixis') through which represented selves are able to enter into language.

To be a fictional character is to be both an agent and an object of discourse; at once a speaker, a person spoken to, and a person referred to—a voiced subject. These are the same conditions as hold for being a person: leaving infancy and becoming a human subject is a process of learning to occupy the spaces of each of the first-, second-, and third-person pronouns, and of understanding oneself as existing at the point of their intersection: I recognize that the 'he' spoken of is the same as the 'I' whom I identify as myself and the 'you' with which I am addressed. Further, I must learn to understand that the 'I', 'you', and 'he' or 'she' refer both exclusively to myself, under certain circumstances, and exclusively to any other person who is in a position to be referred to by them. And, at the same time, I learn that the 'I' is the space of my most intimate being, a metonym of my presence to myself as a person; that the grain of my voice is carried in my speaking this word of myself, my self. For insofar as I experience myself as a person, I am, above all else, a subject of consciousness and will grounded in my bodily being; and that subjectivity is expressed through my occupation of the place of the 'I'. William James writes of this self of experience that it takes place in relation to a field of reference created by the body:

> The individualized self, which I believe to be the only thing properly called self, is a part of the content of the world experienced. The world experienced (otherwise called the 'field of consciousness') comes at all times with our body at its centre, centre of vision, centre of action, centre of interest. Where the body is, is 'here'; when the body acts is 'now'; what the body touches is 'this'; all other things are 'there' and 'then' and 'that'. These words of emphasized position imply a systematization of things with reference to a focus of action and interest which lies in the body... The body is the storm centre, the origin of co-ordinates, the constant place of stress in all that experience-train. Everything

circles round it, and is felt from its point of view. The word 'I', then, is primarily a noun of position, just like 'this' and 'here'...[1]

Yet the 'I' through which we experience and speak the convergence of the world on our bodily position is, in the first instance, no more than a grammatical form, indicating an entity which is in an active relation to a verb. So the crucial question is how the linguistic function is connected to the fact of consciousness, and, more generally, of incarnate selfhood (which we may take to include non-conscious forms of bodily sense and mental activity), while at the same time referring promiscuously to whoever or whatever occupies that place in the sentence and in the context of its use.

One way of exploring this question is to think about what exactly the word 'I' means or designates. Here I follow Maximilian De Gaynesford's account. He expresses the philosophical stakes—and the mutually incompatible underpinnings that the pronoun 'I' provides to them—as follows:

> Descartes had better be right to regard *I* as a referring term and as an expression whose uses are logically guaranteed against reference failure. Otherwise his meditator obtains no release whatsoever from the depths of his methodological doubt. Hume had better be justified in assuming that one can express thoughts using *I* without identifying what is being referred to. Only so can he derive the distinctive feature of his epistemology: that we have no idea corresponding to the self. Kant had better be right that *I* is capable of serving as a completely empty term in the phrase *I think*, one without referential or ascriptive significance. Otherwise his *Transcendental Deduction* cannot account for the possibility of experience.[2]

Gaynesford identifies and argues against a composite of three assumptions that constitute contemporary philosophical orthodoxy about the use of 'I'. They are a Rule Theory, which says that a simple rule is sufficient to give the meaning of the term; an Independence Theory, which says that one can use the term without having to identify who is being referred to; and a Guarantee, which says that the use of 'I' logically guarantees any use of the term against failure to refer. Together these theories respond to the question 'How does *I* refer?' with the answer: 'To the user, directly, and always successfully' (p. 4).

But to say that 'I' refers to the speaker or writer is to attribute meaning to the expression itself rather than its uses; and incorporating the notion of use to say that 'any use of *I* refers to whoever produced it' (p. 2) raises complicated questions about the nature of referring expressions. Descartes's Cogito assumes that 'I' refers to a self, and then infers something about that self (that it thinks and therefore exists): but to say 'I am thinking' may merely be a way of saying that there is some thinking going on. The move from a grammatical to a substantial subject may not

[1] William James, *Studies in Radical Empiricism*, in Bruce Wilshire (ed.), *William James: The Essential Writings* (Albany: SUNY Press, 1971), p. 211, n. 1; misquoted and miscited in Rom Harré, *The Singular Self: An Introduction to the Psychology of Personhood* (London: Sage, 1998), p. 55.

[2] Maximilian De Gaynesford, *I: The Meaning of the First-Person Term* (Oxford: Clarendon Press, 2006), p. 2; hereafter cited in the text.

be warranted. Descartes assumes 'that by the very meaning of the term, any use of *I* is guaranteed to have something, and the right something, to refer to'; and this something must be 'a substance that is entirely distinct from the body and other material objects, simple, indivisible, indestructible, immortal, and numerically identical through time' (p. 13).

This qualification of the subject is successively reduced by subsequent philosophers. Locke takes 'I' to refer to 'something *annexed* to a subject', calling this something 'a *Person*, a thinking item in which ideas are interrelated but which is neither a human being nor any other substance' (p. 13). Hume, more wary still, argues that the referent of 'I' cannot be 'something simple and continued . . . and individual'[3] because such an entity would be observable when one introspects, and he is unable to observe it: all he can observe is perceptions. The term 'I' must therefore be able to be used 'to express thoughts about an item (oneself) without the need to identify what is being referred to'; all one can say of it is that it refers 'to whatever unites a particular series of perceptions, determining them precisely as mine'.[4] For Kant, the 'I' which thinks is not phenomenal, 'for it cannot be intuited or conceived as either a material object with a spatio-temporal location, or a merely spatio-temporal object, or even a purely temporal one. But upon its existence depends the possibility of self-ascribing experiences, itself a precondition of experience under any conception which we can make intelligible to ourselves' (p. 15). But Kant is unable to give an account of the pronoun 'I' that would express this; it is, he says, of indeterminate signification, 'the mere form of consciousness' (p. 15), a completely empty expression.

One way of dealing with this indeterminacy is to deny altogether that 'I' refers; Elizabeth Anscombe extends Wittgenstein's claim not to know what 'I' refers to into a claim that '"I" is neither a name nor another kind of expression whose logical role is to make a reference, *at all*.'[5] But if this seems extreme, we could ask whether pronouns constitute a subclass of names. Gottlob Frege distinguishes two divergent uses of 'I': one as '"the peculiar and primitive way" in which "everyone is presented to himself" and "to no one else"'; and the other a public and communicative use.[6] If 'I' is a kind of name, then it must be a proper name rather than a common name (a noun) because it refers to individuals, not to kinds of individuals; but it differs from proper names in that 'every person can use *I* and refer to himself, while only those called *Abelard* can use that name and refer to themselves' (pp. 19–20). The peculiarity of the personal pronoun is that it seems to refer, but

3 David Hume, *A Treatise of Human Nature*, ed. David Fate Norton and Mary J. Norton (Oxford: Oxford University Press, 2000), 1.4.6 (p. 165) and Appendix (p. 399); cited in Gaynesford, *I: The Meaning of the First-Person Term*, p. 14.

4 Gaynesford, *I: The Meaning of the First-Person Term*, p. 14.

5 G. E. M. Anscombe, 'The First Person', in Quassim Cassam (ed.), *Self-Knowledge* (Oxford: Oxford University Press, 1994), p. 154; cited in Gaynesford, *I: The Meaning of the First-Person Term*, p. 18.

6 Gottlob Frege, 'On Sense and Meaning', trans. Max Black, in P. T. Geach and Max Black (eds), *Translations from the Philosophical Writings of Gottlob Frege* (Oxford: Blackwell, 1980); 'The Thought: A Logical Inquiry', trans. A. and M. Quinton, in P. F. Strawson (ed.), *Philosophical Logic* (Oxford: Oxford University Press, 1967), pp. 24–6; cited in Gaynesford, *I: The Meaning of the First-Person Term*, p. 19.

does so to *varying* referents. It is, in Kripke's terminology, a 'rigid designator', but not a proper name, since its reference is occasional (a factor of a particular context of use) rather than inherent. Alternatively, we could ask whether 'I' is a descriptive term, describing something like 'the subject of the present experience' or 'the person who utters this token', or 'the set of rationally related intentional episodes of which *this* one is a member'.[7] But this is problematic, because, in order to account for the thing described, I must assume an 'I' which precedes the description; such an account is either solipsistic or circular.

The dominant account of 'I', however, regards it as a pure indexical: a referring expression whose meaning is given by a rule specifying that it refers to its user. Thus Strawson, for example, using the case of someone thinking 'I am feeling terrible', writes that

> anyone who is capable of formulating such a thought will have mastered the ordinary practice of personal reference by the use of personal pronouns; and it is a rule of that practice that the first personal pronoun refers, on each occasion of its use, to whoever then uses it. So the fact that we have, in the case imagined, a user, is sufficient to guarantee the reference, and the correct reference for the use.[8]

This argument sets up an unbridgeable gap between 'I', on the one hand, and 'you' and 'he/she', on the other, since on Strawson's account it is only of the first-person pronoun that we can say that its reference is determined by a simple contextual rule (the reference of the second- and third-person pronouns is not given by their use), and thus 'the reference of *You* and *He/She* is not logically guaranteed, and their use to express thoughts is not independent of identification'.[9] Moreover, appeal to the person using 'I' to establish its reference assumes the singularity and simplicity of the instance of enunciation. Gaynesford counters that assumption with the example of a sentence written on the side of a van: 'Phone Oxford 1212 if you wish to complain about me' (p. 42), where the 'user' may be the painter who painted the word 'me', or the owner who caused it to be painted, or whoever happens to be driving the van at the time, regardless of whether or not they are willing to have a complaint made about them. One might say—although Gaynesford doesn't put it like this—that the fact that writing can, in principle, always be displaced and recontextualized (as, more generally, can speech), as well as the inherent complexity of the 'voices' involved in enunciation, mean that no simple rule of this kind will work for any but the simplest acts of speech.

Gaynesford's alternative solution to the problem of how 'I' refers is to say that 'I' is a singular referring expression with varying referents. It is neither a proper name nor a descriptive term, and it is not a 'pure indexical' because 'no rule entirely gives its meaning and sufficiently determines its reference and context' (p. 82). It belongs to the class that linguists call *deictics*: terms which refer to contextually

7 Gaynesford, *I: The Meaning of the First-Person Term*, p. 22.

8 P. F. Strawson, 'The First Person and Others', in Cassam (ed.), *Self-Knowledge*, p. 210; cited in Gaynesford, *I: The Meaning of the First-Person Term*, p. 27.

9 Gaynesford, *I: The Meaning of the First-Person Term*, p. 28.

determined elements in the way that William James specified in the quotation I used earlier: by reference to a time and space and a set of interlocutors located in relation to the coordinates given by my body. Deictic terms cannot answer the 'which' question prior to their use; until they are mobilized in a particular context, 'anyone is a potential referent for *I* or *You*; any male/female for *He/She*' (p. 113). Deictic terms discharge their referential function in their use, and they do so, Gaynesford argues, by making a particular individual referentially *salient*. So 'a *Deictic Term* is one whose uses refer by action of a particular sort; namely *by making an individual salient* in the extra-sentential context' (p. 126). Salience is determined in one of three ways: either there is only one individual who could be referred to; or one individual is the most likely candidate for being referred to; or one individual is pointed out; and in the 'central spoken uses of *I*—where the utterer is the referent and salient as such'—'it is sufficient . . . simply to engage in the act of using the term for its referential function to be achieved' (p. 130). The discrimination of deictic reference requires attention to the circumstances of utterance; and this 'extra-sentential context' involves a complex of features of which we may not be consciously aware, including 'the layout of objects in the environment, the context of antecedent discourse, the actual demonstrata of the utterer's bodily movements, and communication-constraints like principles of economy and relevance' (p. 144): not to mention (Gaynesford doesn't) such things as paratextual cues, genre conventions, and cultural assumptions about personal identity.

Gaynesford's solution is at once satisfying and yet, in a sense, no more than the starting point for a new set of questions. Two problems in particular strike me about his analysis. The first is that, despite his stated intention not to privilege the speech situation over that of writing or performance, he does, in fact, work with a notion of the 'centrality' of 'spoken uses' (p. 130), and thus, by implication, the marginality of written uses of the first-person pronoun. By the notion of 'use', too, he explicitly means '*genuine* use: the competent employment of an expression in an utterance which means something by sincere, reflective, competent, and truthful interlocutors who are also trusting (i.e. they take their partners to be sincere, reflective, competent, and truthful)' (p. 7). As Derrida puts it in his exchange with John Searle, this is to write 'as though literature, theater, deceit, infidelity, hypocrisy, infelicity, parasitism, and the simulation of real life were not part of real life'.[10] (Nor, I should add, is Gaynesford at all interested in the possibility that the force of the 'I' might vary historically and culturally: in the way that, for example, the autobiographical 'I' in the Middle Ages had a far greater latitude than it has today.)[11]

The second problem lies in Gaynesford's reference to 'the extra-sentential context' as the relevant guide to the use of deictic terms. The term is left only vaguely defined. Might it refer to other sentences? Perhaps. Does it refer to a physical context? But this then leaves it unclear what the relevant context is for written

[10] Jacques Derrida, 'Limited Inc a b c . . .', trans. Samuel Weber, in *Limited Inc* (Evanston, IL: Northwestern University Press, 1988), p. 90.

[11] Cf. Leo Spitzer, 'Note on the Poetic and the Empirical "I" in Medieval Authors', *Traditio* 4 (1946), pp. 414–22.

uses of 'I' (the 'I, here, now' of writing refers to no determinate person, place, or time); his definition abstracts physicality from the meanings by which it is organized; and it makes no mention of how the structure of meanings that does the organizing of the 'extra-sentential context' might, in its turn, be organized. What is missing to explicate this term—which is, after all, the key to the book's argument—is something like a concept of *discourse*: the organization of meanings at a level higher than the sentence and in accordance with *typified* contexts of situation where the subjects of utterances are never merely individuals (they wear the masks appropriate to their roles). It is only by means of some such concept that we could approach the conventions that determine the kind of statement we are dealing with, the status of its utterer, the layers of enunciation that might be involved (in citation or mockery or in theatrical performance, for example), and the blurring of enunciation in complex forms of utterance such as free indirect discourse. And all of these matters are central, of course, to thinking about the mode of existence of fictional characters.

II

In order to begin to untangle these questions of deixis, the pronoun system, and the concept of discourse—and the concepts of self, person, and character that they entail—I want to turn now to the way these categories are understood in the work of the French linguist Émile Benveniste, who explored them in a remarkable series of papers written between 1946 and 1969. The first of these, 'Relationships of Person in the Verb', begins by speaking of the tripartite classification of the persons of the verb inherited from Greek grammar, in which 'the inflected verbal forms make up the *prosopa*, the personae, the "figurations" under which the verbal notion is realized'.[12] All languages possessing the verb form distinguish three persons of the verb in the singular, in the plural, and sometimes in the dual. These relationships are, however, lexical, not referential: they say nothing about the logical necessity of the category or of the relations it establishes between the three persons, and it is this set of relations that Benveniste proposes to investigate.

As a first approach to the content of the linguistic distinction of persons, he notes that the Arab grammarians distinguish between 'the one who speaks', 'the one who is addressed', and 'the one who is absent' (p. 197). This categorization reveals the lack of homogeneity of the classification, since it sets the relation of 'I' and 'you' conceptually apart from the third ('absent') person. Benveniste explains the disparity as follows:

> In the first two persons, there are both a person involved and a discourse concerning that person. 'I' designates the one who speaks and at the same time implies an

[12] Émile Benveniste, 'Relationships of Person in the Verb', in *Problems in General Linguistics*, trans. Mary Elizabeth Meek (Coral Gables, FL: University of Miami Press, 1971), p. 195; hereafter cited in the text. Here and elsewhere I have silently romanized the Greek alphabet.

> utterance about 'I'; in saying 'I', I cannot *not* be speaking of myself. In the second person, 'you' is necessarily designated by 'I' and cannot be thought of outside a situation set up by starting with 'I'; and at the same time, 'I' states something as the predicate of 'you'. But in the third person a predicate is really stated, only it is outside 'I–you'; this form is thus an exception to the relationship by which 'I' and 'you' are specified. Consequently, the legitimacy of this form as a 'person' is to be questioned. (p. 197)

Let me note, without yet drawing out the consequences of these comments, that this argument supposes that the category of person is a function of presence in the situation of enunciation (which is assumed to be face to face);[13] that it imports the non-linguistic criterion of 'real' personhood into its analysis; that it accepts the referentiality of 'I' and 'you' (which might, however, be fictions or citations); and that it disregards the possibility that all acts of predication of a third person might have the form: '[I say that] p', which would mean that the third person is not, in fact, external to the 'I'–'you' relation. The consequence that Benveniste draws from his argument is that in the third person, 'the variable and properly "personal" element of these denominations is... lacking', which means that 'the "third person" is not a "person"; it is really the verbal form whose function is to express the *non-person*'.[14] Further, the first and second person forms are characterized by their 'oneness': 'the "I" who states, the "you" to whom I addresses himself are unique each time. But "he" can be an infinite number of subjects—or none' (p. 199). Again, the logic of this escapes me: each and every person of the verb is, to use Roman Jakobson's term, a shifter:[15] a term that can be occupied by 'an infinite number of subjects'—although Benveniste is, I think, correct to say that the third person can also be occupied by *no* subject: that it is the sole form used in so-called 'impersonal' expressions like 'it is raining'. This is also what allows it to be used as a form of address in expressions of respect or contempt, which equally depersonalize the speech situation.

The corollary of the argument that the third person is non-personal is that any *person* who is not 'I' is, by definition, 'you'—'especially, but not necessarily, the person being addressed. "You" can thus be defined as "the non-I person"' (p. 201).[16] The two terms exist within a symmetrical and reciprocal 'correlation of personality' (p. 200).[17] At the same time, however, there is a fundamental *a*symmetry between them, which Benveniste calls the 'correlation of subjectivity':

[13] Cf. Barbara Johnson, *Persons and Things* (Cambridge, MA: Harvard University Press, 2008), p. 6: for Benveniste, '[T]he notion of "person" has something to do with presence at the scene of speech and seems to inhere in the notion of *address*.'

[14] Benveniste, 'Relationships of Person in the Verb', pp. 197–8.

[15] Roman Jakobson, 'Shifters, Verbal Categories, and the Russian Verb', in *Selected Writings II: Word and Language* (The Hague: Mouton, 1971), pp. 130–47. The term was originally used by Otto Jespersen in *Language: Its Nature, Development, and Origin* (1923; rpt. London: Allen & Unwin, 1959).

[16] The English translation incorrectly (and confusingly) runs the last two sentences together. I have altered the translation to accord with the French text in Émile Benveniste, *Problèmes de linguistique générale* (Paris: Gallimard, 1966), p. 232.

[17] Benveniste, 'Relationships of Person in the Verb', p. 200.

> What differentiates 'I' from 'you' is first of all the fact of being, in the case of 'I', *internal* to the statement and external to 'you'; but external in a manner that does not suppress the human reality of dialogue. The second person... is a form which assumes or calls up a fictive 'person' and thereby institutes an actual relationship between 'I' and this quasi-person; moreover, 'I' is always transcendent with respect to you. When I get out of 'myself' in order to establish a living relationship with a being, of necessity I encounter or I posit a 'you', who is the only imaginable 'person' outside of me. These qualities of internality and transcendence properly belong to 'I' and are reversed in 'you'. One could thus define 'you' as the *non-subjective person*, in contrast to the *subjective person* that 'I' represents; and these two 'persons' are together opposed to the 'non-person' form (= he). (p. 201)

The uniqueness and the subjectivity inherent in the 'I' mean that there can be no genuinely plural form of the first person: 'I' allows of no multiplication, and the 'we' form can thus only mean 'I plus you' or 'I plus they'. Many languages have distinctive inclusive and exclusive forms to express those two types of conjunction of the 'I' with the 'non-I'. The exception to this rule is in the undifferentiated first person used by royalty or by orators, where '"we" is not a quantified or multiplied "I"; it is an "I" expanded beyond the strict limits of the person, enlarged and at the same time amorphous' (p. 203).

Benveniste's opposition of two forms of linguistic person to a non-personal form has important precedents, particularly in the work of the psychologist Wilhelm Wundt, for whom the third person has 'an essentially deviant position vis-à-vis the first and second person. Only the first and second person are persons'.[18] (Franz Boas, by contrast, writes that 'logically, our three persons of the pronoun are based on the two concepts of self and not-self, the second of which is subdivided, according to the needs of speech, into the two concepts of person addressed and person spoken of':[19] the first person is thus opposed in his schema to the second/third person.) Paul Forchheimer develops Wundt's argument (together with similar arguments made by Bloomfield and Buehler) as follows:

> The first person, referring to the speaker, is subjective, even though one might make a factual statement about oneself. It refers to the subject, i.e. actor of the act of speech. If, at the same time, he is the grammatical or logical subject of the statement, then his announcement about himself is even more subjective. He originates the action. If the speaker is the object of the action, while still talking about himself, he is not describing what he does but what is done to him. The action is decided by someone else. The form, therefore, is less subjective.[20]

This seems to me to make clear something that is also at work in Benveniste's argument: a conflation of the linguistic with the philosophical (and indeed

[18] '...eine wesentlich abweichende Stellung gegenüber der ersten und zweiten Person. Nur die erste und zweite Person sind Personen.' Wilhelm Wundt, *Völkerpsychologie*, vol. II: *Die Sprache* (Leipzig, 1911), p. 141. Cited in Paul Forchheimer, *The Category of Person in Language* (Berlin: De Gruyter, 1953), p. 5.

[19] Franz Boas, *Handbook of American Indian Languages*, vol. I (Washington: Smithsonian Institution, Bureau of American Ethnology, 1911), pp. 39–40.

[20] Forchheimer, *The Category of Person in Language*, p. 29.

psychological) senses of the word 'subject', just as Benveniste similarly conflates the grammatical term 'person' with its sense of 'human being'.

In a later essay, on 'The Nature of Pronouns', Benveniste returns to the question of person, and here he deals more explicitly with the concept of deixis. 'I' and 'you' belong to the series of deictic indicators located in relation to the here and now of speaking, and they refer differently each time they are used, according to the relationship set up in each instance between 'the indicator (of person, time, place, object shown, etc.) and the *present* instance of discourse'.[21] The 'I' that speaks is thus double—instantiated both as referent and as referee: '*I* signifies "the person who is uttering the present instance of the discourse containing *I*". This instance is unique by definition and has validity only in its uniqueness' (p. 218). The reality to which these personal pronouns refer is thus solely 'a "reality of discourse"': deictic forms 'do not refer to "reality" or to "objective" positions in space or time but to the utterance, unique each time, that contains them, and thus they reflect their own use' (p. 219).[22] They are empty signs which are filled by their employment in discourse and are correlated with a range of demonstrative, adjectival, and adverbial forms, and with agreement of the aspect, tense, gender, and person of the verb with the instance of discourse. Lacking reference to anything other than their own use, they claim nothing and cannot be judged as true or false. This 'reality of discourse,' writes Benveniste, 'is a very strange thing': the uniqueness of the instance of discourse guarantees its value, whereas 'if I perceive two successive instances of discourse containing *I*, uttered in the same voice, nothing guarantees to me that one of them is not a reported discourse, a quotation in which *I* could be imputed to another'.[23]

But nothing, of course, guarantees that *any* instance of 'I' is not being cited or imitated, consciously or not: that the 'I' is fully and authentically my own. 'When Berma plays *Phèdre*, who is saying "I"?'[24] Nothing guarantees it because the language that I speak or write or recite is already full of other voices, is never 'uniquely' mine. Nothing guarantees, for example, that the 'I' in 'If I perceive two successive instances of discourse' is that of Émile Benveniste, since he could as easily have written 'you' or 'one': the instance is not unique. Indeed, Benveniste undoes his argument in the very act of making it by his assumption that repetition is not inherent in those unique instances.

The third-person form, Benveniste continues, by contrast to the first and second, refers not to the instance of discourse but to someone or something external to it which 'can always be provided with an objective reference'.[25] It is characterized by its property of '(1) combining with any object reference [*n'importe*

[21] Émile Benveniste, 'The Nature of Pronouns', in *Problems in General Linguistics*, p. 219; hereafter cited in the text.

[22] The English translation has 'proper use', which is surely the wrong translation of 'leur propre emploi' (*Problèmes de linguistique générale*, p. 254) in this instance.

[23] Benveniste, 'The Nature of Pronouns', p. 218.

[24] Philippe Lejeune, *On Autobiography*, trans. Katherine Leary (Minneapolis: University of Minnesota Press, 1989), p. 9.

[25] Benveniste, 'The Nature of Pronouns', p. 221.

quelle référence d'objet], (2) never being reflective of the instance of discourse, (3) admitting of a sometimes rather large number of pronominal or demonstrative variants, and (4) not being compatible with the paradigm of referential terms like *here, now*, etc.' (p. 222). It belongs, in short, to the system that Benveniste calls *histoire* and which he contrasts with the system of *discours*. The system of *discours* is understood to mean 'every utterance assuming a speaker and a hearer, and in the speaker, the intention of influencing the other in some way. It is primarily every variety of oral discourse',[26] or of writing that imitates oral discourse, and in its use of the perfect tense it 'creates a living connection between the past event and the present'.[27] In the system of *histoire*, however, 'no one speaks...; the events seem to narrate themselves. The fundamental tense is the aorist, which is the tense of the event outside the person of a narrator'.[28]

We shall return a little later to this notion of an utterance which has no speaker. For the moment, though, I want to follow the argument about person and deixis through Benveniste's examination, in two further essays, of the relation between the instance of discourse and the force of performative speech acts.

'It is in and through language,' Benveniste writes, 'that man constitutes himself as a *subject*, because language alone establishes the concept of "ego" in reality, in *its* reality which is that of being.'[29] This subjectivity is 'the capacity of the speaker to posit himself as "subject".' This capacity is different from the feeling of being a self, which is a secondary phenomenon; it is, rather, 'the psychic unity that transcends the totality of the actual experience it assembles and that makes the permanence of the consciousness', and is 'the emergence in being of a fundamental property of language. "Ego" is he who *says* "ego". That is where we see the foundation of subjectivity, which is determined by the linguistic status of "person" '.[30] It is thus in occupying the 'empty' persons of the verb or the personal pronouns, with their accompanying deictic indicators, including the self-referential temporality of discourse, that one becomes a subject in the full sense of the word.

This discursive constitution of the subject is exemplified in the workings of performatives: speech acts such as 'I swear' or 'I promise', which accomplish an action by means of the act itself. More precisely, performative consequence follows from 'the fact that the instance of discourse that contains the verb establishes the act at the same time that it sets up the subject'.[31] By contrast, the third-person form—'he swears', 'he promises'—would merely describe a performative action and would itself be without performative consequence. In a later essay, however, this conclusion is modified: there can indeed be effective performatives couched in the third

[26] Émile Benveniste, 'The Correlations of Tense in the French Verb', in *Problems in General Linguistics*, p. 208.

[27] Benveniste, 'The Correlations of Tense in the French Verb', p. 210.

[28] Benveniste, 'The Correlations of Tense in the French Verb', p. 208.

[29] Émile Benveniste, 'Subjectivity in Language', in *Problems in General Linguistics*, p. 224; here and in the next but one sentence I have modified the English translation which has 'the being'.

[30] Benveniste, 'Subjectivity in Language', p. 224.

[31] Benveniste, 'Subjectivity in Language', p. 230.

person: 'Passengers are requested to cross the line by the footbridge only'; 'The chair in Botany is declared vacant'; 'The meeting is open'.[32] In all of these cases, however, 'the utterance in the third person can... be reconverted into a first person and again assume its typical form'.[33] The reference to a speaker is necessary in order to satisfy the criterion that the utterance carry the authority or commitment of the person who utters it, and that it do so in conditions that are unique: if it is repeated it becomes a simple statement of fact, a constative. An utterance will have performative force, then, to the extent that it '*denominates* the act performed because Ego pronounces a formula containing a verb in the first person of the present: "I *declare* the meeting adjourned"; "I *swear* to tell the truth". Hence a performative utterance must name the spoken performance as well as its performer'.[34]

A performative, then, is an act which is self-referential; an act which is unique; an act which creates the subject in the same movement by which it translates his presence into consequence; and an act whose 'typical' form is that of the first person. Benveniste is fully aware of the ramifications of his analysis: these questions go to the heart of what it means to be a self-identical subject—a subject in the full philosophical sense, and in the legal sense of a person with the capacity to commit themselves to fulfil a promise or a contract.

III

The promise is the exemplary performative speech act, the one to which, for example, John Searle devotes the whole of his analysis of illocutionary acts;[35] from it are derived all of those other commissive acts—the underwriting of a contract, the commitment to another in marriage, the ensuring of commercial trust in a promissory note or in fiduciary currency (bearing the legend 'I promise to pay the bearer')—which involve an affirmation of my integrity as a natural or corporate person, and the continuation of my will through future time. It is the obverse of moral and legal responsibility: that is, my liability for acts committed at an earlier stage of my life, even when—because I have changed morally, or have undergone a conversion or even a physically induced change of personality, or simply no longer have any sympathy with my former self—I am now in some important sense a 'different person'. Yet the law, and my sense of moral responsibility, hold me accountable for those acts: the legal subject 'cannot avoid the legal imputation of a causal relation between past acts and present responsibility'.[36]

More generally, the capacity to take responsibility for the fulfilment of an action in the future is one of the conditions for the historical emergence of the key figure

[32] Émile Benveniste, 'Analytic Philosophy and Language', in *Problems in General Linguistics*, pp. 233, 235, 236.

[33] Benveniste, 'Analytic Philosophy and Language', p. 235.

[34] Benveniste, 'Analytic Philosophy and Language', p. 237.

[35] John Searle, *Speech Acts: An Essay in the Philosophy of Language* (Cambridge: Cambridge University Press, 1969), pp. 54–71.

[36] Peter Goodrich, *Reading the Law: A Critical Introduction to Legal Method and Techniques* (Oxford: Blackwell, 1986), p. 204.

of bourgeois modernity, the subject of contract: the subject, that is, who freely enters into and can be expected to observe a commitment to which he pledges his word, and whose civil status is grounded in that freedom.[37]

This fiction of a self which is continuous and causally self-present through time directly contradicts Hume's observation of the discontinuity of the self posited as the unity of its perceptions, and challenges our ordinary sense of the discontinuities in our being and our intentions. Nietzsche's account of promising in *The Genealogy of Morals* is premised on precisely the fictional nature of this continuity: promising is not a mere passive continuation of the present into the future, an inability to shake off a pledge that has been made, but rather 'an active wishing not to be done with it, a continuing to will what has once been willed, a veritable "memory of the will" ',[38] which can survive all the supervening events and even new acts of will. But in order for this 'long chain of the will' to stretch without breaking between one point in time and another, the person who promises

> must first have learned to separate necessary from accidental acts; to think causally; to see distant things as though they were near at hand; to distinguish means from ends. In short, he must have become not only calculating but himself calculable, regular even to his own perception [*überhaupt rechnen, berechnen können—wie muß dazu der Mensch selbst vorerst* berechenbar, regelmäßig, notwendig *geworden sein*], if he is to stand pledge for his own future as a guarantor does.[39]

This shaping of the character of the one who promises is founded in a long, cruel, and violent history of 'breeding' [*heranzüchten*],[40] which results in the possibility of human 'responsibility': pain breeds consciousness of guilt, which is historically grounded in the notion of debt (Nietzsche here plays on the German *Schuld*, 'guilt', and *schulden*, 'to be indebted').[41] The equivalence between the two 'arose in the contractual relation between creditor and debtor, which is as old as the notion of "legal subjects" itself and which in its turn points back to the basic practices of purchase, sale, barter, and trade'.[42] Here we might take note of the etymology of the term 'responsibility' in the Latin *spondere*, which, according to Giorgio Agamben, means the giving of one's own body as a pledge in a contractual arrangement;[43] Nietzsche alludes to that etymology in the passage above. But we might also note that the calculability of the self on which promising is predicated also requires the calculability of the future; and that calculability—the notion of a temporality which unfolds regularly in ways that can be foreseen—works differently in

[37] Cf. Morton J. Horwitz, 'The Triumph of Contract', in *The Transformation of American Law, 1780–1860* (Cambridge, MA: Harvard University Press, 1977).

[38] Friedrich Nietzsche, *The Genealogy of Morals*, trans. Francis Golffing (New York: Doubleday, 1956), p. 190.

[39] Nietzsche, *The Genealogy of Morals*; the German text is taken from Friedrich Nietzsche, *Zur Genealogie der Moral, Werke*, vol. III, ed. K. Schlechta (1954; rpt. Munich: Hanser, 1969), p. 246.

[40] Nietzsche, *The Genealogy of Morals*, p. 189; *Zur Genealogie der Moral*, p. 245.

[41] Nietzsche, *The Genealogy of Morals*, p. 194; *Zur Genealogie der Moral*, p. 250.

[42] Nietzsche, *The Genealogy of Morals*, p. 195; *Zur Genealogie der Moral*, p. 251.

[43] Giorgio Agamben, *Remnants of Auschwitz: The Witness and the Archive*, trans. Daniel Heller-Roazen (New York: Zone Books, 2002), pp. 21–2.

different cultures. Promising is perhaps a universal phenomenon; but in societies governed by contractual relationships it requires a particular kind of work on the self ('he must have become... himself calculable') which goes not just to a legal bond but to the heart of moral character, and which is bound up with those technologies of control of the future (planning, the setting of targets, or insurance and hedging, for example) that bind together the two halves of Nietzsche's phrase: 'not only calculating but himself calculable'. This self which promises, which calculates its own regular extension into a future which can itself be controlled, is a self abstracted from contingency and time.

The continuity of the self, Paul Ricoeur argues, can take two forms; he calls them *ipse* and *idem*, and they designate two forms of identity through time, the former grounded in variation and the latter in an essential sameness. These two forms of self-identity come together in one of the modes in which the self persists through time, that of character, by which Ricoeur means 'the set of distinctive marks which permit the reidentification of a human individual as being the same'.[44] Character is a set of acquired and enduring dispositions, what Aristotle calls *hexis*, and it is linked to habit: 'Habit gives a history to character, but this is a history in which sedimentation tends to cover over the innovation which preceded it, even to the point of abolishing the latter' (p. 121). But it is also formed by a set of identifications with others whom a person admires and values. Character is thus made up, on the one hand, of a dialectic of innovation and sedimentation, and, on the other, of otherness and internalization; and Ricoeur extrapolates from this 'stable pole of character' (in the sense of 'moral character') the narrative conception of story-character, and thereby identifies selfhood as a narrative construct. The other, and more positive way, in which the self persists in time is through keeping one's word. This mode of identity is the opposite of character and habit because it involves a choice ('The continuity of character is one thing, the constancy of friendship is quite another') (p. 123), and I take it to be equivalent to promising: it is 'keeping one's word in faithfulness to the word that has been given' (p. 123). It involves a moral commitment to the other (of whom the friend is the central example), and thus a stabilization of the self in that commitment; and an imaginative projection of the self into the future, grounded in 'the obligation to safeguard the institution of language and to respond to the trust that the other places in my faithfulness' (p. 124).

For Ricoeur, as for Benveniste, promising is thus an act which projects the self into a future on the basis of its presence to itself in the act of enunciation. It requires, in Nietzsche's phrase, a 'memory of the will' which repeats my formative intention continuously from moment to moment. Yet Derrida's critique of Austin's original formulation of the working of illocutionary and perlocutionary acts, of which the performative act of promising is so central an example, as well as his subsequent polemical engagement with Searle, neatly clarify and undo

[44] Paul Ricoeur, *Oneself as Another*, trans. Kathleen Blamey (Chicago: University of Chicago Press, 1992), p. 119; hereafter cited in the text.

the assumptions underpinning it—which are equally at work in Benveniste's and Ricoeur's accounts—namely, that the performative act is a unique and unrepeatable event; that illocutionary force is grounded in the manifestation of presence and intention in the act of speech; that this manifestation of the presence of a singular self occurs in relation to a context of enunciation which is equally singular; that this self takes the form of a 'plenitude of intentional meaning',[45] a 'fulfilled and actualized intentionality, adequate to itself and to its contents';[46] and that subjectivity is formed in such acts performed in speech and face to face with the other in relation to whom my self is formed. Against the argument for the uniqueness of the subject enunciated in the act of speech, and of its surrogate in writing, the signature, Derrida demonstrates, on the one hand, the internal division of the 'I' (the 'I' who promises repeats the 'I' of the formula 'I promise'; and that formula signals that I speak by virtue of an office, an authorized capacity) and, on the other, the necessary repeatability—the iterability—of the signature, which, in order to produce its effects, 'must be able to be detached from the present and singular intention of its production'.[47]

IV

Charles Fillmore gives the following example of uncertainty in the application of deictic reference: you are a young lady who has just been the recipient of a wolf whistle. You want to reprimand the wolf, but it's not clear who he is or indeed if you are the intended target, and 'to turn around and scowl is to acknowledge that you believe the message was intended for you, and that may be taken as presumptuous'.[48] The uncertainty of reference applies both to the person who whistled and to the young lady, and in both cases we know the *kind* of person who fits the description; it's just that we don't know the particular instances that would fit those generic slots. The example closely resembles Louis Althusser's parable of the interpellation by which we are constituted as subjects: a policeman calls out 'Hey, you there!' in the street and we turn around, (mis)recognizing ourselves as having been called.[49] In each case the form of address—the whistle, the word 'you'—designates in the first place an empty slot, and only after that the particular person who fills it, who recognizes themself in it, who is made salient by it, and who thereby anchors the address in a particular time and place.

Moreover, there is no *simple* sense in which that person is anything other than a fact of language. For language, and the body through which it speaks or towards which it is oriented, are not in a relation of simple externality to each other. Two

[45] Derrida, 'Limited Inc a b c...', p. 58.
[46] Derrida, 'Limited Inc a b c...', p. 64.
[47] Derrida, 'Signature Event Context', in *Limited Inc.*, p. 20.
[48] Charles Fillmore, *Lectures on Deixis* (Stanford: CSLI Publications, 1997), p. 59.
[49] Louis Althusser, 'Ideology and Ideological State Apparatuses', in *Lenin and Philosophy and Other Essays*, trans. Ben Brewster (New York: Monthly Review Press, 1971), p. 163.

recent grammars of English set up a clear contrast between ways of envisaging the anchoring of language use in persons. The *Comprehensive Grammar of the English Language* (1985) defines deixis as referring to 'the extralinguistic situation': the time, place, and participants in the act of speech are external to it.[50] *The Cambridge Grammar of the English Language* (2002), by contrast, says of deixis that 'the reference of certain kinds of expression is determined in relation to features of the utterance-act: the time, the place, and the participants, i.e. those with the role of speaker or addressee'.[51] Time, place, and participants are here understood as 'features' of the act of enunciation. The reference of 'I' is not to something outside language (an 'extra-sentential context') but precisely to that act in which I pronounce the word 'I'. This is why Jakobson defines shifters (the 'persons' of the verb, the personal pronouns, and, more generally, all deictic markers) by their self-referentiality: they are 'code'—lexical items—referring to the 'message'.[52]

Agamben similarly argues that the 'pure shifter "I"... is absolutely without any substantiality and content other than its mere reference to the event of discourse... *The subject of enunciation is composed of discourse and exists in discourse alone*'.[53] But in taking this position Agamben misses something of the complexity of this apparently disembodied figure of speech. Discursive persons are also points of orientation in space and time, and this orientation is given by the speaking body: the deictic adverbs of time and place, the demonstratives, and the mood and tenses of the verb are organized by reference to the location of the body of the speaker or the addressee at a particular time and place (there are complications of this schema in written language, as we shall see). Fillmore suggests that, in addition to three modes of spatial dimensionality (simple location, or 'at'; surface location, or 'on'; and interiority, or 'in'), our sense of the world is structured by three axes of spatial orientation (which may be a function of the vestibular system controlled by the semi-circular canals in the inner ears of human beings): up/down, front/back, and right/left. Each of these can be used deictically: 'left' means 'to my left' unless I correct for your perspective; 'in front of' is relative both to where I stand in relation to an object and where that object stands in relation to a reference object; 'up' depends on where I'm looking from. Similarly, deictic uses of measures of time may involve either non-calendric units (*yesterday, today, now*) or calendric units with deictic markers such as *this* (Tuesday) or *next* (year), which refer to the present of enunciation. Certain verbs are intrinsically deictic: *come* and *bring* indicate motion towards the speaker, *go* and *take* indicate motion away.[54] And the tenses of the verb are staged with reference to the time of enunciation (again, this is complicated in some forms of written language).

[50] Randolph Quirk, Sidney Greenbaum, Geoffrey Leech, and Jan Svartik, *A Comprehensive Grammar of the English Language* (Harlow: Longman, 1985), p. 374.

[51] Rodney Huddleston and Geoffrey K. Pullum, *The Cambridge Grammar of the English Language* (Cambridge: Cambridge University Press, 2002), p. 1451.

[52] Jakobson, 'Shifters, Verbal Categories, and the Russian Verb', pp. 131–2.

[53] Agamben, *Remnants of Auschwitz*, p. 116; Agamben's emphasis.

[54] Fillmore, *Lectures on Deixis*, pp. 82–3.

The 'ease of reference' that Gaynesford notes as a feature of spoken uses of 'I'[55]—the apparently direct coincidence of utterer and referent—should not, however, mislead us into understanding the 'I' as a substantial, embodied particular, a self-identical presence. The person referred to is, as we have seen, the occupant of a semantic place; the space and time for which he or she serves as a reference point are constructed in dense networks of metaphor, and the body that orients that person in space and time is imagined and positioned through these networks; the 'now' and 'here' of enunciation can be shifted in linguistic embeddings from one time to another, one place to another, and, through this reference point, operate a set of rules about social roles and authority, linguistic decorum, and the conditions under which acts of speech may effectively take place.

The 'I' is structurally riven, positional and alienable yet embodied, a reference point in time and space and yet movable from discursive point to point. Part of this dividedness of the 'I' has to do with its lability: Erving Goffman has drawn attention to the changes of 'footing' in which speakers' projected selves are shifted from moment to moment as we manage the way our utterances are produced or received.[56] 'Projected selves' is one way of talking about the *personae* of the speech process, and Goffman's paper is a critique of an orthodox linguistic model of face-to-face interaction which 'takes global folk categories (like speaker and hearer) for granted instead of decomposing them into smaller, analytically coherent elements' (p. 6). The process of interaction, he writes, is never just talk but involves sight and touch, the display of attention or disattention, other activities (playing cards, passing the salt, working on a car), and a frame structured by ritual brackets and an ongoing work of maintenance. The hearer may have the status of a ratified participant, but other 'adventitious participants' (p. 8) may also be present and may be deliberately or accidentally addressed. There may be secondary conversations going on, weaving in and out of the 'main' conversation. In the case of 'platform monologues' interaction between speaker and hearers will take a different form, and the audience may be either live or mediated—in which case the recipients are 'imagined' (p. 12) (but so, in a sense, is every participant in an exchange, as each one makes judgements about the other's roles and understandings).

The speaker is, in the first place, a 'talking machine', the acoustic *animator* of speech, the counterpart of the recipient, 'two terms cut from the same cloth, not social roles in the full sense so much as functional nodes in a communication system' (p. 17). Second, the speaker is an *author*, 'someone who has selected the sentiments that are being expressed and the words in which they are encoded' (p. 17). And finally, the speaker is 'a *principal* (in the legalistic sense)': that is, 'someone whose position is established by the words that are spoken, someone whose beliefs have been told, someone who has committed himself to what the words say'; in this case the speaker is not so much a body or a mind as 'a person active in some particular social identity or role, some special capacity as a member of a group, office, category, relationship, association, or whatever, some socially

[55] Gaynesford, *I: The Meaning of the First-Person Term*, p. 131.

[56] Erving Goffman, 'Footing', *Semiotica* 25: 1/2 (1979), p. 5; hereafter cited in the text.

based source of self-identification' (p. 17); and, of course, this capacity may shift in the course of an interaction. Fillmore discusses the grammatical implications of this capacity in his account of what he calls 'social deixis', including devices for person-marking such as pronouns; separation of speech levels; and linguistic markers of status differences.[57]

These notions—animator, author, principal—make up the 'production format' of the utterance, but other layerings appear within the utterance itself. Crucially, what's spoken may not be the speaker's 'own' words: we can recite or read aloud; we can speak for someone else and in their words, as when we read a deposition or provide a simultaneous translation, with our words standing in for theirs. But, writes Goffman, 'the tricky problem is that often when we do engage in *fresh talk*, that is, the extemporaneous, ongoing formulation of a text under the exigency of immediate response to our current situation, it is not true to say that we always speak our own words and ourself take the position to which these words attest'.[58] The 'I' of utterance is thus further divided whenever our words are more than the simplest of statements (like 'Shut the window') which seem directly to express the will or desire of the 'addressing self'—and even these utterances still express a particular social capacity and the authority that derives from it. Many, and perhaps most, utterances, however, 'are not constructed in this fashion. Rather, as speaker, we represent ourselves through the offices of a personal pronoun, typically "I", and it is thus a *figure*—a figure in a statement that serves as the agent, a protagonist in a *described* scene, someone, after all, who belongs to the world that is spoken about, not the world in which the speaking occurs' (p. 19).

This non-self-identity of the 'I' is most clearly evident in forms like 'I went' or 'I shall go', where we represent ourselves 'through the offices of a personal pronoun', and thus as a figure referring to 'a social capacity we no longer enjoy and an identity we no longer claim' (p. 20); but the same principle holds, by extension, for 'I am' or 'I do', in which the instance of enunciation is subtly different from the referent. Goffman gives the example of the qualification of statements by modal verbs such as 'I wish', 'I think', 'I could', 'I hope', and so on, which introduce a distance between the figure and our statement, and 'indeed, a double distance is produced, for presumably some part of us unconditionally stands behind our conditional utterance, else we would have to say something like "I think that I think..."' (p. 20). The most radical extension of this argument is the claim made by some linguists (Goffman cites John Ross) 'that *any* unadorned utterance implies a higher performative verb and a pronoun, e.g., "I say", "aver", "demand", etc., the implication being that all statements are made by figures mentioned or implied, not by living individuals':[59] that all the selves performed or implied by language are figures of speech, figures of the self, which may, in turn, be embedded in multiple reflexive

57 Fillmore, *Lectures on Deixis*, p. 112.

58 Goffman, 'Footing', p. 18.

59 Goffman, 'Footing', p. 26, n. 8, referring to John Robert Ross, 'On Declarative Sentences', in R. Jacobs and P. Rosenbaum (eds), *Readings in English Transformational Grammar* (Waltham, MA: Ginn and Co., 1970).

layerings, not only in the direct and indirect quotation of others or ourselves but in mockery, in 'taking off' another person, in acting, in the citation of adages or scraps of unattributed speech, in innuendo, and in all the 'keyings' by which we shift from one register to another; from one figuring of the self to another.

V

Spoken discourse provides an apparently simple paradigm of deixis: a coincidence between the speaking subject and the subject of the statement. It offers a guarantee that language is grounded in a situation and a set of participants who are concrete, particular, and singular. We have seen this simple account become more complicated, the 'I' a figure which is, nevertheless, at the same time a point of reference in space and time—but one which is alienable, transposable, never simply present to itself. This is to say that the way deictic markers work in speech is both different from and similar to the way they work in writing.

Fillmore's joking example of 'the worst possible case for a totally unanchored occasion-sentence' is that of a message in a bottle reading: 'Meet me here at noon tomorrow with a stick about this big'.[60] Spoken language would fill these empty slots with a physically present speaker anchoring the place and time, and with a gesture giving content to the deictic phrase 'this big'. Writing of the kind that Benveniste calls *discours*, which imitates many of the features of oral discourse, can reproduce some but not all of these deictic markers (it has difficulty with demonstratives, although it can make use of them in quoted speech.) I can write: 'I heard the blackbird sing yesterday', but not: 'I saw *this* one yesterday'. I can also write: 'Mary heard the blackbird sing yesterday', but only in writing that supposes a relation to the time of utterance: in the system of 'impersonal' narrative that Benveniste calls *histoire* I would write: 'Mary heard the blackbird sing the day before', except in those cases where Mary's point of reference and intonation are built into the sentence and 'colour' it (so-called free indirect discourse, which I shall discuss shortly), where *yesterday* would again become appropriate.

For genres such as the letter, some, but not all, of the deictic markers resemble those of speech. The complication here is that, just as in spoken discourse the deictic centre can switch from the first to the second person ('I'll *come* to your house'), so the tense of the letter can refer either to the time of writing or to the supposed time of reading ('I hope you have'/'I hope you had a good vacation');[61] in Cicero's epistolary Latin, by contrast, 'the writer's activities at writing time were by convention assigned a past tense, the time that is past to the writing time assigned the pluperfect tense'.[62] The *Cambridge Grammar* gives a different example of the shifting deixis of writing: the sentence: 'Now wash your hands', posted in a public

[60] Fillmore, *Lectures on Deixis*, p. 60.
[61] Fillmore, *Lectures on Deixis*, p. 122.
[62] Fillmore, *Lectures on Deixis*, pp. 122–3, drawing on Robin Lakoff, 'Tense and its Relation to Participants', *Language* 46 (1970), pp. 838–49.

toilet, simulates an act of speech contemporaneous with the reader's present;[63] but this 'now' is, of course, a fiction, as is any example of 'I, now, here, this' in writing, where the time of the utterance is neither that of writing (am I tapping my keyboard *now*? Or *now*?) nor that of reading; it floats free of any determinate reference. Searle tries, in his debate with Derrida, to solve the problem of the indeterminacy of written reference by the resolute application of common sense, insisting that if we read the sentence 'On the twentieth of September 1793 I set out on a journey from London to Oxford', then 'to the extent that the author said what he meant and you understand what he said you will know that the author intended to make a statement to the effect that on the twentieth of September 1793, he set out on a journey from London to Oxford...'[64] To which Derrida rejoins that it all depends on the generic frame in which we read it, and the possibilities are endless: do we read it 'as a citation? The beginning of a novel? A proverb? Someone else's secretarial archives? An exercise in learning language? The narration of a dream? A cryptic code—conscious or not? The example of a linguist or a speech act theoretician letting his imagination wander for short distances, etc.?'[65]

Dramatic discourse presents another instance of simulated speech where we might expect the pronouns to demonstrate 'ease of reference'. In fact, the situation with dramatic speech is complex, both because the spoken word is usually a performance of the written word, and because the physical person who speaks is not speaking *in propria persona* and is thus not the referent of the pronouns 'I', 'you', or 'he/she': it is the character they are playing who is such a referent, a character we must imagine as inhabiting the actor's physical body and as *impersonated* by it. As with any form of imitation in speech (even the slightest parody of another person's tone), then, there is a gap between the embodied person and the subject of the utterance—between the 'animator' and the 'author' and 'principal'.

The case of third-person preterite narrative—the system that Benveniste calls *histoire*—seems initially clear: in this 'impersonal' mode tense is determined without reference to the time of narration, and is thus non-deictic. But the tense system deployed in *histoire* is still relative to a reference point, and the narration may use modal verbs and adverbs which are normally classed as deictic ('he might perhaps have felt disinclined to do so, but nevertheless decided to accept the invitation'). Even the most impersonal of narratives implies an act of knowing. Consider the opening of Kleist's *The Earthquake in Chile*:

> In Santiago, the capital of the kingdom of Chile, at the very moment of the great earthquake of 1647 in which many thousands of lives were lost, a young Spaniard by the name of Jeronimo Rugera, who had been locked up on a criminal charge, was standing against a prison pillar, about to hang himself.
>
> [*In St. Jago, der Hauptstadt des Königreichs Chili, stand gerade in dem Augenblicke der großen Erderschütterung vom Jahre 1647, bei welcher viele tausend Menschen ihren*

[63] Huddleston and Pullum, *The Cambridge Grammar of the English Language*, p. 1453.
[64] John R. Searle, 'Reiterating the Differences: A Reply to Derrida', *Glyph* 2 (1977), p. 201.
[65] Derrida, 'Limited Inc a b c...', p. 63.

> *Untergang fanden, ein junger, auf ein Verbrechen angeklagter Spanier, namens* Jeronimo Rugera, *an einem Pfeiler des Gefängnisses, in welches man ihn eingesperrt hatte, und wollte sich erhenken.*][66]

There is knowledge here which is assumed to be shared with the reader ('the' great earthquake), and knowledge about the character, his location, his history, and his intentions. No one, no identified speaker articulates this knowledge, but there is nevertheless an act of enunciation in the full sense of the word, and the narrative proceeds from it.

Jakobson includes tense amongst the forms of deixis, but he then provides two separate accounts of the tense system: one (E^nE^s) relates the narrated event to the speech event; the other (E^nE^n) relates one narrated event to another, and he calls it *taxis*, or the relative order of tenses:[67] in the sentence from Kleist's story above, it would involve the relation between the preterite *stand* (rendered in English as an imperfect, 'was standing'), the 'moment' of the earthquake; the associated event of the loss of life (*ihren Untergang fanden*); and the pluperfect which connects this moment of the past to a preceding event (Jeronimo's imprisonment), as well as a modal preterite (*wollte*, 'wished to') which points towards a future. If we assume, however, that every narrated statement has an implied (but usually invisible and unspecified) point of utterance, then this relative order of tenses is merely shifted back by one degree from that implied act of speech, giving the impression of impersonality or objectivity (Benveniste's 'the events seem to narrate themselves').[68] What becomes of crucial importance, then, is the establishment of a reference point; and speech is like and unlike writing in that both work with a temporal point of reference, but *in writing it is not necessarily equivalent to the time of enunciation.*

In his analysis of the semantics of *come* and *bring*, Fillmore suggests that 'in discourse in which neither speaker nor addressee figures as a character', these verbs indicate 'motion toward a place taken as the subject of the narrative, toward the location of the central character at reference time, or toward the place which is the central character's home base at reference time'.[69] This gets to the heart of the matter: 'impersonal' narration shifts its deictic centre from the situation of utterance which is the norm for spoken language, to the spatio-temporal coordinates corresponding to the central or focalized character, or rather to whichever character is central or focalized at that point in the narrative: the 'third person'. In both

[66] Heinrich von Kleist, 'The Earthquake in Chile', in *The Marquise of O– and Other Stories*, trans. Martin Greenberg (London: Faber and Faber, 1963), p. 251; Kleist, *Das Erdbeben in Chili*, in Roland Reuß and Peter Staengle (eds), *Sämtliche Werke*, II/3 (Basel and Frankfurt am Main: Stroemfeld, 1993), p. 7.

[67] Jakobson, 'Shifters, Verbal Categories, and the Russian Verb', p. 135.

[68] Benveniste, 'The Nature of Pronouns', p. 208.

[69] Fillmore, *Lectures on Deixis*, p. 99. By 'reference time' Fillmore means the time of the narrated event, by contrast with 'coding time', the time of enunciation; in *histoire* they coincide. My somewhat contradictory use of the term 'reference point' is meant to indicate whatever spatio-temporal point (be it that of the enunciation or of the narrated event) governs the order of deictic markers, or of quasi-deictic markers, in both 'personal' and 'impersonal' forms of utterance.

'personal' and 'impersonal' narration, however, an anthropomorphized position—a *figure*, meaning, minimally, a set of projected bodily coordinates—constitutes the point of reference from which the complex networks of grammar and discourse are organized: 'Our folk belief in the unitary nature of experience causes us to construct a deictic center from which to view the unfolding story events, and we use this deictic center as we would use the "I" of face-to-face interaction to anchor our comprehension of the text. The reader tracks the shifted deixis in the text as if placed in that center.'[70] After Jeronimo Rugera's prison has been destroyed by the earthquake that hits Santiago,

> [u]nnerved and at a loss as to how to save himself from the general destruction, he scrambled over rubble and beams, while death snatched at him from every side, toward one of the nearest city gates. Here another house crashed down, hurtling wreckage all around, and drove him into a neighboring street; here the flames were licking out of all the gables, flashing brightly through the clouds of smoke, and frightened him into another; here the Mapocho River, heaved out of its bed, bore down upon him in a flood and swept him with a roar into a third street. Here lay a heap of dead bodies...
>
> [*Besinnungslos, wie er sich aus diesem allgemeinen Verderben retten würde, eilte er, über Schutt und Gebälk hinweg, indessen der Tod von allen Seiten Angriffe auf ihn machte, nach einem der nächsten Thore der Stadt. Hier stürzte noch ein Haus zusammen, und jagte ihn, die Trümmer weit umherschleudernd, in eine Nebenstraße; hier leckte die Flamme schon, in Dampfwolken blitzend, aus allen Giebeln, und trieb ihn schreckenvoll in eine andere; hier wälzte sich, aus seinem Gestade gehoben, der Mapochofluß auf ihn heran, und riß ihn brüllend in eine dritte. Hier lag ein Haufen Erschlagener...*][71]

Mieke Bal describes such descriptions as being 'motivated' by an implicit act of looking on the part of the character.[72] The repeated deictic adverb 'here' refers to a series of successive reference points given by Rugera's body and his frightened gaze, as do the deictic phrases *der nächsten Thore* ('the nearest city Gates') and *auf ihn heran* ('down upon him'), indicating motion towards the point of reference. And behind that reference point lies the unfigured point of narrative utterance: in Bal's terms, a bracketed act of speaking which logically precedes the text's declarative sentences.[73]

[70] David A. Zubin and Lynne E. Hewitt, 'The Deictic Center: A Theory of Deixis in Narrative', in Judith F. Duchan, Gail A. Bruder, and Lynne Hewitt (eds), *Deixis in Narrative: A Cognitive Science Perspective* (Hillsdale, NJ: Lawrence Erlbaum, 1995), p. 131; unfortunately the rest of this essay seems to conflate deictic markers with spatio-temporal coordinates.

[71] Kleist, *The Earthquake in Chile*, p. 253; *Das Erdbeben in Chili*, p. 12.

[72] Mieke Bal, *Narratology: Introduction to the Theory of Narrative* (2nd edn, Toronto: University of Toronto Press, 1997), p. 37.

[73] Bal, *Narratology*, p. 22: 'As soon as there is language, there is a speaker who utters it; as soon as those linguistic utterances constitute a narrative text, there is a narrator, a narrating subject. From a grammatical point of view, this is always a "first person"', so that every narrative utterance can be rewritten in the form '(I say:) I ...' or '(I say:) he...'

VI

The concept of deictic shift in third-person narrative was articulated in 1934 by Karl Bühler (his second mode of *Deixis am Phantasma* involves deictic projection onto a fictional location),[74] but, paradoxically, most fully enunciated by two theorists who dispute the existence of that unfigured point of narrative utterance. Käte Hamburger's *The Logic of Literature* defines fictional narration, properly speaking (that is, narration in the third person and the preterite tense), by the disappearance of the subject of the statement (it has no narrator) and the transfer of the 'real' spatio-temporal coordinates of the statement onto the fictive persons of the narrative. This is to say that there is a shift of the experiential centre from the subject of the statement to the fictional character, and this shift is accompanied by a set of formal features which are characteristic of narration: the use of verbs of inner action in the third person ('she thought'); the presence of *erlebte Rede* or free indirect discourse; and a change in the function of the preterite such that it ceases to designate pastness and instead works as an 'atemporal' tense, which designates 'fictionality' and may be combined with deictic markers referring to the position in space and time of the characters.[75]

Ann Banfield's *Unspeakable Sentences* (1982) makes a similar case that narration can be defined by its formal linguistic features, that it differs from 'ordinary' communicative discourse, and that it develops special techniques for representing the sheer otherness of subjectivity in the 'impersonal' forms of narration.[76] She distances herself from Hamburger by invoking Benveniste's distinction between *histoire* and *discours*: what matters for the definition of *discours* is not the presence of the 'I' but rather the 'I–you' pair (p. 145); and this means that, for Banfield, fiction told in the first person is not excluded (as it is for Hamburger) from the definition of narration. The 'unspeakable sentences' of narration are of two, mutually exclusive kinds: sentences of pure and 'objective' narration (which may have a narrator—that is, a first-person speaker—but which have no addressee and no 'now' of enunciation); and sentences of represented speech and thought, in which the subject of consciousness, and the deictic centre of the sentence, is, by definition, a character. Like Hamburger, Banfield's interest is in the linguistic underpinnings of the paradoxical representation of subjectivity in 'impersonal' narration. The stylistic devices to which she pays most attention are the syntactic and lexical deictic markers of subjectivity; these devices render in the third person the markers of discursive selfhood: the 'here, now' of speech, referring to the orientation of the

[74] Karl Bühler, *Theory of Language: The Representational Function of Language*, trans. Donald Fraser Goodwin (1934; rpt. Amsterdam: J. Benjamins, 1990).

[75] Käte Hamburger, *The Logic of Literature*, trans. Marilynn J. Rose (2nd rev. edn, Bloomington: Indiana University Press, 1973), p. 134. Hamburger contrasts the ontology of fiction to that of the 'reality statement' (a proposition with referential force) defined by the 'statement-subject', who is identical with the speaker or author. First-person narration possesses a 'genuine statement-subject' (a narrator) but merely feigns the form of the reality statement.

[76] Ann Banfield, *Unspeakable Sentences: Narration and Representation in the Language of Fiction* (Boston: Routledge & Kegan Paul, 1982), p. 142; hereafter cited in the text.

character, and expressive formulae (colloquial or dialect forms, exclamation marks, incomplete sentences) characteristic of direct discourse, together with syntactic forms (concordance of tenses and persons) which are closer to those of indirect discourse.

Banfield's argument is pitched against a dominant account of free indirect discourse as a 'dual voice', for which the grammatical anomalies of the style are evidence of the fusion of two distinct centres of subjectivity, that of the narrating instance and that of a character.[77] She formulates her objection as a matter of linguistic principle: for every expression there can be only one subject of consciousness; if there is an 'I', then it constitutes the subject of consciousness, or 'SELF'; in the absence (and *only* in the absence) of a narrating 'I' (the 'SPEAKER' which has logical priority over the 'SELF'), then a third-person pronoun may be interpreted as the subject of consciousness.[78] There can be no duality of voice because there can be no more than one instance of subjectivity in an expression. In a narrative *text*, however, there may be a plurality of different subjectivities; but the necessary condition for this serial polyphony is the possibility of sentences with no speaker, sentences 'in which that central authority of the personal voice of the speaker, interpreting, evaluating, expressing and bestowing coherence and unity on a discourse, is absent'.[79] Equating her account of a decentred plurality of subjectivities with the theory of *écriture* developed by Blanchot, Barthes, and Derrida, Banfield locates the rise of its conditions of possibility in post-Cartesian subjectivity.[80]

Banfield's argument is formulated through the rigorous application of transformational linguistics to the analysis of sentences of free indirect discourse (her category of 'represented speech and thought' also includes examples of 'internal'—character-centred—focalization and thought report). The technical dimensions of her argument have been the subject of a detailed critique in Monika Fludernik's magisterial account of free indirect discourse, *The Fictions of Language and the Languages of Fiction*;[81] briefly, Fludernik argues that Banfield's model works for a historically restricted set of texts (the modernist canon from Flaubert through Joyce, Woolf, and Beckett), but has little relevance to earlier and later textual traditions; that it relies on an absolute disjunction between literary language and natural language use; and that her treatment of free indirect discourse as a matter of the presentation of consciousness 'is inherently misguided' because of its exclusion of the utterances by means of which consciousness is represented.[82] Fludernik adduces

[77] Roy Pascal, *The Dual Voice: Free Indirect Speech and its Functioning in the Nineteenth-Century European Novel* (Manchester: Manchester University Press, 1977).

[78] Banfield, *Unspeakable Sentences*, pp. 93–4.

[79] Ann Banfield, 'L'écriture et le Non-Dit', *Diacritics* 21: 4 (1991), p. 25.

[80] Banfield, 'L'écriture et le Non-Dit', p. 28; *Unspeakable Sentences*, p. 225ff.

[81] Monika Fludernik, *The Fictions of Language and the Languages of Fiction: The Linguistic Representation of Speech and Consciousness* (London: Routledge, 1993), especially ch. 7; cf. also Fludernik, 'The Linguistic Illusion of Alterity: The Free Indirect as a Paradigm of Discourse Representation', *Diacritics* 25: 4 (1995), pp. 89–115.

[82] Fludernik, *The Fictions of Language*, p. 381.

a large corpus of written and spoken texts to demonstrate the prevalence of virtually all of the uses that Banfield's normative account of competence excludes. More generally, Fludernik argues that complex mimetic effects cannot be understood by appeal to the properties of sentences, since they take place at the level of textual processes.[83] Many sentences of free indirect discourse are indistinguishable from other narrative sentences except for the contextual cues that orient a reading tying them to characters. Banfield concedes the point with respect to irony: her model cannot explain it since it is not formally representable within linguistic theory;[84] but that argument applies a fortiori to the relation between language, 'voice', and represented persons, which is worked out at the textual level and which is, in the first place, a matter for a poetics.

Another way of putting this is to say that a theory based on sentence structure (or even on what Banfield understands by the concept of *text*, that is, 'a series of E[xpression]s related by the rules of anaphora and of "concordance of person and tense" ')[85] has no meaningful way of talking about the contextual determination of meaning. Brian McHale thus argues that Banfield's model of reading is linear rather than integrational, and points to the absence in her work of an account of 'vertical' or mimetic context, which he calls the text's 'reconstructed level':

> Among the things readers know how to do with texts is to reconstruct, taking their cue from the actual sentences of the text, entities not actually given by those sentences 'in so many words'. Such entities include characters' psychologies, relationships among characters, fictional worlds, and even attitudes (e.g., irony), themes, and 'ideas' in the largest sense—as well as . . . voices and speaking positions.[86]

These reconstructed entities are mimetic concretizations which are built out of sentences (in Uri Margolin's words, they constitute 'a heterogeneous, heteronomous, and emergent conceptual level with respect to the linguistic means of representation')[87] and, in turn, provide an integrative context for both subsequent and, indeed, earlier sentences: they anchor anaphoric reference ('Emma Woodhouse . . . she'), for example, and provide a ground for the distinction between utterances attributed to the narrative and utterances attributed to characters, as well as more complex attributions of perspective and tone. Whereas Banfield restricts the attribution of expressive elements to a single point of subjectivity (either the narrating 'I' or a character), a theory of the play between text and mimetic reconstruction makes it possible to see how sentences might work with a duality of 'voice'.

Two passages from Joyce's *Ulysses* make the point. The first occurs at a point where the perspective shifts about two-thirds of the way through the Nausicaa episode in a moment of undecidable overlap, where the language continues to be the

[83] Fludernik, *The Fictions of Language*, p. 64.

[84] Banfield, 'L'écriture et le Non-Dit', p. 28.

[85] Banfield, 'L'écriture et le Non-Dit', p. 24.

[86] Brian McHale, 'Unspeakable Sentences, Unnatural Acts: Linguistics and Poetics Revisited', *Poetics Today* 4: 1 (1983), p. 34.

[87] Uri Margolin, 'Characters in Literary Narrative: Representation and Signification', *Semiotica* 106: 3/4 (1995), p. 383.

novelettish prose in which Gertie MacDowell's perceptions are rendered, but the knowledge it displays (that he has just quietly masturbated) can only be Bloom's:

> He was leaning back against the rock behind. Leopold Bloom (for it is he) stands silent, with bowed head before those young guileless eyes. What a brute he had been! At it again? A fair unsullied soul had called to him and, wretch that he was, how had he answered? An utter cad he had been. He of all men! But there was an infinite store of mercy in those eyes, for him too a word of pardon even though he had erred and sinned and wandered. Should a girl tell? No, a thousand times no.[88]

A skilled reader, says McHale, would read these sentences through a double reconstruction of the hypothetical source of the style and the source of their point of view; and only such a reconstruction would enable the two to be held together in however difficult a tension. The second passage is from the Eumaeus episode, where 'it is not a matter of two characters laying joint claim to the same sentences, but a character and someone "behind" or "above" him—a narrator, in fact':[89]

> Preparatory to anything else Mr Bloom brushed off the greater bulk of the shavings and handed Stephen the hat and ashplant and bucked him up generally in orthodox Samaritan fashion, which he very badly needed. His (Stephen's) mind was not exactly what you would call wandering but a bit unsteady and on his expressed desire for some beverage to drink Mr Bloom, in view of the hour it was and there being no pumps of Vartry water available for their ablutions, let alone drinking purposes, hit upon an expedient by suggesting, off the reel, the propriety of the cabman's shelter, as it was called, hardly a stonesthrow away near Butt Bridge where they might hit upon some drinkables in the shape of a milk and soda or a mineral. But how to get there was the rub. For the nonce he was rather nonplussed . . .[90]

Banfield reads this style as being expressive of Bloom's consciousness; but it is quite distinct from his customary modes of speech and thought. McHale's own reading (the style reflects not Bloom's consciousness but his situation: the prose is weary because Bloom is) is not particularly convincing either. What matters here is the duality of perspective, and the reader's sense of a distinctive narrative voice, a generically clichéd style which spins off autonomously from the world of the story in the same way as, in the Oxen of the Sun episode, some thirty historically successive styles (Latinate, Anglo-Saxon, Elizabethan, Miltonic, Carlylean . . .) generate narrative personae which have no 'psychological' relation to the deictic centres (Bloom and Stephen) that they construct.

'Dual voice' is, for various reasons, too simple a way of defining the workings of free indirect discourse. But within the 'integrational' perspective of a poetics it seems clear that Banfield's refusal to allow more than a single centre of subjectivity is inadequate to the facts of narration, and, above all, inadequate to the conventions of mimetic reading established for the classic European novel, which

[88] James Joyce, *Ulysses: The 1922 Text*, ed. Jeri Johnson (Oxford: Oxford University Press, 1993), p. 350.

[89] McHale, 'Unspeakable Sentences', p. 37.

[90] Joyce, *Ulysses*, p. 569.

recognize both a deictic centre located in the third person and a narrative instance, personified or not, which underlies it. Character and narrator are the twin 'illusions of alterity' on which the novel is built.

VII

Free indirect discourse—which Frances Ferguson has called 'the novel's one and only formal contribution to literature'[91] —has become a topic 'of supreme theoretical relevance' in narrative theory.[92] This is so because its fusion of narrative language with the language of characters transgresses the ontological distinction between the level of 'the words of the text in the narrating process and the plot level of the fictional world'.[93] It thus problematizes the dualism of any account of narrative as representation, and yet, in the same movement, makes the understanding of narrative discourse dependent on the mimetic projections and attributions that it requires and enables.[94]

The textbook case of free indirect discourse, one that was given political resonance because of the role played by the device in the prosecution of the novel for obscenity, is *Madame Bovary*. This is a passage cited by the prosecuting attorney Pinard in his indictment:

> But when she saw herself in the mirror she wondered at her face. Never had her eyes been so large, so black, nor so deep. Something subtle about her being transfigured her.
>
> She repeated: 'I have a lover! a lover!' delighting at the idea as if a second puberty had come to her. So at last she was to know those joys of love, that fever of happiness of which she had despaired! She was entering upon a marvelous world where all would be passion, ecstasy, delirium. She felt herself surrounded by an endless rapture. A blue space surrounded her and ordinary existence appeared only intermittently between these heights, dark and far away beneath her.

> [*Mais, en s'apercevant dans la glace, elle s'étonna de son visage. Jamais elle n'avait eu les yeux si grands, si noirs, ni d'une telle profondeur. Quelque chose de subtil épandu sur sa personne la transfigurait.*
>
> *Elle se répétait: 'J'ai un amant! un amant!' se délectant à cette idée comme à celle d'une autre puberté qui lui serait survenue. Elle allait donc posséder enfin ces joies d'amour, cette fièvre du bonheur dont elle avait désespéré. Elle entrait dans quelque chose de merveilleux où tout serait passion, extase, délire; une immensité bleuâtre l'entourait, les sommets du sentiment étincelaient sous sa pensée, l'existence ordinaire n'apparaissait qu'au loin, tout en bas, dans l'ombre, entre les intervalles de ces hauteurs.*][95]

[91] Frances Ferguson, 'Jane Austen, *Emma*, and the Impact of Form', *MLQ* 61: 1 (2000), p. 159.

[92] Fludernik, *Fictions of Language*, p. 3.

[93] Fludernik, *Fictions of Language*, p. 3.

[94] Cf. Moshe Ron, 'Free Indirect Discourse, Mimetic Language Games and the Subject of Fiction', *Poetics Today* 2: 2 (1981), pp. 17–18.

[95] Cited in the 'Appendice: Le Ministère Public contre Gustave Flaubert', Gustave Flaubert, *Oeuvres I*, ed. A. Thibaudet and R. Dumesnil, Bibliothèque de la Pléïade (Paris: Gallimard, 1962), pp. 656–7;

The 'concordance of person and tense' allows the prosecution to read the last two sentences as a complicit evaluation made by the narrator; alternatively, they can be read as shifting the centre of subjectivity from the narrator to Emma. They lack the signals of direct discourse ('So at last I am to know') or indirect discourse ('She said to herself that she was therefore at last to know'), and indeed there is little sense here at all of Emma's *voice*; this is narration that Gérard Genette would call internal focalization,[96] and what pushes it into the realm of the subjective is, above all, the use of the imperfect, the tense that Charles Bally first identified as one of the key indices of the *style indirect libre* in French.[97] But what perhaps marks this passage above all is its stylistic suppleness: it moves from the emotion ('*elle s'étonna*') triggered by the verb of perception ('*en s'apercevant dans la glace*') to an analysis, through Emma's eyes, of how she looks, to her directly quoted (but probably silently uttered) words, and then to the train of thoughts that follow on her delighted '*idée*' and her vision ('*sa pensée*') of the contrast between the heights of ecstasy that await her and the ordinary world that 'appeared' to her only intermittently. The language moves at the boundary between speech and conscious and subconscious perception, with little differentiation between them, and, indeed, between Emma's inwardness and the voice of the detached narrator, whose spatial vision enfolds hers at the end of the passage. Hence M. Pinard's anger: what is scandalous in 1857 is the possibility of *sympathy* for an adulterous woman that this lack of distance and differentiation between the poles of narration and character engenders.

It is the ambivalence of free indirect discourse—technically, the way it functions as a projected voice of the other within a frame with which it is anaphorically aligned but to which it is not connected by verbs of reporting[98]—that allows us to catch a glimpse of the way in which fictional character produces the effect of belonging simultaneously to discourse and to representation, and the reason why the analysis of character tends to shift into irreconcilable linguistic and mimetic domains. To be a character is to be both an object of speech and a subject of speech; in the production of character, language produces fictional representations which, in turn, produce more language. Free indirect discourse—the point of convergence

in the text of the novel the passage appears on p. 473. The English translation is from *Madame Bovary*, trans. Paul de Man (New York: Norton Critical Edition, 1965), p. 116. Cf. also H. R. Jauss, 'Literary History as a Challenge to Literary Theory', in *Toward an Aesthetic of Reception*, trans. Timothy Bahti (Minneapolis: University of Minnesota Press, 1982), pp. 42–4; and Dominick LaCapra, Madame Bovary *on Trial* (Ithaca: Cornell University Press, 1982).

[96] Gérard Genette, *Narrative Discourse*, trans. Jane E. Lewin (Ithaca: Cornell University Press, 1980), p. 189.

[97] Charles Bally, 'Le style indirect libre en français moderne I', *Germanisch-Romanische Monatsschrift* 4 (1912), pp. 549–56.

[98] In 'The Linguistic Illusion of Alterity', pp. 95–100, Fludernik concisely defines free indirect discourse as requiring, at a minimum, the anaphoric alignment of the 'personal' referential expressions in a perceived 'discourse of alterity' to the deictic centre of the reporting instance, and the absence of a verb-plus-complement clause structure; other features which have, historically, been central to defining the style, such as temporal shift, narrative parentheticals, deictic alignment with the reported discourse, and the presence of 'expressive' elements are frequent but not obligatory.

of narrative and figural discourse—involves a second-order assignment of speech to a figure concretized at a first order of narrative discourse. Character is thus produced as a complex effect of the layering of levels of language and representation; and an adequate conceptualization of it might require a similar layering of textual and mimetic theories.

Two exemplary readings of Jane Austen's *Emma* will elucidate some of the problems involved in theorizing character in terms of discourse and discursive effects. The first, Joel Weinsheimer's 'Theory of Character: *Emma*', constitutes an extreme reduction of character to text. The article begins by criticizing mimetic criticism for the fact that, in reading the words 'Emma Woodhouse, handsome, clever, and rich...' it accepts the ontological illusion carried in the unstated predication of existence, and reproduces it in a language which 'appears natural, almost an extension of the novels themselves'.[99] To this Weinsheimer contrasts the language of semiotic criticism, for which 'Emma Woodhouse is not a woman nor need to be described as if it were' (p. 187), where the 'it' polemically stresses the textuality of character: 'Emma' becomes a text within *Emma*. It is the closure of fictional texts, Weinsheimer argues, that allows us to read characters as fictive entities, and semiotic criticism is that metalanguage which *imposes* a closure on the text. Its goal is then to refuse the concretizations that produce the illusory fullness of a novelistic world; instead, it aims at a 'reduced articulation' whereby

> the hard, clear lines which in mimetic criticism differentiate one character from another tend to dissolve. Their temperaments, too, shade off toward continuity like the colors of a rainbow. Imputedly unique character—an identity distinctly one's own—becomes communalized among all the characters; it is distributed throughout the novel rather than limited to one unitary text-segment, a particular character. (p. 194)

In a semiotic criticism characters are read as 'pattems of recurrence, motifs which are continually recontexualized in other motifs. In semiotic criticism, characters dissolve' (p. 195)—dissolve, that is, into text.

This dissolution of character in *Emma* takes place along four planes on which representational differentiation is broken down into textual continuity. These are: the planes of 'the continuity of proper names with writing on the one hand and characteristics on the other; the continuity of familial and social strata; the continuity of voiced and unvoiced utterance; and, finally, the continuity of character independent from other characters' (p. 195). Let me discuss only one of these, the continuity of voiced and unvoiced utterance. The argument is simple: any attempt to discriminate the provenance of voices (for example, to distinguish between narrative discourse and the speech of characters, between 'the "said Emma" and the speech attached to it') obscures 'the essential unbroken continuity between exposition and direct discourse'. From a purely linguistic point of view 'there is no speech in the novel', and we must recognize that 'the presence of speech in a novel

[99] Joel Weinsheimer, 'Theory of Character: *Emma*', *Poetics Today* 1: 1–2 (1979), p. 186; hereafter cited in the text.

is in fact a supposition; it is an enabling supposition of mimetic criticism, to be sure, but wholly dispensable in the kind of criticism I have been calling semiotic. For semiotic criticism, novels contain not speech, only text' (p. 203). But at this point Weinsheimer recognizes that this is 'an untenable conclusion', and the article reveals itself to have been a clever exercise in self-destruction. It now becomes clear that any merely demystificatory critique of mimeticism dismisses the very problem it was trying to solve. And the article finishes by reinstating the argument to ontological and methodological ambivalence: 'Without text we cannot, without world we need not perform literary criticism because it would be pointless. What we require is a Janus-faced critic who can do justice to both texts and persons: to the textualized persons, personified texts that are characters' (p. 208).

My second exemplary reading of *Emma*, Graham Hough's 'Narrative and Dialogue in Jane Austen', starts with that problem of ontological indeterminacy which is Weinsheimer's point of arrival. The genre of the novel is the prime example of Plato's 'mixed style', comprising both narrative and dramatic modes of utterance, in which the latter, the discourse of characters, is embedded within the former. The problem raised by this style is not simply that of the coexistence of different voices; this is equally the case in drama, but there the voices all exist on the same plane: 'The conflict is a conflict between epistemological equals, and a consistent texture, though composed of diverse elements, is fairly easy to achieve.' In the novel, by contrast, the problem 'is partly that of different voices, but far more acutely that different parts of the work occupy different ontological and epistemological levels, one for which the narrator makes himself directly responsible, and the other in which he disappears and the words of the characters are simply reproduced'.[100]

Hough identifies five kinds of discourse in *Emma*. Excluding what he calls, I think mistakenly, 'authorial voice' (which is manifested only in a few gnomic utterances), there is an effective range between the poles of 'objective narrative' (that is, a language which is *conventionally* 'objective' and which is, in *Emma*, 'general, abstract, evaluative and formally correct') (p. 208), and direct discourse. The most interesting forms, however, are the two intermediate ones: what Hough calls 'coloured' narrative, and free indirect style. 'Coloured' narrative is 'narrative or reflection or observation more or less deeply coloured by a character's point of view' (p. 204). In linguistic terms—and this definition goes part of the way towards avoiding the psychologism of the concept of point of view—it is a 'virtual quotation' of the interior monologue or imputed inner speech of a character.[101] Hough's example is this passage from Chapter 4:

> The longer she considered it, the greater was her sense of its expediency. Mr Elton's situation was most suitable, quite the gentleman himself, and without low connections; at the same time not of any family that could fairly object to the doubtful birth

[100] Graham Hough, 'Narrative and Dialogue in Jane Austen', *Critical Quarterly* 12: 3 (1970), p. 201; hereafter cited in the text.

[101] Hough, 'Narrative and Dialogue in Jane Austen', p. 205; cf. Derek Bickerton, 'Modes of Interior Monologue: A Formal Definition', *Modern Language Quarterly* 28: 2 (1967), pp. 229–39.

of Harriet. He had a comfortable home for her, and Emma imagined a very sufficient income; for though the vicarage of Highbury was not large, he was known to have some independent property; and she thought very highly of him as a good-humoured, well-meaning, respectable young man, without any deficiency of useful understanding or knowledge of the world.[102]

The passage moves between impersonal narration and phrases—'quite the gentleman himself, and without low connections; at the same time not of any family...'—which approximate to free indirect discourse. It is the play of this style and of free indirect discourse proper, the 'continual slight shifts in the point of view',[103] that produce the peculiar pleasure effects of *Emma*. These shifts are linguistically operated, and the pleasure they produce surely involves the sliding of desire between representational and represented discourse, between enunciative stability and the threat of its interruption or scattering. This is (quite paradoxically, given their different operating assumptions) close to Barthes' account of the 'plural', a way of listening to the text 'as an iridescent exchange carried on by multiple voices, on different wavelengths and subject from time to time to a sudden *dissolve*, leaving a gap which enables the utterance to shift from one point of view to another'.[104] In its emphasis on differentiation Hough's analysis is quite the reverse of Weinsheimer's movement towards a radical indifferentiation, but, at the same time, it avoids sacrificing a textual explanation to a simply mimetic or psychological conception of character.

Hough's term 'coloured narrative' is similar to what other theorists call 'stylistic contagion' or *Ansteckung*, in which the language of the narration is inflected by figural style,[105] as well as to Mikhail Bakhtin's concept of double-voiced discourse.[106] Arguing that this mutual contamination of authorial and figural styles should serve as a model for Austen's use of free indirect speech in *Emma*,[107] Daniel Gunn calls attention to the way the novel's heroine is herself constantly mimicking the voices of others. After Mrs Elton's first visit to Hartfield, for example, she explodes:

Insufferable woman!...Worse than I had supposed. Absolutely insufferable. Knightley!—I could not have believed it. Knightley!—never seen him in her life before, and call him Knightley!—and discover that he is a gentleman! A little upstart, vulgar being, with her Mr E., and her *cara sposo*, and her resources, and all her airs of pert pretension and under-bred finery.[108]

The same mimicry, the same contagion of an embedding by an embedded discourse is equally evident in Emma's *mise en abyme* here and in the narrative discourse

[102] Jane Austen, *Emma*, ed. Stephen M. Parrish (New York: Norton Critical Edition, 2000), p. 21.
[103] Hough, 'Narrative and Dialogue in Jane Austen', p. 210.
[104] Roland Barthes, *S/Z*, trans. Richard Miller (New York: Hill and Wang, 1974), pp. 41–2.
[105] Dorrit Cohn, *Transparent Minds: Narrative Modes for Presenting Consciousness in Fiction* (Princeton: Princeton University Press, 1978), p. 33; Fludernik, *The Fictions of Language*, pp. 333–4.
[106] Mikhail Bakhtin, *Problems of Dostoevsky's Poetics*, ed. and trans. Caryl Emerson (Minneapolis: University of Minnesota Press, 1984), pp. 185ff.
[107] Daniel Gunn, 'Free Indirect Discourse and Narrative Authority in *Emma*', *Narrative* 12: 1 (2004), pp. 39–40.
[108] Austen, *Emma*, p. 181.

which enfolds it. In this instance, the mimicry is of a particular voice; but free indirect discourse runs along a spectrum from specific to general speech patterns (from idiolect to sociolect) and through the characteristic forms of thought and perception of characters. The concept of voice is no more than a metonym for the forms in which characters are represented as centres of subjectivity; it is that mode specific to verbal art forms for indicating speech, thought, or perception, or an even less formed level of sensation and affect. In the classic European psychological novel the language dances from one point on the scale to another, like the interwoven 'voices' of the instruments of a string quartet, often with very little differentiation. As McHale puts it, the categories of speech 'bleed' into one another and into the reporting of categories of thought or perception which may not be accessible to the character, and which we may assume not to be cast in verbal form.[109]

It is clear that my sympathies lie with the standard case about free indirect discourse—that is, that it involves a dual narrative and figural voice, dual and interlocking centres of reference. There are two arguments against this position. The first is technical: since one mind can't read another, there is a loss of verisimilitude in supposing more than one centre of subjectivity in a single utterance. The transparency of the character's mind *must* entail the effacement of the narrator. This argument, whatever its merits, seems to me to repeat one of the ways in which the novel positions itself historically in the seventeenth and eighteenth centuries in relation to the competing discourses of scientific and historical fact: the speakerless discourses of the depersonalized experiment and the document.[110] The second argument has political overtones: the narrative instance is the locus of discursive control in the text, and the presence of the narrator in relation to figural discourse is then taken to be evidence either of discursive authority or of resistance to it, or, alternatively, the very dispersal of narrative authority in free indirect discourse is taken as evidence of the naturalization of 'a *hegemony* impervious to any resistance a subject might wish to make'.[111] What is at stake in these two arguments is partly a matter of definition: if the narrative instance is understood to exist only through the presence of explicit self-reference (as Fludernik understands it, for example),[112] then the case against dual voice probably holds. But it is perfectly possible to conceive of the narrative instance in a less figural manner without ceasing to acknowledge the ways in which it shapes the flow of information in an unfigured but

[109] Brian McHale, 'Speech Representation', in Peter Hühn, John Pier, Wolf Schmid, and Jörg Schönert (eds), *The Handbook of Narratology* (Berlin: De Gruyter, 2009), p. 442.

[110] Mary Poovey, *A History of the Modern Fact: Problems of Knowledge in the Science of Wealth and Society* (Chicago: University of Chicago Press, 1998), pp. 68, 79–82; Murray Cohen, *Sensible Words: Linguistic Practice in England 1640–1785* (Baltimore: John Hopkins University Press, 1977).

[111] Casey Finch and Peter Bowen, '"The Tittle-Tattle of Highbury": Gossip and the Free Indirect Style in Emma', *Representations* 31 (1990), p. 13.

[112] Fludernik, *The Fictions of Language*, p. 443: what counts as a narrator is 'instances of subjective language that imply a *speaking* subject: the personal pronoun *I*, addresses to the narratee, metanarrative commentary (frequently in conjunction with *I, you,* and *we*) and explicit commentary and evaluation'.

not impersonal way,[113] and without giving up on the insight that, in certain key instances such as free indirect discourse, the reader—for this is entirely a matter of construals made by readers[114]—projects, and identifies with, two distinct and related positions.

'Identifies with' does not necessarily mean 'sympathizes with', since the positioning of the reader in relation to characters flows along a scale that runs from empathy to irony: the point is just that we are placed in the text by being brought to make judgements, to know what the narrator knows and what the character knows, to occupy the positions of 'I' and 's/he' at the same time, in the same movement. The experience of character, as subject and object of discourse, stitches us into the text. The entry into discourse, writes Agamben, 'is a paradoxical act that simultaneously implies both subjectification and desubjectification'.[115] It takes place in the endless occupation of the deictic shifters which at once situate me and render me discontinuous with myself, or rather constitute my self as a site of shifting reference. That passage through the empty places of the pronouns and the persons of the verb is something like a journey through non-being, a constitution of the subject in the experience of absence. The pronoun system, like the characters who occupy it, guarantees identity and the dispersal of identity in the same articulation.

It is therefore only in the first instance that identification, the binding-in of the reader or spectator to a fictional discourse, takes place in relation to what Leo Bersani calls 'that incessant *voice* which, in poetry, prose fiction and the essay, never stops implying the presence of a stable and structured self as the centre to which the world always returns and from which it receives its own reassuringly stable designs',[116] and which in drama and film corresponds to the position of the absent one, the unrepresented frame of reference. As I hope my argument has made clear, no subject position can ever be single and univocal, particularly in the temporal extension of language; and the apparently 'unrepresented' discourse of the absent narrator is always a character-position like any other.[117] Hence the possibility for the reader of sliding to an identification with represented subject positions; and hence the contamination of authorial discourse by other voices: by inflections of represented discourse, folds within the fabric of the text.

[113] Noting the effects of presence associated with rhetorical strategy and figurative language in the novels of Henry James, Richard Aczel argues that the value of the concept of the subject of enunciation 'is that it enables us to make a vital and workable distinction between a voiceless, textually irretrievable, yet theoretically reconstructable, organizing, arranging, juxtaposing subject and the subjects who speak within the text—and may also do their share of organizing, arranging, and juxtaposing—as *enunciated*, textual voice'. Richard Aczel, 'Hearing Voices in Narrative Texts', *New Literary History* 29: 3 (1998), p. 477.

[114] This argument is at the centre of Didier Coste's construal of narrative voice as 'the product of the reader's quest for the origin of the text'. *Narrative as Communication* (Minneapolis: University of Minnesota Press, 1989), p. 164.

[115] Agamben, *Remnants of Auschwitz*, p. 116.

[116] Leo Bersani, *A Future for Astyanax: Character and Desire in Literature* (Boston: Little, Brown & Co., 1976), p. 258.

[117] Cf. Barthes, *S/Z*, p. 179.

6

Name

I

'We seldom name ourselves. We routinely name others...'[1] Names, like but unlike pronouns, inscribe us in the social order, tying bodies to language to make us recognizable as persons or non-persons. They are complex tools for performing a range of social operations, and we come, partly or wholly, to inhabit them: to assume that we are our name. Although naming is, in one sense, just a way of picking out one human animal from all others, it is also always charged with messages about power and solidarity. Naming places us, designating such things as gender, birth-order, clan, geographical provenance, ethnicity, and religion. It may indicate legitimacy and the right to belong to a group; children who die unnamed may be buried without ceremony. The laws of nomenclature structure 'the alliances from within which human beings... end up by creating not only other symbols, but also real beings, who, coming into the world, right away have that little tag which is their name, the essential symbol for what will be their lot'.[2]

Naming practices are never unsystematic but they vary sharply from culture to culture. We can posit a number of dimensions along which names operate. First, they tie social persons to particular bodies. Second, they designate and enact kinship relations, including those that have to do with legitimacy of birth and position, with the transmission of property and status, and with continuity or discontinuity between generations. Third, they establish relations with the world of the ancestors or the spirit world, and thereby bring spiritual forces into play. Fourth, they perform relations of familiarity or formality—of solidarity and intimacy, or of social distance and deference—between speakers. And they distinguish between ascriptive identity and (in the case of nicknames, for example) emergent

[1] Earl Miner, *Naming Properties: Nominal Reference in Travel Writings by Bashō and Sora, Johnson and Boswell* (Ann Arbor: University of Michigan Press, 1996), p. 252.

[2] Jacques Lacan, *The Seminar of Jacques Lacan*, Book II, ed. Jacques-Alain Miller, trans. Sylvana Tomaselli (Cambridge: Cambridge University Press, 1988), p. 20; cited in Gabriella vom Bruck and Barbara Bodenhorn, '"Entangled Histories": An Introduction to the Anthropology of Names and Naming', in Gabriella vom Bruck and Barbara Bodenhorn (eds), *The Anthropology of Names and Naming* (Cambridge: Cambridge University Press, 2006), p. 16. In like manner, the character called 'Dostoevsky' in *The Master of Petersburg* thinks of the moment of baptism as 'the union of a soul with a name, the name it will carry into eternity'. J. M. Coetzee, *The Master of Petersburg* (London: Minerva, 1994), p. 5.

or achieved identity. This is to say that names enact many of the central aspects of a culture.

Let me start by asking what a name is—or, more precisely, where names end and other forms of address or reference begin. Maurice Bloch writes that names are used in conjunction with 'other designating devices' such as 'eye contacts, pronouns, titles, gestures, and kinship terms', all of which can be used as alternatives.[3] Of these, titles and kinship terms may be counted as part of the system of nomenclature;[4] but Bloch's point is that names used vocatively belong to a larger network of signifiers deployed in address and response, and that their function cannot be separated from that network. Names used in address may be of many kinds. Amongst the Nuer we find honorific clan names, used in formal contexts; ox-names, used in salutation by a man or a woman's peers or in flirtation; and dance names, which are embellishments of ox-names and are called out at dances.[5] In the Western world, there is a marked difference between the use of given names, nicknames, and surnames, where the latter may be used either deferentially in association with a title, or insolently without one (although conventions here have shifted), and where the non-reciprocal use of a given name is a clear index of difference in power and status. Discussing the way in which, in contemporary English usage, given names are seen as more 'personal' than surnames (losing the 'Christian' name's connotations of 'admitting the person to a community of souls'),[6] Marilyn Strathern summarizes data from the 1960s showing that 'children are called by their personal names, parents and grand-parents by kin terms, while aunts and uncles are often known by a combination of kin term and personal name', and contrasts this with a shift in the 1980s 'from habitual use of kin terms in addressing close senior kin to a choice between that and the personal name'.[7]

If, as is usually the case, we do not name ourselves, then there is a question to be asked about the source of the names that are 'given' to us. While names are often given at birth, they may also be given or changed at later, liminal stages of life; and when we speak of the moment of birth, we must recognize that naming is one of the ways in which social birth is performed in contradistinction to biological birth. Linda Layne notes that foetuses are now often named during pregnancy (sometimes with joking names), and that there is a clearly marked decoupling of social birth from biological birth when the foetus is lost: 'Whereas biological birth is a one-time event, accomplished by a single individual, and once done cannot be reversed,' she writes, 'the attribution of personhood is a gradual, collaborative

[3] Maurice Bloch, 'Teknonymy and the Evocation of the "Social" Among the Zafimaniry of Madagascar', in vom Bruck and Bodenhorn (eds), *The Anthropology of Names and Naming*, p. 98.

[4] Clifford Geertz's extended analysis of Balinese naming practices lists personal names, birth-order names, kinship terms, teknonyms, status titles, and public titles as components of the system of nomenclature. Clifford Geertz, 'Person, Time, and Conduct in Bali', in *The Interpretation of Cultures: Selected Essays* (New York: Basic Books, 1973), pp. 360–411.

[5] E. E. Evans-Pritchard, 'Nuer Modes of Address', in Dell Hymes (ed.), *Language in Culture and Society: A Reader in Linguistics and Anthropology* (New York: Harper & Row, 1964), pp. 221–7.

[6] Marilyn Strathern, *After Nature: English Kinship in the Late Twentieth Century* (Cambridge: Cambridge University Press, 1992), p. 17.

[7] Strathern, *After Nature*, p. 19.

process, and as the process of pregnancy loss makes so clear, personhood often is only provisionally granted and is frequently revoked if the pregnancy does not end in a live birth.'[8] In a quite different context, Stephen Hugh-Jones contrasts the practices of certain Tukanoan groups who delay the child's naming until its bones are hard, since the name is too 'heavy' for the infant to bear, with those living in another region who name their children soon after birth on the grounds that 'naming "transforms the soul"... of the child, giving it strength and vitality and increasing its chances of survival'. In the latter case, the shaman travels in thought to the group's origin house and, intuiting the child in spirit form, accompanies it and its name to this world as it is translated into material form; it is in this transitional period between two births that 'body-soul' and 'name-soul' are joined.[9]

In the same essay, Hugh-Jones cites a distinction made by Eduardo Viveiros de Castro between 'exonymic' and 'endonymic' Amerindian naming systems, a distinction which illuminates the question of the sources of the name's power. In the first, which in some ways resembles the capture of 'head names' (and the life force that flows from the head) from decapitated enemies amongst the Asmat and the Marind-Anim of Irian Jaya,[10] Viveiros de Castro suggests that 'the typical Tupi-Guarani naming system relies on the extra-social as its source or criterion (gods, enemies, animals, the dead)';[11] a Tupinambá man discards his childhood name only after killing and eating an enemy and, on the strength of this act, naming himself. In the second, 'endonymic' system, names are passed down as heirlooms within closed systems 'in which names connote ritual roles and may be the property of corporate groups, with transmission among the living and name recycling being the norm'.[12] As Hugh-Jones summarizes Viveiros de Castro's finely nuanced analysis, the emphasis in the exonymic Tupinambá system is on 'the individual, heroic *acquisition* of singular and never-to-be-repeated names, which set the bearer apart', while in the endonymic system of other Amazonian groups the emphasis falls on 'collectively sanctioned and ceremonialized inter-vivos *transmission* that keeps a limited stock of names in perpetual circulation. In the former case, names belong to the domain of metaphysics and have an individualizing function; in the latter case they belong to the social order and have classificatory functions'.[13]

The act of naming may mark both a social birth and a social death that precedes it: 'The slave's former name died with his former self.'[14] Slave names given in

[8] Linda Layne, '"Your Child Deserves a Name": Possessive Individualism and the Politics of Memory in Pregnancy Loss', in vom Bruck and Bodenhorn (eds), *The Anthropology of Names and Naming*, p. 38.

[9] Stephen Hugh-Jones, 'The Substance of Northwest Amazonian Names', in vom Bruck and Bodenhorn (eds), *The Anthropology of Names and Naming*, pp. 84–5.

[10] Marilyn Strathern, 'Pre-Figured Features', in *Property, Substance and Effect: Anthropological Essays on Persons and Things* (London: Athlone Press, 1999), pp. 31–2.

[11] Eduardo Viveiros de Castro, *From the Enemy's Point of View: Humanity and Divinity in an Amazonian Society*, trans. Catherine V. Howard (Chicago: University of Chicago Press, 1992), p. 153.

[12] Viveiros de Castro, *From the Enemy's Point of View*, p. 151.

[13] Hugh-Jones, 'The Substance of Northwest Amazonian Names', p. 74.

[14] Orlando Patterson, *Slavery and Social Death: A Comparative Study* (Cambridge, MA: Harvard University Press, 1982), p. 55.

European, Caribbean, and North American chattel slavery were typically impoverished in relation to the complex West African nomenclatures they replaced: slave names were diminutive or ironically grandiose, drew on biblical or classical sources, on place names or on the names of the months, or used mutilated forms of African names (Sambo, Quashy, Cuffee) to indicate an incomplete personhood. But slaves gave names themselves, using them privately and often calling their children after kin; naming was always contested, 'a site of struggle rather than . . . a clear set of dominating practices'.[15]

The act of renaming signals a change of social status; slavery is an extreme case of a process that happens at moments of social rebirth: in marriage, at puberty, on joining a gang, by a cardinal on his election as Pope, by men or women undergoing a change of sex, during sickness, at the death of a relative when their hostile spirit may be seeking to seize on your name . . . The new name is what you become, since names are both intimately part of persons and the part that (along with the face) is recognized by others. W. E. H. Stanner writes of Australian Indigenous naming practices that

> the personal names by which a man is known are something more than names. Native statements suggest that names are thought to partake of the personality which they designate. The name seems to bear much the same relation to the personality as the shadow or image does to the sentient body. To stab a man's shadow with a spear is not a friendly action. Names are not symbols so much as verbal projections of an identity which is well known in the flesh.[16]

A person, writes another ethnographer in a commentary on this passage, 'is not the bearer of a name but its embodiment'.[17] Hence the widespread avoidance of the use of personal names and the widespread prohibition on uttering the names of the dead; Stanner notes the proscription, in the population he is studying, on revealing one's name when others are present and on speaking the names of relatives such as the wife's mother, and the substitution of kinship terms for names in direct address; breaches of these prohibitions cause shame and embarrassment.[18] It is because of the metonymic relation of name to person that names are vulnerable to magical appropriation or attack. 'Liberties taken with the name,' Stanner writes,

[15] Susan Benson, 'Injurious Names: Naming, Disavowal, and Recuperation in Contexts of Slavery and Emancipation', in vom Bruck and Bodenhorn (eds), *The Anthropology of Names and Naming*, p. 191.

[16] W. E. H. Stanner, 'Aboriginal Modes of Address and Reference in the North-West of the Northern Territory', *Oceania* 7: 3 (1937), p. 301.

[17] Franca Tamisari, 'Names and Naming: Speaking Forms into Place', in Luise Hercus, Flavia Hodges, and Jane Simpson (eds), *The Land is a Map: Placenames of Indigenous Origin in Australia* (Research School of Pacific and Asian Studies, Australian National University: Pandarus Books, 2002), p. 95. The identity of name and person is not universal, however; André Iteanu writes that 'Orokaiva, unlike many other well-known ethnographic examples, do not consider personal names as components of the person that partake in its specificity and uniqueness. Rather, like shell jewels and feather headdresses, a name is a valuable that can be given away on account [sc. "on behalf"] of a group. As group wealth, names are only momentarily carried by persons . . .' André Iteanu, 'Why the Dead do not Bear Names: The Orokaiva Name System', in vom Bruck and Bodenhorn (eds), *The Anthropology of Names and Naming*, pp. 64–5.

[18] Stanner, 'Aboriginal Modes of Address and Reference', pp. 301–3.

'are liberties taken with the person and are as much resented, so much so that if it is known that a sorcerer has coupled one's name with his secret rites it is proof that his intentions are lethal.'[19] Conversely, namesakes may share a special relationship; they may have reciprocal obligations or a special joking relationship, or one may be taken to reincarnate the other or to occupy the same position in a kinship network. Stanner describes at length the process by which an initial prohibition on contact between namesakes is followed, at a certain time and after an exchange of gifts, by a particularly intimate relation between them, and Richard Alford writes that 'if someone is murdered among the Dogon, the family of the murderer is responsible for producing a replacement who can be given the same name as the deceased. The replacement then fills the kin roles of the deceased'.[20] The general principle at work in both prohibitions and namesake relations (as well as in the use of secret or sacred names) is that 'names possess spiritual forces'.[21]

Crucially, names engage the body: to its complex singularity corresponds the multiplicity of relations that names evoke. The name shares with the body 'the function of bringing another person into existence and assigning that person's status'.[22] And, as Michael Ragussis argues, fiction makes manifest the 'profound transaction between body and name, in bodies that function to perpetuate a name, bodies that are sacrificed to a name, bodies in which one writes one's own or another's name, bodies in which one reads one's own or another's name, even bodies whose clearest meaning is cancelled out by having a name attached to them...'[23]

II

Philosophical theories of the proper name tend to be concerned with only one of the operations performed by names—the identification of individuals—and they are closely associated with arguments in formal and modal logic about the nature of referring expressions. The modern account is usually dated from John Stuart Mill's argument in *A System of Logic* that the semantic value of a proper name is its referent (the real entity it refers to); on Mill's view, whereas common names (nouns) have connotation—that is, attributes which define them—'Proper names are not connotative: they denote the individuals who are called by them; but they do not indicate or imply any attributes as belonging to those individuals.'[24] They attach to objects rather than their attributes. That account was problematized by

[19] Stanner, 'Aboriginal Modes of Address and Reference', p. 302.

[20] Richard D. Alford, *Naming and Identity: A Cross-Cultural Study of Personal Naming Practices* (New Haven: HRAF Press, 1988), p. 77.

[21] Alford, *Naming and Identity*, p. 78.

[22] Michael Ragussis, *Acts of Naming: The Family Plot in Fiction* (New York: Oxford University Press, 1986), p. 228.

[23] Ragussis, *Acts of Naming*, p. 228.

[24] John Stuart Mill, *A System of Logic, Ratiocinative and Inductive: Being a Connected View of the Principles of Evidence and the Methods of Scientific Investigation* (1843; 8th edn, New York: Harper & Brothers, 1882), 1.ii.5 (p. 40).

Gottlob Frege in an 1892 paper, 'Über Sinn und Bedeutung', which argues that two linguistic expressions (the classic example is 'the morning star' and 'the evening star', both of which refer to the planet Venus seen at different times of the day) may have a different semantic value (*Sinn*) while referring to the same entity.[25] Our understanding of the name 'Walter Scott' seems to be determined by the knowledge we have of this person: that he was, for example, 'the author of *Waverley*'. That argument was later (perhaps improperly) conflated with Bertrand Russell's argument that proper names are to be understood as disguised or abbreviated definite descriptions—such that for the name 'Aristotle', for example, we could substitute 'the teacher of Alexander the Great'[26] —and with a variant of descriptivism which states that the reference of a name is given by a cluster or family of fluctuating descriptions with contextual valence.[27]

The most important, and still perhaps the most persuasive, critique of descriptivism is that made by Saul Kripke, who argues that reference cannot be derived from descriptions, since descriptions are contingent attributions and will thus vary across possible worlds. Proper names, he argues, should be understood as conferring identity upon an object across all possible worlds (that is, across all possible modal states), and thus to be what he calls 'rigid designators'.[28] For example, 'although someone other than the U.S. President in 1970 might have been the U.S. President in 1970 (e.g., Humphrey might have been), no one other than Nixon might have been Nixon. In the same way, a designator rigidly designates a certain object if it designates that object wherever the object exists' (pp. 48–9). The statement 'Nixon is Nixon' is necessarily true, whereas the statement 'Nixon is the person who delivered the Checkers speech in 1952' is only contingently true, since it is possible to imagine a world in which Nixon did not deliver the speech, did not become vice-president and subsequently president, and so on; or to imagine a world in which someone else delivered that speech. Thus a naming expression used to pick out an individual has, in general, nothing to do with whatever it is that we know about the individual or with 'some uniquely identifying marks, some unique properties satisfied by the referent' (p. 106); reference and description are just two distinct functions of language. The cluster theory of names is correct in saying that to every name or designating expression there corresponds a cluster of attributes, but not in saying that one or more of these attributes picks out an individual.

There are two important qualifications that Kripke makes to this general argument, however. The first is that our acts of reference depend not just on what we ourselves think, but on the community of belief within which they occur. The second follows from this: that the reference of names *originates* in a description, in what Kripke calls 'an initial baptism', which then generates a causal chain of

[25] Gottlob Frege, 'On Sense and Meaning', trans. Max Black, in P. T. Geach and Max Black (eds), *Translations from the Philosophical Writings of Gottlob Frege* (Oxford: Blackwell, 1980), pp. 56–78.

[26] Bertrand Russell, 'On Denoting', *Mind* 14: 56 (1905), pp. 479–93.

[27] Cf. John Searle, 'Proper Names', *Mind* 67 (1958), pp. 166–73.

[28] Saul A. Kripke, *Naming and Necessity* (Oxford: Basil Blackwell, 1980), p. 48; hereafter cited in the text.

referring uses which are not themselves descriptive (p. 96). Thus, the argument that a referent is not determined by a description holds true for every use of a name except the first one.

Now, this is a useful starting point for thinking about the status of fictional names. My interests may seem to be different from those of philosophers concerned with the truth value of expressions; but in fact what philosophers tend to be interested in is the conditions under which expressions correspond or fail to correspond to entities in actual *or other modally structured* worlds. They are, thus, in principle (although frequently not in practice) concerned in the same way that literary theorists are with the workings of names in non-actual worlds, whether they be the names of really existing persons—the horn player Buddy Bolden in Michael Ondaatje's *Coming through Slaughter*, for example, or Lee Harvey Oswald in Don DeLillo's *Libra*—or the names of characters who have no existence in actuality but who do (in some sense of the word 'exist') exist in fictional worlds.

Fictional characters are identified above all (but not necessarily) by a name. And the ontological status of names—their existence as 'real' or 'fictional' referents—is a function of the kind of world they figure in. The most fundamental questions to ask about the names of fictional characters, then, have to do with how they are pinned to the quasi-persons of a text (how we come to recognize a name as an index of the textual existence of a character), the kind of information and the quality of coherence attaching to the name, and their relation to a modal world. As Fotis Jannidis notes, however, characters may exist without being named (they may be designated by pronouns or noun phrases, or in drama and film they may be nameless bodies), or they may have multiple names, or the same name may refer to several different characters—which means that it is not the proper name, or its equivalent, that is the key reference point for information about and recognition of a character, but rather a semantic structure at a level higher than the textual; extending the argument made in the previous chapter, we can say that character is not a linguistic but a conceptual unit,[29] or, rather, that it is *a semantic entity which is textually constructed*. The name is a kind of hook on which properties are hung and it is one basis for an imputation of identity, but it is only by an extrapolation from the level of language to the semantic level, and the 'world' figured forth there, that we recognize the quasi-persons of fictional texts.

The semantics of possible worlds gives one well-established way of approaching the non-actual worlds of fiction. In Chapter 1 I cited Uri Margolin's argument that possible-worlds semantics deals with the operations of reference, identification, and differentiation by which properties are ascribed to quasi-persons who are members of some non-actual state of affairs, which may be 'very close or very far from the actual world in terms of properties and regularities'.[30] Fictional character is a textually generated component of a possible but non-actual (and non-actualizable)

[29] Fotis Jannidis, *Figur und Person: Beitrag zu einer historischen Narratologie* (Berlin: Walter de Gruyter, 2004), p. 240; cf. also the argument to this effect on p. 169.

[30] Uri Margolin, 'Character', in David Herman (ed.), *The Cambridge Companion to Narrative* (Cambridge: Cambridge University Press, 2007), p. 71.

world, and the concept of 'world' here refers to a rule-governed semiotic construct in which 'fictional entities are treated as constituents of a higher-order, "emergent" structure, the fictional world'.[31] In Lubomir Doležel's definition, fictional worlds are 'ensembles of nonactualized possible states of affairs', not dependent upon actual prototypes, shaped by specific global constraints including the boundedness of what can be known, and containing 'a finite number of individuals who are compossible'.[32]

Within fictional worlds, and despite their referring to non-existent persons, it is still possible to attribute truth values to propositions about characters: with respect to the world of *Madame Bovary*, it is true that 'Emma Bovary committed suicide' and false that 'Emma Bovary died of tuberculosis'.[33] The condition that Kripke takes to be necessary for any act of reference across modal worlds—that names must have a correlate in reality—thus does not hold for the counterfactual worlds of fiction, where distinctions of truth and falsity, and other modal operations such as believing or wishing or remembering, function as a set of 'modal stratifications' within and relative to the particular ontological domain to which fiction belongs.[34] Names can thus 'rigidly designate entities whether these are real or imaginary, fictional or nonfictional', and 'naming is warranted in fictional contexts as long as referential criteria are adjusted to the nature of fictional discourse'.[35] Characters with 'real' names (Napoleon, Buddy Bolden) occupy a peculiar status within fictional worlds: they are fictional to the extent that they are incorporated into the worlds of *War and Peace* or *Coming through Slaughter*, but bring with them constraints on the uses that can be made of them. Arguing against Doležel's claim for the modal unity of fictional worlds, Catherine Gallagher maintains that switching between semantic modes is 'the peculiar language game of certain kinds of fiction': Napoleon in *War and Peace* is a fictional character, but 'the totality of his persona in *War and Peace* is not fictional because it must obey a rule of noncontradiction with the Emperor's personal history'.[36] That rule may be disregarded: in Simon Leys' *The Death of Napoleon* the deposed Emperor escapes from St Helena, leaving behind a double, and travels through post-Napoleonic Europe, ending up, towards the end of the novella, in an insane asylum full of madmen, all of whom claim to be Napoleon.[37] But the very breaking of the rule of non-contradiction continues to assume it.

The fictionality of fictional worlds is thus not an absolute: they may contain shards of non-fictionality. Conversely, 'non-fictional' texts—texts governed by a

[31] Lubomir Doležel, *Heterocosmica: Fiction and Possible Worlds* (Baltimore: Johns Hopkins University Press, 1998), p. 15.

[32] Doležel, *Heterocosmica*, pp. 16, 20.

[33] Doležel, *Heterocosmica*, p. 3.

[34] Ruth Ronen, *Possible Worlds in Literary Theory* (Cambridge: Cambridge University Press, 1994), p. 41.

[35] Ronen, *Possible Worlds in Literary Theory*, p. 136.

[36] Catherine Gallagher, 'What Would Napoleon Do? Historical, Fictional, and Counterfactual Characters', *New Literary History* 42: 2 (2011), pp. 318, 321.

[37] Simon Leys, *The Death of Napoleon*, trans. Patricia Clancy and Simon Leys (London: Quartet, 1991).

truth function—tell stories or construct states of affairs by selecting materials and imposing boundaries, by adopting a particular temporal and moral perspective, and by deploying protocols of truth which are generically specific—that is, by adopting some of the features that we think of as characteristic of fiction.[38] They may use conditionals and subjunctives, anticipations and memories; they may tell half-truths or incomplete truths, and their truths, too, will be specific to a discursive domain. You could say that the 'real' world is one of many possible fictional worlds that happens to be actual, or that it differs from other fictional worlds in being open-ended rather than bounded. What determines the modal status of a world is not the nature of its referents or of its discursive forms but a conventional and usually tacit contract about that status and its particulars—a contract that is institutional in the sense that it emerges from the mechanisms that sustain discursive formations and the ontological contents that they produce, and conventional in the sense that any one world is defined by its relation to other possible worlds. World is a mode of closure; but closure is never complete.

III

Like the names of persons who really exist, the names of fictional characters have the functions of both reference and description; unlike real names, however, fictional names are made up of nothing but clusters of descriptions, elaborated sequentially through a text.[39] This is the force of the structuralist claim that characters are initially empty proper names which come to be filled with semes or predications.[40] The fullest statement is perhaps this by Roland Barthes in *S/Z*:

> When identical semes traverse the same proper name several times and appear to settle upon it, a character is created. Thus, the character is a product of combinations: the combination is relatively stable (denoted by the recurrence of the semes) and more or less complex (involving more or less congruent, more or less contradictory figures)... The proper name acts as a magnetic field for the semes; referring in fact to a body, it draws the semic configuration into an evolving (biographical) tense.[41]

Names are the nodal points in a narrative network, pulling together actions and descriptions and in turn defined, filled with semantic content, by those actions and descriptions.[42] They may start with a pre-given semantic content (referring, for example, to classical figures or using semantically or onomatopoeically rich

[38] Cf. John Frow, *Genre* (London: Routledge, 2006), pp. 87–99.

[39] Cf. William H. Gass, 'The Concept of Character in Fiction', in *Fiction and the Figures of Life* (New York: Alfred A. Knopf, 1970), p. 50: 'To create a character is to give meaning to an unknown X; it is *absolutely* to *define*; and since nothing in life corresponds to these X's, their reality is borne by their name.'

[40] Tzvetan Todorov, *Grammaire du Décaméron* (The Hague: Mouton, 1969), p. 28.

[41] Roland Barthes, *S/Z*, trans. Richard Miller (New York: Hill and Wang, 1974), pp. 67–8.

[42] Peter W. Nesselroth, 'Naming Names in Telling Tales', in Calin-Andrei Mihailescu and Walid Hamarneth (eds), *Fiction Updated: Theories of Fictionality, Narratology, and Poetics* (Toronto: University of Toronto Press, 1996), p. 133.

lexemes or, as with the Vice or the Humour in medieval morality plays, working as 'moral characteronyms'),[43] or they may be semantically neutral; but the name is no more than the ground on which a figure is built.

If it is the case, however, that fictional characters exist as projections from the proper name onto that 'semic configuration', then the possibility arises of a discrepancy between the name and the character who embodies it, giving rise to what Michael Ragussis calls the 'naming plots' that are so central to the novel as a genre. 'The name,' he writes, 'functions most profoundly in fiction not as a static standard-bearer that reveals character from the beginning, but as the center of a matrix of action, at the center of the plots of fiction.'[44] Gilles Deleuze and Félix Guattari thus speak of the novel as being defined, from its beginnings, by 'the adventure of lost characters who no longer know their name, what they are looking for, or what they are doing, amnesics, ataxics, catatonics'; the knight of courtly love, for example, 'spends his time forgetting his name, what he is doing, what people say to him...'[45]

While Deleuze and Guattari's description of the courtly romance as part of the tradition of the novel seems to me (for reasons I elaborate later) wrong, it is perhaps the case that the romance is the genre in which the force of the proper name is most distinctively explored. At its core is what Ragussis calls 'name magic',[46] the belief that names have a force, a performative power, which is greater than that of designation. This belief is cognate with but distinct from the widespread medieval belief—Ernst Curtius calls it a 'category of thought'[47] —in the use of etymology to trace linguistic multiplicities back to the originary moment in which words most closely resemble things;[48] as Jane Bliss argues, 'name-magic overshadows the question of name meaning because a Name has power in itself even if (especially if) it is a meaningless cipher'.[49] It is the acts performed by names, rather than their intrinsic resemblance to the world, that constitutes their power in the romance: the giving or the revealing or the suppression of a name take us to the heart of a destiny or of the religious mysteries which so closely parallel the worlds of courtly love and combat.

[43] Alastair Fowler, *Literary Names: Personal Names in English Literature* (Oxford: Oxford University Press, 2012), p. 16.

[44] Ragussis, *Acts of Naming*, p. 11.

[45] Gilles Deleuze and Félix Guattari, *A Thousand Plateaus: Capitalism and Schizophrenia*, trans. Brian Massumi (Minneapolis: University of Minnesota Press, 1987), pp. 192, 193.

[46] Ragussis, *Acts of Naming*, p. 198 and passim.

[47] Ernst Robert Curtius, *European Literature and the Latin Middle Ages*, trans. Willard R. Trask (New York: Harper & Row, 1953), p. 495.

[48] That belief finds its fullest expression in Isidore of Seville's early seventh-century compendium of all knowledge, the *Etymologiarum sive originum libri xx*, which seeks 'the places where language comes to a standstill, where meaning becomes intrinsic, where, to adopt his own phrase, the first parts of language, the *primogenia*, "do not draw their origin from somewhere else"', and from which, given the immediacy of language to things, one can at once deduce an ontology. R. Howard Bloch, *Etymologies and Genealogies: A Literary Anthropology of the French Middle Ages* (Chicago: University of Chicago Press, 1983), p. 56.

[49] Jane Bliss, *Naming and Namelessness in Medieval Romance* (Cambridge: D.S. Brewer, 2008), pp. 20–1.

The act of naming is given particular importance in one of the most influential romance texts, Chrétien's unfinished *Le Conte du Graal* (the text that Deleuze and Guattari designate as the beginning of the novel), composed for oral performance towards the end of the twelfth century.[50] Like his mother, the widow of the Desolate Forest ('*la veve dame/De la gaste forest soutaine*'),[51] and his dead father, its hero Perceval is without a name for the first third of the narrative, being known, and knowing himself, only as 'darling son', 'darling brother', or (what he calls his '*droit non*' or 'proper name') 'darling little lord' ('*Biax Filz*', '*Biau Frere*', '*Biau Sire*').[52] This naïveté about the difference between epithets and names belongs to the first of the three modes which govern the story and which correspond roughly to the three phases of Perceval's development: a comic mode, in which Perceval figures as an eager rustic youth; an adventure mode, in which he acts as a knight errant; and a mystical mode corresponding to the gradual revelation of the mystery of the grail and of the kinship networks that tie him to it.

From its opening lines, which set up an analogy between storytelling and the sowing of seed on good soil, *Le Conte du Graal* works with a continuously negotiated tension between the barren and the fertile. Perceval's home is the forest, which is both '*gaste*'—waste, uncultivated, but also ravaged—and '*soutaine*'—solitary, desolate; yet he sets out at the beginning of the story at the height of spring, when everything is 'aflame with joy' ('*de joie aflamme*'),[53] to see his mother's ploughmen sowing oats. Fertility is the natural order of things, yet it depends upon a precarious order of human governance and is thus constantly problematic. The ruin of Perceval's father, wounded 'between the legs' ('*parmi les jambes navrez*')[54] and deprived of his lands and treasure, coincides with the death of King Arthur's father, Utherpandragon, when

> Apovri et desherité
> Et escillié furent a tort
> Li gentil home...
> Les terres furent escillies
> Et les povres gens avillies,
> Si s'en fuï qui fuïr pot.

[*worthy men were unjustly disinherited, impoverished, and exiled, their lands ravaged, and the poor reduced to the lowest condition. All who could flee from there fled.*][55]

[50] Chrétien de Troyes, *Le Roman de Perceval, ou Le Conte du Graal*, ed. Keith Busby (Tübingen: Max Niemeyer Verlag, 1993); hereafter *Le Conte du Graal*. I have used the English translation of David Staines, *The Complete Romances of Chrétien de Troyes* (Bloomington: Indiana University Press, 1990). References are to line numbers of the poem and page numbers of the translation.

[51] *Le Conte du Graal*, ll. 74–5/p. 340.

[52] *Le Conte du Graal*, ll. 349–54/p. 344. The interrogation about his name and his responses occur in a later interpolation, probably by a copyist; cf. *Le Conte du Graal*, p. 427.

[53] *Le Conte du Graal*, l. 73/p. 340.

[54] *Le Conte du Graal*, l. 436/p. 345.

[55] *Le Conte du Graal*, ll. 442–4, 447–9/p. 345.

'Distant land, fallow land, destroyed land,' writes Howard Bloch of the Desolate Forest, 'the Arthurian Wasteland constitutes a landscape and a relation of men to their natural environment characterized by depopulation, the infertility of nature, and a crisis of social order.'[56] Yet that threat of barrenness is always balanced against its opposite, as when the siege of the town of Beaurepaire—surrounded by 'barren and deserted' land ('*la terre gaste et escovee*')[57] and equally desolate within, with the streets empty, the abbeys destroyed, and no milking or baking of bread taking place—is suddenly and almost miraculously relieved by the arrival of a barge full of provisions, giving the townspeople an abundance of food and unleashing both the sexual 'joy' ('*joie*') that Perceval and Blanchefleur find in each other and the 'din of the rejoicing' ('*molt joie et bruit*') of the citizens.[58]

These opposing states are tied together by a kind of underlying magical logic: that of the spell and the breaking of the spell. Magical action in fairy tales and folk tales is often organized in triplets, with two successive failures followed by ultimate success. A number of episodes in *Le Conte du Graal* are structured by repetition of this kind: Perceval is unheard twice by King Arthur when he first enters his court, before being heard at his third attempt; the goose attacked by a falcon sheds three drops of blood on the snow, and of the three knights sent out by King Arthur to fetch Perceval as he stands gazing at these drops of blood, only the third, Gawain, is successful. The structure is like that of guesses at the answer to a riddle, with the third attempt being a kind of refutation of the previous unsuccessful answers. The riddle form does indeed appear in *Le Conte du Graal*, both literally (Perceval encounters a charcoal burner who tells him that King Arthur is at once 'happy and doleful' ('*lié et dolant*'),[59] and then explains this to him) and in the form of the questions that are unanswered because unasked, the questions Perceval fails to ask at the Grail Castle. What he sees there, as he sits at dinner with the Fisher King, is a bleeding lance and a bowl ('*graal*') that passes before him into another room; the questions he fails to ask have to do with the nature of the bleeding lance and who it is who is served from the bowl.

The consequences of that failure are, in turn, revealed to him in three successive stages. In the first, a maiden lamenting her lover, a knight who has been beheaded, tells him that he (Perceval) has spent the night at the house of 'the wealthy Fisher King' ('*le riche Roi Pescheor*'),[60] and that, had he asked the right questions,

> Que tant eüsses amendé
> Le buen roi qui est mehaigniez
> Que toz eüst regaaigniez
> Ses membres et terre tenist,
> Et si grans biens en avenist!
> Ma[i]s or saches que grant anui
> En avenront toi et autrui.

[56] Bloch, *Etymologies and Genealogies*, p. 200.
[57] *Le Conte du Graal*, l. 1750/p. 361.
[58] *Le Conte du Graal*, ll. 2577, 2579/p. 371.
[59] *Le Conte du Graal*, l. 845/p. 350.
[60] *Le Conte du Graal*, l. 3495/p. 382.

[*You would have cured the good king who is infirm. He would have regained use of his limbs and been capable of governing the land. But now be certain that harm will befall you and others.*][61]

She then reveals to him that she is his first cousin, that she was brought up with him in his mother's house, and that his mother has died of grief at his leaving.

In the second stage, a hideous maiden who comes to Arthur's court curses Perceval for his failure, repeating what he has already been told and adding that, if the king is not cured of his wounds and does not hold his land in peace, then

Dames en perdront lor maris,
Terres en seront escillies
Et puceles desconseillies,
Qui orfenines remandront,
Et maint chevalier en morront;
Tot cist mal avenront par toi.

[*Ladies will lose their husbands; hapless maidens will be orphans; many knights will die; and lands will be laid waste. All these ills will result because of you.*][62]

Finally, the hermit repeats what the first maiden had told Perceval, that it was a sin of which he was ignorant, namely causing the death of his mother, that has 'cut off your tongue' ('*la langue te trencha*')[63] when he failed to ask why the lancehead never stops bleeding, or who is served from the bowl. Then the hermit reveals to him one part of the truth about the grail:

Cil qui l'en en sert est mes frere,
Ma suer et soe fu ta mere;
Et del riche Pescheor croi
Que il est fix a celui roi
Qui del graal servir se fait.

[*The man who is served from it was my brother. My sister and his was your mother. And as for that rich Fisher King, he is, I believe, the son of this king who has himself served from the bowl.*][64]

And he adds that Perceval must not imagine that the bowl contains 'pike, lamprey, or salmon' ('*lus ne lamproie ne salmon*');[65] the enfeebled king who is served from the grail sustains his life on a single host each day: that is, on the sacrificial body of Christ (the interview with the hermit takes place on Good Friday).

Perceval's silence is a failure to answer the riddle posed by the grail, and at the same time a failure to guess who he is and what his lineage is; it repeats his

[61] *Le Conte du Graal*, ll. 3586–92/p. 384.
[62] *Le Conte du Graal*, ll. 4678–83/pp. 396–7.
[63] *Le Conte du Graal*, l. 6409/p. 417.
[64] *Le Conte du Graal*, ll. 6415–9/p. 417.
[65] *Le Conte du Graal*, l. 6421/p. 417.

previous lack of interest in his mother's story about the fate of his father. At the very moment when the grail passes before him in the Fisher King's castle, when Perceval keeps his silence both because he has been instructed not to be inquisitive and because he 'feared that if he asked a question, he would be taken for a peasant' ('*Et crient, se il le demandast/Qu'en le tenist a vilonie*'),[66] the narrator intervenes to sound a warning in his own person:

> Si criem que il n'ait damage,
> Por che que j'ai oï retraire
> Qu'ausi bien se puet on trop taire
> Com trop parler a la foie[e].
> Ou biens l'en praigne ou mals l'en chiee,
> Ne lor en quiert, rien ne demande.

[*I fear harm may result, for I have often heard it said that there are times when too much silence is the same as too much speech. Whether for good or ill, he did not ask them any question.*][67]

In Claude Lévi-Strauss's reading of the story, there is a kind of inverted homology here with the elements of the Oedipus myth: on the one hand, a question which, in finding its answer and thus bringing together terms meant to remain separate, has as its consequence incest and an unleashing of natural forces ('the son is joined with the mother, the brother with the sister, in the same way as the answer succeeds, against all expectations, in rejoining its question');[68] on the other, an answer without a question of which the corollary is chastity or impotence and the drying up of animal and vegetable fertility. Too much or too little speech: both bring the harm that devastates the land.[69]

Between Perceval's crippled father and the crippled Fisher King (and perhaps also the Fisher King's father, the absent presence in the Grail Castle) there is an 'uncanny resemblance' and a complex set of doublings:[70] the same wound, the same lack of healing, giving rise to the same devastation of the fertile land. As Perceval comes closer to knowledge of the mystery of the grail he comes closer to knowing his own lineage: first he learns that he is the cousin of the young maiden, then that he is the cousin of the Fisher King and the nephew both of the hermit and of the Grail King, his maternal uncles. It is precisely through his failure to ask the right question (in its turn the consequence of 'a sin of which you are ignorant'

[66] *Le Conte du Graal*, ll. 3210–11/p. 379.

[67] *Le Conte du Graal*, ll. 3248–53/p. 379.

[68] Claude Lévi-Strauss, 'The Scope of Anthropology', in *Structural Anthropology*, vol. 2, trans. Monique Layton (Harmondsworth: Penguin, 1978), p. 23.

[69] Howard Bloch notes, however, the way in which the linking of the riddle to incest consummates that 'dream of wedding the laws of kinship to those of language' which plays so crucial a role in the medieval fascination with 'genealogy conceived along linguistic lines and language conceived along family lines'. Bloch, *Etymologies and Genealogies*, pp. 25, 35.

[70] Irit Ruth Kleiman, 'X Marks the Spot: The Place of the Father in Chrétien de Troyes's *Conte du Graal*', *Modern Language Review* 103 (2008), p. 976.

[‘*I. pechiez dont tu ne sez mot*’])[71] that Perceval is inserted into a structure of kinship that, in a quite extraordinary manner, endows him with a name. At the very moment when he tells the maiden that ‘not a word left my mouth’ (‘*Ainc de ma bouche n’en issi*’),[72] she answers:

— Si m’aït Dieux, de tant valt pis.
Coment avez vos non amis?>>
Et cil qui son non ne savoit
Devine et dist que il avoit
Perchevax li Galois a non,
Ne ne set s’il dist voir ou non;
Mais il dist voir et si nel sot.

[‘*So help me God, that is worse. What is your name, friend?*’
And the youth, ignorant of his name, had a sudden inspiration and replied that his name was Perceval the Welshman. He did not know whether or not he spoke the truth. And though he did not know, he spoke the truth.][73]

Knowledge of the truth of his name—more like a flash of involuntary memory, a recollection of what has always been there,[74] than like that act of ‘initial baptism’ that Kripke posits as the origin of the name’s power of reference[75] —comes to Perceval at the very moment when he becomes aware both of his failure and its dire consequences, and of the death of his mother. The withholding of the question—a question, we might say, about the name of the father—brings to Perceval the knowledge at once of his own identity and of his bitter failure (because of a sin of which, as of his name, he is ignorant). Fredric Jameson notes that it is at the moment of defeat in the combat of arms that the hostile knight yields up his name in a plea for mercy (‘*Sire, Ydiers, li filz Nut, ai non*’):[76] to make one’s name known is to expose oneself to the mercy of the other, since the name is understood to be (magically) a metonym of the person. Perceval finds his name in defeat, when he is at his most vulnerable and at the moment of his greatest testing. We might remember Gawain’s motto: never to withhold his name when it is asked for, and never to offer it without first being asked.[77]

We might remember, too, that the conversation with Perceval’s cousin which elicits the recollection of his name takes place beside the corpse of the maiden’s beheaded lover. Perceval is directly analogous to this dead and nameless knight,

[71] *Le Conte du Graal*, l. 6393/p. 416.
[72] *Le Conte du Graal*, l. 3570/p. 383.
[73] *Le Conte du Graal*, ll. 3571–7/p. 383. The maiden immediately replies that his name is changed, from Perchevax li Galois to Perchevax li chaitis, Perceval the wretched; but this is, of course, a change only of epithet (‘*sournon*’), not of name; cf. Bliss, *Naming and Namelessness*, p. 34.
[74] Cf. Barbara N. Sargent-Baur, ‘Le jeu des noms de personne dans le *Conte du Graal*’, *Neophilologus* 85: 4 (2001), p. 492: ‘*Dans un éclair qui fait penser à la mémoire involontaire explorée par Proust, il retrouve au plus profond de son être, non pas une intuition ni une révélation… mais un souvenir.*’
[75] Kripke, *Naming and Necessity*, p. 96.
[76] Chrétien de Troyes, *Erec et Enide*, l. 1042, cited in Fredric Jameson, *The Political Unconscious: Narrative as a Socially Symbolic Act* (London: Methuen, 1981), p. 119.
[77] *Le Conte du Graal*, ll. 5622–5/p. 408.

whom he brutally dismisses: 'The dead with the dead, the living with the living!' ('*Les mors as mors, les vis as vis*').[78] And both are, in complex ways, analogous to the Son who is worshipped in the church where 'the sacrifice of the body of Jesus Christ occurs' ('*S'i sacrefie l'en le cors/Jhesu Crist le prophete sainte*').[79] It is at the level of this mystical analogy that a final act of magical naming occurs:

> Et li hermites li conseille
> Une oroison dedens l'oreille,
> Si le ferma tant qu'il le sot.
> Et en cele oroison si ot
> Assez des nons nostre Seignor,
> Car il i furent li greignor
> Que nomer ne doit bouche d'ome,
> Se par paor de mort nes nome.
> Quant l'oroison li ot apprise,
> Desfendi lui qu'en nule guise
> Ne la deïst sanz grant peril.

[*And the hermit whispered a prayer in his ear, repeating it until Perceval learned it. This prayer contained many of the names of Our Lord, all the highest and the greatest which the tongue of man never dared pronounce except when in peril of death. When he taught him the prayer, he forbade him to utter it except in times of grave danger.*][80]

The sacred name is powerful and dangerous (precisely the meaning of the Latin *sacer*) because it reveals something of the essence of the god. Perceval's name is, likewise, that core of his being which is intimately bound up with the spell lying over the romance's Fathers and the land they cannot rule. If it is revealed to him in a flash of recollection, it is, nevertheless, the case that his naming proceeds in stages, from the epithet substituting for a proper name, to the name which is immediately stripped of its epithet, to his later confident ability to offer his name when asked. In Michael McKeon's words, 'if romance names are the outward embodiment of an inner or essential truth, romance character development tends to proceed by discontinuous leaps between states of being—by "rebirths"—and to be signified by the successive divulgence or alteration of name'.[81]

IV

Jane Bliss writes of the naming conventions of the medieval romance that 'names not given by history are treated as though they were (real-life names), according to the medieval convention that writers follow "the book". In this sense the romance

[78] *Le Conte du Graal*, l. 3630/p. 384.
[79] *Le Conte du Graal*, ll. 580–1/p. 346.
[80] *Le Conte du Graal*, ll. 6479–90/p. 418.
[81] Michael McKeon, *The Origins of the English Novel, 1600–1740* (Baltimore: Johns Hopkins University Press, 1987), p. 39.

is profoundly different from the novel, whose characters together with their names are by convention created'.[82] The text that definitively initiates that break between the romance and the novel (or rather, that initiates the continuing, genre-defining structural tension between the romance and the novelistic modes) is, nevertheless, one whose hero refers constantly to the authority of the Book. Don Quixote

> can become a knight only by listening from afar to the age-old epic that gives its form to Law. The book is not so much his existence as his duty. He is constantly obliged to consult it in order to know what to do or say, and what signs he should give himself and others in order to show that he really is of the same nature as the text from which he springs.[83]

Yet, as Foucault goes on to argue, it is precisely Quixote's mimetic desire that requires him to put those textual signs to the test, and thus inexorably to allow his reader to discover their lack of correspondence with a disenchanted reality.

That relation between the model taken from the book and the mundane reality that undercuts it is already evident in the hero's initial act of changing his name from what the various 'authors of this true history' conjecture might have been Quixada or Quesada or Quexana, to the nobler-sounding Don Quixote de la Mancha;[84] but it emerges more fully in a second act in which Quixote is given a knightly sobriquet. The baptism is made almost casually by Sancho Panza, who informs the departing priests that if they wish to know 'who the valorous knight was that did them such mischief... it was the famous Don Quixote de la Mancha, who also bears the name of The Knight of the Sad Countenance'.[85] Asked by Quixote why he had called him that, Sancho replies with a literal motivation (an assumption 'that attributes can without loss be exchanged for the subject of whom they are predicated'):[86] it's because Don Quixote has 'the most dismal face I've ever seen', either because of his weariness or because he is losing his teeth. But the hero adduces a quite different reason: '"It is from neither", replied Don Quixote, "but because the sage whose task it is to write the history of my deeds must have thought it right for me to take some title, as all knights did in the olden days."'[87] And he resolves to have the emblem of a sad face painted on his shield—although

[82] Bliss, *Naming and Namelessness*, p. 15. *Le Conte du Graal* is narrated by Chrétien on the authority of 'the story'—the 'book' given him by Philip of Flanders—but also, contradictorily, of his personal testimony: 'This I remember well, and so the story testifies' ('*bien m'en ramembre,/Que l'estoire ensi le tesmoigne*'). *Le Conte du Graal*, ll. 2806–7/p. 374.

[83] Michel Foucault, *The Order of Things: An Archaeology of the Human Sciences* (New York: Random House, 1970), p. 46.

[84] Miguel de Cervantes Saavedra, *The Adventures of Don Quixote*, trans. J. M. Cohen (Harmondsworth: Penguin, 1950), Part I, ch. 19, pp. 31–4; *El Ingenioso Hidalgo Don Quijote de la Mancha, Obras Completas*, ed. Angel Valbuena Prat, vol. II (Madrid: Aguilar, 1970), Part I, ch. 19, pp. 1219–21. Further references will cite part, chapter, and page number for each edition.

[85] *—Si acaso quisieren saber esos señores quien ha sido el valeroso que tales los puso... es el famoso Don Quijote de la Mancha, que por otro nombre se llama el* Caballero de la Triste Figura. *Don Quixote*, I.19.146/I.19.1289.

[86] Jacques Lezra, 'The Matter of Naming in "Don Quixote",' in *Unspeakable Subjects: The Genealogy of the Event in Early Modern Europe* (Stanford: Stanford University Press, 1997), p. 165.

[87] *la mas mala figura, de poco acá, que jamas he visto; —no es esto—respondió Don Quijote—, sino que el sabio a cuyo cargo debe de estar el escribir la historia de mis hazañas le habrá parecido que será*

Sancho assures him that the sight of his own face will be enough to reveal the truth of the name.[88]

Now, this 'sage' who will inscribe Don Quixote into the book he will become is elsewhere described as a 'sage enchanter' ('*algún sabio encantador*'),[89] and his role (he is, of course, the author's ironic double) is ambiguous: he may be either friendly or hostile. In Part II Quixote reflects that 'if the author of that history of my exploits, which they say is now in print, chanced to be some enchanter hostile to me, he has probably changed one thing into another, mingling a thousand lies with one truth, and digressed to narrate actions out of the sequence proper to a faithful history'.[90] Either the world conforms to an order of ideal forms ('God knows whether Dulcinea exists on earth or no, whether she is fantastic or not fantastic. These are not matters whose verification can be carried out to the full. I neither engendered nor bore my lady, though I contemplate her in her ideal form…');[91] or else it is enchanted—that is to say, subject to the malevolent enchantment that changes giants into windmills, the order of the Book into some other genre altogether.

That 'other genre altogether' is the novel, the book of sheep and windmills which reverses the terms of Quixote's universe and of the romance epic from which it draws its authority. From the perspective of the novel it is Quixote's universe that is enchanted, and the task of fiction becomes that of a ruthless *dis*enchantment. Its instrument is comic deflation, the act of self-conscious recognition of what really is. Whereas the romance epic is written by a single sage who is assigned the task of memorializing the deeds of its hero, the story of the adventures of Don Quixote exists in an imperfect manuscript and has an uncertain number of authors drawing on speculative sources; the first section of the text is broken off in a frozen tableau and is resumed by a second author, Cide Hamete Benengeli, a Moor and thus by definition a liar, since Moors 'are all cheats, forgers and schemers'.[92] Moreover, the text we are reading is a translation commissioned by the most recent author from a manuscript in Arabic that he bought in the market at Toledo: the book is a commodity, purchased for half a *real*, rather than the gift of the Muse and of vatic transmission.[93] It is the very opposite of that 'age-old epic that gives its form to Law' on which Quixote models himself and to which he expects the world to conform.

bien que yo tome algún nombre apelativo, como lo tomaban todos los caballeros pasados. Don Quixote, I.1.147/I.1.1289.

[88] A useful account of the complexity of naming practices in *Don Quixote* is E. C. Riley, 'Who's Who in *Don Quixote*? Or an Approach to the Problem of Identity', *MLN* 81: 2 (1966), pp. 113–30.

[89] *Don Quixote*, II.2.484/II.2.1497.

[90] *temo que en aquella historia que dicen que anda impresa de mis hazañas, si por ventura ha sido su autor algún sabio mi enemigo, habrá puesto unas cosas por otras, mezclando con una verdad mil mentiras, divertiéndose a contar otras acciones fuera de lo que requiere la continuación de una verdadera historia. Don Quixote*, II.8.516/II.8.1516.

[91] *Dios sabe si hay Dulcinea o no en el mundo, o si es fantástica o no es fantástica; y estas no son de las cosas cuya averiguación se ha de llevar hasta el cabo. No yo engendré ni parí a mi señora, puesto que la contemplo como conviene que sea… Don Quixote*, II.32.680/II.32.1616.

[92] *todos eran embelecadores, falsarios y quimeristas. Don Quixote*, II.3.485/II.3.1498.

[93] Cf. Marthe Robert, *The Old and the New: From* Don Quixote *to Kafka*, trans. Carol Cosman (Berkeley: University of California Press, 1977), pp. 112–3.

The disenchanted order of novelistic reality has a number of delegates within the novel—in the first instance Sancho Panza, for whom the test of reality is the basic bodily functions (an enchanted reality has no place for eating, pissing, and shitting).[94] Sancho embodies comic laughter. In Part I, Chapter 20, as Don Quixote and Sancho Panza listen in fear to the sound of monstrous blows resounding through the night, the latter relieves himself and is reprimanded by his master. The next morning they ride towards the source of the noise, and

> on their turning a corner, there appeared, clear and visible, the indubitable cause of that horrific and, to them, most dreadful sound, which had kept them all that night in such a state of terror and suspense. It was—do not take it amiss, good reader!—six fulling-hammers whose regular strokes made all that din.
>
> Don Quixote was dumbfounded and utterly abashed at this sight and, when Sancho looked at him, his head hung down on his breast in confusion. But when Don Quixote looked at Sancho and clearly saw from his swollen cheeks and his laughing mouth that he was on the point of exploding, despite his own gloom he could not help laughing at the look of him. And as soon as Sancho saw that his master had begun, he let himself go with such violence that he had to hold his sides for fear of bursting.[95]

The moment of anagnorisis initiated by the text is underwritten by Sancho's explosion of laughter, which his master understands for what it is, an act of violence directed against him and which he therefore reciprocates by beating his servant. Violence is, more generally, the mode in which comic deflation is enforced by the representatives of reality within the text. The Duke and Duchess in particular are brutal in their enforcement of a 'sane' reality against those they take to be deluded: Sancho must agree to whip himself in order to release the pseudo-Dulcinea from her enchantment;[96] Doña Rodriguez and Don Quixote are savagely pinched by unknown assailants, who turn out to be the Duchess and Altisidora, 'in a great fury and spoiling for revenge'.[97] The Duke and the Duchess share their amusement over this; but by the time of the final demystification of Don Quixote by the Bachelor Sampson Carrasco—who defeats him in a mock-courtly joust—the joke has lost its force and Quixote, 'melancholy, sorrowful, brooding and in a bad way',[98] has become a tragic figure.

[94] *Don Quixote*, I.49.433/I.49.1465.

[95] *al doblar de una punta, pareció descubierta y patente la misma causa, sin que pudiese ser otra, de aquel horrísono y para ellos espantable ruido, que tan suspensos y medrosos toda la noche los había tenido. Y eran (si no lo has, ¡oh lector!, por pesadumbre y enojo) seis mazos de batán, que con sus alternativos golpes aquel estruendo formaban.*

Cuando Don Quijote vio lo que era enmudeció y pasmóse de arriba abajo. Miróle Sancho, y vio que tenía la cabeza inclinada sobre el pecho, con muestras de estar corrido. Miró también Don Quijote a Sancho, y vióle que tenía los carrillos hinchados y la boca llena de risa, con evidentes señales de querer reventar con ella, y no pudo su melancolía tanto con él, que a la vista de Sancho pudiese dejar de reírse; y como vio Sancho que su amo había comenzado, soltó la presa, de manera que tuvo necesidad de apretarse las ijadas con los puños por no reventar riendo. Don Quixote, I.20.157–8/I.20.1295–6.

[96] *Don Quixote*, II.35.701/II.35/1628.

[97] *llenas de cólera y deseosas de venganza. Don Quixote*, II.50.790/II.50.1681.

[98] *marrido, triste, pensativo y mal acondicionado. Don Quixote*, II.65.892/II.65.1744.

And something curious happens to these delegates of the novelistic real: their world is gradually contaminated by Quixote's enchanted reality, and, as Cide Hamete notes, 'the mockers were as mad as their victims'.[99] Thus, Sancho, Dorothea, the Duke and Duchess, the priest and the barber, and Sampson Carrasco all begin to produce realities that conform to the Book of Quixote's imagination: the priest and the barber try to persuade Quixote out of his madness by dressing up as a damsel errant ('*doncella andante*') and her squire;[100] Sancho transforms a peasant girl into Dulcinea del Toboso, matching his rhetoric to his master's;[101] Dorothea, crossing effortlessly from the novel's pastoral to its novelistic strand, becomes the Princess Micomicona and imitates strictly the code of courtly romance;[102] the deceptions practised by the Duke and Duchess confirm for Quixote his imagined reality—'this was the first time that he was positively certain of being a true and no imaginary knight errant, since he found himself treated just as he had read these knights were treated in past ages';[103] and Quixote's encounter with the Knight of the Mirrors, whom he considers to be an enchanted double, makes it clear that he has forced the world (in this case, again, Sampson Carrasco) to produce a reality that, in its substance, mirrors his own.

That contamination of mundane reality by Quixote's enchanted counter-world spreads, in Part II of the novel, to the narrative instance itself. Quixote's discovery that he exists in a book (the one we know as Part I of the novel) confirms to him the overriding reality of the order of Literature in which he believes himself to exist; and the discovery that a spurious continuation of his adventures is in circulation (the one really, but 'falsely', written by Avellaneda) serves to confirm the scriptural status of Part I. When Quixote and Sancho encounter at an inn a certain Don Alvaro Tarfe, a character from the spurious Part II, they take out an injunction against him requiring him to recognize them as the real Don Quixote and Sancho Panza—and this legal document convinces Don Alvaro that he must have been deceived, and even 'enchanted, since he had touched two such different Don Quixotes with his own hands'.[104] The novel's assertion of the unreality of literature is thus undercut, since it is now only at a great ironical distance—irony to the second degree—that that assertion can be made. In Foucault's summary:

> The first part of the hero's adventures plays in the second part the role originally assumed by the chivalric romances. Don Quixote must remain faithful to the book that he has now become in reality; he must protect it from errors, from counterfeits,

[99] *Y dice más Cide Hamete: que tiene para sí ser tan locos los burladores como los burlados. Don Quixote*, II.70.916/II.70.1758.

[100] *Don Quixote*, I.26.221/I.26.1334.

[101] *Don Quixote*, II.10.528–9/II.10.1523–4.

[102] *Don Quixote*, I.29.252/I.29.1353.

[103] *aquel fue el primer día que de todo en todo conoció y creyó ser caballero andante verdadero, y no fantástico, viéndose tratar del mesmo modo que él había leído se trataban los tales caballeros en los pasados siglos. Don Quixote*, II.31.667/II.31.1608.

[104] *se dio a entender que debía de estar encantado, pues tocaba con la mano dos tan contrarios Don Quijotes. Don Quixote*, II.72.929/II.72.1766.

> from apocryphal sequels; he must fill in the details that have been left out; he must preserve its truth. But Don Quixote himself has not read this book, and does not have to read it, since he is the book in flesh and blood... Between the first and second parts of the novel, in the narrow gap between those two volumes, and by their power alone, Don Quixote has achieved his reality—a reality he owes to language alone, and which resides entirely inside the words.[105]

It is in this way that the novel, in inventing itself and its act of disenchantment of the epic Name, invents a new and reflexive mode of enchantment.

V

One of the most rigorous and passionate studies of name magic is Marcel Proust's *À la recherche du temps perdu*, where the narrator's struggle against the inability of language to capture meaning takes place through a fantasy, always ultimately defeated, of the immanence of meaning in the proper name. Whereas the common noun is both precise and general, denoting a class of objects ('things chosen as typical of everything else of the same sort'),[106] and having only an arbitrary connection with what it signifies, the proper name, by contrast, is 'sonorous', at once vague and particular, embodying an idealized image which is specific, distinct from all other images, yet fluid and resonant. The signifier and the signified mutually contaminate each other; if the neutral phonetic matter becomes substantial and infuses the idea of the person or place with linguistically motivated value,[107] this idea, in turn, introduces into the name a determination composed of certain simple signs emblematic of the person or place—Parma: violets, Stendhal's novel; Florence: the heraldic red lily, the church of St Marie des Fleurs. In this mutual exchange the name detaches itself from the 'real' Balbec/Parma/Venice, and becomes hermetically closed.[108] And with the loss of this third, referential dimension of the sign a compensatory movement takes place: the name acquires a density, an immutability, and a value improper to signs; it becomes a pure phenomenon, in which meaning is contained but which will not release meaning. It functions, like all ritual language, as a magic password, a self-sufficient litany which, precisely because of its evocative function, must not be reducible to synonyms or to syntax. Its closest equivalent in the novel is perhaps the idiosyncratic phrases of Françoise, or the quasi-operatic cries of the street hawkers, with their 'ritual suspension interposing

[105] Foucault, *The Order of Things*, p. 48.

[106] *choses conçues comme pareilles à toutes celles de même sorte*. Marcel Proust, *Swann's Way*, III, in *In Search of Lost Time*, vol. I, trans. C. K. Scott Moncrieff and Terence Kilmartin, revised D. J. Enright (New York: Modern Library, 2003), p. 551; *Du Côté de chez Swann*, III, in *À la recherche du temps perdu*, vol. I, ed. Jean-Yves Tadié, Bibliothèque de la Pléïade (Paris: Gallimard, 1987), p. 380.

[107] Cf. Gérard Genette, 'Proust and Indirect Language', in *Figures of Literary Discourse*, trans. Alan Sheridan (New York: Columbia University Press, 1982), pp. 239–42.

[108] Marcel Proust, *Within a Budding Grove*, II, in *In Search of Lost Time*, vol. II, pp. 324–5; *À l'ombre des jeunes filles en fleurs*, II, in *À la recherche du temps perdu*, vol. II, p. 21.

a silence in the middle of a word'.[109] It is through this magical force of the proper name that the narrator's relations with almost all of the novel's major characters are mediated.

The 'mythical history' evoked by the name is, at the same time, a real history, a unification of person and place, subject and object, and a preservation of the past within the present, not as dead matter but as a genuine continuity. Genealogy, the temporal dimension of the proper name, 'embod[ies] all our history, immuring it, beetling over it',[110] and it 'restores old stones to life';[111] conversely, place names unite the temporal dimension of the name with a spatial dimension (since 'family names and especially noble family names have this particularity, of being at one and the same time the name of a place and the name of a person'),[112] and it is from this fusion that the name's immediacy stems; as it does the archaeologist, it enables the narrator to perceive a 'historical' essence which, 'in the name given to a rock, in a religious rite, still dwells in the midst of the present, like a denser emanation, immemorial and stable'.[113] Uniting the title and the land it points to that unity of nature and culture that the narrator finds in Elstir's painting.[114]

Elstir's art is, in many ways, exemplary to the narrator's literary ambitions. When the narrator first enters the painter's studio it seems to him like 'the laboratory of a sort of new creation of the world'.[115] He misses the early Elstir paintings with which he is familiar; what he sees is a collection of seascapes, and he makes out that their charm 'lay in a sort of metamorphosis of the objects represented, analogous to what in poetry we call metaphor, and that, if God the Father had created things by naming them, it was by taking away their names or giving them other names that Elstir created them anew'.[116] The 'primal vision'[117] of things for which the paintings strive is effected through the formal intention to 'accustom the

[109] An *arrêt rituel mettant un silence au milieu d'un mot.* Marcel Proust, *The Captive*, in *In Search of Lost Time*, vol. V, p. 149; *La Prisonnière*, in *À la recherche du temps perdu*, vol. III, p. 625.

[110] *enferme toute l'histoire, l'emmure, la renfrogne.* Marcel Proust, *The Guermantes Way*, II, in *In Search of Lost Time*, vol. III, p. 736; *Le Côté de Guermantes*, II, in *À la recherche du temps perdu*, vol. II, p. 826.

[111] *rend la vie aux vieilles pierres.* Proust, *The Guermantes Way*, II, p. 742; *Le Côté de Guermantes*, II, p. 830.

[112] Georges Poulet, *Proustian Space*, trans. Elliott Coleman (Baltimore: Johns Hopkins University Press, 1977), p. 29.

[113] *dans l'appellation donnée à une roche, dans un rite religieux, demeure au milieu du présent comme une émanation plus dense, immémoriale et stable.* Proust, *The Guermantes Way*, II, p. 572; *Le Côté de Guermantes*, II, p. 711.

[114] Marcel Proust, *Sodom and Gomorrah*, II, in *In Search of Lost Time*, vol. IV, p. 446; *Sodome et Gomorrhe*, II, in *À la recherche du temps perdu*, vol. III, p. 321.

[115] *le laboratoire d'une sorte de nouvelle création du monde.* Proust, *Within a Budding Grove*, II, p. 565; *À l'ombre des jeunes filles en fleurs*, II, p. 190.

[116] *consistait en une sorte de métamorphose des choses représentées, analogue à celle qu'en poésie on nomme métaphore, et que si Dieu le Père avait créé les choses en les nommant, c'est en leur ôtant leur nom, ou en leur en donnant un autre qu'Elstir les recréait.* Proust, *Within a Budding Grove*, II, p. 566; *À l'ombre des jeunes filles en fleurs*, II, p. 191.

[117] *vision première.* Proust, *Within a Budding Grove*, II, p. 570, translation modified; *À l'ombre des jeunes filles en fleurs*, II, p. 194.

eyes to not recognising…'[118] The painting that is singled out for description is a representation of the port of Carquethuit, one of a series in which Elstir works by suppressing the demarcation between sea and land. The fusion of town and sea is a base metaphor supporting the more crucial image of the church within the sea: 'for instance, the churches of Criquebec which, in the distance, surrounded by water on every side because you saw them without seeing the town, in a powdery haze of sunlight and crumbling waves, seemed to be emerging from the waters, blown in alabaster or in sea-foam, and, enclosed in the band of a variegated rainbow, to form an ethereal, mystical tableau'.[119] Etymologically, the towns of Carquethuit and Criquebec are identical;[120] and behind these 'church'-towns lies a third church, that of Carqueville, covered in ivy, its trembling foliage hiding the 'idea' of the church and causing the whole building to sway.[121] Similarly, at Marcouville-l'Orgueilleuse 'the great bas-reliefs seemed to be visible only beneath a fluid layer, half liquid, half luminous; the Blessed Virgin, St Elizabeth, St Joachim still swam in the impalpable tide, almost detached, at the surface of the water or the sunlight'.[122]

The source of this image of the church surrounded by the sea doubtless lies—for the narrator—in the Guermantes château 'mirrored in its lake',[123] and in the Combray church, 'almost the color of Virginia creeper', a quasi-organic edifice.[124] Its final incarnation is in Venice, and, supported by Venice, in the church of San Marco.

Venice is 'a Gothic city rising from a sea whose waves were stilled as in a stained-glass window', cut in two by a river which bathes 'an oriental church'.[125] As an iconic figure it stands outside time, fusing movement and stasis, nature and culture, 'an impure soil' and 'a blue and virginal water'.[126] Like Yeats's Byzantium or the New Jerusalem, it is a 'fabulous garden of fruits and birds in coloured stone, flowering in the midst of the sea…';[127] it is at once artificial and natural, 'but of a nature which seemed to have created its works with a human imagination'.[128]

[118] *habituer les yeux à ne pas reconnaître…* Proust, *Within a Budding Grove*, II, p. 568, translation modified; *À l'ombre des jeunes filles en fleurs*, II, p. 192.

[119] *par exemple, les églises de Criquebec qui, au loin, entourées d'eau de tous côtés parce qu'on les voyait sans la ville, dans un poudroiement de soleil et de vagues, semblaient sortir des eaux, soufflées en albâtre ou en écume et enfermées dans la ceinture d'un arc-en-ciel versicolore, former un tableau irréel et mystique.* Proust, *Within a Budding Grove*, II, pp. 567–8; *À l'ombre des jeunes filles en fleurs*, II, p. 192.

[120] Proust, *Sodom and Gomorrah*, II, p. 390; *Sodome et Gomorrhe*, II, p. 282.

[121] Proust, *Within a Budding Grove*, II, p. 401; *À l'ombre des jeunes filles en fleurs*, II, p. 75.

[122] *les grands bas-reliefs semblaient n'être vus que sous une couche fluide, moitié liquide, moitié lumineuse; la Sainte Vierge, sainte Elisabeth, saint Joachim, nageaient encore dans l'impalpable remous, presque à sec, à fleur d'eau ou fleur de soleil.* Proust, *Sodom and Gomorrah*, II, p. 561; *Sodome et Gomorrhe*, II, p. 402.

[123] *reflété dans son lac.* Proust, *The Guermantes Way*, I, p. 9; *Le Côté de Guermantes*, I, p. 315.

[124] *presque de la couleur de la vigne vierge.* Proust, *Swann's Way*, I, p. 86; *Du Côté de chez Swann*, I, p. 62.

[125] *une cité gothique au milieu d'une mer aux flots immobilisés comme sur un vitrail; une église orientale.* Proust, *The Guermantes Way*, I, p. 191; *Le Côté de Guermantes*, I, p. 444.

[126] *une terre impure; une eau vierge et bleue.* Proust, *The Captive*, p. 555; *La Prisonnière*, p. 913.

[127] *jardin fabuleux de fruits et d'oiseaux de pierre de couleur, fleuri au milieu de la mer…* Proust, *The Captive*, p. 556; *La Prisonnière*, p. 913.

[128] *mais d'une nature qui aurait créé ses oeuvres avec une imagination humaine.* Marcel Proust, *The Fugitive*, III, in *In Search of Lost Time*, vol. V, p. 852; *Albertine disparue*, III, in *À la recherche du temps perdu*, vol. IV, p. 208.

Containing within it Tante Léonie's room at Combray and the sea of Balbec, it fuses the two towns into a new symbolic totality, a labyrinth containing a magic domain, which, like the palace of an oriental tale (or like the magic transcendence hidden within narrative—in the *Thousand and One Nights*, for example), will not yield to the disillusioned 'quest' of the morning.[129] It stands for the narrator as an image of his newly won freedom;[130] but, 'as it is written beneath the vaults of St Mark's, and proclaimed, as they drink from the urns of marble and jasper of the byzantine capitals, by the birds which symbolise at once death and resurrection',[131] this freedom is, in essence, a form of death—the disappearance of Albertine. Perhaps because of the completeness of its revelation, Venice is never subject to the disenchantment which most names in the novel—Balbec or Guermantes, for example, which are split into warring or irreconcilable halves—undergo.

More towards the daemonic end of this scale of the fusion of qualities within the proper name is the image of Mélusine, half mermaid and half human, a demi-goddess who both preserves and threatens the name of a family. She is a 'fairy', identical with the 'soul' contained in the name but not in the place or person it refers to;[132] 'hidden in the heart of its name',[133] she corresponds to a desire of the imagination and is transformed in accordance with it: thus, the aura surrounding the duchesse de Guermantes varies both in its nature and its intensity for purely subjective reasons. As the true incarnation of the Guermantes name, the Duchess is closely identified with this figure of the union of human and divine natures: she is 'a sort of goddess of the waters'[134] and occupies an aquatic realm, the 'sombre and transparent realm' of the opera boxes ('baignoires') like 'subaqueous grottoes',[135] where a race of aquatic demi-gods and nereids, similar to Elstir's amphibians at Carquethuit, hold sway in their glaucous element, and where Phèdre/Berma too is bathed in a green light. The origin of the Guermantes race (that is, of the name) is semi-divine, although the divine and natural terms of the mating are interchangeable: either 'the union of a goddess with a bird',[136] or 'the mythological impregnation of a nymph by a divine Bird'[137] (the second union recalls the image, reinforced by Elstir's paintings, of Albertine as both Leda and the swan).[138] Gilberte's parentage is equally semi-divine—Odette and Swann—and one sees 'the two natures of

[129] *recherche*. Proust, *The Fugitive*, III, p. 882; *Albertine disparue*, III, p. 230.

[130] Proust, *The Captive*, p. 545; *La Prisonnière*, p. 905.

[131] *comme il est écrit aux voûtes de Saint-Marc, et comme le proclament, buvant aux urnes de marbres et de jaspe des chapiteaux byzantins, les oiseaux qui signifient à la fois la mort et la résurrection.* Proust, *The Captive*, p. 497; *La Prisonnière*, p. 871.

[132] *fée; âme.* Proust, *The Guermantes Way*, I, p. 3; *Le Côté de Guermantes*, I, p. 311.

[133] *cachée au fond de son nom.* Proust, *The Guermantes Way*, I, p. 3; *Le Côté de Guermantes*, I, p. 311.

[134] *comme une divinité des eaux.* Proust, *Sodom and Gomorrah*, II, p. 191; *Sodome et Gomorrhe*, II, p. 139.

[135] *sombre et transparent royaume; des grottes marines.* Proust, *The Guermantes Way*, I, pp. 44, 4; *Le Côté de Guermantes*, I, pp. 340, 338.

[136] *l'union d'une déesse et d'un oiseau.* Proust, *The Guermantes Way*, I, p. 100; *Le Côté de Guermantes*, I, p. 379.

[137] *la fécondation mythologique d'une nymphe par un divin Oiseau.* Proust, *The Guermantes Way*, II, p. 602; *Le Côté de Guermantes*, II, p. 732.

[138] Proust, *The Fugitive*, I, p. 711; *Albertine disparue*, I, p. 108.

M. and Mme Swann ripple and flow and overlap one upon the other in the body of this Mélusine'.[139]

The male counterpart of Mélusine is the centaur, at one extreme a purely moralistic metaphor of sexuality, but elsewhere revealing semi-divine characteristics. The narrator discovers one day 'the mountainous and marine landscape which Elstir had made the scene of those two admirable water-colours, "Poet meeting a Muse" and "Young Man meeting a Centaur", which I had seen at the Duchesse de Guermantes's'.[140] At the time he saw these paintings the narrator had described them as a series of mythological subjects in which the Muses were represented as 'creatures belonging to a species now fossilised', and in some of which a poet 'of a race that would also have been of peculiar interest to a zoologist (characterised by a certain sexlessness) strolled with a Muse…'[141] In one painting a poet rides on the back of a centaur; the appearance of the Muse is left indistinct, and it is likely (especially since the poet is equated with the young man) that it is identical with the centaur, if not pictorially then at least, for the narrator, mythically. The narrator (whose name may or may not be Marcel) is riding a horse when he 'rediscovers' this Elstirian landscape, and the Muse he encounters, in a sudden concentration of prehistory and futurity, is an aviator, seen as Icarus or 'a demi-god'.[142] The same conjunction of androgyny ('sexlessness') and the centaur occurs in the figures of the two de Surgis brothers, sexually complementary, 'like a pair of allegorical figures',[143] forming a union of opposites; Charlus studies them as though trying to uncover 'the riddle of the sphinx', a variant type of the mating of the human with the non-human; and the face he is concentrating on is a text (a '*grimoire*', a book of spells) made up of two modes of writing: 'sibylline signs' and the 'Table of the Law', writing as revelation and as prohibition.[144] The answer to the problem of writing clearly lies in the realm of the daemonic, and all transcendence appears—at this partially concealed level of meaning—as a form of transgression or miscegenation ('*mésalliance*'), or, rather, as a *product* of miscegenation. The element of transgression is extended in the description of the young Iéna who sleeps beneath a sculpted siren, an arrangement which recalls a third painting to be added to the series: 'Death and the Young Man', by Gustave Moreau (cf. 'Morel').[145] But if the Muse is death it is also clearly conducive to artistic fertility, even if the fusion of separated or tabooed planes leads only to the ambiguous fertility arising from the

[139] *ces deux natures de M. et de Mme Swann onduler, refluer, empiéter tour à tour l'une sur l'autre, dans le corps de cette Mélusine.* Proust, *Within a Budding Grove*, I, p. 190; *À l'ombre des jeunes filles en fleurs*, I, p. 555.

[140] *le paysage montagneux et marin qu'Elstir a donné pour cadre à ces deux admirables aquarelles, 'Poète rencontrant une Muse', 'Jeune homme rencontrant un Centaure', que j'avais vues chez la duchesse de Guermantes.* Proust, *Sodom and Gomorrah*, II, p. 581; *Sodome et Gomorrhe*, II, pp. 416–17.

[141] *des êtres appartenant à une espèce fossile; d'une race ayant aussi une individualité particulière pour un zoologiste (caractérisée par une certaine insexualité), se promenait avec une Muse…* Proust, *The Guermantes Way*, II, p. 577; *Le Côté de Guermantes*, II, pp. 714–5.

[142] *un demi-dieu.* Proust, *Sodom and Gomorrah*, II, p. 582; *Sodome et Gomorrhe*, II, p. 417.

[143] *pareils à deux figures allégoriques.* Proust, *Sodom and Gomorrah*, II, p. 117; *Sodome et Gomorrhe*, II, p. 85.

[144] *l'énigme du Sphinx.* Proust, *Sodom and Gomorrah*, II, p. 120; *Sodome et Gomorrhe*, II, p. 88.

[145] Proust, *The Guermantes Way*, II, p. 713; *Le Côté de Guermantes*, II, p. 810.

queerly normal union of the homosexual man and woman Morel and Léa,[146] or from the joining of the two halves of the hermaphroditic vanilla plant.

At the level of style, the device which corresponds to this fusion of heterogeneous elements is metaphor, immediately a problem because of its inner contradictions. For Gérard Genette, Elstir's Carquethuit style forms a baroque 'esthetic of paradox—but by the same token we are very far from the essentialist intentions of the Proustian esthetic'. Nevertheless, 'it must be admitted...that Elstir's style corresponds faithfully to Proust's idea of his own style and, consequently, of his own vision'.[147] Furthermore, it is an a priori impossibility that metaphor should be the instrument of a vision oriented towards essence, since metaphor involves an alienation of the properties of the object, and the disengaged 'common essence' is an abstraction; essence would lie rather 'on the side that differs and resists, on the irreducible and *refractory* side of things'.[148] Genette is thus led to see a strain at the heart of the work, a conflict between a programmatic 'intention' and 'a sort of obscure, negative will'[149] working itself out in despite of the narrator, and undermining the novel's surface teleology. Genette's analysis of the 'metonymic metaphor' explains in part how the contingency and dispersion of objects is overcome in a fusion more complete than the simple elements allow for: the terms 'must mutually reflect and absorb each other, at once "placed side by side" (contiguity) and "seen the one in the other" (analogy)'.[150] In effect, a process of complication and reinforcement deepens and concentrates the metaphor. But Paul de Man's reading of the insistence of the 'literal' in Proust, and thus of the discontinuities embedded in metaphor, problematizes what he calls 'Genette's model of a reconciled system of metaphor and metonymy'.[151]

At the level of narrative, it is 'character' itself that acts in accordance with principles of fusion and disaggregation in relation to the name. The novel's characteristic technique of the metamorphosis of one named character into another is an extended version of metaphor, but its structure is borrowed from the dream, of which the narrator says that

> it is a mistake to pay too much attention to the appearance of the people one saw in one's dream, who may perhaps have been disguised or have exchanged faces, like those mutilated saints in cathedrals which ignorant archaeologists have restored, fitting the head of one to the body of another and jumbling all their attributes and names. Those that people bear in a dream are apt to mislead us. The person whom we love is to be recognised only by the intensity of the pain that we suffer.[152]

[146] Cf. Leo Bersani's astute analysis in *Marcel Proust: The Fictions of Life and Art* (New York: Oxford University Press, 1965), pp. 72–5.

[147] Gérard Genette, 'Proust Palimpsest', in *Figures of Literary Discourse*, p. 211.

[148] Genette, 'Proust Palimpsest', p. 208.

[149] Genette, 'Proust Palimpsest', p. 218.

[150] Gérard Genette, 'Métonymie chez Proust', in *Figures*, vol. III (Paris: Seuil, 1972), p. 61 (my translation).

[151] Paul de Man, *Allegories of Reading: Figural Language in Rousseau, Nietzsche, Rilke, and Proust* (New Haven: Yale University Press, 1979), p. 61.

[152] *il ne faut tenir compte ni de l'apparence des personnes, lesquelles peuvent être déguisées et avoir interchangés leurs visages, comme ces saints mutilés des cathédrales que des archéologues ignorant ont refaits, en mettant sur le corps de l'un la tête de l'autre, et en mêlant leurs attributs et les noms. Ceux que les êtres portent dans un rêve peuvent nous abuser. La personne que nous aimons doit y être reconnue seulement à*

Both the name and the attributes change; something remains to be recognized as a continuous figure, but its continuity is given only by the affective force of our response. This fragmentation of personality and this incoherence of the proper name stem from the shifting compositional patterns into which characters are placed, patterns which break them apart as 'characters' in the same way as the bodies of the saints are mutilated and recomposed. The effect of this is to emphasize 'the disparity, the incommensurability, the disintegration of the parts of the Search, with the breaks, lacunae, intermittences which guarantee its ultimate diversity'.[153] But this is not merely a matter of the disintegration of stable unities: it is precisely the inscription and the readability of character that is made possible by its compositional function.

These are some of the more salient transformations that run through the novel.

(a) The *drame du coucher*, the daily trauma of separation from the mother played out at Combray, evokes a number of parallels, and according to Michel Butor the scene is the motivating force behind all the activity of transformation in the novel: 'Fixated on his mother ever since the kiss at Combray, Marcel can only find a stable equivalent for her, Mlle de Saint-Loup, by completely transforming the society which was contemporaneous with that kiss; in the course of that transformation sexual aberration will gradually deploy all its colors.'[154] The elements of the scene are displaced throughout the novel and projected incompletely upon different sets of characters. A sudden intervention of the first-person voice in *Swann's Way* connects Swann's dependence on Odette with the narrator's on his mother.[155] The desecration of the mother is repeated at Montjouvain where the narrator, watching through a window, spies upon the insulting of the composer Vinteuil by his daughter and her companion, and that insult is repeated more generally by homosexuals[156] and Jews.[157] His father's abdication of authority leads to the creation of a number of father substitutes—Swann, Bergotte, the duc de Guermantes; and, as the mother recedes into the background, her function is taken over by, above all, the grandmother, but also by the duchesse de Guermantes, by Odette, by Albertine, even by the city of Venice.[158] At one point, when the mother refuses to commit herself to an opinion about Albertine, she slips into the role played by the narrator's father;[159] this can happen only because her figural function is, by now, completely divorced from her appearance as a character. Only once after Combray do the two come together again,

la force de la douleur éprouvée. Proust, *Within a Budding Grove*, I, p. 281; *À l'ombre des jeunes filles en fleur*, I, pp. 618–9.

[153] Gilles Deleuze, *Proust and Signs*, trans. Richard Howard (New York: Braziller, 1972), p. 103.

[154] Michel Butor, *Les oeuvres d'art imaginaires chez Proust* (London: Athlone Press, 1964), p. 43 (my translation).

[155] Proust, *Swann's Way*, II, pp. 419–20, 422; *Du côté de chez Swann*, II, pp. 291, 292.

[156] Proust, *Sodom and Gomorrah*, II, p. 416; *Sodome et Gomorrhe*, II, p. 300.

[157] Proust, *The Guermantes Way*, I, p. 342; *Le Côté de Guermantes*, I, p. 550.

[158] Proust, *The Fugitive*, I, pp. 567, 570; *Albertine disparue*, I, pp. 6, 8.

[159] Proust, *Sodom and Gomorrah*, II, p. 443; *Sodome et Gomorrhe*, II, p. 319.

in Venice, where the narrator attempts to resist 'an imaginary plot woven against me by my parents, who imagined that I would be forced to obey them', and this awakens in him 'that defiant spirit which drove me in the past to impose my will brutally upon the people I loved best in the world, though finally conforming to theirs after I had succeeded in making them yield'.[160] He parts from his mother, and Venice immediately loses its substantiality: the loss of his mother entails a dissolution of his own identity, and so an absence in the reality of what is external to him. But, more usually, the original scene is played out—as it is with Albertine, whose tongue, like the mother's kiss, becomes 'a daily bread'—under 'diametrically opposed conditions, so much so that it seems almost sacrilegious to note the identical nature of the consolations vouchsafed!'[161]

(b) The transfer of the mother's initial function in the novel to the grandmother is succeeded, after the older woman dies, by a metamorphosis of the mother into the grandmother, without her recovering, however, the 'maternal' weight the grandmother was made to carry. In her relationship with her daughter there seems little to indicate why the grandmother identifies so strongly with Mme de Sévigné; but we realize, retrospectively, that a displacement of terms is in effect: Mme de Sévigné is the mother (or better: the mother figure) and the narrator is the real *daughter* of whoever holds that title; when his mother 'becomes' his grandmother, she treats the narrator as a daughter.[162] As a son he fulfils a complementary role, that of Hippolyte. Thus, in Charlus's words: 'What Mme de Sévigné felt for her daughter has a far better claim to rank with the passion that Racine described in *Andromaque* or *Phèdre* than the commonplace relations young Sévigné had with his mistresses.'[163] This relationship, both incestuous and profanatory, is also enacted with Albertine serving as the mother figure. Albertine comes to bear an especially close resemblance to the grandmother once they are both dead;[164] the narrator feels guilty of having murdered both of them,[165] and he remembers Albertine's tongue as 'maternal, incomestible, nutritious, hallowed', and as 'penetrating' him

[160] *un complot imaginaire tramé contre moi par mes parents (qui se figuraient que je serais bien forcé d'obéir); cette volonté de lutte, désir qui me poussait jadis à imposer brusquement ma volonté à ceux que j'aimais le plus, quitte à me conformer à la leur après que j'avais réussi à les faire céder.* Proust, *The Fugitive*, III, p. 883; *Albertine disparue*, III, p. 230.

[161] *un pain quotidien; des conditions différentes, opposées parfois jusqu'au point qu'il y a presque sacrilège apparent à constater l'identité de la grâce octroyée!* Proust, *The Captive*, p. 2; *La Prisonnière*, p. 520.

[162] Proust, *The Captive*, p. 180; *La Prisonnière*, p. 646.

[163] *Ce que ressentait Mme de Sévigné pour sa fille peut prétendre beaucoup plus justement ressembler à la passion que Racine a dépeinte dans Andromaque ou Phèdre, que les banales relations que le jeune Sévigné avait avec ses maîtresses.* Proust, *Within a Budding Grove*, II, p. 468; *À l'ombre des jeunes filles en fleur*, II, p. 122.

[164] Proust, *Time Regained*, in *In Search of Lost Time*, vol. VI, p. 439; *Le Temps retrouvé*, in *À la recherche du temps perdu*, vol. IV, p. 566.

[165] Proust, *The Fugitive*, I, p. 670; *Albertine disparue*, I, p. 78.

with a 'mysterious sweetness':[166] in addition to her motherly role, Albertine is a filial lover, and this role doubles and reverses the incestuous union, since after Albertine's departure the narrator sees himself as Phèdre deserted by Hippolyte:[167] increasingly, his relationship with Albertine is rendered in terms of his being a mother, betrayed or profaned by his 'child'. He feels for her 'the tender charm of an affection at once filial and maternal',[168] and, at Balbec, he waits in fear 'of seeing her depart with that same sense of revolt which I had felt in the past when Mamma left my bedside without bidding me goodnight'.[169] Shortly before his decision to marry Albertine, he sees his mother appear looking like the resurrection of his grandmother; through the window, superimposed upon the sunrise, is an image of the room at Montjouvain in which Albertine has taken the place of Mlle Vinteuil's lesbian friend and is engaged in insulting the onlooker, who is also ('that old monkey') the father (or mother, since Vinteuil is both mother and father to his daughter).[170] In schematic form the series of transpositions could be expressed like this:

I		**II**
Grandmother	←	mother
↑		
mother	←	narrator
↑		
narrator	←	Albertine

But a further variation is played on this scheme. If the narrator can have both a maternal and a filial relationship to Albertine, the relationship is capable of internalization: he can be both la Berma-as-Phèdre, betrayed by her daughter, and the daughter (as Hippolyte) betraying his mother.[171] As an old man he talks of his former self as though 'of the son he has lost',[172] and he later realizes that he still sees himself from his mother's point of view.[173] But the most dramatic expression of this interiorization of the parent/child relationship comes after Albertine's revelation of her friendship with Mlle Vinteuil and the '*amie*':

> an image stirred in my heart... preserved alive in the depths of my being—like Orestes whose death the gods had prevented in order that, on the appointed day, he might return to his native land to avenge the murder of

166 *maternelle, incomestible, nourricière et sainte; la mystérieuse douceur d'une pénétration.* Proust, *The Fugitive*, I, pp. 671–2; *Albertine disparue*, I, p. 79.

167 Proust, *The Fugitive*, I, pp. 618–9; *Albertine disparue*, I, p. 42.

168 *une tendresse à la fois filiale et maternelle.* Proust, *The Captive*, p. 97; *La Prisonnière*, p. 587.

169 *de la voir partir avec cette même révolte que j'avais autrefois quand maman s'éloignait de mon lit sans me redire bonsoir.* Proust, *The Captive*, p. 530; *La Prisonnière*, p. 895.

170 *ce vieux singe.* Proust, *Sodom and Gomorrah*, II, p. 722; *Sodome et Gomorrhe*, II, p. 514.

171 Proust, *Time Regained*, pp. 478–80; *Le Temps retrouvé*, pp. 590–2.

172 *du fils qu'il a perdu.* Proust, *Time Regained*, p. 22; *Le Temps retrouvé*, p. 284.

173 Proust, *Time Regained*, p. 354; *Le Temps retrouvé*, pp. 509–10.

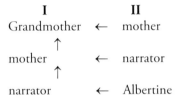

> Agamemnon—as a punishment, as a retribution (who knows?) for my having allowed my grandmother to die; perhaps rising up suddenly from the dark depths in which it seemed for ever buried and striking like an Avenger, in order to inaugurate for me a new and terrible and only too well-merited existence, perhaps also to make dazzlingly clear to my eyes the fatal consequences which evil actions eternally engender, not only for those who have committed them but for those who have done no more, or thought that they were doing no more, than look on at a curious and entertaining spectacle, as I, alas, had done on that afternoon long ago at Montjouvain . . .[174]

The linking of the grandmother's death with Montjouvain, seen in terms of a punishment, is curious, and can only be explained by way of the myth cited: the narrator is the cause of his grandmother's death, and thus corresponds to Clytemnestra, pursued by an avenging son; but as the 'son' both of his mother and his grandmother, he is also Orestes himself, and the scene becomes the expression of the vengeance of the narrator as son upon himself as mother. Montjouvain similarly contains the narrator in several roles: as desecrated mother (Albertine's 'that old monkey'); as son or daughter profaning, or allowing to die, the mother (or his spiritual father, Vinteuil); and as the watcher whose apparent detachment involves him in the scene and both causes and makes him suffer the enacted matricide: as the narrator as judge creates the crime, the narrator as voyeur is what he sees.

(c) Speaking of the portrait of Odette as 'Miss Sacripant', the narrator notes that the artist 'acts in a similar way to those extremely high temperatures which have the power to split up combinations of atoms which they proceed to combine afresh in a diametrically opposite order, corresponding to another type'.[175] It is this process of chemical recombination that is called into play in his own relationship with Odette, who is variously mother and mistress to him (she comes to replace his affection for her daughter Gilberte). Since Miss Sacripant is of uncertain sex,[176] was perhaps the 'mistress' of Charlus,[177] and since the narrator dreams at one point of 'Mme Swann, in the masculine gender and the calling of a

[174] *une image s'agitait dans mon coeur . . . conservée vivante au fond de moi—comme Oreste dont les Dieux avaient empêché la mort pour qu'au jour désigné il revînt dans son pays punir le meutre d'Agamemnon—pour mon supplice, pour mon châtiment, qui sait? d'avoir laissé mourir ma grand'mère; peut-être surgissant tout à coup au fond de la nuit où elle semblait à jamais ensevelie et frappant comme un Vengeur, afin d'inaugurer pour moi une vie terrible, méritée et nouvelle, peut-être aussi pour faire éclater à mes yeux les funestes consequences que les actes mauvais engendrent indéfiniment, non pas seulement pour ceux qui les ont commis, mais pour ceux qui n'ont fait, n'ont cru, que contempler un spectacle curieux et divertissant, comme moi, hélas! en cette fin de journée lointaine à Montjouvain . . .* Proust, *Sodom and Gomorrah*, II, p. 702; *Sodome et Gomorrhe*, II, pp. 499–500.

[175] *agit à la façon de ces températures extrêmement élevées qui ont le pouvoir de dissocier les combinaisons d'atomes et de grouper ceux-ci suivant un ordre absolument contraire, répondant à un autre type.* Proust, *Within a Budding Grove*, II, p. 601; *À l'ombre des jeunes filles en fleur*, II, p. 216.

[176] Proust, *Within a Budding Grove*, II, pp. 584–5; *À l'ombre des jeunes filles en fleur*, II, pp. 203–4.

[177] Proust, *The Captive*, pp. 401–2; *La Prisonnière*, pp. 803–4.

bathing superintendent',[178] she represents, as Albertine does, the figure of a male lover. A similar ambiguity attaches to Swann, who, in the simplest form, acts as the narrator's surrogate father. But in the scene (in the Champs-Elysées) in which the narrator wrestles with Gilberte and ejaculates against her, it is the letter he has written to Swann—a declaration of earnest—which is the real object of his struggle, and perhaps of his pleasure.[179] Later he dreams of Gilberte in the form of a young man who refuses to believe that the narrator's feelings are genuine, just as Swann had rejected his letter; and he equates Gilberte's present antipathy towards him with punishment for his sexual pleasure, which, in fact, was only directed towards her in the first instance.[180] The scene in the park is connected with Odette through Uncle Adolphe: the smell in the toilets, where he is more or less accosted by the attendant, lightens the pain caused by Swann's words because it reminds him of the smell of dampness in his uncle's room at Combray;[181] and it is at this uncle's home that he first meets '*la dame en rose*' in her Miss Sacripant days. The suggested underlying relations with Swann and Odette are not extended into any larger pattern; in abstraction from the characters, however, they contribute to our sense of that 'diametrically opposite order' in accordance with which the book is shaped.

(d) The paths of Albertine and Morel—like that of Gilberte and Saint-Loup—run parallel at many points, converge in a relationship in some ways like those queerly normal relations of Morel to Léa and of Saint-Loup to Gilberte, and at all moments call into question the sexual identity of the narrator. Albertine's name, like Gilberte's, is barely a feminine form—several men in the novel, including Bloch, are named Albert—and the narrator tends to assume a feminine role with her: she first submits to him when she is in a physically dominant position, whereas his earlier attempt to kiss her had failed because 'we had formed a couple symmetrical with but the converse of our present arrangement, for then it had been she who was lying down and I by her bedside'.[182] In moments of distraction Albertine addresses him as she would a lesbian companion,[183] and the narrator extends this after her death in his desire to recreate with Andrée Albertine's sexual experiences with women.[184] She is associated with Odette through the epithet 'pink' repeatedly applied to each of them, and the narrator's nightmares envisage her both as Mlle Vinteuil and as

[178] *dans le sexe masculin et la condition de maître baigneur.* Proust, *Within a Budding Grove*, II, p. 359; *À l'ombre des jeunes filles en fleur*, II, p. 45.

[179] Proust, *Within a Budding Grove*, I, p. 90; *À l'ombre des jeunes filles en fleur*, I, p. 485.

[180] Proust, *Within a Budding Grove*, I, p. 282; *À l'ombre des jeunes filles en fleur*, I, p. 619.

[181] Proust, *Within a Budding Grove*, I, pp. 88, 91; *À l'ombre des jeunes filles en fleur*, I, pp. 483, 485.

[182] *nous formions un couple symétrique mais inverse de celui de l'après-midi actuelle, puisqu'alors c'était elle qui était couchée et moi, à côté de son lit.* Proust, *The Guermantes Way*, II, p. 483; *Le Côté de Guermantes*, II, p. 649.

[183] Proust, *The Captive*, p. 457; *La Prisonnière*, p. 843.

[184] Proust, *The Fugitive*, II, p. 810; *Albertine disparue*, II, p. 179.

her companion. And since Morel's relationship with Charlus parodies Albertine's with the narrator, Charlus is able deliberately to confuse the two: 'for him, the young lady was not Albertine but Morel'.[185]

Morel is protean to the point of having no identity. His first name is Charles, stemming from the same root ('Carolus') as *Charlus*;[186] and *Morel* connects him with Frédéric *Moreau*[187] —that is, with the hero of a Bildungsroman—and with *Marcel*, the putative name of the narrator. Saint-Loup sees Morel as having a kind of common identity with Rachel, and there is perhaps a play on the biblical Rachel and Leah, the wives of Jacob (but the narrator too sees himself as Rachel's son, Joseph).[188] For Charlus, Morel is 'a young David capable of challenging Goliath';[189] earlier, Charlus had asked to see Bloch beating his father, an act which he imagined as a version of that combat. Since Charlus is the 'spiritual father' of Morel, what he admires in him is precisely his capacity for desecrating the father, and after Morel leaves him, Charlus continues to invite this desecration of his fatherliness through the flagellations at the brothel. Similarly, Charlus and Morel form a couple parallel to Mlle Vinteuil and her friend,[190] but Morel's betrayal of Charlus at the Verdurin party, where he is playing the Vinteuil sonata, puts Charlus unmistakably into the position of the composer.[191] The collaboration of Morel and Albertine, finally, in the procurement of young girls corresponds to the collaboration of Mlle Vinteuil and her companion against the memory of Vinteuil; the brunt of this is borne by the narrator, but in the retelling by the narrator the impact is diffused, passed on to Charlus, to the grandmother, to la Berma.

A number of comments suggest the narrator's interest in the role of compositional leitmotifs in organizing narrative texts. In Dostoevsky, 'if...from one novel to another it's the same scene, it's in the compass of a single novel that the same scenes, the same characters reappear if the novel is at all long'.[192] The novelist or musician tends to employ recurrent 'key-phrases' ('*phrases-types*'),[193] like the phrase in Vinteuil's sonata that the narrator is later to transpose to his own work. In Thomas Hardy or Stendhal the leitmotif operates in the form of recurrent structural parallelisms, so that 'all those novels...can be superimposed on one another'.[194] Dostoevsky acts doubly as a model, first because of the essentially

[185] *pour lui, la jeune fille était non pas Albertine, mais Morel.* Proust, *Sodom and Gomorrah*, II, p. 616; *Sodome et Gomorrhe*, II, p. 441.

[186] Proust, *Sodom and Gomorrah*, II, p. 628; *Sodome et Gomorrhe*, II, p. 449.

[187] Proust, *The Captive*, p. 210; *La Prisonnière*, p. 668.

[188] Proust, *Within a Budding Grove*, I, p. 281; *À l'ombre des jeunes filles en fleur*, I, pp. 618–9.

[189] *un jeune David capable d'assumer un combat contre Goliath.* Proust, *Sodom and Gomorrah*, II, p. 355; *Sodome et Gomorrhe*, II, p. 257.

[190] Proust, *The Captive*, p. 352; *La Prisonnière*, p. 768.

[191] Proust, *The Captive*, pp. 424–6; *La Prisonnière*, pp. 820–1.

[192] *si... c'est de roman à roman la même scène, c'est au sein d'un même roman que les mêmes scènes, les mêmes personnages se reproduisent si le roman est très long.* Proust, *The Captive*, p. 509; *La Prisonnière*, p. 880.

[193] Proust, *The Captive*, p. 506; *La Prisonnière*, p. 877.

[194] *tous ces romans [sont] superposables les uns aux autres.* Proust, *The Captive*, p. 507; *La Prisonnière*, p. 879.

identical nature of his female characters and second because of the *content* of the obsessively repeated scenes: parricide, the father's rape of the mother, Smerdiakov's suicide after killing Karamazov.[195] When speaking in his own voice, the narrator is inclined to offer either biological or psychological, rather than literary, explanations of the metamorphosis of characters within the novel. He speaks of the 'mimicry' ('*mimétisme*') by which women take on male characteristics,[196] of the 'coupling of contrary elements' by means of which the narrator comes to resemble his parents,[197] of the genetic transmission of characteristics which splits Gilberte into two people, one dominated by Swann, the other by Odette.[198] His references to the literary aspects of transformation usually concern the distinction between himself as artist and as hero; thus he says of Swann that 'like certain novelists, he had distributed his own personality between two characters, the one who was dreaming the dream, and another whom he saw in front of him...'[199] But these explanations are always too simple in their postulation of the homogeneity of the novel's underlying patterns; those patterns are discontinuous, not an allegory of the self but the play of figures of personhood distributed across the text in such a way that we recognize the continuity of 'characters' only by virtue of 'the intensity of the pain that we suffer' ('*la force de la douleur éprouvée*'):[200] by the affective force that runs beneath and disrupts the surface coherence of the name and of the 'character' that attaches to it.

VI

A narrative begins at the end of a journey, at a place where 'the sea ends and the earth begins. It is raining over the colorless city. The waters of the river are polluted with mud, the riverbanks flooded. A dark vessel, the *Highland Brigade*, ascends the somber river and is about to anchor at the quay of Alcântara'.[201] A passenger disembarks, a certain Doctor Ricardo Reis, aged 48, born in Oporto and arriving from Rio de Janeiro, as we learn when he signs the register at the Hotel Bragança. He has returned to Lisbon after receiving a telegram from a fellow poet, Álvaro de Campos, informing him of the death of their friend Fernando Pessoa. Reading through the newspaper archives, Dr Reis finds an obituary that reports that Pessoa died 'in silence, just as he had always lived', and it adds that '[i]n his poetry he was not only Fernando Pessoa but also Álvaro de Campos, Alberto Caeiro, and Ricardo Reis. There you are', the narrator continues,

195 Proust, *The Captive*, pp. 512–3; *La Prisonnière*, p. 882.
196 Proust, *Sodom and Gomorrah*, II, p. 62; *Sodome et Gomorrhe*, II, p. 47.
197 *l'accouplement des éléments contraires.* Proust, *The Captive*, p. 136; *La Prisonnière*, p. 615.
198 Proust, *Within a Budding Grove*, I, pp. 189–90; *À l'ombre des jeunes filles en fleur*, I, p. 554–5.
199 *comme certains romanciers, il avait distribué sa personnalité à deux personnages, celui qui faisait le rêve, et un qu'il voyait devant lui...* Proust, *Swann's Way*, p. 540; *Du côté de chez Swann*, p. 373.
200 Proust, *Within a Budding Grove*, I, p. 281; *À l'ombre des jeunes filles en fleur*, I, p. 619.
201 José Saramago, *The Year of the Death of Ricardo Reis*, trans. Giovanni Pontiero (London: The Harvill Press, 1992), p. 1. Hereafter cited in the text.

> an error caused by not paying attention, by writing what one misheard, because we know very well that Ricardo Reis is this man who is reading the newspaper with his own open and living eyes, a doctor forty-eight years of age, one year older than Fernando Pessoa when his eyes were closed, eyes that were dead beyond a shadow of a doubt. No other proofs or testimonies are needed to verify that we are not dealing with the same person, and if there is anyone who is still in doubt,

the narrator persists, let him go to the Hotel Bragança and check with the manager, a man of impeccable credentials... (pp. 23–4). Ricardo Reis then visits Pessoa's tomb, where the funeral urn proclaims 'I am here', this is the resting place of 'the decomposing body of a composer of poems who left his share of madness in the world' (p. 28).

Yet a day or two later, on New Year's Eve 1935, Reis returns to his room and finds sitting on the sofa a man whom he recognizes at once although he hasn't seen him for many years; nor does he think it strange that Fernando Pessoa should be sitting there waiting for him. 'He said Hello, not expecting a reply, absurdity does not always obey logic, but Pessoa did in fact reply...' (p. 64). He explains to Reis that he is still allowed to leave 'that place' and wander around as he pleases for nine months—a period symmetrical with that of gestation—since 'apart from exceptional cases it takes nine months to achieve total oblivion' (p. 64). He is not a ghost, he explains at a later moment, but something else. 'What are you then,' asks Reis, and Pessoa answers: 'I can't tell you, a ghost comes from the other world, I simply come from the cemetery at Prazeres. Then is the dead Fernando Pessoa the same as the Fernando Pessoa who was once alive. In one sense yes' (p. 238). Although he has a shadow—his only possession now—Pessoa casts no reflection in the mirror, and no one can see the dead unless they wish to be seen. Reis notes that he is able to see him, and Pessoa replies: 'Because I want you to see me, besides, if you think about it, who are you' (p. 66).

Who indeed is Ricardo Reis? He is the author of a number of largely unpublished poems, some of which are quoted in part in this novel by José Saramago, *The Year of the Death of Ricardo Reis*. The poems are, for the most part, written in the forms of the classical ode in a 'dense, intricate, and highly polished style' which 'enables him to express the most profound concepts with elliptical concision'.[202] Reis is one of the heteronyms of the poet Fernando Pessoa, and, in a biographical note, Pessoa writes that 'Ricardo Reis, educated in a Jesuit high school, is, as I've mentioned, a doctor; he has been living in Brazil since 1919, having gone into voluntary exile because of his monarchist sympathies. He is a formally trained Latinist, and a self-taught semi-Hellenist.' He 'writes better than I, but with a purism I find excessive'.[203]

The letter in which Pessoa describes the genesis and function of his major heteronyms is one of the great documents of modernist literature; Giorgio Agamben

[202] Peter Rickard, 'Introduction', in Fernando Pessoa, *Selected Poems*, ed. and trans. Peter Rickard, Edinburgh Bilingual Library (Austin: University of Texas Press, 1971), p. 33.

[203] Fernando Pessoa, Letter to Adolfo Casais Monteiro, 13 January 1935, *The Selected Prose of Fernando Pessoa*, ed. and trans. Richard Zenith (New York: Grove Press, 2001), pp. 258, 259.

says of it that '[i]n twentieth-century poetry, Pessoa's letter on heteronyms constitutes perhaps the most impressive document of desubjectification, the transformation of the poet into a pure "experimentation ground", and its possible implications for ethics'.[204] Before citing the core passages of this document, let me clarify the distinction that Pessoa makes between heteronymic and orthonymic poetry, on the one hand, and pseudonymic and autonymic poetry on the other. Marilyn Scarantino Jones puts it concisely: 'An author's pseudonymic work differs from his autonymic production only in so far as a different name is attached to it. A heteronym, however, is not merely a name different from the author's but also a separate personality who expresses what the author does not or cannot.'[205]

In addition to the coterie of three major poetic heteronyms—Álvaro de Campos, Alberto Caeiro, and Ricardo Reis—there is a fourth member, who

> is not a heteronym but an orthonym, one who shares the name Fernando Pessoa yet is not the Pessoa who created Caeiro, Reis and Campos. In his notes and diaries, Pessoa carefully distinguished between 'Fernando Pessoa himself' and the orthonymic Fernando Pessoa, the former being the creator of poet-characters while the latter is merely another member of the coterie.[206]

Pessoa's heteronyms and his orthonym are thus not *personae*, masks through which the poet speaks; they are autonomous figures which allow him to take on quite distinct personalities in his writing. Alain Badiou writes that, in this sense, heteronymy can be construed as 'a *dispositif* for thinking, rather than as a subjective drama'.[207] In a passage which might perhaps have sparked Saramago's novel, Pessoa writes:

> In the vision that I call inner merely because I call the 'real world' outer, I clearly and distinctly see the familiar, well-defined facial features, personality traits, life stories, ancestries, and in some cases even the death of these various characters. Some of them have met each other; others have not. None of them ever met me except Álvaro de Campos. But if tomorrow, travelling in America, I were to run into the physical person of Ricardo Reis, who in my opinion lives there, my soul wouldn't relay to my body the slightest flinch of surprise; all would be as it should be, exactly as it was before the encounter.[208]

The genesis of Pessoa's major poetic heteronyms is described in detail in the letter that he wrote to Adolfo Casais Monteiro in January 1935, the year of his own death. Ever since he was a child, he says,

[204] Giorgio Agamben, *Remnants of Auschwitz: The Witness and the Archive*, trans. Daniel Heller-Roazen (New York: Zone Books, 2002), p. 117.

[205] Marilyn Scarantino Jones, 'Pessoa's Poetic Coterie: Three Heteronyms and an Orthonym', *Luso-Brazilian Review* 14: 2 (1977), p. 254.

[206] Scarantino Jones, 'Pessoa's Poetic Coterie', p. 254.

[207] Alain Badiou, 'A Philosophical Task: To Be Contemporaries of Pessoa', in *Handbook of Inaesthetics*, trans. Alberto Toscano (Stanford: Stanford University Press, 2005), p. 43.

[208] Fernando Pessoa, 'Aspects' (the projected preface to the first volume of his collected heteronymic works), in *The Selected Prose of Fernando Pessoa*, p. 4.

> it has been my tendency to create around me a fictitious world, to surround myself with friends and acquaintances that never existed. (I can't be sure, of course, if they really never existed, or if it's me who doesn't exist. In this matter, as in any other, we shouldn't be dogmatic.) Ever since I've known myself as 'me', I can remember envisioning the shape, motions, character and life story of various unreal figures who were as visible and as close to me as the manifestations of what we call, perhaps too hastily, real life. This tendency, which goes back as far as I can remember being an I, has always accompanied me, changing somewhat the music it enchants me with, but never the way in which it enchants me.[209]

As a young child he used to write letters addressed to himself from 'a certain Chevalier de Pas', and there was another figure who was a kind of rival to the Chevalier. This tendency to create an alternative world peopled with imaginary figures persisted through his adult life. Thus, he writes, 'I elaborated, and propagated, various friends and acquaintances who never existed but whom I feel, hear and see even today, almost thirty years later. I repeat: I feel, hear and see them. And I miss them' (p. 255).

In 1912 Pessoa sketched out a few poems with irregular verse patterns and written from a pagan perspective—and then forgot about them. But 'a hazy, shadowy portrait of the person who wrote those verses took shape in me. (Unbeknownst to me, Ricardo Reis had been born.)' (p. 256). A year and a half or so later he tried to invent 'a rather complicated bucolic poet' and spent a few days trying to envision him. Then:

> One day when I'd finally given up—it was March 8th, 1914—I walked over to a high chest of drawers, took a sheet of paper, and began to write standing up, as I do whenever I can. And I wrote thirty-some poems at once, in a kind of ecstasy I'm unable to describe. It was the triumphal day of my life, and I can never have another one like it. I began with a title, *The Keeper of Sheep*. This was followed by the appearance in me of someone whom I instantly named Alberto Caeiro. Excuse the absurdity of this statement: my master had appeared in me. That was what I immediately felt, and so strong was the feeling that, as soon as those thirty-odd poems were written, I grabbed a fresh sheet of paper and wrote, again all at once, the six poems that constitute 'Slanting Rain', by Fernando Pessoa. All at once and with total concentration... It was the return of Fernando Pessoa as Alberto Caeiro to Fernando Pessoa himself. Or rather, it was the reaction of Fernando Pessoa against his nonexistence as Alberto Caeiro.
>
> Once Alberto Caeiro had appeared, I instinctively and subconsciously tried to find disciples for him. From Caeiro's false paganism I extracted the latent Ricardo Reis, at last discovering his name and adjusting him to his true self, for now I actually *saw* him. And then a new individual, quite the opposite of Ricardo Reis, suddenly and impetuously came to me. In an unbroken stream, without interruptions or corrections, the ode whose name is 'Triumphal Ode', by the man whose name is none other than Álvaro de Campos, issued from my typewriter. (p. 256)

Thus, he continues, 'I created a nonexistent coterie, placing it all in a framework of reality. I ascertained the influences at work and the friendships between them,

[209] Pessoa, Letter to Adolfo Casais Monteiro, pp. 254–5. Hereafter cited in the text.

I listened in myself to their discussions and divergent points of view, and in all of this it seems that I, who created them all, was the one who was least there' (p. 257).

Now, this account is partly mythical—there is manuscript evidence that the Caeiro poems were written over several weeks rather than in one ecstatic sitting—but it goes to the heart of the radical enunciative strategy that Pessoa develops in that body of work that was largely unpublished at his death, and in which something like seventy-two distinct heteronyms have been identified. The names of these heteronyms, I should note, are no more arbitrary than those of Pessoa's English and French alter egos, Alexander Search, C. R. Anon, and Jean Seul. The 'rather complicated bucolic poet' who turned out to be Alberto Caeiro, author of the volume entitled *The Keeper of Sheep*, began his journey into being as a joke on Pessoa's friend Mario de Sá-Carneiro; '*carneiro*' in Portuguese is 'sheep', and 'Caeiro', as Richard Zenith points out, is '*Carneiro*' without the '*carne*', the flesh. (We might note, too, the play of these two names in the title of the collection of poems that Pessoa planned for his orthonym: *Cancioneiro*, 'songbook'.) Alberto Caeiro died at the age of twenty-six; Sá-Carneiro committed suicide just short of his twenty-sixth birthday. The name of Caeiro's disciple, de Campos, means 'from the fields'—'where Alberto tended his imaginary or metaphorical sheep'.[210] And the surname of the monarchist Ricardo Reis means, in Portuguese, 'kings'. There is thus a certain magical fusion of names and persons in Pessoa's heteronymy.

I want now to begin exploring the significance of Pessoa's relation to his heteronyms by citing three commentaries on his account of that moment of ecstatic otherness in which—like Rainer Maria Rilke hearing the voice that dictated to him the opening lines of the Duino elegies, or waking up one morning to find that his handwriting had completely altered—he is possessed by the spirit of Alberto Caeiro. The first is that of Agamben, who focuses on the alternation, in this 'incomparable phenomenology of heteronymic depersonalization', between Caeiro and the Pessoa who responds to him. Agamben writes:

> Not only does each new subjectification (the appearance of Alberto Caeiro) imply a desubjectification (the depersonalization of Fernando Pessoa, who submits himself to his teacher). At the same time, each desubjectification also implies a resubjectification: the return of Fernando Pessoa, who reacts to his non-existence, that is, to his depersonalization in Alberto Caeiro. It is as if the poetic experience constituted a complex process that involved at least three subjects—or rather, three different subjectifications-desubjectifications, since it is no longer possible to speak of a subject in the strict sense.[211]

The context for this argument in *Remnants of Auschwitz* is Agamben's discussion of the constitution of subjectivity in the double movement (active and passive) of auto-affection and its underlying form as shame; the analogue he cites is Keats's description of the 'poetical Character' as 'not itself—it has no self—it is every thing

[210] Richard Zenith, 'Introduction: The Birth of a Nation', in Fernando Pessoa, *A Little Larger than the Entire Universe: Selected Poems*, ed. and trans. Richard Zenith (London: Penguin, 2006), p. xxi.

[211] Agamben, *Remnants of Auschwitz*, p. 119.

and nothing—It has no character'; and of the poetic experience as fundamentally shameful, since 'not one word I ever utter can be taken for granted as an opinion growing out of my identical nature—how can it, when I have no nature?' 'Even now,' Keats adds, 'I am perhaps not speaking from myself: but from some character in whose soul I now live.'[212] In the case of Pessoa, says Agamben, what happens in the process of successive depersonalizations is the emergence of 'a new poetic consciousness, something like a genuine *ēthos* of poetry' in which the poet understands 'that he must respond to his own desubjectification', and yet does so in a way that goes beyond the simple assertion of a subject form that has now become problematic.[213]

The second commentary is Pessoa's own, in a prelude to the account of the moment of genesis of Caeiro. This account is clinical—Pessoa uses the term 'psychiatric'. 'My heteronyms,' he writes,

> have their origin in a deep-seated form of hysteria. I don't know if I'm afflicted by simple hysteria or, more specifically, by hysterical neurasthenia. I suspect it's the latter, for I have symptoms of abulia [that is, lack of will, indecisiveness] that mere hysteria would not explain. Whatever the case, the mental origin of my heteronyms lies in my relentless, organic tendency to depersonalization and simulation. Fortunately for me and for others, these phenomena have been mentally internalized, such that they don't show up in my outer, everyday life among people; they erupt inside me, where only I experience them. If I were a woman (hysterical phenomena in women erupt externally, through attacks and the like), each poem of Álvaro de Campos (the most hysterically hysterical part of me) would be a general alarm to the neighbourhood. But I'm a man, and in men hysteria affects mainly the inner psyche; so it all ends in silence and poetry...[214]

Hysteria and neurasthenia, as these terms are used at the time, are gendered versions of the same neurosis, the former flamboyant and manifested on the body, the latter more diffuse and taking the form both of non-specific aches and pains and of more deep-seated psychological disorders. Pessoa is describing both a pathology and the work of sublimation that keeps it turned inward and productive of poetry, and this sublimation involves both a loss of self and a deep identification with his alter egos. Asking himself how he writes 'in the name of these three', Pessoa answers:

> Caeiro, through sheer and unexpected inspiration, without knowing or even suspecting that I'm going to write in his name. Ricardo Reis, after an abstract meditation that suddenly takes concrete shape in an ode. Campos, when I feel a sudden impulse to write and don't know what. (My semiheteronym Bernardo Soares, who in many ways resembles Álvaro de Campos, always appears when I'm sleepy or drowsy, such that my qualities of inhibition and logical reasoning are suspended; his prose is an endless

[212] John Keats, Letter to John Woodhouse, 27th October 1818; cited in Agamben, *Remnants of Auschwitz*, pp. 112–3.
[213] Agamben, *Remnants of Auschwitz*, p. 119.
[214] Pessoa, Letter to Adolfo Casais Monteiro, p. 253.

reverie. He's a semiheteronym because his personality, although not my own, doesn't differ from my own but is a mere mutilation of it.)[215]

In each case it is a form of suspension of consciousness that makes possible the sudden, unexpected event of poetic creation.

The third commentary is that of Greg Mahr, who writes that Pessoa 'became a great poet only after a powerful dissociative experience involving the creation of other identities, an event strongly reminiscent of dissociative identity disorder. In this case, though, dissociation appeared to resolve for Pessoa certain tensions implicit in the modernist sensibility, and allowed him new possibilities of creative freedom'.[216] Specifically, the welling up in Pessoa of the unreflexive, 'naïve' poet Alberto Caeiro offers a solution to the modernist compulsion to reflexivity and to 'sentimentality' in Friedrich Schiller's sense of the word. Caeiro's 'vigorous lyrical voice seems to come from a different sensibility than that of the self-critical, diffident, and painfully self-aware modernist':[217] the painful self-awareness (or rather awareness of the absence of self) that characterizes both the orthonymic Fernando Pessoa of *Cancioneiro* and the semi-heteronym Bernardo Soares to whom the authorship of the extraordinary collection of fragments that make up *The Book of Disquiet* is attributed.

Let me suggest, however, that it is possible to think about the use and function of the heteronyms in another way, one that would see them not as an episode in the history of the subject or as a more or less resolved or mitigated pathology but rather as a rhetorical strategy. On this reading, the work done by Pessoa's use of the names of others is to provide a solution to the modernist problem of the impossibility of speaking *in propria persona*, of speech that would not at once be caught up in the already-said, in the clichés of expression or representation. The speech of the heteronyms is language to the second degree, belonging neither to the figures who author them nor to the poet standing behind those figures but to the floating space of a metapoetics which is yet not distinct from the poems: the space within which the multiple voices of *Ulysses* or the fragmented voices of 'The Waste Land' take place, for example, or the unauthored voices of surrealist automatic writing, or Gertrude Stein's automatized prose, or the language of infelicitous translation through which Ezra Pound makes his Propertius speak.

In this sense, Pessoa's heteronyms belong very specifically to the history of modernist depersonalization: a history that includes, say, Eliot's claim that '[p]oetry . . . is not the expression of personality, but an escape from personality';[218] or Jorge Luis Borges' attack on 'the exceptional pre-eminence now generally awarded to the self' and his counter-claim that '[t]here is no whole self', the self is a mirage, no more than a rhetorical move, 'a few muscular sensations' and the sight of the branches

[215] Pessoa, Letter to Adolfo Casais Monteiro, pp. 258–9.
[216] Greg Mahr, 'Pessoa, Life Narrative, and the Dissociative Process', *Biography* 21: 1 (1998), p. 24.
[217] Mahr, 'Pessoa, Life Narrative, and the Dissociative Process', p. 29.
[218] T. S. Eliot, 'Tradition and the Individual Talent', in *Selected Essays* (3rd edn, London: Faber, 1961), p. 21.

that the trees place outside his window.[219] Depersonalization, in this history, is not a psychological phenomenon, a matter of the zeitgeist, but a rhetorical strategy of writing in and through the names of others; and this, I suggest, is how we should read the thematization of the absence or fragmentation of self throughout Pessoa's work.

In an alternative account of this moment of genesis of the heteronyms and of his relation to them, Pessoa writes:

> Today I have no personality: I've divided all my humanness among the various authors whom I've served as literary executor. Today I'm the meeting-place of a small humanity that belongs only to me.
>
> I subsist as a kind of medium of myself, but I'm less real than the others, less substantial, less personal, and easily influenced by them all. I too am a disciple of Caeiro . . .[220]

And elsewhere he adds that '[t]he human author of these books knows no self whatsoever within himself. When, for whatever reason, he senses a self within him, he quickly sees that it's a being very different from himself although having some resemblances'.[221]

Numerous passages from *The Book of Disquiet* pick up this topos of the fragmentation of the self under its reflexive scrutiny.[222] Let me quote a few, almost at random:

> . . . as an ironic spectator of myself, I've never lost interest in seeing what life brings . . . I am, in large measure, the selfsame prose I write. I unroll myself in sentences and paragraphs, I punctuate myself.[223]
>
> Whatever I feel is felt (against my will) so that I can write that I felt it. Whatever I think is promptly put into words, mixed with images that undo it, cast into rhythms that are something else altogether. From so much self-revising, I've destroyed myself . . . I spend my life wondering if I'm deep or not, with no remaining plumb except my gaze that shows me—blackly vivid in the mirror at the bottom of the well—my own face that observes me observing it. (p. 170)
>
> Each of us is several, is many, is a profusion of selves. So that the self who disdains his surroundings is not the same as the self who suffers or takes joy in them. In the vast colony of our being there are many species of people who think and feel in different ways . . . my entire world of all these souls who don't know each other casts, like a motley but compact multitude, a single shadow—the calm, bookkeeping body with

[219] Jorge Luis Borges, 'The Nothingness of Personality', in *The Total Library: Non-Fiction 1922–1986*, ed. Eliot Weinberger, trans. Esther Allen, Suzanne Jill Levine, and Eliot Weinberger (London: Penguin, 2007), pp. 3–4.

[220] Fernando Pessoa, 'Another Version of the Genesis of the Heteronyms', in *The Selected Prose of Fernando Pessoa*, p. 262.

[221] Fernando Pessoa, unpublished preface to the heteronyms, in *Poems of Fernando Pessoa*, trans. Edwin Honig and Susan M. Brown (San Francisco: City Lights, 1998), p. 149.

[222] Jerome Maunsell describes it as an 'intensely self-aware wreck of a book'; Jerome Boyd Maunsell, 'The Hauntings of Fernando Pessoa', *Modernism/modernity* 19: 1 (2012), p. 125.

[223] Fernando Pessoa, *The Book of Disquiet*, ed. and trans. Richard Zenith (London: Penguin, 2001), p. 169. Hereafter cited in the text.

> which I lean over Borges's tall desk, where I've come to get the blotter that he borrowed from me. (pp. 327–8)

'Borges' here is presumably no more than a fellow clerk, not the writer who speaks in remarkably similar ways of the division of the self, who is 'not sure which of us it is that's writing this page';[224] but we shall return to that Borges. This thematization of the unhappy consciousness in its specific relation to writing is equally to be found in the work of all of Pessoa's major heteronyms; it is present by way of its negation in Caeiro's calm refusal of reflexivity and his rigorous nominalism; in the later, more introspective poetry of Álvaro de Campos; in the measured anguish of the orthonym Fernando Pessoa; and even in the calm classicism of Ricardo Reis, in a poem such as this, written shortly before his return to Portugal following Pessoa's death:

> *Countless Lives Inhabit Us*
> Countless lives inhabit us.
> I don't know, when I think or feel,
> Who it is that thinks or feels.
> I am merely the place
> Where things are thought or felt.
>
> I have more than just one soul.
> There are more I's than I myself.
> I exist, nevertheless,
> Indifferent to them all.
> I silence them: I speak.
>
> The crossing urges of what
> I feel or do not feel
> Struggle in who I am, but I
> Ignore them. They dictate nothing
> To the I I know: I write.[225]

One of the ways in which the heteronyms and the orthonym are distinguished from 'Fernando Pessoa himself' is that the heteronyms cannot themselves have heteronyms: there can be no infinite spiral of multiplying and named selves. (This is also true for the orthonym 'Fernando Pessoa'.) The description of the 'countless lives' of Reis's poem takes one step towards that possibility, although it is met with a philosophical refusal. The same step is taken more firmly in Saramago's *The Year of the Death of Ricardo Reis*, where the heteronym Ricardo Reis starts both to take on a life of its own and to become aware of the other selves it contains. Unpacking his documents when he arrives at the Hotel Bragança, Reis comes across a recent manuscript—the one just quoted, but in this translation the first

[224] Jorge Luis Borges, 'Borges and I', in *Collected Fictions*, trans. Andrew Hurley (New York: Viking, 1998), p. 324.
[225] Fernando Pessoa & Co., *Selected Poems*, ed. and trans. Richard Zenith (New York: Grove Press, 1998), p. 137.

lines read '*Innumerable people live within us. If I think and feel, I know not who is thinking and feeling, I am only the place where there is thinking and feeling*'; and the narrator continues, 'though they do not end here, it is as if everything ends, for beyond thinking and feeling there is nothing'.[226] Reading over these lines, Reis reflects: 'Who is using me in order to think and feel, and among the innumerable people who live within me, who I am...what thoughts and feelings are the ones I do not share because they are mine alone?' The answer to the first of these questions is that the one who is using Ricardo Reis to think and feel is Fernando Pessoa, but also the reader, who occupies the position of his 'I' in the act of reading; and the second question is answered towards the end of the book, when Reis asks Fernando Pessoa: 'Is there anything that belongs only to me', and is told, 'Probably not' (p. 313): again, both because Reis is a creature of writing and because he is possessed (perhaps in both senses of the word) by those who read him.

Selves are innumerable, discontinuous, and virtual. After falling asleep one afternoon, Reis wakes up to find on the table a sheet of paper with two lines of poetry he had written earlier ('*All I ask of the gods is that I should ask nothing of them*', p. 35; emphasis in original). Annoyed, he reflects that '[i]t never occurs to people that the one who finishes something is never the one who started it, even if both have the same name, for the name is the only thing that remains constant' (p. 37). This is Alberto Caeiro's position: names designate a contingent and discontinuous content. They contain multitudes. On another afternoon,

> Ricardo Reis did not go out to dine. He had some tea and cakes on the large table in the living room surrounded by seven empty chairs. Under a chandelier with seven branches and two bulbs he ate three small sponge cakes, leaving one on his plate. He counted again and saw that the numbers four and six were missing. He soon found the four, the corners of the rectangular room, but for six he had to get up and look around, which resulted in eight, the empty chairs. Finally he decided that he himself would be six, he could be any number if he was innumerable. (p. 204)

Later, when his idealized beloved, Marcenda, visits him, he has to decide which room to take her to, 'into the dining room would be absurd, in which of the chairs around that long table would they sit, side by side or facing, and how many would be seated there, he being innumerable, and she is certainly more than one...' (p. 209).

If one's selves are innumerable, they also exist—as the heteronym Ricardo Reis does—independently of their author or of whatever might be designated as a primary self. At one point Reis reflects that 'already Rio de Janeiro is like a distant memory, perhaps of some other life, not his, one of those innumerable lives. Yes, at this very moment another Ricardo Reis may be dining in Oporto or lunching in Rio de Janeiro, if not farther afield' (p. 197). The best way of explaining this actualization of virtual selves in an endless set of other possible worlds is by reference to the primary intertext of *The Year of the Death of Ricardo Reis*, a novel by Herbert

[226] Saramago, *The Year of the Death of Ricardo Reis*, p. 13; emphasis in original.

Quain called *The God of the Labyrinth*, which Reis has accidentally taken with him from the ship's library, where

> [t]he tedium of the voyage and the book's evocative title had attracted him. A labyrinth with a god, what god might that be, which labyrinth, what labyrinthine god. In the end it turned out to be a simple detective story, an ordinary tale of death and investigation, the murderer, the victim, and finally the detective, all three accomplices to the crime. In my honest opinion, the reader of a mystery is the only real survivor of the story he is reading, unless it is as the one real survivor that every reader reads every story. (p. 12)

Reis reads this novel intermittently, struggling to make sense of it and at times falling asleep over it; he finally takes it with him when, at the end of the novel, he departs this world along with Fernando Pessoa, whose nine months are now up. Now, *The God of the Labyrinth* is one of the texts that Borges describes in his story 'A Survey of the Works of Herbert Quain', recalling from memory—since he has lost his only copy—a plot which contains 'an incomprehensible murder in the early pages of the book, a slow discussion in the middle, and a solution of the crime toward the end'.[227] But then a long paragraph in the novel's final pages introduces the sentence: '*Everyone believed that the chessplayers had met accidentally*' (emphasis in original), which forces the reader to infer that the proposed solution is erroneous and so to discover another solution—just as it is left to the reader, in the story of the numbers in Reis's dining room, to work out that the unmentioned number five is that of the branches of the chandelier which have no bulbs. Even more directly relevant, however, is the next work of Quain's described in this story, *April March*, in which successive chapters describe an event and then a series of preceding events, each of which is an alternative version of what might have led up to it, and each of which, in turn, has a series of virtual antecedents; the structure is precisely that of the Chinese novel described in Borges' story 'The Garden of Forking Paths', a work which is literally a labyrinth where each of the ramifying branches of any event is simultaneously actualized within 'an infinite series of times, a growing, dizzying web of divergent, convergent, and parallel times'.[228] It is within such a universe, and only such a universe, that Pessoa's heteronyms can, in turn, generate heteronyms in a nesting of reality and fiction that extends to infinity.

The insanity that seems to characterize the narrator of *The Year of the Death of Ricardo Reis*, a novel in which 'absurdity does not always obey logic', is perhaps a necessary corollary of the novel's literalization of Pessoa's dissociative vision. At its mildest this madness takes the form of a supposition that the world is shaped according to human need: 'Fortunately,' the narrator notes at one point, 'he cannot see himself in the mirror clouded by steam, this must be the compassion shown by mirrors at certain critical moments';[229] and again:

[227] Jorge Luis Borges, 'A Survey of the Works of Herbert Quain', in *Collected Fictions*, p. 108.
[228] Jorge Luis Borges, 'The Garden of Forking Paths', in *Collected Fictions*, p. 127.
[229] Saramago, *The Year of the Death of Ricardo Reis*, p. 247.

> If all the seconds and minutes were exactly the same, as marked on the clock, we would not always have time to explain what takes place in them, the substance they contain, but fortunately for us the episodes of greatest significance tend to occur in seconds of long duration and minutes that are spun out, which makes it possible to discuss at length and in some detail without any serious violation of the most subtle of the three dramatic unities, which is time itself. (p. 181)

That charming confidence is matched by moments of radical uncertainty when the narrator accuses himself of saying something untrue, or puzzles over how much detail the reader will require, or—more frequently—alternates between blunt assertions of fact and a disclosure of ignorance, the former often masking the latter, as when he describes Marcenda in passing as a virgin, for

> although this has not been mentioned and she herself does not declare it, Marcenda is a virgin, a wholly private matter, even a fiancé, should she ever have one, will not dare to ask, Are you a virgin. For the time being and in this social ambiance one assumes that she is. Later, at the opportune moment, we may discover with some indignation that she wasn't after all. (p. 110)

But the madness of the narrator is perhaps, above all, a matter of our inability to distinguish his commentary from the fantasies of the characters he describes. At one point, for example, the police informer Victor encounters Ricardo Reis and his invisible dead creator, and 'as Ricardo Reis crossed the street followed by Fernando Pessoa, the police informer had the impression there were two shadows on the ground. These are the effects of reflected light, an illusion, after a certain age the eyes are not capable of distinguishing between the visible and the invisible' (p. 237). Just as the novel's dialogue, which lacks quotation marks and any demarcation of speakers, often can't be precisely allocated, and just as its lack of interrogation marks makes it hard to distinguish question from statement, so sentences like this are free-floating: they might be the comment of a naïve narrator, or they might be Victor's thoughts; there's no way of knowing.

That multilayered enunciative force is a component of the novel's strategy of layering the opposition of the fictive to the real through a series of hierarchically ordered levels, none of which is final and definitive. Reflecting on theatrical mimesis, Ricardo Reis concludes that 'only a different reality, whatever it is, may be substituted for the reality one wishes to convey. The difference between them mutually demonstrates, explains, and measures them, reality as the invention it was, invention as the reality it will be' (p. 89). Reality is, as the narrator puts it, 'all false and at the same time all true' (p. 168). Consider this dialogue between Reis and Pessoa:

> Soon you will be telling me that life and death are the same. Precisely, my dear Reis. In the space of one day you have stated three quite different things, that there is no death, that there is death, and now that life and death are the same. There was no other way of resolving the contradiction of the first two statements. And, as he said this, Fernando Pessoa gave a knowing smile. (p. 239)

For 'life' and 'death' in this dialogue we can substitute the words 'reality' and 'fiction': that is surely the meaning of Pessoa's 'knowing smile'. The real and the fictive meet in that paradoxical area that D. W. Winnicott called transitional, an area 'which is not challenged, because no claim is made on its behalf except that it shall exist as a resting place for the individual engaged in the perpetual human task of keeping inner and outer reality separate yet inter-related'.[230]

At the very end of the novel Ricardo Reis finds himself beginning to fade away physically: 'In the morning he cannot rise without first identifying himself with his own hands, line by line, what he can still find of himself, like a fingerprint partially obliterated by a large scar':[231] he identifies himself 'line by line' because he is made of writing, his 'I' inhabited and possessed by his creator Fernando Pessoa (whose name in Portuguese means 'person') and by the reader, by whatever reader is left for his unpublished poems, locked away in a trunk in Fernando Pessoa's rooms. In this drama of mirrors and names, of heteronyms and orthonyms and of an author who is doubled between them, observing himself observing himself and all his others, the reader, finally, is the only true other, 'the one real survivor', the only character without a name.

[230] D. W. Winnicott, 'Transitional Objects and Transitional Phenomena', in *Collected Papers: Through Paediatrics to Psychoanalysis* (London: Tavistock, 1958), p. 230.

[231] Saramago, *The Year of the Death of Ricardo Reis*, p. 309.

7
Face

I

Name and pronoun are inscriptions and identifications of personhood or quasi-personhood in language. But pronouns and names are necessarily articulated with bodies: that articulation (and the further articulation of bodies with mental states) constitutes the schematic matrix of personhood that is mimed by fictional character. In this chapter I explore the face as a semiotic medium, before moving, in the final chapter, to think about real and represented bodies.

Kōbō Abe's novel *The Face of Another* tells the story of an unnamed scientist whose face has been so badly burned by liquid oxygen that he must wear bandages, dark glasses, and a surgical mask to conceal the 'leech-like mass . . . swollen and distended, red and black, intertwining' that it has now become.[1] The novel takes the form of a prefatory letter addressed by 'I' to 'you', his wife, and then three notebooks, Black, White, and Grey, which he asks her to read. They recount his isolation from both his colleagues and his wife behind his 'false face' (the reference is to a drawing by Klee of a cruelly inscrutable bandaged figure), and his decision to construct a mask which will fit like a skin over his face and fully resemble a face—but not his own. Yet he hesitates, unwilling to accept that the loss of his face is a kind of loss of self, at least in relation to others: a mask would pose 'a challenge to the face and to the authority of the face' (p. 31), and yet it must differ from his own (former) face in order not to be a meaningless simulacrum.

Once he decides to proceed, two issues confront him. The first is a set of technical problems, which he solves by constructing a metal cast of his damaged face onto which the mask will fit exactly; by buying a sample of skin to act as a template for texture and resilience; by modelling the face in an elastic synthetic material laid over a spongy resin base and, in order to allow for movement, anchored on strips of tape corresponding to the lines of the facial muscles (the Langer lines); and by painstakingly colouring the surface, inserting facial hairs, and using steam heating to set wrinkles into the mask along the Langer lines in accordance with a predetermined set of affect ratios. The result is a 'soft gelatinous membrane' (p. 95) which he can apply to his face with a mild glue.

[1] Kōbō Abe, *The Face of Another*, trans. E. Dale Saunders (Harmondsworth: Penguin, 1972), p. 14. Hereafter cited in the text.

The second issue he faces, the second issue that faces him (the metaphor of oppositional positioning is inescapable), is the terrible freedom imposed on him by having to choose what kind of face his mask will be. From the work of a (seemingly fictitious) French physiologist, Henri Boulan, he draws a model of four facial types which he correlates with four basic Jungian personality types. The choice he finally makes, of the fourth, extravert type, is determined by his anguish at the unreachable otherness of his wife: he desires, he realizes, both to reach her and to destroy her, and the face he has chosen is that of a hunter; and the question he must then answer is whether this is 'the negation of my real face or actually a new face'. At this point he has not yet posed a third alternative: that this mask is indeed his real face.

Before he reaches this decision two events have moved him to meditate on the relation of the face to the mask. The first occurs when he retreats from the crowded streets into a cinema where a close-up of a woman's face is shown in such distorting detail that it loses all meaning as a face. Immediately after this he enters an exhibition of Noh masks, which, in their bare immobility, seem to him to be a rejection of life. One in particular resembles a skull with a thin membrane applied to it, and he generalizes from it to ask whether there wasn't 'in the radical method of the Noh mask some fundamental principle which made the face an empty container, some law applicable to every mask, every expression, every face? The face,' he concludes, 'is made by someone else; one doesn't make it oneself...' (p. 69).

This is the beginning of his recognition that the face is itself a mask, not the 'window of the soul' (p. 103), and that his facelessness had been a kind of freedom. The mask he wears, conversely, is at once a new way of being and a loss. Looking at his masked self in the mirror for the first time, he sees a stranger staring back at him, and 'When it smiled it was full of the feeling of death' (p. 96).[2] It is as though he were seeing his own shadow disappear. Yet almost at once this mirror self comes to feel like a living face, into which he slips without resistance. So much himself does it become that it takes over his will, acting in ways that are out of character with his former self and ignoring the plans he has made for it. Gradually it becomes objectified into an other self that he calls 'the mask': like the digital alt in *Second Life*, or like Golyadkin's alter ego in Dostoevsky's *The Double*, it acts out fantasies that he would not formerly have entertained.[3]

Chief among these is the fantasy of seducing 'you', his wife, a 'shameless' erotic fantasy with strong overtones of violence that 'I' at once encourages and deeply resents;[4] his jealousy leads to a 'desperate duel' between himself and the mask

[2] In the 1959 film directed by Georges Franju, *Les Yeux sans Visage*, a doctor reconstructs his daughter's damaged face using grafts taken from young women whom he then murders; looking at herself in the mirror, the daughter sees 'someone who looks like me but comes from far away'. The grafts fail, and for much of the movie we see Christiane wearing a dead, expressionless mask and moving like a marionette.

[3] Kubrick uses a similar trope in *Eyes Wide Shut*, when the Tom Cruise character (Dr Bill Hartford) returns home to find his wife sleeping next to a mask lying on his pillow: a mask which is a figure at once of his own face and of her fantasy lover, and a representative both of the masked figures at the menacing and erotic gathering where he wore it the previous night and of the horde of men she dreamed he had watched her fucking. Stanley Kubrick, dir., *Eyes Wide Shut* (1999).

[4] Abe, *The Face of Another*, p. 137.

(p. 138). When, to his despair, his wife submits to the seduction, he finds himself in a triangular relationship in which he plays two parts: 'I was a cuckold present at his wife's adultery' (p. 183). At the same time, he realizes that she herself has no singular dimension of being: 'Just as I had a double existence, you did too. If I was another person wearing a stranger's mask, you were another person wearing a mask of yourself' (p. 179). The counterpart to this realization is the recognition that 'I had not made a mask at all. The mask had become my real face, and thought itself in fact real' (p. 201).

At the end of the third notebook we return to the novel's beginning: a rented room where he has left a letter and the three notebooks for his wife to read. In the cupboard he has left 'the corpse of the mask' (p. 201) and an elaborately made button that the wife had given to her lover—a token of the identity of 'I' and the mask. He himself will wait for her at home. But he waits in vain. When he goes to the room, fearing that she may have killed herself, he finds, in place of his own letter, a letter that she has addressed to him, in which she writes that 'It was not the mask that died... but you': she had always known that he was the masked stranger, and had assumed that he knew that she knew: 'You knew and yet demanded that we go on with the play in silence' (p. 210)—out of delicacy towards her, she had thought. Her words go to the core of their misunderstanding:

> In a happy frame of mind, I reflected that love strips the mask from each of us, and we must endeavour for those we love to put the mask on so that it can be taken off again. For if there is no mask to start with, there is no pleasure in removing it, is there?... At first you were apparently trying to get your own self back by means of the mask, but before you knew it you had come to think of it only as your magician's cloak for escaping from your self. So it was not a mask, but somewhat the same as another real face, wasn't it?... It was not the mask, but you yourself. It is meaningful to put a mask on, precisely because one makes others realize it is a mask (p. 211)—

but he had not known how to treat it, how to inhabit it, how to own its actions. And, she adds, 'Since the mask will not come back, there is no reason for me to return either' (p. 212).

II

It is that dialectic explored in Abe's novel, between the face as mask and the face as window to the soul, that I shall begin exploring here. Michael Taussig uses precisely these words when, in a book on publicly known but unacknowledged secrets, he describes the face as

> the figure of appearance, the appearance of appearance, the figure of figuration, the ur-appearance, if you will, of secrecy itself as the primordial act of presencing. For the face itself is a contingency, at the magical crossroads of mask and window to the soul, one of the better-kept public secrets essential to everyday life.[5]

[5] Michael Taussig, *Defacement: Public Secrecy and the Labor of the Negative* (Stanford: Stanford University Press, 1999), p. 3.

Structured into the face, and into its role as public secret, is a fetish effect which works by means of a 'strategic ignorance', whereby we deny the mask when we look at the window, and vice versa.[6] We cannot see them together; indeed, their coexistence is impossible, although it is necessary and true.

Now, what is immediately at stake in this relation of the face to the mask, this masking of the face's transparency or this discovery that the face is itself opaque, is the categorical opposition of surface to depth, and the opposition of illusion to truth inscribed within it. Here the face stands in an immediate or masked relation to the spirit which lies behind it, and which it makes available through an act of 'presencing' (or which, as mask, it conceals). Taussig uses the paradox of the open secret as a way of trying to understand that act of presencing, with the effect at once of containing the act and of playing (or flirting) with its metaphysical dangers. We can glimpse a more purely metaphysical form of the understanding of the face as presence in an essay by Georg Simmel on the aesthetic significance of the face. That significance, writes Simmel, 'is described only in very general and approximate terms when it is said that in the features of the face the soul finds its clearest expression'.[7] Of all the elements of the body, the face has the highest degree of inner unity, and thus 'appears to be pervaded by mind'.[8] Not only does it symbolize the spirit, however; the naked face, the heir to a body which is now clothed, also expresses 'an unmistakable personality':[9] 'In the face alone, emotion first expressed in movement is deposited as the expression of permanent character.'[10] Character is sedimented emotion etched into the mask of the face, 'hardly more than gestures,' writes Proust, 'which force of habit has made permanent'.[11]

The face must thus first be severed from the body (the naked from the clothed) in order to gain its expressive force. But it is not the face as a whole, but, above all, the eye which, in its mobility and in its structuring of space through the gaze, 'epitomizes the achievement of the face in mirroring the soul', and gives an intimation of the possibility that 'appearance' might 'become the veiling and unveiling of the soul'.[12] A progressive division thus cuts the face off from the body and then separates one feature from its characteristic inner unity. It is the eyes which function as the window, where we look *through* the face to the soul behind. But we may not always look through this window: direct gaze into another's eyes is a contravention of social codes except in situations of intimacy or where it is licensed by such things

[6] Taussig, *Defacement*, p. 225.

[7] Georg Simmel, 'The Aesthetic Significance of the Face', trans. Lore Ferguson, in Kurt H. Wolff (ed.), *Georg Simmel, 1858–1918: A Collection of Essays, with Translations and a Bibliography* (Columbus: Ohio State University Press, 1959), p. 276.

[8] Simmel, 'The Aesthetic Significance of the Face', 276.

[9] Simmel, 'The Aesthetic Significance of the Face', p. 278.

[10] Simmel, 'The Aesthetic Significance of the Face', p. 279.

[11] *Les traits de notre visage ne sont guère que des gestes devenus, par l'habitude, définitifs.* Marcel Proust, *Within a Budding Grove*, II, in *In Search of Lost Time*, vol. II, trans. C. K. Scott Moncrieff and Terence Kilmartin, revised by D. J. Enright (New York: Modern Library, 2003), p. 667; *À l'ombre des jeunes filles en fleur*, II, in *À la recherche du temps perdu*, vol. II, ed. Jean-Yves Tadié, Éditions de la Pléïade (Paris: Gallimard, 1988), p. 262.

[12] Simmel, 'The Aesthetic Significance of the Face', p. 281.

as public performance or superior power (in interrogation, for example).[13] And what of the other expressive elements of the face? What of the mouth, through which the spirit gives utterance? What of the lines of affect drawn and mobilized by the facial muscles? And what of the fact that there is not one window but two, and that it is impossible to look into and through both of them at once? Look at a face too closely and its 'inner unity' dissolves into fragmented pieces. '*The face, what a horror*. It is naturally a lunar landscape, with its pores, planes, matts, bright colors, whiteness, and holes: there is no need for a close-up to make it inhuman; it is naturally a close-up, and naturally inhuman, a monstrous hood.'[14]

Deleuze and Guattari's account of the close-up draws directly on cinema, but it is also perhaps indebted to the most extended literary account of the visual surface of the face, the running thread of analysis of Albertine's face in *À la recherche du temps perdu*. In opposition to a conception of the human face as the singular, unified, and unique expression of an underlying and singular personality, Proust offers a reading of a face that is not unique, is not singular, is not the property or the manifestation of its wearer, and is neither spatially nor temporally coherent.

Albertine is at first an indeterminate figure, a member of the little group of adolescent girls the narrator gets to know at Balbec, whose faces

> were for the most part blurred with this misty effulgence of a dawn from which their actual features had not yet emerged. One saw only a charming glow of colour beneath which what in a few years' time would be a profile was not discernible. The profile of today had nothing definitive about it, and could be only a momentary resemblance to some deceased member of the family to whom nature had paid this commemorative courtesy.[15]

That momentary resemblance is, nevertheless, the expression of a more fundamental determinism: although faces change too slowly for us to perceive the transformations they undergo, one has only to see these girls standing next to a mother or an aunt to realize, not only how they would age but how they would come to conform to an atavistic type, when 'a coarse nose, a protruding jaw, a paunch' would appear, apparently from nowhere but 'actually in the wings, ready to come on, unforeseen, inevitable...'[16]

[13] Paul Ekman and Wallace V. Friesen, *Unmasking the Face* (Englewood Cliffs, NJ: Prentice Hall, 1975), p. 16.

[14] Gilles Deleuze and Félix Guattari, 'Year Zero: Faciality', in *A Thousand Plateaus: Capitalism and Schizophrenia*, trans. Brian Massumi (Minneapolis: University of Minnesota Press, 1987), p. 190; cf. Siegfried Kracauer, *Theory of Film: The Redemption of Physical Reality* (Oxford: Oxford University Press, 1960), p. 48, speaking of Griffith's use of the cinematic close-up of the face as an end in itself: 'Any huge close-up reveals new and unsuspected formations of matter; skin textures are reminiscent of aerial photographs, eyes turn into lakes or volcanic craters.'

[15] *Pour la plupart les visages mêmes de ces jeunes filles étaient confondus dans cette rougeur confuse de l'aurore d'où les véritables traits n'avaient pas encore jailli. On ne voyait qu'une couleur charmante sous laquelle ce que devait être dans quelques années le profil n'était pas discernable. Celui d'aujourd'hui n'avait rien de définitif et pouvait n'être qu'une ressemblance momentanée avec quelque membre défunt de la famille auquel la nature avait fait cette politesse commémorative.* Proust, *Within a Budding Grove*, II, p. 662; *À l'ombre des jeunes filles en fleur*, II, pp. 258–9.

[16] *un gros nez, une bouche proéminente, un embonpoint... prêt à entrer en scène, imprévu, fatal.* Proust, *Within a Budding Grove*, II, p. 644; *À l'ombre des jeunes filles en fleur*, II, p. 245.

Emerging from that 'stream of ductile matter, continuously moulded by the fleeting impression of the moment',[17] Albertine only gradually takes form, and indeed is unrecognizable from one encounter to the next. What we see is both a singular person slowly separating from her companions, and a figure constructed through a multiply retrospective view. Isolating what he takes to be the same girl from the various others from whom she is barely distinguishable, the narrator seeks to fix a particular impression as a definitive moment against which her later forms of appearance are assessed:

> Thus it is, coming to a halt, her eyes sparkling beneath her polo-cap, that I still see her again today, silhouetted against the screen which the sea spreads out behind her, and separated from me by a transparent sky-blue space, the interval of time that has elapsed since then—the first impression, faint and tenuous in my memory, desired, pursued, then forgotten, then recaptured, of a face which I have many times since projected upon the cloud of the past in order to be able to say to myself of a girl who was actually in my room: 'It is she!'[18]

Emblematic of this frustrated attempt to fix the material reality of Albertine's face is the tiny mole which wanders around it, appearing first on her cheek, below her eye (p. 618/p. 228), then later on her chin (p. 622/p. 230), only to come to rest finally on her upper lip, just below her nose (p. 625/p. 232). Just as Albertine herself, as Genette notes, is successively uncovered in different personae, so her face 'alters from one day to the next, not only in its expression, but also in its very form and material'.[19] The most extraordinary, and the most painterly, description of that changing materiality is the following:

> On certain days, thin, with a grey complexion, a sullen air, a violet transparency slanting across her eyes such as we notice sometimes on the sea, she seemed to be feeling the sorrows of exile. On other days her face, smoother and glossier, drew one's desires on to its varnished surface and prevented them from going further; unless I caught a sudden glimpse of her from the side, for her matt cheeks, like white wax on the surface, were visibly pink beneath, which was what made one so long to kiss them, to reach that different tint which was so elusive. At other times, happiness bathed those cheeks with a radiance so mobile that the skin, grown fluid and vague, gave passage to a sort of subcutaneous glaze which made it appear to be of another colour but not of another substance than the eyes; sometimes, when one looked without thinking at her face punctuated with tiny brown marks among which floated what were simply two larger, bluer stains, it was as though one were looking at a goldfinch's egg, or

[17] *un flot de matière ductile pétrie à tout moment par l'impression passagère qui les domine.* Proust, *Within a Budding Grove*, II, p. 662; *À l'ombre des jeunes filles en fleur*, II, p. 259; hereafter cited in the text.

[18] *C'est ainsi, faisant halte, les yeux brillants sous son 'polo' que je la revois encore maintenant, silhouettée sur l'écran que lui fait, au fond, la mer, et séparée de moi par un espace transparent et azuré, le temps écoulé depuis lors, première image, toute mince dans mon souvenir, désirée, poursuivie, puis oubliée, puis retrouvée, d'un visage que j'ai souvent depuis projeté dans le passé pour pouvoir me dire d'une jeune fille qui était dans ma chambre: 'C'est elle!'.* Proust, *Within a Budding Grove*, II, p. 558–9; *À l'ombre des jeunes filles en fleur*, II, p. 186.

[19] Gérard Genette, 'Proust Palimpsest', in *Figures of Literary Discourse*, trans. Alan Sheridan (New York: Columbia University Press, 1982), p. 215.

perhaps at an opalescent agate cut and polished in two places only, where, at the heart of the brown stone, there shone, like the transparent wings of a sky-blue butterfly, the eyes, those features in which the flesh becomes a mirror and gives us the illusion of enabling us, more than through the other parts of the body, to approach the soul. But most often it too showed more colour, and was then more animated; sometimes in her white face only the tip of her nose was pink, and as delicate as that of a mischievous kitten with which one would have liked to play; sometimes her cheeks were so glossy that one's glance slipped, as over the surface of a miniature, over their pink enamel, which was made to appear still more delicate, more private, by the enclosing though half-opened lid of her black hair; or it might happen that the tint of her cheeks had deepened to the mauvish pink of cyclamen, and sometimes even, when she was flushed or feverish, with a suggestion of unhealthiness which lowered my desire to something more sensual and made her glance expressive of something more perverse and unwholesome, to the deep purple of certain roses, a red that was almost black; and each of these Albertines was different, as is each appearance of the dancer whose colours, form, character, are transmuted according to the endlessly varied play of a spotlight.[20]

Where is Albertine in this? In the writing itself, of course, for she exists nowhere else, as no other written character exists elsewhere than in the writing. Each successive face, in this description, is richly endowed with the attributes of material existence, but the total effect—as Genette again notes—'is not a transparent depth, but an overloading, a textual plethora in which the face becomes bogged down, engulfed, and finally disappears'.[21]

But Albertine exists too in a kind of geometry which Proust characteristically expresses through the notion of multiple perspectival planes, and, more concretely, of the array of buildings in a townscape. Thus, the moral qualities that a person

[20] *Certains jours, mince, le teint gris, l'air maussade, une transparence violette descendant obliquement au fond de ses yeux comme il arrive quelquefois pour la mer, elle semblait éprouver une tristesse d'exilée. D'autres jours, sa figure plus lisse engluait les désirs à sa surface vernie et les empêchait d'aller au-delà; à moins que je ne la visse tout à coup de côté, car ses joues mates comme une blanche cire à la surface étaient roses par transparence, ce qui donnait tellement envie de les embrasser, d'atteindre ce teint différent qui se dérobait. D'autres fois le bonheur baignait ses joues d'une clarté si mobile que la peau, devenue fluide et vague, laissait passer comme des regards sous-jacents qui la faisaient paraître d'une autre couleur, mais non d'une autre matière que les yeux; quelquefois, sans y penser, quand on regardait sa figure ponctuée de petits points bruns et où flottaient seulement deux taches plus bleues, c'était comme on eût fait d'un oeuf de chardonneret, souvent comme d'une agate opaline travaillée et polie à deux places seulement, où, au milieu de la pierre brune, luisaient comme les ailes transparentes d'un papillon d'azur, les yeux où la chair devient miroir et nous donne l'illusion de nous laisser plus qu'en les autres parties du corps, approcher de l'âme. Mais le plus souvent aussi elle était plus colorée, et alors plus animée; quelquefois seul était rose, dans sa figure blanche, le bout de son nez, fin comme celui d'une petite chatte sournoise avec qui l'on aurait eu envie de jouer; quelquefois ses joues étaient si lisses que le regard glissait comme sur celui d'une miniature sur leur émail rose qui faisait encore paraître plus délicat, plus intérieur, le couvercle entrouvert et superposé de ses cheveux noirs; il arrivait que le teint de ses joues atteignît le rose violacé du cyclamen, et parfois même, quand elle était congestionnée ou fiévreuse, et donnant alors l'idée d'une complexion maladive qui rabaissait mon désir à quelque chose de plus sensuel et faisait exprimer à son regard quelque chose de plus pervers et de plus malsain, la sombre poupre de certaines roses d'un rouge presque noir; et chacune de ces Albertine était différente, comme est différente chacune des apparitions de la danseuse dont son transmutées les couleurs, la forme, le caractère, selon les jeux innombrablement variés d'un projecteur lumineux.* Proust, *Within a Budding Grove*, II, pp. 718–9; *À l'ombre des jeunes filles en fleur*, II, pp. 298–9.

[21] Genette, 'Proust Palimpsest', p. 215.

presents to us on the surface of the face are said to 'rearrange themselves in a totally different order if we approach them from a new angle—just as, in a town, buildings that appear strung in extended order along a single line, from another viewpoint are disposed in depth and their relative heights altered'.[22] This is a matter of optics, indeed of 'optical errors'[23] which need to be continually corrected without any hope of a final correct view, since all that is available to us is the multiplicity of perspectival orderings. Juxtaposition, Georges Poulet writes—the simultaneity of successive moments, rather than the superimposition of more recent upon older temporal layers—is the heart of Proust's method, a spatialization of time which is the direct opposite of Bergsonian *durée*.[24] On this account, 'the human face is indeed, like the face of the God of some oriental theogony, a whole cluster of faces juxtaposed on different planes so that one does not see them all at once'.[25]

The most radical, perhaps the most famous, and certainly the most comic of these exercises in perspectival play is the episode of the kiss of Albertine's cheek, when the narrator seeks to establish his knowledge of her face on a 'new plane' ('*ce plan nouveau*'):

> At first, as my mouth began gradually to approach the cheeks which my eyes had recommended it to kiss, my eyes, in changing position, saw a different pair of cheeks; the neck, observed at closer range and as though through a magnifying-glass, showed in its coarser grain a robustness which modified the character of the face... I can think of nothing that can to so great a degree as a kiss evoke out of what we believed to be a thing with one definite aspect the hundred other things which it may equally well be, since each is related to a no less legitimate perspective. In short, just as at Balbec Albertine had often appeared different to me, so now—as if, prodigiously accelerating the speed of the changes of perspective and changes of colouring which a person presents to us in the course of our various encounters, I had sought to contain them all in the space of a few seconds so as to reproduce experimentally the phenomenon which diversifies the individuality of a fellow-creature, and to draw out one from another, like a nest of boxes, all the possibilities that it contains—so now, during this brief journey of my lips towards her cheek, it was ten Albertines that I saw; this one girl being like a many-headed goddess, the head I had seen last, when I tried to approach it, gave way to another...[26]

[22] *se rangent selon une formation tout autre si nous l'abordons par un côté différent—comme dans une ville les monuments répandus en ordre dispersé sur une seule ligne, d'un autre point de vue s'échelonnent en profondeur et échangent leur grandeurs relatives.* Proust, *Within a Budding Grove*, II, p. 619; *À l'ombre des jeunes filles en fleur*, II, p. 228.

[23] *les erreurs optiques.* Proust, *Within a Budding Grove*, II, p. 619; *À l'ombre des jeunes filles en fleur*, II, p. 229.

[24] Georges Poulet, *Proustian Space*, trans. Elliott Coleman (Baltimore: Johns Hopkins University Press, 1977), pp. 105–6.

[25] *Le visage humain est vraiment comme celui du Dieu d'une théogonie orientale, toute une grappe de visages juxtaposés dans des plans différents et qu'on ne voit pas à la fois.* Proust, *Within a Budding Grove*, II, pp. 677–8; *À l'ombre des jeunes filles en fleurs*, II, pp. 269–70.

[26] *D'abord au fur et à mesure que ma bouche commença à s'approcher des joues que mes regards lui avaient proposé d'embrasser, ceux-ci se déplaçant virent des joues nouvelles; le cou, aperçu de plus près et comme à la loupe, montra, dans ses gros grains, une robustesse qui modifia le caractère de la figure... je ne vois que cela qui puisse, autant que le baiser, faire surgir de ce que nous croyions une chose à aspect défini, les cent autres choses qu'elle est tout aussi bien, puisque chacune est relative à une perspective non moins légitime. Bref, de même qu'à Balbec, Albertine m'avait souvent paru différente, maintenant, comme si, en*

In contrast to the painterly impressionism of the previous passage describing the changing materiality of Albertine's face, here we have something closer to a cubist figuration of the simultaneity of distinct planes of vision. It is grounded in the fact that the human face offers itself to view from multiple angles; the tension between a frontal and a profile view has not merely a visual force but that of a moral incommensurability:

> When she was lying completely on her side, there was a certain aspect of her face (so sweet and so beautiful from in front) which I could not endure, hook-nosed as in one of Leonardo's caricatures, seeming to betray the malice, the greed for gain, the deceitfulness of a spy whose presence in my house would have filled me with horror and whom that profile seemed to unmask.[27]

That 'phenomenon which diversifies the individuality of a fellow-creature' of which the narrator speaks is the virtual multidimensionality that, over time, generates its discrepant realizations whilst appearing at any one moment as a single thing. The work of the artist is no more than this 'experimental' unlocking of a multiplicity where we had thought to find a unity.

It is, finally, in the face of Albertine in sleep that we find a different order of decomposition of the face, returned now to a kind of pre-human existence:

> By shutting her eyes, by losing consciousness, Albertine had stripped off, one after another, the different human personalities with which she had deceived me ever since the day when I had first made her acquaintance. She was animated now only by the unconscious life of plants, of trees, a life more different from my own, more alien, and yet one that belonged more to me. Her personality was not constantly escaping me, as when we talked, by the outlets of her unacknowledged thoughts and of her eyes... [T]hose lowered lids gave her face that perfect continuity which is unbroken by the eyes. There are people whose faces assume an unaccustomed beauty and majesty the moment they cease to look out of their eyes.[28]

accélérant prodigieusement la rapidité des changements de perspective et des changements de coloration que nous offre une personne dans nos diverses rencontres avec elle, j'avais voulu les faire tenir toutes en quelques secondes pour recréer expérimentalement le phénomène qui diversifie l'individualité d'un être et tirer les unes des autres, comme d'un étui, toutes les possibilités qu'il enferme, dans ce court trajet de mes lèvres vers sa joue, c'est dix Albertines que je vis; cette seule jeune fille étant comme une déesse à plusieurs têtes, celle que j'avais vue en dernier, si je tentais de m'approcher d'elle, faisait place à une autre... Marcel Proust, *The Guermantes Way*, II, in *In Search of Lost Time*, vol. III, pp. 498–9; *Le Côté de Guermantes*, II, in *À la recherche du temps perdu*, vol II, pp. 660–1.

[27] *Il n'y avait que, quand elle était tout à fait sur le côté, un certain aspect de sa figure (si bonne et si belle de face) que je ne pouvais souffrir, crochu comme en certaines caricatures de Léonard, semblant révéler la méchanceté, l'âpreté au gain, la fourberie d'une espionne, dont la présence chez moi m'eût fait horreur et qui semblait démasquée par ces profils-là.* Marcel Proust, *The Captive*, in *In Search of Lost Time*, vol. V, p. 97; *La Prisonnière*, in *À la recherche du temps perdu*, vol. III, p. 587.

[28] *En fermant les yeux, en perdant la conscience, Albertine avait dépouillé, l'un après l'autre, ses différents caractères d'humanité qui m'avaient déçu depuis le jour où j'avais fait sa connaissance. Elle n'était plus animée que de la vie inconsciente des végétaux, des arbres, vie plus différente de la mienne, plus étrange et qui cependant m'appartenait d'avantage. Son moi ne s'échappait pas à tous moments, comme quand nous causions, par les issues de la pensée inavouée et du regard... ces paupières abaissées mettaient dans son visage cette continuité parfaite que les yeux n'interrompent pas. Il y a des êtres dont la face prend une beauté et une majesté inaccoutumées pour peu qu'ils n'aient plus de regard.* Proust, *The Captive*, pp. 84, 86; *La Prisonnière*, pp. 578–9.

There is, of course, a kind of fetishistic possessiveness in the narrator's admiration, as there is in his entire relationship with Albertine. And if Albertine here seems to shed the layered perspectival planes through which he has known her, it is not to return to some primordial simplicity, however much the narrator might wish to grasp a core of her being which cannot escape him and from which she cannot return his gaze. Rather, 'I, who was acquainted with many Albertines in one person, seemed now to see many more again reposing by my side. Her eyebrows, arched as I had never noticed them, encircled the globes of her eyelids like a halcyon's downy nest. Races, atavisms, vices reposed upon her face.'[29]

III

The human face is a piece of skin with holes in it, what Deleuze and Guattari call the 'white wall/black hole system'.[30] These holes form a collection of disparate sensory organs arrayed across the upper head and the muzzle: the eyes an extended stalk running from the optic nerve and the visual cortex; the lips a turning outwards of the mucous membrane; the nose and mouth an opening to lungs and gut; the ears small flaps of flesh channelling sound deep into the temporal lobe. As a whole, this skin can be peeled back from the skull to reveal muscle, flesh, nerves, and bone, and it is nourished by blood vessels and sweat glands. As a whole, too, however, it forms a gestalt, the expressive configuration that reveals 'an unmistakable personality' (Simmel). That configuration is no more an illusion than is the character effect; it is a central component of the person effect, the 'front' by which we recognize others and relate to them.

In evolutionary terms, the face is at once a sensory receptor and a screen for the display of attitudes and intentions vis-à-vis the other. That display may be understood as the expression of an underlying emotion, or even as constituting the emotion; or it may be understood as a signalling process. Here the foundational text is Charles Darwin's *The Expression of the Emotions in Man and Animals* (1872), which argues for the universality of facial expressions of emotion across the human species and, to some extent, between animal species. The argument is, of course, directed against notions of the independent creation of humans and animals: such facial expressions as 'the bristling of the hair under the influence of extreme terror, or the uncovering of the teeth under that of furious rage', or the use of the same facial muscles in laughter as are used by monkeys, are indicative of 'descent from a common progenitor'.[31] Given the fleeting and subtle nature of facial expressions,

[29] *Moi qui connaissais plusieurs Albertine en une seule, il me semblait en voir bien d'autres encore reposer auprès de moi. Ses sourcils arqués comme je ne les avais jamais vus entouraient les globes de ses paupières comme un doux nid d'alcyon. Des races, des atavismes, des vices reposaient sur son visage.* Proust, *The Captive*, p. 87; *La Prisonnière*, p. 580.

[30] Deleuze and Guattari, 'Year Zero: Faciality', p. 167.

[31] Charles Darwin, 'Introduction to the First Edition', in *The Expression of the Emotions in Man and Animals*, with an Introduction, Afterword and Commentaries by Paul Ekman (1872; 3rd edn, London: HarperCollins, 1998), p. 19. Hereafter cited in the text.

however, as well as the sympathetic and imaginative involvement of the observer, Darwin sets out a series of methodological safeguards: he has studied infants, who 'exhibit many emotions, as Sir C. Bell remarks, "with extraordinary force"; whereas in after life, some of our expressions "cease to have the pure and simple source from which they sprang"' (p. 20); he studies the insane, 'as they are liable to the strongest passions and give uncontrollable vent to them' (p. 20); he has shown photographs of the faces of a galvanized patient to 'above twenty educated persons of various ages and both sexes, asking them, in each case, by what emotion or feeling the old man was supposed to be agitated', finding that some of the expressions were recognized by almost all his informants and thus 'may, I think, be relied on as truthful' (p. 21); he has *not* relied on paintings or sculptures, since their object is beauty, and 'strongly contracted facial muscles destroy beauty' (p. 22); he has circulated a printed questionnaire to a number of British colonists, including missionaries and 'protectors of the aborigines' (p. 24), 'to ascertain whether the same expressions prevail...with all the races of mankind, especially those who have associated but little with Europeans'—concluding that

> whenever the same movements of the features or body express the same emotions in several distinct races of man, we may infer, with much probability, that such expressions are true ones—that is, are innate or instinctive. Conventional expressions or gestures, acquired by the individual during early life, would probably have differed in the different races, in the same manner as do their languages. (p. 22)

Finally, he has observed 'the expression of the several passions in some of the commoner animals' (p. 24).

Darwin writes against a tradition of physiognomic analysis which attributes character traits to the structure of the face rather than to its habitual movements. His book is one of the earliest to use photographic evidence, and it is innovative both in its evolutionary perspective and in the range of forms of evidence it employs. Its methodological flaws are readily apparent, however. Darwin employs a Lamarckian model of the inheritance of acquired characteristics to explain the evolutionary transmission of patterns of expression. The photographs he uses to elicit descriptions of emotion are given no context, and the expressions they depict are strongly exaggerated. His questionnaire asks leading questions ('Is astonishment expressed by the eyes and mouth being opened wide, and by the eyebrows being raised?') (p. 22). He attributes emotions to animals in an unproblematized manner, and the concept of 'states of mind' is vague enough to fit any model of emotion. His assumption that infants, the insane, and non-European peoples most directly express truthful emotional states, and that conventional expressions mask them, sets up too simple a dichotomy between the natural and the cultural. And, perhaps most importantly, he fails to pose the question of the evolutionary advantage of the involuntary expression of inner states.

The central issue here is whether facial 'expression' is, in fact, expressive of an inner state, or whether we should think of some more complex relation between mental states, social interactions, and facial display (which can, of course, only heuristically be abstracted from bodily display and language). The dominant paradigm of psychological analysis in the Darwinian tradition, represented by the affect-program (or facial expression program) theorists Silvan Tomkins, Paul Ekman, and Carroll Izard, is ambivalent about this: Izard writes that 'Emotion at one level of analysis *is* neuromuscular activity of the face',[32] or else that it is the consequence of proprioceptive feedback from that activity. Similarly, Tomkins describes the affects as

> sets of muscle, vascular, and glandular responses located in the face and also widely distributed through the body, which generate sensory feedback which is inherently either 'acceptable' or 'unacceptable'. These organized sets of responses are triggered at subcortical centers where specific 'programs' for each distinct affect are stored. These programs are innately endowed and have been genetically inherited.[33]

In some sense, however, the relation between affect and face is causal: affect programs are the force which drives and controls the neuromuscular activity of the face and can be read from it. Conventional, culturally learned display rules may mask the underlying affects,[34] but the assumption of these theorists is, as Ruth Leys puts it, 'that there is a "state" inside the individual that, in the natural course of things, will show itself on the outside, especially the face, and that when it does it is a true exhibition of the emotion'.[35] Indeed, the explicit goal of the facial expression program is to develop a facial hermeneutics capable of mapping the correspondence between facial displays and a limited, pancultural, and discrete set of basic emotions,[36] understood as 'natural kinds and semantic primitives',[37] and tautologically defined (with some qualifications) by their distinctive facial display.[38] Tomkins thus distinguishes nine 'innate affects' and their facial correlates in this way:

> The positive affects are as follows: first, *interest* or *excitement*, with eyebrows down and stare fixed or tracking an object; second, *enjoyment* or *joy*, the smiling response; third, *surprise* or *startle*, with eyebrows raised and eyes blinking. The negative affects are the following: first, *distress* or *anguish*, the crying response; second, *fear* or *terror*, with eyes frozen open in fixed stare or moving away from the dreaded object to the side, with skin pale, cold, sweating, and trembling, and with hair erect; third, *shame*

[32] Carroll Izard, *The Face of Emotion* (New York: Appleton-Century-Crofts, 1971), p. 188; cited in James A. Russell and José Miguel Fernández-Dols, 'What Does a Facial Expression Mean?', in James A. Russell and José Miguel Fernández-Dols (eds), *The Psychology of Facial Expression* (Cambridge: Cambridge University Press, 1997), p. 4.

[33] Silvan Tomkins, 'Affect as the Primary Motivational System', in M. B. Arnold (ed.), *Feelings and Emotions: The Loyola Symposium* (New York: Academic Press, 1970), pp. 105–6; cited in Ruth Leys, *From Guilt to Shame: Auschwitz and After* (Princeton: Princeton University Press, 2007), p. 136. Note that Ekman and Izard tend to use the term 'emotion' to translate Tomkins's more rigorous concept of 'affect'.

[34] Paul Ekman, Wallace V. Friesen, and Phoebe Ellsworth, *Emotion in the Human Face: Guidelines for Research and an Integration of Findings* (New York: Pergamon Press, 1972), p. 23.

[35] Leys, *From Guilt to Shame*, p. 142.

[36] Ekman, Friesen, and Ellsworth, *Emotion in the Human Face*, p. 166.

[37] Russell and Fernández-Dols, 'What Does a Facial Expression Mean?', p. 13.

[38] Paul Ekman, 'Facial Expression and Emotion', *American Psychologist* (April 1993), pp. 386–7, 388–90; Ekman here admits the theoretical possibility of 'nonsignal emotions', although he finds no definitive evidence for them.

> or *humiliation*, with eyes and head lowered; fourth, *contempt*, with the upper lip raised in a sneer; fifth, *disgust*, with the lower lip lowered and protruded; sixth, *anger*, or *rage*, with a frown, clenched jaw, and red face.[39]

These discrete and innately patterned responses are driven by innate activators which he understands as degrees of density of neural firing and which occur pre-cognitively.[40]

In a canonical experiment testing the cross-cultural commonality of expressions, Ekman and Friesen filmed one set of subjects in California and another set in Tokyo, showing each person while seated alone a short film with a 'positive' content (scenery) and another with 'negative' content (sinus surgery). When facial movements were assessed they were found to be closely correlated across the two groups at identical moments in the films.[41] In the second part of the experiment, a scientist was introduced into the room with the subject while additional stressful film was shown, on the hypothesis that the presence of an authority figure in Japan might lead the subject to mask their negative affect with a smile, whilst in the United States it might tend to its amplification rather than concealment; in the event, 'measurement of the facial movements showed no overlap in the facial behavior of the Japanese and Americans'; and Ekman concludes that 'in private, when no display rules to mask expression were operative, we saw the biologically based, evolved, universal facial expressions of emotion. In a social situation, we had shown how different rules about the management of expression led to culturally different facial expressions'.[42] Nature and culture are related as truth to falsity.[43]

One objection to the methods employed by these theorists has to do with their use, in experimental situations, of decontextualized images, frozen at a moment in time into an allegorical mask.[44] This objection goes to the heart of how facial displays are conceived: if they are seen as socially structured displays of motive and intent rather than as (true or masked) expressions of an inner state, then their context is integral to how they function, and their relation to an emotional state may be relatively adventitious.[45] Alan Fridlund thus argues that facial displays must be understood to

[39] Silvan Tomkins, 'Affect Theory', in Klaus R. Scherer and Paul Ekman (eds), *Approaches to Emotion* (Hillsdale, NJ: Lawrence Erlbaum, 1984), pp. 167–8.

[40] Tomkins, 'Affect Theory', pp. 168–9.

[41] Paul Ekman, 'Universals and Cultural Differences in Facial Expressions of Emotion', in J. Cole (ed.), *Nebraska Symposium on Motivation 1971* (Lincoln: University of Nebraska Press, 1972), pp. 207–25.

[42] Paul Ekman, 'Expression and the Nature of Emotion', in *Approaches to Emotion*, p. 321.

[43] And indeed Ekman has developed techniques and training programmes to unmask lying and for use in counterterrorism programmes: Paul Ekman, *Telling Lies: Clues to Deceit in the Marketplace, Politics, and Marriage* (New York: W.W. Norton, 2009).

[44] Cf. José Miguel Fernández-Dols and James M. Carroll, 'Is the Meaning Perceived in Facial Expression Independent of its Context?', in Russell and Fernández-Dols (eds), *The Psychology of Facial Expression*, pp. 275–94; Alan Fridlund has criticized the cross-cultural studies of Ekman and others for their use of 'pre-selected posed facial expressions, forced-choice response format, within-subject design, and lack of contextual information' (Alan J. Fridlund, *Human Facial Expression: An Evolutionary View* (San Diego: Academic Press, 1994), p. 251).

[45] Daniel Gross argues that we should, in fact, read Darwin as foregrounding 'the inherent rhetoricity of emotion', and charges Ekman with obfuscating this rhetorical dimension of Darwin's work in favour of an 'expressivist model of evolutionary biophysiology'. Daniel M. Gross, 'Defending

have provided an evolutionary advantage in signalling to others; that 'vigilance for and comprehension of signals' must have 'co-evolved with the signals themselves'; and that this 'could occur only if displays provided reliable, graded, mutually beneficial signals of contingent future action'.[46] Rather than there being a limited number of expressions of fundamental emotions, displays are calibrated to a situation and to the identities and relationship of the interactants, and will vary accordingly. The facial displays we make when we are alone are not evidence of an inner truth which we mask in public, because solitude is not the absence of social interaction: when we are alone we often treat ourselves as interlocutors, or we project imaginary others or act as though others were present, or we imagine ourselves into future scenarios, or we treat animals or inanimate objects as though they were persons. In short, 'the physical presence of others is one of the *least* important ways of assessing the sociality of facial displays'.[47] On this reading, deceptive signalling is not the culturally learned concealment of an authentic emotion but is omnipresent in the natural world as a way of negotiating dangerous or ambivalent situations by means of mimicry or bluffing: 'nonhuman displays seem as thoroughly embedded in social relations as the faces we make ourselves'.[48] And we might add that facial displays need not, in any sense, be a matter of intent: our constant and acute awareness of the gaze of others—of the flash of white around the iris that tells us where another person is directing their gaze—is an alertness to a signal that is neither willed nor conscious but is built into the very fabric of interaction in the human group.

IV

The contrast I have been exploring between the expressive and display functions of the face can be recast at a quite different level of abstraction as a contrast between an ethical conception of the face and the sociological concept of facework. 'The face,' write Ekman and Friesen, 'is *commanding* because of its very visibility and omnipresence.'[49] Emmanuel Levinas describes the face of the Other (*Autrui*) as being positioned, not in front of me ('*en face de moi*') but above me: it is 'verticality and uprightness; it spells a relation of rectitude'.[50] It *commands* me not to allow the other to die alone, 'as if to do so were to become an accomplice in his death. Thus the face says to me: you shall not kill.'[51] Or rather, as Judith Butler notes, the face

the Humanities with Charles Darwin's *The Expressions of the Emotions in Man and Animals* (1872)', *Critical Inquiry* 37: 1 (2010), pp. 35, 44.

[46] Alan J. Fridlund, 'The New Ethology of Human Facial Expressions', in Russell and Fernández-Dols (eds), *The Psychology of Facial Expression*, pp. 104–5; this essay usefully condenses material from Fridlund's *Human Facial Expression*.

[47] Fridlund, 'The New Ethology of Human Facial Expressions', p. 119.

[48] Fridlund, 'The New Ethology of Human Facial Expressions', p. 114.

[49] Ekman, Friesen, and Ellsworth, *Emotion in the Human Face*, p. 1.

[50] Emmanuel Levinas and Richard Kearney, 'Dialogue with Emmanuel Levinas', in Richard Cohen (ed.), *Face to Face with Levinas* (Albany: SUNY Press, 1986), pp. 23–24.

[51] Levinas and Kearney, 'Dialogue with Emmanuel Levinas', p. 24.

is at once an incitement to murder and the call not to.[52] Like the man in Kafka's parable of the Law who comes to a gate which he can never enter and which only he could ever have entered, it is only the Other whom I can wish to kill and whom I must not kill, since 'I can wish to kill only an existent absolutely independent, which exceeds my powers infinitely, and therefore does not oppose them but paralyzes the very power of power.'[53] The face is an epiphany which 'brings forth the possibility of gauging the infinity of the temptation to murder, not only as a temptation to total destruction, but also as the purely ethical impossibility of this temptation and attempt'.[54]

Why is it the face that offers this epiphany, and at what level of abstraction is the concept of face pitched? Derrida insists that the face in Levinas should not be read either allegorically or as prosopopeia: the other is given 'in person' only in the face, at once substance and presence; 'the face does not signify, does not present itself as a sign, but *expresses itself*, offering itself *in person*, in itself, *kath'auto*'.[55] Its ethical force is triggered by the sight of 'nose, eyes, a forehead, a chin', but 'what is specifically the face cannot be reduced to that',[56] and particularly not to vision. It is clear, too, that face can take the form of something other than the human face; Levinas gives an example, taken from Vasily Grossman's novel *Life and Fate*, of the relatives of political prisoners standing in a queue and able to see only each other's backs, each of which is deeply expressive of their suffering: here the back *is* the face, the 'extreme precariousness of the other'.[57] The face is thus something like the expressive essence of the human, and yet it is at once more and less than human, defined both by its radical particularity and by its absolute nakedness and destitution; it 'shivers in its nudity. It is a distress', and thus a supplication which 'imposes itself upon me without my being able to be deaf to its call or to forget it, that is, without my being able to suspend my responsibility for its distress'.[58] This ethical absolute, this solicitation, is manifested in the form of an epiphany or a 'visitation' or a 'disclosure', but 'the visitation of the face is not the disclosure of the world': it '*enters* into our world from an absolutely foreign sphere, that is, precisely from an ab-solute, which in fact is the very name for absolute strangeness. The signifyingness of a face in its abstractness is in the literal sense of the term extra-ordinary, outside of every order, every world'.[59]

[52] Judith Butler, *Precarious Life: The Powers of Mourning and Violence* (London: Verso, 2004), p. 134.

[53] Emmanuel Levinas, *Totality and Infinity: An Essay on Exteriority*, trans. Alphonso Lingis (The Hague: Martinus Nijhoff, 1979), p. 198.

[54] Levinas, *Totality and Infinity*, p. 199.

[55] Jacques Derrida, 'Violence and Metaphysics: An Essay on the Thought of Emmanuel Levinas', in *Writing and Difference*, trans. Alan Bass (London: Routledge & Kegan Paul, 1978), p. 101.

[56] Emmanuel Levinas, 'The Face', in *Ethics and Infinity: Conversations with Philippe Nemo*, trans. Richard A. Cohen (Pittsburgh: Duquesne University Press, 1985), pp. 85–6.

[57] Emmanuel Levinas, *Alterity and Transcendence*, trans. Michael B. Smith (London: The Athlone Press, 1999), p. 140.

[58] Emmanuel Levinas, 'Meaning and Sense', in *Basic Philosophical Writings*, ed. Adriaan T. Peperzak, Simon Critchley, and Robert Bernasconi (Bloomington: Indiana University Press, 1996), p. 54.

[59] Levinas, 'Meaning and Sense', p. 53.

That absolute alterity makes itself known to me, above all, in the fact that the face speaks, and is solicited in speaking. Speaking cannot be reduced to the mouth, and is not specifically human, since the word that emanates from the face is the word of the Other which 'proceeds from the absolutely Absent',[60] one name for which is God. Although the Other can be spoken of, is presented as a 'theme', a content, it nevertheless evades this objectification insofar as it is itself an interlocutor which 'upsurges inevitably behind the said'.[61] Echoing Mikhail Bakhtin's ethics of dialogue, Levinas argues that the 'welcome of the face' is generated 'in the opposition of conversation and sociality',[62] where 'opposition' means the form of the face-to-face. The speaking face—the face acting in speech rather than seized upon by vision—makes possible an authentic relation to the Other; 'it is discourse and, more exactly, response or responsibility which is this authentic relationship'.[63] Yet this ethical relation subtending speech is not an emanation of the I, but rather calls it into question, since I am the other of my other; it is the face-to-face discourse of this mutually asymmetrical dyad which constrains my capacity to kill.

The face precedes any ontic determination of Being; it is that which cannot be contained, comprehended, encompassed, expressed in number or concept; 'it is neither seen nor touched—for in visual or tactile sensation the identity of the I envelops the alterity of the object, which becomes precisely a content'.[64] It is incommensurate with any exercise of power, 'be it enjoyment or knowledge'.[65] It has no propositional value since it is an ethical absolute and the plane of the ethical precedes ontology. And although a face can be used to deceive,

> deceit and veracity already presuppose the absolute authenticity of the face—the privileged case of a presentation of being foreign to the alternative of truth and non-truth... To seek truth I have already established a relationship with a face which can guarantee itself, whose epiphany itself is somehow a word of honor.[66]

The nakedness of the face puts it beyond (outside and prior to) representation; it is *pure* signification, that which makes any sign system possible;[67] 'the face with which the Other turns to me is not reabsorbed in a representation of the face'.[68] It 'is not a character within a context', not a set of attributes, but 'meaning all by itself'.[69] Absolute, prior to culture, history, and ontology, the face is an epiphany

[60] Levinas, 'Meaning and Sense', p. 60.
[61] Levinas, *Totality and Infinity*, p. 195.
[62] Levinas, *Totality and Infinity*, p. 197.
[63] Levinas, 'The Face', p. 88.
[64] Levinas, *Totality and Infinity*, p. 194.
[65] Levinas, *Totality and Infinity*, p. 198.
[66] Levinas, *Totality and Infinity*, p. 202.
[67] This, I think, is the basis for Deleuze and Guattari's critique of the face, or rather the abstract machine of faciality, as the site of the two semiotic systems of *signifiance* and subjectification; their critique seems to me to be weakened by their valorization of the mask 'in primitive societies' as a becoming-animal which 'assures the head's belonging to the body'. Deleuze and Guattari, 'Year Zero: Faciality', p. 181.
[68] Levinas, *Totality and Infinity*, p. 215.
[69] Levinas, 'The Face', p. 86.

which entails neither a concealment nor a revelation, for if it did then 'the face would be one with a mask'.[70]

If it is face-to-face discourse that constrains my capacity to kill, however, then we might ask what becomes of mediated communities and mediated discourse. Is it writing—which obviates the face-to-face—that initiates murder? What of represented faces—in the icon, the portrait, in photography, in film, on Facebook? Are these no more than poses, dissimulations? What of the mirrored face? What of the face that is *posed* even in face-to-face immediacy? Levinas writes that 'there is an essential poverty in the face; the proof of this is that one tries to mask this poverty by putting on poses, by taking on a countenance':[71] as it is for Ekman, the inner truth of the face is *disguised* by the pose, the false face. But which face does not pose itself, present itself, render itself expressive, simulate itself in its presentation? And what, finally, of communication which does *not* take place 'without violence, in peace with this absolute alterity'?[72] Can one be at peace with alterity, rather than being disturbed by it? For what is missing in Levinas's account is a lack of any sense of the *strangeness* of the face of the other, that absence or that multiplicity and ambiguity of meaning that we find in the face of Albertine; and a lack, too, of a sense of the otherness of *my* face in the mirror: any sense of bewilderment at my face appearing to me as other, as my other self.

Agamben notes that the Greek *prosōpon*, face, 'etymologically signifies "what stands before the eyes, what gives itself to be seen"'.[73] The English word 'face', from the Latin *facies*, a surface or aspect, has the same sense: the face is the front that we present to the world, and it governs our sense of frontality, our positioning vis-à-vis those others who, in turn, face us, front-on.

The Chinese concept of *mien* similarly designates the physical face as well as the surface of an object, a direction, a view, but from the fourth century BC develops the figurative sense of social 'front', social prestige; about a thousand years later the literal meaning begins to be gradually displaced by the term *lien*, which also takes over some of the figurative senses, while '*mien*, with the meaningless syllable *-tzu* attached, had developed different connotations'.[74] Hsien Chin Hu distinguishes the current usage of the terms (although this varies regionally) as follows: '*mien-tzu*...stands for the kind of prestige that is emphasized in this country [the United States]: a reputation achieved through getting on in life, through success and ostentation', whereas *lien* 'is the respect of the group for a man with a good moral reputation...*Lien* is both a social sanction for enforcing moral standards and an internalized sanction.' While *lien* is 'maintained or lost as a whole', *mien-tzu* 'can be borrowed, struggled for, added to, padded—all terms indicating a gradual increase in volume'.[75]

[70] Levinas, 'Meaning and Sense', p. 60.
[71] Levinas, 'The Face', p. 86.
[72] Levinas, *Totality and Infinity*, p. 197.
[73] Giorgio Agamben, *Remnants of Auschwitz: The Witness and the Archive*, trans. Daniel Heller-Roazen (New York: Zone Books, 2002), p. 53.
[74] Hsien Chin Hu, 'The Chinese Concepts of "Face"', *American Anthropologist*, n.s., 46: 1 (1944), pp. 45–6.
[75] Hu, 'The Chinese Concepts of "Face"', p. 61.

Face in either of these figurative senses

> is not a face that can be washed or shaved, but a face that can be 'granted' and 'lost' and 'fought for' and 'presented as a gift'...Abstract and intangible, it is yet the most delicate standard by which Chinese social intercourse is regulated...Face cannot be translated or defined. It is like honor and is not honor. It cannot be purchased with money, and gives a man or a woman a material pride. It is hollow and yet is what men fight for and what many women die for. It is invisible and yet by definition exists by being shown to the public...It is amenable, not to reason but to social convention.[76]

Face is what is at stake in 'the only human relationships that really count, those between persons of unequal status—and *everyone* is unequal'.[77] What is crucial in social interactions is finding an appropriate balance between insisting on one's own *mien-tzu* and respecting and protecting that of others, within a complex and emotionally charged network of relations between kin, between members of different age groups, between business partners, and between friends, where loss of face or shaming can irreparably damage both the person and the relationship. Saving face is thus a primary social obligation, as is concern for one's own face: not to want *lien* (*pu-yao lien*) is to be shameless, and thus to breach one of the primary conditions of social order.[78]

Erving Goffman's concept of facework draws heavily on the Chinese concept of face, applies it to Western societies, and teases out some of its implications. The term *face*, he writes, 'may be defined as the positive social value a person effectively claims for himself by the line others assume he has taken during a particular contact', where a *line* is 'a pattern of verbal and nonverbal acts by which he expresses his view of the situation and through this his evaluation of the participants, especially himself'.[79] This is a carefully complicated definition: the claim to face, to 'positive social value', is made in relation to others' evaluations of one's own evaluation of a situation and the actors in it, including those assessing one's evaluation, and especially oneself. The interlocking play of perspectives mimes the fraught nature of social interaction, and Goffman emphasizes its affective force: 'A person tends to experience an immediate emotional response to the face which a contact with others allows him; he cathects his face; his "feelings" become attached to it' (p. 6). Yet these feelings never belong in any simple way to the individual: 'while his social face can be his most personal expression and the center of his security and pleasure, it is only on loan to him from society; it will be withdrawn unless he

[76] Y. T. Lin, *My Country and My People* (New York: The John Day Co., 1939), pp. 199–200; cited in Hui-Chin Chang and G. Richard Holt, 'A Chinese Perspective on Face as Inter-Relational Concern', in Stella Ting-Toomey (ed.), *The Challenge of Facework: Cross-Cultural and Interpersonal Issues* (Albany: SUNY Press, 1994), p. 99.

[77] L. Stover, *The Cultural Ecology of Chinese Civilization* (New York: Pica Press, 1974), pp. 247–8; cited in Ron Scollon and Suzie Wong Scollon, 'Face Parameters in East–West Discourse', in Ting-Toomey (ed.), *The Challenge of Facework*, p. 138.

[78] Hu, 'The Chinese Concepts of "Face"', p. 51.

[79] Erving Goffman, 'On Face-Work: An Analysis of Ritual Elements in Social Interaction', in *Interaction Ritual: Essays in Face-to-Face Behavior* (1967; rpt. New Brunswick, NJ: Aldine Transaction, 2005), p. 5. Hereafter cited in the text.

conducts himself in a way that is worthy of it' (p. 10). The attachment to face, and the ever-present risk that it might be lost, ensures my commitment to maintaining and saving face as well as my involvement in the face of others: 'One's own face and the face of others are constructs of the same order; it is the rules of the group and the definition of the situation which determine how much feeling one is to have for face and how this feeling is to be distributed among the faces involved' (p. 6).

Depending on the circumstances, I may be either *in face* or *out of face*. The former is the more usual situation since most lines I may take are of an institutionalized kind, and taking a particular line allows me to present an internally consistent image that is supported by contextual judgements and evidence, as well as by consistency between my present line and actions I have taken or not taken in the past. When these conditions are in place, 'the person's face clearly is something that is not lodged in or on his body, but rather something that is diffusely located in the flow of events in the encounter' (p. 7), and it entails a further set of implicit attributes or entailments which will usually pass without examination. The taken-for-grantedness of face becomes a matter of notice only when the events become subject to interpretation. If face cannot be sustained (if I have no usable line to resort to), I am embarrassed or shamed: I lose face. But I am constrained not only to save my own face but to be considerate of the face of others, and to be disinclined 'to witness the defacement of others' (p. 10). If I am capable of casually witnessing someone else's humiliation I am said to be heartless; someone who can casually take part in their own defacement is said to be shameless. The convention that each person provisionally accepts each other person's line is the condition of possibility for social interaction.

Facework is, in Goffman's usage, the set of actions a person undertakes 'to make whatever he is doing consistent with face' (p. 12); it is thus a set of meta-actions, and it goes by the names of 'tact' or 'social skill' or '*savoir-faire*'. Its primary function is to deal with threats to face: unintentional gaffes, spite, or unintended offence. It may involve tactics of avoidance, or of a deliberate overlooking which maintains the fiction that no threat to face has occurred; or it may take the form of correction, the 'righting of ritual disequilibrium' ('ritual' because 'one's face... is a sacred thing, and the expressive order required to sustain it is therefore a ritual one') (p. 19). The sequence of face-saving acts which restore equilibrium Goffman calls an interchange, and there are four classic moves: the challenge by which misconduct is signalled; an offering, by which the offender is invited to express contrition or to explain away the offence, or to provide compensation, or to agree to punish himself; the acceptance of the offering; and, finally, a display of gratitude by the person forgiven. There are, of course, a range of possible deviations from this sequence, as when the challenge is refused and face is brought into question on each side. In all of these responses emotions play a role; but 'these emotions function as moves, and fit so precisely into the logic of the ritual game that it would seem difficult to understand them without it' (p. 23). These are the positive uses of facework; but facework may be performed in an aggressive or self-serving way, turning it into a contest, the purpose of which 'is to preserve everyone's line from an inexcusable contradiction, while scoring as many points as possible against one's adversaries and making as many gains as possible for oneself' (p. 24). Typical moves here are snubs, digs, bitchiness, and comebacks.

All societies mobilize their members to be 'self-regulating participants in social encounters' by acquiring the feelings, the moral qualities, and the sense of self that attach to face: they are taught 'to have pride, honor, and dignity, to have considerateness, to have tact and a certain amount of poise' (p. 44). These are some of the elements of character that we refer to as universally human; but, Goffman concludes, 'universal human nature is not a very human thing. By acquiring it, the person becomes a kind of construct, built up not from inner psychic propensities but from moral rules that are imposed upon him from without' (p. 45). While Goffman's account of face is starkly opposed to that of Levinas, it is yet curiously convergent with it in its recognition of the non-humanity of face. The Levinasian face is an ethical absolute prior to all social, historical, cultural determination; it speaks from an immense inner distance, whereas face for Goffman is entirely relational, entirely social, entirely a construct of display. For each of them, however, the surface that mediates the human relation to otherness takes on something like the strangeness of a mask; a self-strangeness that is the condition of my relation to the stranger.

V

At the very beginning of his career, in a passage from the *Cogitationes Privatae* that we know only from a copy made by Leibniz, the young Descartes writes: 'Actors, taught not to let any embarrassment show on their faces, put on a mask [*personam*]. I will do the same. So far, I have been a spectator in this theatre which is the world, but I am now about to mount the stage, and I come forward masked [*larvatus prodeo*].'[80] The internet blogger who goes by the name 'larvatus' comments on the strangeness of Descartes' choice of words here: the mask he dons is not the theatrical mask (*personam*) but the *larva*, a word that means both 'mask' and 'ghost'; the past participle *larvatus* has the sense of 'bewitched' or 'enchanted' (and, according to Norman Brown, of 'possessed by demons') as well as 'masked'.[81] The notion conveyed by this phrase 'is of a ghost issuing from the grave, just as an actor issued masked from the sides or back of the stage'.[82] And the blogger refers to a passage from Apuleius's *De deo Socratis* which explains the nature of the *larvae*.

It is worth pausing to look at the context of this passage, which occurs in an account of the class of *daemones*.[83] Apuleius is seeking to explain two things: first, how there can be intercession in human affairs on the part of the gods, who are

[80] René Descartes, *The Philosophical Writings of Descartes*, vol. I, trans. John Cottingham, Robert Stoothoff, and Dugald Murdoch (Cambridge: Cambridge University Press, 1985), p. 2.

[81] *Larvatus's journal*, available at <http://larvatus.livejournal.com/5889.html> Last accessed 28 June 2013. The reference to Norman O. Brown is to *Love's Body* (1966; rpt. Berkeley: University of California Press, 1990), p. 66.

[82] Brown, *Love's Body*, p. 66.

[83] This is the Latin spelling of the Greek *daimones*; the text uses both forms interchangeably.

remote from humanity; and second, the nature of the personal *daimon* who speaks to Socrates and whom Socrates reveres. The explanation he offers (in part by ventriloquizing Plato) has to do with the existence of 'certain intermediate divine powers' situated between the highest heaven and the earth, in the region of the *aer*: that is, the thicker, moister air nearest the earth and lying beneath the thinner, more fiery *aether*. These *daemones* bear prayers upwards to the gods and convey benefits downwards, and each of them is assigned particular tasks—

> whether constructing dream visions, or marking prophetic entrails, or directing divinatory bird-flight, or teaching oracular bird-cry, or launching thunder-bolts, or inspiring seers, causing clouds to flash, or indeed every other activity through which we try to make out the future.[84]

Just as later theologians will have to solve the dilemma of the mode of materiality of angels, Apuleius proposes that these intermediate entities have a small degree of weight to stop them ascending to the heavens and yet are light enough to prevent their falling to earth; their bodily mass is akin to that of thick clouds. Just as the shades of the dead in Dante are made of aerial bodies, the *daemones* 'are assembled from the purest, liquid, and clear element of the *aer*, and are consequently not easily visible to any man, unless they vouchsafe a sight of themselves on the gods' instructions' (p. 204). And, again because of their intermediate status, they have 'immortality in common with the gods above, and susceptibility in common with man below' (p. 205).

Yet, in another sense, the *daemon* can be thought of as either equivalent to the character of the individual, or as the guardian spirit (Latin *genius*) which watches over each person and bears witness, both here and in the afterlife, to their actions and thoughts; this is the *daimon* that Socrates hears speaking to him, in a voice unlike any human voice.[85] The obverse of these beneficial spirits is the class of *daemones* which formerly lived as men—and this is the passage larvatus quotes:

> I find that this [species] is commonly referred to in the ancient Latin language as a *Lemur*. And of these *Lemures*, the type which has as its assigned province the care of its descendants and holds possession of the house by means of its placated and peaceful power, is called the *Lar familiaris*; while the type which from its bad behaviour in life is punished by having no fixed abode, and by a kind of exile of uncertain wandering, only a mild terror for virtuous humans, but harmful to the evil—that type most people call *Larvae*. When it is truly uncertain which sphere of operation belongs to any individual spirit and whether it is a *Lar* or a *Larva*, they call it by the name of *deus Manis*... (p. 211)

Descartes, the great rationalist whose writings refer so frequently to dreams, hallucinations, simulacra, and the world of imaginary entities, has clothed himself in

[84] Apuleius, 'On the God of Socrates', in *Apuleius: Rhetorical Works*, trans. Stephen Harrison, John Hilton, and Vincent Hunink, ed. Stephen Harrison (Oxford: Oxford University Press, 2001), p. 200. Hereafter cited in the text.

[85] P. 211; cf. Plato, *Phaedrus* 242c2, trans. R. Hackforth, in Edith Hamilton and Huntington Cairns (eds), *The Collected Dialogues of Plato* (Princeton: Princeton University Press, 1961), p. 489.

the mask of the wandering spirits of the dead; the Cartesian ego which is secured by the act of thought is, at its heart, other than itself.

The English word 'mask' probably derives from the post-classical Latin *masca*, an evil spirit or spectre; masks are in general closely associated with the spirit world. I should like to isolate two questions here: first, why does this association exist? And second—the question that has been developing throughout this chapter—what is the relation between the mask and the human face? We can perhaps get a little closer to answering the latter question by way of an intermediate form, the facial tattoo.

In a consideration of split representation in a number of distinct cultures (that is, representations in which an animal or human figure is considered as though bisected lengthwise and then joined in such a way as to present a double, symmetrical profile viewed frontally), Claude Lévi-Strauss notes that amongst the Maori, as amongst the Caduveo Indians of southern Brazil, facial tattoos, which reproduce many of the features of split representation, are not only insignia of rank but also 'messages fraught with spiritual and moral significance'.[86] For these cultures,

> the design *is* the face, or rather it creates it. It is the design which confers upon the face its social existence, its human dignity, its spiritual significance. Split representation of the face, considered as a graphic device, thus expresses a deeper and more fundamental splitting, namely that between the 'dumb' biological individual and the social person whom he must embody.[87]

In an earlier essay on mask cultures Levi-Strauss had spoken of certain dance masks 'which opened suddenly like two shutters to reveal a second face, and sometimes a third one behind the second, each one imbued with mystery and austerity'.[88] Here he returns to

> [t]hose masks with louvers, which present alternately several aspects of the totemic ancestor—sometimes peaceful, sometimes angry, at one time human, at another time animal—[which] strikingly illustrate the relationship between split representation and masquerade. Their function is to offer a series of intermediate forms which insure the transition from symbol to meaning, from magical to normal, from supernatural to social. They hold at the same time the function of masking and unmasking. But when it comes to unmasking, it is the mask which, by a kind of reverse splitting, opens up into two halves, while the actor himself is dissociated in the split representation, which aims... at flattening out as well as displaying the mask at the expense of the individual wearing it.[89]

Thus, split representation on a flat surface is only a special case of its appearance on a three-dimensional surface. And there is one three-dimensional surface

[86] Claude Lévi-Strauss, 'Split Representation in the Art of Asia and America', in *Structural Anthropology*, trans. Claire Jacobson and Brooke Grundfest Schoepf (London: Allen Lane The Penguin Press, 1968), p. 257.

[87] Lévi-Strauss, 'Split Representation in the Art of Asia and America', p. 259.

[88] Claude Lévi-Strauss, *The Way of the Masks*, trans. Sylvia Modelski (Seattle: University of Washington Press, 1982), p. 5, citing his own 1943 essay 'The Art of the North West Coast' in the *Gazette des Beaux-Arts*, vol. 24.

[89] Lévi-Strauss, 'Split Representation in the Art of Asia and America', p. 262.

in particular where decoration and form cannot be separated, either physically or socially: the surface of the human face. The answer to the question Lévi-Strauss had initially raised about the peculiarity and yet the broad cultural distribution of the occurrence of split representation is thereby answered: 'split representation results from the projection of a three-dimensional mask onto a two-dimensional surface'.[90]

Now this seems to me at once illuminating and wrong: illuminating in its understanding that the face is created by the tattoo and the mask, and that unmasking is not the revelation of the naked face since the face is never naked; but wrong in its deployment of a Durkheimian (and Maussian) dualism of nature and culture which, like Goffman's opposition of 'inner psychic propensities' to 'moral rules imposed from without',[91] sets the biological against the social, the actor against the role. The figure of the mask lends itself all too readily to a dichotomy of inner truth and conventional exterior; that of the masks which open only onto other masks, however, goes some way towards a complication of that dualism. We go forth masked: but this is truly our face.

VI

The association of the mask with the sacred and with the spirits of the dead testifies to its power to capture the spectral forms of the departed. We can see this clearly in the Roman *imago*, the wax mask moulded on the face of the dead ancestor, which Mauss identifies as one of the central components of the Roman *persona*.[92]

In Florence Dupont's account, the great Roman families possessed the distinctive right to *imagines*, and thus a right to construct a material genealogy. The painted wax death masks were a direct impression of the deceased person's face, metonymically linked to it and thus not distinct from the face they represent and whose person they preserve; their function is like that of the English word *stamp* or the Greek *kharakter*: at once the instrument and the mark it leaves. After the funeral the *imago* was locked in a chest in the family atrium, where 'it was used to trace vast genealogical trees, in which only the illustrious men of the family appeared'.[93] It was normally never seen: what was visible was the *tituli*, signs hung from the chests indicating the personal fame (*nomen*) and the collective glory (*honos*, the offices held) of the deceased. The *imagines* represented merely personal identity, but they had 'a reality beyond that of appearance and resemblance, a reality that did not function through recognition of a model' (p. 410): rather, they

[90] Lévi-Strauss, 'Split Representation in the Art of Asia and America', p. 263.
[91] Goffman, 'On Face-Work', p. 45.
[92] Marcel Mauss, 'A Category of the Human Mind: The Notion of Person; The Notion of Self', trans. W. D. Halls, in Michael Carrithers, Steven Collins, and Steven Lukes (eds), *The Category of the Person: Anthropology, Philosophy, History* (Cambridge: Cambridge University Press, 1985), pp. 16–17.
[93] Florence Dupont, 'The Emperor-God's Other Body', trans. Brian Massumi, in Michael Feher (ed.), *Fragments for a History of the Human Body, Part Three* (New York: Zone Books, 1989), p. 409. Hereafter cited in the text.

were effectively the dead person. And they represented him at the funerals of his descendants, when they were removed from the chest and worn on the face of an actor dressed in the robes of the highest office attained by the dead person; these masked figures were paraded from the home to the forum for the funeral oration, where they sat in the audience in their seats of office, and then to the city's outskirts for the cremation and burial.

The *imago*, metonymically tied to the person, is at once incorruptible and mortal:

> Since the *imago* is a material form, it is not a soul, much less an immortal one. The *imago* is a religiously pure body because it can remain on the surface of the earth without staining heaven or men, but it is nevertheless a mortal form. If its wax support disappears, if the family that looks after the *imagines* dies out or loses interest, then the ancestral forms will die. Nothing is more vulnerable than an *imago*, which is even more fragile than its wax support. For the *imago* is, strictly speaking, neither the wax mask nor the wax of the mask, but... a form detached from the corpse and transmitted to the wax. (p. 414)

It is this incorruptible and yet mortal form that becomes the immortal body of the deified emperors, the incarnation of their numinous force. The religious problem that had to be resolved was this: the death of a man or woman 'was the presence on the earth's surface of a body that stained and paralysed the community. In order to be able to act again, to sacrifice, to read auspices, the community had to purify itself and complete its mourning' (p. 401), and this was done by creating a *sepulcrum* outside urban boundaries where the *ossa*, literally the bones, whatever remained over from the cremation, were buried. This place of burial was both present in and separate from the world of men; and it was precisely his burial that stood in the way of the consecration of the dead emperor, since his sepulchred body 'tied him to a religious place from which it would be impious to remove him, but where it was impossible to treat him as a god' (p. 402).

The ritual solution to this obstacle to the apotheosis of the emperor was to produce two bodies, the first of which (his human body) was cremated and buried. The second body was the *imago*, a wax mask of the dead man's face, which was then given a funeral in its own right. Thus, in the second funeral of Septimius Severus in 211 AD, a wax *imago* was placed on the funeral bed, painted yellow 'to give it the pallor of sickness' (p. 204), treated by doctors for seven days, each day pronounced worse, and on the last day proclaimed dead. Funeral rites were then conducted for the 'corpse'. It is this second body that, in disappearing without trace in the flames, is transferred to the space of the gods to become the immortal body of the deified ruler.

The legal condition for the creation of this second body was that it must be a *part* of the dead man's body; and Roman law did indeed recognize metonymic presence as 'a real presence of the thing, not a fictional presence' (p. 407). That condition holds equally for the early Christian icon.

Hans Belting cites the cult image of the Virgin of Nicopeia, seized by the Venetians from Byzantium in 1203 and installed as a protective icon of the city.

This image, read as an authentic portrait of Mary, 'led a unique existence, even a life of its own. At state ceremonies, it was received as if it were an actual person. The image, as object, demanded protection, just as it in turn granted protection as an agent of the one whom it depicted'.[94] The authenticity of the iconic image is given in one of two ways: it may be 'unpainted' (that is, it is of heavenly origin, or else it comes about by a direct transfer of substance in the impression of the model's face on a cloth); or it may be painted by St Luke or by the painter brought to Bethlehem by the three wise men and then transferred, in a direct line of transmission, to later, faithful copies. But authenticity is also guaranteed by its ability to appear to people in dreams or to work miracles; it possesses a power of its own, and is used not only as an object of veneration but 'for very tangible purposes, from the repulsion of evil to healing and the defence of the realm' (p. 44). An authenticity of origins, then, and an authenticity of effects: in each case the image is conceived not as a representation but as presence; 'the image *was* the person it represented, at least that person's active, miracle-working presence, as the relics of saints had previously been' (p. 47). More broadly, the holy portrait is evidence of the presence of God in human life, a trace of the sacred within mundane time and carrying the auratic force of that trace.

The early medieval icon is thus neither a conventional representation nor a metaphor; it is literally the presence of the holy person, just as the consecrated host is literally the body of Christ. The image partakes of the person it represents, mirroring the form of its archetype and borrowing from it its supernatural power. In this sense the image is not an aesthetic creation but is 'more or less the property—indeed the product—of its model' (p. 153). This auratic power of the image is under threat from the beginning, however, from the authority of the word and from the iconoclasm, common to all the monotheistic religions, that seeks to distance God from any presence in sensual representation. The banning of cult images in the Reformation introduces a distinction between the public and private functions of representation, and corresponds to a more general crisis of the image. That crisis has to do, in part, with the privatization of the image, and in part with a new professionalization of painting. Belting gives the example of Jan van Eyck's representation of the *vera icon* or 'Veronica'—an 'authentic' image of Christ's face imprinted on cloth. Van Eyck's painting is a portrait modelled on the cloth image, and the guarantee of its authenticity is now the painter's infallible eye, which assures a perfect match between model and likeness.[95] This is a 'holy portrait', in which 'the immobile frontality preserves the aura of the icon, but the close-up simulates the physical appearance of a living person sitting in an interior whose windows are reflected in Jesus' eyes. In the competition between the genres, two separate functions of the picture have been reconciled' (p. 430). Representational

[94] Hans Belting, *Likeness and Presence: A History of the Image before the Era of Art*, trans. Edmund Jephcott (Chicago: University of Chicago Press, 1994), p. 4. Hereafter cited in the text.

[95] There are two versions, from 1438 and 1440; both are signed, but the later painting also refers to Van Eyck as the 'inventor', and adds the motto *als ich chan*, 'as well as I can'. Belting, *Likeness and Presence*, p. 430.

accuracy, on the one hand, and mastery of the laws of optics on the other, govern the transition from a religious to an aesthetic regime, where 'the new presence *of* the work succeeds the former presence of the sacred *in* the work' (p. 459). It is this presence of the informing idea of art that brings the secular portrait into being.

In the aftermath of the iconic tradition, writes Catherine Soussloff, 'Christian religious art no longer bore the full weight of the burden of immanent sacredness... Yet in the case of portraiture, the lingering cultural belief in the immanence of the subject's presence remained',[96] a belief which has much to do with the spiritual significance attributed to the face. The origins of portraiture (including the religious icon) lie in funerary art, and the shift from private memorial icons to cult images of a saint 'took place in the realm of tombs, much as the cult of saints itself grew out of the funeral practices of the previous age'.[97] James Breckenridge describes such images of the dead as 'instruments of magic: magic for the protection of the living, magic for the sustenance of the departed, and often both at once'.[98] It is arguable that that inheritance never disappears from portraiture, including the photographic likeness.

What exactly does a portrait represent? A face, we might think; but many 'official' portraits show a monarch or some other powerful person full-length and in full costume.[99] Breckenridge is scathing about classical Greek artists for their failure to understand that the head and face are 'the essential elements, the only indispensable means, for establishing individual identity', and for 'placing the core of the personality elsewhere than in the head. They seem almost perverse in this refusal to acknowledge that the head, the evident site of all the localized senses, deserved special emphasis when indicating the seat of consciousness.'[100] This is the face as window to the soul, of course; but the Greeks are excused their perversity in the light of the emergence in Greece of the portrait as 'a work of art portraying the single individual for his own sake'.[101] This 'single individual' must be a definite person, not a class or type, and the portrait 'must render the personality, i.e., the inner individuality, of the person represented in his outer form'.[102] In this (deeply normative) sense the portrait would present an image that corresponds to the proper name and the concrete particular it represents—and would thus correspond in

[96] Catherine M. Soussloff, *The Subject in Art: Portraiture and the Birth of the Modern* (Durham, NC: Duke University Press, 2006), p. 11.

[97] Belting, *Likeness and Presence*, p. 88.

[98] James D. Breckenridge, *Likeness: A Conceptual History of Ancient Portraiture* (Evanston, IL: Northwestern University Press, 1968), p. 7.

[99] Berenson calls such a representation of a public role an 'effigy' rather than a portrait; his assumption is that the portrait in some sense represents a 'private' self. Bernard Berenson, 'The Effigy and the Portrait', in *Aesthetics and History* (London: Constable, 1950), pp. 188–9.

[100] Breckenridge, *Likeness*, p. 10. Marcia Pointon notes that Western art before the sixteenth century, and many other non-Western cultures, do not prioritize the head in this way. Pointon, *Hanging the Head: Portraiture and Social Formation in Eighteenth-Century England* (New Haven: Yale University Press, 1993), p. 7.

[101] Breckenridge, *Likeness*, p. 14.

[102] Bernhard Schweitzer, 'Griechische Porträtkunst', in *Acta Congressus Madvigiani Hafniae MDMLIV*, III: *Portraiture* (Copenhagen, 1957), pp. 8ff, as translated by B. V. Bothmer, *Egyptian Sculpture of the Late Period, 700 BC to AD 100* (Brooklyn: Brooklyn Museum, 1960), p. 118; cited in Breckenridge, *Likeness*, p. 4.

some sense to the form of character that we know from the European novel, with the essential difference that portraiture has no category of fiction.

But it is not unproblematic to speak of the portrait as a referential rather than a fictional genre, as Wendy Steiner, amongst many others, does when she speaks of the tension between the referential particularity of portraiture and the requirements of aesthetic generality.[103] Against this assumption, Soussloff distinguishes two discrepant claims about the portrait: 'The truth claims of an indexical exteriority, or resemblance, to the person portrayed simultaneously coexists in the genre with a claim to the representation of interiority, or spirituality. Both of these are said to reside in the portrait representation itself and in the eyes of the beholder.'[104] That truth claim relates to an identifiable individual; but likeness is not given ontologically, and in practice recognition tends to act as a substitute for likeness. By the same token, many portraits work powerfully without our having any knowledge of the person represented, or even whether such a person existed; attributing a proper name to the image is doubtless always a temptation but is in no way essential to the aesthetic (as opposed to the documentary) work of the portrait.

If the dominant topos of the portrait genre is its claim to give a faithful rendition of an individual physiognomy, its deeper claim is that its rendition of the body, and especially of the face, will reveal, as through a window, the inner depths of character. In this it works with a kind of folk physiognomy which attributes meaning—'character'—to facial structure and expression, reading them as the index of a habitus. Yet portraits characteristically make use of coded emblems of character to reinforce that reading,[105] and 'are filled with the external signs of a person's socialized self, what Erving Goffman referred to as the "front" of an individual'.[106] These may be props and cues indicating a status-laden possession, or they may take the form of clothing and jewellery coding for a social position. In the form of portraiture that Berenson calls 'effigies'—dynastic or nationalistic collections, corporate portraits, state portraits on coins or statues or representations of the two bodies of the sovereign—the codes of power turn face and body into pure typological emblems of authority.

The paradox of the portrait—stemming perhaps from its origins in funerary practices and in the death mask—is its capture of a sense of the presence of a model whom it will outlast. Rendering an appearance in the brief moment caught by pencil or brush, it commemorates a present that has passed, and thereby draws attention to its own production. A different form of this paradox is found in the self-portrait, a genre that came into being at the same time as the free-standing

[103] Wendy Steiner, *Exact Resemblance to Exact Resemblance: The Literary Portraiture of Gertrude Stein* (New Haven: Yale University Press, 1978), pp. 4–5.

[104] Soussloff, *The Subject in Art*, p. 5.

[105] Cf. Ann Jensen Adams, *Public Faces and Private Identities in Seventeenth-Century Holland: Portraiture and the Production of Community* (Cambridge: Cambridge University Press, 2009), p. 47.

[106] Shearer West, *Portraiture* (Oxford: Oxford University Press, 2004), p. 30, citing Erving Goffman, *The Presentation of Self in Everyday Life* (New York: Anchor Books, 1959), p. 22.

secular portrait in the late fifteenth century and that depends on the availability of flat mirrors, which were largely unavailable outside Venice before this time; here the doubling of artist and model relies on a doubling of the image, with that on the canvas reproducing the suppressed but indispensable image in a mirror. Derrida puts it like this:

> In order to form the hypothesis of the self-portrait of the draftsman as self-portraitist, *and seen full face*, we, as spectators or interpreters, must imagine that the draftsman is staring at one point, at one point only, the focal point of a mirror that is *facing* him; he is staring, therefore, from the place that *we* occupy, in a face to face with him: this can be the self-portrait of a self-portrait only *for the* other, for a spectator who occupies the place of a single focal point, but in the center of what should be a mirror. The spectator replaces and then obscures the mirror...[107]

Yet this stare of the draftsman embodies another impossibility, that of looking into the mirror and into the canvas at the same time. Consider the self-portrait by Renée Sintenis in Figure 7.1.[108] Here the artist's partial nudity is that of a model in a life class, a woman whose role is to be looked at and drawn. But this model is drawing, and we assume that she is drawing the image we are seeing: we stand where she would look were she to raise her eyes from her pad. But her eyes are lowered; she does not see the model that she is drawing, and indeed, as Derrida observes, it is only by hypothesis that we imagine that we see the artist 'doing the self-portrait of the draftsman doing the self-portrait of the draftsman'.[109] She might, indeed, be drawing *us*, or any other random thing. Were she, conversely, to be looking (in the image) straight at us—that is, at the mirror that we replace—she would not see to draw. It is that slight disjunction between the gaze and the hand that constitutes the radical impossibility of the self-portrait. But there is another ambiguity here as well: we do not know whether the model represented is left-handed or right-handed: viewed directly, front-on, or, let us say, through a window, she is left-handed; since the image must have been seen and then remembered as she looked into a mirror and down again to the pad, however, we must assume that it is the right hand that is doing the sketching. (Her other arm and hand are, of course, curiously truncated.) The disturbance in the field of vision created by the invisible mirror 'can haunt the visible as its very possibility'.[110]

The mirror reflects me to myself, at once whole and other, allowing me to know myself as though I were another person, to know myself *as* another person, as the other of that other whom I see facing me, regarding me knowingly. That knowledge has historical and technological conditions of existence: the long development of

[107] Jacques Derrida, *Memoirs of the Blind: The Self-Portrait and Other Ruins*, trans. Pascale-Anne Brault and Michael Naas (Chicago: University of Chicago Press, 1993), pp. 61–2.

[108] Renée Sintenis, *Nude Self-Portrait, 1917*. Pencil, 26.8 X 20 cm. Städtische Kunsthalle, Mannheim/ photo Margita Wickenhäuser/©DACS 2004. I take the image from West's *Portraiture*.

[109] Derrida, *Memoirs of the Blind*, p. 61.

[110] Derrida, *Memoirs of the Blind*, p. 45.

Fig. 7.1. Renée Sintenis, 'Nude Self-Portrait', 1917.
Source: © RENEE SINTENIS/BUS—Bildkonst Upphovsrätt i Sverige. Licensed by Viscopy, 2013.

mirror technology, from the polished copper and tin alloys or thin bronze sheets of the ancient Mediterranean civilizations through the Romans' use of polished obsidian and the long quest for flat, thin, clear glass which would not shatter under the impact of a coating of hot metal, comes to fruition only in the early sixteenth century when the glassmakers of Murano found a formula for silicate of potash and lime and improved the mirror's silvering by combining tin and mercury, thus making possible 'a process in which clarity [is] distilled from matter'.[111] It is at least another century before the dissemination of mirrors across the middle-class population occurs, and not until the 1830s that they are mass-produced, making the image of our own face commonplace.

Imperfect mirrors show the world 'through a glass, darkly', rather than in that state of future clarity that St Paul calls 'face to face';[112] their use in Paul's Corinth may have been primarily for the purpose of divination rather than for self-inspection. The clarity of the modern plane mirror, the translucent perfection of the image it casts back to us, nevertheless darkly conceals certain problems of resemblance: the reversal of left and right, the lack of any perspective other than the frontal (except in the multiplication of mirrors which then dizzyingly multiplies the reflected world), and an illusory depth which seems to extend back beyond a surface which cannot, however, be crossed. 'Form without substance, subtle and impalpable',[113] the mirror image 'escapes every sense but vision, and in particular touch, which forms the basis of our tangible reality',[114] creating thereby 'a tiny gap in the heart of resemblance'.[115] Hence the fantasies with which it is imbued: that it captures souls, in particular those of the recently dead; that it creates a double which can escape me. My face in the mirror is a doubling of the same, an identity of my self with my illusory other.

VII

The naked face is disguised by the mask: this topos is at the heart of Western theatrical convention from the Renaissance onwards. The theme of the masquerade, the notion that 'the world's all face',[116] gives rise to an endless play of illusion and deception, to 'countless episodes of mistaken identity, misplaced trust, and misdirected suspicion',[117] and to recognition scenes which reverse the disorders of loss and disguise.[118] The very notions of theatricality and 'acting' have the same effect: Diderot's requirement that the actor be a 'cold and calm spectator' of his

111 Sabine Melchior-Bonnet, *The Mirror: A History*, trans. Katharine H. Jewett (New York: Routledge, 2001), p. 18, quoting a memorandum written by Volcyr de Sérouville, the secretary to the Duke of Lorraine.

112 *blepomen gar arti di esoptrou en ainigmati, tote de prosōpon pro prosōpon*, 'For now we see through a glass, darkly, but then face to face', 1 Corinthians 13: 12. The 'glass' may be the polished bronze mirrors for which Corinth was known, or a lens or window. Cf. Mark Kauntze, 'Seeing Through a Glass Darkly: The Interpretation of a Biblical Verse in Augustine of Hippo', in Miranda Anderson (ed.), *The Book of the Mirror: An Interdisciplinary Collection Exploring the Cultural Story of the Mirror* (Newcastle: Cambridge Scholars, 2008), pp. 60–9.

113 Melchior-Bonnet, *The Mirror*, p. 102.

114 Melchior-Bonnet, *The Mirror*, p. 104.

115 Melchior-Bonnet, *The Mirror*, p. 224.

116 Dror Wahrman, *The Making of the Modern Self: Identity and Culture in Eighteenth-Century England* (New Haven: Yale University Press, 2004), p. 168.

117 Jean-Christophe Agnew, *Worlds Apart: The Market and the Theater in Anglo-American Thought, 1550–1750* (Cambridge: Cambridge University Press, 1986), p. 112.

118 Cf. Terence Cave, *Recognitions: A Study in Poetics* (New York: Oxford University Press, 1988).

role, and that, like Garrick, he play upon his face as an instrument, reinforces that disjunction between surface and depth, the false face and the naked face.[119]

But the relation between face and mask has an older and more complex history; let me illustrate it by way of a discussion of the masking theatre of the New Comedy. The plot formulae, the conventions and devices, and the characters of the Hellenistic and early Roman genre of the New Comedy form the central comic tradition in the Western world,[120] from Menander, Plautus, Terence, and the late Hellenistic prose romances to Jonson, Shakespeare, Molière, Dickens, Oscar Wilde, and most of the corpus of cinematic comedy and musicals. The basic plot, which W. Thomas MacCary describes as 'nubile',[121] is simple: a young man falls in love with a young woman; the young woman is unobtainable (because she is of low birth or a slave or apparently not a virgin), and the union of the lovers is blocked by a heavy father or his surrogate, who may be an older and wealthier rival. There is then a plot reversal which reveals the girl's parentage to be suitable (and often restores broken kinship ties: the reuniting of the girl with her father is a common theme); this revelation takes place by means of tokens such as a ring, or through recognition by an older character such as a nurse of a physical mark revealing the girl's identity. The plot ends with a marriage, often more than one if the basic plot is multiplied, and/or with festivities marking the transition from the old, 'blocking' society based on law, convention, and prohibition, to the 'congenial' society which, in Menander, is both literally and thematically Athens, 'the political community which receives and judges a new play, which receives and accepts a new *oikos* (household). When the play ends, the marriage is cemented with the ritual formula: "I plight my daughter for a harvest of legitimate [i.e. citizen] children." The central action of the play is that which permits the community to reproduce itself'.[122] In the phrase that many critics use of Hollywood's comic genres, the plot consists in the *formation of the couple*,[123] and its function is to move the social

119 Denis Diderot, 'Paradoxe sur le comédien', in F. C. Green (ed.), *Diderot's Writings on the Theatre* (Cambridge: Cambridge University Press, 1936), pp. 253–4, 272.

120 Hunter dates the genre from the Greek plays written between the death of Alexander in 323 BC and the end of the following century, and Latin adaptations of Greek comedies presented at Roman public festivals between 240 and 160 BC. Until substantial papyrus discoveries in the twentieth century, Menander's plays were known to later periods only through fragments and through the adaptations of Plautus and Terence. R. L. Hunter, *The New Comedy of Greece and Rome* (Cambridge: Cambridge University Press, 1985), p. 1.

121 W. Thomas MacCary, 'The Comedy of Errors: A Different Kind of Comedy', *New Literary History* 9: 3 (1978), pp. 525–36.

122 David Wiles, *The Masks of Menander: Sign and Meaning in Greek and Roman Performance* (Cambridge: Cambridge University Press, 1991), p. 28.

123 Rick Altman writes of the musical that 'the couple is the plot': everything moves towards its formation, and that formation drives and resolves all other plot issues. *The American Film Musical* (Bloomington: Indiana University Press, 1987), p. 35. The phrase seems to have entered English-language critical discourse from Janet Bergstrom's interview with Raymond Bellour, 'Alternation, Segmentation, Hypnosis: Interview with Raymond Bellour', *Camera Obscura* 1–2 (1979), p. 88, where, in fact, it refers to the genre of the western and to 'an art of narrative founded on representation, conflict, enigma, hermeneutics, suspense' (p. 89). Cf. also Virginia Wright Wexman, *Creating the Couple: Love, Marriage, and Hollywood Performance* (Princeton: Princeton University Press, 1993).

order from one generation to the next. (Underlying that two-generation structure, as Northrop Frye argues, is an implicit or explicit three-generation structure, in which the reversal of the law of the Father, the *senex*, restores a lost golden age: in Dickens, as I argued in Chapter 4, often represented by the benevolent uncle.)[124]

The transformation of a social order happens through the transformation of families, and that is where the focus of New Comedy lies: on the household and its relations of power and knowledge. The need to shift knowledge rapidly at the end of the play accounts, perhaps, for the formulaic and arbitrary nature of the genre's conventions (although, using a distinction I make elsewhere, it's more properly called a mode than a genre).[125] Julius Caesar Scaliger sarcastically remarks that 'in New Comedy... marriages and love affairs are the chief subjects. There are many jealous rivalries. Virgins are bought from bawds so that they may be free; some may be discovered to be free by a ring, by rattles or amulets, by a nurse, recognized by a father, mother, lover, or brother, always to the great discomfort of the bawds'.[126] And Robert Miola summarizes the influence of New Comedy conventions on Shakespeare by noting his use of stylized localities such as the sea, the brothel, and the temple, the pattern of paired but contrasting characters, the climactic recognition scene, dramatic devices such as the locking-out of the lover, disguise, and eavesdropping, as well as 'familiar New Comedic configurations: the blocking father, his daughter, her lover; the clever slave and master; the importunate lover and worldly courtesan; the reunion of parent and child'.[127]

To formulaic conventions corresponds a highly stylized cast of characters, of which the most important have dual roles as social or generational figures and as members of the household: the *senex*, the old man (who may be a miser or a misanthrope) is also a father (typically a *pater durus* or *iratus*, a heavy or choleric father, but also, at times, a rival to the son, *pater amans*); the *adulescens*, the young man, who may be dissolute or weak-willed, is also a son in conflict with his own or his beloved's father; the young woman, *virgo* or *pseudo-virgo*, is also a daughter; the changeling is someone's child, and the identical twins are at once siblings and offspring; the *matrona*, the middle-aged woman, is also a wife and mother; and the various forms of the slave (*servus callidus*, the tricky slave; *servus stultus*, the stupid slave; *nutrix*, the nurse, and so on), the parasite, the garrulous cook, and even the courtesan (*hetaira* or *meretrix*) are members of or adjuncts to the household. To this list we should add the stock types of the boastful soldier (*miles gloriosus*), the pimp (*leno*) or bawd (*lena*), the rustic, the shrew, the quack doctor, and the pedant. Menander drew, in part, on the types represented in the *Characters* of his teacher Theophrastus, Aristotle's successor as head of the Lyceum: in particular, those of

124 Northrop Frye, *Anatomy of Criticism: Four Essays* (1957; rpt. New York: Atheneum, 1965), p. 171.

125 John Frow, *Genre* (London: Routledge, 2006), pp. 63–7; my usage follows that of Alastair Fowler, *Kinds of Literature: An Introduction to the Theory of Genres and Modes* (Cambridge, MA: Harvard University Press, 1982).

126 Julius Caesar Scaliger, *Poetices* 148; quoted in Robert S. Miola, *Shakespeare and Classical Comedy: The Influence of Plautus and Terence* (Oxford: Clarendon Press, 1994), p. 140.

127 Miola, *Shakespeare and Classical Comedy*, p. 18.

the *eiron*, or dissembler; *alazon*, or boaster; and *kolax*, or flatterer.[128] Plautus drew both on the Greek tradition and on the Fabula Atellana, a farce tradition from the Naples area which relied on 'a set number of fixed characters who were catapulted into a whole series of new situations', and of which the stock figures 'were Maccus, the fool; Bucco, the braggart or glutton; Pappus, the foolish old man; and Dossennus, the wily one'[129] —characters who survive, more or less intact, into the *commedia dell'arte* and English pantomime. As for Terence, his rejection of the stock characters of Plautus is expressed in the Prologue to *Heautontimoroumenos*, where he writes: 'Give me the chance to be allowed to put on, without interruption, a play which contains more talk than action. That way an old man won't for ever continually have to play the running slave, the angry old man, the greedy parasite, the shameless swindler and the grabbing pimp...'[130]

Northrop Frye uses the account given in the Byzantine *Tractatus Coislinianus*, which may be a commentary on the lost second book of Aristotle's *Poetics*,[131] to schematize this character set. 'With regard to the characterization of comedy,' he writes,

> the *Tractatus* lists three types of comic characters: the *alazons* or impostors, the *eirons* or self-deprecators, and the buffoons (*bōmolochoi*). This list is closely related to a passage in the *Ethics* which contrasts the first two, and then goes on to contrast the buffoon with a character whom Aristotle calls *agroikos* or churlish, literally rustic. We may reasonably accept the churl as a fourth character type, and so we have two opposed pairs. The contest of *eiron* and *alazon* forms the basis of the comic action, and the buffoon and the churl polarize the comic mood.[132]

Frye's schema groups the *senex iratus* and the boastful soldier (as surrogate heavy father) in the *alazon* group; in the opposed *eiron* group he places both the hero (because 'the dramatist tends to play him down and make him rather neutral and unformed in character'),[133] the heroine because of her frequent use of disguise, and the tricky slave, who is reincarnated in later comedy as the scheming valet or the *gracioso*: Figaro, Leporello, and Jeeves. Amongst the characters who 'polarize the comic mood', he assigns the parasite and the cook to the group of buffoons, and the gull, the straight man, and the malcontent to the group of churls. All of this is, in its range of learned application, insightful, but both reductive and conceptually problematic: the *Tractatus* lists *alazon, eiron*, and *bōmolochus* as examples, not as an exhaustive list; *alazon* has a primary meaning of boaster rather than impostor, and *eiron* may have a stronger meaning of 'dissembling' as well as the sense of

[128] J. Michael Walton and Peter D. Arnott, *Menander and the Making of Comedy* (Westport, CT: Greenwood Press, 1996), pp. 97–8.
[129] Walton and Arnott, *Menander and the Making of Comedy*, p. 123.
[130] Quoted in Netta Zagagi, *The Comedy of Menander: Convention, Variation and Originality* (Bloomington: Indiana University Press, 1995), p. 41.
[131] For a full account of the textual history and an attempted reconstruction of Book II of the *Poetics*, cf. Richard Janko, *Aristotle on Comedy: Towards a Reconstruction of* Poetics *II* (London: Duckworth, 1984).
[132] Frye, *Anatomy of Criticism*, p. 172.
[133] Frye, *Anatomy of Criticism*, p. 173.

self-deprecation.[134] In any case, the downplaying of the hero in no way makes him an *eiron*, and the gulf between the relatively formless hero of New Comedy and the forcefulness of the tricky slave makes it difficult to see how they can belong to the same category.

The crucial fact about the New Comedy, in both its Greek and Roman versions (although in different ways in each) is that it is a *masked* comedy. The editor of the Loeb edition of Menander writes that the dramatist

> apparently inherited a drama of conventional type-figures—braggart soldier, greedy parasite, garrulous cook, spineless lover, choleric father, selfish courtesan and the like—immediately identifiable by the audience from the masks these characters wore and the names they were given. These enabled an experienced member of the audience to predict the total personality of a character on his first entrance, provided the playwright had made it conform to type.[135]

The key argument was made by MacCary: there is, he writes, 'substantial evidence that Menander's characters were not only "typed" but were indeed, to a degree, identical in play after play. If these characters were consistent in this sense, one would expect the same mask to have been assigned to the same character for each appearance'.[136] Thus if the name Smikrines always designates a miser, Moschion is known for his willingness to rape, and Chairestratos has a predilection for harp girls, it is likely that each is known as a generic mask. The ten Menandrean slaves named Daos 'probably wore the same mask, Pollux no. 22 or 27, "leading slave with roll of red hair" or "leading slave with wavy hair" '.[137] In short, the system of types is a system of masked figures who are characterized by the interplay between a rigid and stylized designator of the face, and the complexities of movement and voice which animate it.

David Wiles' seminal work on Menander picks up on this thesis, arguing that, for the New Comedy, 'the dominant sign system is the mask, the ancient emblem of Dionysus'.[138] His analysis of this system extrapolates a series of assumptions about acting from Greek rhetorical theory, of which the most directly relevant is number (iv): 'In respect of character types, the standard term is *prosōpon*, or mask. The character type represented and the mask worn are indisseverable' (p. 23). What are the implications of this fusion?

[134] In the *Nicomachean Ethics* (1127b25) Aristotle identifies *eironeia* and *alazoneia* as opposed forms of dissembling in relation to an ethical mean of plain truth; cf. P. W. Gooch, 'Socratic Irony and Aristotle's *Eiron*: Some Puzzles', *Phoenix* 41: 2 (1987), pp. 95–104.

[135] Geoffrey Arnott, 'Introduction', in *Menander*, vol. I, Loeb Classical Library (Cambridge, MA: Harvard University Press, 1979), pp. xxxii–iii; quoted in Wiles, *The Masks of Menander*, p. 70.

[136] W. Thomas MacCary, 'Menander's Characters: Their Names, Roles and Masks', *Transactions and Proceedings of the American Philological Association*, 101 (1970), p. 278. For a dissenting view, cf. P. G. McC. Brown, 'Masks, Names and Characters in New Comedy', *Hermes* 115: 2 (1987), p. 183: 'If the ethos of a character can change from play to play, what do we gain by regarding him as one character making eight appearances rather than as eight different characters who happen to have the same name?'

[137] W. Thomas MacCary, 'Menander's Slaves: Their Names, Roles, and Masks', *Transactions and Proceedings of the American Philological Association*, 100 (1969), p. 285.

[138] Wiles, *The Masks of Menander*, p. 17. Hereafter cited in the text.

In Theophrastus' work on acting (*hypokrisis*) the key distinction is that between *ēthos* and *pathos*, (moral) character and feeling, where *ēthos* represents a fixed moral disposition and *pathos* is the transient emotion felt by the character. Thus, '*ēthos* is signified by the unchanging element in theatrical communication, the mask, the *prosōpon*, the character type. *Pathos* is expressed by that which is of the moment, the voice' (p. 24), with the actor's body as the point where the two intersect. Unlike classical tragedy, where moral character emerges from the action of the play, in the New Comedy the mask is designed to be read frontally and to convey maximum information about the character. The mask is fixed; the voice, by contrast, is dynamic, working as 'a musical instrument activated by the *psychē*. The breath gave direct access to the roots of feeling. In Hellenistic theatre, where all the roles were shared amongst three actors, one voice, albeit slightly differentiated, served for many characters. The purpose of vocal technique was not to individuate and clarify character, but to individuate and clarify specific emotions' (p. 24).

Although it is fixed, the mask of New Comedy is, nevertheless, semiotically complex, in a way that is true neither of the leather phallus and padded stomach of Aristophanic comedy nor of the neutral mask of classical tragedy, which invites a judgement of actions rather than of appearance. Through a painstaking reading of Pollux's *Onomasticon*, which gives a detailed description of forty-four New Comedy masks grouped into the four genera of humankind (old man, young man, slave, woman), together with the pottery reproductions of masks excavated from the island of Lipari,[139] Wiles seeks to reconstruct the system of differential features (hair style and colour, forehead, eye shape and eyebrows, mouth, beard, and skin colour) which together make up a stylized characterology. Thus, the polyvalent mask of Daos, the scheming (but also anguished) servant, bears a fixed grimace which may express either of these emotions depending on how the mask is held: 'The typical slave traits of raised brows, furrowed forehead, and grinning mouth eloquently express mischief when the face is raised and a grimace of pain when the mask is lowered';[140] the mask expresses not an individual psychology but 'a complex of typical traits' (p. 98) corresponding to a social status. As Patrizia Magli notes, there is an 'odd coincidence' between the 'stiff facial masks of ancient actors, which set expressions according to a few symbolic representations, recognizable even at a distance, and ancient physiognomics, with its interest in the stable and lasting traits of a face, as separate from the passions that might move it'.[141] That science of physiognomy is detailed in two separate treatises from the Aristotelian school which suppose the interdependence of the soul and its external manifestations: 'Just as there is a dialectic between body and *psychē* in physiognomic theory, so there must be a dialectic between word and mask in Menander's theatre.'[142]

[139] Julius Pollux, *Onomasticon*; L. Bernabò-Brea, *Menandro e il teatro greco nelle terracotte liparesi* (Genova: SAGE, 1981).
[140] Wiles, The Masks of Menander, p. 95.
[141] Patrizia Magli, 'The Face and the Soul', in Michael Feher (ed.), *Fragments for a History of the Human Body, Part Two* (New York: Zone Books, 1989), pp. 90–1.
[142] Wiles, *The Masks of Menander*, p. 87. Hereafter cited in the text.

The four genera of masks described by Pollux are directly correlated with the four elements that, in Aristotelian psychology, form the human person:

old man	cold and dry
young man	hot and wet
slave	hot and dry
woman	cold and wet (p. 152)

The system of Greek New Comedy masks is built around these polarities, and around the distinctions of young and old, male and female, free and slave—that is, the relations of father and child, man and wife, and master and slave—which Aristotle takes to be the core structural elements of the social order. When the New Comedy is transplanted to Rome, however, these distinctions cease to work: the opposition of free citizens to slaves is inapplicable to the dependent clients of the wealthy, whose status is similar to that of manumitted slaves; Roman women, especially those without fathers and husbands, have the capacity to be powerful and to move freely in male society; and in the Roman gerontocracy the father has the power of life and death over his household. Thus, 'while the young hero in Menander seems to be moving steadily towards maturity, the young hero in Plautus is concerned only with immediate gratification. Father and son have an absolute conflict of interests, and there can be no sense that between them lies a golden mean' (p. 162).

Hellenistic drama is written for three actors, whose persons disappear in the succession of roles. Yet it is precisely in that disappearance that the structural tension that marks the New Comedy—the play of *ēthos* and *pathos*, of rigid character mask and the dynamics of voice and movement—emerges to mark out the thematic structure of concealment and revelation that lies at the core of the New Comedy plot. That structure takes two main forms. The first is a structure of *error*: mistakes of identity which are resolved through an act of recognition. Miola notes that 'the resolution of classical *errores* occurs variously through a chance that sometimes hints at larger design. Perhaps the earliest surviving New Comedic errors play, Menander's *Perikeiromene*, presents lost children with tokens, separated twins, confusions about identity, and a final recognition'.[143] The second is a structure of *intrigue*, in which it is the deceiver who is unmasked in order to resolve the order of knowledge. Frye puts this structure of concealing and revealing, masking and unmasking in terms of a movement between the two modes of comic thought (*dianoia*): opinion (*pistis*) and proof (*gnosis*):

> the movement from *pistis* to *gnosis*, from a society controlled by habit, ritual, bondage, arbitrary law and the older characters to a society controlled by youth and pragmatic freedom is fundamentally, as the Greek words suggest, a movement from illusion to reality. Illusion is whatever is fixed and definable, and reality is best understood as its negation: whatever reality is, it's not *that*. Hence the importance of the theme of

[143] Miola, *Shakespeare and Classical Comedy*, p. 19.

> creating and dispelling illusion in comedy: the illusion caused by disguise, obsession, hypocrisy, or unknown parentage.[144]

Frye also notes 'the curious feature of doubled characters which runs all through the history of comedy',[145] attributing it to an ambivalence between the powers of Eros and the moral order. But the twinnings, pairings, and doublings that run through this comic tradition surely have at least as much to do with the visual puns that result from the use of identical masks: they are part of what Miola calls 'the New Comedic principle of binary construction that developed naturally from the limited repertory of classical masks and character types'.[146]

The masking traditions of Greek and Roman New Comedy are interestingly like and unlike other traditions of masked drama. The closest line of continuity—perhaps because of a rather direct line of descent from Atellan Farce and a symbiotic relation with the scripted *commedia erudita* based in New Comedy models—is with the *commedia dell'arte*, with its limited repertory of stock characters in recognizable costumes and half-masks. The *commedia* is a carnivalesque tradition, whose masked characters—Arlecchino, Pantalone, Pedrolino, Pulcinella, Brighella, Colombina—invert the social, sexual, and linguistic hierarchies that the unmasked characters represent. In tracing the connection between this tradition and that of the Roman mask, Wiles emphasizes the concern with the afterlife manifested in the Roman death cults: 'While the Greek who put on a mask created a new form of life,' he argues, 'the Roman who put on a mask resurrected a dead being.'[147] And the Plautine mask, like that of Arlecchino with its rounded eyes or of Pantalone's hooked nose and phallic beard, 'seems to take on animal and infernal attributes. It is not an imitation of observed human features, but a symbol. Like all carnivalesque *commedia* masks, it liberates the wearer from the hierarchical, sexual, gravitational, and ontological constraints of normal existence'.[148]

The Greek mask is a surface which offers no prospect of a hidden interior. In the Roman mask, structurally differentiated from the civic *imago* or death mask, there is an implicit tension between the surface and the person of the actor, as there is with the half-mask of the *commedia*. In a very different tradition, that of the Japanese Noh theatre, the mask is placed slightly forward, leaving the outline of the actor's face visible: that gap expresses the Buddhist concept of an inner space which has precedence over the body, as well as the tension between the requirement, on the one hand, that the actor should breathe life into the character he plays, and, on the other, that he should conform to a set of conventions, according to which each intonation and gesture is closely prescribed, his facial expressions are masked, and the role itself—an old woman, a warrior, a god—is apparently insubstantial.[149] The organization of performance signs in these traditions differs in key

[144] Frye, *Anatomy of Criticism*, pp. 169–70.
[145] Frye, *Anatomy of Criticism*, p. 181.
[146] Miola, *Shakespeare and Classical Comedy*, p. 155.
[147] Wiles, *The Masks of Menander*, p. 129.
[148] Wiles, *The Masks of Menander*, p. 141.
[149] Peter Lamarque, 'Expression and the Mask: The Dissolution of Personality in Noh', *Journal of Aesthetics and Art Criticism*, 47: 2 (1989), p. 158.

respects from that of naturalistic theatre, where it is the face that is used to express emotion (*pathos*) and the voice to express character (*ēthos*). In modern Western theatre, the mask conceals the face and the soul: 'If the modern audience searches to reconstruct a soul beneath the mask of characterization, then a physical mask must necessarily be an impediment to that search. The nature of such a soul cannot be deduced from external signs, it can only be inferred. With a different concept of self, the Hellenistic audience did not find the mask a hindrance but an essential guide';[150] in the theatre of modernity the face itself becomes a mask.

[150] Wiles, *The Masks of Menander*, p. 114.

8
Body

I

Thomas Mann's story 'The Transposed Heads' (1940) tells of the complex relationship between Sita of the beautiful hips and two youths, Shridaman and Nanda, who are 'little different in age and caste, but very unlike in body'.[1] The close friendship between the two young men is based on a series of contrasts in their social status and their personality: Shridaman is a merchant and of learned Brahmin stock, whereas Nanda is a smith and a cowherd, 'a son of the people, simple and blithe, a Krishna-manifestation, dark of skin and hair'.[2] Nanda is powerfully built, whereas Shridaman is fair and soft-limbed: his 'was a body proper to serve as adjunct and appendage to a noble and knowledgeable head-piece, that was of course head and front of the whole, whereas with the whole Nanda the body was, so to speak, the main thing, and the head merely a pleasing appendage'.[3] The two are 'like Siva in his double manifestation'—and yet, 'after all, they were not like Siva', who encompasses all oppositions: they are rather like reflections of each other.[4] To use Schiller's terms (the story doesn't, but the reference is clear), Shridaman and Nanda represent the poles of the sentimental and the naïve.

On a walking tour together, the two youths stop at a shrine on the bank of a river. Here a young girl, Sita, comes to bathe. For Nanda, she is a 'person', whom he has known as a young girl on a swing; for Shridaman she has a 'higher meaning', is an incarnation of the great goddess.[5] Nanda argues for the unity of seeming and

[1] *Wenig verschieden an Jahren und Kastenzugehörigkeit, aber sehr ungleich nach ihrer Verkörperung.* Thomas Mann, 'The Transposed Heads', in *Stories of a Lifetime*, vol. II, no translator listed (London: Mercury Books, 1961), p. 214; Thomas Mann, 'Die vertauschten Köpfe: Eine indische Legende', in *Die Erzählungen*, vol. 2 (Frankfurt am Main: Fischer Bücherei, 1967), p. 549. Further page references are to these editions.

[2] *ein Sohn des Volks und von lustiger Einfalt, eine Krischna-Erscheinung* (p. 215/p. 550).

[3] *Es war ein Körper, wie er wohl einem edlen und wissenden Haupt, welches bei dem Ganzen eben die Hauptsache, als Zubehör und Anhängsel dient, wohingegen bei dem ganzen Nanda sozusagen der Körper die Hauptsache war und der Kopf bloß ein nettes Zubehör* (p. 216/p. 551). Mann uses both of the commonly used German words for head (*Haupt* and *Kopf*) and both of the commonly used words for body (*Leib* and *Körper*), punning particularly, as in this passage, on *Haupt* as both 'head' and 'chief' or 'main' or 'most important' (*Hauptsache*).

[4] *Alles in allem waren die beiden wie Schiwa, wenn er sich verdoppelt; Da sie jedoch nicht eins waren wie Schiwa... so waren sie einander wie Schaubilder* (p. 216/p. 551).

[5] *Person; den höheren Sinn einer solchen Erscheinung* (p. 229/pp. 563–4).

being, Shridaman for their disparity, since the essence of things resides in the name or soul rather than the appearance. But Nanda notes that Shridaman has been sexually moved by the sight of the girl, and indeed he becomes lovesick for her. Nanda undertakes to make representations on his behalf, and the marriage is arranged. At this point, however, the narrator cautions the reader not to be mistaken about the true nature of this tale, which now turns its face away for a short time; when it turns back it is changed, Medusa-like, into 'a face [literally: 'a mask'] of horror'.[6]

Six months after the wedding of Shridaman and Sita, who had 'granted to her narrow-nosed husband the full enjoyment of wedded bliss',[7] they travel with their friend Nanda back to Sita's village, each of them conflicted by complicated sexual feelings. As night falls they lose their way in the forest; and when day dawns they find themselves at a shrine of Devi-Durga, 'the terrible and unapproachable, Kali the dark Mother'.[8] Here Shridaman has a vision of death, of blood, of darkness, of sexuality, of nothingness, and realizes that he must sacrifice himself to the goddess. Seizing a sword from the bloody floor, he beheads himself—an act, the narrator observes, which would seem 'quite common and natural' but which is, in fact, so difficult as to be 'scarcely credible at all'.[9] Nanda discovers the body and, not knowing which part of it to address, opts for the head, expressing his guilt for his feelings about Sita, saying that he is guilty not because of any act he has performed but 'by my very existence in the flesh',[10] and deciding that he too must behead himself.

Sita then discovers the pair. Assuming that they have fought and killed each other, and that she will be held to blame, she prepares to hang herself from a vine, when she hears a voice: 'no other, of course, than the voice of Devi-Durga the Unapproachable, Kali the dark, the voice of the World-Mother herself', saying 'Will you just let that be for a minute, you silly ape!'[11] Scolding her—'you goose'[12]—the goddess points out to Sita that she has missed her last two periods and is expecting a son, and forces her to confess an attachment to Nanda which had begun when he wooed her on behalf of another man. What Sita had felt in her conjugal relations with Shridaman was a sense that 'desire did not become my noble husband Shridaman, it became neither his head nor his body';[13] whereas with Nanda it would have been a very different matter. Indeed—in a passage that recalls the central moment of fantasmatic adultery in Goethe's *Elective Affinities*—Sita confesses that at those moments when she made love to Shridaman, she would

[6] *zu einer gräßlichen Maske verzerrt* (p. 238/p. 572).

[7] *ihrem schmalnasigen Gatten den Vollgenuß ehelicher Lust gewährte* (p. 238/p. 572).

[8] *ein Heiligtum der Dewi, Durgâ's der Unnahrbaren und Gefahrvollen, Kâlî's, der dunklen Mutter* (p. 240/p. 574).

[9] *etwas Gewohntes und Natürliches*; the fact that Shridaman did this must *mit fast ungläubigem Staunen hingenommen werden* (p. 242/pp. 576–7).

[10] *wenn ich schuld bin einfach durch mein Dasein im Fleische* (p. 245/p. 579).

[11] *die Stimme Durgâ-Dewi's, der Unnahbaren, Kâlî's, der Dunklen, die Stimme der Weltenmutter selbst; Willst du das wohl augenblicklich sein lassen, du dumme Ziege?* (p. 249/pp. 583–4).

[12] *du Pute* (p. 249/p. 584).

[13] *Die Liebeslust stand Schridaman, meinem edlen Gemahl, nicht zu Haupt, und nicht einmal zu seinem Körper* (p. 252/p. 586).

grow pale with sorrow and close her eyes in order to imagine that it was Nanda whom she embraced.

In reply, the goddess, who is Disorder, proclaims the need for order in the institution of marriage, and commands Sita to make good the double sacrifice by replacing the heads on the bodies. This she does, and the blood flows back into them; but in her confusion she transposes the heads. In this manner 'they lived who had been sacrifices. But they lived transformed; the body of the husband dwelt with the head of his friend, the body of the friend with the husband's head'.[14]

How is Sita then to tell which of them is which? Ignoring their bodies, she addresses herself to their heads; and this decision turns out to be the right one,

> for it was definitely by these that their I- and my-feelings were conditioned. He who on narrow, light-complexioned shoulders bore the simple head of Garga's son knew himself to be Nanda. And equally the other, with the head of the grandson of Brahmins on top of a broad, bronze-coloured frame, knew and comported himself as Shridaman.[15]

Each is pleased with their new body, though Shridaman regrets the loss of the other whom he has admired; Nanda, for his part, is not surprised that these opposites were attracted when Sita recomposed them, since their friendship had already united these very different men in a kind of elective affinity. The trouble that now arises between them, however, has to do with the question of who is married to Sita. Nanda asserts that, since 'to me my body is my main point',[16] and the narrow-shouldered body he now possesses has fathered the child that Sita is carrying, it is thus he who is the husband. Shridaman challenges this assertion of identity: the other is clearly Nanda, and therefore not Sita's husband. To which the latter replies: 'I am Nanda…But as truly as I call this wedded body mine and use the word "I" of it, just so truly is Sita of the lovely curves my wife and her fruit of my begetting.'[17] To this Shridaman then replies that 'it was not that body she really embraced, as I learned to my sorrow when she muttered in her sleep. Instead it was the one I now call my own'.[18] Paternity, and a fortiori marital status, follow the body; but the actual body is not the real body.

In this situation the decision as to the identity of her husband is left to Sita; she, however, cannot decide between them. They therefore seek out a holy man, Kamadamana, to identify the true husband. Nanda leads the way into the forest, but is uncertain of the path, since when he had come this way before 'he had done

[14] *Die Geopferten lebten, aber sie lebten vertauscht: der Leib des Gatten mit dem Haupt des Freundes, des Freundes Leib mit dem Haupte des Gatten* (p. 257/p. 591).

[15] *denn nach diesen ging es, nach den Köpfen bestimmten sich unzweifelhaft die Ich- und Meingefühle, und als Nanda fühlte und wußte sich derjenige, der das volkstümliche Haupt des Sohnes Garga's auf schmalen und hellen Schultern trug; als Schridaman gebärdete sich mit Selbstverständlichkeit jener, dem auf prächtigen, dunklen Schultern das Haupt des Brahmanenenkels saß* (p. 258/p. 592).

[16] *Mir ist mein Leib die Hauptsache* (p. 259/p. 593).

[17] *Ich bin Nanda… aber so wahr ich diesen Gattenleib mein eigen nenne und von ihm Ich sage, so wahr ist die ringsum schöngliedrige Sita mein Weib und ihr Früchtchen ist mein Erzeugnis* (pp. 259–60/p. 594).

[18] *Denn nicht er war es, wie aus ihrem Flüstern und Lallen zu meinem unendlichen Leide hervorging, den sie in Wahrheit umarmte, sondern er, den ich nunmehr mein eigen nenne* (p. 260/p. 594).

so in another body, and this hampered his intuition and sense of locality'.[19] When they eventually find him, Kamadamana delivers a double verdict, opting first for the body (Sita is 'the wife of him who has his friend's head on his shoulders'—that is, Nanda) and then for the head ('Husband is, who wears the husband's head').[20] Nanda then departs to become a hermit, and Sita promises to love and cherish the body that was once his. Shridaman now has a body corresponding to the passion his head had conceived, and to which his own former body had been inadequate; Sita is in full possession of the body she had secretly desired; and the narrator hints that Sita's mistake in transposing bodies and heads had perhaps not been altogether a mistake.

Yet, for all her happiness, Sita 'had not foreseen—nor in her happiness would at first admit it—that the Nanda-body, when combined with the narrow-nosed Shridaman-head, the thoughtful, mild eyes and cheeks covered with soft fan-shaped beard, was no longer Nanda's lively body but another altogether'.[21] Within a short space of time, and 'under the influence of the head and the laws of the head, it gradually became like a husband-body'.[22] Shridaman no longer anoints his body, as Nanda had, with mustard oil; he sits in a more refined pose, and, because he engages in no physical labour, his arms begin to lose their strength, his chest becomes narrower, and fat gathers on his belly. The refinement of his head extends to his body: his hands and feet become more delicate, his complexion lightens, and, in short, his body becomes an appendage to his head. But this change is not unilateral, and a reciprocal influence extends from the body to the head; once Shridaman has been given a beautiful body to accompany his noble head, 'his mind straightway found something sad in the fact that the strange had now become his and was no longer an object of admiration—in other words, that he was not himself that after which he had yearned'.[23] And now his lips begin to thicken, his nose to become fleshly, and 'the final product was a Shridaman with a finer Nanda-body and a coarser Shridaman-head'.[24] Sita thus concludes that a corresponding change will have taken place with Nanda:

> The lonely and doubtless beautified husband-body hovered before her, wearing a pathetically refined Nanda-head, and suffering spiritually from the long separation.

[19] *denn hatte auch Nanda schon früher einmal den Weg durchs Weglose zu ihm gefunden, so hatte er's doch mit anderem Körper getan, was seine Ortserinnerung und Findigkeit einschränkte* (pp. 263–4/p. 598).

[20] *die Frau dessen, der des Freundes Haupt auf den Schultern trägt; Gemahl ist, der da trägt des Gatten Haupt* (p. 269/p. 603).

[21] *sie hatte nicht vorbedacht, und ihr Glück wollte es vorerst nicht wahrhaben, daß der Nanda-Leib in Einheit mit dem schmalnäsigen Schridaman-Haupt, seinen gedankensanften Augen und dem milden, fächerförmigen Bart um die Wangen nicht mehr derselbe, nicht länger Nanda's fröhlicher Leib, sondern ein anderer war* (p. 274/p. 608).

[22] *indem er sich unter dem Einfluß des Hauptes und seiner Gesetze nach und nach ins Gattenmäßige wandelte* (p. 274/p. 608).

[23] *da er Geist besaß, war ihm gleich so gewesen, als liege etwas wie Traurigkeit darin, daß das Fremde nun sein geworden und kein Gegenstand der Bewunderung mehr war—mit anderen Worten: daß er nun selber war, wonach ihn verlangt hatte* (p. 276/pp. 610–11).

[24] *Es war auf die Dauer ein Schridaman mit verfeinertem Nanda-Leib und vergröbertem Schridaman-Kopf* (p. 277/p. 611).

> Longing and pity for him so far away were born and grew in her, so that she closed her eyes in Shridaman's wedded embraces and in lust waxed pale for very woe.[25]

(Again the text refers almost directly to the fantasmatic adultery scene in *Elective Affinities*, where 'imagination ... asserted its rights over reality' and, while she is in Eduard's arms, 'the Captain hovered back and forth before the soul of Charlotte'.)[26] From this point on the plot moves quickly. A son is born to Sita and her husband—however we are to understand that term. Sita decides to show him to his body-father, Nanda the hermit; meeting him she sees 'that his arms were strong like those that had swung her up to the sun',[27] and that his face is not unrefined; and for a day and a night the pair enjoy 'wedded bliss'.[28] Shridaman arrives, without anger; his natural jealousy 'was lightened by the knowledge that this was his former body with which Sita was now renewing her marriage vows—an act that might as well be called faithfulness as the reverse';[29] who she sleeps with, indeed, is unimportant, 'since even though one of them had nothing from it, she always did it with both of them'.[30] Shridaman then, as the wisest of the three, announces the decision he has come to: that since only death can put aside the divisions that have come between them, the two men must die, each struck to the heart by the other's sword; in this way Sita will be able to commit herself honourably to the flames. This they do; and the child Andhaka, uniting the beauty and the wisdom of his two fathers, lives to become a reader to the King of Benares.

II

No such brief summary of Mann's story can do anything like justice to the depth of its philosophical playfulness, the parodic complexity of its analysis of the relations of body to mind. Nor can it do anything like justice to its account of triangular desire in this story of the exchange of a woman between two men and of the sexual complexities inherent in all triangular relations—as, it suggests, all sexual relations are.

[25] *Der einsam verschönte Gattenleib schwebte ihr vor, wie er im Zusammenhang mit dem armen, verfeinertem Freundeshaupt auf eine geistige Weise unter der Trennung von ihr litt; und ein sehnsüchtiges Mitleid mit dem Fernen wuchs in ihr auf, so daß sie die Augen schloß in Schridamans ehelicher Umarmung und in der Lust vor Kummer erbleichte* (p. 277/pp. 611–2).

[26] Johann Wolfgang von Goethe, *Elective Affinities*, trans. R. J. Hollingdale (Harmondsworth: Penguin, 1971), p. 106. Cf. Goethe, *Die Wahlverwandtschaften, Werke*, vol. III (Frankfurt am Main: Insel-Verlag, 1966), p. 415: '*... behauptete die Einbildungskraft ihre Rechte über das Wirkliche. Eduard hielt nur Ottilien in seinen Armen; Charlotten schwebte der Hauptmann näher oder ferner vor der Seele.*'

[27] *daß seine Arme wacker waren wie die, die sie zur Sonne geschaukelt* (p. 280/p. 614).

[28] *das Ehe-Glück* (p. 281/p. 615).

[29] *Denn seine Eifersucht... war durch das Bewußtsein geläutert, daß es sein eigener ehemaliger Leib war, mit dem Sita die Ehe wieder augenommen hatte, was man ebensowohl einen Akt der Treue wie einen solchen des Verrates nennen konnte* (p. 282/p. 616).

[30] *da sie es, mochte auch der eine weiter nichts davon haben, immer mit ihnen beiden tat* (p. 282/p. 616).

But my interest is less in the story's analysis of sexual exchange than in the clarity with which it sets up one of those thought experiments about bodies and heads that have been so central to philosophical reflection on the relation between bodies and minds, and which, translated into folk wisdom, so directly underpin our understanding both of personhood and of fictional character. These thought experiments go back at least as far as the speculations by the Stoic philosopher Chrysippus on whether 'two individuals with distinctive qualities...could occupy the same substance (*ousia*)',[31] and they are repeated in a number of late twentieth-century thought experiments about separation, fusion, fission, and exchange, designed to puzzle out precisely that question of the nature of identity in the relation between heads (or brains) and bodies that Mann explores. Derek Parfit, for example, imagines a teletransportation device that would scan every cell in my body, destroying them in the process and then reconstituting them by means of a Replicator on Mars, so that my identity, without being physically continuous, is nevertheless preserved in its entirety; then he complicates this by imagining a more advanced version of the device that leaves me intact but mortally damaged on earth while replicating a healthy version of me on Mars. Is this Replica, he asks, identical to me, or is it someone else who has been made to be identical to me? In the second case, my Replica consoles me for my imminent death, and then

> assures me that he will take up my life where I leave off. He loves my wife, and together they will care for my children. And he will finish the book that I am writing. Besides having all of my drafts, he has all of my intentions. I must admit that he can finish my book as well as I could. All these facts console me a little. Dying when I know that I shall have a Replica is not quite as bad as, simply, dying. Even so, I shall soon lose consciousness forever.[32]

Although the normal assumption might be that this second case is just about as bad as dying, Parfit argues that it is not: it is just about as good as ordinary survival, since although my numerical identity perishes, my qualitative identity is continued. The case, he says, is like a theory of resurrection which assumed that God could reassemble all the scattered or vaporized bits of matter that make up my body to create an exact Replica of me in the afterlife. On this account, being a person is a contingent fact rather than something that is distinct from my body and my brain. Again, Parfit imagines the case of a pair of identical twins, each of them injured, such that they have between them one healthy brain and one healthy body. If a surgeon were able to transplant the brain into the body, who would the resulting person be? This, says Parfit, is not a difficult question to answer: 'If all of my brain continues both to exist and to be the brain of one living person, who is psychologically continuous with me, I continue to exist. This is true whatever happens to the rest of my body', since 'receiving a new skull and a new body is just the limiting case of receiving a new heart, new lungs, new arms, and so on'.[33]

[31] Richard Sorabji, *Self: Ancient and Modern Insights about Individuality, Life, and Death* (Chicago: University of Chicago Press, 2006), p. 83.

[32] Derek Parfit, *Reasons and Persons* (1984; 2nd edn, Oxford: Clarendon Press, 1986), p. 201.

[33] Parfit, *Reasons and Persons*, p. 253.

Bernard Williams similarly imagines a number of different versions of the fusion or fission of identity in the exchange of brains and bodies. One, which he cites from Sydney Shoemaker, is that of two people whose brains are replaced in each other's bodies, and where judgements of personal identity follow the transferred character and memory traits;[34] there is then a complication of this (following David Wiggins) in which a single brain is split between two bodies, giving rise, apparently and paradoxically, to two distinct but identical persons.[35] Finally, Williams imagines that all of the information contained by a brain could be removed from it into an information-storage device and then transferred to another brain in another body, such that we could then 'print off more than one person in accordance with these conditions'.[36] In this case the difficulty of the identity of two or more non-identical entities is resolved by the conclusion that these new entities would, in the first instance, be types of the prototype person from whom they derive—type persons rather than token persons—although they would then increasingly diverge from the prototype and from each other as they underwent different experiences, becoming 'copies which are increasingly blurred or written-over'.[37]

Although both Parfit and Williams allow, to some extent, for the kind of mutual shaping and transformation of mind and body that is so central to Mann's 'The Transposed Heads', the dominant metaphor is, nevertheless, that of what Fernando Vidal calls a 'neurophilosophical reduction' of body to brain, such that 'if the brain of person A is transplanted into the body of person B, then A undergoes a body transplant rather than B a brain transplant':[38] persons are their character and their memories before they are their bodies. The crudest version of that reduction is perhaps the widespread metaphor of the brain in a vat, which John Searle expresses like this: 'Each of our beliefs must be possible for a being who is a brain in a vat because each of us is precisely a brain in a vat; the vat is a skull and the "messages" coming in are coming in by way of impacts on the nervous system.'[39] I shall return to that reduction of body and person to brain shortly; but first let me discuss what is, to my mind, the most compelling account in the analytic literature (that is, in the strictly philosophical literature) of the relation of persons to material bodies. This is P. F. Strawson's argument in the first half of *Individuals* (1959) that material bodies and persons are to be taken as basic and interdependent particulars.

By 'particulars' Strawson means such things as 'historical occurrences, material objects, people and their shadows', but not 'qualities and properties, numbers and

[34] Sydney Shoemaker, *Self-Knowledge and Self-Identity* (Ithaca: Cornell University Press, 1963), pp. 23ff., cited in Bernard Williams, 'Are Persons Bodies?', *Problems of the Self: Philosophical Papers 1956–1972* (Cambridge: Cambridge University Press, 1973), p. 77.

[35] David Wiggins, *Identity and Spatio-Temporal Continuity* (Oxford: Basil Blackwell, 1967), cited in Williams, 'Are Persons Bodies?', pp. 52ff.

[36] Williams, 'Are Persons Bodies?', p. 80.

[37] Williams, 'Are Persons Bodies?', p. 81.

[38] Fernando Vidal, 'Brains, Bodies, Selves, and Science: Anthropologies of Identity and the Resurrection of the Body', *Critical Inquiry* 28: 4 (2002), p. 938.

[39] John R. Searle, *Intentionality: An Essay in the Philosophy of Mind* (New York: Cambridge University Press, 1983), p. 230; cited in Shaun Gallagher, *How the Body Shapes the Mind* (Oxford: Oxford University Press, 2005), p. 135.

species'.[40] We identify particulars by means of identifying references (proper names or pronouns, certain descriptive phrases, demonstratives, and so on), and each of us possesses a unifying knowledge framework which allows us to fit the stories told by other people, as well as our own, into a single experientially grounded spatio-temporal system containing the particulars that make up our world and which, despite discontinuities of attention to them, we are able to recognize as different occurrences of the same thing. Material bodies, which are at once three-dimensional (and thus available to observation), diverse, complex, stable, and enduring, satisfy the criteria required of the 'basic particulars' on which the identification of others depends (p. 39), and do so better than other candidates such as processes, events, states, or conditions, since they 'secure to us one single common and continuously extendable framework of reference, any constituent of which can be identifyingly referred to without reference to any particular of any other type' (p. 54).

When we use language to refer to the world we tend not to undertake an elaboration of a complete referential framework but to use shortcuts such as proper names; and 'the bearers *par excellence* of proper names are persons and places. It is a conceptual truth... that places are defined by the relations of material bodies; and it is also a conceptual truth that persons have material bodies' (p. 58). But does this matter? Could we envisage an alternative universe in which material bodies were not the basic particulars?

Strawson's example of such a universe is one in which our experience was purely auditory, and he assumes that such a universe would give us no spatio-temporal grounding. What is not clear is how, in this no-space universe, I could distinguish between states of myself, on the one hand, and what is not myself or a state of myself on the other: it is not clear, that is to say, how the notion of a subject of perception of sound could develop that would be different from sound itself; how there could be a distinction between the subject's experiences and the idea of that which has them.

In forming an idea of what we ourselves are, we ascribe to ourselves both the kinds of enduring properties that we would normally ascribe to material bodies (height, colouring, shape, weight, and so on) and other properties (actions and intentions, sensations, thoughts, feelings, memories, and so on) which are relatively transient. What needs explanation here is 'that one's states of consciousness, one's thoughts and sensations, are ascribed *to the very same thing* to which these physical characteristics, this physical situation, is ascribed' (p. 89); and, indeed, we need to explain why one's states of consciousness are or should be ascribed to anything at all. One possible answer to these questions would have to do with the unique role the body plays in perceptual experience (at the most basic: the 'impacts on the nervous system' that feed information to the brain in a vat); but that experience is complex and in some ways contingent: we could imagine the different modalities

[40] P. F. Strawson, *Individuals: An Essay in Descriptive Metaphysics* (London: Methuen, 1959), p. 15; hereafter cited in the text.

of sensation (sight, smell, touch, hearing, and so on) each feeding in contradictory information. Certainly my body is unique to me, both as a source and as an object of perception, but this does not explain 'why I should have the concept of *myself* at all, why I should ascribe my thoughts and experiences to *anything*' (p. 93).

One response to this question—that of Descartes and perhaps, at one point, of Wittgenstein—would be that our conflation of states of consciousness with certain bodily characteristics is the effect of an illusion that there is an underlying self common to both sets of predicates (Parfit, too, comes close to a similar conclusion). For Descartes, as for Locke following him, the substance of the self or the person can be dissociated from the substance of the body. Another response would just be to say that experiences cannot be 'owned' by a self. Each of these responses seems to posit 'that there are two uses of "I", in one of which it denotes something which it does not denote in the other' (p. 98). If we think that this denial is faulty, however, then it will necessarily follow that one can ascribe states of consciousness to oneself only if and insofar as one can ascribe them to other people; and one can identify others only if those others are something more than just the possessors of states of consciousness.

Getting away from the aporias of dualism thus requires acknowledging 'that a necessary condition of states of consciousness being ascribed at all is that they should be ascribed to the *very same things* as certain corporeal characteristics, a certain physical situation etc.' (p. 102); it is in this sense that 'the concept of a person is logically prior to that of an individual consciousness. The concept of a person is not to be analysed as that of an animated body or an embodied anima' (p. 103); it is a conceptual primitive, and in that sense it undermines the notion of *embodiment* that has shaped so much of the current neurophilosophical turn.

III

That turn can perhaps most economically be described by telling the story of the shift from one paradigm to another. The convergence, in the postwar period, of neuroscience and computational science in the study of artificial intelligence gave rise to a model of mental activity which was computational and functional: cognitive systems were studied in terms of the logical processes that drove them, regardless of whether they took place in human brains or silicon chips. The role of bodies in this model is to be represented in the somatosensory cortex or to feed in the raw data of sensation on which cognition operates;[41] the business of mind is the manipulation of symbols formed on the basis of registered sensations in order to create representations of an external world.

That model has been gradually but inexorably displaced in the cognitive sciences by a range of models of embodied cognition which posit the interdependency

[41] Cf. Raymond W. Gibbs, *Embodiment and Cognitive Science* (Cambridge: Cambridge University Press, 2005), pp. 2, 5.

of mind, body, and environment. Thus Francisco Varela, Evan Thompson, and Eleanor Rosch argue, in a seminal text, that the principal activity of brains is not the representation of a given world but the making of continuous modifications of their own states; they are autonomous, self-organizing systems, and 'instead of *representing* an external world, they *enact* a world as a domain of distinctions that is inseparable from the structure embodied by the cognitive system'.[42] Extrapolating from a case study of colour perception, they argue that perception should be understood neither as a recovery of the properties of the world nor as the projection onto it of the categories of the observer but rather as a mutual specification of perceiver and perceived. Cognition is embodied action in the sense that it 'depends upon the kinds of experience that come from having a body with various sensorimotor capacities',[43] and that those capacities are, in turn, embedded in and interact with an environment with which they have co-evolved. It follows from this formulation that perception is an active process, an *offering* of attention, 'not simply embedded in and constrained by the surrounding world' but contributing to 'the enactment of this surrounding world'.[44] For theorists of embodied cognition consciousness is an emergent property of brain states but is not reducible to them. Evan Thompson argues, against Daniel Dennett, that 'the mind does not reside in the brain *per se*: it resides in the embodied organism embedded in the world';[45] and, in Andy Clark's formulation, while there should be no questioning of 'the basic materialist vision of mind as emerging fully and without residue from physical goings-on', it is also the case that some of these goings-on 'don't stay neatly in the brain', or even in the biological body: much cognition goes on in 'hybrid ensembles of neural, bodily, and environmental elements'.[46]

The story of the shift away from a computational paradigm which had reached the limits of its usefulness is allegorized in Richard Powers' novel *Galatea 2.2*. Its protagonist, 'Richard Powers', is the Humanist-in-Residence at the Center for the Study of Advanced Sciences and an assistant to Philip Lentz, a cognitive neurologist seeking to model the human brain through a cumulative series of neural networks that will eventually learn to interpret and comment on any literary text in the examination taken by Masters students in English for admission to PhD candidacy. (The project is probably modelled on the Cyc project, developed from 1984 by Douglas Lenat as an encyclopaedic database of common sense knowledge designed to allow intelligent systems to reason like human beings.)[47] As the neural network develops through eight successive implementations, A to H, each of

[42] Francisco J. Varela, Evan Thompson, and Eleanor Rosch, *The Embodied Mind: Cognitive Science and Human Experience* (Cambridge, MA: MIT Press, 1991), p. 140.
[43] Varela, Thompson, and Rosch, *The Embodied Mind*, p. 173.
[44] Varela, Thompson, and Rosch, *The Embodied Mind*, p. 174.
[45] Evan Thompson, 'The Mindful Body: Embodiment and Cognitive Science', in Michael O'Donovan-Anderson (ed.), *The Incorporated Self: Interdisciplinary Perspectives on Embodiment* (Lanham, MD: Rowman & Littlefield, 1996), pp. 132–3.
[46] Andy Clark, *Supersizing the Mind: Embodiment, Action, and Cognitive Extension* (Oxford: Oxford University Press, 2008), p. xxviii.
[47] Cf. Andy Clark, *Being There: Putting Brain, Body, and World Together Again* (Cambridge, MA: MIT Press, 1998), pp. 2–3.

which incorporates the previous stage as a subsystem of an increasingly distributed and interdependent emergent system, the novel charts a progressive hierarchy of human knowledges from the formal to the very informal.

Thus, Implementation A, which is fed massive vocabulary lists, learning to recognize words and to parse rudimentary syntax, fails just because of the power of its ability to recognize fixed verbal patterns: it learns and retains too much and, like Borges' Funes with his photographic memory of particulars, is therefore unable to move from data to generalization. Its successor, Implementation B, is taught how to forget, and moves from A's pattern recognition to a form of computational linguistics which allows it to answer a riddling nursery rhyme (the one about the man going to St Ives with seven wives), but to do so only because of its 'unfailing literal-mindedness'.[48] B can generalize to cases but cannot move from cases to rules; it is replaced by Implementation C, set up as a structure of parallel processing between distributed subsystems, which can generalize about its own generalizations but which opens up, by its shortcomings, a further dimension of knowledge acquisition. For it to understand a word like 'ball' it must not only process an almost infinite number of predicates and exceptions, but must compensate for its lack of referential and affective knowledge: its incomprehension of what a ball feels like in the hands and in relation to a human body. C cannot match its verbal knowledge with visual, haptic, and kinetic knowledges, nor can it understand objects as part of physical and social interaction with others, grounded in time and in complex structures of exchange.

It is with Implementation H, however, that the linkages between learning, sociality, and embodiment are most fully explored. Implementation H is the first of the neural networks to have a name: she is called Helen, and she is also the entity which most crucially feels its lack of embodiment, with all the consequences this entails for semantic understanding. She 'sorted nouns from verbs, but, disembodied, she did not know the difference between thing and process, except as they functioned in clauses' (p. 195). This is to say that, whereas for humans conceptualization is rooted in bodily perception and precedes language, Helen must work back from words to the experience they convey. 'She had trouble with values, because she had no fear of self-preservation, no hierarchy of hard-wired pain. She had trouble with causality, because she had no low-level systems of motion perception from which the forms of causality are thought to percolate' (p 250); she 'could neither feel nor gauge herself. Hungry-full; warm-cold; up-down: she worked these as abstract axes, not as absolutes of need' (p. 243).

Yet it is important to be clear about what exactly it is that she lacks. In a perceptive essay on the novel, Katherine Hayles writes that

> Rick refers to Helen as 'disembodied', but this is of course true only from a human perspective. The problem that Helen confronts in learning human language is not that she is disembodied (a state no presence in the world can achieve!) but rather that

[48] Richard Powers, *Galatea 2.2* (London: Abacus, 1996), p. 95; hereafter cited in the text.

> her embodiment differs significantly from that of humans. There is nothing in her embodiment that corresponds to the bodily sensations encoded in human language. For her there is no 'body in the mind', as Mark Johnson has called it, no schemas that reflect and correspond to her embodied experience in the world.[49]

This passage is a part of Hayles' larger argument against the Platonic dream of a separation of information from material embodiment: 'It can be a shock,' she writes, 'to remember that for information to exist, it must *always* be instantiated in a medium.'[50] But instantiation is not the same as, or is not what we mean by, embodiment. The point about silicon-based information is that it can be transferred without loss of organization from instance to instance and from medium to medium: it is not tied to any one incarnation.

There are two points of comparison here with human embodiment. First, the body can itself be understood as an information system, in which, or in relation to which, secondary information systems are embedded. Second, human consciousness can likewise be transferred from one medium to another, in the sense that thought can be materialized as writing or image or sound in such a way that it extends beyond and is independent of the thinking body. What is distinctive about human embodiment is not the fact of instantiation but the nature of human learning: the emergence of concepts from bodily experience, and the fact that, as the narrator of *Galatea* puts it, 'Human knowledge is social. More than stimulus-response. Knowing entails testing knowledge against others. Bumping up against them'.[51]

Hayles notes the consequences in the novel for learning machines: since the post-human Helen 'does not have a body in anything like the human sense of the word', she 'approaches meaning from the opposite direction taken by humans', for whom 'incarnation precedes language... Concepts about what it means to be an embodied creature must evolve for her out of linguistic signification'.[52] She achieves, at best, what Lentz calls 'functional equivalence'. But we can put this even more strongly: it is not just concepts about what it means to be an embodied creature that Helen struggles with, but conceptuality itself, to the extent that all concepts emerge from the experience of embodiment. Hayles' reference to Mark Johnson's notion of the 'body in the mind' is central here: Johnson and George Lakoff have argued through a series of books that the semantic primitives that underlie all human conceptualization correspond directly to the experience of spatially situated human bodies: metaphors of front and back, of spatial containers and boundaries, of motion through space, of grasping and ingesting, and of the relation of one body to another form the substrate for all conceptual apprehension

[49] N. Katherine Hayles, *How We Became Posthuman: Virtual Bodies in Cybernetics, Literature, and Informatics* (Chicago: University of Chicago Press, 1999), p. 265.
[50] Hayles, *How We Became Posthuman*, p. 13.
[51] Powers, *Galatea 2.2*, p. 148.
[52] Hayles, *How We Became Posthuman*, p. 263.

of the world.[53] Human thought is at once contained and structured by the boundaries of the body and its relation to lived space.[54]

IV

Now, how that containment and structuring works *in detail* is the subject of the turn to embodiment in the disciplines of neuroscience and cognitive science, and in those areas of the philosophy of mind that draw on them. Here I want to explore two concepts which seem to me central to this turn: the concept of the body schema, and Antonio Damasio's closely related concept of the proto-self.

In thinking about the concept of the body schema, I follow Shaun Gallagher's careful distinction between the questions of how the body appears as an intentional object in the perceptual field, and how it constrains or shapes that field. The concept of the *body image* answers the former question; the concept of the *body schema*, by contrast, designating 'a system of sensory-motor capacities that function without awareness or the necessity of perceptual monitoring',[55] answers the latter. Yet there is a long history of confusion of the two: by psychoanalytic theorists like Paul Schilder, for example, who equates the 'postural' model of the body, developed by the neurologist Henry Head as an account of cortical representations of motor changes, with conscious representations of the positional and symbolic dimensions of the body.[56] Maurice Merleau-Ponty, while more careful about distinguishing the two concepts, still leaves unexplained the relation of the body schema to marginal body awareness; and later feminist theorists like Moira Gatens and Elizabeth Grosz, who depend closely on Schilder and Merleau-Ponty, tend to pass without differentiation from an account of functions that operate below the level of intentional awareness to the intentional states and dispositions that constitute body image, with the phenomenon of the phantom limb acting for each as a template of the possibility of that passage.[57]

In Head's pioneering account, the schema is a preconscious function which registers constantly shifting proprioceptive and kinaesthetic information from all of the systems that give feedback about the state and position of the body.[58]

[53] George Lakoff and Mark Johnson, *Metaphors We Live By* (Chicago: University of Chicago Press, 1980); Mark Johnson, *The Body in the Mind: The Bodily Basis of Meaning, Imagination, and Reason* (Chicago: University of Chicago Press, 1987); George Lakoff, *Women, Fire, and Dangerous Things* (Chicago: University of Chicago Press, 1987); George Lakoff and Mark Johnson, *Philosophy in the Flesh: The Embodied Mind and its Challenge to Western Thought* (New York: Basic Books, 1999).

[54] Cf. also the important work of Horst Ruthrof on the corporeal basis of semantics: *Semantics and the Body: Meaning from Frege to the Postmodern* (Toronto: University of Toronto Press, 1997), and *The Body in Language* (London: Cassell, 2000).

[55] Gallagher, *How the Body Shapes the Mind*, p. 24.

[56] Paul Schilder, *The Image and Appearance of the Human Body* (New York: Wiley, 1950), p. 11: 'The body schema is the tri-dimensional image everybody has about himself. We may call it "body image".'

[57] Moira Gatens, 'A Critique of the Sex/Gender Distinction', in *Imaginary Bodies: Ethics, Power and Corporeality* (London: Routledge, 1996), p. 12; Elizabeth Grosz, *Volatile Bodies: Toward a Corporeal Feminism* (Bloomington: Indiana University Press, 1994), p. 73.

[58] Henry Head, W. H. R. Rivers, James Sherren, Gordon Holmes, Theodore Thompson, and George Riddoch, *Studies in Neurology*, 2 vols (London: Oxford University Press, 1920).

Specifically, it is made up of feedback from receptors on the skin or beneath its surface about pressure, temperature, and friction; feedback about movement and spatial position from receptors in the joints; feedback about balance, direction, and posture from the vestibular system in the inner ear, from the relative dispositions of head and trunk, and from pressure on parts of the body in contact with gravity-resisting surfaces; feedback from skin stretch about bodily disposition and volume; feedback from receptors in the inner organs about nutrition and homeostasis; feedback from muscles about the expenditure of effort; and feedback about levels of energy and fatigue from central systems sensitive to the composition of the blood.[59] Brian Massumi groups these into proprioceptive, tactile, and visceral systems, where tactility is 'exteroceptive', visceral sensation is 'interoceptive', and proprioception, which 'folds tactility into the body, enveloping the skin's contact with the external world in a dimension of medium depth: between epidermis and viscera', has the task of translating 'the exertions and ease of the body's encounters with objects into a muscular memory of relationality. This is the cumulative memory of skill, habit, posture', a kind of 'sixth sense directly attuned to the movement of the body':[60] absolutely central to our experience of spatial position and motion, and thus to our mapping of and interaction with the world around us. Without these schemata, Head and his collaborator, Gordon Holmes, write, 'we could not probe with a stick, nor use a spoon unless our eyes were fixed upon the plate. Anything which participates in the conscious movement of our bodies is added to the model of ourselves and becomes part of these schemata: a woman's power of localization may extend to the feather in her hat'.[61] The body schema is thus not bounded by the body: the car in which I drive, the spade with which I dig, the clothes I wear, the game controller which guides me into a digital world are incorporated into my sense of my body's dynamic positioning in space, my sense of embodied selfhood.

That sense is not normally available to my attention: it is the effaced sense—a constant and continuous pre-reflective awareness—of my body accomplishing an action; Gallagher speaks of it as 'a prenoetic performance of the body', a fitting of the body to its actions and its world without the need for 'a reflexive conscious monitoring directed at the body'.[62] Although the body schema can be modified by training or by conscious attention, and although, conversely, long-term aspects of body image can come to function prenoetically, it is normally the case that my proprioceptive awareness 'is not itself a perception of the body as an object'; it is 'a non-perspectival awareness of the body',[63] an awareness *in* rather than *of* action. Although it provides the basis for an egocentric spatial framework for perception, it is not itself situated in space: it is, rather, that which brings space and spatial

[59] Gibbs, *Embodiment and Cognitive Science*, p. 28.

[60] Brian Massumi, *Parables for the Virtual: Movement, Affect, Sensation* (Durham, NC: Duke University Press, 2002), pp. 58–9.

[61] Henry Head and Gordon Holmes, 'Sensory Disturbances from Cerebral Lesions', *Brain* 34 (1911), p. 188; cited in Grosz, *Volatile Bodies*, p. 66.

[62] Gallagher, *How the Body Shapes the Mind*, p. 32.

[63] Gallagher, *How the Body Shapes the Mind*, pp. 137–8.

perspective into existence. And it involves but is not reducible to neurological functioning: it is a form of sense-making, but at a pre-reflective level.

The sense it makes is intermodal: a knitting together of motor space, proprioceptive space, and perceptual space. Although until recently the consensus in psychology had been that the relation between intero- and exteroceptive systems developed only between the third and sixth months of the child's life, and that an intermodally organized body schema therefore developed at a correspondingly late stage, more recent research on neonate imitation of adult facial expressions seems to indicate some degree of innate body schema, and posits that intermodal translation between the senses is operative from birth—or, more precisely, that 'no "translation" or transfer is necessary because it is already accomplished in the embodied perception itself, and is already intersubjective'.[64] If proprioception is a form of embodied awareness, then we can ask the further question as to whether it constitutes a form of pre-reflective consciousness; and Gallagher answers that, to the extent that it involves an intermodal patterning and a differentiation of self from non-self, there is a real sense in which it does.[65]

The crucial point here is just that proprioceptive awareness is non-intentional (it has no object apart from its own performance). A somewhat different form of this question about the emergence of consciousness in relation to bodily feedback systems is posed by Antonio Damasio. At the heart of his argument is the thesis that the brain has two distinct functions: a representational function concerned with mapping the world, and a cybernetic function concerned with monitoring the organism's internal chemical profile and correcting any detected changes of state. We could think of this as a kind of *mise en abyme*, in which part of what the brain models is its own non-conscious activity.

That cybernetic activity has as its object the homeostatic regulation, within a narrow range of variation, of the endocrine, immune, and autonomic nervous systems governing temperature, oxygen concentration, and pH levels in the body. Damasio understands changes in the state of these systems as the equivalent of emotions, and sees emotions, conversely, as devices regulating responses to an external situation or to the internal state of the organism; they do so, for example, by 'providing increased blood flow to arteries in the legs so that muscles receive extra oxygen and glucose, in the case of a flight reaction, or changing heart and breathing rhythms, in the case of freezing on the spot'.[66] In the course of the experience of an emotion, neurons located in the hypothalamus, the basal forebrain, and the brain stem send commands, either by way of chemical molecules transmitted directly through the bloodstream, or by way of electrochemical signals sent along neuron pathways to act on other neurons or on muscular fibres or organs,

[64] Gallagher, *How the Body Shapes the Mind*, p. 80.

[65] Gallagher, *How the Body Shapes the Mind*, pp. 105–6.

[66] Antonio Damasio, *The Feeling of What Happens: Body and Emotion in the Making of Consciousness* (Orlando, FL: Harcourt, 1999), p. 54; hereafter cited in the text. Damasio's argument about the emergence of consciousness was first expounded in *Descartes' Error: Emotion, Reason, and the Human Brain* (New York: Putnam, 1994), but is more fully developed here.

which then release their own chemicals into the bloodstream; these signals bring about a global change of state in the organism, including in the brain itself, and thereby induce changes in behaviour. In addition to these humoral and neural signals, which Damasio calls a 'body loop', changes of state may be effected by what he calls an 'as-if body loop', where 'the representation of body-related changes is created directly in sensory body maps, under the control of other neural sites', such as the prefrontal cortices—'as if' the body had really been changed (p. 80).

What Damasio calls 'core consciousness'—a state that precedes reflexive consciousness, and which is not dependent on conventional memory, working memory, reasoning, or language—is a deep-seated, non-verbal sense 'of the very existence of the individual organism in which that mind is unfolding and of the fact that the organism is engaged in interacting with particular objects within itself or in its surroundings' (p. 89). It is coextensive with the emotions, and perhaps shares the same neural substrate; and it can be distinguished from whatever inferences we may draw about the contents of our state of consciousness, since it is no more than 'the unvarnished sense of our individual organism in the act of knowing' (p. 125). Core consciousness is grounded, in turn, in what Damasio calls the proto-self: that is, precisely that ensemble of neurological patterns that stand in for the body and which are the effect of the organism's activity of self-monitoring. The body's somatosensory apparatus constitutes the proto-self as an activity of first-order mapping of the organism. The argument about the emergence of a basic form of ('core') consciousness follows then from the duality of the brain's modelling functions: as it maps the world (an object which may be either external to the organism or internal to it—a remembered object, for example), the brain registers the disturbances of its own state caused by this mapping, and this process then generates a second-order reflexive mapping. A kind of story is told here: '*that of the organism caught in the act of representing its own changing state as it goes about representing something else*. But the astonishing fact is that the knowable entity of the catcher has just been created in the narrative of the catching process' (p. 170; emphasis in original). Consciousness is a kind of by-product of the brain's somatic self-representation as a moment of its representation of the world.

This is an ingenious account, and it has several virtues: it grounds consciousness in bodily processes and in their emotional correlates, and it does so without conceiving of bodily processes and consciousness as ontologically distinct (Catherine Malabou's objection that it leaves the process of translation between the 'neuronal' and the 'mental' obscure thus seems to me to miss the point);[67] it gets around the problem of postulating a pure moment of origin; and it allows for a description, on the basis of this degree-zero of core consciousness, of the more complex, 'extended'

[67] Catherine Malabou, *What Should We Do With Our Brain?* (New York: Fordham University Press, 2008), p. 62. Malabou's more extended treatment of the relations between the cerebral and the psychic in *The New Wounded: From Neurosis to Brain Damage*, trans. Steven Miller (New York: Fordham University Press, 2012), seems to me a more open and interesting account of what a neuropsychoanalysis might be.

modes of consciousness that correspond to an autobiographical self, embedded and constituted in the systems of the pronoun and the name.

If it has a parallel in the psychological literature, it is perhaps—for all their differences—with Freud's notion of the ego as being, in the first instance, a bodily ego. The key passage occurs in 'The Ego and the Id' (1923). Describing the differentiation of these two entities, Freud notes the duality of our perception of the body: the body, and, above all, its surfaces, 'is a place from which both external and internal perceptions may spring. It is seen like any other object, but to the touch it yields two kinds of sensations, one of which may be equivalent to an internal perception'.[68] Thus, the ego is 'first and foremost a bodily ego [*Körper-Ich*]; it is not merely a surface entity, but is itself the projection of a surface';[69] and in a later note Freud adds: 'I.e. the ego is ultimately derived from bodily sensations, chiefly from those springing from the surface of the body. It may thus be regarded as a mental projection of the surface of the body, besides, as we have seen above, representing the superficies of the mental apparatus.'[70] The ego emerges from representations of the body's sensory apparatus, and it is only in part conscious; Didier Anzieu describes it as a 'skin ego', emerging from that interface between inside and outside, 'inner' and 'outer' sensation, and providing 'the anaclitic grounding for all the psychical functions'.[71] In this model, too, psychic functions are derived from the body's sensory systems, in a process of projection which is conceptually close to Damasio's account of the body's nested self-representation.

V

'We invent with our bodies, and thereby reinvent those bodies. Unlike other animals, we have a relation to our bodies, a relation that we invent, and a relation that is our bodies.'[72] We imagine our bodies; and the *body image* is one name for that imagined body. Yet the concept of body image is beset with problems.

One that I have already signalled has to do with what we might call the psychologization of the body schema. The central case here involves the phenomenon of the phantom limb—that is, the sensation of persistent movement and feeling in an amputated limb. Thus Warren Gorman, for example, writes that

> the phantom is the result of a psychic striving by the individual to replace a missing part of the body image, after that missing part has been diseased or traumatized. No physical cause that is regularly reproducible has yet been identified... The psychiatric significance of the phantom of any part... appears to be that the phantom constitutes

[68] Sigmund Freud, 'The Ego and the Id', in *The Standard Edition of the Complete Psychological Works of Sigmund Freud* XIX, trans. James Strachey (London: Hogarth Press, 1955), p. 25.
[69] Freud, 'The Ego and the Id', p. 26.
[70] Freud, 'The Ego and the Id', p. 26, n. 1 (added 1927).
[71] Didier Anzieu, *The Skin Ego*, trans. Chris Turner (New Haven: Yale University Press, 1989), p. 21.
[72] Steven Connor, *The Book of Skin* (London: Reaktion Books, 2004), p. 30.

> an attempt at restitution of the missing part, a denial of its absence, or a somatic substitute for mourning over its loss.[73]

And for Elizabeth Grosz, 'the phantom limb is the narcissistic reassertion of the limb's presence in the face of its manifest biological loss, an attempt to preserve the subject's narcissistic sense of bodily wholeness'.[74] The question is whether what is at issue is a matter of body schema or body image: of a deeply bedded sense of motor action, or of a representation or percept so vivid that it allows one to forget that the limb is missing. Gallagher suggests that the argument to vividness of perception is contradictory, since it would involve 'not simply a perceptual presence alongside a conceptual acknowledgement of absence, which is in some regards the mark of a phantom, but this, together with a forgetting of the conceptual acknowledgement'.[75] A more parsimonious explanation would be that 'forgetting is normal and possible precisely because motor behavior does not ordinarily require that my limbs be included in my perceptual awareness': I move my legs or reach out to grasp something not because I have a perception of the activity of my limbs but because, 'thanks to the coordinated processes of body schemas, movement usually takes care of itself'.[76] Forgetting is a usual, indeed constitutive, component of the body schema, and the phantom thus seems to be an element of the schema.

A different sort of problem with the concept of the body image is that it has been trivialized by being stripped of its fantasmatic dimension, or that dimension is measured against a truth of which the image is a distortion. Gallagher's definition of the body image as consisting of 'a system of perceptions, attitudes, and beliefs pertaining to one's own body'[77] locates it—despite the passing concession that 'conceptual and emotional aspects of body image no doubt inform perception and are affected by various cultural and interpersonal factors'[78] —in a realm in which desire and fantasy have no place. The common use of the concept to describe the relation of the anorexic to her body, by contrast, recognizes the fantasy but understands it as a false consciousness, a distortion of what the body really is.

An adequate theory of the body image should thus not conflate it with the schemata that underpin motor activity, and should engage the experiential and fantasmatic dimensions of body awareness. The question is one about the appropriate metaphors with which to conceptualize a relation at once of discontinuity and of a certain kind of continuity with the body schema; and one possibility would be to say that the body image *appropriates* that 'body-model in the brain' which Thomas Metzinger describes as the 'phylogenetically oldest part of the human self-model' and which is not attentionally available;[79] on this account, the body image—what

[73] Warren Gorman, *Body Image and the Image of the Brain* (St Louis, MI: Warren H. Green, Inc., 1969), p. 99.

[74] Grosz, *Volatile Bodies*, p. 73.

[75] Gallagher, *How the Body Shapes the Mind*, p. 91.

[76] Gallagher, *How the Body Shapes the Mind*, p. 91.

[77] Gallagher, *How the Body Shapes the Mind*, p. 24.

[78] Gallagher, *How the Body Shapes the Mind*, p. 26.

[79] Thomas Metzinger, *Being No One: The Self-Model Theory of Subjectivity* (Cambridge, MA: MIT Press, 2003), p. 439.

Metzinger calls the 'phenomenal self-model'—makes the body schema 'available for attention and motor control',[80] and thus translates my non-perspectival awareness of my body into a *knowledge* that this is *my* body.

The body schema, registering changes in bodily position and movement in space, maps a spatiality which is entirely relative to the body's dynamic orientation and interaction. Indeed, Massumi suggests that the body's proprioceptive referencing is constitutive of spatial experience in a way that cognition based on visual cues is not: rather than movement being indexed to position, 'position emerges from movement, from a relation of movement to itself'.[81] Our understanding of space is not, in the first place, perceptual or cognitive but a matter of pragmatic action within and upon it. Perception and cognition are thus, in the first instance, active ways of dealing with a spatial environment. Raymond Gibbs notes that 'perceiving an object without touching it partly involves imagining how it may be physically manipulated...This perception-action coupling suggests that perceiving an object requires people to conjecture something that if pulled would bend, if thrown would knock something else aside, and if turned would reveal another side'.[82] And this is the force of Merleau-Ponty's argument for the priority of an active and interactive over an instrumental model of perception: 'My body has its world, or understands its world, without having to make use of any "symbolic" or "objectifying" function.'[83] It conceives of its world in action, and it is from this pragmatic relation to the world that every more complex understanding of spatiality develops.

The grasping of space through our bodily situation gives us an orientation which yields a set of basic spatial coordinates: we conceive it as up/down, in front/behind, inside/outside, moving forward/backwards/sideways, being central/peripheral, and so on. The 'front' of a house is that part which has its 'face' to me, or, if I am inside it, that part from which I would face those who would approach it; I live 'in' time, 'on' a street, 'under' certain conditions. These are the 'image schemata', the 'dynamic analogue representations of spatial relations and movements in space'[84] that provide the foundation for the basic conceptual categories by which the world is organized—or, to put this more cautiously, let me say with Mark Turner that it is plausible, but not demonstrable, 'that our understanding of social, mental, and abstract domains is formed on our understanding of spatial and bodily stories'.[85] At the same time, the body itself is structured as the locus of overlapping symbolic dimensions: my back, for example,

> is simultaneously a spatial designation, a rarely seen part of the body, a sector associated with anal functions, that which 'faces away' from people, an area difficult to defend, a source of unique kinesthetic sensations, a locale particularly activated by

[80] Metzinger, *Being No One*, p. 486.
[81] Massumi, *Parables for the Virtual*, p. 180.
[82] Gibbs, *Embodiment and Cognitive Science*, p. 64.
[83] Maurice Merleau-Ponty, *Phenomenology of Perception*, trans. Colin Smith (1962; rpt. London: Routledge, 2002), p. 162.
[84] Gibbs, *Embodiment and Cognitive Science*, p. 90.
[85] Mark Turner, *The Literary Mind* (New York: Oxford University Press, 1996), p. 51.

> certain emotions, a favorite site for the administration of punishment by one's parents, and so on.[86]

Steven Connor similarly speaks of the voice as charging the relation between my body and space with a dense phenomenal force:

> More even than my gaze, my voice establishes me in front of things and things in front of me...As I speak, I seem to be situated in front of myself, leaving myself behind. But if my voice is out in front of me, this makes me feel that I am somewhere behind it. As a kind of projection, the voice allows me to withdraw or retract myself. This can make my voice a persona, a mask, or sounding screen.[87]

But, equally, my voice emanates from an inside and establishes a relation between that inside and an outside, and the possibilities of passage from one to the other. This symbolic order of the body is what I call its fantasmatic dimension, and what Moira Gatens calls the imaginary body. It is constructed from 'evanescent and fragmentary evidence derived from multiple sensory systems such as vision, proprioception and hearing';[88] and its key coordinates are the boundaries between the inside and the outside; between the self and the other; between male and female; between the clean and the polluted; and between the living and the dead. (These, of course, are the polarities that make up much of the affective force of religion.) Gatens describes the imaginary body as the effect of a 'system of exchange, identification and mimesis' in which I shape my sense of myself by way of an incorporation of the bodies of others.[89] It may, at times, have about it 'an eerie anonymity and otherness', and it allows us to be 'objects, for ourselves and to ourselves: recipients of our own sadism/masochism; esteem/disdain; punishment/reward; love/hate. Our body image is a body double that can be as "other" to us as any genuine "other" can be.'[90] It is through this imaginary body that our fundamental fantasies about who we are and how we engage with others are shaped.

VI

In Richard Powers' *The Echo Maker*, which tells the story of a man suffering from Capgras syndrome (a neurologically based delusion that the people one is emotionally close to are impostors or replicants), one of the central characters, an Oliver Sacks-like figure called Gerald Weber, reflects on the simplest and most unsettling insight he has gained: that

[86] Seymour Fisher, *Body Experience in Fantasy and Behavior* (New York: Appleton-Century-Crofts, 1970), p. 570.

[87] Steven Connor, *Dumbstruck: A Cultural History of Ventriloquism* (Oxford: Oxford University Press, 2000), p. 5.

[88] V. S. Ramachandran, 'Consciousness and Body Image: Lessons from Phantom Limbs, Capgras Syndrome and Pain Asymbolia', *Philosophical Transactions of the Royal Society of London B*, 353 (1998), p. 1854.

[89] Gatens, *Imaginary Bodies*, p. 31.

[90] Gatens, *Imaginary Bodies*, p. 35.

> baseline experience was simply wrong. Our sense of physical embodiment did not come from the body itself. Several layers of brain stood in between, cobbling up from raw signals the reassuring illusion of solidity...[91]
>
> Even the intact body was itself a phantom, rigged up by neurons as a ready scaffold. The body was the only home we had, and even it was more a postcard than a place. We did not live in muscles and joints and sinews; we lived in the thought and image and memory of them. No direct sensation, only rumours and unreliable reports.
>
> And yet the ghost was real. People with lost feet, asked to tap their toes, lit up that part of the motor cortex responsible for walking. Even the motor cortex of intact people flashed, when they simply imagined walking... Sensing and moving, imagining and doing: phantoms bleeding one into the other.[92]

And in Vikram Chandra's *Sacred Games* an old intelligence agent, K. D. Yadav, suffering from Bonnet's syndrome, in which visual impairment leads to hallucinations, thinks to himself:

> We are built like this only, to see apparitions, to construct a vision of the world inside this lonely palace of bones, to live in this dream and be terrified of dying out of it, to suffer this nightmare made from impressions as if it were real. A rat's vision of reality is as real as mine, as yours, as ours. But we live and die and kill in this ghostly phantasmagoria of mirroring narratives.[93]

The imaginary body is that phantasmagoria: that place where the real and the remembered and the imagined merge.

VII

While many fictional plots are naming plots, all fictional plots are body plots: stories about birth and death, sexual desire, pain, ageing, struggle, eating, touching, excreting, blushing, speaking, seeing and being seen, feeling, becoming... *Elective Affinities* is about the coming together and the separation of bodies in processes that are likened to chemical or magnetic attraction, and about a single adulterous act that takes place with different partners in the body and the imagination. *Pale Fire* turns the metaphor of the king's two bodies into the basis of a story about mirrored, multiplied, and distorted selves, and, like *Robinson Crusoe*, it thematizes the fantasy about eating and being eaten that drives Kinbote and Crusoe deeper into their imaginary worlds. *Tristram Shandy* is a long joke about castration and the fear of sexuality, and *Clarissa* is the representation of a prolonged struggle to the death over its heroine's bodily integrity, but also of the reader's bodily response to her plight. Dante's *Inferno* and *Purgatorio* are centrally concerned with the bodily status and the bodily torments of the disembodied shades of the dead, and the *Paradiso* with the body reassembled at the resurrection. *Hamlet* is centrally about bodily corruption and sexual loathing, the bodily basis of the temperaments, and

[91] Richard Powers, *The Echo Maker* (London: William Heinemann, 2006), p. 258.
[92] Powers, *The Echo Maker*, p. 260.
[93] Vikram Chandra, *Sacred Games* (London: Faber, 2006), p. 318.

the positioning on a stage of the bodies of actors and of the characters who double them; and the novels of Dickens portray the daemonic energy that structures the family romance and drives the metabolic conversion of bodies into things. Bodies are named, and name themselves as an 'I'; names and pronouns settle on bodies, pass from one body to another, struggle to assert themselves in relation to bodies: to be named, to name oneself, is to find or take a place within a kinship network or a social order which is, at the most basic level, an order of bodies.

Yet bodies are never just bodies: they are a component of an assemblage made up of bodily sensation, bodily appearance, and bodily habitus; of the complex status of the person within kinship networks, cultural networks, social networks; of the fantasies through which the imaginary body works out its relation to other people, other bodies, to the bodies of the dead and its own, unimaginable death; and of the temporality that governs the passage of a body through a plot or a life. My body represents me, grounds my sense of being an embodied self, myself and no other, a self relative to other selves and the world I inhabit; the scale of my body is my measure of that world; and yet it is never simply identical with me. I am and am not my body, and that ambiguity highlights some of the problems that beset the concept of embodiment: that it supposes an immediacy of the body to consciousness rather than allowing for the complex mediations and disjunctions between them; that, as Strawson's argument makes clear, it reinscribes a dualism in the very act of seeking to overcome it (since 'something' is there to be embodied); and that it conceives of 'the body' as a general human form, whereas there is no body that is not marked by its sex, its age, its skin colour, its ability or disability: those specificities that map out a social place.[94]

Fictional bodies may be grafted onto the bodies of actors (in film or drama), or drawn as still or animated figures, or verbally described, or merely implied. All such descriptions or impersonations—all representations of fictional bodies—go directly to the social and moral force of character.

Let me take as an extended example the General Prologue to Chaucer's *Canterbury Tales*, which announces that the author will give a description of each of the twenty-nine pilgrims making up the company travelling from The Tabard in Southwark to Canterbury. He thinks it appropriate

> To telle yow al the condicioun
> Of ech of hem, so as it semed me,
> And whiche they weren and of what degree,
> And eek in what array that they were inne...[95]

Towards the end of the Prologue, he informs us that he has described

> Th'estaat, th'array, the nombre, and eek the cause
> Why that assembled was this compaigny... (716–7)

[94] Cf. Gatens, *Imaginary Bodies*, pp. vii–viii.

[95] Geoffrey Chaucer, 'The General Prologue', in *The Canterbury Tales*, ed. Jill Mann (London: Penguin, 2005), p. 4, ll. 38–41; further line references are given in the text.

The semantic value of 'condicioun' flows between the particularity of the pilgrims' characters and the generality of their social standing; and 'array' (which covers clothing but also weapons and jewellery) has to do with the correspondence (and at times the disjunction) between social condition and social display. 'Condicioun' is a term based in the doctrine of the estates (the three major social groupings of the Church, the nobility, and the peasantry), but it corresponds more closely with trade, profession, and vocation. Each condition has its own peculiar status, its own forms of knowledge and practice, forms of dress appropriate to it, in some cases its own tools of trade, and a particular bodily habitus.[96] This complex of features stands at the heart of each of the descriptions given in the General Prologue: an assemblage of characteristics to do with social standing, social occupation, the presentation of self, and bodily and facial appearance and habitus.

The description of the Merchant (ll. 270–84) balances most of these characteristics. We begin with a physical description: he has 'a forked berd', is dressed 'in mottelee' (cloth of mixed colour), and sits high on his horse—perhaps a metaphor for his attempt to elevate his status. He wears 'a Flaundrissh bevere hat', and his boots are tied 'faire and fetisly' (neatly). Then we move to his speech: he delivers his opinions 'ful solempnely', lets everyone know about the profit he makes, and wants the seas kept free for trade. Finally, we learn about his skill as a merchant, which includes making advantageous sales of foreign currency ('Wel koude he in eschaunge sheeldes selle'), and using his intelligence as well as his dignified demeanour so that no one knows that he operates on credit ('that he was in dette') because of the bargains he drives and his 'chevisaunce': his usurious money-lending. The portrait ends by applying the carefully platitudinous epithet 'worthy' to the merchant, and with the admission that the narrator doesn't know what his name is ('But sooth to seyn, I noot how men him calle').

The most complex descriptions are those that play with ambiguity of judgement. Let me single out three, of which the first is that of the Prioress (ll. 118–62). There are a number of indications of a tension between Madame Eglentine's calling as a nun and her worldly interests, from her devotion to matters of etiquette, her elegant (but not Parisian) French, her small dogs which she feeds on roast meat and white bread, her 'conscience and tendre herte' towards animals (but not, apparently, towards human beings), her pleated wimple and her coral rosary beads, and the ambiguous motto on her golden broach, 'Amor vincit omnia'. What I want to draw particular attention to is a series of negations that are made so insistently as to force a contrary sense. They have to do with eating:

> At mete wel ytaught was she withalle;
> She leet no morsel from hir lippes falle,
> Ne wette hir fingres in hir sauce depe.

[96] Elizabeth Fowler notes that 'in one direction, habitus alters the human body; in the other, it clings to the social person. These two roles of habitus provide the structure of the portrait'. Elizabeth Fowler, *Literary Character: The Human Figure in Early English Writing* (Ithaca: Cornell University Press, 2003), p. 67.

> Wel koude she carye a morsel and wel kepe
> That no drope ne fille [fell] upon hir brest;
> In curteisye was set ful muche hir lest [etiquette... delight].
> Hir over-lippe wiped she so clene,
> That in hir coppe ther was no ferthing [drop] sene
> Of grece, whan she dronken hadde hir draughte;
> Ful semely after hir mete she raughte [reached]...

The repetitions affirm what they deny: greasy lips, greed, the hungering body that the Prioress strives so nicely to negate.

In the case of the Monk and the Friar, there is no ambiguity of moral judgement (the Monk is worldly and self-indulgent, the Friar corrupt in his womanizing, his willingness to trade absolution for bribes, and his contempt for the poor and sycophancy towards the wealthy); rather, there is a tension between explicit (if ironically expressed) moral judgement and the vitality of the worlds built around these two men. For the Monk (ll. 165–207), it is a world consisting of the hunt, of horses, fish, fowl, greyhounds, and hares; the religious texts that would constrain him he dismisses as not worth 'a pulled [plucked] hen' or 'an oystre'; and he himself is glowing with life:

> His heed was balled [bald], that shoon as any glas,
> And eek his face, as he hadde been enoint;
> He was a lord ful fat and in good point [condition].
> Hise eyen stepe [eyes prominent], and rollinge in his heed,
> That stemed as a forneis of a leed...
> [That gleamed like a fire under a cauldron]
> He was nat pale as a forpined goost [tormented spirit].
> A fat swan loved he best of any roost...

As for the Friar (ll. 208–69), his vitality is that of a salesman: a convivial, easy-going man who can milk coins out of a penniless widow, give a pleasant penance to those who can pay, sing merrily in company, and who, when he is in song, has eyes that twinkle 'as doon the sterres [stars] in the frosty night'.

While each of the portraits in the General Prologue contains elements of moral character, physical appearance, and social status, three in particular are emphatic about bodily characteristics. The first is that of the Wife of Bath (ll. 445–76), whose portrait mixes together biographical details (her skill in cloth-making, her extensive pilgrimages); moral characterization (on the one hand, her insistence on taking precedence in church, and the way she is put 'out of alle charitee' if someone goes before her; on the other, her laughing and gossiping and her knowledge of 'remedies of love' and 'of that art the olde daunce'); and description of her fine clothing and of her face and body: she is somewhat deaf (the result of being beaten by her fifth husband, as we learn in the Prologue to her own tale);[97] her face is 'boold... and fair, and reed of hewe'; and she is 'gat-tothed' (gap-toothed), something she herself associates later with 'the preente of Seinte Venus seel' (the imprint

[97] 'The Wife of Bath's Prologue', in *The Canterbury Tales*, p. 233, ll. 634–6.

of St Venus's seal),[98] and broad-hipped. She is a formidable and fully sexualized being, and the General Prologue's portrait is only the beginning of the account she later gives of her own vivid sexuality.

The second is that of the Miller (ll. 545–66), a 'stout carl', 'ful big...of brawn and eek of bones', and a champion wrestler:

> He was short-sholdred, brood, a thicke knarre [a thick-set man];
> Ther was no dore that he nolde heve of harre [would not heave off its hinges],
> Or breke it at a renning with his heed.
> His berd as any sowe or fox was reed,
> And therto brood as though it were a spade.
> Upon the cop [tip] right of his nose he hade
> A werte [wart], and theron stood a tuft of heris [hairs],
> Reed as the bristles of a sowes eris [ears].
> His nosethirles [nostrils] blake were and wide;
> A swerd and bokeler bar he by his side.
> His mouth as greet was as a greet fourneis...

It's an astonishingly precise and detailed description of a kind of uncontrolled animal physicality, supplemented by an account of the Miller's dishonesty and his coarse storytelling. This is what his character is: bodily being, physical violence, and the sort of ethical disposition that (as we are supposed to know) goes with these things.

The animal references here—the sow and the fox—carry something of the iconographic force that the images of hare, goat, gelding, and mare do in the case of the Pardoner: that of sexualized representations of an animal vitality. In the third portrait that emphasizes physical characteristics, that of the Summoner (ll. 623–68), the simile spells it out: 'As hoot he was and lecherous as a sparwe [sparrow]'. Like the Miller, the Summoner is described in terms of facial flaws. He

> hadde a fir-reed [fiery-red] cherubinnes face,
> For saucefleem he was with eyen narwe...
> [he was covered with pimples and had narrow eyes]
> With scaled [scabby] browes blake and piled [scrubby] berd;
> Of his visage children were aferd.

No medication, even the most astringent, is available

> That him mighte helpen of his whelkes [pimples] white,
> Nor of the knobbes [lumps] sittinge on his chekes.
> Wel loved he garlek, oinons and eek lekes,
> And for to drinke strong win, reed as blood...

The second half of the portrait then describes the Summoner's particular habits of corruption: he will accept the bribe of a quart of wine to let some 'good felawe'

[98] 'The Wife of Bath's Prologue', p. 232, ll. 603–4.

keep his concubine for a year; he translates the 'ercedekenes curs' of excommunication into something that can be bought off with money; and he knows the secrets of the young people of the diocese and has power and influence over them. His moral ugliness, that is to say, matches his physical ugliness; he is defined at once by his office and by the abuse of that office.

The 'condiciouns' that the General Prologue describes are social offices embodied in individuals who are, to different degrees, physically particular. As a general principle, the 'straight' characters are described in ethical rather than physical terms: the Parson and the Plowman are given no particularizing description at all; the Knight is given only one line ('And of his port as meke as is a maide', l. 69). The more grotesque or comic or morally flawed a character is, the greater the extent to which he or she is physically individuated. 'Embodiment' in each of these portraits is something more, however, than a physical description of the body. It includes the face as both a part of and distinct from the body; and clothing, jewellery, weapons, and the horse and manner of riding are all included as dimensions of bodily being. From these particulars a bodily habitus is inferred which 'helps fit the body to the social person'.[99] Without that 'fixing', that assemblage of physical, moral, and social elements in the social office or social person, the bodies that we take to be the primary stuff of being are little more than random fragments—a wart, gaps between the teeth, a carefully wiped upper lip. 'Social persons,' writes Elizabeth Fowler, 'have a kind of creative ontological priority over the bodies that fiction presents as prior to them.'[100] And over the bodies that we are.

Only one character is not described in the General Prologue: Chaucer himself. Yet he is present as one of the pilgrims, and it is from the perspective of his judgements ('a worthy man withalle'; 'a good felawe') that we view the other travellers. When he does eventually make an appearance, in Fragment VII (Group B^2), as something other than the narrating 'I' casually introduced in line 20 of the General Prologue, it is to be invited by 'oure Hoost', Harry Bailly, to tell a story of his own—which he does so badly, with the tale of 'Sir Thopas', that he is forced by the Host to stop telling it ('Mine eris aken of thy drasty speche!'; 'thy drasty ryming is nat worth a tord' [turd]);[101] he then offers instead (since he doesn't know any other tales in verse) 'a litel thing in prose', the wearisome 'Tale of Melibee'. Chaucer, in short, is the worst storyteller in the group. But it is at the moment when he is invited by Harry Bailly to tell a story that Chaucer is directly, and sarcastically, described: 'What man artow?' says our Host:

> Thow lookest as thow woldest finde an hare,
> For evere upon the ground I se thee stare.[102]

[99] Fowler, *Literary Character*, p. 11.
[100] Fowler, *Literary Character*, p. 70.
[101] Chaucer, 'The Thopas–Melibee Link', in *The Canterbury Tales*, p. 509, ll. 923, 930.
[102] Chaucer, 'The Prioress–Thopas Link', in *The Canterbury Tales*, p. 500, ll. 696–7.

Harry Bailly then jokes to the others about Chaucer's girth and perhaps about his sexuality:

> He in the wast [waist] is shape as wel as I;
> This were a popet [a dainty little person] in an arm t'enbrace
> For any woman smal [slender] and fair of face! (ll. 700–2)

Finally, he notes that Chaucer is unsociable ('For unto no wight dooth he daliaunce', l. 704) and that there is something otherworldly about him:

> He semeth elvvish by his contenaunce. (l. 703)

'Elvvish' suggests the daemonic other, the 'associated' and uncanny figure of the paredros: the familiar who accompanies a group, 'the third who walks always beside you',[103] the figured absence from which all narrative figuration emerges.

VIII

Nowhere is the centrality of bodies to fictional plots more striking than in those media—theatre, film and television, comic books, manga, digital games—in which the visibility of real or represented bodies constitutes the very stuff of the medium and the primary point of identification of characters. Their texts are made out of bodies positioned in space, bodies that touch each other, that look at each other, pass each other by, embrace or strike each other, seek to destroy each other or to possess each other; bodies clothed and unclothed, made up and coiffed, twirling a cane and tripping over their own feet, balanced and unbalanced, in control or out of control, torn apart by bullets or by cars...

In the theatre and the cinema, those bodies are at once the bodies of the actor and the body of the character: the actor is simultaneously herself and another, imaginary person, the two fused into a single yet, paradoxically, divided entity. Theatrical bodies are 'immediately' present to us (we could, in theory, touch them, although in fact an invisible mediation separates them from us); cinematic bodies are made of light and shadow, fictions of presence constructed through multiple takes, the editing of those takes into sequences, the use of body doubles, digital effects which further manipulate the filmed shots—a whole complex machinery of magic. Yet these bodies engage us with a kind of immediacy. Lesley Stern poses as follows the question of how this happens:

> The argument is sometimes made that in theatre, in live performance, actors are able to generate and transmit energy because the audience occupies the same space-time continuum as the actors, whereas the cinema is struggling always to create and sustain an illusion of presence. In fact the argument can be made that the audience in live

[103] T. S. Eliot, 'The Waste Land', in *Collected Poems 1909–1962* (London: Faber and Faber, 1963), p. 77, l. 359.

> theatre needs to fictionalise the solid three-dimensional bodies of the actors in order to enter into the dramatic fiction, to effect a performative exchange... The challenge is to understand *how* the body in cinema can produce affects and transmit energy when it is an unreal or fictional body: always figured out, spatialised by the camera, lighting, framing, cutting, and temporalised too—cut up, dispersed, faded in, speeded up, slowed down.
>
> We can approach this conundrum by remembering that even though the cinematic body is insubstantial, ephemeral, it is also indexical of the real, and it is in this tension (between the indexical and the fictional) that mimetic engagement is generated.[104]

This is a version of the tension that I identified in Chapter 1 between thinking of characters as pieces of writing or imaging, and thinking of them as person-like entities; and what I identified in Chapter 2 as the challenge 'of holding together in a single frame at once the ontological discontinuity which allows us to distinguish a representational act from other acts, and the ontological continuity that binds them to each other'. In cinema that tension is concretely realized in the ontological hybridity of the filmed body: when I watch *Blade Runner* I see the embodied persons of Harrison Ford, Sean Young, Rutger Hauer, and so on;[105] but I read them as Rick Deckard, Rachael, Roy Batty, and other named and unnamed characters.[106]

These bodies put into play, by way of the opposition of human persons to replicants, a direct problematization of the distinction between persons and fictional characters. When Zhora is killed by Deckard we witness the body of a woman, hunted down by a man with a gun, lying lifeless and bloody amongst smashed plate glass. It *looks* like an ugly and brutal murder; yet in one sense it is not, because Zhora is a replicant, a machine built for service, a non-person. At the level of story this death is merely the elimination of a bioengineered entity—'it', as Deckard refers to Rachael when he discovers that she is a replicant—that happens to look and behave like a human being. But the body that is killed—or rather, the body that is killed in simulation—is that of a human person.[107] The actress Joanna Cassidy at once represents and, necessarily, fails to represent the non-personhood of a replicant: there *is no difference* between the simulated bodies of the replicants

[104] Lesley Stern, 'From the Other Side of Time', in *The Cinema of Michael Powell: International Perspectives on an English Film-Maker*, ed. Ian Christie and Andrew Moor (London: BFI, 2005), p. 45.

[105] Ridley Scott, dir., *Blade Runner* (Theatrical Release, 1982; Director's Cut, 1992; Final Cut, 2007). The 1981 version of the screenplay by Hampton Fancher and David Peoples can be found at: <http://www.dailyscript.com/scripts/blade-runner_shooting.html>, and a reconstruction of the final shooting script, including variant readings of the Workprint, Original International Theatrical Release, and Director's Cut versions (but not of the Final Cut, the only version over which Scott had full control), at <http://www.brmovie.com/Downloads/Docs/BR_Scripts.htm>. Both accessed 28 May 2013.

[106] Jean-Louis Comolli argues that it is not that the body of the actor appears to us as an attribute of the character, but rather that the character 'has for us the value of an attribute of the actor's body': 'first to appear will be the body, the body as an *empty mask*, and the character will only appear later and bit by bit as effects of this mask'. Jean-Louis Comolli, 'Historical Fiction: A Body Too Much', trans. Ben Brewster, *Screen* 19: 2 (1978), p. 43.

[107] 'The body filmed is not an imaginary body, even if the fiction refers it to some purely invented character and whatever the phantasies for which it is the support.' Comolli, 'Historical Fiction', p. 42.

and 'real' human bodies; at the level of the body (real or represented) there is no difference between the fictions and the persons.[108]

The character Pris is a particularly rich vehicle for reflection on the hybridity of the cinematic body. Carrying less metaphysical baggage than Roy Batty, who physically resembles Blake's Satan and indeed, in the scene with the eye-maker Chew, (mis)quotes Blake's *America* ('Fiery the angels fell. Deep thunder roll'd/Around their shores... burning with the fires of Orc'),[109] or than Zhora, 'Miss Salome', the castrating snake-dancer 'trained for an Off-World kick-murder squad', Pris is played for the menacing ambiguity of an animated marionette. The key scene takes place in the rooms of J. F. Sebastian, a genetic designer who lives with his mechanical dolls. As Deckard enters, gun in hand, Pris, dressed in high-punk, with bedraggled hair and blackened eyes, sits mute and motionless amongst the dolls and mannequins, her head covered by a transparent veil. And then, with a violent scream, she comes to life, somersaulting through the air to land on Deckard's head, clamping it hard between her thighs and trying to break his neck. When Deckard shoots her, she dies screaming and flailing like a broken machine.

That somersault, as Stern points out, repeats an earlier one in Sebastian's apartment, when Pris demonstrates why she's not a computer by doing a quick, easy back-flip. Her body here 'is a body that simultaneously moves (through human agency) and is moved (mechanically, through cinematic means)'.[110] The uncanny force of that later somersault has to do at once with the effect of repetition (the reappearance of the same as other) and with the play between the mechanical and the organic; the uncanny, Freud wrote, is triggered by doubling, by repetition, and by 'waxwork figures, ingeniously constructed dolls and automata'.[111] We might think of Kleist's essay on the puppet, which, affected neither by the force of gravity nor by self-consciousness, offers an image of a superhuman grace, akin to that of the gods[112]

[108] Michael Wood makes a related point about the fact that 'no image on the screen can be entirely untrue'. When we watch a dream sequence (his example is a flash-forward in Visconti's *Death in Venice*) its modal status cannot simply be undercut as it could in a novel: 'You see what you see'. Noel King, '"Giving Time to Images": Michael Wood on Film,' *Metro Magazine* 135 (2002), p. 135.

[109] The lines from Blake's *America a Prophecy* are:

> Fiery the Angels rose, & as they rose deep thunder roll'd
> Around their shores: indignant burning with the fires of Orc
> And Bostons Angel cried aloud as they flew thro' the dark night.

William Blake, *The Complete Poetry and Prose of William Blake*, ed. David V. Erdman (rev. edn, Berkeley: University of California Press, 1982), plate 11, ll. 1–3, p. 55. Cf. Christiane Gerblinger, '"Fiery the Angels Fell": America, Regeneration, and Ridley Scott's *Blade Runner*', *Australasian Journal of American Studies* 21: 1 (2002), pp. 19–30.

[110] Lesley Stern, 'I Think, Sebastian, Therefore... I Somersault: Film and the Uncanny', *Paradoxa* 3: 3–4 (1997), p. 352.

[111] Sigmund Freud, 'The Uncanny', *Standard Edition* XVII, p. 226; cited in Stern, 'I Think, Sebastian, Therefore... I Somersault', p. 353.

[112] '... grace will be most purely present in the human frame that has either no consciousness or an infinite amount of it, which is to say either in a marionette or in a god'. Heinrich von Kleist, *Selected Writings*, ed. and trans. David Constantine (London: Dent, 1997), p. 416; Heinrich von Kleist, *Berliner Abendblätter* I, *Sämtliche Werke*, II/7, ed. Roland Reuß and Peter Staengle (Basel and Frankfurt am Main: Stroemfeld, 1997), pp. 330–1.

(Victoria Nelson writes of the way the 'automated Neoplatonic daemons of puppet, robot, cyborg, and virtual entity... still carry for us, below the level of consciousness, that uncanny aura the unacknowledged "holy" characteristically assumes in a secular context').[113] The puppet's exemplary otherness has the form of 'a fiction of wholeness that the subject will strive to resemble',[114] a *thing* that the self will always, necessarily, fail to become. It may thus be the case that the structure of human subjectivity must be thought, as Barbara Johnson puts it, in terms of our ability to be or to be like a thing, that 'identity is an object... without which there would be no subject'.[115] The paradox of the replicant is that it models and undoes the privilege of the human.

Blade Runner relentlessly thematizes vision and its relation to personal identity: the Voight-Kampff test administered to subjects to test whether they are human or replicant works by measuring pupil dilation in response to emotionally laden questions, and the film's opening sequence, cutting from a view of Hades to the testing of Leon, is mediated by the close-up of an eye, possibly, but not certainly, the eye of Holden, the blade runner who is administering the test. That scene ends with Leon murdering Holden ('My mother?... Let me tell you about my mother'), and it is repeated (with slight variations in the dialogue) as a 'movie' when a recording of it is screened in Bryant's office. The optical device that measures pupil dilation and screens it on a monitor is later repeated in the device (the Esper machine) with which a photograph from Leon's room is analysed into three dimensions. The flat photograph shows only an empty room with a curved elbow at one side and a convex mirror (side-lit, in a manner that recalls Van Eyck or Vermeer)[116] at the rear; scanned and converted (impossibly!) into three dimensions, it reveals perspectives not available in the photograph, including an image of a sleeping woman reflected in the mirror and then a close-up of her face. Two things happen here. First, Deckard follows an indexical trace of the real through the photograph's registration of a moment of frozen time; the photograph functions here as evidence and has the phenomenological structure of the clue. Second, in the successive scans of the photograph its temporality is transformed: 'This inert object, a mere trace of the past, becomes multidimensional and is suddenly possessed of the present-tense modality of cinema. Deckard issues commands like a film director ("Track right... Now pull back...") and the frozen moment of the photograph is granted a new temporality.'[117]

The photograph nails down identity by linking it indexically to a past. What gives Rachael the assurance of being human is her memories, which are anchored in photographs of herself as a child with her mother. This is the classically Lockean view of the continuity of personhood through time: '... as far as... consciousness can be

[113] Victoria Nelson, *The Secret Life of Puppets* (Cambridge, MA: Harvard University Press, 2001), pp. 30–1; cited in Barbara Johnson, *Persons and Things* (Cambridge, MA: Harvard University Press, 2008), p. 86.

[114] Johnson, *Persons and Things*, pp. 58–9.

[115] Johnson, *Persons and Things*, p. 181.

[116] Scott Bukatman, *Blade Runner*, BFI Modern Classics (London: BFI, 1997), p. 46.

[117] Bukatman, *Blade Runner*, p. 46.

extended backwards to any past Action or Thought, so far reaches the Identity of that *Person*; it is the same *self* now it was then; and 'tis by the same *self* with this present one that now reflects on it, that that Action was done'.[118] But Locke's account allows for the possibility of discontinuity of identity: in cases of forgetting, 'our consciousness being interrupted, and we losing sight of our past *selves*, doubts are raised whether we are the same thinking thing; *i.e.* the same substance or no'.[119] This is the converse of Parfit's case of the Replica created by scanning every cell of my body and recreating a self that is psychologically continuous with me: for Rachael, the terrible doubt created by Deckard is that her memories are not her own memories, that the photographs are fakes, and thus that she is not continuous with herself.

But it is not only Rachael's identity that is called into question: the figure of the replicant undermines the grounding of all human identity either in memory or in the indexical link between representation and the body. Elissa Marder suggests that the 'memories' that Deckard narrates to Rachael, telling her they belong not to her but to Tyrell's niece, may, in fact, be his own: Rachael is not, she suggests, recognizing the memories, because she has never had them.[120] Whether or not this is the case, it is certainly true that after this scene Deckard lingers over his own photographs on the piano, which are disparate and which may equally be unrelated to him. Is there a picture of his mother here? The only woman we see clearly is from a different era, and in any case, in *Blade Runner* 'the figure of the mother refuses to guarantee that one is born, and not made, human'.[121] The film's open secret is that Deckard himself is or may be a replicant. Scott Bukatman stresses its ambiguity about this, whereas for Slavoj Žižek it is precisely Deckard's replicant status that forces us to see the replicant not as a simulation of the human but as its paradigm: not only my body but my most personal memories belong to the Other, and 'it is only when, at the level of the enunciated content, I assume my replicant-status, that, at the level of enunciation, I become a truly human subject'.[122] That possibility is then, in turn, undercut: knowing the term of their own mortality, replicants 'are ultimately the impossible fantasy-formation of us human mortals: the fantasy of a being conscious of itself qua Thing...'[123]

The still photograph gives us, supposedly, a still life, a trace of frozen time: the memory of who we are. Cinema arranges still photographs in sequence to produce the illusion of movement and of presence. As Deckard holds in his hands the picture of Rachael with her mother, the image—for just a moment, and ever so slightly—flickers within the frame. Fiction, illusion, magic, it comes to a kind of life.

[118] John Locke, *An Essay Concerning Human Understanding*, ed. Peter H. Nidditch (Oxford: Clarendon Press, 1975), Book II, ch. 27, §9, p. 335.

[119] Locke, *An Essay Concerning Human Understanding*, Book II, ch. 27, §10, p. 336.

[120] Elissa Marder, '*Blade Runner*'s Moving Still', *Camera Obscura* 27 (1991), p. 99.

[121] Marder, '*Blade Runner*'s Moving Still', p. 105.

[122] Slavoj Žižek, *Tarrying with the Negative: Kant, Hegel, and the Critique of Ideology* (Durham, NC: Duke University Press, 1993), p. 41.

[123] Žižek, *Tarrying with the Negative*, p. 42.

IX

'Nothing tells memories from ordinary moments; only afterwards do they claim remembrance on account of their scars.'[124] Paris has been destroyed by a global nuclear war. The survivors live underground in prison camps, and the victors rule over a civilization of rubble. One man, the one about whom this story is told, is chosen for an experiment which sends him through time, since that is the only path to survival—chosen because of the strength of his obsessive but unclear childhood memory of a moment on the observation deck at Orly Airport: he remembers a woman, a moment of shock, a death. He travels back in time; he meets a woman, recognizes her; they meet each time he returns, like a ghost (this is what she calls him), a *revenant*. After their last meeting he is sent into the future, to a flourishing but alien civilization; he is given a source of energy which will allow his ruined world to be rebuilt. Then, he knows, having accomplished his task, he will be executed. Travellers from the future appear to him and offer to take him with them; instead, he asks to be allowed to return to the past, to the 'twice-lived fragment of time' that he remembers. He is on the observation deck at Orly; he sees the woman, and runs towards her; an official from the camp has trailed him to the past, and he realizes, as he dies, that there is no way out of time; that this haunted moment he had been granted to see as a child was the moment of his own death.

The action takes place through a filmed sequence of still photographs, succeeding each other at different speeds, sometimes by means of a fade or a dissolve, and with the film camera at times moving in on an image or panning back. There is a voice-over narration, and some whispered dialogue in German when he is being injected with the drugs that send him backwards and forwards in time. There is an occasional musical soundtrack, and the beating of his heart. At one moment, and only one moment, the still photos of the woman lying in bed, succeeding each other more urgently, suddenly and briefly come to life—to *cinematic* life—as the woman smiles and her eyes blink.[125]

The film takes place in linear time; the story takes place in the reversible time which is proper only to memory, to the projection of a future, and to textuality.[126]

The linear succession of images (the film is called a 'photo-roman') generates a story through intersecting layers of time. We see a character emerge, as figure from ground: 'this was the man whose story we are now telling'; and then another. In the movement of her face, we see (but this is, perhaps, first of all her lover's vision, our proxy in the represented world) the moment of animation that gives her life—as we witness, at the film's end, as he himself does, the moment that finally removes him from his textual existence.

[124] Chris Marker, dir., *La Jetée* (1962).

[125] Vivian Sobchack notes that the suddenness of this blink 'speaks more to surprise at an unexpected and radical shift in the ontological status of the image and our relation to it than to a more superficial narrative or formal surprise'. Vivian Sobchack, *Carnal Thoughts: Embodiment and Moving Image Culture* (Berkeley: University of California Press, 2004), p. 145.

[126] Cf. John Frow, *Time and Commodity Culture* (Oxford: Clarendon Press, 1997), p. 229.

X

To be a character is to have a textual existence and, momentarily, to appear to exist beyond it.

To be a person is to inhabit a physical and fantasmatic body, to wear the mask which is truly your face, to speak with the voices of others—to be defined at your very heart by the non-personal; and, at any moment, to appear to have a life that exists beyond it.

Bibliography

Aarseth, Espen J., 'Nonlinearity and Literary Theory', in George P. Landow (ed.), *Hyper/Text/Theory* (Baltimore: Johns Hopkins University Press, 1994), 51–86.

Aarseth, Espen J., *Cybertext: Perspectives on Ergodic Literature* (Baltimore: Johns Hopkins University Press, 1997).

Abe, Kōbō, *The Face of Another*, trans. E. Dale Saunders (Harmondsworth: Penguin, 1972).

Aczel, Richard, 'Hearing Voices in Narrative Texts', *New Literary History* 29: 3 (1998), 467–500.

Adams, Andrew A., 'Virtual Sex with Child Avatars', in Charles Wankel and Shaun Malleck (eds), *Emerging Ethical Issues of Life in Virtual Worlds* (North Carolina: Information Age Publishing, 2010), 55–72.

Adams, Ann Jensen, *Public Faces and Private Identities in Seventeenth-Century Holland: Portraiture and the Production of Community* (Cambridge: Cambridge University Press, 2009).

Adorno, Theodor W., 'The Essay as Form', in *Notes to Literature*, vol. 1, trans. Shierry Weber Nicholsen (New York: Columbia University Press, 1991), 3–23.

Agamben, Giorgio, *Stanzas: Word and Phantasm in Western Culture*, trans. Ronald L. Martinez (Minneapolis: University of Minnesota Press, 1993).

Agamben, Giorgio, *Remnants of Auschwitz: The Witness and the Archive*, trans. Daniel Heller-Roazen (New York: Zone Books, 2002).

Agamben, Giorgio, 'What is an Apparatus?', in *What is an Apparatus and Other Essays*, trans. David Kishik and Stefan Pedatella (Stanford: Stanford University Press, 2009), 1–24.

Agamben, Giorgio, *The Sacrament of Language: An Archaeology of the Oath*, trans. Adam Kotsko (Stanford: Stanford University Press, 2011).

Agnew, Jean-Christophe, *Worlds Apart: The Market and the Theater in Anglo-American Thought, 1550–1750* (Cambridge: Cambridge University Press, 1986).

Alford, Richard D., *Naming and Identity: A Cross-Cultural Study of Personal Naming Practices* (New Haven: HRAF Press, 1988).

Althusser, Louis, *Lenin and Philosophy and Other Essays*, trans. Ben Brewster (New York: Monthly Review Press, 1971).

Altman, Rick, *The American Film Musical* (Bloomington: Indiana University Press, 1987).

Andersen, Peter Bogh, *A Theory of Computer Semiotics: Semiotic Approaches to Construction and Assessment of Computer Systems* (Cambridge: Cambridge University Press, 1990).

Anon, 'Note: What We Talk About When We Talk About Persons: The Language of a Legal Fiction', *Harvard Law Review* 114: 6 (2001), 1745–68.

Anscombe, G. E. M., 'The First Person,' in Cassam (ed.), *Self-Knowledge*, 140–59.

Anzieu, Didier, *The Skin Ego*, trans. Chris Turner (New Haven: Yale University Press, 1989).

Apperley, Tom, *Gaming Rhythms: Play and Counterplay from the Situated to the Global*, Theory on Demand #6 (Amsterdam: Institute of Networked Cultures, 2010).

Apter, Emily, 'Technics of the Subject: The Avatar-Drive', *Postmodern Culture* 18: 2 (2008), n.p.

Apuleius, 'On the God of Socrates', in *Apuleius: Rhetorical Works*, trans. Stephen Harrison, John Hilton, and Vincent Hunink, ed. Stephen Harrison (Oxford: Oxford University Press, 2001), 185–216.

Arcand, Bernard, *The Jaguar and the Anteater: Pornography Degree Zero*, trans. Wayne Grady (London: Verso, 1993).

Aristotle, *Poetics (De Poetica)*, trans. Ingram Bywater, in *The Basic Works of Aristotle*, ed. Richard McKeon (New York: Random House, 1941).

Arnott, Geoffrey, 'Introduction', in *Menander*, vol. 1, Loeb Classical Library (Cambridge, MA: Harvard University Press, 1979), xiii–xlv.

Auerbach, Erich, *Mimesis: The Representation of Reality in Western Literature*, trans. Willard R. Trask (Princeton: Princeton University Press, 1953).

Auerbach, Erich, *Dante: Poet of the Secular World*, trans. Ralph Manheim (Chicago: University of Chicago Press, 1961).

Auerbach, Erich, 'Figura', trans. Ralph Manheim, in *Scenes from the Drama of European Literature* (Minneapolis: University of Minnesota Press, 1984), 11–76.

Augé, Marc, *Non-Places: Introduction to an Anthropology of Supermodernity*, trans. John Howe (London: Verso, 1995).

Austen, Jane, *Emma*, ed. Stephen M. Parrish (New York: Norton Critical Edition, 2000).

Babb, Lawrence, *The Elizabethan Malady: A Study of Melancholia in English Literature from 1580 to 1642* (East Lansing: Michigan State College Press, 1951).

Badiou, Alain, 'A Philosophical Task: To be Contemporaries of Pessoa', in *Handbook of Inaesthetics*, trans. Alberto Toscano (Stanford: Stanford University Press, 2005), 36–45.

Bakhtin, Mikhail, *Problems of Dostoevsky's Poetics*, ed. and trans. Caryl Emerson (Minneapolis: University of Minnesota Press, 1984).

Bal, Mieke, *Narratology: Introduction to the Theory of Narrative* (2nd edn, Toronto: University of Toronto Press, 1997).

Bally, Charles, 'Le style indirect libre en français moderne I', *Germanisch-Romanische Monatsschrift* 4 (1912), 549–56.

Balzac, Honoré de, 'Avant Propos', in *La Comédie Humaine* I, Bibliothèque de la Pléïade (Paris: Gallimard, 1951), 7–20.

Banfield, Ann, *Unspeakable Sentences: Narration and Representation in the Language of Fiction* (Boston: Routledge & Kegan Paul, 1982).

Banfield, Ann, 'L'écriture et le Non-Dit', *Diacritics* 21: 4 (1991), 20–31.

Barker, Francis, *The Tremulous Private Body: Essays on Subjection* (London: Methuen, 1984).

Barraud, Cécile, Coppet, Daniel de, Iteanu, André, and Jamous, Raymond, *Of Relations and the Dead: Four Societies Viewed from the Angle of their Exchanges*, trans. Stephen J. Suffern (Oxford: Berg, 1994).

Barthes, Roland, *S/Z*, trans. Richard Howard (New York: Hill and Wang, 1974).

Barthes, Roland, *Sade/Fourier/Loyola*, trans. Richard Miller (Berkeley: University of California Press, 1976).

Bateson, Gregory, *Steps to an Ecology of Mind* (Chicago: University of Chicago Press, 2000).

Batman, Stephen, *Batman upon Bartholme, His Book De Proprietatibus* (London, 1582).

Becker, George J. (ed.), *Documents of Modern Literary Realism* (Princeton: Princeton University Press, 1963).

Belting, Hans, *Likeness and Presence: A History of the Image before the Era of Art*, trans. Edmund Jephcott (Chicago: University of Chicago Press, 1994).

Benjamin, Walter, *The Origins of German Tragic Drama*, trans. John Osborne (London: New Left Books, 1977).

Benson, Susan, 'Injurious Names: Naming, Disavowal, and Recuperation in Contexts of Slavery and Emancipation', in vom Bruck and Bodenhorn (eds), *The Anthropology of Names and Naming*, 178–99.

Bentham, Jeremy, *Principles of Penal Law, The Works of Jeremy Bentham*, vol. 1, ed. John Bowring (Edinburgh: William Tait, 1843).
Benveniste, Émile, *Problèmes de linguistique générale* (Paris: Gallimard, 1966).
Benveniste, Émile, *Problems in General Linguistics*, trans. Mary Elizabeth Meek (Coral Gables, FL: University of Miami Press, 1971).
Berenson, Bernard, 'The Effigy and the Portrait', in *Aesthetics and History* (London: Constable, 1950), 188–9.
Bergstrom, Janet, 'Alternation, Segmentation, Hypnosis: Interview with Raymond Bellour', *Camera Obscura* 1–2 (1979), 70–103.
Bernabò-Brea, L., *Menandro e il teatro greco nelle terracotte liparesi* (Genova: SAGEP, 1981).
Bernstein, Charles, *The Sophist* (Los Angeles: Sun & Moon Press, 1987; rpt. Cambridge: Salt Publishing, 2004).
Bersani, Leo, *Marcel Proust: The Fictions of Life and Art* (New York: Oxford University Press, 1965).
Bersani, Leo, *A Future for Astyanax: Character and Desire in Literature* (Boston: Little, Brown & Co., 1976).
Berthaud, Jacques, 'Shandeism and Sexuality', in Myer (ed.), *Laurence Sterne: Riddles and Mysteries*, 24–38.
Bible: Authorized King James Version (Oxford: Oxford University Press, 1997).
Bickerton, Derek, 'Modes of Interior Monologue: A Formal Definition', *Modern Language Quarterly* 28: 2 (1967), 229–39.
Biocca, Frank, 'The Cyborg's Dilemma: Progressive Embodiment in Virtual Environments', *Journal of Computer-Mediated Communication* 3: 2 (1997), n.p.
Black's Law Dictionary (4th edn, St. Paul, MN: West Publishing Company, 1968).
Blackwell, Mark (ed.), *The Secret Life of Things: Animals, Objects, and It-Narratives in Eighteenth-Century England* (Lewisburg: Bucknell University Press, 2007).
Blake, William, *The Complete Poetry and Prose of William Blake*, ed. David V. Erdman (rev. edn, Berkeley: University of California Press, 1982).
Blanchot, Maurice, 'Everyday Speech', *Yale French Studies* 73 (1987), 12–20.
Bliss, Jane, *Naming and Namelessness in Medieval Romance* (Cambridge: D.S. Brewer, 2008).
Bloch, Howard, *Etymologies and Genealogies: A Literary Anthropology of the French Middle Ages* (Chicago: University of Chicago Press, 1983).
Bloch, Maurice, 'Teknonymy and the Evocation of the "Social" among the Zafimaniry of Madagascar', in vom Bruck and Bodenhorn (eds), *The Anthropology of Names and Naming*, 98–114.
Boas, Franz, *Handbook of American Indian Languages*, vol. 1 (Washington: Smithsonian Institution, Bureau of American Ethnology, 1911).
Boehrer, Bruce, 'Animal Characters and the Deconstruction of Character', *PMLA* 124: 2 (2009), 542–7.
Boehrer, Bruce, *Animal Characters: Nonhuman Beings in Early Modern Literature* (Philadelphia: University of Pennsylvania Press, 2010).
Boellstorff, Tom, *Coming of Age in Second Life: An Anthropologist Explores the Virtually Human* (Princeton: Princeton University Press, 2008).
Boethius, Anicius Manlius Severinus, 'A Treatise Against Eutyches and Nestorius', in *Boethius: The Theological Tractates and The Consolation of Philosophy*, trans. H. F. Stewart and E. K. Rand, Loeb Classical Library (Cambridge, MA: Harvard University Press, 1968), 73–127.
Boldy, Steven, *The Novels of Julio Cortázar* (Cambridge: Cambridge University Press, 1980).
Borges, Jorge Luis, *Collected Fictions*, trans. Andrew Hurley (New York: Viking, 1998).

Borges, Jorge Luis, *The Total Library: Non-Fiction 1922–1986*, ed. Eliot Weinberger, trans. Esther Allen, Suzanne Jill Levine, and Eliot Weinberger (London: Penguin, 2007).

Bourdieu, Pierre, *The Logic of Practice*, trans. Richard Nice (Stanford: Stanford University Press, 1990).

Boureau, Alain, 'Droit et Théologie au XIIIe siècle', *Annales. Histoire, Sciences Sociales* 47: 6 (1992), 1113–25.

Boyd, Brian, *Vladimir Nabokov: The American Years* (Princeton: Princeton University Press, 1991).

Boyd, Brian, *Nabokov's* Pale Fire*: The Magic of Artistic Discovery* (Princeton: Princeton University Press, 1999).

Bradley, A. C., *Shakespearean Tragedy* (1904; rpt. London: Macmillan, 1962).

Breckenridge, James D., *Likeness: A Conceptual History of Ancient Portraiture* (Evanston, IL: Northwestern University Press, 1968).

Bright, Timothy, *A Treatise of Melancholy. Containing the Causes Thereof, And Reasons of the strange effects it untieth in our minds and bodies: with the Physick Cure, and spiritual consolation for such as have thereto adjoined afflicted Conscience* (1586; rpt. London: William Stansby, 1615).

Brown, Beverley, 'A Feminist Interest in Pornography: Some Modest Proposals', *m/f* 5–6 (1981), 5–18.

Brown, Norman O., *Love's Body* (1966; rpt. Berkeley: University of California Press, 1990).

Brown, P. G. McC., 'Masks, Names and Characters in New Comedy', *Hermes* 115: 2 (1987), 181–202.

Brown, Peter, *The Body and Society: Men, Women, and Sexual Renunciation in Early Christianity* (New York: Columbia University Press, 1988).

Bruner, Jerome, 'Life as Narrative', *Social Research* 54 (1987), 11–32.

Bruyère, Jean de La, *Les Caractères ou les moeurs de ce siècle, Oeuvres Complètes*, ed. Julien Benda, Bibliothèque de la Pléïade (Paris: Gallimard, 1951).

Bruyère, Jean de La, *Characters*, trans. Henri van Laun (Oxford: Oxford University Press, 1963).

Bühler, Karl, *Theory of Language: The Representational Function of Language*, trans. Donald Fraser Goodwin (Amsterdam: J. Benjamins, 1990).

Bukatman, Scott, *Blade Runner*, BFI Modern Classics (London: BFI, 1997).

Burn, Andrew, and Schott, Gareth, 'Heavy Hero or Digital Dummy? Multimodal Player–Avatar Relations in *Final Fantasy 7*', *Visual Communication* 3: 2 (2004), 213–33.

Burstyn, Varda (ed.), *Women against Censorship* (Vancouver: Douglas & McIntyre, 1985).

Burton, Robert, *The Anatomy of Melancholy* (London: J.M. Dent, 1932).

Butler, Judith, *Precarious Life: The Powers of Mourning and Violence* (London: Verso, 2004).

Butor, Michel, *Les oeuvres d'art imaginaires chez Proust* (London: Athlone Press, 1964).

Bynum, Caroline Walker, *The Resurrection of the Body in Western Christianity, 200–1336* (New York: Columbia University Press, 1995).

Callon, Michel, 'Some Elements of a Sociology of Translation: Domestication of the Scallops and the Fishermen of St Brieuc Bay', in John Law (ed.), *Power, Action and Belief: A New Sociology of Knowledge* (London: Routledge & Kegan Paul, 1986), 196–223.

Caplan, Jane, and Torpey, John, 'Introduction', in Jane Caplan and John Torpey (eds), *Documenting Individual Identity: The Development of State Practices in the Modern World* (Princeton: Princeton University Press, 2001), 1–12.

Carrithers, Michael, Collins, Steven, and Lukes, Steven (eds), *The Category of the Person: Anthropology, Philosophy, History* (Cambridge: Cambridge University Press, 1985).

Cassam, Quassim (ed.), *Self-Knowledge* (Oxford: Oxford University Press, 1994).

Castle, Terry, *Clarissa's Ciphers: Meaning and Disruption in Richardson's 'Clarissa'* (Ithaca: Cornell University Press, 1982).

Cave, Terence, *Recognitions: A Study in Poetics* (New York: Oxford University Press, 1988).

Cervantes Saavedra, Miguel de, *The Adventures of Don Quixote*, trans. J. M. Cohen (Harmondsworth: Penguin, 1950).

Cervantes Saavedra, Miguel de, *El Ingenioso Hidalgo Don Quijote de la Mancha, Obras Completas*, ed. Angel Valbuena Prat (Madrid: Aguilar, 1970).

Cetina, Karin Knorr, 'Sociality with Objects: Social Relations in Postsocial Knowledge Societies', *Theory, Culture and Society* 14: 1 (1997), 1–30.

Chandra, Vikram, *Sacred Games* (London: Faber, 2006).

Chang, Hui-Chin, and Holt, G. Richard, 'A Chinese Perspective on Face as Inter-Relational Concern', in Ting-Toomey (ed.), *The Challenge of Facework*, 95–132.

Chatman, Seymour, *Story and Discourse: Narrative Structure in Fiction and Film* (Ithaca: Cornell University Press, 1978).

Chaucer, Geoffrey, *The Canterbury Tales*, ed. Jill Mann (London: Penguin, 2005).

Chrétien de Troyes, *The Complete Romances of Chrétien de Troyes*, trans. David Staines (Bloomington: Indiana University Press, 1990).

Chrétien de Troyes, *Le Roman de Perceval, ou Le Conte du Graal*, ed. Keith Busby (Tübingen: Max Niemeyer Verlag, 1993).

Cixous, Hélène, 'The Character of "Character"', trans. Keith Cohen, *New Literary History* 5: 2 (1974), 383–402.

Clark, Andy, *Being There: Putting Brain, Body, and World Together Again* (Cambridge, MA: MIT Press, 1998).

Clark, Andy, *Supersizing the Mind: Embodiment, Action, and Cognitive Extension* (Oxford: Oxford University Press, 2008).

Coetzee, J. M., *The Master of Petersburg* (London: Minerva, 1994).

Coetzee, J. M., 'The Harms of Pornography: Catherine MacKinnon', in *Giving Offense: Essays on Censorship* (Chicago: University of Chicago Press, 1996), 61–82.

Cohen, Murray, *Sensible Words: Linguistic Practice in England 1640–1785* (Baltimore: Johns Hopkins University Press, 1977).

Cohn, Dorrit, *Transparent Minds: Narrative Modes for Presenting Consciousness in Fiction* (Princeton: Princeton University Press, 1978).

Comolli, Jean-Louis, 'Historical Fiction: A Body Too Much', trans. Ben Brewster, *Screen* 19: 2 (1978), 41–54.

Condren, Conal, *Argument and Authority in Early Modern England: The Presupposition of Oaths and Offices* (Cambridge: Cambridge University Press, 2006).

Connor, Steven, *Dumbstruck: A Cultural History of Ventriloquism* (Oxford: Oxford University Press, 2000).

Connor, Steven, *The Book of Skin* (London: Reaktion Books, 2004).

Cooper, Robbie, *Alter Ego: Avatars and their Creators* (London: Chris Boot, 2007).

Corblin, François, 'Les désignateurs dans les romans', *Poétique* 54 (1983), 199–211.

Cortázar, Julio, *Rayuela* (Buenos Aires: Editorial Sudamericana, 1963).

Cortázar, Julio, *Hopscotch*, trans. Gregory Rabassa (London: Collins and Harvill Press, 1967).

Cortázar, Julio, *62: Modelo para armar* (Buenos Aires: Editorial Sudamericana, 1968).

Cortázar, Julio, *62: A Model Kit*, trans. Gregory Rabassa (1972; rpt. New York: Bard Books, 1973).

Cortázar, Julio, 'The Broken Doll', in *Around the Day in Eighty Worlds*, trans. Thomas Christensen (San Francisco: North Point Press, 1986), 201–10.

Coste, Didier, *Narrative as Communication* (Minneapolis: University of Minnesota Press, 1989).

Crogan, Patrick, *Gameplay Mode: Between War, Simulation and Technoculture* (Minneapolis: University of Minnesota Press, 2011).

Culler, Jonathan, *Structuralist Poetics* (Ithaca: Cornell University Press, 1975).

Culpepper, Jonathan, *Language and Characterisation: People in Plays and Other Texts* (London: Longman, 2001).

Curtius, Ernst Robert, *European Literature and the Latin Middle Ages*, trans. Willard R. Trask (New York: Harper & Row, 1953).

Damasio, Antonio, *Descartes' Error: Emotion, Reason, and the Human Brain* (New York: Putnam, 1994).

Damasio, Antonio, *The Feeling of What Happens: Body and Emotion in the Making of Consciousness* (Orlando, FL: Harcourt, 1999).

Dante Alighieri, *The Divine Comedy*, 6 vols, trans. Charles S. Singleton, Bollingen Series LXXX (Princeton: Princeton University Press, 1973).

Darwin, Charles, 'Introduction to the First Edition', in *The Expression of the Emotions in Man and Animals,* with an Introduction, Afterword and Commentaries by Paul Ekman (1872; rpt. London: HarperCollins, 1998), xxi–xxxvi.

De Grazia, Margreta, Hamlet *without Hamlet* (Cambridge: Cambridge University Press, 2007).

De Man, Paul, *Allegories of Reading: Figural Language in Rousseau, Nietzsche, Rilke, and Proust* (New Haven: Yale University Press, 1979).

Defoe, Daniel, *Robinson Crusoe*, ed. Michael Shinagel (2nd edn, New York: Norton Critical Edition, 1994).

Deleuze, Gilles, *Proust and Signs*, trans. Richard Howard (New York: Braziller, 1972).

Deleuze, Gilles, *Francis Bacon: The Logic of Sensation*, trans. Daniel W. Smith (Minneapolis: University of Minnesota Press, 2003).

Deleuze, Gilles, and Guattari, Félix, *A Thousand Plateaus: Capitalism and Schizophrenia*, trans. Brian Massumi (Minneapolis: University of Minnesota Press, 1987).

DeLillo, Don, *Point Omega* (London: Picador, 2010).

DeLillo, Don, 'Midnight in Dostoevsky', in *The Angel Esmeralda: Nine Stories* (New York: Scribner, 2011), 119–45.

Derrida, Jacques, 'Violence and Metaphysics: An Essay on the Thought of Emmanuel Levinas', in *Writing and Difference*, trans. Alan Bass (London: Routledge & Kegan Paul, 1978), 79–153.

Derrida, Jacques, 'Limited Inc a b c...', trans. Samuel Weber, in *Limited Inc* (Evanston, IL: Northwestern University Press, 1988), 29–107.

Derrida, Jacques, *Memoirs of the Blind: The Self-Portrait and Other Ruins*, trans. Pascale-Anne Brault and Michael Naas (Chicago: University of Chicago Press, 1993).

Descartes, René, *The Philosophical Writings of Descartes*, vol. 1, trans. John Cottingham, Robert Stoothoff, and Dugald Murdoch (Cambridge: Cambridge University Press, 1985).

Dever, Carolyn, *Death and the Mother from Dickens to Freud: Victorian Fiction and the Anxiety of Origins* (Cambridge: Cambridge University Press, 1998).

Dibbell, Julian, *My Tiny Life: Crime and Passion in a Virtual World* (New York: Henry Holt & Co., 1998).

Dickens, Charles, *Bleak House*, ed. George Ford and Sylvère Monod (New York: Norton Critical Edition, 1977).

Dickens, Charles, *David Copperfield*, ed. Jerome H. Buckley (New York: Norton Critical Edition, 1990).

Dickens, Charles, *Great Expectations*, ed. Edgar Rosenberg (New York: Norton Critical Edition, 1999).

Diderot, Denis, 'Paradoxe sur le comédien', in *Diderot's Writings on the Theatre*, ed. F. C. Green (Cambridge: Cambridge University Press, 1936), 249–317.

Diderot, Denis, 'Éloge de Richardson', in *Contes et romans*, ed. Michel Delon, Bibliothèque de la Pléïade (Paris: Gallimard, 2004), 897–911.

Dolbier, Maurice, 'Books and Authors: Nabokov's Plums', *New York Herald Tribune*, 17 June 1962, 2–6.

Doležel, Lubomir, *Heterocosmica: Fiction and Possible Worlds* (Baltimore: Johns Hopkins University Press, 1998).

Donnerstein, Edward, Linz, Daniel, and Penrod, Steven, *The Question of Pornography: Research Findings and Policy Implications* (New York: The Free Press, 1987).

Dowling, William C., 'Who's the Narrator of Nabokov's *Pale Fire*?', <http://www.rci.rutgers.edu/~wcd/palenarr.htm>. Last accessed 28 June 2013.

Dupont, Florence, 'The Emperor-God's Other Body', trans. Brian Massumi, in Michael Feher (ed.), *Fragments for a History of the Human Body, Part Three* (New York: Zone Books, 1989), 397–419.

Eagleton, Terry, *The Rape of Clarissa: Writing, Sexuality and Class Struggle in Samuel Richardson* (Oxford: Basil Blackwell, 1982).

Ekman, Paul, 'Universals and Cultural Differences in Facial Expressions of Emotion', in J. Cole (ed.), *Nebraska Symposium on Motivation 1971* (Lincoln: University of Nebraska Press, 1972), 207–25.

Ekman, Paul, 'Expression and the Nature of Emotion', in Scherer and Ekman (eds), *Approaches to Emotion*, 319–43.

Ekman, Paul, 'Facial Expression and Emotion', *American Psychologist* (April 1993), 384–92.

Ekman, Paul, *Telling Lies: Clues to Deceit in the Marketplace, Politics, and Marriage* (New York: W.W. Norton, 2009).

Ekman, Paul, and Friesen, Wallace V., *Unmasking the Face* (Englewood Cliffs, NJ: Prentice Hall, 1975).

Ekman, Paul, Friesen, Wallace V., and Ellsworth, Phoebe, *Emotion in the Human Face: Guidelines for Research and an Integration of Findings* (New York: Pergamon Press, 1972).

Eliot, T. S., *Selected Essays* (3rd edn, London: Faber and Faber, 1961).

Eliot, T. S., *Collected Poems 1909–1962* (London: Faber and Faber, 1963).

Ellis, John, 'Photography/Pornography/Art/Pornography', *Screen* 21: 1 (1980), 81–108.

Emmott, Catherine, *Narrative Comprehension: A Discourse Perspective* (Oxford: Oxford University Press, 1997).

Engels, Friedrich, draft letter to Margaret Harkness (April 1888), in Karl Marx and Friedrich Engels, *On Literature and Art* (Moscow: Progress Publishers, 1976), 89–92.

Epstein, A. L., *Ethos and Identity: Three Studies in Ethnicity* (London: Tavistock, 1978).

Esposito, Roberto, 'The Dispositif of the Person', *Law, Culture and the Humanities* 8: 1 (2012), 17–30.

Evans-Pritchard, E. E., 'Nuer Modes of Address', in Dell Hymes (ed.), *Language in Culture and Society: A Reader in Linguistics and Anthropology* (New York: Harper & Row, 1964), 221–7.

Fabian, Johannes, *Time and the Other: How Anthropology Makes its Object* (New York: Columbia University Press, 1983).

Fanning, Christopher, 'On Sterne's Page: Spatial Layout, Spatial Form, and Social Spaces in *Tristram Shandy*', in Marcus Walsh (ed.), *Laurence Sterne* (London: Pearson Education, 2002), 178–200.

Felski, Rita, 'The Invention of Everyday Life', *New Formations* 39 (1999), 13–31.

Ferguson, Frances, 'Jane Austen, *Emma*, and the Impact of Form', *MLQ* 61: 1 (2000), 157–80.

Ferguson, Frances, *Pornography the Theory: What Utilitarianism Did to Action* (Chicago: University of Chicago Press, 2004).

Fernández-Dols, José Miguel, and Carroll, James M., 'Is the Meaning Perceived in Facial Expression Independent of its Context?', in Russell and Fernández-Dols (eds), *The Psychology of Facial Expression*, 275–94.

Ficino, Marsilio, *De Studiosorum Sanitate Tuenda, De Vita Libri Tres* I (1482–9).

Field, Andrew, *Nabokov: His Life in Art* (Boston: Little, Brown, 1967).

Fielding, Henry, *Joseph Andrews*, ed. R. F. Brissenden (Harmondsworth: Penguin, 1977).

Fillmore, Charles, *Lectures on Deixis* (Stanford: CSLI Publications, 1997).

Finch, Casey and Bowen, Peter, '"The Tittle-Tattle of Highbury": Gossip and the Free Indirect Style in *Emma*', *Representations* 31 (1990), 1–18.

Fisher, Seymour, *Body Experience in Fantasy and Behavior* (New York: Appleton-Century-Crofts, 1970).

Fitzgerald, Michael, 'Character Evidence and the Literature of the Theophrastan Character: A Phenomenology of Testimony', *An Aesthetics of Law and Character: Texts, Images, Screens, Studies in Law, Politics, and Society* 34 (2004), 133–53.

Flaubert, Gustave, *Oeuvres I*, ed. A. Thibaudet and R. Dumesnil, Bibliothèque de la Pléïade (Paris: Gallimard, 1962).

Flaubert, Gustave, *Madame Bovary*, trans. Paul de Man (New York: Norton Critical Edition, 1965).

Fludernik, Monika, *The Fictions of Language and the Languages of Fiction: The Linguistic Representation of Speech and Consciousness* (London: Routledge, 1993).

Fludernik, Monika, 'The Linguistic Illusion of Alterity: The Free Indirect as a Paradigm of Discourse Representation', *Diacritics* 25: 4 (1995), 89–115.

Fokkema, Aleide, *Postmodern Characters: A Study of Characterization in British and American Postmodern Fiction* (Amsterdam: Rodopi, 1991).

Forcheimer, Paul, *The Category of Person in Language* (Berlin: De Gruyter, 1953).

Foucault, Michel, *The Order of Things: An Archaeology of the Human Sciences* (New York: Random House, 1970).

Foucault, Michel, 'The Confession of the Flesh', in *Power/Knowledge: Selected Interviews and Other Writings, 1972–1977*, ed. Colin Gordon, trans. Colin Gordon, Leo Marshall, John Mepham, and Kate Soper (New York: Pantheon, 1980), 194–228.

Foucault, Michel, 'Technologies of the Self', in Luther H. Martin, Huck Gutman, and Patrick H. Hutton (eds), *Technologies of the Self: A Seminar with Michel Foucault* (Amherst: University of Massachusetts Press, 1988), 16–49.

Foucault, Michel, 'Governmentality', in *Power: Essential Works of Foucault, 1954–1984*, vol. 3, ed. James D. Faubion, trans. Robert Hurley et al. (London: Penguin, 2002), 201–22.

Foucault, Michel, *The Hermeneutics of the Subject: Lectures at the Collège de France 1981–1982*, trans. Graham Burchell (New York: Picador, 2005).

Foucault, Michel, *Security, Territory, Population: Lectures at the Collège de France, 1977–1978*, ed. Michel Senellart, trans. Graham Burchell (New York: Palgrave Macmillan, 2007).

Foucault, Michel, *The Birth of Biopolitics: Lectures at the Collège de France, 1978–1979*, ed. Michel Senellart, trans. Graham Burchell (New York: Palgrave Macmillan, 2008).

Fowler, Alastair, *Kinds of Literature: An Introduction to the Theory of Genres and Modes* (Cambridge, MA: Harvard University Press, 1982).
Fowler, Alastair, *Literary Names: Personal Names in English Literature* (Oxford: Oxford University Press, 2012).
Fowler, Chris, *The Archaeology of Personhood: An Anthropological Appraisal* (London: Routledge, 2004).
Fowler, Elizabeth, *Literary Character: The Human Figure in Early English Writing* (Ithaca: Cornell University Press, 2003).
Freccero, John, 'Manfred's Wounds and the Poetics of the Purgatorio', in Rachel Jacoff (ed.), *Dante: The Poetics of Conversion* (Cambridge, MA: Harvard University Press, 1986), 195–208.
Frege, Gottlob, 'The Thought: A Logical Inquiry', trans. A. and M. Quinton, in P. F. Strawson (ed.), *Philosophical Logic* (Oxford: Oxford University Press, 1967), 17–38.
Frege, Gottlob, 'On Sense and Meaning', trans. Max Black, in P. T. Geach and Max Black (eds), *Translations from the Philosophical Writings of Gottlob Frege* (Oxford: Blackwell, 1980), 56–78.
Freud, Sigmund, *The Origins of Psychoanalysis: Letters to Wilhelm Fliess, Drafts and Notes: 1887–1902*, ed. Marie Bonaparte, Anna Freud, and Ernst Kris, trans. Eric Mosbacher and James Strachey (New York: Basic Books, 1954).
Freud, Sigmund, *The Standard Edition of the Complete Psychological Works of Sigmund Freud in 24 vols*, trans. James Strachey (London: The Hogarth Press, 1955).
Freud, Sigmund, *Beyond the Pleasure Principle*, in *Standard Edition* XVIII, 1–64.
Freud, Sigmund, 'A Child is Being Beaten', in *Standard Edition* XVII, 175–204.
Freud, Sigmund, 'The Ego and the Id', in *Standard Edition* XIX, 1–66.
Freud, Sigmund, 'Family Romances', in *Standard Edition* XIX, 235–41.
Freud, Sigmund, *Group Psychology and the Analysis of the Ego*, in *Standard Edition* XVIII, 65–143.
Freud, Sigmund, *The Interpretation of Dreams, in Standard Edition* IV, 1–338, and V, 339–627.
Freud, Sigmund, *Introductory Lectures on Psychoanalysis*, in *Standard Edition* XV, 3–239, and XVI, 243–476.
Freud, Sigmund, 'Mourning and Melancholia (1917)', in *Standard Edition* XIV, 239–58.
Freud, Sigmund, 'On Narcissism: An Introduction (1914)', in *Standard Edition* XIV, 73–102.
Freud, Sigmund, 'Two Encyclopaedia Articles (1923)', in *Standard Edition* XVIII, 235–59.
Freud, Sigmund, 'The Uncanny', in *Standard Edition* XVII, 217–56.
Fridlund, Alan J., *Human Facial Expression: An Evolutionary View* (San Diego: Academic Press, 1994).
Fridlund, Alan J., 'The New Ethology of Human Facial Expressions', in Russell and Fernández-Dols (eds), *The Psychology of Facial Expression*, 103–29.
Friedman, Ted, '*Civilization* and Its Discontents: Simulation, Subjectivity, and Space', in Greg M. Smith (ed.), *On a Silver Platter: CD-ROMs and the Promises of a New Technology* (New York: New York University Press, 1999), 132–50.
Frow, John, 'Spectacle, Binding: On Character', *Poetics Today* 7: 2 (1986), 227–50.
Frow, John, 'The Last Things Before the Last: Notes on *White Noise*', in Frank Lentricchia (ed.), *Introducing Don DeLillo* (Durham, NC: Duke University Press, 1991), 175–91.
Frow, John, *Time and Commodity Culture: Essays in Cultural Theory and Postmodernity* (Oxford: Clarendon Press, 1997).

Frow, John '"Never Draw to an Inside Straight": The Critique of Everyday Reason', *New Literary History* 33: 4 (2002), 623–38.

Frow, John, *Genre* (London: Routledge, 2006).

Frye, Northrop, *Anatomy of Criticism: Four Essays* (1957; rpt. New York: Atheneum, 1965).

Frye, Northrop, 'Dickens and the Comedy of Humours', in *The Stubborn Structure: Essays on Criticism and Society* (London: Methuen, 1970), 218–40.

Frye, Roland Mushat, 'Ladies, Gentlemen, and Skulls: Hamlet and the Iconographic Traditions', *Shakespearean Quarterly* 30: 1 (1979), 15–28.

Gallagher, Catherine, *Nobody's Story: The Vanishing Acts of Women Writers in the Marketplace, 1670–1820* (Berkeley: University of California Press, 1994).

Gallagher, Catherine, 'The Rise of Fictionality', in Franco Moretti (ed.), *The Novel,* vol. I: *History, Geography, and Culture* (Princeton: Princeton University Press, 2006), 336–63.

Gallagher, Catherine, 'What Would Napoleon Do? Historical, Fictional, and Counterfactual Characters', *New Literary History* 42: 2 (2011), 315–36.

Gallagher, Shaun, *How the Body Shapes the Mind* (Oxford: Oxford University Press, 2005).

Galloway, Alexander R., *Gaming: Essays on Algorithmic Culture* (Minneapolis: University of Minnesota Press, 2006).

Garvey, James, 'Characterization in Narrative', *Poetics* 7 (1978), 63–78.

Gass, William H., 'The Concept of Character in Fiction', in *Fiction and the Figures of Life* (New York: Alfred A. Knopf, 1970), 34–54.

Gatens, Moira, *Imaginary Bodies: Ethics, Power and Corporeality* (London: Routledge, 1996).

Gaynesford, Maximilian de, *I: The Meaning of the First-Person Term* (Oxford: Clarendon Press, 2006).

Gazzard, Alison, 'The Avatar and the Player: Understanding the Relationship Beyond the Screen', in *2009 Conference in Games and Virtual Worlds for Serious Applications* (IEEE Computer Society 2009), 190–3.

Gee, James Paul, 'Video Games and Embodiment', *Games and Culture* 3: 3–4 (2008), 253–63.

Geertz, Clifford, 'Person, Time, and Conduct in Bali', in *The Interpretation of Cultures: Selected Essays* (New York: Basic Books, 1973), 360–411.

Geertz, Clifford, 'From the Native's Point of View: On the Nature of Anthropological Understanding', in *Local Knowledge: Further Essays in Interpretive Anthropology* (New York: Basic Books, 1983), 55–70.

Gellert, Bridget, 'The Iconography of Melancholy in the Graveyard Scene of "Hamlet"', *Studies in Philology* 67: 1 (1970), 57–66.

Gelley, Alexander, 'Character and Person: On the Presentation of Self in the Novel', in *Narrative Crossings: Theory and Pragmatics of Prose Fiction* (Baltimore: Johns Hopkins University Press, 1987), 58–78.

Genette, Gérard, 'Métonymie chez Proust', in *Figures* III (Paris: Seuil, 1972), 41–63.

Genette, Gérard, *Narrative Discourse,* trans. Jane E. Lewin (Ithaca: Cornell University Press, 1980).

Genette, Gérard, *Figures of Literary Discourse,* trans. Alan Sheridan (New York: Columbia University Press, 1982).

Gerblinger, Christiane, '"Fiery the Angels Fell": America, Regeneration, and Ridley Scott's *Blade Runner*', *Australasian Journal of American Studies* 21: 1 (2002), 19–30.

Gibbs, Raymond W., *Embodiment and Cognitive Science* (Cambridge: Cambridge University Press, 2005).

Gilson, Étienne, 'Dante's Notion of a Shade: *Purgatorio* XXV', *Mediaeval Studies* 29 (1967), 124–42.

Ginsberg, Warren, *The Cast of Character: The Representation of Personality in Ancient and Medieval Literature* (Toronto: University of Toronto Press, 1983).

Glaudes, Pierre, and Reuter, Yves, *Le Personnage* (Paris: PUF, 1998).

Goethe, Johann Wolfgang von, *Die Wahlverwandtschaften: Ein Roman, Werke*, vol. III (Frankfurt am Main: Insel-Verlag, 1966).

Goethe, Johann Wolfgang von, *Elective Affinities*, trans. R. J. Hollingdale (Harmondsworth: Penguin, 1971).

Goffman, Erving, *The Presentation of Self in Everyday Life* (New York: Anchor Books, 1959).

Goffman, Erving, 'Footing', *Semiotica* 25: 1–2 (1979), 1–29.

Goffman, Erving, 'On Face-Work: An Analysis of Ritual Elements in Social Interaction', in *Interaction Ritual: Essays in Face-to-Face Behavior* (1967; rpt. New Brunswick, NJ: Aldine Transaction, 2005), 5–45.

Gooch, P. W., 'Socratic Irony and Aristotle's *Eiron*: Some Puzzles', *Phoenix* 41: 2 (1987), 95–104.

Goodrich, Peter, *Reading the Law: A Critical Introduction to Legal Method and Techniques* (Oxford: Blackwell, 1986).

Gordon, Paul Scott, 'Disinterested Selves: *Clarissa* and the Tactics of Sentiment', *ELH* 64: 2 (1997), 473–502.

Gorman, Warren, *Body Image and the Image of the Brain* (St Louis, MI: Warren H. Green, Inc., 1969).

Gragnolati, Manuele, *Experiencing the Afterlife: Soul and Body in Dante and Medieval Culture* (Notre Dame, IN: University of Notre Dame Press, 2005).

Greenblatt, Stephen, *Renaissance Self-Fashioning: From More to Shakespeare* (Chicago: University of Chicago Press, 1980).

Greenblatt, Stephen, *Hamlet in Purgatory* (Princeton: Princeton University Press, 2001).

Greenblatt, Stephen, *Will in the World: How Shakespeare Became Shakespeare* (London: Pimlico, 2004).

Greimas, A. J., 'Réflexions sur les modèles actantiels', in *Sémantique structurale* (1986; Paris: Larousse, 1966), 172–91.

Grivel, Charles, *Production de l'intérêt romanesque* (The Hague: Mouton, 1973).

Gross, Daniel M., 'Defending the Humanities with Charles Darwin's *The Expressions of the Emotions in Man and Animals* (1872)', *Critical Inquiry* 37: 1 (2010), 34–59.

Grosz, Elizabeth, *Volatile Bodies: Toward a Corporeal Feminism* (Bloomington: Indiana University Press, 1994).

Gunn, Daniel, 'Free Indirect Discourse and Narrative Authority in *Emma*', *Narrative* 12: 1 (2004), 35–54.

Haakonssen, Knud, *Natural Law and Moral Philosophy: From Grotius to the Scottish Enlightenment* (Cambridge: Cambridge University Press, 1996).

Halperin, David M., *How To Be Gay* (Cambridge, MA: Harvard University Press, 2012).

Hamburger, Käte, *The Logic of Literature*, trans. Marilynn J. Rose (2nd rev. edn, Bloomington: Indiana University Press, 1973).

Hamon, Philippe, 'Pour un statut sémiologique du personnage', in Roland Barthes, Wolfgang Kayser, Wayne Booth, and Philippe Hamon, *Poétique du récit* (Paris: Seuil, 1977), 115–80.

Hamon, Philippe, *Le Personnel du roman: Le système des personnages dans les* Rougon-Macquart *d'Emile Zola* (Geneva: Droz, 1983).

Harkin, Maureen, 'Smith's *The Theory of Moral Sentiments*: Sympathy, Women, and Emulation', *Studies in Eighteenth-Century Culture* 24 (1995), 175–90.

Harré, Rom, *The Singular Self: An Introduction to the Psychology of Personhood* (London: Sage, 1998).

Hayles, Katherine N. *How We Became Posthuman: Virtual Bodies in Cybernetics, Literature, and Informatics* (Chicago: University of Chicago Press, 1999).

Hayot, Eric, *On Literary Worlds* (New York: Oxford University Press, 2012).

Head, Henry, and Holmes, Gordon, 'Sensory Disturbances from Cerebral Lesions', *Brain* 34 (1911), 102–254.

Head, Henry, Rivers, W. H. R, Sherren, James, Holmes, Gordon, Thompson, Theodore, and Riddoch, George, *Studies in Neurology*, 2 vols (London: Oxford University Press, 1920).

Heath, Stephen, 'Difference', *Screen* 19: 3 (1978), 51–112.

Heath, Stephen, 'Body, Voice', in *Questions of Cinema* (London: Macmillan, 1981), 176–93.

Hegel, G. W. F., *Vorlesungen über die Ästhetik III, Werke in zwanzig Bänden* (Frankfurt am Main: Suhrkamp Verlag, 1970).

Heller, Agnes, *Everyday Life*, trans. G. L. Campbell (London: Routledge & Kegan Paul, 1984).

Hertz, Robert, *Death and the Right Hand*, trans. Rodney and Claudia Needham (Glencoe: The Free Press, 1960).

Hirst, Paul, 'Introduction to Edelman', in Bernard Edelman, *Ownership of the Image: Elements for a Marxist Theory of Law*, trans. Elizabeth Kingdom (London: Routledge & Kegan Paul, 1979), 1–18.

Hobbes, Thomas, *Leviathan*, ed. Noel Malcolm (Oxford: Clarendon Press, 2012).

Hochman, Baruch, *Character in Literature* (Ithaca: Cornell University Press, 1985).

Hollis, Martin, 'Of Masks and Men', in Carrithers, Collins, and Lukes (eds), *The Category of the Person*, 217–33.

Horwitz, Morton J., *The Transformation of American Law, 1780–1860* (Cambridge, MA: Harvard University Press, 1977).

Hough, Graham, 'Narrative and Dialogue in Jane Austen', *Critical Quarterly* 12: 3 (1970), 201–29.

Hu, Hsien Chin, 'The Chinese Concepts of "Face"', *American Anthropologist*, n.s., 46: 1 (1944), 45–64.

Huddleston, Rodney and Pullum, Geoffrey K., *The Cambridge Grammar of the English Language* (Cambridge: Cambridge University Press, 2002).

Hugh-Jones, Stephen, 'The Substance of Northwest Amazonian Names', in vom Bruck and Bodenhorn (eds), *The Anthropology of Names and Naming*, 74–96.

Hulme, Peter, *Colonial Encounters: Europe and the Native Caribbean, 1492–1797* (London: Methuen, 1986).

Hume, David, *A Treatise of Human Nature*, ed. David Fate Norton and Mary J. Norton (Oxford: Oxford University Press, 2000).

Hunter, Ian, 'Reading Character', *Southern Review* 16: 2 (1983), 226–43.

Hunter, Ian, *Rival Enlightenments: Civil and Metaphysical Philosophy in Early Modern Germany* (Cambridge: Cambridge University Press, 2001).

Hunter, Ian, Saunders, David, and Williamson, Dugald, *On Pornography: Literature, Sexuality and Obscenity Law* (London: Macmillan, 1993).

Hunter, J. Paul, *The Reluctant Pilgrim: Defoe's Emblematic Method and Quest for Form in* Robinson Crusoe (Baltimore: Johns Hopkins University Press, 1966).

Hunter, R. L., *The New Comedy of Greece and Rome* (Cambridge: Cambridge University Press, 1985).

Iteanu, André, 'Why the Dead do not Bear Names: The Orokaiva Name System', in vom Bruck and Bodenhorn (eds), *The Anthropology of Names and Naming*, 52–72.

Izard, Carroll, *The Face of Emotion* (New York: Appleton-Century-Crofts, 1971).
Jakobson, Roman, 'Shifters, Verbal Categories, and the Russian Verb', in *Selected Writings II: Word and Language* (The Hague: Mouton, 1971), 130–47.
Jakobson, Roman, 'Notes marginales sur la prose de Pasternak', in *Questions de Poétique* (Paris: Seuil, 1973), 127–44.
Jakobsson, Mikael, 'Rest in Peace, Bill the Bot: Death and Life in Virtual Worlds', in Schroeder (ed.), *The Social Life of Avatars*, 63–76.
James, Henry, 'The Altar of the Dead', in *The Short Stories of Henry James*, ed. Clifton Fadiman (New York: Modern Library, 1945), 319–57.
James, William, *The Essential Writings*, ed. Bruce Wilshire (Albany: SUNY Press, 1971).
Jameson, Fredric, *The Political Unconscious: Narrative as a Socially Symbolic Act* (London: Methuen, 1981).
Janko, Richard, *Aristotle on Comedy: Towards a Reconstruction of* Poetics *II* (London: Duckworth, 1984).
Jannidis, Fotis, *Figur und Person: Beitrag zu einer historischen Narratologie* (Berlin: Walter de Gruyter, 2004).
Jauss, H. R., 'Interaction Patterns of Identification with the Hero', in *Aesthetic Experience and Literary Hermeneutics*, trans. Michael Shaw (Minneapolis: University of Minnesota Press, 1982), 152–88.
Jauss, H. R., 'Literary History as a Challenge to Literary Theory', in *Toward an Aesthetic of Reception*, trans. Timothy Bahti (Minneapolis: University of Minnesota Press, 1982), 3–45.
Jespersen, Otto, *Language: Its Nature, Development, and Origin* (1923; rpt. London: Allen & Unwin, 1959).
John, Juliet, *Dickens's Villains: Melodrama, Character, Popular Culture* (Oxford: Oxford University Press, 2001).
John, Juliet, *Dickens and Mass Culture* (Oxford: Oxford University Press, 2010).
Johnson, Barbara, *Persons and Things* (Cambridge, MA: Harvard University Press, 2008).
Johnson, D. Barton, *Worlds in Regression: Some Novels of Vladimir Nabokov* (Ann Arbor: Ardis, 1985).
Johnson, Mark, *The Body in the Mind: The Bodily Basis of Meaning, Imagination, and Reason* (Chicago: University of Chicago Press, 1987).
Johnson, Samuel, *The Rambler*, Issue no. 4 (1750).
Jones, Ernest, *Hamlet and Oedipus* (1949; rpt. New York: W.W. Norton, 1976).
Jones, Marilyn Scarantino, 'Pessoa's Poetic Coterie: Three Heteronyms and an Orthonym', *Luso-Brazilian Review* 14: 2 (1977), 254–62.
Jonson, Ben, *Every Man Out of His Humour*, ed. Helen Ostovitch, The Revels Plays (Manchester: Manchester University Press, 2001).
Josipovici, Gabriel, 'The Body in the Library', in *Writing and the Body* (Brighton: The Harvester Press, 1982), 1–33.
Jouve, Vincent, *L'effet-personnage dans le roman* (Paris: PUF, 1992).
Joyce, James, *A Portrait of the Artist as a Young Man* (London: Penguin, 1960).
Joyce, James, *Dubliners* (Harmondsworth: Penguin, 1993).
Joyce, James, *Ulysses: The 1922 Text*, ed. Jeri Johnson (Oxford: Oxford University Press, 1993).
Juul, Jesper, 'Introduction to Game Time', in Wardrip-Fruin and Harrigan (eds), *FirstPerson*, 131–42.
Kantorowicz, Ernst, 'The Sovereignty of the Artist: A Note on Legal Maxims and Renaissance Theories of Art', in *Selected Studies* (Locust Valley, NY: J. J. Augustin, 1965), 352–65.

Kauntze, Mark, 'Seeing Through a Glass Darkly: The Interpretation of a Biblical Verse in Augustine of Hippo', in Miranda Anderson (ed.), *The Book of the Mirror: An Interdisciplinary Collection Exploring the Cultural Story of the Mirror* (Newcastle: Cambridge Scholars, 2008), 60–9.

Keen, Suzanne, *Empathy and the Novel* (Oxford: Oxford University Press, 2007).

Keller, James R., *Princes, Soldiers and Rogues: The Political Malcontent of Renaissance Drama* (New York: Peter Lang, 1993).

Kerr, Lucille, 'Betwixt Reading and Repetition (apropos of Cortázar's *62: A Model Kit*)', in Carlos J. Alonso (ed.), *Julio Cortázar: New Readings* (Cambridge: Cambridge University Press, 1998), 91–109.

Keymer, Thomas, *Sterne, the Moderns, and the Novel* (Oxford: Oxford University Press, 2002).

Kinder, Marsha, *Playing with Power in Movies, Television, and Video Games: From Muppet Babies to Teenage Mutant Ninja Turtles* (Berkeley: University of California Press, 1993).

King, Noel, '"Giving Time to Images": Michael Wood on Film', *Metro Magazine* 135 (2002), 134–8.

King, Ross, '*Tristram Shandy* and the Wound of Language', *Studies in Philology* 92: 3 (1995), 291–310.

Kitzes, Adam H., *The Politics of Melancholy from Spenser to Milton* (New York: Routledge, 2006).

Kleiman, Irit Ruth, 'X Marks the Spot: The Place of the Father in Chrétien de Troyes's *Conte du Graal*', *Modern Language Review* 103 (2008), 969–82.

Kleist, Heinrich von, 'The Earthquake in Chile', in *The Marquise of O– and Other Stories*, trans. Martin Greenberg (London: Faber and Faber, 1963), 251–67.

Kleist, Heinrich von, *Das Erdbeben in Chili*, in Roland Reuß and Peter Staengle (eds), *Sämtliche Werke*, II/3 (Basel and Frankfurt am Main: Stroemfeld, 1993).

Kleist, Heinrich von, *Berliner Abendblätter I*, in Roland Reuß and Peter Staengle (eds), *Sämtliche Werke*, II/7 (Basel and Frankfurt am Main: Stroemfeld, 1997).

Kleist, Heinrich von, *Selected Writings*, ed. and trans. David Constantine (London: Dent, 1997).

Klibansky, Raymond, Panofsky, Erwin, and Saxl, Fritz, *Saturn and Melancholy: Studies in the History of Natural Philosophy, Religion and Art* (London: Thomas Nelson, 1964).

Koselleck, Reinhart, 'On the Anthropological and Semantic Structure of *Bildung*', in *The Practice of Conceptual History: Timing History, Spacing Concepts*, trans. Todd Samuel Presner et al. (Stanford: Stanford University Press, 2001), 170–207.

Kracauer, Siegfried, *Theory of Film: The Redemption of Physical Reality* (Oxford: Oxford University Press, 1960).

Kripke, Saul A., *Naming and Necessity* (Oxford: Basil Blackwell, 1980).

Kula, Witold, *Measures and Men*, trans. R. Szreter (Princeton: Princeton University Press, 1986).

Kundera, Milan, *The Unbearable Lightness of Being*, trans. Michael Henry Heim (London: Faber, 1984).

Lacan, Jacques, 'Desire and the Interpretation of Desire in *Hamlet*', *Literature and Psychoanalysis: The Question of Reading: Otherwise, Yale French Studies* 55/56 (1977), 11–52.

Lacan, Jacques, *The Seminar of Jacques Lacan*, Book II, ed. Jacques-Alain Miller, trans. Sylvana Tomaselli (Cambridge: Cambridge University Press, 1988).

Lacan, Jacques, 'The Mirror Stage as Formative of the *I* Function as Revealed in Psychoanalytic Experience', in *Écrits*, trans. Bruce Fink, in collaboration with Héloïse Fink and Russell Grigg (New York: Norton, 2006), 75–81.

LaCapra, Dominick, Madame Bovary *on Trial* (Ithaca: Cornell University Press, 1982).

Laclos, Pierre Choderlos de, *Les Liaisons Dangereuses*, trans. P. W. K. Stone (London: Penguin, 1961).

Lakoff, George, *Women, Fire, and Dangerous Things: What Categories Reveal About the Mind* (Chicago: University of Chicago Press, 1987).

Lakoff, George, and Johnson, Mark, *Metaphors We Live By* (Chicago: University of Chicago Press, 1980).

Lakoff, George, and Johnson, Mark, *Philosophy in the Flesh: The Embodied Mind and its Challenge to Western Thought* (New York: Basic Books, 1999).

Lakoff, Robin, 'Tense and its Relation to Participants', *Language* 46 (1970), 838–49.

Lamarque, Peter, 'Expression and the Mask: The Dissolution of Personality in Noh', *Journal of Aesthetics and Art Criticism* 47: 2 (1989), 157–68.

Lamb, Jonathan, *Sterne's Fiction and the Double Principle* (Cambridge: Cambridge University Press, 1989).

Lamb, Jonathan, 'Things as Authors', in *The Things Things Say* (Princeton: Princeton University Press, 2011), 201–29.

Laplanche, J., and Pontalis, J.-B., *The Language of Psychoanalysis*, trans. Donald Nicholson-Smith (New York: Norton, 1973).

Laplanche, Jean, *Life and Death in Psychoanalysis*, trans. Jeffrey Mehlman (Baltimore: Johns Hopkins University Press, 1976).

Laqueur, Thomas, *Making Sex: Body and Gender from the Greeks to Freud* (Cambridge, MA: Harvard University Press, 1990).

Larvatus's journal <http://larvatus.livejournal.com/5889.html>. Posted 24 December 2004. Last accessed 28 May 2013.

Latour, Bruno, *We Have Never Been Modern*, trans. Catherine Porter (Cambridge, MA: Harvard University Press, 1993).

Laurel, Brenda, *Computers as Theatre* (Reading, MA: Addison-Wesley, 1991, 1993).

Laurentius, Andreas, *A Discourse of the Preservation of the Sight: of Melancholick Diseases: of Rheumes, and of Old Age*, trans. Richard Surphlet (London, 1599).

Lawrence, D. H., *The Letters of D. H. Lawrence*, vol. II: *June 1913–October 1916*, ed. George J. Zytaruk and James T. Boulton (Cambridge: Cambridge University Press, 1981).

Layne, Linda, '"Your Child Deserves a Name": Possessive Individualism and the Politics of Memory in Pregnancy Loss', in vom Bruck and Bodenhorn (eds), *The Anthropology of Names and Naming*, 32–50.

Le Goff, Jacques, *The Birth of Purgatory*, trans. Arthur Goldhammer (Chicago: University of Chicago Press, 1984).

Leavis, F. R., *The Great Tradition* (1948; rpt. Harmondsworth: Penguin, 1972).

Lejeune, Philippe, *On Autobiography*, trans. Katherine Leary (Minneapolis: University of Minnesota Press, 1989).

Lévi-Strauss, Claude, 'The Art of the North West Coast', *Gazette des Beaux-Arts* 24 (1943), 175–82.

Lévi-Strauss, Claude, 'Split Representation in the Art of Asia and America', in *Structural Anthropology*, trans. Claire Jacobson and Brooke Grundfest Schoepf (London: Allen Lane, The Penguin Press, 1968), 245–73.

Lévi-Strauss, Claude, 'The Scope of Anthropology', in *Structural Anthropology*, vol. 2, trans. Monique Layton (Harmondsworth: Penguin, 1978), 3–32.

Lévi-Strauss, Claude, *The Way of the Masks*, trans. Sylvia Modelski (Seattle: University of Washington Press, 1982).

Levinas, Emmanuel, *Totality and Infinity: An Essay on Exteriority*, trans. Alphonso Lingis (The Hague: Martinus Nijhoff, 1979).

Levinas, Emmanuel, 'The Face', in *Ethics and Infinity: Conversations with Philippe Nemo*, trans. Richard A. Cohen (Pittsburgh: Duquesne University Press, 1985), 85–92.

Levinas, Emmanuel, 'Meaning and Sense', in Adriaan T. Peperzak, Simon Critchley, and Robert Bernasconi (eds), *Basic Philosophical Writings* (Bloomington: Indiana University Press, 1996), 33–64.

Levinas, Emmanuel, *Alterity and Transcendence*, trans. Michael B. Smith (London: The Athlone Press, 1999).

Levinas, Emmanuel, and Kearney, Richard, 'Dialogue with Emmanuel Levinas', in Richard Cohen (ed.), *Face to Face with Levinas* (Albany: SUNY Press, 1986), 13–33.

Lévy-Bruhl, Lucien, *Primitive Mentality*, trans. Lilian A. Clare (New York: Macmillan, 1923).

Lévy-Bruhl, Lucien, *How Natives Think*, trans. Lilian A. Clare (Princeton: Princeton University Press, 1985).

Leys, Ruth, *From Guilt to Shame: Auschwitz and After* (Princeton: Princeton University Press, 2007).

Leys, Simon, *The Death of Napoleon*, trans. Patricia Clancy and Simon Leys (London: Quartet, 1991).

Lezra, Jacques, *Unspeakable Subjects: The Genealogy of the Event in Early Modern Europe* (Stanford: Stanford University Press, 1997).

Lin, Y. T., *My Country and My People* (New York: The John Day Co., 1939).

Liu, Alan, *The Laws of Cool: Knowledge Work and the Culture of Information* (Chicago: University of Chicago Press, 2004).

Locke, John, *An Essay Concerning Human Understanding*, ed. Peter H. Nidditch (Oxford: Clarendon Press, 1975).

Locke, John, *The Second Treatise of Civil Government, Two Treatises of Government*, ed. Peter Laslett (Cambridge: Cambridge University Press, 1988).

Loewen-Schmidt, Chad, 'Pity, or the Providence of the Body in Richardson's *Clarissa*', *Eighteenth-Century Fiction* 22: 1 (2009), 1–28.

Lotman, Jurij, *The Structure of the Artistic Text*, trans. Ronald Vroon (Ann Arbor: Michigan Slavic Contributions, University of Michigan, 1977).

Luhmann, Niklas, *The Reality of the Mass Media*, trans. Kathleen Cross (Stanford: Stanford University Press, 2000).

Lukács, Georg, *Studies in European Realism* (New York: Grosset & Dunlap, 1964).

Lukács, Georg, 'Über die Besonderheit als Kategorie der Ästhetik', in *Probleme der Ästhetik, Werke*, vol. 10 (Neuwied: Luchterhand, 1969), 539–789.

Lukács, Georg, *The Theory of the Novel: A Historico-Philosophical Essay on the Forms of Great Epic Literature*, trans. Anna Bostock (Cambridge, MA: MIT Press, 1971).

Lukes, Steven, 'Conclusion', in Carrithers, Collins, and Lukes (eds), *The Category of the Person*, 282–301.

Lynch, Deirdre Shauna, *The Economy of Character: Novels, Market Culture, and the Business of Inner Meaning* (Chicago: University of Chicago Press, 1998).

Lyons, Bridget Gellert, *Voices of Melancholy: Studies in Literary Treatments of Melancholy in Renaissance England* (London: Routledge & Kegan Paul, 1971).

MacCary, Thomas W., 'Menander's Slaves: Their Names, Roles, and Masks', *Transactions and Proceedings of the American Philological Association* 100 (1969), 277–94.

MacCary, Thomas W., 'Menander's Characters: Their Names, Roles and Masks', *Transactions and Proceedings of the American Philological Association* 101 (1970), 277–90.

MacCary, Thomas W., 'The Comedy of Errors: A Different Kind of Comedy', *New Literary History* 9: 3 (1978), 525–36.

McHale, Brian, 'Unspeakable Sentences, Unnatural Acts: Linguistics and Poetics Revisited', *Poetics Today* 4: 1 (1983), 17–45.

McHale, Brian, 'Speech Representation', in Peter Hühn, John Pier, Wolf Schmid, and Jörg Schönert (eds), *The Handbook of Narratology* (Berlin: De Gruyter, 2009), 434–46.

Macintyre, Alasdair, *After Virtue: A Study in Moral Theory* (3rd edn, Notre Dame, IN: University of Notre Dame Press, 2007).

McKee, Alan, Albury, Katherine, and Lumby, Catharine, *The Porn Report* (Melbourne: Melbourne University Press, 2008).

McKeon, Michael, *The Origins of the English Novel, 1600–1740* (Baltimore: Johns Hopkins University Press, 1987).

McKeon, Michael, *The Secret History of Domesticity: Public, Private, and the Division of Knowledge* (Baltimore: Johns Hopkins University Press, 2005).

Mackinnon, Catherine A., *Feminism Unmodified: Discourses on Life and Law* (Cambridge, MA: Harvard University Press, 1987).

Mackinnon, Catherine, *Toward a Feminist Theory of the State* (Cambridge, MA: Harvard University Press, 1989).

Magli, Patrizia, 'The Face and the Soul', in Michael Feher (ed.), *Fragments for a History of the Human Body, Part Two* (New York: Zone Books, 1989), 86–127.

Mahr, Greg, 'Pessoa, Life Narrative, and the Dissociative Process', *Biography* 21: 1 (1998), 24–35.

Maitland, Frederic, 'Moral Personality and Legal Personality', in *The Collected Papers of Frederic William Maitland*, ed. H. A. L. Fisher (Cambridge: Cambridge University Press, 1911), vol. 3, 304–20.

Malabou, Catherine, *What Should We Do With Our Brain?* (New York: Fordham University Press, 2008).

Malabou, Catherine, *The New Wounded: From Neurosis to Brain Damage*, trans. Steven Miller (New York: Fordham University Press, 2012).

Mallarmé, Stéphane, 'Le Tombeau d'Edgar Poe', in *Oeuvres complètes*, vol. I, ed. Bertrand Marchal, Bibliothèque de la Pléïade (Paris: Gallimard, 1998), 38.

Mann, Thomas, 'The Transposed Heads', in *Stories of a Lifetime*, vol. 2, no translator listed (London: Mercury Books, 1961), 214–87.

Mann, Thomas, 'Die vertauschten Köpfe: Eine indische Legende', in *Die Erzählungen*, vol. 2 (Frankfurt am Main: Fischer Bücherei, 1967), 549–620.

Manning, Susan, 'Did Human Character Change? Representing Women and Fiction from Shakespeare to Virginia Woolf', *Partial Answers* 11: 1 (2013), 29–52.

Manovich, Lev, *The Language of New Media* (Cambridge, MA: MIT Press, 2001).

Marder, Elissa, '*Blade Runner*'s Moving Still', *Camera Obscura* 27 (1991), 89–107.

Margolin, Uri, 'Introducing and Sustaining Characters in Literary Narrative: A Set of Conditions', *Style* 21: 1 (1987), 107–24.

Margolin, Uri, 'Structuralist Approaches to Character in Narrative: The State of the Art', *Semiotica* 75: 1/2 (1989), 1–24.

Margolin, Uri, 'Individuals in Narrative Worlds: An Ontological Perspective', *Poetics Today* 11: 4 (1990), 843–71.

Margolin, Uri, 'Characters in Literary Narrative: Representation and Signification', *Semiotica* 106: 3/4 (1995), 373–92.

Margolin, Uri, 'Characters and their Versions', in Mihailescu and Hamarneh (eds), *Fiction Updated*, 113–32.

Margolin, Uri, 'Naming and Believing: Practices of the Proper Name in Narrative Fiction', *Narrative* 10: 2 (2002), 107–27.
Margolin, Uri, 'Character', in David Herman, Manfred Jahn, and Marie-Laure Ryan (eds), *Routledge Encyclopedia of Narrative Theory* (London: Routledge, 2005), 52–6.
Margolin, Uri, 'Character', in David Herman (ed.), *The Cambridge Companion to Narrative* (Cambridge: Cambridge University Press, 2007), 66–79.
Mark, Gregory A., 'The Personification of the Business Corporation in American Law', *University of Chicago Law Review* 54 (1987), 1441–83.
Marriott, McKim, 'Hindu Transactions: Diversity without Dualism', in Bruce Kapferer (ed.), *Transaction and Meaning: Directions in the Anthropology of Exchange and Symbolic Behaviour* (Philadelphia: Institute for the Study of Human Issues, 1976), 109–42.
Martin, Raymond, and Barresi, John, *The Rise and Fall of Soul and Self: An Intellectual History of Personal Identity* (New York: Columbia University Press, 2006).
Massumi, Brian, *Parables for the Virtual: Movement, Affect, Sensation* (Durham, NC: Duke University Press, 2002).
Maunsell, Jerome Boyd, 'The Hauntings of Fernando Pessoa', *Modernism/modernity* 19: 1 (2012), 115–37.
Maus, K., *Inwardness and Theater in the English Renaissance* (Chicago: University of Chicago Press, 1995).
Mauss, Marcel, *Sociologie et anthropologie* (1950; rpt. Paris: PUF, 1973).
Mauss, Marcel, *Sociology and Psychology: Essays*, trans. Ben Brewster (London: Routledge & Kegan Paul, 1979).
Mauss, Marcel, 'A Category of the Human Mind: The Notion of Person; The Notion of Self', trans. W. D. Halls, in Carrithers, Collins, and Lukes (eds), *The Category of the Person*, 1–25.
Meadows, Mark Stephen, *I, Avatar: The Culture and Consequences of Having a Second Life* (Berkeley: New Riders, 2008).
Meissner, W. W., 'Notes on Identification 1: Origins in Freud', *The Psychoanalytic Quarterly* 39 (1970), 563–89.
Melchior-Bonnet, Sabine, *The Mirror: A History*, trans. Katharine H. Jewett (New York: Routledge, 2001).
Mercer, Peter, Hamlet *and the Acting of Revenge* (London: Macmillan, 1987).
Merleau-Ponty, Maurice, *Phenomenology of Perception*, trans. Colin Smith (1962; rpt. London: Routledge, 2002).
Metzinger, Thomas, *Being No One: The Self-Model Theory of Subjectivity* (Cambridge, MA: MIT Press, 2003).
Mihailescu, Calin-Andrei and Hamarneh, Walid (eds), *Fiction Updated: Theories of Fictionality, Narratology, and Poetics* (Toronto: University of Toronto Press, 1996),
Mill, John Stuart, *A System of Logic, Ratiocinative and Inductive: Being a Connected View of the Principles of Evidence and the Methods of Scientific Investigation* (1843; rpt. New York: Harper and Brothers, 1882).
Miller, J. Hillis, *Charles Dickens: The World of His Novels* (1958; rpt. Bloomington: Indiana University Press, 1969).
Miller, J. Hillis, *Ariadne's Thread: Story Lines* (New Haven: Yale University Press, 1992).
Miner, Earl, *Naming Properties: Nominal Reference in Travel Writings by Bashō and Sora, Johnson and Boswell* (Ann Arbor: University of Michigan Press, 1996).
Miola, Robert S., *Shakespeare and Classical Comedy: The Influence of Plautus and Terence* (Oxford: Clarendon Press, 1994).

Morgan, Robin, 'Theory and Practice: Pornography and Rape', in Laura Lederer (ed.), *Take Back the Night* (New York: William Morrow Co., 1980), 134–40.

Morgentaler, Goldie, *Dickens and Heredity: When Like Begets Like* (London: Macmillan, 2000).

Moss, Roger B., 'Sterne's Punctuation', *Eighteenth-Century Studies* 15: 2 (1981–2), 179–200.

Mullan, John, *Sentiment and Sociability: The Language of Feeling in the Eighteenth Century* (Oxford: Clarendon Press, 1988).

Mulvey, Laura, 'Visual Pleasure and Narrative Cinema', *Screen* 16: 3 (1975), 6–18.

Murphet, Julian, 'The Mole and the Multiple: A Chiasmus of Character', *New Literary History* 42: 2 (2011), 255–76.

Myer, Valerie Grosvenor (ed.), *Laurence Sterne: Riddles and Mysteries* (London: Vision Press, 1984).

Myer, Valerie Grosvenor, 'Tristram and the Animal Spirits', in Myer (ed.), *Laurence Sterne: Riddles and Mysteries*, 99–112.

Nabokov, Vladimir, *Pale Fire, Novels 1955–1962* (1962; rpt. New York: The Library of America, 1996).

Ndalianis, Angela, *The Horror Sensorium: Media and the Senses* (Jefferson, NC: McFarland, 2012).

Nelson, Victoria, *The Secret Life of Puppets* (Cambridge, MA: Harvard University Press, 2001).

Nesselroth, Peter W., 'Naming Names in Telling Tales', in Mihailescu and Hamarneth (eds), *Fiction Updated*, 133–43.

Newman, James, 'The Myth of the Ergodic Videogame', *Game Studies* 2: 1 (2002), n.p. <http://www.gamestudies.org/0102/newman>. Last accessed 28 June 2013.

Nicholas, Barry, *An Introduction to Roman Law* (Oxford: Clarendon Press, 1962).

Nietzsche, Friedrich, *The Genealogy of Morals*, trans. Francis Golffing (New York: Doubleday, 1956).

Nietzsche, Friedrich, *Zur Genealogie der Moral*, in K. Schlechta (ed.), *Werke*, vol. 3 (1954; rpt. Munich: Hanser, 1969).

Nutton, Vivian, 'Humoralism', in W. F. Bynum and Roy Porter (eds), *Companion Encyclopedia of the History of Medicine*, vol. I (London: Routledge, 1993), 281–91.

Oprisky, Robert L., *Honor: A Phenomenology* (London: Routledge, 2012).

Paiva, Ana, Andersson, Gerd, Höök, Kristina, Mourão, Darío, Costa, Marco, and Martinho, Carlos, 'SenToy in FantasyA: Designing an Affective Sympathetic Interface to a Computer Game', *Personal and Ubiquitous Computing* 6 (2002), 378–89.

Pajaczkowska, Claire, 'The Heterosexual Presumption: A Contribution to the Debate on Pornography', *Screen* 22: 1 (1981), 79–92.

Parfit, Derek, *Reasons and Persons* (1984; rpt. Oxford: Clarendon Press, 1986).

Pascal, Roy, *The Dual Voice: Free Indirect Speech and its Functioning in the Nineteenth-Century European Novel* (Manchester: Manchester University Press, 1977).

Paster, Gail Kern, *The Body Embarrassed: Drama and the Disciplines of Shame in Early Modern England* (Ithaca: Cornell University Press, 1993).

Paster, Gail Kern, *Humoring the Body: Emotions and the Shakespearean Stage* (Chicago: University of Chicago Press, 2004).

Patterson, Orlando, *Slavery and Social Death: A Comparative Study* (Cambridge, MA: Harvard University Press, 1982).

Pearce, Celia, 'Towards a Game Theory of Game', in Wardrip-Fruin and Harrigan (eds), *FirstPerson*, 143–53.

Perlin, Ken, 'Can There Be a Form Between a Game and a Story?', in Wardrip-Fruin and Harrigan (eds), *FirstPerson*, 12–18.
Pessoa, Fernando, *Selected Poems*, ed. and trans. Peter Rickard, Edinburgh Bilingual Library (Austin: University of Texas Press, 1971).
Pessoa, Fernando, *Poems of Fernando Pessoa*, trans. Edwin Honig and Susan M. Brown (San Francisco: City Lights, 1998).
Pessoa, Fernando, *The Book of Disquiet*, ed. and trans. Richard Zenith (London: Penguin, 2001).
Pessoa, Fernando, *The Selected Prose of Fernando Pessoa*, ed. and trans. Richard Zenith (New York: Grove Press, 2001).
Pessoa, Fernando, *A Little Larger than the Entire Universe: Selected Poems*, ed. and trans. Richard Zenith (London: Penguin, 2006).
Pessoa, Fernando, & Co, *Selected Poems*, ed. and trans. Richard Zenith (New York: Grove Press, 1998).
Peters, Laura, *Orphan Texts: Victorian Orphans, Culture and Empire* (Manchester: Manchester University Press, 2000).
Phillips, Adam, 'Keeping it Moving: Commentary on Judith Butler's "Melancholy Gender/Refused Identification"', in Judith Butler, *The Psychic Life of Power: Theories in Subjection* (Stanford: Stanford University Press, 1997), 151–9.
Pinch, Adela, *Strange Fits of Passion: Epistemologies of Emotion, Hume to Austen* (Stanford: Stanford University Press, 1996).
Plato, *The Collected Dialogues of Plato*, ed. Edith Hamilton and Huntington Cairns (Princeton: Princeton University Press, 1961).
Pointon, Marcia, *Hanging the Head: Portraiture and Social Formation in Eighteenth-Century England* (New Haven: Yale University Press, 1993).
Poovey, Mary, *A History of the Modern Fact: Problems of Knowledge in the Sciences of Wealth and Society* (Chicago: University of Chicago Press, 1998).
Poovey, Mary, *Genres of the Credit Economy* (Chicago: University of Chicago Press, 2008).
Pope, Alexander, 'Of the Characters of Women', *Moral Essays*, 'Epistle II: To a Lady', in *The Poems of Alexander Pope*, ed. John Butt (1963; rpt. London: Methuen, 1965), 559–69.
Porter, Roy, 'Introduction', in Roy Porter (ed.), *Rewriting the Self: Histories from the Renaissance to the Present* (London: Routledge, 1997), 1–14.
Pottage, Alain, 'Introduction: The Fabrication of Persons and Things', in Pottage and Mundy (eds), *Law, Anthropology, and the Constitution of the Social*, 1–39.
Pottage, Alain, and Mundy, Martha (eds), *Law, Anthropology, and the Constitution of the Social* (Cambridge: Cambridge University Press, 2004).
Poulet, Georges, *Proustian Space*, trans. Elliott Coleman (Baltimore: Johns Hopkins University Press, 1977).
Powers, Richard, *Galatea 2.2.* (London: Abacus, 1996).
Powers, Richard, *The Echo Maker* (London: William Heinemann, 2006).
Pratt, Branwen Baily, 'Dickens and Father: Notes on the Family Romance', *Hartford Studies in Literature* 8: 1 (1976), 4–22.
Price, Martin, *Forms of Life: Character and Moral Imagination in the Novel* (New Haven: Yale University Press, 1983).
Priest, Graham, *Towards Non-Being: The Logic and Metaphysics of Intentionality* (Oxford: Clarendon Press, 2005).
Propp, Vladimir, *Morphology of the Folktale*, trans. Lawrence Scott (2nd edn, Austin: University of Texas Press, 1968).

Proust, Marcel, *À la recherche du temps perdu*, ed. Jean-Yves Tadié, 4 vols, Bibliothèque de la Pléïade (Paris: Gallimard, 1987).

Proust, Marcel, *In Search of Lost Time*, trans. C. K. Scott Moncrieff and Terence Kilmartin, revised by D. J. Enright, 6 vols (New York: Modern Library, 2003).

Pushkin, Aleksandr, *Eugene Onegin, a Novel in Verse*; translated from the Russian, with a Commentary, by Vladimir Nabokov, Bollingen Series (New York: Pantheon, 1964).

Quirk, Randolph, Greenbaum, Sydney, Leech, Geoffrey, and Svartik, Jan, *A Comprehensive Grammar of the English Language* (Harlow: Longman, 1985).

Ragussis, Michael, *Acts of Naming: The Family Plot in Fiction* (New York: Oxford University Press, 1986).

Ramachandran, V. S., 'Consciousness and Body Image: Lessons from Phantom Limbs, Capgras Syndrome and Pain Asymbolia', *Philosophical Transactions of the Royal Society of London B* 353 (1998), 1851–9.

Richardson, Samuel, *Clarissa, or The History of a Young Lady*, ed. Angus Ross (1747–8; rpt. London: Penguin, 1985).

Rickard, Peter, 'Introduction', in Pessoa, *Selected Poems*, 1–61.

Ricoeur, Paul, *Oneself as Another*, trans. Kathleen Blamey (Chicago: University of Chicago Press, 1992).

Riley, E. C., 'Who's Who in *Don Quixote*? Or an Approach to the Problem of Identity', *MLN* 81: 2 (1966), 113–30.

Rimmon-Kenan, Shlomith, *Narrative Fiction: Contemporary Poetics* (London: Methuen, 1983).

Robert, Marthe, *The Old and the New: From* Don Quixote *to Kafka*, trans. Carol Cosman (Berkeley: University of California Press, 1977).

Ron, Moshe, 'Free Indirect Discourse, Mimetic Language Games and the Subject of Fiction', *Poetics Today* 2: 2 (1981), 17–39.

Ronen, Ruth, *Possible Worlds in Literary Theory* (Cambridge: Cambridge University Press, 1994).

Rorty, Amélie Oksenberg, 'A Literary Postscript: Characters, Persons, Selves, Individuals', in Amélie Oksenberg Rorty (ed.), *The Identities of Persons* (Berkeley: University of California Press, 1976), 301–23.

Rose, Nikolas, *Governing the Soul: The Shaping of the Private Self* (London: Routledge, 1989).

Ross, John Robert, 'On Declarative Sentences', in R. Jacobs and P. Rosenbaum (eds), *Readings in English Transformational Grammar* (Waltham, MA: Ginn and Co., 1970), 222–72.

Russell, Bertrand, 'On Denoting', *Mind* 14: 56 (1905), 479–93.

Russell, James A., and Fernández-Dols, José Miguel (eds), *The Psychology of Facial Expression* (Cambridge: Cambridge University Press, 1997).

Russell, James A., and Fernández-Dols, José Miguel, 'What Does a Facial Expression Mean?', in Russell and Fernández-Dols (eds), *The Psychology of Facial Expression*, 3–30.

Ruthrof, Horst, *Semantics and the Body: Meaning from Frege to the Postmodern* (Toronto: University of Toronto Press, 1997).

Ruthrof, Horst, *The Body in Language* (London: Cassell, 2000).

Ryan, Marie-Laure, 'Will New Media Produce New Narratives?', in Marie-Laure Ryan (ed.), *Narrative Across Media: The Languages of Storytelling* (Lincoln: University of Nebraska Press, 2004), 337–59.

Ryan, Marie-Laure, *Avatars of Story* (Minneapolis: University of Minnesota Press, 2006).

Sacks, Oliver, *The Man Who Mistook his Wife for a Hat* (London: Duckworth, 1985).

Sade, Donatien-Alphonse-François, Marquis de, *Justine, Philosophy in the Bedroom, and Other Writings*, trans. Richard Seaver and Austryn Wainhouse (New York: Grove Press, 1965).

Sage, Victor, '"[T]he privileged horror ... of the constellation": Cortázar's use of the Gothic in *62: A Model Kit*', *E-rea* 5: 2 (2007), 1–12.

Saramago, José, *The Year of the Death of Ricardo Reis*, trans. Giovanni Pontiero (London: The Harvill Press, 1992).

Sargent-Baur, Barbara N., 'Le jeu des noms de personnes dans le *Conte du Graal*', *Neophilologus* 85: 4 (2001), 485–99.

Scherer, Klaus R., and Ekman, Paul (eds), *Approaches to Emotion* (Hillsdale, NJ: Lawrence Erlbaum, 1984).

Schilder, Paul, *The Image and Appearance of the Human Body* (New York: Wiley, 1950).

Schlicke, Paul, *Dickens and Popular Entertainment* (London: Allen & Unwin, 1985).

Schroeder, Ralph (ed.), *The Social Life of Avatars: Presence and Interaction in Shared Virtual Environments* (London: Springer, 2002).

Schweitzer, Bernhard, 'Griechische Porträtkunst', in *Acta Congressus Madvigiani Hafniae MDMLIV*, III: *Portraiture* (Copenhagen, 1957), 8ff., as translated by B. V. Bothmer, *Egyptian Sculpture of the Late Period, 700 BC to AD 100* (Brooklyn: Brooklyn Museum, 1960).

Scollon, Ron, and Scollon, Suzie Wong, 'Face Parameters in East-West Discourse', in Ting-Toomey (ed.), *The Challenge of Facework*, 133–57.

Searle, John, 'Proper Names', *Mind* 67 (1958), 166–73.

Searle, John, *Speech Acts: An Essay in the Philosophy of Language* (Cambridge: Cambridge University Press, 1969).

Searle, John R., 'Reiterating the Differences: A Reply to Derrida', *Glyph* 2 (1977), 199–208.

Searle, John R., *Intentionality: An Essay in the Philosophy of Mind* (New York: Cambridge University Press, 1983).

Seigel, Jerrold, *The Idea of the Self: Thought and Experience in Western Europe since the Seventeenth Century* (Cambridge: Cambridge University Press, 2005).

Serres, Michel, *The Parasite*, trans. Lawrence R. Schehr (Baltimore: Johns Hopkins University Press, 1982).

Shakespeare, William, *Henry IV, Part 2*, ed. A. R. Humphreys, The Arden Shakespeare, Second Series (London: Methuen Drama/Bloomsbury Publishing, 1981).

Shakespeare, William, *Hamlet*, ed. Ann Thompson and Neil Taylor, The Arden Shakespeare, Third Series (London: Thomson Learning, 2007).

Shoemaker, Sydney, *Self-Knowledge and Self-Identity* (Ithaca: Cornell University Press, 1963).

Sidney, Sir Philip, *An Apology for Poetry, or The Defense of Poesy*, ed. Geoffrey Shepherd (London: Thomas Nelson, 1965).

Simmel, Georg, 'The Aesthetic Significance of the Face', trans. Lore Ferguson, in Kurt H. Wolff (ed.), *Georg Simmel, 1858–1918: A Collection of Essays, with Translations and a Bibliography* (Columbus: Ohio State University Press, 1959), 276–81.

Sinfield, Mark, 'Uncle Toby's Potency: Some Critical and Authorial Confusions in *Tristram Shandy*', *N&Q* 223 (1978), 54–5.

Siraisi, Nancy G., *Medieval and Early Renaissance Medicine: An Introduction to Knowledge and Practice* (Chicago: University of Chicago Press, 1990).

Smeed, J. W., *The Theophrastan 'Character': The History of a Literary Genre* (Oxford: Clarendon Press, 1985).

Smith, Adam, *The Theory of Moral Sentiments*, ed. Knud Haakonssen (Cambridge: Cambridge University Press, 2002).

Sobchack, Vivian, *Carnal Thoughts: Embodiment and Moving Image Culture* (Berkeley: University of California Press, 2004).

Sontag, Susan, 'The Pornographic Imagination', in *Styles of Radical Will* (New York: Dell, 1970), 35–73.

Sorabji, Richard, *Self: Ancient and Modern Insights about Individuality, Life, and Death* (Chicago: University of Chicago Press, 2006).

Soussloff, Catherine M., *The Subject in Art: Portraiture and the Birth of the Modern* (Durham, NC: Duke University Press, 2006).

Spitzer, Leo, 'Note on the Poetic and the Empirical "I" in Medieval Authors', *Traditio* 4 (1946), 414–22.

Springer, Mary, *A Rhetoric of Literary Character: Some Women of Henry James* (Chicago: University of Chicago Press, 1978).

Spurgeon, Caroline, *Shakespeare's Imagery and What it Tells Us* (1935; rpt. Cambridge: Cambridge University Press, 1952).

Stanner, W. E. H., 'Aboriginal Modes of Address and Reference in the North-West of the Northern Territory', *Oceania* 7: 3 (1937), 300–15.

Starr, G. A., *Defoe and Spiritual Autobiography* (Princeton: Princeton University Press, 1965).

States, Bert O., Hamlet *and the Concept of Character* (Baltimore: Johns Hopkins University Press, 1992).

Steiner, Wendy, *Exact Resemblance to Exact Resemblance: The Literary Portraiture of Gertrude Stein* (New Haven: Yale University Press, 1978).

Stern, Lesley, 'I Think, Sebastian, Therefore...I Somersault: Film and the Uncanny', *Paradoxa* 3: 3–4 (1997), 348–66.

Stern, Lesley, 'From the Other Side of Time', in Ian Christie and Andrew Moor (eds), *The Cinema of Michael Powell: International Perspectives on an English Film-Maker* (London: BFI, 2005), 36–59.

Stern, Lesley, *Dead and Alive: The Body as Cinematic Thing* (Montreal: Caboose, 2012).

Sterne, Laurence, *Letters of Laurence Sterne*, ed. Lewis Perry Curtis (1935; rpt. Oxford: Clarendon Press, 1965).

Sterne, Laurence, *The Life and Opinions of Tristram Shandy, Gentleman*, ed. Melvyn New and Joan New (London: Penguin, 2003).

Stover, L., *The Cultural Ecology of Chinese Civilization* (New York: Pica Press, 1974).

Strathern, Marilyn, *The Gender of the Gift: Problems with Women and Problems with Society in Melanesia* (Berkeley: University of California Press, 1988).

Strathern, Marilyn, *After Nature: English Kinship in the Late Twentieth Century* (Cambridge: Cambridge University Press, 1992).

Strathern, Marilyn, 'Pre-Figured Features', in *Property, Substance and Effect: Anthropological Essays on Persons and Things* (London: Athlone Press, 1999), 29–44.

Strawson, Galen, 'Against Narrativity', *Ratio*, n.s., 17 (2004), 428–52.

Strawson, P. F., *Individuals: An Essay in Descriptive Metaphysics* (London: Methuen, 1959).

Strawson, P. F., 'The First Person—and Others', in Cassam (ed.), *Self-Knowledge*, 210–15.

Surmelian, Leon, *Techniques of Fiction Writing: Measure and Madness* (New York: Doubleday, 1968).

Sussman, Herbert, and Joseph, Gerhard, 'Prefiguring the Posthuman: Dickens and Prosthesis', *Victorian Literature and Culture* (2004), 617–28.

Tamisari, Franca, 'Names and Naming: Speaking Forms into Place', in *The Land is a Map: Placenames of Indigenous Origin in Australia*, ed. Luise Hercus, Flavia Hodges,

and Jane Simpson (Canberra: Research School of Pacific and Asian Studies, Australian National University/Pandarus Books, 2002), 87–102.
Taussig, Michael, *Defacement: Public Secrecy and the Labor of the Negative* (Stanford: Stanford University Press, 1999).
Taylor, Charles, *Sources of the Self: The Making of the Modern Identity* (Cambridge, MA: Harvard University Press, 1989).
Taylor, T. L., 'Living Digitally: Embodiment in Virtual Worlds', in Schroeder (ed.), *The Social Life of Avatars*, 40–62.
Taylor, T. L., *Play between Worlds: Exploring Online Game Culture* (Cambridge, MA: MIT Press, 2006).
Theophrastus, *The Characters*, trans. Philip Vellacott (1967; rpt. Harmondsworth: Penguin, 1973).
Thomas, Yan, 'Le sujet de droit, la personne et la nature', *Le Débat* 100 (1998), 85–107.
Thomas, Yan, 'Le sujet concret et sa personne: Essai d'histoire juridique rétrospective', in Olivier Cayla and Yan Thomas, *Du droit de ne pas naître: À propos de l'affaire Perruche* (Paris: Gallimard, 2002), 91–170.
Thompson, Ann, and Thompson, John O., *Shakespeare: Meaning and Metaphor* (Brighton: The Harvester Press, 1987).
Thompson, E. P., 'The Moral Economy of the English Crowd in the Eighteenth Century', in *Customs in Common* (London: Penguin, 1993), 185–258.
Thompson, Evan, 'The Mindful Body: Embodiment and Cognitive Science', in Michael O'Donovan-Anderson (ed.), *The Incorporated Self: Interdisciplinary Perspectives on Embodiment* (Lanham, MD: Rowman & Littlefield, 1996), 127–44.
Ting-Toomey, Stella (ed.), *The Challenge of Facework: Cross-Cultural and Interpersonal Issues* (Albany: SUNY Press, 1994).
Todorov, Tzvetan, *Grammaire du Décaméron* (The Hague: Mouton, 1969).
Tomashevsky, Boris, 'Thematics (1925)', in L. Lemon and M. Reis (trans. and eds), *Russian Formalist Criticism* (Lincoln: University of Nebraska Press, 1965), 61–95.
Tomkins, Silvan, 'Affect as the Primary Motivational System', in M. B. Arnold (ed.), *Feelings and Emotions: The Loyola Symposium* (New York: Academic Press, 1970), 101–10.
Tomkins, Silvan, 'Affect Theory', in Scherer and Ekman (eds), *Approaches to Emotion*, 163–95.
Trevor, Douglas, *The Poetics of Melancholy in Early Modern England* (Cambridge: Cambridge University Press, 2004).
Turner, Mark, *The Literary Mind* (New York: Oxford University Press, 1996).
Tychsen, Anders, Hitchens, Michael, and Brolund, Thea, 'Character Play: The Use of Game Characters in Multi-Player Role-Playing Games across Platforms', *ACM Computers in Entertainment* 6: 2 (2008), article 22, 1–24.
Van Ghent, Dorothy, 'The Dickens World: A View from Todgers's', in George H. Ford and Lauriat Lane, Jr. (eds), *The Dickens Critics* (Ithaca: Cornell University Press, 1961), 213–32.
Vance, Carole S. (ed.), *Pleasure and Danger: Exploring Female Sexuality* (1984; rpt. London: Pandora Press, 1992).
Vande Berg, Michael, '"Pictures of Pronunciation": Typographical Travels through *Tristram Shandy* and *Jacques le Fataliste*', *Eighteenth-Century Studies* 21: 1 (1987), 21–47.
Varela, Francisco J., Thompson, Evan, and Rosch, Eleanor, *The Embodied Mind: Cognitive Science and Human Experience* (Cambridge, MA: MIT Press, 1991).

Varro, Marcus Terentius, *Rerum Rusticarum Libri Tres*, in Marcus Porcius Cato and Marcus Terentius Varro, *On Agriculture*, trans. William Davis Hooper, Loeb Classical Library (Cambridge, MA: Harvard University Press, 1967), 160–529.

Vidal, Fernando, 'Brains, Bodies, Selves, and Science: Anthropologies of Identity and the Resurrection of the Body', *Critical Inquiry* 28: 4 (2002), 930–74.

Vitek, William, *Promising* (Philadelphia: Temple University Press, 1993).

Viveiros de Castro, Eduardo, *From the Enemy's Point of View: Humanity and Divinity in an Amazonian Society*, trans. Catherine V. Howard (Chicago: University of Chicago Press, 1992).

Vom Bruck, Gabriella, and Bodenhorn, Barbara (eds), *The Anthropology of Names and Naming* (Cambridge: Cambridge University Press, 2006).

Vom Bruck, Gabriella, and Bodenhorn, Barbara, '"Entangled Histories": An Introduction to the Anthropology of Names and Naming', in vom Bruck and Bodenhorn (eds), *The Anthropology of Names and Naming*, 1–30.

Wahrman, Dror, *The Making of the Modern Self: Identity and Culture in Eighteenth-Century England* (New Haven: Yale University Press, 2004).

Walton, J. Michael, and Arnott, Peter D., *Menander and the Making of Comedy* (Westport, CT: Greenwood Press, 1996).

Wardrip-Fruin, Noah, and Harrigan, Pat (eds), *FirstPerson: New Media as Story, Performance, and Game* (Cambridge, MA: MIT Press, 2004).

Wark, McKenzie, *Gamer Theory* (Cambridge, MA: Harvard University Press, 2007).

Warner, William, *Reading* Clarissa*: The Struggles of Interpretation* (New Haven: Yale University Press, 1979).

Waters, Catherine, *Dickens and the Politics of the Family* (Cambridge: Cambridge University Press, 1997).

Watt, Ian, *The Rise of the Novel: Studies in Defoe, Richardson, and Fielding* (1957; rpt. Harmondsworth: Penguin, 1963).

Watt, Ian, 'The Comic Syntax of *Tristram Shandy*', in Howard Anderson and John S. Shea (eds), *Studies in Criticism and Aesthetics 1660–1800: Essays in Honour of Samuel Holt Monk* (Minneapolis: University of Minnesota Press, 1967), 315–31.

Weimann, Robert, *Shakespeare and the Popular Tradition in the Theater: Studies in the Social Dimension of Dramatic Form and Function*, ed. Robert Schwarz (Baltimore: Johns Hopkins University Press, 1978).

Weinsheimer, Joel, 'Theory of Character: *Emma*', *Poetics Today* 1: 1–2 (1979), 185–211.

Weinstein, Arnold, *Fictions of the Self: 1550–1800* (Princeton: Princeton University Press, 1981).

West, Shearer, *Portraiture* (Oxford: Oxford University Press, 2004).

Wexman, Virginia Wright, *Creating the Couple: Love, Marriage, and Hollywood Performance* (Princeton: Princeton University Press, 1993).

Wiggins, David, *Identity and Spatio-Temporal Continuity* (Oxford: Basil Blackwell, 1967).

Wiles, David, *The Masks of Menander: Sign and Meaning in Greek and Roman Performance* (Cambridge: Cambridge University Press, 1991).

Williams, Bernard, 'Are Persons Bodies?', in *Problems of the Self: Philosophical Papers 1956–1972* (Cambridge: Cambridge University Press, 1973), 64–81.

Williams, Linda, *Hard Core: Power, Pleasure, and the 'Frenzy of the Visible'* (Berkeley: University of California Press, 1989).

Winnicott, D. W., 'Transitional Objects and Transitional Phenomena', in *Collected Papers: Through Paediatrics to Psychoanalysis* (London: Tavistock, 1958), 229–42.

Wolfendale, Jessica, 'My Avatar, My Self: Virtual Harm and Attachment', *Ethics and Information Technology* 9 (2007), 111–19.

Wolff, Martin, 'On the Nature of Legal Persons', *Law Quarterly Review* 14 (October 1938), 494–521.

Woloch, Alex, *The One vs. the Many: Minor Characters and the Space of the Protagonist in the Novel* (Princeton: Princeton University Press, 2003).

Wundt, Wilhelm, *Völkerpsychologie*, vol. 2: *Die Sprache* (Leipzig, 1911).

Zagagi, Netta, *The Comedy of Menander: Convention, Variation and Originality* (Bloomington: Indiana University Press, 1995).

Zenith, Richard, 'Introduction: The Birth of a Nation', in Pessoa, *A Little Larger than the Entire Universe*, xiii–xxxii.

Žižek, Slavoj, *Tarrying with the Negative: Kant, Hegel, and the Critique of Ideology* (Durham, NC: Duke University Press, 1993).

Zola, Émile, 'The Experimental Novel', in Becker (ed.), *Documents of Modern Literary Realism*, 162–96.

Zola, Émile, 'On the Rougon-Macquart Series', in Becker (ed.), *Documents of Modern Literary Realism*, 159–61.

Zubin, David A. and Hewitt, Lynne E., 'The Deictic Center: A Theory of Deixis in Narrative', in Judith F. Duchan, Gail A. Bruder, and Lynne Hewitt (eds), *Deixis in Narrative: A Cognitive Science Perspective* (Hillsdale, NJ: Lawrence Erlbaum, 1995), 129–55.

FILMS

Franju, Georges, dir., *Les Yeux sans Visage* (1959).

Hitchcock, Alfred, dir., *Psycho* (1960).

Kubrick, Stanley, dir., *Eyes Wide Shut* (1999).

Marker, Chris, dir., *La Jetée* (1962).

Scott, Ridley, dir., *Blade Runner* (Theatrical Release, 1982; Director's Cut, 1992; Final Cut, 2007).

WEBSITES

Blade Runner script, <http://www.dailyscript.com/scripts/blade-runner_shooting.html> accessed 28 May 2013; <http://www.brmovie.com/Downloads/Docs/BR_Scripts.htm> accessed 28 May 2013.

Larvatus's journal, <http://larvatus.livejournal.com/5889.html> accessed 28 June 2013.

<http://en.wikipedia.org/wiki/Omar_Little> accessed 28 May 2013.

Index